CULTURE AND BEHAVIOR OF THE SEBEI

CULTURE AND BEHAVIOR OF THE SEBEI

A Study in Continuity and Adaptation

BY WALTER GOLDSCHMIDT

With the assistance of Gale Goldschmidt

A Contribution to the Studies
in Culture and Ecology

Edited by Walter Goldschmidt

UNIVERSITY OF CALIFORNIA PRESS
Berkeley • Los Angeles • London

University of California Press
Berkeley and Los Angeles, California

University of California Press, Ltd.
London, England

ISBN: 0-520-02828-7

Library of Congress Catalog Card Number: 74-82848
Copyright ©1976 by The Regents of the University of California

Printed in the United States of America

DEDICATED TO

The Sebei People

Contents

Appendixes

Illustrations

Albums

Tables

Preface

Culture and Behavior of the Sebei is the second contribution to the Culture and Ecology in East Africa Project. It is thus part of a collaborative effort designed to study the adaptive processes of change in culture, society, and individual behavior. The first volume in the series was *The Individual in Cultural Adaptation* by Robert B. Edgerton. Four other monographs are projected:

> Francis P. Conant, *The Pokot People*
> Symmes C. Oliver, *The Kamba of Kenya*
> Philip W. Porter, *The Ecology and Environment of East Africa*
> Edgar V. Winans, *Hehe Local Neighborhoods*

The broad purpose of the project was to determine whether alterations took place in institutionalized behavior, in customary procedures of both ceremonial and everyday life, in cultural values, and in patterns of individual behavior in response to altered economic circumstances under aboriginal conditions. The general strategy of the research program was to study four tribes, each of which had sectors devoted largely or wholly to pastoral pursuits and other sectors devoted to hoe farming, and to examine the social, cultural, and behavioral attributes of two communities (one pastoral and one farming) in each of the four tribes. The research tools of the project included questionnaires, tests and the usual anthropological methods of intimate observation, and the questioning of informants. Information on the geographical circumstances, the resource potential, and the man-land relationships in the four tribal areas was obtained by the geographer. An anthropologist obtained the social and cultural data for each tribe.

The present work examines in close detail the adaptive process as it has been reconstructed for the Sebei, a Southern Nilotic people of Uganda. Because very little is presently known of their culture, the work is also a general ethnography, seeking to understand life activities and perceptions, as well as institutional forms. Above all, I want to acknowledge my indebted-general ethnography, seeking to understand life activities and perceptions, as well as institutional forms.

I want above all to acknowledge my indebtedness to the Sebei, among whom I spent so many pleasant and interesting days, and among whom I count many friends — far too many to list here, so I must thank them anonymously. I owe a particular debt to my able and patient interpreters, Richard Bomet and Yovan Chemtai, and to Gale's interpreters, Susanna Koko and Lovina Ndege. Many other Sebei helped in clerical capacities, as occasional interpreters, and in other tasks, and they also have my gratitude. I want also to express my appreciation to the old chief, Yunusu Wandera, and to his successor, Aloni Muzungyo, and to the late A. Y. Chemonges, member of the Uganda Legislature. Many political leaders in Sebei were also helpful and have my thanks, including especially A. S. Ngokit, G. W. Cheborion, D. P. Arapta, and Stanley Salimu.

Even more important were the many neighbors in Binyinyi, Sasur, and Kapsirika. I want to mention in particular Psiwa Kapchemesyekin and his sons and Lewendi Satya and his sons in Sasur; Salimu Kambuya and his brothers Ndiwa and Andyema in Kapsirika; and some particularly honorable informants, Kapsilut, Musani, Chilla, and Baita.

I am indebted to the late Sir Andrew Cohen, governor of the Uganda Protectorate, for having steered me to the Sebei, to Audrey Richards who was helpful when I was a neophyte Africanist, and to John Lindsell, district commissioner, Bugisu, in 1954.

It is with special pleasure that I express my indebtedness to the research team of the Culture and Ecology Project; Francis Conant, Robert Edgerton, Symmes Oliver, Philip Porter, and E. V. Winans helped more than they know in the formulation of my thoughts about cultural adaptation. Edgerton and Porter deserve particular thanks for their more substantive contribution to this volume. The team included my wife, Gale Goldschmidt; she has contributed substantially to the data recorded here, and her role is recognized on the title page.

Diverse persons helped the manuscript take shape in various ways, and I want to thank Hillarie Kelly, Anne Lapides, Otomi Nagano, Mary Schaeffer, Nancy Strowbridge, and my colleagues John Kennedy, Thomas Weisner, and Edgerton, Porter, and Winans, whose comments on drafts of the manuscript have been most helpful. The photographs were taken by Gale and me, except for the picture by Gedge, which was supplied me by the late H. B. Thomas. The pictures were printed by Terry Lichtenstein.

Finally, I owe a more tangible debt to a number of agencies who supported various phases of my work. My first visit was made possible by a Fulbright Research Scholarship and ancillary grants from the Social Science Research Council and the Wenner-Gren Foundation for Anthropological Research. The Culture and Ecology Project was supported by grants from the National Science Foundation (Grant G11713) and from the National Institute of Mental Health (Public Health Service Grant MH-04097). A Senior Scientist Award from NIMH afforded me the free time for work on this book.

To all the above, and to many others not specifically mentioned, I dedicate this work as a token of my appreciation.

W. G.

Introduction
The Theory and Practice of Ethnography

One does not buy judgeship with cattle; one buys it with the ears.

Sebei proverb

ETHNOGRAPHY AS GENRE

It has long been my conviction that every anthropologist owes to the world, for the privilege of having been an anthropologist, at least one good ethnography. But I now realize that the price is too great — not out of any disenchantment with my discipline, but because the task is impossible. All that one can ask is that the anthropologist try to write a good ethnography. I offer this book as an earnest on that indebtedness.

Ethnography as a genre came into being in a more innocent era. We are apt to think of it as Boasian, for the students of Boas made much of ethnographic data, but it is pre-Boasian — a product of the amateur scholar, the more erudite missionaries, the local officials, and the presuffragette feminists — and best represented, as Lévi-Strauss has somewhere pointed out, in the old Annual Reports of the Bureau of American Ethnology.

Ethnography has two defining characteristics, beyond the obvious fact that it deals with community life. The first is that it seeks to encompass the whole of life, from the methods of childbirth to the fate of the soul.

The second hallmark of ethnography is that it regards the customary as more important than the actual. Thus, ethnography is a construct of the social order, but, when properly done, it is the natives' construct and not the ethnographer's. The organization of expectation, rather than the regularities of daily existence, is the center of attention. These two features in conjunction lead to the conceptualization of culture, to an awareness of how the totality of life is perceived by the actors themselves and how culture governs, or more accurately monitors, their conduct.

Anthropological theory of the nineteenth and early twentieth century was built on ethnography. In the United States, the dominant pattern for three decades was the study of Indian tribal life. For the most part, this meant

1

salvage ethnography. In salvage ethnography, the natives' constructs are recorded because the realities of everyday life are dominated by the demands of their political rulers. As long as theories were designed to explain traditions and customs, rather than everyday realities, this dependence on native constructs did not appear to be disadvantageous as it manifestly was if anthropology was ever to become more than merely the science of custom.

The professionalization of anthropology, though dependent upon the ethnography at the outset, succeeded in destroying ethnography as a literary form. Scholars, particularly those with a scientific orientation, entered the field with particularistic questions about facets of the behavioral system. To answer such questions, they had to reach into the daily lives of the people they studied. In so doing, they penetrated the crust of custom and entered into deeper strata of human existence, finding new sets of potentially meaningful interrelationships. In the process, they also sensitized later field workers to involvements of which earlier reporters had remained innocent; a process that started very early with Lewis Henry Morgan in the area of kinship. As more and more areas were thus illuminated, the impossibility of total reportage became increasingly evident.

The professionalization of the anthropologist had another effect on a more mundane level. As a professional, the anthropologist's personal life was in the academy; he went to the field for a brief stint, encompassing his work within a limited sabbatical or fellowship period. Caught in the status system of the scholarly community and holding the economic expectations of Western life, he found that his production was also measured in these terms. The first ethnographic field experience has the attributes of a Plains Indian vision quest, a liminal period of suffering and hardship from which the successful future warrior returns with new knowledge and power. Sometimes, it might be said that, like the quest of Crashing Thunder, the vision appears to have been more fake than real.

Other factors contributed to changing the nature of the genre. Natives increasingly became less native as Western customs became universalized. Modern transportation and the growing cadre of anthropologists made it no longer improbable that years would pass before another scholar would visit the area; therefore, it was less imperative to apprehend the totality of life.

The inherent difficulty in "doing" an ethnography led to a tendency toward denial — a psychological justification for not aspiring to the impossible. Denial has taken many forms, such as the focus on a single aspect of behavior, community studies, the concern with culture change ("acculturation"), and the like. One form deserves further attention: the denial of the very existence of culture. Two groups, both heavily influenced by sociology, have sought this path. The British sector, under the influence of Durkheim, tries to explain the patterned behavior of tribal life in terms of structural principles responding to functional needs. By penetrating deeper into the social order in efforts to understand primitive sociology, they ironically presented us with excellent ethnographic accounts, marred only by the

self-imposed limitations on their areas of interest, while their "explanations," which were their expressed aim, have proved of more limited value.

The second group, influenced by the methodologies of American sociology, endeavors to focus on the actualities of behavior. So far, most of its work
has been limited either to highly acculturated peoples in the United States,
or to social systems in which native life has been amalgamated and subordinated to external dominance. In contrast to both traditional ethnography
and British social anthropology, they find less salience to the "organization
of diversity" aspect of the social order, less concern for the moral impera-
tives of the community, and hence less need to attend to the patterns of
expectation, rather than the manifestation of actuality. The movement has
made two contributions to the study of exotic social behavior and hence also
to the difficulties inherent in ethnography as genre. First, it has reawakened
interest in the individual as an individual, as distinct from his role in society
(as in British social anthropology), or as a type (as in American psychologi-
cally-oriented anthropological studies). Second, it has demanded methodological sophistication, validation of data, methods, probabilities, and the
like.

One must accept the positive contribution of both schools, but one must
object to their denial of the concept of culture. Inasmuch as one of the
major intellectual revolutions of the past century is the substitution of
cultural explanations of human behavior for biological ones, the denial of
culture would have serious consequences if these scholars did not, in fact,
regularly slip cultural explanations into their discourse.

The increased specialization of knowledge has required the development
of ethnographic specialists who deal exclusively with law, economics, religion, art, and so on. Specialization has resulted in the codification of a basic
error of perception, against which ethnography is a necessary counterforce.
The specialists' compartmentalization of knowledge, which is so characteristic of academic thought and has been institutionalized by university cur-
ricula, is a misrepresentation of social reality. Man does not live leisure on
Saturday, religion on Sunday, and economics the other five days of the
week; what he believes, what he does, and how he feels are all of a piece —
not merely in the sense of interconnection but on a much deeper level. To
lose sight of this fact is to deny the essential contribution of anthropology
and to make it a second-rate replica of more specialized social disciplines. If
the concept of culture has no reality basis, anthropology has no reason to
exist.

Culture is the shared perception of reality, the taken-for-granted metaphysical order that is seen to shape human events, the perceptions and
presuppositions that guide the sentiments and influence the actions of each
individual in the course of his everyday life. Man's perceptions guide his
actions when he is wresting his livelihood from his environment, resolving
conflicts, participating in ritual action, playing, or fantasizing. Because the
individual is generally not aware of his perceptions and presuppositions, they

must be indirectly perceived by the ethnographer rather than seen. They manifest themselves phenotypically, in the consistencies that underlie the diversity of behavior.

Ethnography is unique in that it must seek to portray the totality of the life patterns of a people in a way that will make them comprehensible and meaningful to the reader. An ethnographer's work is very much like that of a novelist in that he presents significant details that evoke the complexity of the whole but differs from that of the novelist in that the ethnographer must endeavor to portray an external reality, not one of his own making, and with events seen or heard about, not ones he contrived. The construct is a model of how thousands of people spend hundreds of thousands of hours and of how they perceive the way they spend them. It is built from scraps of information — like the reconstruction of a Grecian urn from a few shards. To accomplish this, the ethnographer must do more than detail the customs; he must show the people in action, preserving their expression so that the reader can perceive what these actions mean to the actors. He must place these actions and expressions in the context of meaningful problems that his subjects must face. By the close of an ethnography, there should be no surprises but a sense of understanding, recognition, and consistency.

The ethnographer has other responsibilities as well; he must take cognizance of the needs of others in cross-cultural research, must record for the social anthropologist the kin and other relationships among the actors, for the student of symbolism the pesky details of ceremonial behavior, for the culture-historian the clues to similarities with neighboring and distant peoples, and so on. Because he is likely to be the last to deal with many matters, he has a responsibility to the theoretician of as yet unformulated interests. He cannot meet all these responsibilities fully, yet he must meet them where he can. Finally, of course, he has responsibilities to the subjects of his study: to provide an honest appraisal, to preserve their dignity, and to protect them from harm.

Despite all the difficulties, I believe that a good ethnography is an appropriate ideal. I do not enter this arena with the innocence of earlier reporters, though I may share their naïveté. I come armed with — or perhaps burdened by — many of the realizations and sensitivities of the intervening century, and I take these more detailed analyses, methodological problems, and concerns with individual variation very much to heart. The result is a book flawed by limitations that cannot be obscured. Among them are the omission of some areas and the lack of penetration into others. In the realm of material culture, I recorded relatively little and used less, in part because of the Sebei's own lack of interest and virtuosity in technology. I did no work on language, music, or dance because of my own limitations. Many other specific subjects are lightly touched on or overlooked. Yet, the essence of my approach has been to cast my net as widely as possible, with all the difficulties and limitations this presents. I cannot disengage myself from the costs of eclecticism because my intellectual interests involve the interface between several standard theories.

In what follows, I have taken what might be called a multimedia approach (though I cannot escape the linearity of language), bringing to bear upon each class of events all the various kinds of pertinent information available to me. Informants' statements have been juxtaposed with descriptions of observed events, pieced out with pertinent statistics, given immediacy with snippets of conversations or excerpts from songs, and, where possible, illustrated with photographs.

The problem of time is always a difficult one in ethnography, particularly when change is a central consideration. The problem is exacerbated when one is trying to see spatial variances that reflect temporal changes, and made more difficult yet when one's ethnographic work has extended over two decades. The present tense is used for continuing cultural practices, whether observed or communicated by informants, though in many instances these customs are no longer practiced precisely as they had been prior to the arrival of Europeans; the past tense is used to describe actual events or to refer to events in the distant past. I hope in this way to avoid casting the whole book in the past tense while preserving a sense of historical accuracy.

THE CULTURE AND ECOLOGY PROJECT

This book endeavors to be a general ethnography of the Sebei; it also develops a central thesis. Because I have set forth the basic strategy for this research elsewhere (Goldschmidt, 1965) and explained the underlying theoretical orientation in my introduction to the first of the volumes on Culture and Ecology Project (Goldschmidt, 1971b), I will merely summarize these considerations here.

The central thesis is that institutions are adaptive mechanisms designed to organize social action in terms of the situational requisites in which a people must operate. Behavior, whether individual or institutionalized, is responsive to the external environment: old forms are reshaped to meet new exigencies; there is continuity as well as change; and tradition exerts a powerful influence on the particular forms that exist at any one time.

The Sebei inspired this thesis. Twenty years ago, when I first visited them on a Fulbright grant, my aim was to record the customary behavior of a tribe as yet unstudied. In those days, the concept of tribe was still intellectually (and socially) acceptable; the issue of the delineation of an entity had not been raised. While I was ready to accept the Sebei as a tribe, or a unified amalgam of tribes, I rapidly became aware that my understanding of them was impaired by the fact that they were internally differentiated. On the basis of theoretical predilections already formulated (Goldschmidt 1959), I assumed that the internal differentiation related to basic ecologic variables and considered this proposition worthy of testing. I saw the demonstration of such an adaptive process as a contribution to the understanding of cultural evolution, for a modern theory of evolution does not concern itself with grand schemas, but with the minutiae of adjustments in the social order to new modes of economic exploitation arising from changes in either the environment, the technological apparatus, or both.

The internal variance in Sebei attitudes and orientations was perceived as being responsive to the diverse opportunities for economic exploitation, particularly as between cattle-keeping pastoralism and the cultivation of plantains, maize, and other crops. Because much of Africa is devoted to some kind of admixture of these two economies, a consistent effort to examine the concomitant internal variations in tribal cultures seemed worthwhile. The Culture and Ecology Project was established under my direction to explore this thesis. The project was designed to discover what regularities in behavioral and institutional adaptation could be found in a series of tribes, each of which had sectors primarily engaged in farming and others primarily engaged in pastoralism. In 1961, a team of six of us studied four tribes; I was in Sebei from June of that year to November 1962, except when I was involved with the administration of the project as a whole.

Our strategy involved three kinds of investigation, carried out collaboratively on four separate tribes, all within East Africa: two Kalenjin-speaking tribes (Sebei and Pokot) and two Bantu (Kamba and Hehe). Since, in our theoretical structure, the environment was the external variable to which each of the several cultures had to adapt, a geographer, Philip Porter, was included on the team. His specific charge was to examine the potentialities of the landscape for human exploitation and the manner in which such exploitation was accomplished.

Because we believed that institutional changes begin to take place when a people feel discomfitted by old patterns, we had to examine individual attitudes and values. To this end, our research team included Robert Edgerton, an anthropologist specially competent in the psychological aspects of social behavior. The results of his structured investigation have been published (Edgerton, 1971, henceforth referenced as RBE), and the data did, in large measure, conform to our expectations.

The third kind of investigation was more traditional. In each of the four tribes, an ethnographer studied in detail not only the general character of cultural expectations but the specific manifestations of social behavior in each of two communities: one in a farming and the other in a pastoral sector. I served as one of the four ethnographers.

The general problem, then, was to examine the internal diversity within four East African tribal peoples, each of which had made adaptations to diversities in the environment. This book reports the details of the adaptive process among the Sebei.

In order to understand the process of social change, it is necessary to recognize two interrelated orders of reality: first, continuing actions and interactions and, second, the perceptions, whether unconscious or consciously formulated, that a people share about the nature of their social world and the purpose of their actions. The two orders are closely interrelated, for each constantly influences the other. Those who deny the role of culture, who would study only manifest events, would fail to understand the distinction, for example, between polygyny and bigamy, for divested of cultural meanings, the behavior would be the same. Yet, those who concern themselves only with custom would fail to perceive the conflicts that polygamy — or, for that matter, monogamy — may create. Where adaptation and change are involved, the relation between the norms and behavior takes on central importance. As new circumstances arise, a tension develops between cultural expectation and existential realities. An understanding of the adaptive process therefore requires an awareness of these cultural orientations.

Thus there are two central themes in this book: continuity, the internal consistency that characterizes traditional Sebei culture; and adaptation, a process that takes place over time.

METHODOLOGIES

Spatial variation was central to the Culture and Ecology thesis. Because this kind of variance is the result of a process of adaptation and because processes have, by their very nature, a temporal dimension, I have been impelled to examine alterations through time as well.[1] My theoretical orientations, and the character of my problem, have also forced me to take cognizance of individual variance in behavior, to see the actualities of daily life against the background of the standards of expectation and moral order within which they operate. These varied demands made it necessary to utilize diverse techniques for obtaining data.

Informants' statements. The testimony of individual Sebei men and women (and occasionally children) was an essential source of information on both current and past practices, as well as those intrapsychic events that find but partial expression in overt behavior. I frequently brought a number of people together to discuss common topics, such as a group of clansmen to recount clan histories. I talked to scores of people from all parts of Sebei, some more extensively than others, usually on matters with which they had the greatest familiarity.

Observation. While no ethnography can adequately portray the native scene without observation, even the most gifted observer can see only what happens in front of him. Observation is most fruitful when it deals with standardized and repeated events, such as ritual acts and recurrent everyday events. We made no effort to standardize observational procedures.[2]

In studying Sebei life, I benefitted from others' observations and perceptions. The most important supplement was provided by my wife Gale, whose participation has enriched this work in many ways. Some specific passages were taken directly from her material, but her contribution extends far

---

1. The Culture and Ecology thesis treats spatial variation as an expression of temporal change, but this must be done with caution.

2. In the abstract, I regret this decision. It was motivated in part by my desire to maximize the freedom of choice of each ethnographer and in part by the difficulty of standardizing any cross-cultural observational procedure.

beyond these details. Of particular value were her insights into individual personalities and motivations — insights derived from both her natural talent and her training in psychiatric social work.

A very different talent is represented by Philip Porter, for he could perceive aspects of the natural environment, and of man's use of environment, that escaped me. His observations have informed many pages of this work, particularly in chapters 2, 6, and 7.

Edgerton's observations, as well as his detailed data, have also been helpful, and several items from his general notes and much of his statistical information appear in these pages.

I have not used the phrase "participant observation," which I think is a ritualistic phrase intended to imply much more than is in fact the case. Of course, we participated in those activities where we were welcome, from beer parties to a retaliatory raid, but at best such participation is superficial, for the depths of involvement are not available to the outsider, whose motivation and perceptions not only are, but must be, other than those of the community members.

Encounters. With the help of Yovan Chemtai, a remarkable interpreter, I developed a technique of recording the interaction between individuals in situations of conflict or confrontation, using a form of data that I call the ethnography of encounters (Goldschmidt, 1969, henceforth referenced as *KC;* 1972a). The record of such encounters reveals the expectations, styles of interaction, personality, and values expressed in everyday crisis situations. Excerpts of available encounters appear where appropriate throughout the text.

Questionnaire data. In order to provide data on individual variation, it is necessary to obtain statistical counts. Several separate questionnaires were used. The sample base for them comprised the two communities of Sasur in Sipi Gombolola, the farming village, and Kapsirika in Ngenge Gombolola, the pastoral site. Our sampling procedure was, first, to find representative communities of the two economic patterns; second, to delimit these units in terms of Sebei perceptions of community boundaries; and third, to obtain a saturation sample of household heads.

We had five separate schedules. They were usually taken at the same time, usually but not always from the household head, most often by myself but some (usually from women) by Gale. The Sasur schedules were mostly recorded in October-November 1961; the Kapsirika ones chiefly in February-March 1962. The schedules deal, respectively, with demography, livestock, land ownership and use, cash involvements, and brideprice. They are analyzed in subsequent chapters, and details of their form, content, and the like are discussed in conjunction with their use.

In addition to the questionnaires, the sample provided a basis for the special questionnaire and test administered by Robert Edgerton, who interviewed 33 men and 31 women in Sasur and 31 men and 33 women in Kapsirika. He presents details of the sampling procedures in his book

(RBE:49-52). I have used data from this investigation to illuminate many points.

In 1954, Gale also took a questionnaire from an opportunity sample of 20 women, largely in the Binyinyi area. These data give us insight into women's attitudes with respect to husbands and co-wives and their behavior relative to the treatment of children; the data appear largely in chapters 8 and 9. (A questionnaire I took in 1954 was, unfortunately, destroyed in a fire.)

Geography and land use. Philip Porter made analyses of climate, soils, and patterns of land use, which he presents in detail in his monograph (Porter, n.d.), but much of this information illuminates matters in the present work as well. The maps reproduced here not only are based upon data Porter obtained but were prepared by him. Particularly useful are the detailed maps of the two communities subjected to intensive study and of the land holdings of several farmers. Our joint effort to map the lands of Psiwa Kapchemesyekin and his sons yielded much unanticipated but valuable information. Information on land values was dependent upon this kind of detailed investigation.

Standardized statements. In this work, I found songs had the greatest usefulness as standardized statements about social behavior, for they frequently reveal specific attitudes (such as toward crying at circumcision) more eloquently than anything else. Also included in this rubric are proverbs, stories, and symbolic expression in rituals. The Sebei are relatively impoverished in their imaginative verbal expressions. Adults do not normally tell stories and generally disavow any knowledge of them. Gale recorded translations of stories taken from children in 1954; even the children were reluctant, though sometimes accomplished, storytellers. Unfortunately, not all these tales survived the fire. A few are recorded in this book, at points where they seem particularly informative about attitudes.

Photographs. The Sebei are excellent photographic subjects; on the one hand, they have no objection to the camera and, on the other, they do not pose in front of it, except for the children. This, together with Gale's perception — for she took most of the pictures — has made photography an important source of information and reportage on Sebei behavior.

Miscellany. The ethnographer must, it seems to me, be both imaginative and opportunistic in acquiring information that will lead to insights and evidence — as well as obtuse, nosy, and intrusive. In one instance, I used role-playing as a means of data collection (on brideprice bargaining, Chapter 8), and I believe this to be an inadequately utilized technique. My recording of the geneologies of cattle not only provided insight into attitudes and values but generated statistical information of great importance (Chapter 5; also *KC;* Goldschmidt, 1972c). Both innovative techniques owe more to chance than prescience.

I also used native clerks at various times, primarily in gathering clan histories (Chapter 1) and market data (Chapter 7).

I regret that I did not find it possible to learn Sebei, for I am fully aware that many nuances of cultural attitudes and behavior have escaped me as a result of this disability. In 1954, virtually all interpretation was done for me by Richard Bomet, son of Chilla, a man then about forty, who had gone to a missionary school, was fluent in Swahili and Luganda as well as in English and Sebei, and has subsequently played an important role in Sebei public life (plate I:12). He also worked with me from time to time in my later visit and was a good informant. Bomet identified strongly with the Sebei, was interested in and anxious to learn more about traditional culture, and actively sought knowledgeable informants. He did not like to discuss the seamier aspects of life or to translate gossip on interpersonal relationships. In 1961-62, my chief interpreter was Yovan Chemtai (Plate I:11), a man then in his late thirties, who had served as a court reporter. More alienated than Bomet from his culture, he was less interested in customary matters but more interested in patterns of on-going behavior and thus ideally suited for the more sociological purposes of my second visit.

Gale worked with the help of Susanna Koko in 1954 (Plate I:14), one of two young girls who spoke English, and with Lovina Ndege in 1961-62 (Plate I:13). Others helped us from time to time, but all the quotations in this book were translated by one of these four, with only the slightest need to edit in conformity with standard English usage. I did record in text some materials, particularly songs and sayings, but have not reproduced texts here.

I have adopted a number of conventions and practices. Spelling of Sebei words is, insofar as possible, in accord with practices currently adopted by the Sebei Committee on Orthography. Place names, however, are spelled as they appear on maps. (In these matters, I have been assisted by Dr. Christine Montgomery, though she should not be blamed for any errors.) English spellings have involved only the addition of the tailed n (ŋ, as in si*ng*) and the use of the tilde as in Spanish, especially for final consonants (Sapiñ). The sounds represented by d, k, p, and t may be voiced, not voiced, or, frequently, partially voiced. I have tried to use a minimum of Sebei terms, and have provided a glossary for those I have used throughout.

The age-set system has provided me with the basis for determining the age of older persons (assuming circumcision at age eighteen) and provides the Sebei with a means of dating events, particularly those of the nineteenth century. The times and periods may be read from the diagram of the cycling system (Figure 7) or in the chronology (Appendix A).

Names of persons have been changed, without particular note being taken, when I felt some damage might be done to the individual's reputation; sometimes names have merely been obscured with initials.

All monetary values are expressed in East African shillings, which exchanged at the rate of seven for a dollar ($0.14) during the period of the study.

Chapter 1
History: The Broader Context of Sebei Culture

The Sebei are easy to be converted to new fashions . . .

Yunusu Wandera, ex-*saza* chief

CULTURAL BACKGROUND

Modern Sebei consists of three formerly independent but closely interrelated tribes living on the northern and northwestern slopes of Mount Elgon (and on the plains below) in eastern Uganda. The term Sebei has come into use in modern administrative parlance, and the descendants of these three tribes now identify themselves as Sebei. Etymologically, Sebei (variously Sabei, Sapei, and so on) is a corruption of Sapiñ, the name of one of the tribes. The other two tribes are the Mbai and the Sor.[1] Their territory was curtailed by the drawing of the Kenya-Uganda border, for Sapiñ formerly extended into modern Kenya on the eastern side of the mountain and onto the Uasin-Gishu Plateau. In language and culture, the Sebei are closely affiliated to the people on the southern slopes of Elgon; indeed, modern politics largely severed these close ties, though a good deal of intermarriage and movement between the territories and some psychological identity remain. This last has been reinforced by modern political leaders, who formed the Sabaot Union (people who use the greeting, *supay*) as a pressure group. The union includes the three Sebei tribes in Uganda and their sister tribes on the Kenya side of the border, Bok, Kony, and Boŋom (Kipkorir, 1973:71). The research reported in this volume, however, applies only to the three tribes in Uganda who identify themselves as Sebei.

The circum-Elgon Sabaot tribes are a closely affiliated cluster of the group of tribes now known as Kalenjin. Tucker and Bryan (1962:137) define this term as follows:

---

1. These and other tribal names (e.g., Boŋom) are often given in the literature in their pluralized form (*-yek* or *-isiyek* suffix), as the Sebei often so use them. I have consistently adopted the simplified form in conformity with anthropological usage of the collective singular.

> The name "Kalenjin" is a group name recently adopted by the speakers of two non-Bantu languages of Kenya — Nandi and Kipsigis — to cover these and neighbouring languages and dialects and their speakers also. Its meaning in Nandi is "I tell you." This name has since been taken over in the field of African linguistics as a useful label to cover an entire language group. . . .[2]

Tucker and Bryan divide the estimated 600,000 speakers of Kalenjin into three groups, the Päkot (or Pokot, formerly known as Suk), the Tatog (including the Tatoga, Barabaig, and Tatura) spoken in the Northern and Central districts of Tanzania, and the Nandi-Kipsigis, in which they include the Sabaot cluster. The Tatog, or Tatoga are now considered a separate subgroup from Kalenjin (Sutton, 1968:81). According to Sebei, Nandi-Kipsigis is intelligible to them when carefully spoken; Pokot requires some experience before it can be understood. The Kalenjins are a part of the ethnic group formerly called Nilo-Hamites, a term that is objectionable on several grounds and has now been generally replaced by the term Southern Nilotes.

Joseph Greenberg in his classification of African languages (1955:62) originally put Nandi-Suk (i.e., Kalenjin) in one sector of the Great Lakes division ("Nilo-Hamitic" of the older literature) of the Southern branch of the Eastern Sudanic family of languages. He subsequently (1963) slightly rearranged the relationships, putting all the Kalenjins in a southern sector of the Nilotic branch of the Eastern Sudanic family, which he sees as a part of the Chari-Nile group.

The Nilotes must be considered one of four major cultural influences in East Africa. The first is an old layer of hunters and gatherers now represented by rapidly disappearing remnants of Dorobo or Bushmanoid peoples. The second, also represented by only a remnant population of Iraqw and closely related groups, is Cushitic-speaking. The third is the Bantu, who entered the area from the south and the west; and the fourth is the Nilotes.

George P. Murdock (1959:332-33) has reconstructed the early history of these peoples: Cushitic descendants of the "Sidamo" people occupied the Lacustrine area when Bantu speakers arrived from the west at a time when the Nilotes were backward agricultural peoples, who subsequently (presumably in the seventh century A.D.) "developed a full-fledged pastoral complex, which they could either combine with their traditional agricultural pursuits or detach from the latter and practice independently when the geographic environment did not permit extensive cultivation." With this economy, the Nilotes "expanded with explosive force," taking land from the Cushitic peoples and penetrating into Bantu territory on the northeast shores of Lake Victoria, as well as taking land from Bushmanoid hunters. "There thus resulted a mixed population speaking a Nilotic language with strong Cushitic increments and exhibiting a culture which combined Nilotic and Cushitic elements."

---

2. B. E. Kipkorir (1973:70-73) gives more detail on the etymology of the term.

Christopher Ehret (1971) has recently sought to work out the history of these relationships in much greater detail by examining language similarities and the amount and character of word borrowing and cultural uniformities, with occasional use of archeological evidence. He places the origin of this cultural development much further in the past than does Murdock and sees three major thrusts in which Nilotic people entered the area formerly occupied by the Cushites and the hunters and gatherers. The earliest migrants were the ancestral Kalenjins, the later two groups were the ancestral Masai and the closely related Karamojong-Luo, whose expansion as far south as northwestern Kenya is quite recent.

Ehret's reconstruction is the most comprehensive effort to date to present this history, though in many details it is conjectural and uncertain. He dates the beginnings of this culture, which he calls pre-Southern Nilote, as far back as 2000 B.C. or earlier, and finds its origins in the interaction between Nilotes and Cushites in the Kenya-Ethiopia-Sudan corner.[3] On the basis of ethnographic similarities, he postulates that by 2000 B.C. the culture included the following traits still found among the Sebei: (1) age-sets (though they were then non-cycling), (2) individual family homesteads, (3) extraction of upper incisors, (4) absence of any tabu against women handling cattle, and (5) absence of hereditary chieftancy. He believes (on the basis of word borrowing) that these people took over from Cushitic neighbors the practice of circumcision for both sexes, the tabu on eating fish, and the cycling pattern of age-sets. (Ehret, 1971:36)

At about the time of Christ, Ehret argues, the Southern Nilotes were in the Western Highlands of Kenya, along with Bantu who came from the south and Cushite remnants, inhabiting the area between Mount Elgon and Lake Victoria and elsewhere. It was at this time that iron and humped cattle were introduced.

> The pre-Southern Nilotes who were spread over so large an area of East Africa at the beginning of the Christian era were both herders and cultivators. As vocabulary attributable to late pre-Southern Nilotic indicates, they kept cattle including humped breeds, goats, and donkeys. They branded their cattle, and they knew of at least two East African grains, sorghum and eleusine. Evidence is lacking, however, that they planted either bananas or root crops.
>
> By the end of late pre-Southern Nilotic times they knew of iron, but it seems improbable that they ever made use of the iron hoe.... [Ehret, 1971:44]

During the latter part of this period, at least, they were collecting honey and making beer but probably acquired the cylindrical beehive from the Bantu.

> The proto-Southern Nilotes had, among other such items, the large oval shield still used today, cowries, copper for rings, pots, and at least one kind of

---

3. Recent archeological evidence from Norasura (Odner, 1972:77) indicates that cows were milked and that agriculture probably was practiced. The finds are dated at between 900 and 400 B.C. (Odner, 1972:72).

leather sack. In their subsistence practices they made use of their cattle's
blood: there was a proto-Southern Nilotic word for the special kind of arrow
used to bleed cattle. [Ehret, 1971:44-47]

The ancestral Kalenjins, he feels, were influenced by the Southern Cushites in the area, as well as by the Bantu; their culture was formulated in the
Western Highlands of Kenya, and they spread into the Elgon area at the
expense of Southern Cushites and other Nilotes between 400 and 1000 A.D.
The Masai, descendants of Eastern Nilotes, entered the area rather late,
borrowed from and absorbed many of the Southern Nilotes, and expanded
early in the present millenium to push back and break up Kalenjin strength.
The closely related Karamojong and Luo expanded southward much later,
pushing through Uganda and west of Mount Elgon to reach the shores of
Lake Victoria just prior to European penetration of the area.

This history has several salient and relevant aspects: it gives great antiquity
to the basic and central feature of Kalenjin-Southern Nilotic culture; it
expresses the identification of this culture with the drier highlands of eastern
Africa to which it was a fundamental adaptation, and it expresses the reality
of a basic territoriality in the constant conflicts that might otherwise be seen
as mere raiding or sport. It perhaps pays inadequate attention to the adaptive
character of the culture, which Murdock has forcefully expressed. This last
point is given documentation, not only for the Sebei, but for other African
peoples in studies of the Turkana-Jie (Gulliver, 1955), and the Arusha-Masai
(Gulliver, 1963), the Tumbuka (Murdock, 1959:302), the Sukuma (Malcolm, 1953:44-45), and the Hehe (Winans, 1965).

Though the economic commitment is truly ambivalent, the social commitment among the Kalenjin tribes is stronger toward the livestock sector
than toward farming; livestock in general and cattle in particular have greater
and more dramatic involvement in the social and ritual life than do land and
crops. Of all the Southern Nilotes, the Sabaot Kalenjins are unique in that
they have become involved with the cultivation of plantains, which they
have clearly obtained from their Bantu neighbors.

The fact that most of the Dorobo and other remnant hunting and
gathering groups occupied many of the forest uplands and mountain areas of
East Africa suggests that the Mount Elgon area also contained such populations. There is no evidence of any such remnant, however, as John Roscoe
discovered as early as 1919 (Roscoe, 1924:85-86), nor of any such influences on the specifics of Sebei culture.

Matters are not quite so simple with respect to the existence of Cushitic
influences. The architectural form (see Chapter 3), of rectangular, sod roofed
houses found high on the mountain, in the area called *Masop,* is similar to
that found among the remnant Southern Cushites in Tanzania; it is so
outstandingly different, and so much more elaborate, than the houses found
elsewhere among the Nilotes that it is difficult not to regard it as a remnant
element of this old Cushitic culture. To be sure, there is a good environmental reason for the persistence of this tradition, for the tightly-sealed

low-roofed houses shared nightly by people and livestock retain warmth in the extremely cold nights at this high altitude. The Sebei say that the flat-roofed houses formerly were found on the escarpment and disappeared only in very late prehistoric times. The first Europeans to reach Sebei did not report houses of the flat-roofed type but reported that "their houses, however, are quite different, being round instead of oblong [in contrast to the Wa-kuavi, or agricultural Masai of Lake Baringo], and made of strong wickerwork plastered inside with mud, and having a nearly flat roof covered with earth." (Ravenstein, 1891:202)

It also seems likely that the irrigation systems found sporadically in East Africa are a remnant of this old culture, the more particularly in that the Pokot and Marakwet, who use them, claim they found the system in operation when they arrived in their present territory (Hennings, 1951:202). But of such works I found no evidence in present Sebei, either on the ground or in their tradition. I think we may say that the Sebei have been little influenced by this ancient tradition and that, despite their partial retention of this old architectural form, this absence of Cushitic influence applies to the people of Masop as well as to those of the escarpment.

The existence of house pits (and other earthworks) called "Sirikwa holes," which are identified with a recurrent mythic reference by Kalenjin to a departed people called Sirikwa, are identified by some with the Cushites. The Sebei have a widely told tale of a diaspora from Sebei in some past period, as well as a clan called Kapsirikwa, and these two are sometimes linked by informants; thus J. M. Weatherby, for instance, believes the archeological features to be linked with the flat-roofed houses and the diaspora story, giving evidence of an ancient population (Weatherby, 1964). J. E. G. Sutton (1964, 1966), on the basis of more extensive examination of the archeological evidence, expresses skepticism about this hypothesis and is supported by data from a recent excavation made on the eastern edge of Mount Elgon (Chapman, 1966).

THE DYNAMICS OF SEBEI PROTOHISTORY

Our major interest in Sebei history has to do with the dynamic process of adaptation to the variant environmental aspects of modern times. While the Sebei are not notably historically minded, there is adequate evidence in accounts of clan migrations and recent wars and raids to piece together a reasonable reconstruction of the late prehistoric period.

In the eighteenth century, the Sabaot tribes occupied the whole of Mount Elgon, utilizing with variant emphases the old Kalenjin dual economy of livestock and grains; by the beginning of the nineteenth century, if not earlier, they were pressed from all quarters. They were subject to constant raiding by people the Sebei identify as Masai[4] and their Kalenjin relatives,

---

4. i.e., Maa-speaking peoples, presumably the "Uasin-Gishu Masai."

the Nandi, which had the effect of reducing the Sebei population and creating extreme hardships. The attacks were augmented by the action of other Nilotes from the north, particularly the Karamojong, and later the Sebei kinsmen, the Pokot. Meanwhile, the Bantu peoples (presumably in response to Luo pressure) began pushing from the south. There were twin results from this pressure; the Sebei adopted the cultivation of plantains (very likely giving in return the practice of male circumcision), and they were pushed out of most of the moister area, a process that was continuing at the advent of European overrule.

When Sebei are asked about their origins, either they have nothing to say or they take the mythic view that they are descendants of Masop, the mountain personified as the son of the first being.

The myth is a simple genealogical charter, expressing the relationship among the several Kalenjin tribes, and the closer one among tribes within the Sabaot group, all descended from a personified representation of Mount Elgon, Musobo, the son of the original prophet, Kingo. I have grave doubts that this is an old myth; no old men ever told it to me, despite frequent

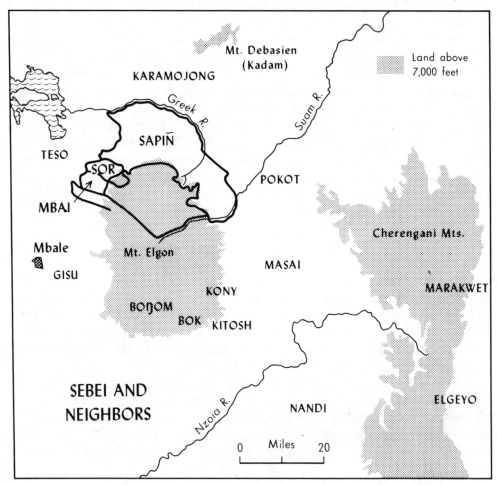

inquiries, but I heard it in political speeches and was told parts of it by younger, politically oriented men. It is also current among the Kony (Were, 1967a: 19-20). The summary in Figure 1 is adapted from a political tract designed to assert the Sebei's right to Mount Elgon.

When a Sebei is asked about the genealogy of his clan, he normally starts with the eponymous founder and his several "sons," who are the eponymous founders of its several lineages; he then traces descent to himself and others of the clan. He sometimes embellishes this genealogical record with place names and movements, and this, more than anything else, gives us a sense of Sebei history. For two or three generations prior to his own, he will be able to give the age-set of his ancestors and may be able to add such details as why they moved and the situation upon their arrival at the present location. In the process, we get some sense of origins, migrations, wars, and the circumstances of the late prehistoric period.[5] I should add, however, that these genealogies do not come tripping off the tongues of even the best informants on the subject; they are in varying degrees inadequately remembered and reconstructed with difficulty.

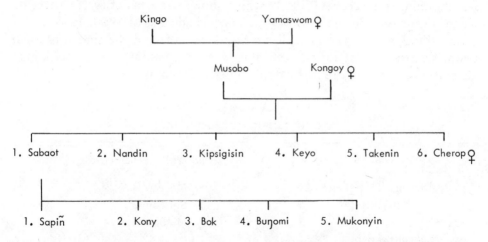

Figure 1. Genealogical Myth of Sebei Origins. *Source:* Adapted from *Memorandum Submitted by the Sebei Kok Committee to the Commission of Inquiry in Bugisu District* (mimeographed, circa 1960).

Perhaps the most satisfactory in terms of coherence and detail was the genealogy given to me for the Kapsombata clan, a large clan that settled in Chema, has a village named after it as a result of that settlement, and was well represented in Sasur, our farming village. The following account was given me in 1961 by Mukware, a Maina II man. His information suggests that the invasion of the Chema area of Sebei must have begun in Nyonki times and continued through the Maina period (i.e., lasted from the 1870s to the 1890s).

> Sombata, the eponymous founder, came from Sengwer in the Cherengani Hills of the Elgeyo District in Kenya, where a clan of that name still lives. He

---

5. Were (1967a) reports similar diversity of origin among the clans of Abaluyia.

was of Kaplelaich pinta, which means he was born in the first quarter of the nineteenth century. The Sombata clan left, for reasons unknown, travelling south of Mount Elgon through the lands of the Kony and Bok and settled in a place called Simotwet ap Kobugosa, in what later became South Bugisu. At that time, there were no Gisu people on the slopes of Elgon. The Bagisu started pushing, however, so Sombata moved to Budadiri in North Bugisu, leaving some clan members "who have now become Bagisu." With continued pressure from the Bagisu, Sombata, or by now certainly his sons, went on to Butadinga Hill near Siroko, west of present Sebei territory.

Chemongoyi, one of Sombata's grandsons, was the first to settle in the Chema area, moving from Legene where his father Chemon lived. The Kapsombata were the second of the Mbai clans to enter this area, which was then Sor territory. The Kapsombata clan came in great numbers and fought the Kabunga clan, who left, and the Kapsombata took their land. Many other clans scattered. The people from Mbai brought plantains into the area; before that, the crops were millet and sorghum.

The Kapsombata clan, in its migrations from the Cherengani Hills to Sebei via the southern side of Mount Elgon, was accompanied by other clans, including the Kapchesi, Kapchai, and Kapkoykoy. I obtained outline histories on about sixty clans (Table 1) which show that a majority (68 percent) claim origins outside the territory the Sebei claimed as of 1900. Table 1 also shows the close ties with the Elgeyo-Marakwet area and the spread of Mbai peoples eastward. The longest genealogical record I obtained went back nine generations, but there are many doubtful elements in it.

TABLE 1
Place of Origin of Sebei Clans

From outside Sebei		From within Sebei territory	
Cherengani-Sengwer	19	Mbai[b]	9
North Bugisu	5	Sor/Sapiñ	2
Bok	3	Masop	4
Bukedi/Bagwere	2		
Other[a]	3		
Totals	32		15

[a]Baringo, Debasien, and "beyond Busia."

[b]Including territory west of present Sebei that Sebei claim had been theirs.

Data recorded by Sebei clerks interviewing clan elders.

We turn next to a consideration of military conflicts. J. M. Weatherby (1962a) has published a paper on Sebei warfare based upon discussions with Sebei informants. He indicates there were six Nandi "wars" between 1850 and 1904, two Masai conflicts (1820 and 1850), two Pokot "wars" (1830 and 1869), and six Karamojong "wars" (1830-94). Whether or not his details are accurate, his material emphasizes the fact that throughout the nineteenth century the Sebei were repeatedly harassed by the pastoral peoples on their northern and eastern flanks. He errs in the false specificity of his dating and in treating the raiding patterns as wars in the sense known to Western society; these people were after cattle rather than territory, which does not mean that the harassment had no geopolitical effects. We know that the Sebei abandoned their use of the plains north of Mount Elgon as a result of the raids, retreating to the relative safety of the mountains, and for a time also abandoned the Kabruron area on the north face of the mountain. Pokot raiding (which is virulent today) did not often occur in early times, because the Pokot and Sebei recognized their close relationship; the Karamojong, Nandi, and Uasin-Gishu Masai were the more insistent and virulent attackers.

Military actions in the western and southern sectors (which Weatherby unaccountably does not discuss) were more important in the geopolitical sense. The Gisu, Teso, and Kitosh were after land and not cattle; i.e., were expansionist (LaFontaine, 1959:11). Fighting with the Gisu was started, one Chumo man told me, "by our fathers and grandfathers." Another said, "the Gisu were more in numbers and managed to push the Sebei back bit by bit." The pressure from the south began to be felt by the Sebei in Nyikeao times (mid-nineteenth century), when they were at a place the Sebei call Simotwet ap Kobugusu on the Mananjwa River on the southern face of Elgon. The pitched battles of the late nineteenth century took place on the plains near the present site of the town of Siroko. One informant concluded his description as follows: "The Gisu came as far as Amagol and wanted to occupy that area, but the Kaptui, Kapkedya, Kamnurongo, and some of the other clans around there fought them and drove them back. This was from Nyonki to Maina times [from the 1860s to the 1880s]." Were (1967a: *passim*) documents a similar relationship between the Gisu and the Sebei but puts the clashes somewhat earlier.

Two things were happening: the Sebei were acquiring cultigens and associated agricultural techniques from their Bantu neighbors and, in the process, must have become increasingly populous. At the same time, the Gisu were exploiting contiguous territories and were also becoming more numerous, undoubtedly at a greater rate since they had better control of the necessary agricultural techniques, and were expanding farther and farther into the well-watered Mount Elgon area by means of military action. Having become plantain cultivators under the tutelage of their enemies, with whom they also intermarried, the Sebei seem to have fallen back in two stages. First, they retreated to the Kigule-Legene area on the present Gisu-Sebei boundary on the western escarpment; a generation later, they responded to the continuing pressure by moving on to the north slope, bringing with them their newly acquired agricultural arts. Here they must have been received with mixed feelings. On the one hand, they brought new cultivation techniques well suited to the area and added numbers that strengthened the Sebei against the pastoralists' raiding. On the other, they competed for the available resources.

A second threat developed in the west in the form of the agriculturalized Teso, who, according to Were (1967a:53), arrived in the area early in the eighteenth century. The Teso, an Eastern Nilotic group related to the

Karamojong, had become agriculturalists in the well-watered plains north-west of Mount Elgon, across the Siroko River, which had been the western boundary of the Sebei. The Teso, whom the Sebei call Komom, sought to expand their holdings into the lands which, though Sebei territory, remained unoccupied as a result of pastoralists' depradations. These pressures from the west apparently affected the relationships between the Sebei tribes. As these tribes considered themselves one people, a fight between tribes was not considered a war, yet the following account indicates that internal peace did not always prevail.

> The Mbai people were very proud that they were more numerous than the Sapiñ. Sapiñ women went to buy plantains when there was a shortage of food, for the Mbai were the only people who had bananas. The Mbai wanted to steal these women, so they planned to take things by force: women, pots, sheep and goats, and yams and other food in the fields and the granaries. They came with their women, saying, "The Sapiñ people are very few and we won't mind about them." The Sapiñ people called an alarm, attacked the Mbai, and drove them out so that the pots they had collected fell and were broken and the grass was mowed down by the speed of their going. Many Mbai men were killed, but leaders said not to kill them all, but only to threaten them. If it had been the Karamojong, they would have killed them. Those who killed Mbai couldn't mark the shoulders because they were also Sebei.
>
> I was a boy [late 1890s] and stood on the rocks where I could watch the battle.

Because of my concentration on the Sebei in Uganda, I know less of what was taking place on the south side of the mountain, but the indications are that events there were very similar. Just as the northwest slope is divided between the more pastorally oriented Sapiñ and the thoroughly agricultural Mbai, with the Sor as buffer in between, so, too, on the south there were the pastoral Kony and the plantain growing Bok, with the Boŋom as a third group. Furthermore, the tribes on the south face were also subjected to pressures from the Bantu people we now know as Kitosh. The following narrative of the conflicts in this region is drawn from accounts by Chilla (of Maina III), the father of my interpreter Richard Bomet, and Chilla's friend, Masop arap Kisa (also Maina III) a man of Bok.

> Sebei and Bok are one; their ancestors were one; the grandfather of Sebei and Bok was one. Some sons went south of the mountain and others remained on this side. When we went to Bok, we became farmers and lived mainly on bananas and millet. Then one time the cattle died and the Bok people saved the Kony people who had no food. At that time, there were no Kitosh people; we were alone in the area. The first to raid the Bok were the Nandi. Many people were killed because the Bok had no arrows but only spears and shields while the Nandi had arrows. This one [and he showed me one he had brought] was smeared with poison, but it's all fallen off now; I have kept it to show to my grandsons. My father got it from the Nandi.
>
> After the Nandi had gone, the Masai came. They had spears only. By that time, the Maina were young and ready for fighting and the Masai were driven away. Since then, the Masai have never come back to attack the Bok.

Then the Kitosh came in great numbers, even the women. By this time, we recognized the power of the Kony prophet, Kyonge. The Bok had forts made of mud. The Kitosh said, "We will finish them in an hour." Then Kyonge fell asleep [presumably to have a dream by which he would make a prophesy]. The military leader asked Kyonge, "How will we manage to fight the Kitosh?" Kyonge told them to wait until afternoon, when it would start to rain.

In the afternoon, there was much rain and the men came out of the fort and started fighting. They fought until their spears were broken, and then they used swords. Even now you can find skulls of Kitosh men. I was a child in the fort at this time.

Earlier, before the Masai war, the Kitosh were troublesome and the Bok and Kony sent a man named Soito to make peace with the Kitosh at Kikai's fort. Before peace could be arranged, the young people killed Soito, even though he had been given safe passage. The Bok and the Kony people wanted to get revenge, but they were too few in number, so they asked the Pokot to help them. The Pokot and some Sebei came and attacked Kikai's fort. One Sebei climbed trees and shot people with arrows. The Kitosh had no arrows. After a while, the Sebei shot burning arrows and set the fort on fire. Then the Kitosh people opened the gate, and so all the people were killed except a very few who escaped.

This account involves several separate conflicts, but the one of particular interest was fought with the Kitosh "who came in great numbers — even the women." It is notable that the Kalenjin groups united in their efforts to repel this external threat. In the Kony-Bok relationship, we see also the dual adaptation to pastoralism and farming and the mutual benefit that resulted from it.

The Sebei do not take a heroic stance in their accounts of intertribal warfare. Occasionally they win; occasionally they lose; more often they appear as the victims of predatory raiders who steal their cattle and kill indiscriminately. The general import of their sparse narratives of military operations is that they were on the defensive. One informant says: "We never carry our war to other areas; we just defend our territory." There are repeated accounts of hiding the women, children, and livestock in caves as a protection against raiders, leaving only the young men out to defend themselves. Even today, the Sebei are more raided against than raiding. The younger men on the escarpment have only fear of fighting and no desire or cultural encouragement to do battle against their harassers.

Social changes were also occurring. The Sebei abandoned their brush-enclosed, concentrated settlements (*manyattas*) and scattered over the land. Older informants pointed out the location of such settlements, but historical accounts from the late nineteenth century do not report them. The age-set declined in importance as an element in military activity and social control. The prophets, particularly in the west, acquired additional authority over secular matters and took on the trappings, if not the power, of rulers. Using a ceremony called *chomi ntarastit,* which had not existed before, they instituted a form of community law.

The Sebei suffered periodically from severe famines. These are recorded for modern times (1918, 1933), for the late precontact period (Maina I through Maina III; 1880s and 1890s) and for periods further back in time. These famines, and the resulting fluctuations in the population of the area, have had important implications for the dynamics of Sebei demography. The early importance of this environmental condition appears in accounts of an ancient diaspora associated with the Sirikwa. It is presumably an historic event, but is described with a kind of mythic quality.

> There was a big outflow from Sebei; the people went away to the east, the young men and women. I think it was in Kaplelaich [1825-45] or Nyikeao [1845-65] time; it was before the Gisu came. That was the time the older people were locked in the caves. Very few remained here. They left because of famine. They went by way of a place called Tambul below the Sipi River onto the plains. The women and the old people were left behind and made a great mourning. They mourned their sons and daughters, but those who departed didn't turn back. The first group did not take cattle, but the second did.

Some say those left behind were sealed into caves for their protection but were never released. In 1954, I was importuned to blast open a "cave" (a broken formation that looked like stonework) west of Kapchorwa by men whose clan ancestors were thought to be sealed there and making trouble. Interested in the rituals that they might perform, I induced some workmen to blast the rock. My curiosity was not satisfied, for the rock did not yield and no ceremonials were performed.

Two other events were significant. First, at some time during the 1890s, the Sebei acquired the cultivation of maize, which came to them from the east, preceding the Europeans. It was a very hard kernel grain and was later replaced by better varieties. In 1897, Austin (1903:74) reported: "The numerous spurs and banks of the many mountain torrents... are thickly cultivated with bananas, Indian corn, mtama (or dura), beans, pumpkins, yams and various other foodstuffs...." Maize was not noted by the Frederick Jackson party in 1890.

The second item involves the immigration of a small group of Bagwere onto the western slope of Elgon, which allegedly took place in Nyikeao times. These people are now called Bumachek; they retain Bagwere as their domestic language but all speak Sebei and regard themselves as Sebei. They have adopted many Sebei customs and are much intermarried with Sebei, yet are culturally distinctive (RBE:286-87). There is no evidence of overt hostility between the two ethnic groups, nor are there any data on why these people migrated or how they were received over a century ago.

Let me now summarize these data with a series of general statements that I think they sustain.

1. The Sebei are heirs to a cultural tradition dating back two millennia, in which the basic institutional forms were adapted to the dry plains of East Africa.

2. About two centuries ago, the Sabaot peoples occupied the whole circum-Elgon area, adapting their basically Kalenjin economy to its variant

environments, but retaining their primary interest in livestock and their secondary interest in the cultivation of grains.

3. If at that time there were still either Dorobo or Cushitic people on the mountain, they either disappeared entirely or were absorbed, leaving only the distinctive house type as a visible surviving feature.

4. The Sebei adopted from their neighbors the cultivation of plantains and root crops and the construction of conical thatched-roof houses and became increasingly sedentary in their habits, though never giving up their commitment to livestock.

5. Their relationships with other Kalenjins remained essentially friendly, and people moved back and forth between tribal areas. But as time went on, the Sebei were increasingly subjected to raiding, first by other pastoralists (Uasin-Gishu Masai and Karamojong) and then by Nandi and other Kalenjin neighbors.

6. Pressure from the Bantu (Gisu and Kitosh), who sought land for cultivation and therefore were engaged in territorial expansion, deprived the Sebei of a large sector of highly productive land. Similar pressure from the agriculturalized Teso was successfully repulsed.

7. Gisu pressure had repercussions, as the by now partly Bantuized Sebei fell back, first to the Legene area and then to the north face of the mountain, bringing increased population and new forms of agriculture and architecture, which they had learned from their tormentors. The local Sebei, in turn, scattered farther eastward (or even across the mountains) into areas that had been largely vacated by the continuing depredations of pastoral raiders.

8. These movements spread the cultivation of plantains throughout Sebei territory, thereby extending the sedentarization of the population.

EARLY CONTACTS

The Swahili caravan routes produced the first direct contact between the Sebei and the Western world. For a decade or more before Europeans entered the area, the Swahili had used Sebei as a base camp and provisioning station for caravans seeking ivory and other products of the northern Uganda plains. There is no indication whatsoever that the Sebei were touched by the slave trade. A Maina III informant said:

> The first men to come into Sebei were Swahili. That was when I was about eight or ten years old [i.e., early 1880s]. They came to seek food. They came first to the Kony area. They brought thin wires to trade. I took flour, bananas, and yams to trade for wire. The Swahili couldn't get enough food in Kony so they came to Sebei.
>
> The Sor of Cheptui attacked the Swahili and tried to get their cattle. The Swahili didn't want war. Some people were killed because the Swahili had guns. The Sebei thought the Swahili were traveling along like women with nothing but hollow things like a bamboo pole, so they attacked them and learned that the hollow things were guns.

The Swahili established a permanent provisioning base in the area, first at Atar, then farther west at Kapchorwa, later at Sasur, and finally in Legene. The Sebei bought iron wire and "americani" cloth from them in exchange for food. "One piece of wire extending from the finger to the elbow was exchanged for about three gallons of millet flour." The relationships were mostly cordial over the years; they called one another uncle. The first Sebei woman to marry a Swahili man has been remembered in a song. The Swahili stayed on and later helped the Sebei fight the Baganda but ultimately moved their base to Teso.

The first known contact of Europeans with Sebei was the expedition of F. J. Jackson and E. Gedge in February 1890. Of this visit, the following account has the richest available description of the Sebei.

> On January 29th, Mr. Jackson left the Angalul with a view to obtaining a fresh supply of provisions in the district of Save, which lies to the north of Mount Elgon, and of proceeding across the very top of that ancient volcano on his return journey to Mumiya's. An ascent of about 2000 feet (from 4372 to 6346 feet) brought the explorers from the northern foot of the mountain to Save, the inhabitants of which dress like the Wa-kuavi. Their houses, however, are quite different, being round instead of oblong, and made of strong wickerwork plastered inside with mud, and having a nearly flat roof covered with earth. They cultivate wimby, pumpkins, bananas, yams, and a small species of sweet potato. Honey is plentiful and the wealth in cattle, sheep, and goats appears to be considerable. But notwithstanding these great natural advantages of their present abode, the inhabitants talked of removing themselves elsewhere, as they were continually being harassed by Masai and Wa-Nandi. Even whilst the caravan was present in the district the latter invaded its western portion, carrying off some 200 head of cattle, besides killing a lot of people and burning their villages. Iron wire are the only barter goods which are demanded by these people, and ivory they decline to part with altogether, excepting for cattle. [Ravenstein, 1891:202]

Jackson, in his reminiscences (1930), gives us no information on the Sebei, nor does his companion Gedge in an unpublished diary (Gedge, n.d.). The late H. B. Thomas, the noted historian of the early colonial period of Uganda, kindly supplied me with the excerpts from this diary, as well as some photographs taken by Gedge.[6] Though the party remained on the escarpment from February 4 to 13, 1890, Gedge records little about the Sebei. His entry for the 5th reads:

> Natives brought in fair quantity of food and some plantains. Beads are no use here but they take cowries and iron wire. The Country has been raided lately by the Masai & Nandi who have cleared off nearly all the cattle, besides killing a good number & burning the villages. I wish they would come while we are here. They'd catch it hot.

On the 9th, he notes:

> Report in middle of night that the Nandi have come on a raiding expedi-

---

6. Among these photographs, some show the use of caves but have little detail; one of a young man is reproduced here (Plate I:1).

tion ... all the women, cattle, etc. have been cleared out & stowed themselves away.

On the 10th, these reports are confirmed:

> A message that attack had commenced on the villages ... The raiders were
> Nandi about 1,000 strong ... and had ... killed many Save people, burnt
> villages & carried off about 300 cattle. Seeing us encamped here prevented
> them attacking this side. The Save people caught one of the Nandi up a tree
> and killed him, ... stuck as full of arrows as a pin cushion besides subsequent
> mutilation. These Save people must have a miserable time of it. ... and will
> soon be exterminated. They have no unity — it is everyone for himself.

The second known contact with Sebei was by C. W. Hobley (1929:94-95),
who made a circuit of the mountain in 1896. He gives us no information on
the area.

Chilla, a Maina III informant, gives an account of the first contact with
Europeans as follows. (In terms of dates, this could well be Jackson and
Gedge, though he specifically speaks of only one man.)

> Before they made the route through the Suk country, one white man came
> into this area. He spent the night near the present Ngenge bridge on the upper
> side. The next morning he went on to Ngenge and shot buffalo and different
> kinds of game and brought horns. As soon as he left, the rinderpest attacked
> the game. The game spread the rinderpest to the cattle. I was not then yet
> initiated, being about thirteen or fourteen years old. My father lost very
> many cattle. The rinderpest spread as far as Kenya. The first Maina had been
> initiated [late 1880s], and it was when the first of them were being married
> that the cattle began to die. The Swahili people came in here before Maina
> started initiating. The Swahili brought cattle to trade for ivory, and there
> were raids and the Swahili were killed. Those who survived brought the white
> man through the Boita gate. They went to a place called Chesumwo by the
> Atar River. There was just one white man and his *askaris.* By this time,
> Maina III had been initiated. This is now the second white man to come here.

This must be Herbert H. Austin, who accompanied Lieutenant Colonel
J. R. L. Macdonald in the important and controversial Juba Expedition into
northern Uganda and Kenya, was involved in the Nubian rebellion, and
established a camp and provisioning base in Sebei which lasted from November 1, 1897 to December 20, 1898. Austin writes:

> On November 1 we experienced a long and trying day [climbing the escarp-
> ment] before we reached the populated district of Save, as the porters found
> the stiff climb almost beyond their powers in their present weak state. The
> higher we ascended, the more glorious became the view and fresher the air,
> and the more charming our surroundings; but we had little leisure to enjoy
> these, as our immediate desire was to get everybody into camp before dark.
> Eventually we reached the Swahili traders' stockade, the occupants of which
> came out to meet us in spotlessly clean flowing robes, which formed a
> marked contrast to the ragged, bedraggled appearance of our hard-worked
> porters. Osborn had already pitched camp on the opposite bank of the stream
> to that on which the stockade existed, and, looking down from the higher

ground on to our camp, I thought I had seldom seen so lovely a spot, and in truth I had seen many a lovely one in Europe, Asia, Africa, and America before that day. The Swahili traders supplied us with three and a half bags of flour the same evening for our weary men, and I commenced negotiations with them regarding the purchase of some 600 bags more for the expedition. [Austin, 1903:72-73]

Austin describes the Sebei as follows:

The natives in many respects are not unlike the Wa-Kikuyu, as they smear their bodies over with the same chocolate-coloured clay, liberally mixed with fat, and work their hair into the similar mop-head style. Their ears are, however, not distended to quite so great an extent, and they wear few ornaments beyond a little iron chain and iron wire round their necks and wrists, and perhaps an ivory bracelet in addition round their biceps, whilst a leather belt, adorned with cowrie shells round the waist, is also very generally worn by the young bloods. A small goat-skin, well cured and greased, and soft as chamois leather, is thrown jauntily over one shoulder, whilst in his hand the young warrior carries either a long-handled spear with a small blade or bow and arrows, and a long, narrow, oval-shaped shield of thick hide.

The elder women wear two hides, and are satisfied with a ring or two of iron wire round the neck, and similar ornaments round the wrists. They are great smokers, and, like the elderly ladies of Kavirondo, strut about with pipes, consisting of small earthenware bowls, to which are attached long wooden stems.

. . . The young unmarried girls wear a very simple costume, consisting of a ring or two of iron wire round the neck and a small leather apron 8 to 9 inches square, or a fringe of beads, not unlike rosaries, of the same size, which depends in front from a girdle round the waist, whilst a similar, though somewhat larger, covering of hide falls behind. In the Save district, where we now were, beads appeared to be absolutely never worn by the natives except a few of a black variety, which seemed to take the place of iron wire . . . [Ibid., pp. 75-76].

The total Juba Expedition, according to Austin, involved 7 Europeans, 27 Sikhs, 69 Sudanese, 482 Swahili, 32 Masai, 3 Indians and 43 "Sudanese women and followers." There were two columns in the north, with one European and more than 200 others left at the Sebei base. The Sapiñ area was inadequate to supply such a massive population, and Austin began to tap the Mbai area.

By dint of long and slow bargaining we had succeeded in obtaining some twenty bags of flour [in Sapiñ] for dispatch to the Marich garrison, so I decided to split up our camp next day at Save. Tracy and Osborn, therefore, proceeded on the 9th with a party of some thirty-five men to Mbai, carrying trade goods and so on in order to open out a market; this proved an unqualified success in course of time, and from here, at various periods during the next year, some 4,000 loads of banana flour, chiefly, were obtained. [Ibid., p. 77]

The following July, Austin returned to the Sebei base from the west (through Bugisu) and describes Mbai as follows:

Many natives thronged out to meet us as we passed through endless banana groves, and the difference between them and those we had lately been amongst was most striking. Instead of the poverty-stricken looking crowd we had become accustomed to, these men were smartly got up, their bodies nicely oiled and dyed, their hair neatly worked, and altogether bearing a sleek, well-groomed appearance. Cowrie shells were conspicuous everywhere, thanks to the quantities expended by Tracy in the purchase of banana flour. So popular were these little shells that one cowrie purchased about 1.5 pounds of flour, or, in other words, one load of cowries, numbering about 12,000, purchased close on 300 loads [50 to 60 pounds] of flour. [*Ibid.,* pp. 131-32]

All this commerce was not accomplished without conflict: Both Austin's account and those given to me by informants agree that it was the Sor who objected to the demand for food, sought to stop the passage of the caravans, brought about several skirmishes in which a number of Sebei and one or two of the Juba Expedition askaris were killed, and ultimately capitulated — only again to raise difficulties as the pressure of these constant purchases began to tell on the Sebei. Toward the end, the expedition found not only that the prices of goods became higher, but also that the Sebei were increasingly reluctant to trade at all. One informant said:

As soon as they left, there was an outbreak of famine. There were no rains. This is called the famine of Maina III. The famine lasted for two years [1898-99]. The Europeans stayed for only one year. On the third year, when rain came, the Chepilat were circumcised.

This must have been 1901. The following informant's statement must refer to the patrol initiated by Sub-Commissioner William Grant, together with the local commander of the King's African Rifles, in 1902 (see below).

After the people of Siron went away, other Europeans (very many with lots of porters) came through the Kapturu Gate, bringing many, many cows with them. They settled at Burkoyen, or Boi. As they had no food, their porters spread all over Sebei, snatching sheep and goats and slaughtering them. These people are called Kapchang (locusts). After about two or three days, they returned the way they came. As soon as they left, the Baganda people arrived.

The Baganda brought the Sebei into the administrative orbit in one of the many bizarre chapters of African colonial history. The Juba Expedition was not concerned with administering or "pacifying" the Sebei; it was merely exploiting its resources for its own ulterior purposes. When it left, as an informant said, it left for good. It had been, by the standards of the time, a mild experience in Afro-European contact with relatively little bloodshed and animosity on either side. The same cannot be said for what followed.

The British administration, after the general disturbances of the Sudanese mutiny, utilized Muganda general Semei Lwakilenzi Kakunguru to bring the northeastern portions of Uganda under control. In the spring of 1900,

Kakunguru set up headquarters in the Mbale area and, with a large army of Baganda followers, proceeded to bring Bugisu under control. Though the British officially took over direct control in 1902, Kakunguru continued to exercise much power. In December 1902 William Grant, with a company of King's African Rifles under a Lieutenant Tidmarsh, patrolled as far as Sebei. Kakunguru with 204 guns (an indication of his still considerable following) accompanied them. (Thomas, 1937:134) In January 1904, Kakunguru was made *saza* (county) chief and his domain included Sebei.

Yunusu Wandera, the first appointed chief of Sebei, describes Kakunguru as "a tall, slim, very tough man. Had he been a European, he would have been a famous person, like Churchill. He was clever and wise . . . a man who was brave and knows how to judge. Even today in Sebei we use some of his knowledge." But of his rule, Wandera says, "When Kakunguru sent out his officers, they were very fierce people. Many of the Sebei ran away as far as Pokot country. People had to carry loads. Even when Mwanga [the last Muganda chief in Sebei] was county chief, he made people carry his children."

One informant described matters thus:

> When the Baganda came they settled just east of Kapchorwa at a place called Kikwopmoria. There were no Europeans among this group. The Sebei said, "Let's fool these people and take them to a bushy place so they can't steal the cattle," but the Baganda nevertheless took our cattle to Karamoja and exchanged them for donkeys. They needed these donkeys because the people refused to be porters for the Baganda. Then they started attacking the people and managed to kill many because they had guns. These people were called Kakunguru and the officer in charge was called Katikiro.
>
> The Kaptanya people fought them every day so they moved into the heart of the Kaptanya *saŋta* and went on fighting. One man, Sendet Kapyesengich, killed a Muganda; his mother had been shot by the Baganda. When these people were still there, a European officer came and moved them to Kapchorwa and built a big fort there. They stayed in Kapchorwa until the officer returned and appointed chiefs at Sebei.

The depredation of the Baganda not only caused Sebei to flee and subjected the remainder to humiliation and bloodshed, it also considerably disrupted their institutions. It appears that no circumcision took place between the Chepilat (*circa* 1901) and the Chumo I (1909 or 1910) when the Baganda had been superseded by British officials. The influence of the prophets also declined. The prophet Matui had inspired the refusal of the Chema people to withhold food from Austin, but we do not hear of any later action, and by the 1920s Matui was without power or function. The erosion of the role of prophet lessened the sense of Sebei unity, always tenuous at best. When the British colonial administration took over direct control, they were viewed as protectors rather than conquerors, and by the beginning of World War I a number of Sebei enlisted in the King's African Rifles and served in distant parts of Uganda.

RECENT HISTORY

One of these soldiers was Yunusu Wandera (Djumo I). He was appointed a chief in Sebei in 1927, serving under a Muganda County chief, Daudi Musoke, whose headquarters were in Budadiri (Bugisu). In 1934, Wandera was made *saza* chief of the newly created Saza Sebei. He was retired 1948 and replaced by Aloni Muzungyo, who remained *saza* chief of Sebei, except for a brief period in the late 1950s, until Sebei became an independent district in 1962.

Ironically, the British presence did not protect the Sebei from either of the two kinds of external harassment that had historically been their lot — the depredation of pastoralists' raids and the pressure from their agricultural neighbors.

Cattle raids have been a continued scourge for the Sebei, abating for a while but increasing in intensity in recent years. My first visit to the plains early in 1954 was to observe a conference between the commissioners of Bugisu, Karamoja, and West Suk (Kenya) districts, who were seeking to bring together tribal representatives and formulate something that could be called an amnesty. My chief impression of the meeting was that of watching three captive cocks, held captive awaiting the cook, establish their pecking order, just as the three tribes under colonial domination were concerned with theirs. I also remember the Bugisu District commissioner or one of his aides quietly expressing the bureaucratically improper wish that the Sebei would more aggressively take matters in their own hands. (As recently as 1972, the issue of raids was presented to President Idi Amin as a major problem during his brief helicopter stop at Kapchorwa.) In 1962, when Uganda acquired its independence from the British, many Sebei, fearing that the Pokot of Kenya would take advantage of their celebration to launch a massive raid, established a military bivouac as a protective measure. A mimeographed document, *A Report from Chepsukunya Police on 2/8/61*, (anonymous, 1961?), prepared by the Sebei, analyzed records of 116 raids between April 1957 and June 1961 in which 11 Sebei were killed, 4,548 cattle were stolen, 115 small stock and 4 donkeys taken, one house burned and maize stolen. (By 1972, the raiding had so escalated that the entire plains area from Chepsukunya to Greek River, nearly 50 square miles, had been evacuated. At least two of my Kapsirika friends had been speared to death, most of the cattle and other stock taken, and the population either moved to the shadow of the police post with the remnants of their herds or dispersed over the mountain. There were no signs of human occupation where the village of Kapsirika, one of the two communities analyzed in detail in this report, had once flourished in the middle of this now abandoned stretch.)

The pressure of the Gisu was no longer military, but it continued to be effective. History and geography conspired to give them a central place within the political structure established by the colonial government, which above all gave them access to the schooling necessary to train the cadres of chiefs and other officials. Gisu pressure took three basic forms:

(1) Infiltration into Sebei territory generally, so that within it they constituted 27 percent of the population by 1959. Sebei attitudes contributed to this; they loaned, rented, sold, or just allowed occupancy of the land. The Gisu, still more clearly oriented to farming and pressed for adequate resources, simply took advantage of the situation.

(2) Erosion along the edges of traditional Sebei territory and successful annexation of the western and southern sectors. The area west of present Sebei District toward which the Gisu were pushing before the Europeans arrived was used chiefly for grazing and hunting, like the rest of the Sebei plains, and was largely unoccupied. A document prepared anonymously by Sebei living in these areas, *Memorandum of Sebei People in North Bugisu to the Minister of Local Government* (Entebbe, 1960?), describes how the Gisu took over.

> At that time there were some Sebei in Muyembe ... One [District Commissioner] Bugisu called Perryman requested [the Sebei] to allow him to bring some Bagisu ... to live together with the Sebei in Muyembe ggombolola because there were few Sebei there and because the Bagisu in Bududa ... were overcrowded ... The Sebei rejected the D.C.'s request because they knew that if the Bagisu came, there would not be enough room for grazing their cattle and cultivating their food and the game would die off quickly ... After few years the Bagisu came, and the Sebei kept peace as the D.C. instructed them.... Many Bagisu immigrated to Muyembe with the purpose of robbing land from the Sebei by force, using the administrative powers.... After Sebei County had been created, many Sebei ... moved to Sebei [County] because of the bad treatment they received. ...

(3) Harassment and deprivation of the Sebei through political and social institutions. This technique took place on two levels; in the local areas where the Gisu managed to obtain the administrative posts and at the district government level. Regarding the former, the same document lists a number of specific complaints, including the following:

Not allowing the Sebei to circumcise their girls; imprisoning, fining, and giving corporal punishment to those who did.

Taking over the chieftancies.

Refusing to teach Sebei children in the schools.

Not giving the Sebei time to pay fines imposed by the court, but attaching their property, which was "sold to Bagisu chiefs."

Tricking Sebei by leaving stolen cattle in front of their houses so that when these were "found" the owner of the house would be severely beaten and even imprisoned.

Torturing suspects or persons who had not paid their taxes quickly by making them stand six or more hours in the sun, with the result that one man and three women died.

On the district level, the council was dominated by the Gisu. A Sebei Kok Committee document, *Memorandum Submitted by the Sebei Kok Com-*

mittee to the Commissioner of Inquiry in Bugisu District (1960?) sets forth a number of grievances, including failure to provide schools, medical facilities, and roads; job discrimination at all levels; judicial discrimination particularly with respect to land cases; and numerous others.

The growing concern over internal control was reinforced by the realization that the imminent departure of the British would leave the Sebei unprotected. In 1959, the Sebei leaders made demands for changes in the organization and administration of Bugisu District. Though British officials told me privately that they felt the Sebei complaints were justified, the council did not make the changes, and in 1960 most of the twelve Sebei members boycotted the Bugisu District Council. That November, with still no action on the part of the government, the Sebei blocked the road just east of Sipi in an act of civil disobedience. Several leaders were arrested and jailed for this act but were released the following January. These actions, together with the political influence exerted by A. Y. Chemonges in Kampala, led to the establishment of a separate Sebei District early in 1962, just a few months before Uganda became independent. Sebei's own Uhuru (Independence Day) was observed with a massive celebration in Kapchorwa, which became the district headquarters.

SOME GENERALIZATIONS ON SEBEI HISTORY

The old ex-*saza* chief Wandera once said to me, "The Sebei are easy to convert to new fashions — not like other tribes." He is absolutely right. This remarkable feature of Sebei culture expresses itself in matters both large and small. When Sir Frederick Jackson described the Sebei, he said they had mudded coiffures; twenty years later, the missionary ethnologist John Roscoe reported no such thing; the custom had been abandoned as a result of Baganda attitudes. I found that the dress of the Sebei, aside from reflecting affluence, expressed generation changes: skin robes; old blankets; *kanzu* (man's white robe), khaki shirts and shorts, slacks and shirt. In Benet, I saw a field riddled with the burrows of some species of ground rat. I was told that rats had become plentiful since the Sebei had stopped eating them as a result of missionary disapproval. These early shifts make it understandable that Edgerton found less consistency in Sebei responses to his questions than in responses from any other tribes studied in the Culture and Ecology Project (RBE:122), including even the Kamba whom Symmes C. Oliver (1965) found so culturally uncommitted.

Lest we think such inconsistency involved only trivial things, attention should be called to the matter of the prophets. The Sebei prophet, standing at the juncture between the organization of the secular society and the religious belief system, organized both ceremonial and mundane affairs. The last great prophet, Matui, ceased to function in the decades before he died, and the Sebei took no action to resurrect the social role — which they should have done by disinterring his bones so that his spirit could enter one of his clansmen — until twenty-five years had passed.

Chemonges, the most powerful Uganda political leader from the back country until his untimely and mysterious death, once said to me that the Sebei would be the future political leaders of the world because they were peculiarly suited to the political role. I think he was expressing, from a different perspective, the same evaluation that Wandera had made.

The Sebei are heir to an ancient cultural tradition forged in the arid grasslands of East Africa, a social and economic system peculiarly suited to the exploitation of that environment. Over two or more millennia and throughout this vast area, only the Sabaot group, so far as we know, endeavored to adapt this dry grasslands culture to a totally different environment and economy, a wet upland region suitable for the cultivation of plantains. Evidence indicates that the change began with the grandparents or great-grandparents of the senior men I knew. It was underway on the north escarpment of Elgon when Jackson and Gedge and the Baganda entered the scene, bringing new technologies and new institutions and once again changing the course of Sebei history and the very meaning of environment.

Thus, the Sebei were caught in mid-stride, fixed by external events at a time when they were undergoing, or attempting to undergo, a major change in their way of life. They were adapting old institutions to new situations. Thus disengaged from some of their ancient verities, they had not yet become accustomed, let alone committed, to new ones.

Chapter 2
The Environmental Context

Greet me, Masop;
Regrets, coldness of the mountain —
that does not want the fat man,
that does not want the weak man,
that does not want the cowardly man.
Where speaks the merewet?
Where speaks the bird?

From a hymn to Mount Elgon (Masop)

IMPRESSIONS

Mount Elgon is not a mountain to be viewed from the distance. Though it rises more than 10,000 feet above the plains, its great breadth and gradual slope form a flat cone that can rarely be seen from below. Rather, it is a mountain to be on, for it offers vistas of exciting beauty.

One reaches Sebeiland by driving northward from Mbale, the capital of the Eastern Province of Uganda, over undulating land planted in cotton and plantains. After crossing the Siroko River, the road cuts directly to the right just before reaching the sub-county headquarters of Muyembe. Occasionally, glimpses of the higher upland grasses of Mount Elgon are seen but the sheer red cliffs and the waterfalls in the middle distance dominate the view. The summit usually remains obscured in a cover of cloud.

A series of switchbacks up the sheer cliff brings one into Bulegene, formerly Mbai territory but now held by the Gisu. The road continues northward, cutting red gashes in the soil and crossing cold mountain streams as it winds through land heavily cultivated to plantains. Entry into Sebei territory, across the Muyembe River, brings no visual change either in physical landscape or in cultural characteristics. Some three miles farther, another series of switchbacks leads upward from the lower plateau to the escarpment, suddenly displaying the community of Sipi, lying at an elevation of about 6,000 feet, with its scattering of tin-roofed *dukas* (shops) and, just beyond, two of the three waterfalls on the Sipi River, one a sheer drop and

SEBEI COUNTRY
NORTHERN PART OF MT. ELGON

TO UASIN GISHU PLATEAU

GRASS DOV
FOREST ZO

TO SUAM RIVER,
KITALE AND TRANS-NZOIA

KORTEK EL. 9033 FT.

RIWA   BUKWA

CHESOWERI

TO CHERANGANI HILLS

POKOT

KABRURON   MOUNT

TO KACHELIBA
AND KARASUK

GREEK RIVER

BINY

Sundet R.

UPE COUNTY   DRY SEASON   KAPSIRIKA

GRAZING   Cheborom R.

KAMAYINDI

Tabok R.

Ngenge R.

NGENGE   KON

MESOZOIC VOLCANICS INCLUDING
CARBONATES AND SOME BASAL SEDIMENTS

TO MOROTO   CHEPSUKUNYA

ELGON   SEBEI DISTRICT
AGGLOMERATE   PYROXENE GNEISS   Greek R.

KARAMOJA

COUNTRY

Atar R.

0   1   2   3
SCALE   5   10   10   MILES
1   2   3   4   5   10   15   KILOMETE

AN ISOMETRIC
BLOCK DIAGRAM

VERTICAL EXAGGERATION 1:1.67

CONSTRUCTED BY P.W. PORTER AND DRAFTED BY S. HAAS
DEPARTMENT OF GEOGRAPHY, UNIVERSITY OF MINNESOTA
MAY, 1975

KONY   BOK   BONOM

KITOSH GROUPS SOUTH OF THE
MOUNTAIN EXTENDING TO
LAKE VICTORIA

SABAOT GROUPS LIVING ON SOUTH SIDE
OF MT. ELGON

TO SUMMIT AND CRATER OF MT. ELGON
9 MILES, EL. 14,175 FT.

EL. 11,250 FT.

LAKE VICTORIA LIES 75 MILES
TO THE SOUTHWEST

BENET

SASUR AND KAMINGONG

DENSE PLANTAIN CULTIVATION
(NO DATA)

CENTRAL

FOREST

RESERVE

GISU TERRITORY

KAPCHORWA

BUGINYANYA

5700 FT.

KOPTOKOI R.

CHEBONET   SIPI FALLS   SIPI EL. 5939 FT.

SIPI

BULEGENE

TO MBALE

CHEPTUI R.

BUYAGA

CHEPTUI

CHEBONET R.

MUYEMBE

FT.

NORTH BUGISU COUNTY

EL. 3400 FT.

PIAN COUNTY

ALLUVIUM

PRECAMBRIAN BASEMENT COMPLEX UNDIFFERENTIATED ACID GNEISSES

NORTH

PART OF LAKE OKOLITORUM
WHICH DRAINS INTO LAKES
SALISBURY AND KYOGA

FORESTS

PLANTAINS - EACH SYMBOL
EQUALS 16 ACRES

ESCARPMENT

ROAD

POLITICAL BOUNDARY

STUDY AREA

MINOR SETTLEMENT

the other a fan of white water over red rocks. This escarpment is the heartland of the Sebei. Dotted through the banana plantations are round grass-thatched houses and occasionally a rectangular one with a tin roof, while off to the north lie the vast plains.

Behind one of the three spectacular falls on the Sipi River is a deep grotto where the Sebei obtained salt and hid their cattle in times of raids, as they did in many another cave on the mountain. Across a second small stream lies the village of Sasur, the agricultural community of our study. The land seems covered with the rich green plantain. Occasionally, glimpses can be had of red bluffs or of the plains 2,500 feet below, now sere, now touched with a light green, depending upon the season. In the distance, Lake Salisbury shimmers in the last rays of the sun.

The road continues onward, either deeply rutted and muddy or heavy with dust, again depending upon the season. It rounds each spur and cuts back toward the mountain and downward to cross each stream, turning beyond the bridge sharply back to the left and around the next spur in seeming endless repetition. The colors gradually change, the deep greens and reds turning to pastel shades, the grasses and acacia interspersed with cultivated gardens of maize or millet replacing the plantains that are now limited to pockets in the valleys. In color and in line, the mountain recalls repeated scenes from ancient Chinese paintings, reducing man to scale. The plain below is now more often grey than green, with small angular peaks jutting up like rocks from the sea, while in the distance the beautiful and ever-changing shape of Mount Debasien (or Kadam) rises sheer out of the flat plain (Plate II:22). Few houses stand close to the road, but there are occasional groups of shops offering kerosene, soap, razor blades, cigarettes and yardage goods. Kapchorwa, the district headquarters of Sebei, faces north. Except for the whitewashed rocks lining the driveway to the official buildings, Kapchorwa presents a picture of a sleepy African town, busy only when the Sebei District Council meets.

Binyinyi lies eight miles farther; it was our research headquarters at the time of our first visit. From here, mountaineers climb to the summit, up a trail that for the first mile leads past houses, sometimes directly through a compound. At a constant but easy climb, one reaches the forest reserve, where Sebei are no longer allowed to dwell. The path passes Arkak Cave, which was once inhabited by a famous prophet but is now used only by occasional transients, and continues on up the slippery and sloping rock through a *Pygeum* montane (interspersed with tall bamboo) forest to the community of Benet, where the first Masop people can be seen. The trail leads on to the summit past occasional old-fashioned, rectangular, sod-roof houses. Interspersed with forest areas are open grassy downs, which offer glimpses of the treeless summit.

Eastward from Binyinyi along the escarpment, the population has grown more sparse; where plantains formerly gave way to maize, now maize increasingly gives way to bush; and cattle and goats are more frequently seen. The terrain is more rugged, the distance between streams is greater, and the road descends and rises more steeply at each crossing. The view of the plains is dominated by Riwa, the rocky outlier of Mount Elgon to the northeast. Finally, the road rises in a series of switchbacks over a high pass below Korteg Hill and then descends into the Bukwa Valley, again richly cultivated and populous. The road eases off southward to the Kenya border. Here the landscape is largely divided into fields of maize, and these are frequently fenced, for cultivation practices have been influenced by the European farmers of the Kenya highlands.

It is sometimes possible to take a steep and challenging road down from Bukwa through Karasuk to the plains. After passing through flat, thorn-busy country occupied by the Pokot of Kenya, it reaches Greek River and thus returns to Uganda and Sebei territory. These are the Sebei plains, lying between the foot of Elgon and the westward flowing Greek River. They had been empty until just before World War I, when a military post was put at the Greek River crossing, offering a protection that enabled Sebei to reoccupy territory they had abandoned because of the military depredations of the Pokot and Karamojong. A few miles farther on, the narrow track crosses the Sundet River; to the south lies Kapsirika, the pastoral community of our study. The grandeur of Debasien on the north overwhelms the much larger Mount Elgon to the south. A few dozen giraffe, an occasional herd of zebra, and more rarely some eland may be seen. From the road, it is easy to believe this land uninhabited and uncultivated, but an air view displays scattered houses and kraals and herds of cattle, and the bushland is interspersed with plots cultivated in the long straight furrows made by ox-drawn plows. The round houses with thatched roof, similar to those on the escarpment, are subtly different, often not mudded at all, and the workmanship is less elegant, for it is warmer here and the houses are more readily abandoned.

The track continues westward until it reaches the main road extending to the Karamoja, on across the Ngenge River and past the *gombolola* headquarters, where cattle auctions are held twice each month. It then swings southward passing Muyembe and then the turnoff leading to the escarpment, by means of which our earlier ascent to Sebei territory was made.

PHYSIOGRAPHIC ZONES

The lands of the Sebei are readily divided into three major life zones: (1) the highland area lying well above 9,000 feet on Elgon in an area the Sebei call Masop; (2) the plains spreading between the foot of Elgon and the Greek River, with brush and grasslands below 4,000 feet; and (3) the escarpment, the Sebei heartland where most of the population live between the 5,000-foot and 7,000-foot contours. This last zone is diverse and must be divided into three separate regions, the boundaries of which are graded rather than clearly demarcated. The differentials are largely a product of differences in precipitation, from nearly 80 inches to less than 40 inches (see map) as one moves eastward; to some extent, they are also the product of differences in soil and topography.

We must stop to examine the concepts of Masop and Soi, as the Sebei use the terms. Masop has several distinct meanings. It is the name of Mount Elgon and of the personification of that mountain as an ancestor of the Sebei people (and, as Masaba, was adopted by the Gisu). By extension, the inhabited area high on the mountain is also referred to as Masop and the people of that area are called Masopesiyek, even though they are not thought of as a different tribe. Similarly, the plains are referred to as Soi and one occasionally hears the people referred to as Soyisyek. Masop and Soi are also used by the Sebei to mean upward and downward, respectively. A man in Masop who is going to the escarpment will speak of going to Soi, whereas a man travelling from the plains to the inhabited upper reaches would say he is going to Masop. (I have here adopted the term Masop to refer to the inhabited upper reaches, because there is no other easy way to refer to this area without confusion.)

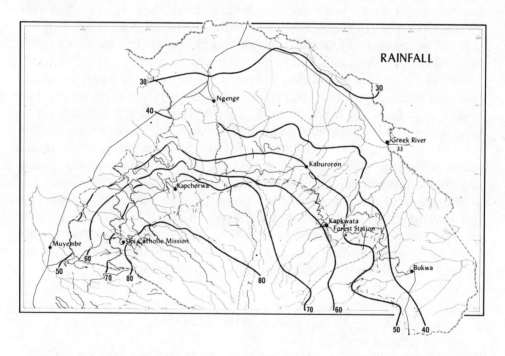

Masop. Before British occupation, the Sebei lived scattered through the forest but were expelled by the colonial administration in order to preserve this cover. They continue to live above the area of thick forest, where large patches of open, grass-covered downs are interspersed with forest areas which, the Sebei claim, are encroaching on the grasslands. The mixed *Pygeum* moist montane forest consists of *Pygeum africanum* and many small evergreen cedars and mahoganies. The canopy is broken and the ground enveloped by a dense understory of ferns and shrubs, while the trees are covered with a tangle of climbing vines. In the drier areas, such as at the community of Benet at 9,500 feet, the *Pygeum* gives way to other forms and ground cover is more sparse. Farther up the northern slope, the forest gives way to a subalpine, herb-rich grassy moorland, in which tree heather competes with *Stoebe kilimandscharica* and grasses, which have been extended by man-made fire and grazing. There are also areas of bamboo forest, either closely massed small-stemmed or more dispersed large-stemmed stands, depending upon the stage in the growth cycle.

The region is often covered with cloud, with a high level of precipitation. The nights are regularly cold and the days frequently so, though when the sun shines, it may be warm and even hot. The area is, however, frost-free.

Fewer than a thousand Sebei live in this area, scattered in dispersed communities between the 9,000- and about 10,000-foot contours, where the open grasslands provide food for their cattle and sheep (the government has forbidden goats) and where they can cultivate. They use a form of house that presumably dates from antiquity (Plate I: 19) and is not found at lower levels, and they are generally more isolated from Western cultural influences. It is a mistake, however, to assume that these people represent some kind of aboriginal Sebei condition, for they have acquired new elements and made many special adaptations to the particularities of their environment (see, for instance, changing women's dress, Plates I: 3-5). Indeed, the retention of their tightly sealed, low-roofed houses, with sectors set aside for their stock, is itself an adaptation to the cold nights and the need for warmth and protection for their animals.

The economy of the region is divided between stock-keeping and gardening, supplemented chiefly by gathering wild honey (which is more important here than elsewhere in Sebei) and the manufacture of baskets (Plate II:12) and mats of bamboo, which are exchanged for foodstuffs and sold to the people on the escarpment. The Sebei distinguish the *Pygeum* forest (*woket*) from the grassy heaths (*kewet*), which are interspersed with the forest, and generally place their houses on the borders between them. The gardens, which tend to be small and are crudely fenced against depredations of bush pigs, are established by cutting back the forest. As the total acreage of gardening represents the merest fraction of available land, there appear to be no restrictions on the right to use it. The major crop is English potatoes (Plate I:2), but peas and other garden vegetables are also grown. Neither plantains nor maize grows in the area. A government-sponsored program proved wheat was a feasible crop, but its cultivation was abandoned because of the depredations of birds. The growing season extends virtually the year around, so that the small plots can be double-cropped and planting and harvesting spread out.

Cultivation of crops is not the only economic activity. Livestock are fully as important as crops to the Masop people. They graze on the *kewet* for most of the year but find forage in the forest during the dry season (January-March). Sebei informants vaguely indicate that private rights to grazing land were acquired patrilineally, but non-kinsmen let their animals graze together and where the cattle graze usually is determined by the location of the owner's house. The cattle do not require herding, but boys tend the calves and sheep, and all animals are put into the rear section of the houses at night. The Sebei also set beehives out in the forest, clearly proclaiming the private right to specified portions of the forest. The honey is chiefly made into beer but is also sold.

The economy of the area is enriched by trade, abetted by the use of donkeys as beasts of burden. The chief products sent below are the bamboo baskets and mats fabricated by the women, honey, and some livestock. In exchange, the people obtain maize, dried sweet potatoes, and dried plantains, as well as such products of Western manufacture as they can afford. Philip Porter estimated that one man, who seems to have been particularly active in this mercantile role, imported more than 2 metric tons of food per year. These exchanges play a significant role in the economy of Masop.

Soi. The Sebei claim to have owned all the plains north and northwest of the mountains as far as Greek River (Keriki, in Sebei) to the north and the Siroko River (Ciok in Sebei) to the west. A century or more ago, they grew gardens on this land, which they tended in groups for mutual protection from animals and enemies and then and later used for hunting. They virtually abandoned the area as a result of increased military operations in the latter half of the nineteenth century, retreating to the mountains and the increased cultivation of plantains and maize. They returned to these lowlands when the British established a garrison at Greek River, and the area north of Elgon was peopled by former residents of the escarpment. The western sector was settled by Gisu and is not a part of Sebei District now, though some Sebei dwell there.

This area is savanna, mostly grass but some shrub east of the Sundet River (Plates I:17-18). Part of the area is classified as thicket, and some of the region is swampy. Mount Elgon breaks sharply, and the plains slope very gently to the Greek River. The lower slopes of the mountain, sparsely covered with brush and acacias, offer neither homesite or cultivable land, but they are used for grazing and the very occasional hunting of small game. The plains once abounded in game; there are still giraffe, zebra, and eland; lion are seen by the Sebei as a regular threat and the howl of the hyena is heard almost nightly.

The 1959 population of Ngenge Gombolola (the sub-county is coterminous with the Sebei plains) was listed as 6,759, of whom just over half (3,662) were Sebei, 2,327 were Gisu (living chiefly on the western edge of the area), and the remainder a variety of tribal groups, including a number of representatives of the Sabaot peoples from the Kenya side of the mountain. Thus, about 11 percent of the Sebei people live on the plains, though there is a larger percentage of non-Sebei than in any other sub-county.

While the plains Sebei are cattlemen and think of themselves as pastoralists rather than farmers, agriculture has been a part of their economy since the earliest settlements in the area and is of increasing importance. In the early 1920s, an effort was made to induce them to raise cotton but, as in Masop, wildlife depredations discouraged the operation. They do grow maize, some of which they sell, millet, and some sorghum. All farming, other than kitchen gardens and tobacco cultivation, involves the ox-drawn plow, which became prevalent only in the early 1950s.

Livestock plays a more important role than farming in the cultural life, if not the economy, of the plains Sebei, and the per capita ownership of cattle is the greatest of any section of Sebei. Cattle are far more important than small stock, though most people have some sheep and goats, which they graze along with the calves. During the rainy season, the animals can be watered at nearby streams and returned to the kraals daily; during the dry seasons, the animals must be taken to Greek River every second day, and herdsmen must remain with the cattle overnight. Occasionally, the surface water of Greek River disappears and wells must be dug in the sandy river bottom. Each stockman determines independently each day where his herd will go for grass. Indeed, often the herds are attended by boys or appear to be untended, though the former is against the law, and the latter not recommended in view of depredations and raids.

The Escarpment. Nearly 90 percent of the Sebei, and about 85 percent of Sebei District population, live on the escarpment above the 5,000-foot contour and below the forest reserve, the lower boundary of which is at about 7,000 feet. Physiographically, climatically, and culturally, it is far from homogeneous, however. The changes as one moves eastward derive from differences in rainfall and soils and are compounded by the influence of altitude, for the climate differs between the upper and lower reaches of the mountain face.

This latter variation can be seen in the study of natural vegetation zones made by I. Langdale-Brown, H. A. Osmaston, and J. G. Wilson (1964), from which the following quotations are abstracted. These zones, which relate to rainfall probabilities, form a series of concentric rings around the summit, lying lower on the western side and rising higher on the eastern slope. The inhabited escarpment area consists essentially of two such rings; the upper reaches consist of forest savanna mosaics and moist *Combretum* savannas.

> The most important and abundant element of this [forest savanna] mosaic is a savanna-like community which consists of a mixture of forest remnants and incoming savanna trees and a grass layer dominated by *Pennisetum purpureum* (Elephant grass). This is the result of partial clearing of the original forest and a subsequent succession under the influence of repeated cultivation, cutting and grass fires. The proportions of forest and savanna trees vary according to previous land-use history. [p. 52]

In the *Combretum* savanna:

> deciduous broad leaved trees of the *Combretaceae* make up the bulk of the woody cover . . . which is characterised in the grass layer by *Hyparrhenia*

> *rufa.* Tree cover is light to moderate, 10 to 40 feet high, with abundant *Combretum molle, Terminalia glaucescens* and *Albizia zygia.* . . . It is subjected to the effects of annual grass fires, the cutting of wood for fuel, and periodic clearing for cultivation. [p. 57]

This zone is broadest in the western sectors, narrows east of Kapchorwa, and occasionally disappears altogether, reappearing in a narrow band just below the forest line. Taken together, these two physiographic zones essentially constitute the area of plantain cultivation; between 80 and 90 percent of all plantain acreage is found within them.

Below these two bands is the dry *Combretum* savanna, with varying plant dominances. The open grasslands:

> are all either fire climax communities or communities influenced by fire, with a significant proportion of broad leaved deciduous species. There are, however, considerable variations in composition and origin. . . . Small thicket clumps of mixed deciduous and evergreen species are common in these communities which suggests that they are related to a thicket climax. . . . [Some] communities have appreciable admixtures of *Acacia* and other dry species and owe their present composition and appearance to the cumulative effects of burning, overgrazing, compaction, run-off and erosion. It is thought that these communities are degraded forms of a combretaceous savanna woodland climax. [p. 59]

Acacia is absent in the western area but appears as one rounds the mountain.

Farther to the east, on the northeastern corner, the lower reaches are covered by dry acacia savanna.

> These communities are either tree savannas or savanna woodlands with a maximum tree height of 20 feet. *Acacia gerrardii* var. *gerrardii, Themeda triandra* and *Setaria incrassata* are the dominant species. They occur on free draining clays and clay loams in the northwest of Karamoja at elevations of 3,500 to 5,000 feet. These areas are heavily populated by game animals and tsetse flies. Grass fires are annual occurrences so the community is probably some kind of fire and grazing climax. [p. 63]

The area devoted to *Combretum* savanna is utilized largely for grains and stock in varying mixtures, with plantains in pockets having moisture retention and wind protection. The acacia savanna is devoted chiefly to stock raising.

CULTURAL GEOGRAPHY OF THE ESCARPMENT

While physiographic variations relate primarily to altitude, cultural entities tend to cut across the escarpment and extend up to Masop and down to the plains. This is no accident, for Sebei economic strategy involved the exploitation of these diverse ecological areas.

The vertical orientation of Sebei social geography has been considerably altered by historic events. The road across the escarpment has changed the axis of social interaction; there is now much more east-west traffic, abetted by the growing use of lorries, buses, and private cars. The empty zone of the forest has also further isolated the people of Masop. Moreover, while the plains were formerly utilized by escarpment peoples who went there for the day or brief periods, they have now become populated by permanent residents, reducing but not eliminating usage by those on the escarpment. Despite these changes, the traditional north-south (or, more accurately, up-down) pattern of land use continues. It is useful, therefore, to distinguish three geographical areas of the escarpment based on economic patterns: a western or Sipi area, a central area, and an eastern or Bukwa area.

The western or Sipi area extends from the Muyembe border on the southwest as far as the Cheseper River, comprising all of Sipi Gombolola and the Miruka (division of a subcounty) of Tegeres beyond. The area is extremely well watered, with a rainfall average at Sipi Mission station of nearly 80 inches. The short dry season (December to February) does not impede plant growth. There is 100 percent probability of adequate rainfall for one crop per season and a very high probability for a second cropping season (Plates I:15-16). It is the area of greatest population density, includes most of the land devoted to plantains and coffee, and has the highest per capita amount of land in other crops. Cattle, sheep, and goats are kept in the area only in small numbers. More than a third of the population in the area (mostly on the western edge) are Gisu, but there are very few people from other tribes, except for the Bumachek, who identified themselves for census purposes as Sebei. The village of Sasur, one of the communities we studied, lies in this region.

The central area extends eastward from the Cheseper River to the spur beyond the Siti River. It shades from a situation not far removed from the Sipi region to one in which cropland is sparse. The rainfall drops to 65 inches at Kapchorwa and 44 inches at Kabruron. The dry seasons are longer, somewhat later, and prevent the cultivation of plantains except in sheltered spots. The population densities decline in this central area to about 100 persons per square mile; the area in cropland (other than plantains and coffee) drops to 0.4 acres per capita in the western half of this region and 0.2 in the eastern half. This was the old Sapiñ heartland; it was less influenced by the Bantu peoples and by the incursion of plantains before Europeanization. The region has essentially the same mixed economy as that of Sipi but with lower densities and differing ratios: fewer plantains and less coffee, proportionately more maize and root crops, and more involvement with livestock.

The Bukwa area lies at the eastern edge of Sebei territory, around the spur of the mountain. Prior to European influence, it must have been culturally and economically very similar to the north slope as well as to the Kony pastoralists in Kenya to the south. The region is drier and more open. Rainfall at Bukwa averages about 37 inches per year. There are very few acres in plantains, and maize has become the major crop, with more land (both absolutely and per capita) in such cultivation. There is no coffee.

Livestock numbers are large. The area is marked by heavy European influence, with fenced fields, a few tractor-drawn plows, and a pattern of marketing maize in Kenya. Cultural practices in general are also influenced by Kenya tribal peoples. It must have been sparsely populated in aboriginal times and heavily stock-oriented, but when the Sebei were subjected to Baganda overrule, many moved from the Kapchorwa area to Bukwa and established homes there. Now population densities reach 250 per square mile in the Suam Miruka.

TERRITORIAL UNITS

The Sebei originally consisted of three tribes, Mbai, Sor, and Sapiñ. Mbai occupied the western area as far as the Chebonet River and thus coincided with the area of intensive cultivation. The Sor were a smaller group occupying the region of economic transition between the Chebonet and the Cheseper rivers. Sapiñ territory, extending as far as the Suam River and beyond, was an area of mixed economy in which grains were the chief crop and livestock played a far more important role in the economy than in the other two regions, though plantains were cultivated in small pockets. Mbai territory spread at the expense of Sor.

These tribes, in turn, divided into a series of geographically based local polities called *pororisyek* (*pororyet*, sing.), which formed the basic Sebei

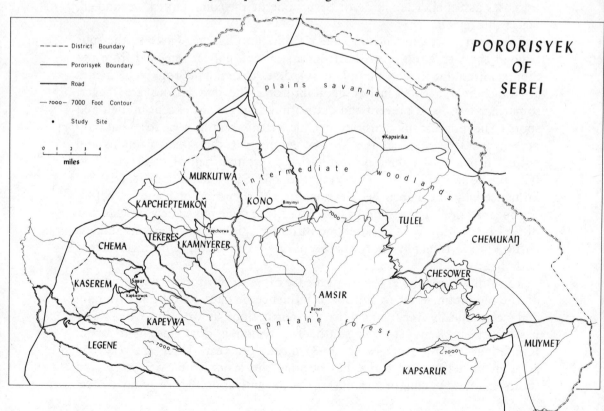

ALBUM I
People and Places

1 Photograph taken by Gedge on February 28, 1890, near Kapchorwa. The man was identified as Chemengich.

2-5 People of Masop: the monkey skin cape (2) is unique. The dress of the three generations of Benet women displays the change in fashion from the skin robe of the blind old woman (Benet, 1954).

6-10 People of the escarpment, all taken in 1954 in the Kapchorwa-Binyiniyi area.

11-14 Interpreters: (11) Yovan Chemtai, 1962; (12) Richard Bomet, 1954; (13) Lovina Ndege, 1962; (14) Susanna Koko, 1954.

15-16 Landscapes in Sipi.

17-18 Landscapes of the plains: (17) Kapsirika landscape; Mount Debasien in background; (18) aerial view of Kapsirika showing houses, granaries and plowed fields.

19-22 Sebei houses: (19) flat-roofed house of Masop; (20) houses in the Nyelit *manyatta* on the plains; (21) the *Sikerointe* of another Chemengich in Sasur; (22) constructing a house by *moyket*.

1

3   4

6

8

9

7

10

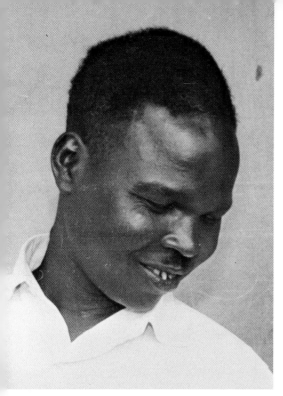

11

12

13   14

15

16

17

18

19

20

21

22

geographical community. Most of the boundaries between *pororisyek* were streams. The upper and lower boundaries generally are indistinct.

The *pororisyek*, running from west to east, are as follows:

Mbai:

1. Legene, between the Simu and the Muyembe (Yembek, in Sebei) rivers.
2. Kapeywa, between the Muyembe and the Chebonet rivers, occupying the western sector of the upland country and the higher escarpment lands above the cliffs.
3. Kaserem, below the lands occupied by Kapeywa.

Sor:

4. Chema, between the Chebonet and the Cheptui rivers.
5. Tegeres, between the Cheptui and the Cheseper rivers, including some territory to the east of the latter. (Some informants spoke of a third Sor *pororyet,* Keyeberi, extending above the forest line above Tegeres, but this is uncertain. I do not know the *pororyet* status of the area between the Sipi and the Chebonet prior to the Mbai incursions.)

Sapiñ:

6. Kapcheptemkoiñ, from the Cheseper to Kaptokoi rivers, in the lower reaches.
7. Kamnyerer, between the same streams in the upper area. (These two *pororisyek* were not entirely separate; it was said that the latter "finished off" the Kapcheptemkoñ and would help protect the territory in case of attack.)
8. Murkutwa, between the Kaptokoi and Atar rivers.
9. Kono, between the Atar and Tabok rivers.[1]
10. Tulel, a broad area between the Tabok and Siti rivers.
11. Amsir, the upper reaches of the mountain on the east side. (The boundary between Kapeywa of Mbai and Amsir is not clear, nor are the boundaries between these two *pororisyek* and those of the escarpment sharply defined. The forest, now unoccupied, was never very densely settled, and the terrain and economic circumstances suggest that boundaries were of relatively little importance.)
12. Chesower, between the Siti and Bukwa rivers below the forest line but limited to the upper reaches.
13. Chemukaŋ (now called Kabei), the lower portion of this region, including the present Riwa and Mutagiet.
14. Kapsarur, the upper area between the Bukwa and Suam rivers.
15. Muymet, the lower reaches between these two rivers.

Kony, which lies to the south and east of Sebeiland, included the following *pororisyek* mentioned by one or more informants: Kapeywa, Keperyir, Kyepekos, Psartuk, Kamatempei, and Kipurit.

---

1. The map reproduced in *Sebei Law* (p. xv) has Kono and Tulel reversed.

There were no separate *pororisyek* on the plains; the land there was claimed, though not occupied, by the people above. By the time the plains were occupied, aboriginal political structure had deteriorated to the extent that *pororisyek* were not formed, the area having been pioneered by Sebei from all parts of the territory.

The Sebei social landscape was further divided into smaller geographical units, which the Sebei call *saŋta* (*soŋmwek*, pl.). These I have called villages. The boundaries, which are generally formed by streams and cliffs or steep areas, are clearly known, even though they are sometimes quite artificial. *Soŋmwek* vary in size, depending partly on the density of population, and generally include between twenty and forty households. They appear to split when population growth intensifies. Villages were delimited on the plains, probably in response to the needs of the administration, for Sebei give minor social importance to village affiliation.

The colonial government superimposed upon this system its own pattern of administrative units, adopting elements of the Baganda structure and Luganda terminology. Until Sebei became a separate district in 1962, the area delineated as Sebei by the administration constituted a single county (*saza*) with an appointive chief and council. It was divided into five sub-counties (*gombololas*), each of which had its own chief and council. (The number and boundaries of these units changed from time to time.) These were: Sipi, which conformed rather closely to the old Mbai territory; Kaptanya, headquartered at Kapchorwa, which was also the center of *saza* administration; Kabruron; Bukwa; and Ngenge (on the plains). These were in turn divided into lesser official units, which also had paid appointive chiefs, and councils, and again into *miruka*.

SASUR AND KAPSIRIKA

Our project research involved the detailed examination of behavior in two villages, one representative of the intensive agricultural sector and the other of the cattle-keeping sector. The villages initially chosen were Sasur in Sipi Gombolola and Kapsirika in Ngenge Gombolola. Because we required for statistical purposes a base sample of at least thirty household heads, we expanded our units to include contiguous communities — Kamingong in Sipi and Kamayindi in Ngenge. Kamingong had been a part of Sasur until 1941, when it was recognized as a separate village. The movement of people between Kapsirika and Kamayindi is such that the distinction is not readily recognized by the inhabitants. For simplicity's sake, I will refer to each of the paired villages as Sasur and Kapsirika, respectively, unless there are special reasons to preserve the internal distinction.

Sasur occupies 0.4 square miles of land. It lies about 2 miles beyond the market town of Sipi on a bench that lies at an elevation of about 6,100 feet, with considerable local relief. The western edge is formed by an abrupt escarpment, the south and east are marked by streams that are cut in gorges, the north by steep slopes and small cliffs. About 75 percent of the land is cultivated. The mountain road cuts through the southern portion of the village, and the school established by the Native Anglican Church, and operated now by the government, lies within the village. Sasur has a pleasant climate. During the year's record, the temperature reached 84° F only once and the night temperatures never fell below 52° F. The mean for the year was 65.7° F, with but little variation from month to month. The diurnal range was consistent throughout the year, averaging 19° F — the lowest occurring in May (16.3° F) when 11.3 inches of rain fell, the highest occurring in December (21.5° F) when only .8 inches of rain fell. The total rainfall in 1961 was 106.3 inches, but this was the year of record-breaking rains. The average rainfall at the Sipi Mission station over the preceding 19 years had been 78 inches. There is a short dry season in January and February. It is an area ideally suited to the cultivation of plantains and coffee.

The Sebei live scattered over the land in Sasur, as they do elsewhere, each person putting his house or houses on his land. The distribution of houses is indicated on the attached map prepared by Porter on the basis of observation and aerial photographs. There is a tendency for members of each clan to occupy contiguous land.

Kapsirika occupies an area of roughly 12 square miles, but the Kapsirikans' economic activities extend both north and south of the community boundaries to lands otherwise unoccupied. The village lies along the road extending from Chepsukunya, where the police station is, to the border and marketing town of Greek River. Beyond Greek River live the Karamojong. The villagers view the community boundaries as marked by the mountain break on the south, the Sundet River on the east, the road on the north, and an almost imperceptible and vaguely defined watershed on the west. The lower slopes of the mountain are used for grazing small stock. The lands to the east and west belong to the villagers of Nyelit and Nobokuta, respectively, but the Kapsirikans utilize salt licks within their village boundaries.

Kapsirika lies on the gentle alluvial slope that extends northward at an inclination of about 50 feet per mile. At the lower northern edge, the land is flat and featureless, easily flooded and often swampy. The natural vegetation varies from south to north. The mountainside consists of an open fire climax sparsely covered tree savanna, excessively well drained, with a low potential for grazing and cultivation. The southern portion of the plains is covered with savanna woodland; the clay loams are well drained. Along the Sundet River is a galerie forest; the stream does not flow throughout the year and supplemental water has been made available by a bore hole, which also is not entirely reliable. On the flatter lands to the north, the clay fraction in the soil increases and the tree cover disappears, leaving only a few types, mostly stunted "whistling thorn" (*Acacia drepanolobium*) in open grassland. Further north is a mosaic of open grassland, thorn thicket, and swamp. This south-to-north axis extends about 6 miles.

Kapsirika lies at an altitude of about 3,500 feet. Its climate stands in strong contrast to that of Sasur. The highest temperature recorded in our

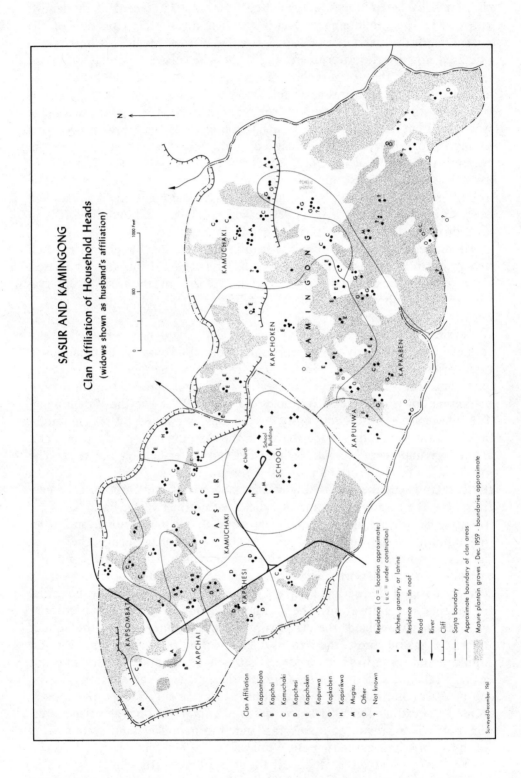

SASUR AND KAMINGONG

Clan Affiliation of Household Heads
(widows shown as husband's affiliation)

Clan Affiliation
A Kapsombata
B Kapchai
C Kamuchaki
D Kapchesi
E Kapchoken
F Kapunwa
G Kapkaben
H Kapsirikwa
M Mugisu
O Other
? Not known

Residence (O = location approximate:)
(u.c. = under construction)
Kitchen, granary, or latrine
Residence — tin roof
Road
River
Cliff
Sanja boundary
Approximate boundary of clan areas
Mature plantain groves · Dec. 1959 · boundaries approximate

Surveyed December 1961

1000 Feet

500

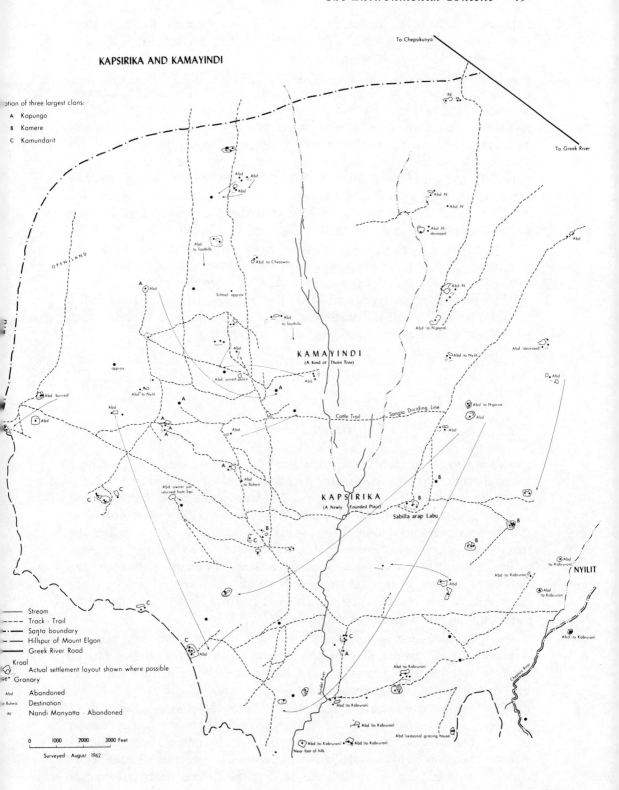

KAPSIRIKA AND KAMAYINDI

To Chepsikunya

To Greek River

...ation of three largest clans:

A Kapungo

B Kamere

C Kamundarit

OPENLAND

Abd
Abd
Abd

Abd .N
Abd .N

Abd .N
deceased

Abd

Abd
to foothills

Abd to Chesower.

A Abd

School approx

Abd .N

Abd
to foothills

KAMAYINDI
(A Kind of Thorn Tree)

Abd to N'gornai

Abd to Nyilit

Abd .deceased

approx

Abd

Abd joined police

Abd to Nyilit

A

A

Abd to Nyilit

A

Cattle Trail

Sangta Dividing Line

Abd to N'gornai

Abd

Abd

D. Abd

B

Abd burned!

Abd

C

C

A

A

A

A

Abd

Abd
to Bukwa

KAPSIRIKA
(A Newly Founded Place)

B

B

B

Sabilla arap Labu

B

Abd owner just
returned from Sipi

C

C

C

C

B

Abd
to Kabruron!

NYILIT

Abd to Kabruron

Abd
to Kabruron

Abd

Abd

C

C

A

Abd to Kabruron

Abd (to Kabruron)

Stream

Track - Trail

Sangta boundary

Hillspur of Mount Elgon

Greek River Road

Kraal   Actual settlement layout shown where possible

se' Granary

Abd   Abandoned

to Bukwa   Destination

.N   Nandi Manyatta - Abandoned

0   1000   2000   3000 Feet

Surveyed · August 1962

Abd (to Kabruron)

Abd (seasonal grazing house)

Abd (to Kabruron)   Abd (to Kabruron)
Near foot of hills

Sundet River

Chepton River

field season was 98° F; the lowest, 52° F. The annual mean, 74.7° F, suggests that, as an average, it is always 9° F hotter on the plains than it is in Sasur. Cool night temperatures, partly the result of air drainage off the mountain, lead to phenomenal diurnal ranges in the dry season. The mean diurnal range in February was nearly 34° F, and the average was 25.4° F at Chepsukunya, about 3 miles to the west, where we established a weather station. The average precipitation recorded at Ngenge, farther to the west, was 35 inches, and that at Kapsirika is probably little different. Though this is but half the precipitation of Sipi, it would be sufficient for crops were it not for the much greater amount of sunshine, which creates greater water needs to sustain crops such as maize and millet. As a result, only one crop a season is possible; planting must wait until May; and there is a much higher probability of crop failure, even in this single season, than in Sasur.

The people of Kapsirika, like those of Sasur, live scattered over the land, also building on plots they consider their own. Fellow clansmen also tend to live near one another, though not with the same degree of contiguity. In the neighboring village of Nyelit, most of the people changed this pattern in response to the continued harassment of the Karamojong and Pokot raiders and gathered together in a brush-enclosed *manyatta.*

DEMOGRAPHY

The diversity of the Sebei landscape and its attendant economic potential under aboriginal exploitative techniques have resulted in considerable variation in the distribution of population. The west is the most densely populated area, with the whole Miruka of Kapeywa having a density of more than 700 persons per square mile. The population thins out as one crosses the escarpment, reaching as low as 64 in the Miruka of Kabruron, and rising again to more than 250 in the most easterly Miruka of Suam. Populations are still lower on the plains; the highest population concentration is twenty times that of the lowest. These data are set forth in Table 2 and presented graphically on the accompanying map.

More detailed demographic information was developed for Sasur and Kapsirika, based upon a demographic schedule constructed to give data on the following items: (1) name, age-set, birthplace, clan affiliation, and previous residences of the household head; (2) name, age-set affiliation, and birthplace of his mother and father, and whether these were living or dead; (3) name, age-set, clan, birthplace of each wife, whether she had previously been married, and whether she was living or dead; (4) name, sex, age, marital status, education, religious affiliation and current residence of each wife's children, whether they were living or dead at the time of interview, and an estimate of age at death of those deceased; (5) name, sex, relation to head,

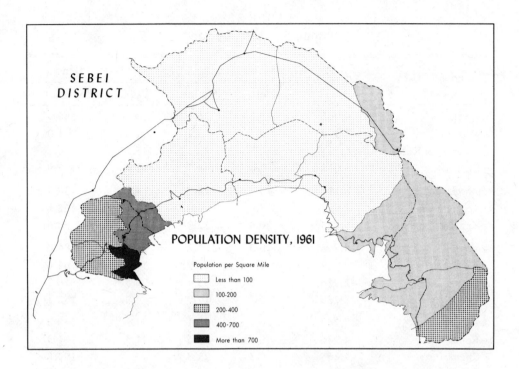

SEBEI
DISTRICT

POPULATION DENSITY, 1961

Population per Square Mile

☐ Less than 100

▤ 100-200

▦ 200-400

▨ 400-700

■ More than 700

and role of all other persons currently in the household. (There were also data on the household head's religious affiliation, education, travel, and other social factors, from which Edgerton constructed evidence on level of acculturation.)

This schedule was taken from a saturation sample of the four villages, though not all households are represented. I think these data are accurate within the limitations generally applicable to schedule data, with a few minor reservations. Frequently, if the data seemed inadequate, a question would reveal their accuracy.[2]

A household is defined as all persons sharing a compound, and may consist of one or several separate dwelling units. Included in such households will be older widowed or divorced women, when they are living in conjunction with their son or son-in-law, and unmarried men when they are living in conjunction with their fathers. A few unmarried men had separate households. The results are presented in Table 3. The data from our samples are extrapolated to the total village by using the household size corrected for known instances where single women were dwelling alone. I have here given the data separately for each of the villages that constitute our farming sample, as well as the combined figure, but not for the two units that constitute the pastoral village, as these were not treated as separate entities

---

2. Residents are defined as all persons dwelling within village confines at the time of enumeration. A man with a wife living outside the village was recorded as a resident (and as polygynous), but his wife and her children were not recorded as residents of the village. The three or four men more or less permanently employed outside the village, who had residences and wives within it, were included.

TABLE 2
Population Distribution

Gombolola and miruka	Population[a]		Area[b]		Density
	No.	Pct	Sq. mi.	Pct	Pop. sq. mi.
Sipi: total	14,061	26.2	36.4	8.8	386.3
Kapeywa	3,575	6.9	5.1	1.2	701.0
Kaserem & Kobil	6,453	12.5	23.2	5.6	278.1
Chema[c]	4,033	7.8	8.1	2.0	497.9
Kaptanya: total	8,117	15.7	58.7	14.1	138.3
Tegeres	2,962	5.7	6.4	1.5	462.8
Kaptaret	5,155	10.0	52.3	12.6	98.6
Kabruron: total	8,505	16.5	101.2	24.4	84.0
Kabruron	3,067	5.9	47.9	11.6	64.0
Kono	2,716	5.3	35.4	8.5	76.7
Chesoweri	2,722	5.3	17.9	4.3	152.1
Bukwa: total	13,782	26.7	87.1	21.1	158.2
Kabei	4,746	9.2	46.6	11.3	101.3
Chepkwasta	4,268	8.3	21.8	5.3	195.8
Suam	4,768	9.2	18.7	4.5	255.9
Ngenge: total	7,101	13.7	130.8	31.6	54.3
Kapkwot	2,849	5.5	75.3	18.2	37.8
Sundet[c]	2,330	4.5	43.2	10.4	53.9
Greek River	1,922	3.7	12.3	3.0	156.3
Sebei Total	51,566	100.0	414.2	100.0	124.5

[a]1959 census population increased by .4 percent per annum to give 1961 estimates.
[b]Planimeter readings made by P. W. Porter. Area excludes uninhabited forest reserves.
[c]Includes communities of intensive study, Sasur and Kapsirika.

TABLE 3
Demographic Data on Sasur and Kapsirika

	Sasur	Kamingong	Sasur-Kamingong	Kapsirika
Total structures	53	80	133	Unknown
Households	32	45	77	54
Sample	29	31	60	50
Average household size	5.69	5.93	5.82	6.49
Total population	168	232	400	279
Area (Sq. mi.)	......	......	0.4	12
Population density	......	......	1000	25
Acres per household			3.3	142

SOURCE: Data for Tables 3-10 are based on demographic questionnaires taken in 1961-62.

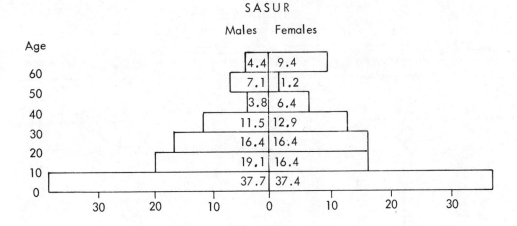

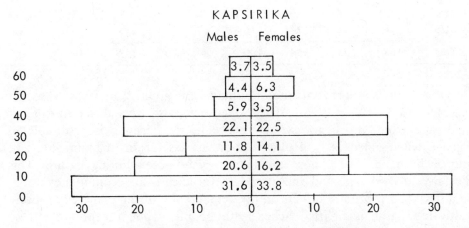

Figure 2. Population Pyramids: Sasur and Kapsirika

by the Sebei. The table shows the essential consistency in village population size and demonstrates the dramatic differential in population density.

The age distribution of the population in the two areas varies slightly, with a somewhat greater population of small children and older people in Sasur and a slightly higher proportion of people in their reproductive years in Kapsirika (Table 4). These data are summarized graphically in Figure 2. These differences reflect the lower Kapsirika birthrate and, I believe, a tendency for old people to move away from the plains whenever the opportunity is available. (It should be noted that the estimates of age, based upon the circumcision data for older people, particularly is subject to error, especially the relative ages of men and women. I believe the anomaly in the older bracket for Sasur is explainable on this basis.)

SUMMARY

Sebei environment shows remarkable variation in its small territory. The contrasts between the well-watered mountain slopes of Sipi and the rela-

TABLE 4
Sasur and Kapsirika Populations by Age and Sex

| | Sasur | | | | Kapsirika | | | |
| | | | Totals | | | | Totals | |
Age	M	F	No.	Pct	M	F	No.	Pct
0 - 4	40	37	77	21.8	28	29	57	20.5
5 - 9	29	27	56	15.8	15	19	34	12.2
10 - 14	16	17	33	9.3	18	15	33	11.9
15 - 19	19	11	30	8.5	10	8	18	6.5
20 - 29	30	28	58	16.4	16	20	36	12.9
30 - 39	21	22	43	12.1	30	32	62	22.3
40 - 49	7	11	18	5.1	8	5	13	4.7
50 - 59	13	2	15	4.2	6	9	15	5.4
60 - Up	8	16	24	6.8	5	5	10	3.6
Totals	183	171	354	100.0	136	142	278	100.0

tively dry plains north of the mountain are great. Sipi is as lush and productive an area as any in Africa, but Ngenge is a very different kind of landscape from which to extract a livelihood. Farming is profitable in Ngenge when aided by the plow but is far less certain than in Sipi, and animal husbandry is a more satisfactory way of exploiting nature. This diversity in landscape and the attendant variance in its economic exploitation have had profound effects on the demography of the two areas. Closely cultivated Sasur is tightly packed with people, while the population of Kapsirika is widely dispersed, leaving ample space for cattle to graze. This differential will be found reflected in diverse ways as we examine the details of Sebei culture and how it is manifested in the two communities.

Chapter 3
The Sebei Polity

A poor man who is clanless shall live in peace

Chomi ntarastit ritual

Leadership in traditional Sebei society rested largely on personal qualities. Men who spoke wisely and effectively in councils became known as judges; some attained wide recognition and were called from great distances to hear disputes. Men who had killed an enemy in battle and shown themselves to be brave and capable of leadership became the military leaders. Men of wealth also had influence because prosperity demonstrated their ability and gave them a measure of de facto authority. None of these roles was highly formalized, and none gave men control over others in this essentially individualistic society. The most formal role was that of prophet. Prophets also were largely self-selected, and their influence ultimately depended upon the evidence of their capacity accurately to predict the outcome of wars, hunting expeditions, and other matters that were put before them.

An orderly social system was maintained through the operation of three sets of institutions: clans, age-sets, and territorial units. These institutions continue, with considerable modification and dilution, to perform such functions. The clan is a jural entity in major disputes and is responsible for its own internal harmony. Age-sets serve as a grading system in a society that recognizes the importance of seniority. These two aspects of Sebei social organization will be set forth in the next chapter.

The focal element in the spatial divisions is the *pororyet* (*pororisyek*, pl.), a territorial unit of about five to ten square miles with a population of about two thousand. In military matters, these units are independent. Each *pororyet* has a council (*kok*), which meets informally as occasion demands. They are grouped into three tribes, which have no formalized unity, and in turn the three tribes are unified through recognition of a single prophet, the coordination of major ceremonies, and the general awareness of their commonality, but not by any institutionalized system of decision-making. The *pororisyek* are divided into villages (*saŋta*), a demarcated area of varying size

55

giving a sense of unity to about thirty households. Villages also have councils to hear minor, domestic matters but no formal leadership. The households, consisting of a man, his wives, and their children, may be seen as the minimal social unit. This chapter will examine these units in detail, starting with the institutionalization of the Sebei-wide unity and concluding with an examination of the households, taking into account some of the changes and variations that these institutions display.

PROPHETS

The Sebei, like most Southern Nilotic people, have traditionally recognized the existence of specially endowed persons called *workoyontet*, prophets. Past prophets had special powers for predicting events, and people came to them for advice on diverse matters, such as hunting expeditions and warfare. Their close association with supernatural powers was also expressed in their role in determining when certain ceremonies should begin and in some aspects of the organization of such rites.

The prophet supplied, in a limited way, some of the functional elements of political leadership, utilizing his esoteric knowledge to establish a measure of secular power. Older informants recalled some half dozen prophets, but the institution came in direct confrontation with established political power in the Baganda period (1903-10). Older Sebei, idealizing this aspect of the prophet's power, often speak as if he were a ruler, but this was not the case, though where the prophet combined his divination with charismatic qualities he could exert a good deal of public influence. This was particularly the case with Matui.

Matui was the last great prophet, a man of Nyonki I *pinta* (age-set) who died in 1938. His son, Mangusho Arap Matui, also endeavored to serve as prophet, was arrested in 1931 and exiled for a period of about twelve years and died in 1946. These men were the last to perform as prophets. They belonged to the Kapchai clan, which occupied the lower portion of the Sipi area known as Kapchai or Kobil and provided a line of prophets extending far back in time. According to information received from a number of men and a document prepared by the oldest living son of Matui, there were eleven prophets in this line,[1] beginning with Kupchai, presumably the clan founder.

On the last day of our stay, November 18, 1962, the Sebei had a great ceremony of digging up the bones of the prophets Matui and Mangusho (Plates III:34-35). One man, in a speech delivered at a meeting arranging for this ceremony, reported on Matui's death as follows:

---

1. These are as follows: Kupchai; Kurye Wataŋara; Mukuŋ Kumwal; Kumar Arap Mukuŋ; Aramar; a second Kumar; Namume, Kwoimet age-set; Chepet Latyao, Nyikeao age-set; Matui, Nyonki I age-set, and Mangusho Arap Matui, Chepilat age-set. (Weatherby indicates there were two prophets named Matui, but this is in direct contradiction to all the information I obtained.) This line of prophets originated in the Cherangani Hills.

In 1938, soon after I was circumcised, Matui called us at about four in the afternoon and said, "I am old enough, and I am dying." He said in the old days prophets were not buried in the ground but placed on an anthill. "But now, as it is the time of having government, you must bury me. But let me sleep on my back, bringing a konduwet [type of plantain] leaf and cover my eyes with it and put earth on me, and then put sumotwet [bark cloth tree] on my feet and another on my head. When authorized by chiefs to do this, you are to take up the bones and press them in an anthill, where they should have been put if there had been no government." He died on January 1, 1938 and was buried on January 2.

The Sebei had feared to undertake this act, which seems innocent enough until one realizes that the purpose of such disinterment and reburial is to release the spirit so that it can enter into another man of the clan and thus continue the line of prophets. Only after the establishment of a separate Sebei district and the imminent independence of Uganda did talk of such disinterment begin to take place, and then fearfully and, I suspect, without fulfillment had it not been for my urging. In the process of planning the affair, there was much discussion of Matui's role, numerous public speeches about Matui, and a document prepared by Salimu Chemaswet, the son of Matui (Chemaswet, 1962). From this material, I gained additional insight into the manner in which the prophet Matui operated, but the data must be used with caution, as they both idealize and enlarge the scope of Matui's activities.

Matui was recognized as a prophet from the Mutalla River in the southwest to the Suam River in the east. He had several wives and a large retinue of persons who helped him — as messengers, assistants, and menials. Ordinary diviners would determine minor matters, leaving the important ones for Matui. As one man who had consulted him when young said, "You go there thinking you are going alone, but when you get there you find many people have already gathered." It was Matui's practice not to appear until a group had gathered. He wore a leopard skin robe to which iron circles were attached, so that people could hear the jingle of his coming. Women and children were not permitted to be present during these consultations. Men who came for advice brought gifts, usually livestock, which had been garlanded with sinentet vines. Special colored animals were appropriate for these gifts. Men came to be advised on matters such as military expeditions and hunting forays, and he would tell them when and where they should go, who (usually identified by age-set) would make the kills, and what game they would find. He had medicines he gave to hunters or warriors to assure success. He would, for instance, put medicine on one man's spear and order him to be the first to throw his spear, and this would prevent the enemy from throwing their spears. He was brought some of the kill, a leopard's skin, or an elephant tusk, as appropriate, by the successful hunters. Girls captured in military ventures were also brought to him. Matui was not a curer — this was not appropriate to a prophet — but he did prognosticate the occurrence of epidemic diseases, as well as other disasters, and would order appropriate ceremonials to deter such catastrophes. When a girl became ill with smallpox, he ordered the scabs from her sores placed in an anthill, and this caused the disease to disappear, though the girl died.

Matui also heard litigations, though under what circumstances and by what authority is not clear. An informant said:

> If people quarreled over the kill in hunting, they would bring the case before Matui; it was like the government. The one against whom Matui charged would have to lie down and be whipped, so Matui was halfway like government and halfway like a prophet. Cases were brought to other prophets too, but they were not so powerful as Matui.

Matui not only responded to the inquiries made by his visitors, he also initiated action. Such action appears to have been taken in response to dreams, after which he would order certain ceremonies performed. He had two sources of secular power. One was the ritual of *chomi ntarastit*, a rite that established community law in Sebei. The second was his apparently exclusive knowledge — at least exclusive to his clan — of an ordeal medicine used to determine guilt or innocence in accusations of witchcraft. Through these two activities, the Sebei found in Matui a source of order and adjudication that was quite different from the general patterned action of their lives. No other prophet is associated with *chomi ntarastit* or the administration of the poison ordeal, nor did any other surround himself with similar pomp and circumstance.

Matui's endeavors to stop the trading of Austin and his party led to bloodshed. According to Chemaswet, his father went into hiding when the Baganda came, so that another man was made chief of the area. The Baganda unsuccessfully sought Matui in the cave Kakarwa, then burned down his house and granaries, and later, in further search for him, one of the officers was killed, though not by Matui. This situation appears to have left Matui powerless and must certainly also be responsible for the rapid decline of most of those Sebei rituals that had to be initiated by the prophets.

Mangusho, the son of Matui, began to act as a prophet in 1922. Some informants claim that his father objected to Mangusho's taking on this role, as it is not considered right for a son to do so while his father is still alive. Nevertheless, in 1927, Mangusho did correctly prophesy a plague of locusts and advised the Sebei not to plant. Chemaswet wrote:

> He further said that time was approaching for the white people to go back to their home land, and that they would go away gradually and peacefully without the people having to wage war against them, and that they would be leaving at night. After their leaving, he continued, the power would then be returned to the 'hereditary rulers' of each tribe. In Sebei, the people would be loyal to Mangusho, and would work for him; but they would be disloyal to the Government. [Chemaswet, 1962]

At about the same time, Mangusho became involved with the protection of a murderer, or was so accused, and was also accused of witchcraft when this murderer stabbed the chief, Wandera, during the attempt to arrest him.

The details of these encounters vary somewhat with the teller, but the essential fact is that Mangusho came in direct confrontation with colonial authority. According to Wandera, Mangusho continued to prognosticate the imminent departure of the Europeans, to deprecate their appointive chiefs, and to refuse to appear before the district commissioner as ordered. Five others were arrested for "carrying Mangusho's message," though the single survivor of this incident denied he had any such involvement. (Efforts to obtain court records proved entirely unrewarding.) The outcome was Mangusho's arrest and deportation and the final elimination of prophets from the Sebei scene.

Arrangements for the disinterment of Matui and Mangusho were initiated in the fall of 1962 in two lengthy public meetings devoted chiefly to eulogizing the deceased and justifying the act. Other private meetings must have been held to determine the course of action, because an elaborate ritual was set, for which there could have been no model based upon experiences of living Sebei. The public aspect of the ritual consisted in the presentation of cattle and sheep, beer, and other gifts by various citizens of Sebei to the eldest living son of Matui, Salimu Chemaswet, who was dressed in a leopard robe decorated with iron rings and an ostrich-plumed leopard hat, presumably after the fashion of his distinguished father (Plates III:33-34).

Two other Sebei prophets, Arapkuprukoin and Arapkoipot, were operating contemporaneously with Matui, but neither of them is remembered with the same reverence. I do not know how these three prophets interrelated with one another; there does not appear to be any kind of territorial division, for the two former ones lived in the Sapiñ area, while Matui, who lived in Mbai, is said to have extended his influence over the whole of Sebei. Arapkuprukoin was a member of Kapchepkisa clan and was probably of Kaplelaich age-set. He was born deformed, lived in the cave called Arkak above Binyinyi on the trail to Benet, from which he announced his prophecies, and is credited with having predicted the coming of the Europeans. In 1898, he was killed, as described in detail by Weatherby (1962a:206), in his cave during a Nandi raid, along with many Sebei who were using the cave as a hiding place.

Arapkoipot was a man of Kapchepkoiñ clan and of the Nyonki I *pinta*, and lived in Kirwogo. He is famous for having prophesied the occurrence of a disease of the penis and advising the postponement of the circumcision. Many Sebei did not heed this advice and suffered as a result. The death of Arapkoipot was described to me in circumstantial detail.

> Arapkoipot lived between Kapchorwa and Binyinyi and was killed at Kirwogo. They killed him because he did bad things. It was in the second year of the famine, after the last Maina had been circumcised, but before the Chepilat circumcision, and the people were suffering very much. He told the people not to expect rain and that they would get trouble from enemy raids. They thought he was unhappy because the people did not give him gifts, so he was given bullocks and she-goats that he might give a prophecy of rain. Later he told the people that there would be no raids and they could go to collect salt. They went to a cave for salt, and while the men were there the Karamojong

raided the area of goats and sheep, as there was no one to call the alarm. By
the time the men returned, the Karamojong were far away and the people
were too weak to chase after them.

Arapkoipot prophesied again that floods were coming down from the
mountain and would sweep away the home of Kamasa and that a monkey-
skin hat was lost at a place called Kapao. The first meant that the Karamojong would take all Kamasa's possessions; the second that my father's
younger brother, the man who owned the hat, would be killed at Kapao. The
people became annoyed with Arapkoipot, thinking that he was working
against them, so they planned to kill him.

When Arapkoipot returned some time later, the people got word of his
coming, as he was an important man. Arapkoipot joined some men inside a
house, and the young men gathered outside. They feared to attack the
prophet, as he was a very big man with thighs like those of a cow, and very
strong. My uncle, though much older, said, "If you have fear, let me spear
him, for this man is working against the people and wants to spoil the
country." He went to the door to grab the prophet but was pulled inside by
him instead. He called to the young men for help and they pulled Arapkoipot
out of the house. He clung to the doorposts until they were uprooted. When
they had him outside, people held him by his arms and legs and beat him on
his head and neck until he was dead. While he was being beaten, he said he
wanted to say something to the people, but they would not let him.

After Arapkoipot was killed, they slaughtered a ram and placed some of
the chyme and tail fat in the prophet's mouth to prevent him from causing
more deaths. They put his body out for the animals to devour, and he was so
huge that it took three days for the vultures to consume his body. When my
brother and I were herding the cattle, we went to see the dead body; it was
something that scared us.

Aramakor did not die; the floods did not happen; the Karamojong did not
come. That's why they killed the prophet, because he caused these bad
things. Perhaps these prophets are the ones who cause the raiding of people in
the country.

Prophets played an important secular role based on their supernatural
powers. There is no indication that the Sebei hold any theories with respect
to how the prophet gains his prescience beyond the vague "it is given to him
by God." or "he inherited the power in his clan." In the case of the Kapchai
clan, there was (as in other specializations such as ordinary diviners and
smiths) a clan continuity, with the general assumption that when one
member died another would acquire his powers, but the prophet's role was
not a clan monopoly. It was the essence of the role of the prophet that he
establish his position through successful auguries and that he retain it by
continuing to make accurate predictions. When his prophesy failed, or
perhaps when it was too negative, he not only lost favor but could lose his
life. While the prophets did not have police and judicial power, Matui (and
perhaps also the other prophets) did exert a strong force for unity and
amity.

I find the differences between Matui and the other prophets particularly
intriguing. I had anticipated that farmers would tend to place greater weight
on political office and hereditary title, while pastoralists would depend more

heavily upon the interaction among clans and the role of prominent personalities in matters of governance. It is therefore significant that descent was so
important to the prophets in the agricultural area of Mbai and that they took
a more active role in public affairs than prophets in other areas, surrounded themselves with the accoutrements of power, displayed their status
with leopard robes and other symbols, and organized community law.

RITUAL UNITY AND *CHOMI NTARASTIT*

The most important force for social unity of the Sebei people was the
integration of their ceremonial activities. They did not perform their rituals
together as one people, but their major ceremonies were orchestrated by the
prophet so that they took place in proper sequence. This reinforced the
sense of internal amity and interdependence. All major ceremonies were
initiated at the behest of the prophet, or by him at the request of self-
selected elders; they started in the east and moved westward *pororyet* by
pororyet, across the face of the mountain.[2] In a more specific Durkheimian
sense, these rituals reinforced the *pororyet* as a social entity, for the rituals
brought the membership together physically and spiritually. The most interesting and most political of these rituals was the *chomi ntarastit* (eating the
law), which interpreters gloss as "passing the law."

The *ntarastit* rite was initiated by the prophet Matui at irregular intervals,
informants variantly estimating at from two to five years, whenever he felt
that lawlessness had reached such proportions as to require its reenactment.
Wandera and other older Sebei said it was first inaugurated by the prophet
Namume, the grandfather of Matui, and must therefore have been instituted
about 1850. It was an oath of allegiance, using oath in the Sebei sense rather
than in our watered-down meaning, for, unlike the other community-
oriented ceremonies, it was built directly on the conceptual apparatus and
ritual performance of the oath when used as a means of direct redress. It has
not been performed since Kakunguru's forces subjected the Sebei to Baganda
overrule, but elderly informants had witnessed the last occurrence.

The ritual was held after the millet had sprouted but before it was ready
for harvest. The people of each territory assembled at the meeting place for
each *pororyet*, being called together by the sounding of a horn.

The ceremony involved the lighting of a ritual fire and the erection of an

---

2. The places in the order in which the ceremony was held are: (1) Chemukuŋ: Muymet *pororyet;*
(2) Kapsarur: Kapsarur *pororyet;* (3) Kapkwata: Cheseper and Amsir *pororisyek;* (4) Kabruron: Kono
pororyet; (5) Binyinyi: Tulel *pororyet;* (6) Kirwogo: Murkutwa *pororyet;* (7) Bugoyen: Kapcheptemkoñ and Kamnyerer *pororisyek;* (8) Kwamo; Chema and Tegeres *pororisyek;* (9) Kapkwirwok: Sowis
and Kapeywa *pororisyek;* (10) Amagol: Kaserem *pororyet;* (11) Kwembe: Sowis (see below) and part
of Legene *pororisyek;* and (12) Kobur: remainder of Legene *pororyet.* Some but not all informants
spoke of a Sowis *pororyet* as separate from Kapeywa; it presumably was separate prior to the
disruptions caused by Gisu pressure.

oathing altar. According to one informant, the fire should be lit from embers passed on from the fire of the preceding ceremony to the east. Into this fire were thrown branches or leaves of a variety of plants (see Appendix E). An altar was built on a major path by implanting certain very hard posts, which do not easily rot, and tying them together with special vines. On top of this was placed, according to one informant, the skull of a hyena or, according to another, a large onion-shaped plant called tororumwet, which has a very irritating juice and into which chicken feathers had been stuck. A stem of plantains was placed on or by the altar. The Sebei utilize native plants as symbols, and these are generally divided into those associated with oathing and those that are used to placate the spiritual forces and remove evil (see Chapter 11). The plants used for the *chomi ntarastit* altar were drawn from both categories (see Appendix E).

Toward sundown, the men of the *pororyet* would gather around the altar, naked, and, holding their spears in their left hand against the object on top of the altar, they all would swear a series of oaths asserting that if any wrong were done, this law would take effect, mentioning a wide variety of matters, such as arson, theft, murder, and the like. Their chant would be led by an old man who would assert each act, while a chorus of the men around the altar repeated each item. Among the things specifically mentioned by informants were: "If there is a poor man who is clanless, he shall live in peace," and "If a big clan steals from a small clan, they will be guilty." After completing these statements, an old man would start a song, which could not be translated, as follows

> *Cheboye, chebo, hoo chebo*
> *Kirisoye, kirisoy, hoo kirisoy*

At the close of each line, the group of men would lunge at the altar with their spears and then turn their spears to the west and start in that direction, closing the ritual.

The purpose of the ritual is explicitly stated: to establish rules of conduct and to sanction the right of the community to take punitive action against any member who fails to live up to them. The punitive actions took the form of plundering their stores and killing their stock (*vide Sebei Law* 1967 [hereafter *SL*], 106-107 *et passim*). the purposes of the ritual are sociologically so obvious as to form a textbook case of a ritual affirmation of community solidarity. The sanctions do not replace clan loyalty and the negotiation of legal matters between clans but superimpose upon them the right of the community to punish those who disobey the law and therefore explicitly stress the protection of the weak against the strong.

Ntaristit is built on the ritual of the oath and thus calls forth the effects of the curse upon those who fail to maintain the peace. At the same time, it creates a legitimate use (and some instances also suggest abuse) of the power of the people as a whole, whose application of the sanctions is thus protected against legitimate retaliation by those against whom the sanctions are taken. It does not rest on curative or prophylactic sacraments but calls forth powerful maledictions of the very kind that the Sebei regularly use as a court of last resort in their vendettas. Despite this powerful basis, however, the sanctions lack staying power. Informants repeatedly said the ritual's effects waned with time and that when the prophet saw that the people were "no longer obeying the law," i.e., respecting the oath, he would call for the ritual to be performed and so invoke its sanctions once again. Hence the uncertain periodicity of this ritual. Though the ritual was performed by each *pororyet* independently, sanctions could be applied across *pororyet* lines.

TRIBES

The distinction that the Sebei make between the three constituent tribes remains enigmatic to me. There is no evidence in any of my notes of any organizational or ritual element that overtly expresses this social entity. Yet, despite the lack of organizational and ritual reenforcement, tribal names and tribal boundaries are regularly expressed and, indeed, the Mbai and Sapiñ people also express mutual distrust and prejudice. The tribal names, Mbai, Sor, and Sapiñ also appear in the earliest accounts of the Sebei, notably Austin's. There also are dialectical variations that are more or less coterminous with the tribal boundaries.

Three recognized Sabaot tribal groups with close linguistic, cultural and social ties are also found in modern Kenya; Kony, which lies just southeast of the Sebei, Bok, and Boŋom. There is a good deal of friendly moving back and forth, as well as intermarriage, but the ties between the Sebei and those in Kenya are not so close as among the three that fall within Uganda and have been further weakened by the international boundary.

THE *PORORYET*

The *pororyet*, in contrast, was the focal element in the territorially based social groups among the Sebei, though its function has been superseded by territorial divisions established by the colonial government. Each man was specifically a member of one *pororyet*, to which he owed allegiance, and each *pororyet* therefore had not only a clear geographical delimitation but also a social boundary. Each *pororyet* had a ceremonial center and a meeting place (usually under a large fig tree). It had its own judges or elders (*kirwokik*), and, most important of all, its own military. Each *pororyet* formed a battalion or regiment in military operations, fighting under its own leaders. Indeed, the term *pororyet* in other Kalenjin tribes has reference to the military unit. Weatherby (1962a:201) says: "The territorial military divisions of the tribe are known as Bororiosiek. Bororiet . . . is related to a word 'Boriet' which implies 'fighting.'" Huntingford (1953:8) equates the word with the Masai word for age-set, *ol-poror,* and the Luo word for "to be equal," *porore*. For the more closely related Nandi, he says that *pororyet* "originally denoted a group of people who formed a fighting unit, all such people having equal status as warriors of the same age-set. In this sense it may be translated 'regiment.' Later the term was extended to cover the land on which the members of the regiment lived . . ." It is entirely in keeping with the Sebei situation that the same semantic evolution should have taken place. In major military actions, the *pororyet* was the unit of operation — indeed, more importantly so than either clan or age-set.

The *pororyet* also had a measure of political authority in the form of a council (*kok* or *kokwet*) and of elders or judges (*kirwokintet kirwokik*), which met at a place specially set aside for such activity (*SL*:163-68). Neither the *kokwet* nor the role of *kirwokintet* appears to have been highly formalized. All circumcised men could participate in *kokwet* discussions, and young men were enjoined to attend; women and uncircumcised children could listen but were not normally allowed to speak. Such councils served as courts in which disputes were heard and resolved, either in peaceable encounters between clans, or in actions taken under the aegis of *chomi ntarastit*. Presumably, such administrative matters as decisions regarding the performance of rituals were subject to such discussion.

The *kirwokik* were men whose ability to speak and judgment were highly regarded. Though some informants spoke of them as being elected, it would seem rather that the requisite qualities emerged in them in the course of time. Some of these men (*kirwokik ñewo*, big judges) were known widely throughout Sebei and were called to distant parts to proffer their wisdom in matters of importance; while others, sometimes called their assistants, were known as *kirwokik ñe miniŋ*, small judges. This form of leadership was not dependent upon wealth, number of wives, or hereditary station, though undoubtedly such elements entered into their reputation. "Judgeship," the Sebei say, "is bought with the ear, not with cattle." The names of important *kirwokik* of pre-Baganda times are still remembered. When the Sebei reoc-cupied the plains area, they did not formulate new *pororisyek* there, but each man reckons his *pororyet* affiliations patrilineally from his place of origin. Perhaps the failure to reconstitute or formalize the *pororyet* in Ngenge is an expression of the degree to which this unit had lost functional relevance during the period of Baganda domination.

The importance of the *pororyet* as a social unit was best expressed by the fact that, though a person could transfer his allegiance from his natal *pororyet* to another, he did so by means of a special ceremony; membership was thus not casual. A man's *pororyet* affiliations were normally those of his father; if he married a woman of another *pororyet*, she joined his. (No marital regulations applied to *pororyet* affiliation.) A man might wish to transfer his allegiance either because of developing enmity with others, or because a series of deaths or other disasters made him feel a need to change his fortune. A proper person making such a change gave a beer party, announced his departure, and made his farewell: "If he fails to do this, the *pororyet* people may send bad words after him and he will find bad luck where he goes and will have to return to the *pororyet* and beg forgiveness." I was told that a man might also be ostracized, but no instances were cited. Some time after a man took up residence in a new *pororyet*, he was expected to slaughter a bull and invite the members of the *pororyet*. He was also expected to marry a woman of the *pororyet*.

When a whole clan moved into an area, the ceremonial demands were greater. When the Kapsombata *aret* (clan) moved into the Chema *pororyet* (in the 1870's), a three-day feast was held, with the *pororyet* and the Kapsombata clan each furnishing two bulls and the latter also many rams. The entire *pororyet* held a *korosek* ceremony. The new members were sprinkled with fresh milk, using palm frond ribs and other branches, with appropriate recitation of words indicating that they were united together and living in peace.

Korosek is a general term for a *pororyet*-centered ceremony of purification or amity. These ceremonials, having the manifest function of cleansing the world and eliminating disease and drought, have the latent function of reinforcing the *pororyet* unity. The harvest *korosek* was held annually after the start of the harvest. The last one was held in Bukwa in 1928; there was one reported for the Binyinyi area in 1920, but it had already lost its continuity and had disappeared earlier in the west. The prophet selected three men in each *pororyet* to serve as ritual leaders, one to provide the bull (black) for slaughtering, one to light the fire, and the third, who must be an old man, to cut up the bull. The ritual was held by a large tree (supulyontet, mowet, or simotwet, each of which exudes milky sap) near the house of the man who provided the sacrificial animal.

The fire, a central element in the ritual, was made with fire sticks; an old man began the process and a younger one took it over. The fire was caught in desiccated cow dung. The fire sticks were not to be used again but were kept in the house of the man who started the fire. Upon the fire were placed a number of branches and leaves (which had to be broken off and not cut) of a variety of plants which together constitute the *korosek* group of plants (see Appendix E). All the women of the *pororyet* brought to the fire some of each crop — millet, maize, beans, sweet potatoes, yams, and tobacco (to name the plants mentioned), milk from the morning's milking, milk from lactating women, and a piece of firewood taken from the fire-rack inside the house — and placed these on the fire. The content of the intestines of the bull was also placed on this fire, producing much smoke, but the chyme was taken home by the women, who put a bit into their pots when they cooked the new crop. All the people of the *pororyet* together with their cattle and small animals, gathered around this fire (men and boys to the east, women and girls to the west) and breathed the smoke. The meat of the bull was roasted and consumed, as no part could be taken from the ceremonial grounds. The skin was cut into small rings and worn by all the people; men on their right middle finger, women on their iron necklaces. The bones were thrown into the fire.

At sunset of the first day of the ceremony, the women would take a coal on a piece of wood and throw it away with their left hand, saying, "Go away!" for "they are sending away disease, famine, and all kinds of bad luck." They also would say, "Let us enjoy the food that will make us strong." That evening, they took coals to their homes, using it to start a new fire in the hearths they have cleaned of ashes. This fire had to remain for the four days of the ceremony.

During the four days of the ceremony, there was to be neither work nor sexual intercourse, for everyone "must respect the ceremony." Nobody was supposed to enter or leave the *pororyet* during this period (they could go through it if they did not stop to eat or drink), but visitors could join the ceremony if they remained through the four days.

Another *korosek* ceremony was also performed by each *pororyet* in turn during epidemics to eliminate disease, as during a smallpox epidemic at the beginning of this century. This, too, was organized by the prophet, who appointed a person in each *pororyet* to slaughter an animal (a bull or ram, but not a goat) by stabbing it with a knife. Pieces of meat from all parts of the animal were skewered on two sticks and taken by about ten selected persons at sunset to the west across the stream that marked the *pororyet's* western boundary, where the sticks were planted in the ground, slanting to the westward. Thus the diseases of smallpox, dysentery, ulcers, "strong cough," and an illness called *kotap mahindi*, i.e., "Indian disease," were expelled from the *pororyet*. As the ceremony moved to the westernmost *pororyet* the people would throw the ritual meat into the Siroko River and say, "Disease, go with this water to the land of the Teso." This ritual involved the same *korosek* plants and appears to be a modification of the annual rite, which has essentially the same function.

The purpose of the third ritual involving the *pororisyek* was to bring rain; it was performed during a drought. For this, there was neither beer nor feasting, but the people danced during the day at the pool in a stream where the ceremony was held. In the afternoon, a precircumcision *tekeryontet* (see Chapter 9) girl would enter a stream, carrying a palm frond and a ball of "dried beer" made from sorghum and followed by a man leading a ewe that had not reproduced. The girl would beat the water with the palm frond and throw the ball of beer mash into the water, singing a song, one version of which was rendered as follows:

> Thunder, thunder; may it bring rain to the land
> Thunder, thunder at Kaptambul [a location].

A somewhat variant description indicated that all the children who were *tekeryontet* would enter the pool, be dipped in the water four times, and later smeared with mud from the pool.

MILITARY OPERATIONS

The existence of external threats and/or the opportunity to exploit neighbors through military action is a situational factor of major significance for an understanding of the organization of a society. In resisting the dual pressures upon them from the pastoralists in the north and east and the farmers in the south and west, the Sebei took an essentially defensive posture; they retreated from the plains to the north and from the mountainside to the south. They frequently hid themselves and their cattle in caves to avoid confrontation, though they did engage in battle from time to time and did take aggressive action occasionally. Weatherby (1962a) discusses Sebei warfare and deals with some of the organizational characteristics.

Each *pororyet* was an independent entity; it could choose whether or not to join an aggressive operation or aid other *pororisyek* when they were attacked. (There was an exception in that Kamnyerer and Kapcheptemkoñ operated together under what appears to have been a mutual agreement.) Military action was not in the domain of either the age-set or the clan. "Among the Sebei, unlike the Nandi, all the age-sets go to war together: The Sebei do not go raiding but are defenders."

In general, Sebei military activity is not associated with clans, but in descriptions of fighting in the western sector against the Gisu and Teso reference was made to particular clans having responsibility for engaging the enemy. I believe that this pattern represents a significant cultural variation, expressing the greater importance of clans in the internal structure of Sebei polity as a temporary response to sedentarization in this area.

Each *pororyet* had its own military leader, *nyikanet* (*nyikonik* pl.) or *aletairion* (from Masai *olaitoriani*). These were men who had proved themselves to be good warriors and bore the shoulder cicatrices that indicated they had killed men in battle. A *nyikanet* also had to demonstrate that he had the qualities of leadership, including the ability to speak to the people. He consulted the prophets and interpreted their orders, as well as led in battle, determined tactics, and maintained order. He was also expected to maintain an attitude of battle-readiness during times of peace. There is no evidence that he had any policing powers within the *pororyet*. The position was not hereditary. Outstanding leaders are remembered by older informants as generally having been young men, but not all of the same age-set. They led a battalion, called *luket*.

Prior to engaging in a battle, all or some of a number of events might take place. A prophet might be consulted regarding the conduct and outcome of the battle or might predict an imminent raid and advise men to be ready. The men would be called to arms by the blowing of an *aryemput* a kudu (antelope) horn. If time permitted, the men might be prepared for action in a number of ways. Medicine known to certain persons would be smeared upon them to make them invincible or to render the enemy's spears useless. An ox might also be slaughtered and its meat consumed by the warriors after the entrails had been read for auguries. Old men also encouraged fighters with speeches, pep talks, and a kind of *récitatif* to which the soldiers reply in refrain.

Medicine from a plant called silelyet was used to make men fearless. After it had been either smoked or crushed, it was put into water and the filtered infusion taken through the nostrils. It is said to make a person "a bit mad" and so fearless that he would go right up to the enemy, with an effect likened to marijuana. A warrior took it on his own initiative. He then became *sirimoito*, an emotional state in which the heart beats very strongly, with strong feelings of resentment, a desire to meet the enemy, and a heightened physical ability so that he would be in danger of harming himself. Such men were apt to be killed in battle.

The conduct of warfare varied with diverse situations, from defensive tactics, to secret night raids, to pitched battles. In the more organized expeditions, the men formed into separate units, the older ones staying in a kind of base camp and the younger ones leading the foray. In open battles, men with shields and spears would be interspersed with bowmen, who were unprotected, unless they were behind the spearmen. Spears were thrown and only occasionally thrust. Enemy spears that missed their mark were often picked up and used as weapons. Arrows were sometimes tipped with poison. Pitched battles would start in the morning and last until mid-afternoon. "By that time, everybody is really very tired and both sides start blowing their horns to stop the fighting until the next day." Cease-fires were arranged by the opposing leaders. While the soldiers were returning to their homes, another horn (*kontit*) would be blown.

Women sometimes accompanied men to battle and often shouted to urge the warriors on: "I think you are becoming a woman"; "If you are afraid of fighting, let us change the sexes"; "You are losing our country by letting the enemies come in." Sometimes women went out in front, and then the men had to go forward, or they would be shamed before their wives.

Trophies were taken — spears, shields, hats, or even dogs, but not parts of slain bodies. The spears and shields of slain fellows were returned to their wives, and, if the battle was not too distant, the body would be brought back. The Sebei deny cannibalistic actions, but some claim that the Gisu or other Bantu people practiced cannibalism.

A warrior who had killed an enemy was decorated with cicatrices cut in rows across the shoulder. The first person to spear a victim received these in five rows reaching from the right shoulder to the breast; the second man to spear the victim got them on the left shoulder. If the original warrior killed a second man, the scars were continued down the back; if a third man, the scars were placed under the arm. Any person, of any age-set, who had killed an enemy could make the cuts. The cicatrices were made with a sharp arrow and rubbed with goat chyme. They had no ceremonial purpose but were marks of valor, "like medals." A warrior who had killed a man was honored in other ways, such as by privileges around the beer pot.

Any man who has killed a person is endangered and must undergo a cleansing ceremony, lest he contract a disease called *kulelekey*. This causes such severe itching that he will scratch himself to death. If he has killed an enemy, a white male goat is slaughtered in the bush and a ringlet of skin from its chest is cut and worn on the killer's right middle finger. The goat meat may be eaten only by old men who are about to lose their teeth; a young man who eats it will lose his teeth. Before the killer can again drink milk, he must also be blessed by having milk spat on him. I am not certain whether a warrior who has killed an enemy must undergo the ritual cleansing demanded of a person who has murdered a man, as informants disagreed on this point. The ritual for a murder is in many ways like that for twins. The murderer is secluded either in the bush, in a cave, or in an old woman's house, and the *yotunet* (release) ceremony is performed at the close of seclusion by a man who has undergone the rite. The ceremony takes place with the whole *saŋta* present. A pregnant ewe is slaughtered and the amniotic fluid given him to drink. He also eats a dung beetle after pinching its head. The medicines given him are those given to the mother of twins. There is no singing, but the axe and pick are struck together (as in circumcision and other rituals). The ewe must be consumed by the murderer (and presumably the ritualist); no one who has not killed a person may eat any part of the animal. The murderer must not drink milk for a long time, and when he does, it must be from a cow who is about to wean her calf.

Though warfare as an organized activity was eliminated with the establishment of European rule, military operations remain a part of Sebei plains life as a result of the continued raiding across the borders by Karamojong and Pokot. In 1962, alarms on the plains were so severe that they spread up to the escarpment, and people fled down the road. We could find no evidence of invaders but learned that the young men of Sipi retained no desire to engage in battle and denigrated their relatives on the plains for living in such a dangerous and foolish situation. These attitudes were again expressed later in the year when people of Kapsirika tried to recruit Kabruron men to help ward off an anticipated Pokot attack. So far as I could discover, only one man from the escarpment responded.

This fear of attack came when rumors spread that the Pokot, who live in Kenya, were going to take advantage of the Uhuru celebrations at the time of Uganda independence. As a military tactic, instigated by the local chief, the men of Kapsirika established a camp on the banks of the Sundet, which was manned for several nights. There was no attack, but a raid on one of the kraals took place on the third night. While this event was hardly a recapitulation of ancient military practices, it does give rise to some relevant observations and insight into attitudes. While the Kapsirikans did not relish fighting, they prepared to engage the enemy — a contrast to the flight behavior on the escarpment.

There was an air of nervous excitement among the men and a good deal of heated discussion as to who was to be there and why others did not participate. The first thing I noticed was that the younger ones took off many of their clothes, stripping to shorts and a cloth tied across their shoulders. There was a good deal of sexual and schatological talk as well — condemning men who just wanted to go home to their wives, or whose bowels were full because they had eaten plantains or maize mush and not just milk and meat. ("Can people eat meat with their mouth and maize with their ass?" was one man's way of complaining about the breach of the rule against eating both together.) Some of the older men did not relish spending an uncomfortable night in the bush, and they were criticized on the grounds that their advice was needed, but ultimately most of them were excused as some were willing to stay. A good deal of the discourse had to do with the acquisition of animals for slaughter. The first night, Salimu Kambuya offered an animal. Actually, he gave a heifer to his brother Andyema, who provided the bullock for slaughter, under a contractual arrangement called *namanya* (see Chapter 5). The next two nights, there was far more difficulty; when one man finally offered a *namanya* it was refused, because he was known not to meet his obligations. When finally it was decided that one man not present should give the animal, a group of the warriors went with sticks of wood to his kraal, put them on the fence, and sat silently in a circle, waiting for him to agree. (Had he not agreed to give the ox, for which he was to get a *namanya* heifer, it would have been taken anyway.)

The entrails of the animal slaughtered the first night were read for omens by the senior man present, Kapsilut, who found them favorable. In the middle of the night, he made further inquiries by the method of tossing sandals (KC:26-27) and the men then in camp gathered round and appeared much relieved that the sandals had also given a favorable augury. The next morning, all the men lined up and faced the east as the sky was turning pink, and a prayer was led by Kapsilut and another old man. Later, the men held court over a young man who had taken Salimu's spear, leaving Salimu "like a woman." They found the young man guilty and gave him eight lashes.

While patrols were formed and sent in different directions throughout the night, it was clear that these plainsmen were no longer warriors by 1962. Many of the elders complained that the men shouted "like boys after bush pigs" and laughed through the night, that they failed to follow proper food tabus, that, when the raid finally came, many turned back rather than ford Greek River, and that those who followed lost the trail and had to wait for dawn. The track ultimately led through a kraal belonging to a Pokot family, whose denials were accompanied by expressions of innocence. The men complained bitterly the next day that the young men had been enjoying the beef but were not doing their duty.

Military failure in modern Sebei is not surprising, for the Sebei have what approaches a tradition of defeat. They have come to utilize the mountain and its caves as a bastion, though it proves an inadequate fortress. They have largely lost the taste for raiding that characterizes their Kalenjin cousins and have thereby lost both men and territory. Their military operations seem never to have been well organized, and what organization did exist has withered away in the past half century. Attitudes toward military prowess do vary, however, and, despite the failures of the bivouac on the Sundet and the unseemly deportment of some young men, the people of Kapsirika do appreciate military prowess and bravery. Some young men take pride in their reputation for having killed a number of their enemy and are honored for it. They receive special privilege at the beer pot even if they can no longer wear the scarification of a successful warrior. They do not disdain fighting as the young men of Sasur do, even if they are not organized for it.

THE *SAŊTA*

The *pororisyek* were subdivided into smaller, spatially defined social units called *saŋta*. Unlike the *pororyet*, the *saŋta* continues as a social unit today. *Saŋta* is also the term for the area within a man's compound where the family gathers for discussion; I presume that the use of the term for village is derivative or, more likely, that both derive from the time when more than a single family lived within an enclosure. This etymology suggests that the concept of village has its origin in the meaning of a center of discourse, rather than being a geographically delimited space. Such a semantic shift would parallel that for *pororyet*, altering older terms for social actions into spatially defined units.

The whole of Sebei is a mosaic of such units, and their boundaries tend to be small streams or cliffs. The distinctions between villages are not evident to an observer, for houses are scattered over the landscape, each man building upon his own land. There is nowadays no central place for meeting nor any clear internal system of communication, though formerly each *saŋta* had such a center. Membership depends upon residence, and residence is freely moved. The wives of polygynous men often reside in separate villages. Villages vary in size from about 100 acres to several square miles, but their population seems to be fairly consistent in size, ranging from twenty to forty households.

In some ways, the *saŋta* is a miniature *pororyet*. It has its own council (*kokwet*) and its own meeting place. It has its elders or judges (*kirwokik*), who hold council on matters of local concern — chiefly family quarrels or minor disputes between neighbors. The *saŋta* manifestly is of less importance to the Sebei than the *pororyet*; it plays no role in military activity, and, although one informant said that each *saŋta* has a cave in which to hide its women, children, and livestock, this is not universally the case.

One ritual (*chepserer*) centered on the *saŋta* is no longer performed. It symbolized and reinforced the unity of the village, though it was performed to rid the community of witchcraft. It was chiefly directed at women, who are thought to engage in sorcery against men and other women, but was also expected to act on men engaged in witchcraft and, according to one informant, was also a protection against the evil eye. *Chepserer* took place at a pool created by damming up a stream. A green snake would be killed and dropped in the pool, and the people gathered would place a curse on any villager engaged in acts of sorcery. They would then release the water, once again dam it, and express a similar malediction on men engaged in wizardry.

Although there was a tendency in the western part of Sebei for clansmen to settle together and though some villages were constituted virtually of single clans, such identity between clan and village nowhere exists today and is not part of the structural system. There is evidence for such settlement, however, in the tendency of clansmen to live in close contiguity, whether because they settled that way historically (as in Sasur) or because men preferred to place their houses near other clansmen (as in Kapsirika). A measure of population mobility is offered in tables 5 and 6, which give the birthplace of household heads, their wives, and their parents, and the present residence of their married or independent children. These tabulations demonstrate the greater stability of the Sasur population, as compared with Kapsirika. This measure of stability is not seriously altered when Sasur and Kamingong are treated separately.

Looking first at Sasur, we see that more than three-quarters of the household heads were born in the combined villages and their sons settled there, while nearly half of their fathers were from the community. If we expand the area to the nearby cluster of villages, which once formed a *pororyet* these proportions measurably increase. The western source of the parental population, particularly the fathers, is also shown. The women generally do not come from the same village, but most of them are from nearby. In contrast to the sons, the daughters tend to scatter, a point often made by parents who recognize that daughters are lost to them when they grow up. These ratios do not reflect marital rules as such, for there are no regulations regarding whence a man must obtain a wife, but reflect other circumstances. Men tend to remain near their fathers because it is from them that they get their land. They marry women from nearby villages, the orbit within which their social contacts are formed. The Sebei told me that women tend to marry men who live further east, but the data do not sustain this notion, for nearly as many mothers and wives came westward to Sasur as came eastward; nor does there appear to be any marked difference in the direction the daughters have moved.

Very few household heads were born in Kapsirika, and only three had fathers born there; nor were many additional men born on the nearby plains. Many of the fathers were born on the central escarpment — the area just above the Ngenge plains — and a large proportion of the household heads were also from this area. Fewer plainsmen came from the area of concentrated plantain cultivation in the western escarpment (only one was actually from Sipi). Many of the men came from Kenya, chiefly from the closely related Bok and Kony territories. A few of these identify themselves as Bok or Kony ("I am a true Bok man"), but most of them are Sebei, descendants of Sebei men who fled to Kenya to escape the excesses of Baganda officials.

The women, whether mothers or wives, show more diverse origins, and the daughters are more widely scattered than the sons. We find no Gisu wives on the plains, but a good many came from the plantain area of the west. The pattern of Sebei children who have married and established households in Kapsirika is quite like that of Sasur, suggesting a tendency to establish a continuing line of patri-oriented descent.

Table 7 further develops the mobility of the Kapsirika population, for it indicates how long household heads have dwelled in the community. Of the 35 not born in Kapsirika, information was obtained from 33 and, of these, 21 had arrived since 1940. The mobility of the Kapsirika population is also expressed by internal movement and the abandonment of homesteads. Of the 95 homesteads located on aerial photographs made in 1959, 39 had been

TABLE 5
Population Mobility: Sasur

	Birthplace						Residence					
	Fathers[a]		Mothers[a]		Hshld head		Wives		Sons		Daughters	
Area	No.	Pct	No.	Pct	No.	Pct	No.	Pct	No.	Pct	No.	Pct
Sasur/Kamingong	24	42.9	4	7.1	47	77.0	16	19.8	20	76.9	6	25.0
Nearby villages[b]	10	17.9	28	50.0	4	6.6	30	37.0	3	11.5	6	25.0
Western area[c]	14	25.0	6	10.7	7	11.5	9	11.1	0		3	12.5
Chebonet area	2	3.6	12	21.4	1	1.6	10	12.3	1	3.8	4	16.7
Eastern Sebei[d]	2	3.6	4	7.1	1	1.6	8	9.9	1	3.8	4	16.7
Ngenge (plains)	0		0		0		0		0		0	
Masop	0		0		0		1	1.2	0		0	
Other tribal areas	4	7.1	2	3.6	1	1.6	7	8.6	1	3.8	1	4.2
Totals	56	100.1[e]	56	99.9[e]	61	99.9[e]	81	99.9[e]	26	99.8[e]	24	100.1[e]

[a]The number of household heads with fathers/mothers born in area, not the actual number of persons.
[b]A cluster of contiguous villages between the Sipi and the Cheptui rivers.
[c]Sebei territory west of the Sipi River, including Legene.
[d]Escarpment area east of Chebonet.
[e]Not 100 percent because of rounding.

TABLE 6
Population Mobility: Kapsirika

Area	Birthplace								Residence			
	Fathers[a]		Mothers[a]		Hshld head		Wives		Sons		Daughters	
	No.	Pct	No.	Pct	No.	Pct	No.	Pct	No.	Pct	No.	Pct
Kapsirika	3	7.5	0	0	9	20.5	5	6.1	11	73.3	5	23.8
Elsewhere on plains	1	2.5	6	15.4	2	4.5	7	8.5	0		3	14.3
Western escarpment[b]	9	22.5	8	20.5	3	6.8	14	17.1	0		0	
Central escarpment[c]	12	30.0	9	23.1	9	20.5	12	14.6	1	6.7	8	38.1
Eastern escarpment[d]	0		1	2.6	4	9.1	11	13.4	1	6.7	3	14.3
Masop	2	5.0	1	2.6	0		0		0		0	
Other tribal areas[e]	13	32.5	14	35.9	17	38.6	33	40.2	2	13.3	2	9.5
Totals	40	100.0	39	100.1[f]	44	100.0	82	99.9[f]	15	100.0	21	100.0

[a] The number of household heads with fathers/mothers born in area, not actual number of persons.
[b] Including Tegeres.
[c] Kapchorwa and Kabruron.
[d] Chesower and Bukwa.
[e] Mostly Sabaot groups.
[f] Not 100 percent because of rounding.

abandoned by August 1962. It was claimed that 7 were abandoned because of normal wear and decay, 1 due to fire and 2 because of death; the remaining families left Kapsirika because of incessant Karamojong and Pokot raiding. Of those 23 for whom the destination was known, 8 had moved to new houses in Kapsirika, 2 had moved to the neighboring *saŋta* of Nyelit, 3 had returned to Nandi and 10 had moved onto the escarpment. The fact that many of the moves were in response to the heightened incidence of inter-tribal raiding undoubtedly influenced the rate of mobility but does nothing to diminish the important underlying fact that these pastoral plainsmen feel free to move about. (By 1972, the entire *saŋta* had been abandoned, many residents moving to the escarpment but some taking up residence in more protected parts of the plains.)

TABLE 7

Time of Arrival in Kapsirika of Household Head

	Household heads	
Time	No.	Pct
Born in Kapsirika	9	21.4
Before 1920	1	2.4
1920-29	3	7.1
1930-39	8	19.0
1940-49	10	23.8
1950-62	11	26.2
Total	42	99.9[a]

[a]Not 100 percent because of rounding.

With a population as mobile as this, and with land so freely held, there can be hardly any meaning to the notion of clan neighborhoods, but there was a marked tendency for sons to remain in close proximity to their fathers. We have noted the location of households belonging to the three most populous clans in Kapsirika on the map prepared by Porter. These show the tendency of the Kabungo to cluster in the central area, with the Kamare to the east, and the Kamundarit in the southwest. But these are not contiguous areas, for other units are sometimes interspersed. Old informants said that the Sebei formerly lived in age-grade organized *manyattas*, in parts of Sapiñ as recently as Maina times, and south of the mountains even later. (Neither Jackson and Gedge nor Austin mentions this form of settlement pattern, so it must have disappeared by that time.)

The most detailed description of these *manyattas* upon which the attached schematic map (Figure 3) is based, was given to me by a man from the Kenya Sabaot. The *manyatta* is a roughly circular enclosure with a brush fence (*sityet*) divided into a right (*tai*) on the east and a left (*let*) side (the former for married men and the latter for the bachelors' house, or *siker-*

ointe) by a brush fence or an imaginary line. In the center is a fire, and the place is called *kok*, where discussions are held. The rectangular houses, like those of Masop, are built around the peripheries, with their doors facing to the center. Each side is again divided into a right and a left side (as one faces the fire); right being for the senior age-set and the left for the junior. A main gate is indicated on the married men's side, but its orientation is said not to be important. There are other gates, as well. Within the enclosure are kraals for the animals. I was told such a *manyatta* would house about two hundred persons.

In about 1960, a group of families in the village of Nyelit, which lies on the eastern border of Kapsirika, resettled in an enclosed *manyatta* as a protective measure against raiding. Though I was told it was patterned after the old style, it was not structured in the manner just described. Only ten of the families of Nyelit preferred the relative safety of the fenced area to the greater personal freedom of scattered dwellings. Clan membership did not figure in the selection or location of individual houses.

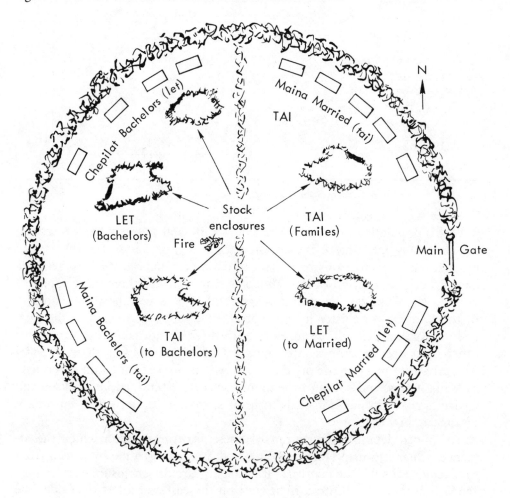

Figure 3. Old Style *Manyatta*.

The entire area was an oval about 300 yards in length and a little more than half that in width. The ten families had at the time built a total of twenty-six houses and about eight smaller structures for sheep and goats. There were seven separate cattle enclosures, some of which were shared by two men. The larger gate opened to the east and was closed at night by putting thorn bush across the opening; there was a small exit on the west side as well. The houses were not limited to the peripheries; there was no central fire; there was no grouping by clans. The several houses belonging to individual men were adjacent, but the houses of other men were sometimes just as close, so that one could not observe even such groupings. In short, spatial arrangements reflected no obvious social parameters other than the integrity of the compound families created by polygyny and a tendency for widowed mothers and unmarried sons to build close to the household to which they were attached. After three generations of living in dispersed villages, the structural integrity of the ancient *manyatta* residence pattern had been destroyed.

THE HOUSEHOLD

The smallest unit in Sebei social behavior is the individual household, consisting of a man, his wife or wives, their unmarried children, other relatives who may share household resources and activities, and occasionally non-relatives. The existence of polygyny means that there may be compound households. The husband is the recognized head of this social unit; he owns the basic resources and is, theoretically at least, charged with responsibility for their management. Among the kindred who are frequently part of such units are widowed mothers and circumcised but unmarried sons, who normally have their own house and not infrequently their own gardens and economic activities.

The household may consist of a single dwelling unit or of several. A polygynous man is expected to build a separate house for each wife, and he almost always does so; he also prefers to have a house of his own, but does not always do so. He almost always does if he has a daughter above the age of four or five, for he should not sleep in the same house with such a girl. A widowed mother who lives with her son (more rarely her daughter) will always have a separate house, for a man cannot sleep in the same house with either his mother or his mother-in-law.

There is a normal and expected evolution of the household. When a man marries, he may bring his bride to his *sikerointe* the separate house he built after circumcision as a bachelor (Plate I:21). Often he has established a permanent liaison with her before the marriage arrangements are made. He will, however, want to build a separate house for her by the time the first child arrives and will probably set up his establishment at a greater distance from his parental home than before. When the first child gets to be of crawling age, his wife will want a helper, and unless there is one nearby — as for instance a younger sister or half-sister of the head — she will bring in a girl of eight or ten years to serve as *mwet* (child servant). It is at about this time that a man begins to think of taking a second wife, for only rarely are wives of the same age group. Thus, the household grows larger and additional houses are built for each wife. Ultimately, his sons will establish a separate *sikerointe* in turn and frequently after his father dies his mother will build a house near his and become a part of that household. In due course, the unit will progressively decline in size, leaving ultimately an old couple, who may, to avoid loneliness, bring in grandchildren to help with the domestic chores.

On the plains, the Sebei often enclose the several houses to form a compound. A brush fence, enclosing an area known as *kienkut*, has two gateways, a large one known simply as *aret* (pathway), or *aretaptoka* (cattle path), and a smaller one (*mokotut*), which is used for calves and is easier to open and close. In front of the door of each house is an area known as the *saŋta* (the same word as used for village) where the outdoor work is done and people sit and talk; a mudded outside floor (*kitawet*, literally flat rock) on which grain is dried, and to the north and lower side the *kapterok*, the kitchen garden area where the sweepings and trash are thrown. Between the area where the granaries are located (*kapchoken*) to the south of the house, and the *saŋta* is a place called *kaitameteu* (literally the place of the head of the home), where the beer pot is set at times of a work party. In some compounds, there may be one such place for each wife. Within the enclosure, but separately fenced off, are the kraals for the cattle (*peiwut*) and often another for the calves, sheep, and goats (*kweyo*), though such small stock may be kept in a special house (*muntyor*) built like the dwellings. The houses face either east or west; their doors often open directly across from one another. The several wives' houses have no set relationship either to that of the husband, if he has a separate one, or to each other. The only major consideration regarding orientation has to do with the place of the granaries to the south (up-slope) and the trash area to the north (down-slope).

Such an arrangement is not found on the escarpment. In Sasur, there will usually be a grassy area outside, a pounded surface where grain can be set to dry, and a place to set the beer pot. Cooking is not usually done outdoors, except for heating water for beer, but much food preparation goes on outside, or on the veranda.

Sebei houses fall into three types: (a) the rectangular house now found only in the mountain area (Plate I:19); (b) the round wattle and daub house with conical thatched roof, which is the prevalent form of Sebei structure both on the escarpment and on the plains (Plates I:20,22), and (c) the rectangular, multiroomed house with corrugated iron roof which is of growing importance among the more acculturated and opulent Sebei.

The flat-roofed house, *klalmet*, is constructed of mud and wattle. It is a long, narrow rectangle; an interior wall separates the roughly one-third devoted to living quarters from the remainder, which houses livestock. An overhang over the front entrance forms a small veranda on which wood, beehives, and the like may be stored. There is a side entrance for animals.

There are no windows in the dwelling portion, but sometimes an opening is left for ventilation in the animal quarters, as well as drains for animal urine. The dark, smoky interiors offer protection against the cold nights in this mountain area. Informants state that just before Europeans arrived the houses on the escarpment were of this type in Sapiñ, but not in Mbai, and that the people from Chema eastward started to copy the round houses of their Bantu neighbors in Maina times. The arrangement of the residential part of the interior is shown in Figure 4 (see also Thomas, 1963:115).

Round houses vary in size from as little as ten feet in diameter to more than twenty. Larger ones have a center pole; the smaller ones do not. Whatever their size, they are consistent in structure and arrangement, except that there may or may not be a screened-off back area in which sheep, goats, and calves are kept.

Certain recognized and standard areas characterize the interior of a Sebei house (Figure 5). To the right of the door is an area called *meteu* where the household head sits; to the left is an area called *kapterpey* where guests sit. Toward the back and at the left is the fireplace behind which is a wood rack for drying the fuel. At the rear of the house is a storage area, unless it has been walled off to house small stock. Milk gourds and other objects of use hang from the posts. Nowadays, there may be a wooden bedframe at the back or at the right side of the house, but many Sebei still sleep on cowhides, which are rolled out of the way during the day. The houses on the plains differ only in detail from those on the escarpment. On the rainy and relatively cold mountainside, houses are more firmly constructed and heavily thatched, whereas on the plains they are often left unmudded so that the air can circulate freely.

The modern rectangular house normally has a central room, which the man uses to entertain his guests, and a series of rooms leading from it, one for each wife. Its construction requires considerable additional investment, not only for the cost of the corrugated iron, but because such a roof requires much firmer construction, larger timbers, several doors and windows, and, as a consequence, additional costs for the labor of the carpenter. A few also have cement floors. This form of house remains a rarity in Sebei and is a mark of status; most men of political importance have such houses. In view of the frequent expressions of hostility among co-wives dwelling under separate roofs, one may reasonably wonder at the effect of such close and enforced proximity, but I have no information on the matter.

The household as a social entity also has a clear structure; the man is head, his wives subordinate directly to him and fundamentally independent of one another, with each responsible for her children. The senior wife has certain privileges and responsibilities, best exemplified by the fact that she is supposed to care for him when he is ill; it is in her house that he should die. She is also expected to act as mentor to the junior wives, teaching them domestic chores and receiving deference in return. The essential independence of each wife is, however, reinforced by the fact that each has her own land to cultivate and her own cows to milk. Each also cooks separately,

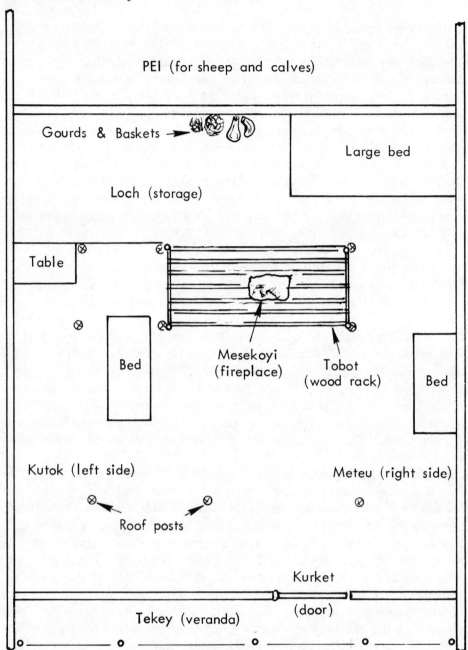

Figure 4. Residential Area of Rectangular House

feeding her children and her husband when he is there. A man is supposed to share himself with each wife and not show favoritism in any way.

All household chores, including the hauling of wood and water, most farming chores, and the milking of cows, are women's work. Other care of livestock and some agricultural tasks are done by men. Girls from the age of five are inducted into women's work; boys from the age of six or seven will herd small stock.

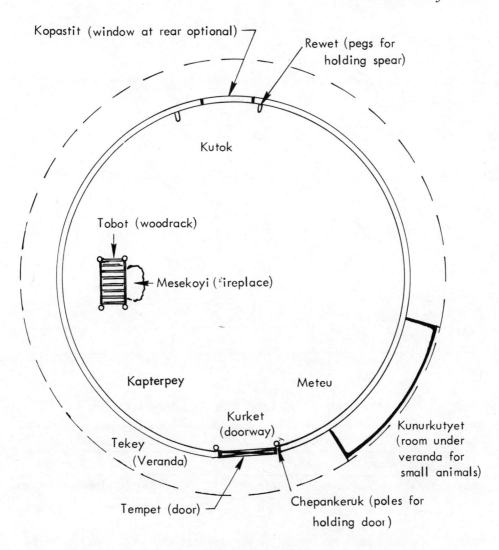

Kopastit (window at rear optional)

Rewet (pegs for holding spear)

Kutok

Tobot (woodrack)

Mesekoyi (fireplace)

Kapterpey

Meteu

Kurket (doorway)

Tekey (Veranda)

Kunurkutyet (room under veranda for small animals)

Tempet (door)

Chepankeruk (poles for holding door)

Figure 5. Round House

The census data developed in our schedules indicate a wide range in household size (Table 8). The higher frequency of smaller households in Kapsirika expresses, I think, the lower fertility and higher infant mortality there; the higher frequency of larger households reflects the greater incidence of polygyny (Table 9). In Sasur, 17 percent of the men currently are living with two or more wives; in Kapsirika 37 percent. (Actual polygyny is greater but impossible to calculate with accuracy; many of the women no longer in the household are legally married to their husbands. The rate of polygyny would be less than the total number of reported marriages for the men.) Many Sebei women have had more than one husband, though never more than one at a time (Table 41), for which the rates in Sasur and Kapsirika are virtually identical. Only four women in the total sample of 165 had been inherited — one from a father and three from brothers.

TABLE 8
Household Units by Size: Sasur and Kapsirika

No. in household	No. of household units	
	Sasur	Kapsirika
1	2	1
2	3	2
3	3	4
4	12	9
5	9	6
6	6	5
7	14	2
8	4	5
9	1	1
10	4	1
11-16	2	7
Total units	60	43
Average per household	5.90	6.47

TABLE 9
Plural Marriages among Sebei Men: Sasur and Kapsirika

No. of Wives	Currently in household				Ever married by head			
	Sasur		Kapsirika		Sasur		Kapsirika	
	Hshlds	Women	Hshlds	Women	Hshlds	Women	Hshlds	Women
0	2	0	2	0	2	0	0	0
1	48	48	25	25	37	37	18	18
2	8	16	8	16	18	36	13	26
3	2	6	8	24	3	9	7	21
4							2	8
5							2	10
6							1	6
Totals	60	70	43	65	60	82	43	89

In a third of Sasur households, there are persons who are not related as wife or child. Such outside members may be serving as a mother's helper (*mwet, mwenik*, pl.; glossed as child servant by the Sebei), as workers, as dependents, or as guests of indefinite duration. Table 10 gives the kin relationship of these outsiders; a clear (but not exclusive) emphasis on patrilineal relationship, is somewhat greater in the farming than the pastoral community, in keeping with the broader mobility patterns of the pastoral

TABLE 10
Extraneous Household Members: Sasur and Kapsirika

Relationship	Sasur[b]	Kapsirika[c]
To head		
Mother	9	3
Brother[a]	10	9
Sister[a]	7	5
Others	0	7
Total	26	24
To wife		
Mother	0	2
Brother[a]	3	4
Sister[a]	3	
Others	0	1
Total	6	7
Descendants of both		
Sons[a]	3	0
Daughters[a]	2	2
Total	5	2
No kin		
Workers	0	6
Others	1	2
Total	1	8
Grand total	38	41

[a]These categories include spouse and descendants of such kin.

[b]60 Sasur households reporting.

[c]43 Kapsirika households reporting.

group. Particularly striking is the differential frequency with which widowed mothers join their son's households and the complete absence of the mother-in-law of the head in Sasur. This reflects not so much a pattern of caring for the aged as it does the pattern of residence: sons have taken over some of their mother's land in the farming area; they do not move on to the land belonging to their mothers-in-law. In Kapsirika, land acquisition is not crucial and there are two instances in which a widow is part of the household of her son-in-law. There were five *mwenik* in Sasur and three in Kapsirika; they are all kin but related in diverse ways. The kin who are part of a household share its tasks and rewards, but the widowed mothers in Sasur have virtually independent economies and the adult sons have varying degrees of economic independence, because they are in a period of transition. The hired workers in the plains have a dependent relationship; they may be paid in cash or kind or both (*KC*:43-44, 59).

COMPARISONS

The most obvious contrasts between Sasur and Kapsirika lie in the greater population density, the importance of land as resource, and the permanency of settlement in the farming area as against the sparsity of population, the open availability of land, and the recency of settlement and fluctuating population in the pastoral community. In Sasur, also, fewer clans are represented in the larger population and they tend to be settled in more clearly contiguous units. In both communities, there is a sense of belonging to one's village of residence, despite the fact that membership is secondary to residence, that place of residence can be changed, and that some men have households in different villages. (There were no persons dwelling in both Kapsirika and a neighboring village, but two men had a wife in Kapsirika and another wife in Bukwa.) In neither community do the clans constitute structural divisions of the community; they are different orders of social organization. Affairs that belong to the local sector of the clan are not directly relevant to the community, and community matters that arise are not mediated through the clan. It may have been otherwise under aboriginal conditions. (These comparisons are summarized in Table 11.)

It may seem surprising that Kapsirika, with its newer and more mobile population, should display more community action than Sasur, as the available evidence strongly suggests. While I observed no action in Sasur that had as its focus the community as such, two events in Kapsirika were community-oriented. One was a moot at which one man threatened to make an oath against his neighbor, who, he felt, had aided and abetted some Pokot raiders who twice took cattle from his kraal. The moot was presided over by the appointive chief but (as it involved oathing) was not an official action. About fifteen or twenty Kapsirika men, and only Kapsirika men, were present, because it was considered a meeting of the *saŋta*, and a matter of village-wide concern. The second instance was the formation of a military defense against the threat of Pokot raids described in the section on warfare. The neighboring plains village of Nyelit had taken this a step further in establishing the permanent *manyatta*.

Though there is compelling evidence in Edgerton's comparison of farmers' and pastoralists' questionnaires and tests that the pastoralists are more individualistic than the farmers and readier to take direct personal action, there is also evidence of a greater sense of community among pastoralists. In my epilogue to his book (*RBE*:299), I wrote:

> The pastoralists' responses show a sense of community loyalty; the farmers' the negative aspects of community interaction. This cohesion is directly expressed in the pastoralists' preference for clansmen and kinsmen and their more frequent resort to cooperation, as well as in their greater display of respect for authority. It is also expressed indirectly in their stronger sense of guilt and shame, and in their greater concern with wrongdoing. The centri-fugal force among farmers stands in sharp contrast. It is revealed directly in their expression of hatred and their disrespect for authority, in their seeking

TABLE 11
Summary of Demographic and Social Comparisons

Sasur	Kapsirika
High population density (1000 persons per sq. mi.)	Low population density (25 persons per sq. mi.)
Close contiguity with neighboring villages	Separation from neighboring villages
Continuity of residence	Recency of residence
Permanence of residence; little movement	Impermanence of residence; much movement
Fewer and stronger clans with considerable contiguity	Many clans, none with large members and less contiguity
No village-wide social action	Some village-wide social action

personal ties (friends) rather than formalized ones, in their litigiousness, their verbal aggression, and their greater jealousy of wealth.

There are several reasons why the pressure toward community action should exist: threatening actions by an external enemy, against which an internal solidarity becomes a functional necessity; relative isolation from persons outside the community; and fewer sources of friction among pastoralists who still have abundant land available to them.

Chapter 4
Clan, Kin, and Age-Set

Oh, here is drink for all of us; even our grandfathers, even our fathers; all the old women and all the old men; even our uncles who have gone below. Drink ye! Watch over us that we may love, that the people should be in peace. Even the cows and goats should increase and have long life. You who are evil, you drink and go away; do not return to this house. Away!

Sebei prayer to the good and evil spirits

The remaining elements in the formal structuring of Sebei society are the kin-based organizational units, clan and lineage; the kinship terminology and the patterning of interpersonal relationship based on consanguinity and marriage; and the age-set structure. In dealing with each of these subjects, our attention will be directed both to its traditional organization (as it existed at the time of first European contact) and to its present operation, examining the structural elements, the functional use, and the psychological involvements of these institutions.

CLAN AND LINEAGE

Each Sebei belongs to a clan (*aret, arosyek*, pl.), a patrilineal, strictly exogamous, named social entity. *Aret* membership is the most important affiliation in a man's life; it is the first thing a person wants to know about a stranger. A man cannot change clan affiliation, except as clans may split apart. Clans have a strong spiritual hold on their members and are even seen as having a kind of genetic inheritance of traits.

There are some two hundred separate clans among the Sebei, though a definitive list cannot be made. Each clan is composed of the descendants of a single founder, and usually its name is formed by prefixing the syllable *kap* (descendants of) to the founder's name. Some, however, have names derived from mythic accounts or some habit or practice attributed to the founder.

Most clans are divided into lineages (*kota*, *korik*, pl., literally house) constituted of the descendants of the founder. Lineages are also named after their founders using the prefix *kap-*.

The Sebei speak of clan leaders, using the terms *kirwokintet* (as for the judges in *pororyet* matters) and of clan councils (*kokwet*). Leadership is essentially informal and generally based on seniority. The term *kirwokintet* does not signify a special office or incumbent, but rather an individual whose capacities as a speaker and whose personal judgment is generally appreciated. Seniority is calculated not in terms of a person's age, but by the seniority of his lineage within the clan, and of ancestry within the lineage. The leader has no formal powers.

Clan councils are held to plan retaliation or negotiation over offenses committed against the clan, adjudicate internal matters such as quarrels among members, chastise a troublesome member, or initiate necessary ritual acts that would prevent further deaths brought about by sorcery or the displeasure of the spirits of the dead. Clans continue to function in such matters, most frequently in hearings in conjunction with funerals (*KC*: *passim*; Goldschmidt, 1973b). I have witnessed clan meetings regarding problems deriving from suspected witchcraft and oathing and more mundane matters, but such meetings are officially disapproved.

Clan membership is strictly patrilineal. A man does have some special involvement with related clans, including the natal clan of his mother and his father's mother, but this does not imply membership. The Sebei specifically believe that a person belongs to the clan of his genitor, not his father, and that it is bad for a man who is not properly a member of the clan to partake of ritual clan food and beer and participate in its funeral rites. It is said that if he is allowed to do so, he will prosper and the clansmen will become poor and die out. As the Sebei adopt children, the issue may be raised in this context as well as in·regard to illegitimacy, as the following incident indicates:

> A boy named Cheperoin was roaming about. One of the men of our *aret* took this little boy and treated him as his own son. He arranged to have the boy circumcised ,and paid property for his brideprice. After that man was married, the men of the *aret* said that they would accept him as a member of their *aret*, but they would not share two things: first, they would not join with him in a funeral ceremony and, second, when cattle, goats or sheep were slaughtered, he should not be allowed to eat of the heart. This boy now has many descendants and his *aret* is called Kapcheperoin.

Women take the clan affiliation of their fathers, but Sebei men assert that upon marriage they take the clan affiliation of their husbands. The matter is ambiguous. The marriage ritual makes little symbolic expression of such a change, though it certainly expresses the wife's subordination to the husband's clan. The concept does receive strong affirmation in the funeral rituals, for a married woman is a chief mourner for her husband, and for the clansmen of her husband, but not for her own clansmen. On the other hand, if a woman commits a murder, vengeance or compensation is exacted from her father's clan, not her husband's, and she is subject to revenge for a crime committed by a man or woman of her natal clan. If a woman has difficulties with her husband, she seeks support from her natal clansmen. To Sebei men (but I believe women would agree), a woman's clan affiliation seems relatively insignificant. For instance, clan safety is endangered when a boy is fathered by a man of a different clan, but is not indangered if the child is a girl as this causes no spiritual harm, since she will never partake of the ritual food expressive of clan unity.

The clans are not totemic, as are other Kalenjin peoples' such as the Kipsigis, (Peristiany, 1939:117-24), Nandi (Huntingford, 1953:20-21), and Marakwet (Kipkorir, 1973:6-9), despite Roscoe's assertion (1924:82). A few clans have food tabus. The Kaptui do not eat buffalo nor the Kapchepkoin hippopotami, "Because they are members of our clan, and we get sick if we do." The Kapkwech do not eat sheep, because their founder was born when his mother was herding sheep and was therefore named Kwech (lamb). These are the only specific clan food tabus I learned. Some clans are named after a preferred food. Dietary involvements are found in about one clan in ten.

The Sebei do not have lengthy genealogies. Out of twenty-six instances in which I endeavored to trace the male line back to the founder, only fourteen respondents could do so. Of those who could not, most could recall the names of their grandfathers or great-grandfathers. While one man recorded a depth of nine generations to the clan founder, most gave depths of three or four. There is no way of knowing how accurate these records are; the essential fact is that they show little sense of continuity and little mythification of the clan. The age-set of the great-grandfather is rarely known, and never beyond that generation.

While some clans had settled in particular areas and informants would speak of clans and lineages as if they resided in a particular area, in fact, they are now widely scattered. I obtained what purported to be a complete genealogy of one lineage (Kapkuyot) of the Kamuchaki clan, in Sasur. Of thirty-five household heads listed, thirteen lived in Sasur and another seven elsewhere in Sipi. The remainder were widely scattered, with three near Kapchorwa, two in Kabruron, five in Bukwa, three in Ngenge, and one each in Pokot and an unspecified place in Kenya.

When clans are divided into lineages, these units are universally thought to have been established by the sons of the clan head. Lineage seniority is in terms of the relative age of their founders. The number of lineages per clan varies; of the fifty-two clans for which I obtained information, one had five *korik*, four had four *korik*, twenty-nine had three, fifteen had two, and there were three for which no subdivisions existed.

Lineages are natural lines of cleavage in Sebei, as elsewhere. The investigation of some sixty clan units evoked data on seventeen fissions that had taken place in the past, involving forty different clans.[1] There appear to be two basic reasons for the separation of clans. One may be called migration; clans move apart and lose a sense of unity, and this appears to have been the case in five of the seventeen instances. The other is that there is a quarrel and a more-or-less formal separation, and this accounts for six instances. (No explanation was adduced for the other six cases.)

An example of migration is given in the following mythic account:

> There was a man who had five sons. Famine broke out. One of the sons said, "I shall go down to Soi and look for mushrooms (*arok*)," so we call those people Kaparok. Another said, "I will go to the forest and hunt ground rats (*pundyei*)," so we call his descendants Kapundyei. A third son said, "I will not leave, but will stay here and starve and wither (*yus*)," but he managed to survive and we call his people Kapyus. Another son ran away, leaving his son (named Mwey) and they are called Kapchemwey. The last one heard that there was land with much food, and though he was warned that the people were ugly (*sankut*), he said, "I will go there even if they are ugly, provided they will feed me," so we call his people Kapsankut.

Under such a separation, the clans remain linked to one another and retain a formalized relationship; they may share the heart of a slaughtered animal or share the beer brought by a suitor to his future father-in-law, and they are enjoined from intermarriage. "But it was only a few years ago that one of the sons of the Kapyus clan married a woman of Kapundyei clan. That was a very big shame."

A similar mythic basis was described for the split between Kapchemekwen and Kapchoken clans. The informant who gave this account said:

> There were two brothers. One of them went to Masop in search of firewood (*kwenik*), and he finally came to Kapchorwa. The leader of this clan was Chemekwen. But the other said he wanted to make granaries (*choken*), and moved to the present Sipi looking for material to make them, and founded the Kapchoken clan.

The second account of this separation is more matter-of-fact:

> Chemekwen, the founder of our clan was older brother to Choken. They lived on Mount Debasien in Karamoja District. When famine broke out in the country, they went to look for food and came to the cave called Kaptum, near Sipi falls. After some time Chemekwen decided to move east and went to Kaptaret, in Kaptanya. Choken left the cave, but remained in Sipi. He then formed his own clan.

---

1. In one instance, the fissions formed a genealogical relationship (not noted by the Sebei informants) as follows:

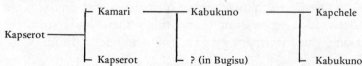

Here again, the rules of exogamy were breached. The informant goes on to say that in Nyonki times a man of Kapchoken married one of our daughters. "This sort of action annoyed us Kapchemekwen very much, but we have not married Kapchoken's daughters. But if we happen to get a Kapchoken girl, we will have our revenge."

Formal separation can occur when hostility develops between the *korik* of a clan. This may be the result either of some direct confrontation between the *korik*, or because one clansman is causing trouble as a murderer and bringing revenge against the whole clan. Such a separation is formalized by an oathing. The clansmen are called together under a korkorwet (Uganda coral or red hot poker) tree, which is, among other things, the appropriate tree for suicides. The men climb the tree and jump down, saying, "We are no longer members of this *aret*." Later, they spear the tree to seal a further oath (see *SL*:110-11). Henceforward, the two clans cannot share clan beer or the heart of an animal; presumably they could intermarry, but the mutual sentiment would preclude this for some time.

I sat in on discussions concerning the possible separation of *korik* among members of the Kaptui clan in 1962. Some persons in the clan thought that the recurrent deaths were being caused by the fact that one man was not legitimately a member of the group, being an illegitimate child "brought on the back of the mother" when married into the clan. This child, a Chepilat *pinta* man, was dead, but there was feeling among some that his *kota* should be expunged. General opinion held that, if this were to be done, it should have been undertaken long ago, that jealousy was at the root of the desire of some to undertake this separation, and that other causes were the source of the deaths. Their opinion prevailed.

The relationship between such clans is not forgotten, and there appears to be recurrent pressure for them to unite. In one instance described, two *korik* were willing but a third refused. The informant who described the oath of separation went on to say:

> The Kapkurot and Kapchemo clans are talking about forming together again now. A man of Chumo *pinta*, whose brother lost three children in one day, himself lost two children within a week. They went to the diviner, who ordered that the clans reunite. If they have the ceremony, it must be done at the tree just west of Kapchorwa, where the separation ceremony took place. They don't know the real tree to work on, but they will select one and uproot it. They will have to dig out all the roots or else it might grow up again. They will then sprinkle beer upon each other and claim friendship again.

A ceremonial reunification is described in *Sebei Law* (110-11).

Not all fissions that derive from disputes are formalized with an oath, but where there has been open expression of hostility, there must still be a ritualized peacemaking. One informant gave the following description:

> Chehira of the Kapet clan was a ruthless murderer and killed many Gisu and was one of those who increased the friction between the Sebei and the Gisu. He was hot-tempered and would not hesitate to commit murder. Therefore

his brother, Chelombu, asked Chehira to go away, and he went to Bok, while Chelombu and Kwareŋ, another brother, went to Amagol and started the Kapkwareŋ clan, and later settled in Chema.

The Kapet and Kapkwareŋ clans cannot intermarry. But in the old days, the two clans would get together. The Kapet would slaughter a white uncastrated bull and the Kapkwareŋ a red ram. The two clans would be on opposite sides of the river, and they would take the chyme from the animals to the opposite side; afterwards they would eat the uncooked fat of the ram's tail and the cooked chest portion of the bull. This would establish fellowship between them, and they could eat and drink together. This ceremony is done when, for instance, a person of the same clan but a different *kota* kills repeatedly, leading to a feeling of separation between the lineages, but the people later want to become reconciled.

Clans that perform the oath ceremony become entirely separate, but those that have separated because of migration or other reasons retain a linkage (*arapañ*, from *pañ*, meat). They are called meat clans because the men may share the heart of animals slaughtered. Although they are not supposed to intermarry, they occasionally do so. There is no evidence that clans linked together owe one another mutual protection, nor will an oath against one clan have effect upon the other. As they share bridal beer, so they say, they cannot marry, for then the in-laws would be drinking their beer together.

While these clans, lineages, and linked clans give the appearance of a segmentary system of the kind described elsewhere in Africa and Southwest Asia, the social meaning and function of each of the three levels is entirely different. There is none of the standard opposition that characterizes the segmentary system, and the Sebei system does not provide a basis for increasingly extended social order as is the case, for instance, with the Nuer (Evans-Pritchard, 1940a:192-203) or the Somali (Lewis, 1961:*passim*). On the contrary, the essential and focal element in Sebei thought and action is the clan; it is the true jural unit. The linked clans have no jural authority at all; they are merely matters of sentiment based on remembered (or imputed) history, expressed in a sense of exogamy and the propriety to share certain ceremonial foods.

Until a lineage splits from others in the clan, it has neither psychological potency nor political clout. Only when there are disputes internal to the clan do the *korik* take on the characteristics of the clan itself, bringing *korik* members into closer cohesion and spiritual unity. Because it is apt to have a more concentrated social existence and closer remembered ties as a result of its shorter history, the *kota* is the unit of immediate access. Marital disputes or other forms of family discord and other legal matters of an essentially trivial kind may be handled by the *kota* — or even some segment thereof.

If the clan is structured for major legal purposes as the jural unit, it follows that it plays a leading role in the settlement of legal matters. I have discussed this role in *Sebei Law*.

> The law of violence is essentially clan law, and acts of harm against a person are viewed as being either actually or potentially against his clan. Legal actions in redress of such wrongs are therefore actions by the clan. Similarly,

the act is seen as being an act of the clan as a whole and not merely of the individual who actually performed the injury; retaliation is therefore against the clan and not the individual. [*SL*:81]

One informant stated the role of the clan in these terms:

I want to make clear to you what the major laws about killing are. First, it was the law that you should not kill a person, because some member of your clan will be killed and, second, everybody in the clan must suffer if compensation is to be paid. If neither revenge nor compensation is had, then they will have to do sorcery, and this is a most dangerous thing, because it is more serious and is not forgotten. The clan who has not paid compensation or been avenged — their children will all die, and even nowadays you can see people doing ceremonies to get rid of these curses so that people can live.

After a dispute between clans that had involved a killing, a ceremonial assertion of amity is requisite. Rituals of amity vary considerably but all involve the slaughter of an animal jointly by representatives of the two clans. For instance, a settlement finally took place some two years after the quarrel that led to the killing of one man. In the presence of representatives of the two clans, a man of the lineage of the murderer and another from that of the victim held between them a ram. They each stabbed at it with knives and as it lay dying ran off to a nearby stream to bathe together as a sign of friendship. When they returned, the ram had been skinned and the people had dispersed. The two men then took the right thigh and cut it as a further expression of amity. The clan that was to receive the compensation (30 cattle and 30 small stock) provided the ram, which was eaten by the clan that was to pay the compensation.

The sanction that enforces these contributions lies in the power of the oath, for if the injured clan should resort to this form of retaliation, any person in the clan is liable to be the victim — indeed, all may be. It behooves a clan to rid itself of persons whose repeated behavior causes such problems, as they may do by simply killing him or allowing others to kill him (*SL*:107-108), or by separating his *kota* from others, as already indicated.

Although the clan as a whole has a claim on its members to furnish stock, the clan does not hold property. (There are some indications to the contrary, in that cattle earmarks are clan marks, not individual brands, and in western Sebei the clans tended to settle in concentrated areas and spoke of clan lands; yet, an examination of actual transactions shows that neither herd management nor land management is a clan prerogative, but entirely an individual matter.) Rather, the clan has a moral and legal claim on members of the clan as persons, and this claim may result in demands for goods, as well as services, and this may impair some of the personal freedom of its members (*SL:* 159-60).

Continuing clan concerns for mutual protection are expressed in occasional meetings designed to remove causes that are presumed to be responsible for their decline in numbers. In 1972, I witnessed a meeting of clansmen organized for such purpose.[2] The meeting involved about forty or fifty persons, seated on folding chairs or on the grassy slope edged by a plantain *shamba* near the chairman's house. There were, in addition to clansmen and women, one "advisor," an outsider, a neighbor who was wealthy and whose judicial advice was valued. The clan consists of two *korik*, both of which were represented. Six separate matters were discussed, not including one initiated by a woman but declared to be "not a part of the agenda" and therefore set aside.

The issues were as follows:

1. An oath made by one *kota* against the other for the murder of some children, placed by their mother. A diviner had advised compensation, but the woman had refused. She had died, but oathing substance had been transmitted to her daughter, who was willing to have the *korosek* ceremony for removal of the oath, but demanded compensation. There was a lengthy discussion on how to raise the money and furnish grain for beer.

2. A curse placed upon the Kapsamsama clan for the theft of a cow. No Kapsamsama representative was present, and nothing was decided "because it is they who are dying."

3. A curse placed on the meat of a stolen cow by its owner without warning his clansmen, with a bleeding arrow borrowed from a neighbor. The arrow was hidden in a cave and transmitted to the owner's son. As both clans were losing members, the advisor said there should be no compensation but only a slaughtered ram and beer.

4. A curse by a married daughter of the clan who had been beaten to death. Before she died, she said, "If you kill me, let my blood live and kill all your family." Her father beat her grave with a goat skin, reinvoking the oath. The death of two clan brothers was seen as a result of this oath. The matter was internal to the clan and *kota*, so a *korosek* ceremony was ordered to be performed.

5. A curse made by a man against his brother-in-law, who was keeping some of his cattle. The brother-in-law had used them for his brideprice and claimed they had been stolen. The man cursed his brother-in-law by shooting a bleeding arrow borrowed from a neighbor into the middle of his kraal, and members of that family were dying. As the principals in the original theft and curse had died, the clan feared that the curse would act reciprocally upon them. It was suggested that *korosek* be performed, with only a goat for compensation, and that the man who received the goat pay 5 shillings to the neighbor who had furnished the arrow.

6. An oath against another clan for murder of one of the first clan's members, which was dismissed since, "We are not the ones that are dying; let them come to us."

I find it surprising that the great force of clan identification exists with practically no ritual reinforcement other than the *korosek* rites to remove

2. This is the same clan that was concerned with the problem in 1961 (*SL*:83-84).

the power of a curse. There are no clan rituals that create a sense of amity separate from external threat. This is not only true today; there are no such rituals in Sebei memory. Other ritual acts express clan amity, but they do not bring the clan together. When a man dies, only clansmen (and their wives) may be shaved. When an animal is slaughtered, only clansmen may partake of the heart. On certain ritual occasions, notably in marriage negotiations, certain pots of beer are for clan members alone. These acts express clan identity and reinforce the sense of personal affinity, but there is no great outpouring of spirit nor verbal reaffirmations.

The sense of clan unity is furthered by Sebei beliefs about the spirits of the dead (*oyik, oynatet* sing.). These spirits are essentially harmful, and they must regularly be placated with beer and bits of food. No beer is consumed without a proper libation, mentioning the names of dead clan ancestors, hence repeated reference to the continuity of the clan. Other ritual occasions for placating or honoring the clan *oyik*, such as the naming of a child and occasionally the dedication of an animal, clearly reinforce the individual's sense of belonging to the clan and his continuity with its ancestry, but do not celebrate the sense of clanhood.

Clans are said to have certain innate tendencies. I was given a list of six clans said to have a tendency to leprosy and of eight that had the evil eye. Some clansmen said that there was a tendency for their clan's children to be born with half-arms or other crippling defects; one clan tended to have twins who prospered, another, twins who died, and a third's children all tended to die. Temperamental elements were also among these clan traits: "We are a polite people"; "Our clan is hot-tempered." One said, "We are a polite people, but due to the fact that we have married girls from other hot-tempered and warlike clans, some of our clan members have adopted their uncles' habits. I think their uncles' blood has entered into them." The existence of a diviner or minor curing prophet in the Kapsongen *aret* was explained by the fact that his mother had been a member of Kapchai, the clan of the prophet Matui, "so the *oynatet* of his mother's clan Kapchai went to him. . . . When he died [the informant continued], the spirit of our grandmother's clan came to me, and I am now doing that work."

Certain social roles also are clan-associated. Only two clans know the special witchcraft called *kankanet*; certain clans are prophets, smiths, and, according to some, circumcisors. Some clans also spoke, historically at least, of having been cattle-keepers or cultivators and in one instance of having been hired herdsmen for others, as they were poor. Occasionally, a clan reputation is denied, as when one informant said "people complain that we are bewitchers, but we are not." In one instance, the warlike tendency was asserted for a single *kota* rather than the whole clan.

In summary, the clan must be seen as a jural unit, a nonproperty-owning corporate entity, in which each person is imbued with a strong sense of mutual obligation, sanctioned by deep conviction concerning spiritual forces. The importance of this jural unity lies in the fact that it protects the individual. Under ancient conditions, a person without clansmen was in constant jeopardy and might be summarily killed. I was told that this was particularly true in the agricultural west, though cultural expression indicates it was also true throughout Sebei. There is a special word for a "clanless man," *pananet*. It was particularly in the interest of justice to such persons, I was told, that Namume instituted the *chomi ntarastit* establishing a measure of legal protection for those who had no clansmen. The psychological force of clan identity has not been destroyed with the passage of time, despite the decline of its legal function. This is not merely because clan identity is sanctioned in belief and expressed directly and indirectly in the minor rituals of daily life; it is also because the clan plays a continuing role in maintaining social relationships.

KINSHIP TERMINOLOGY AND USAGE

The classifications expressed in the pattern of kin term usage are of the Omaha type; that is, mother and mother's sister are equated, father and father's brother are equated, and there are separate terms for father's sister and for mother's brother, and the term for mother's brother applies to the sons and son's sons of the mother's brother. Details of the terminology are presented in Appendix C; here we will discuss certain features and problems that characterize terminological usages.

Mother's brother. The term for the mother's brother, *mama*, is applied to his male descendants and to all men of the mother's clan, except the grandfather. The clan is referred to as *kamama*, as is that portion of the brideprice that goes to the mother's brother.

Father's sister. The term *senke* is applied not only to all the women father calls sister, but women also use this term for their brothers' children; i.e., it is reciprocal. It may also be used for father's mother's sister's daughter and for father's father's sister.

Siblings. The most commonly used term for siblings, *yeya*, does not differentiate between the sexes and applies to parallel cousins on both the mother's and father's side. Another pair of terms differentiates siblings by sex, *mutapiya* and *chepiya*, which together have the same extension as *yeya*. *Chepiya* is also used for daughter. Finally, there is a term that is considered very polite (*wonyo*) that is used by women to address their brothers.

Parents. The word for father (*papa*) is extended to apply not only to his brothers and his age-set mates, but also to the husband of any *senke*, and the husband of the mother's brother's daughter. It is used as an especially polite means of addressing others, such as son-in-law and father-in-law. Another term (*kwan*) is used only in reference for the actual father. The term for mother (*yeyo*) applies to all the wives of the father, to the sisters of the mother, the father's brother's wives, and to the mother's brother's wife and daughter, and by extension and as a polite form to other women such as the mother-in-law and the wives of the father's age-set. A second word, *kamet*, is used similarly to *kwan*.

Cousins. As already indicated, all parallel cousins are equated with siblings (*yeya*) and mother's brother's son is equated with mother's brother (*mama*); mother's brother's daughter is equated with mother (*yeyo*). Father's sister's child is called *lekwetaplekwet*, child of my child or *wiritapchepto*, son of my daughter.

Children. There is a sexually undifferentiated term, *lekwet*, for child, which is widely applied, and a differentiated pair, *weri* for boys and *chepiy* or *chepiya* for girls.

Second generation terms. There are two terms for grandparent or grand-child. The word *kuko* is a reciprocal term between grandchild of either sex and grandfather; *koko* is similarly used reciprocally between grandchild and grandmother. These terms are generally used also for siblings of these grandparents, but not for spouses of grandchildren. Another term, *mucho-koret*, is used only for grandchild.

Third generation. A self-reciprocal term (*kasanya*), undifferentiated by sex, is used for great grandparents and great grandchildren.

Spouse. The words for husband, *pontoni*, and wife, *chepyos*, are not properly used in public after the couple have children, when they should address one another as father/mother of their oldest living child and later as grandfather/grandmother of their oldest living grandchild. There is a second term for wife, *korkoni*, which is highly disrespectful, usually used in anger. Co-wives may address one another by either of three terms (and may also call one another sister), of which *chemnyo* is the most usual and *sentenyu* the most polite, and often applied to the wives of the husband's age-set mate as well.

In-laws. The term *kapikoi* is applied to both sister's husband and spouse's brother. An alternate form, *alaptani*, has been borrowed from the Bok and appears mostly in the east. Chemtai thought it may be a corruption of *araptani* but was certain that the old people pronounced it as recorded. Alan Jacobs (personal communication) suggests that this may be derivative from Masai *olaputani*, which is used to refer to any male of the mother's clan, more particularly mother's brother, and derives from the verb *aputan*, "to establish affinal relations." Both terms are extended to siblings and to the in-laws of one's own siblings, and also to father's sister's husband and to wife's brother's son.

The term *pukot* for sister-in-law is applied comparably to *kapikoi* but may also be used by a woman for her father's sister's husband. The term *limenyu* used between siblings of spouses is found in the east and *arawe* (or *arowo*) is similarly used in Mbai. The words for parents-in-law, *pontetapikoi* and *chepyosyetapikoi* are extended to the parents of the men and women married to one's siblings. The parents of a man and woman married to one another use the term *pomwai*, which was said to be of Bok origin.

The son-in-law may be called *kapikoi* or *santani* or addressed as *apo*, all terms of respect. The daughter-in-law may be called *lekwani*, my child, or daughter- or wife-of-my-son. The spouses of a man's sister's children may be addressed as *koko*.

For some kin, there are a variety of words from which choice is made, while for other kin there is only one word that is proper. The former tends to be the case for the more intimate and freer relationships (child, grandchild, spouse, sibling); the latter for those that are more clearly role-defined (*mama, senke*) or where age-status tends to formalize the expected behavior (father, mother, grandparent). There is also a tendency to spread certain terms that connote respect to other kin as an expression of deference. Some kin one must always address by kin term; others, such as a man's daughter-in-law, must not be addressed by kin term. The context of the situation and the emotional involvements may govern the choice of terms used for wife.

> I call my wife by the name she received at circumcision and I can call her by the Yap-name [i.e., teknonymously] she received when she had a child. I call her by that name when there are people around. When I am angry, I call her by her circumcision name. I call her *korkoni* (wife) in two situations: first, when I am resting or having friends or am tired. I will say, "Wife, untie my shoes," or "Wife, bring me something." The other time is when I am angry and say, "What is wrong with this wife?" The polite way to call her is to use her name, but if she waits too long, I might call her "wife." She usually calls me by my circumcision name, but if people are around she calls me "father of Chemingich" [the eldest son]. This is a particularly polite way of addressing me.

Associated with these kin roles are expected forms of behavior. Certain kin of opposite sex stand in a relationship called *tekso*, which was variantly glossed as one of fear or respect (the word is the same in Sebei) and was said to derive from the verb *tek*, to defend oneself. The degree of restraint varies in intensity, being most important between a man and his mother-in-law and a man and his daughter.

> When I go to my mother-in-law's house, she goes to the far part of the house and covers herself carefully. She greets me in a quiet voice. There is a special place for me to sit and a special place for her to sit.

Tekso applies to the following relations of a man: all women of his mother's clan, including the mother; all women of his wife's mother's clan and generation; his daughters, the daughters of his age-mates, his brother's daughters, and his father's sister's daughters. A "mild" *tekso* relationship exists between a man and his *senke*. A breach of *tekso* relationships requires an apology and ceremonial removal of the "bad birds" that derive from the breach.

The most stringent regulation with respect to incest applies to a man and his daughter. A girl never sleeps in the same house with her father after she has reached the age of five or six. The restriction on behavior is extended to her husband; he is addressed in highly polite form. The restriction not only applies to all women so classified, but extends to the daughters of one's age-mates. The relationship applies as well between a man and the wives of his son; the wife is called daughter of my child or daughter of the house, for to refer to her as son's wife is indelicate. No *tekso* applies to persons called *koko*, *kuko* (grandparents), *kesenyontet* (great grandparents), brothers-in-law or sisters-in-law. The wife's sister's husband and the wife's sister's daughter are "free relationships." A mild joking relationship exists between a man and his wife's sisters: "They do not speak of sexual matters aloud but go about whispering to one another." A man may not, however, marry his wife's sisters.

The mother's brother, though set off by the all-important Sebei differential of age, is, in general, a friendly or easy relationship. "My *mama* was always kind to me and chastised me only once. He would take my part against my father. If he and my father agreed on something, then I would have to agree too."

The relation between brothers is ambivalent, for they are enjoined on all occasions to be friendly and cooperative and are, of course, fellow clansmen and hence tied into the system of mutual support, yet they also are in direct competition. Fratricide is not an infrequent occurrence. Rivalry between brothers is endemic; it is they who will share the often scarce resources of the father. On the plains, it appears that the greater rivalry is between full brothers (*KC:passim*) while in the farming sector the sons of different mothers show the greater antagonism.

The relation between brothers and sisters is also characterized by antagonism, for the brother is deeply concerned with the marriage of his sister and, along with the father, may seek to force a liaison on her on the basis of his desires rather than hers. This situation, together with the generic pattern of male dominance, often creates a direct confrontation in which the brother beats his sister into submission. Sisters, on the other hand, are not put into a rivalrous relationship over property. The only expression of strong bonds that we observed between siblings was between sisters. When they marry, they are separated, but they frequently visit and regularly give gifts of food to one another when they do so.

The Sebei extend the idea of kinship to people who are not related by consanguinity or affinity, but with whom they have some other established and more-or-less permanent bond. The most important of these is the *pinta*-mate. This bond is so important that it may function as a connecting relation and it has been necessary to include it in the kinship chart (Appendix C). *Pinta*-mates are equated as brothers. A man has a mild joking relationship with his *pinta*-mates' wives and a strict tabu with his daughters. Also, kin terms are regularly extended to a man's age-mate, particularly by his wives. A person calls his father's age-mates as he does his father, this man's wife as mother, and an age-mate's daughter as daughter. A woman will refer to her son's age-mate as son and to her husband's age-mate as husband. A man calls his own *pinta*-mate *pintenyu*, *chorwenyu* (referring to their having grown up together), or *serichenyu*, (which has reference to the thighs).

Special terms of address, with quasi-kinship implications are also used in other circumstances. A close neighbor (*latyet*) is called *latenyu*, and a man is particularly enjoined from having sexual relations with the wife of his *latyet*.

When two men enter into a cattle contract they become *tilyet* to one another, and address each other and their respective wives as *tilyenyu*. They incur with this an obligation of mutual respect and must share beer and food on all occasions, and again sexual relations are tabu.

If a man furnishes an animal for an age-mate's son or daughter at the time of initiation, the two men and their respective wives call one another by a special name: *posupen* if it is an ewe, *ntowo* if a heifer, and *pomonko* if it is a bullock. "The children will then be like mine and the wife of my *pomonko* will be respected; we don't have *tekso*, but still I avoid talking about sexual matters." An initiate will also call his sponsor (*moteriyontet*) *moteriyenyu*. These relationships also carry behavioral obligations, usually restraint in sexual conduct with the relative's wives (who share the designation) and obligations to entertain or share food.

There is a structural relationship between clans that derives from genealogical relationship and that sets off eight clans with respect to any ego into four categories: First, ego's own clan, with its all-important implications. Next is ego's mother's clan, referred to as the mother's brother's clan, *kamama*. A person may not marry into the *kamama* clan. Third, the clans ego refers to as *kapkuka*, the clans of his father's mother and his mother's mother, or perhaps more accurately the clans that his parents call *kamama*. Marriage into the *kapkuka* clans is permissible and, indeed, is said to be the preferred marriage "but we are leaving that now." (Since a man is not supposed to marry two women of the same clan or into the clan to which his full brother is married, I do not see how that form of marriage could be statistically very high, though that does not impair the notion of preference.) Finally, there are the four clans of his great-grandmothers, the clans that his mother and father call *kapkuka*, and which he calls *kapsenyis* or *kasenyis*. A person should not marry a member of this clan, lest he become thin and waste away from a disease called *kalelekei*, from which he will eventually die — "but now we have forgotten that." The relationship between these clans is indicated in Figure 6.

In addition to these clans, there are others the Sebei refer to as the clan of their aunts — that is, the ones into which their father's sisters have married. If the pattern of marriage between *kapkuka* clans were followed, these then would, in fact, be the *kapsenyis* clans, but this fact was not pointed out to me by the Sebei. (The term is not, according to Chemtai, related to the word *senke*, but to *kasan*, to carry on one's back.) *Kapkuka* and *kapsenyis* clans are not involved in ceremonial relationships or in property transfer.

In addition to the specific restrictions on marriage to certain clans, there are other relationships in which marriage or extramarital intercourse is forbidden. A man must not marry a woman of the same clan as a living wife, a true sister of a deceased wife, or a woman of the clan of his wife's mother. He should not marry into the clan of his brother's wife, particularly of the "brother he will bury"; i.e., the one whose wives he should inherit. He is also not permitted to marry the daughter of an age-mate, who stands in relation to him as daughter. Nowadays, men argue over whether this restriction

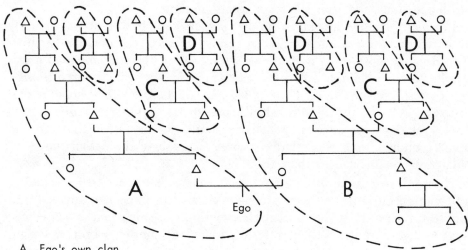

A. Ego's own clan

B. Ego's mother's brother's clan (kamama)

C. Ego's grandparental clans (kapkuka)

D. Ego's great grandparental clans (kasenyis)

Figure 6. Clans Standing in Special Relation to Ego.

applies to the entire *pinta* or just a subset (*KC*:68-69) and I believe that the rule will die out.

While kinship plays an important role in the patterning of interpersonal relationships, it is my no means a dominant factor in organizing social life. The very fact that age-mates, neighbors, and partners in cattle contracts take on simulated kinship roles suggests that other determinants have significant influence on daily social behavior. Aside from clansmen on the one hand, and the intimate relationships of the domestic ménage — parent-child and husband-wife — there are not many standardized kin-based role demands. Important kin-specific roles are found only in the twin ceremony, marriage and funeral rites, and to a lesser extent in circumcision and in the harvest ritual called *misisi*. The important symbolic act of exchanging bracelets on a bride is done by the groom's brother, and the even more important act of burying the dead is a brother's role. A brother should also participate in the twin ceremony and appear at circumcisions of his brother's children, but he has no special role. The mother's brother receives an animal in brideprice and should also be present at the circumcision of his sister's children but again has no ritual role. The aunt (*senke*) of the bride has minor ritual involvement with the marriage. Brothers, sons, unmarried sisters, and daughters and wives of brothers and sons are mourners at a funeral. Of all ceremonials other than these rites of passage, the only one to center on kindred is the family harvest thanksgiving of *misisi*, where mother's brother, daughter's husband, wife's father, and wife's brother participate along with the closer family relatives. Such quasi-kin as neighbor, age-mates, and *tilyet* have almost as frequent ritual roles, while the actual ritualist is usually an unrelated person who has been the principal in a similar ritual at some earlier time. Even the blessings, accompanied by spewing milk, as on a bride, or smearing chyme, as on an initiate, may be done by any old person, not necessarily a kinsman.

In one set of actions, however, kinship plays a dominant role — in the division of the meat when a bullock is slaughtered. Certain portions of the animal are given to particular kin categories or other particular classes of persons. I have listed these in Table 12. Not all informants agreed on details, and some regional differences are unclear to me (I never observed such a division). When sheep and goats are slaughtered, the rules of division are not enforced, though persons are sometimes given the appropriate cuts as a social gesture, if they are present.

The heart of the bullock is sacred to clan brothers. It and the hump (also shared among clansmen) are viewed as prime cuts. Among the kindred specifically having a right to the animal are sisters, wives, and men who call the owner *mama* and *kuko*, and the brothers-in-law and fathers-in-law. There is no special part for the man who is the owner's *mama*, however. Some of the selections have direct symbolic meaning, such as the pancreas (which Sebei say looks like a kraal) and the lower intestines, which are given to the women, for they clean the dung out of the kraal. Certain muscles of the lower leg are not to be eaten by young men, as they would impair the ability to run. As ceremonial slaughtering generally involves an animal taken under contract, there is a special portion for the man whose bullock it was and for the wife from whom the *namanya* heifer is to be given in return. There are other nonkin categories whose rights are also recognized, notably the men of the *pororyet*, the neighbor, the herdsmen, and the man who is a specialist in delivering calves when there is difficulty. His right does not depend upon his having performed this service, for he may be called upon at some future date. The portion that goes to the *pororyet* and the lungs are roasted and eaten at the time of slaughtering.

The Sebei have extended the notion of rights to certain portions of a slaughtered animal to rights to enjoy a share of beer. They use the term "meats" (*payento*) for these rights, which are listed in Table 13. Only four of these meats must go to kin, while a number go to reward persons for real or potential services of various kinds. These services are related to the activities of cattle-keeping, even though the beer has been provided for services to agriculture. The exceptions are the midwife and the *terekok* (meat of the burden), which was explained as a new form adopted after the introduction of the burdens (especially headloads) imposed by a foreign bureaucracy.

I believe the differences between the meats of slaughtering and the

TABLE 12

Distribution of Meats from Slaughtered Animals

Portion	Term	Persons sharing meat
Heart	*Mukuleyto*	Clan brothers share with owner
Thigh (right)	*Kwisto*	Clan brothers share with owner
Hump	*Kapyoket*	Real brothers
"Waist"	*Swet*	Clan Sisters
Rump	*Lepit*	Father-in-law or brother-in-law
Throat	*Pintapmak*	Father, sister, son
Cheeks	*Kwarimatet*	Grandfather (must be male)
Sweetbreads Lower intestine	*Chesapeiwut*	Wives and their children (because they clean dung from kraal)
Inside hind legs	*Katiŋisyet*	Father; old man (part of flesh from which son came)
Side and ribs	*Kelanyantet*	*Tilyet* (man who furnished animal)
Foreleg	*Chulanet*	Wife whose animal was slaughtered
Neck	*Katit*	Neighbor (not person of clan)
Back of neck	*Malanyet*	To herdsman
Part of rump	*Paswet*	
Back	*Peynetap komoy*	"Meat of veterinarian" for specialist in delivering calves
Chest (*takatet*) Ribs (*Koroswek*) Liver (*koito*)	*Pinya tap mat*	"Meat of fire," cooked and eaten by men of *pororyet*
Lungs	*Makta*	To children

"meats" of beer may be read to indicate an important shift in the ordering of Sebei social life. While beer is an ancient Southern Nilotic culture trait, it has certainly taken on greater importance as Sebei became more sedentarized. In the process, it would seem, the patterning of interactions and obligations changed, with a lessening of particularistic kinds of kinship and increased involvement with obligations of other kinds — the neighbor, the friend, the helper. This must, however, remain an untestable speculation.

THE AGE-SET SYSTEM

The Sebei share the Southern Nilotic system of cycling age-sets. Each man, at the close of the initiation rituals that start with circumcision, is inducted

TABLE 13
Distribution of "Meats" of the Beer Pot

Portion term	Recipient
Muntwet (meat of libation)	Father or other old clansman who pours libation gives this meat to a friend
Kotkotin	Old man who "sets the beerpot." *Kotkot* is the divination for naming children.
Kalenkin	Brother who will bury host
Kapchuket (hump)	Recipient chosen by brother who has received *kalenkin*
Kwameret (cheek)	Father's sister's son or grandfather
Koikapmok (neck)	For sister's son
Kolama	Person who keeps fire going during fermenting process; originally for man who lights fire at harvest *korosek*
Pororyet	A young man who is able to protect the cattle in time of raids
Peynetap komin (meat of the midwife)	A woman who has special midwifery knowledge
Peynetap komoy (meat of veterinarian)	A man who specializes in delivering calves
Teitapoino (cow of the river)	Person who has rescued cow from river mud
Korotowit (cow of the rock)	Person who has rescued cow caught between rocks (this and preceding are alternate concepts of same meat)
Yuwatet (summer rains)	Person who is far from home and caught in rain
Terekok (meat of the burden)	Person who has assisted host. (Derives from the time when Baganda and Europeans made Sebei carry headloads.)
Kapyoket	Person whom host once improperly kept from beer
Kuptumwoi (knees)	Old man who must use his knees struggling in intercourse
Peynetap latyet (meat of the neighbor)	Available only when beer is furnished under *kwolyo* contract
Konkechisawek (farewell)	An old man who will leave the beer early, saying a special prayer as he does so

into the particular subdivision of a particular age-set (*pinta*) that is currently open. The cycle consists of eight *pinta* each divided into three subsets. The entire cycle requires about 160 years to complete. The names and order of these units is indicated in Figure 7. The circumcision years (which for earlier

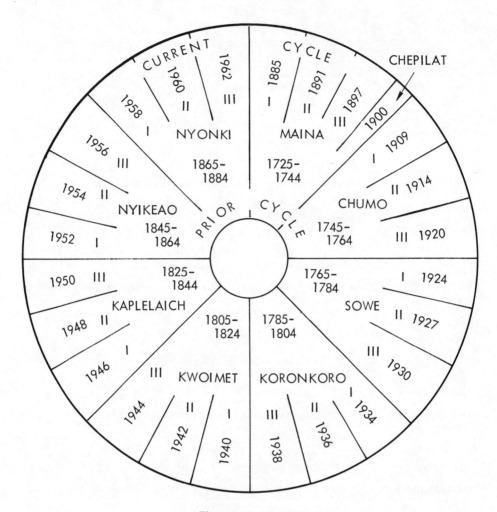

Figure 7. Age-Set Cycle

years are necessarily approximated) are indicated for the cycle completed in 1962; the period during which the age-set was being circumcised is indicated for the preceding cycle.

In olden days, the time for initiation was set by the prophets in response to requests made by fathers whose sons wanted to be circumcised. The prophet determined the propitious time by the life cycle of a plant (*Mimulopsis* sp.) called variantly syetet or nuka, varieties of which grow in the forest and high on the mountain. The vine has the characteristic of flowering and dying back (like an annual) every five to seven years. It is considered harmful to the initiates to circumcise them when the plant is in flower, so they wait until the dormant stage. Thus, circumcision takes place every five to seven years. Each circumcision period is associated with one of the subdivisions; three successive ones establish an age-set. Normally, the ages of age-set members span a period of about twenty years. The Sebei date events by age-sets, referring to the period during which it was open to initiates.

There appears to be a vague sense of identity between successive age-sets of the same name, expressed chiefly in a sense that the character of the two periods will be similar.

Although the *pinta* is a clearly bounded social group and affiliation involves important personal social ties, it is not now nor has it been within memory a salient element in the organization of political, legal, or military affairs. This is indicated both by the absence of age-set function and the absence of age-set structure. It is reasonable to assume that at one time the *pinta* did have military or governmental significance among the Sebei, as it had with other Southern Nilotes.

As noted earlier, Sebei once lived in *manyattas* consisting of two age-sets, each with its own quarters. Such a pattern must certainly have had some relationship to military or governmental functions, but this pattern of settlement seems to have disappeared entirely by the time of historic contracts. I doubt that it ever was characteristic of the western sector — certainly not by the time they had adopted the cultivation of plantains.

Although the Sebei distinguish warriors (*moran, moranik*, pl.; a Masai term) from elders (*poynatet, poyik*, pl.), the change from one to another is gradual, and although seniority of elders over warriors is recognized, there is no clear point of transition from one grade to another. Thus, there is no ceremonial closing of an age-set group, nor any ceremonial transition subsequent to initiation. Furthermore, unlike the practice among other Kalenjin peoples, the existing group makes no effort to hold back the initiation of the next group.[3]

> We are not like the Kony and Nandi, where one *pinta* quarrels with another. An uncircumcised fellow is troubled in many ways by those who have been initiated, but once a man is circumcised, he is regarded as a man and cannot be troubled by another. Among the Uasin-Gishu and Kony people, a man of one *pinta* does not dare to pass near the house of others. We don't have that system, for in Sebei each group goes to war. The Sebei were not going out raiding but were defenders; you find brave people among the elders and the young men.

So the new age-set did not have the duty of warfare, and as the above quotation makes clear, this was because defensive warfare required the full support of all able-bodied and capable men.

Nor did age-sets have any formal role in governance. To be sure, seniority played a part in a person's authority but no man assumed the right to control over others by virtue of an age-set role. Indeed, seniority was always relative; it was incremental, and men gradually assumed the role of respected elder ("He would become somewhat more *poynatet*").

---

3. Among the Kony, the *pinta* establishes the time when its unit is closed to further entry by a ceremony called *tamokyet*. All the men of the *pinta* in each *pororyet* gather together in the bush where they remain for ten days. There they slaughter a white ox, from the skin of which they make ringlets for each man, who wears it on the middle finger of the right hand. There are no songs or dances, but they "pretend they are having the final circumcision ceremony." After this, the next *pinta* may circumcise.

Though age-sets spanned about a generation, there was no rule as to the age-set affiliations of father and son, except that the two could not belong to the same *pinta*, which would be a physiological impossibility. A man's first son might be in the next age-set, but the child of a late marriage might well be in the third following.

The age-set is structured only in the sense that the *pinta* has three subdivisions established through successive initiations. There are no formalized roles within the structure, either military, political, or ritual. There is no distinction in function or authority between the subdivisions. The smaller units are named ordinally: *ŋapirek*, first, *oyperek*, following, and *ŋeteywek*, last. (I have adopted the convention of identifying them with Roman numerals.) There is some vague sense of difference between the first one and the two others, chiefly expressed in beer and feasting. Thus, when a man furnishes beer for his *pinta* at the time his child is being initiated, the father should supply one pot for the first group and a second for the other two. When a man establishes blood brotherhood (which is done only among the Kenya Sabaot), he should do so with the opposite sector based upon the same duality. But I found no important ritual or secular involvement between the two sectors, such as occurs elsewhere in Nilotic age-set patterns.

So far as my observations and information indicate, primary loyalty is to the *pinta* as a whole and to the subset only secondarily — very much as with clan and lineage and with *pororyet* and *saŋta*. The social obligations extend to the whole *pinta* not to the lesser unit, though here the Sebei themselves argue the matter (*KC*:65-69). The second and third subsets are sometimes named after some event of the time, but the first section is never given such a nickname. Among the nicknames of recent subsets (they do not cycle, but sometimes reappear) are the following:

> Chepsaket. Maina II (*saket*, mud) it rained very much and was muddy.
> Chepsaror. Nyonki III (*saror*, tail) there was a comet in the sky just before this group was circumcised.
> Cheripko. Nyonki II (*ripko* refers to watching inside the house) The harvest was heavy and the people were too busy to build men's houses for the initiates, so they had to stay with their mothers.

While the age-set system conforms to the general pattern of this institution among the Southern Nilotes, it has little to do with the functioning of the legal or governmental operations within the memory of living Sebei. Fellow members of age-sets are not expected to be involved in mutual protection or in retaliation for homicide, as they are in other tribes with age-set organization. This reduction of the age-set was not a direct or indirect product of acculturation influence but was a natural evolution of the Sebei social order (see Chapter 12). The significance of the *pinta* has further declined because of the change in the periodicity of initiation. Nowadays, the initiation for boys takes place biennially during the school holiday (December) to minimize the disruption to education.

The first known disruption in the regularity of circumcision started at the first contact with the outside, though the two events were not directly related. The last Maina age-set had been initiated just before Austin arrived in 1897, for they were healing at the time. This group, however, was ill-fated. The prophet Arapkoipot had warned that circumcision should not take place. It is said that a boy named Arapsowet fell in love, but his sweetheart insisted that he be circumcised before she would marry him and would not wait. He besought his father, who refused. Arapsowet went after his father with a spear but killed a goat instead. The father then gave in, and thus the Maina III circumcision began in the east. When the ritual was undertaken against the prophet's orders, the boys began to suffer from a disease of the penis ("the end of the penis fell off") and many of them committed suicide. Circumcision continued as far as Chema, when it was stopped by the prophet Matui. The Maina III were nicknamed Chemutwa, after *mutwa*, the foreshaft of a compound arrow. Two or three years later, the circumcision was resumed, forming a group named Chepilat, never properly tied into the cycle. ("If they want to marry a Maina daughter, they call themselves Chumo" and the other way around.)

The next circumcision did not take place until 1909 or 1910. I credit this delay chiefly to disruption by the Baganda, whose unbridled control of Sebei lasted until about 1908, when the first British officials began to control this part of Uganda. Thereafter, the period became shorter and shorter until finally it was standarized. The shortened span did not so much reduce the size of the unit, for the Sebei population was increasing rapidly, but rather narrowed the age range of the group. This has undoubtedly further reduced any latent tendency to see events in terms of age-sets, as the overlap in age between successive groups is almost as great as the normal range within a group.

Pinta affiliation retains a strong hold on personal attitudes and influences interpersonal relationships. Every man knows his age-set and that of his father and other important men in his life, and the age-set affiliations of important historic figures are as apt to be noted as their *pororyet* and almost as readily as their clans. Age-grading formulates a fraternal bond. Men are expected to be solicitous and polite with their age-set fellows;[4] often I had to wait while by interpreters went through the proper formalities with their age-mates. I was often asked my own affiliation to place me in terms of seniority, for seniority is a basic principle in the ordering of interaction among the Sebei. Some seniority is calculated genealogically (by relative age of the connecting relative), but it may be calculated by age-set. Thus, "when sitting around the beer pot, the youngest circumcised men sit on the east side and the older ones on around, according to *pinta*, so the old men are to the west. If a young man comes and sits in the old men's area, they will say that it is not fit for him. ('Those who are sitting here are about to die.')"

---

4. Sexual hospitality is extended to age-set mates among the Kony but not the Sebei. The guest is obliged to accept this privilege.

Such rules of etiquette and kinship reinforce the sense of *pinta* affiliation, but they do not provide it with significant function.

Women, too, are circumcised and inducted into the same age-sets — or rather counterpart groups with the same name. Their affiliation does not appear to be important either in the organization of the society or in ordinary social intercourse. Some women profess not to know their *pinta*. A woman's social involvements are with her husband's *pinta*, not hers; she does not invite her *pinta*-mates to beer, but her husband's; does not observe marriage tabus regarding her (or her mother's) *pinta*, but those of the men; no kin terms are extended to her *pinta*-mates. Coinitiation certainly creates and cements personal bonds among the women, but these are fractured if a woman's marital residence is at a distance from her home, and no sodality is created by the initiation.

Authority and deference are based on age and seniority; a set of attitudes laid down by the fact that any initiated man has authority over, expects obedience from, and may rightfully chastise any uninitiated child. This also sets up age-based antagonism. These attitudes affect current political activities. In 1962, there appeared to be four cadres of political leadership distinguished fundamentally on the basis of age. First, there were a few remaining old men who had been leaders during the transition of power from the Baganda back to the Sebei in the second and third decades of this century — men like Yunusu Wandera (Chumo I *pinta*), who still had a good deal of power though no formal authority. Next there were the senior leaders, men generally of Koronkoro *pinta*, like the *saza* chief Aloni Muzungyo, my interpreter and aide, Richard Bomet, and the head of the judicial system in the *saza*, Stanley Salimu. (These were men about fifty years old.) In 1962, this age group was being much pressed by men some ten years younger, led by the late Chemonges, who was the first Sebei to become a member of the Uganda Legislature. The younger leaders successfully pressed for a separate Sebei District and were pushing to remove the older group from the center of power and put them in special "advisory" roles. They were aided by quite young men, just finished with their schooling, who were pressing to have important roles in the newly created district — and often with success.

While I never heard these men identify themselves or others in terms of age-set affiliation, I did hear a good deal of prejudicial remarks in terms of age levels — "those young men," "he is too old." and the like. Though there is a tendency for age-based antagonism to emerge under conditions of rapid acculturation and differential levels of education, traditional age-attitudes seem more important in Sebei politics. In 1962, the young men were not generally better educated or more acculturated than the older ones and they did not make this the point of contention. At any rate, age identification is an attribute of Sebei sentiments and expresses itself in public as well as in private life.

SUMMARY AND CONCLUSIONS

There are three central parameters to the structures of traditional Sebei society: space kindred, and age. These are represented by three sets of social groups: tribe, *pororyet*, and *saŋta*; clan and lineage; and age-sets and their subdivisions. Each man has an affiliation with each such unit; together, they place him in the structure of Sebei society.

To these, we may add a fourth parameter not represented by social units: the individual as a set of personal and economic capabilities. Salient elements in the social order are the private right to property and the recognition that a person's status is dependent, in an important measure, on his manipulations of events by persuasion, guile, and economic clout. A Sebei man may be rich or poor. He may be rich in cattle, *mokoriyontet*; in land, *manoŋteyontet*; or in family, *meywontet*. He may be viewed as wise and therefore asked to serve as judge, *kirwokintet*, or he may be viewed as a nobody, *payanet*, and his words ignored in public debate. In this highly individualized social order, much of the public regard that a man enjoys will be responsive to these personal qualities.

These four elements are found both among the farmers and the pastoralists; they are continuous in time as far back as our data give any information. Any variation that may be seen as cultural adaptation must therefore be in the relative emphasis that each receives, or in details of their involvement. At the close of the preceding chapter, I pointed out that the spatial units have historically taken on increased importance and attributed this fact to the involvement with agriculture, the attendant sedentary patterns of life, and the defensive posture for protecting these assets that characterized Sebei military operation. In this chapter, we have seen the obverse of that coin in the decline of the age-set. The age-set is ideally suited to the purposes of creating a military cadre for the aggressive raid-and-run operations appropriate to cattle pastoralism, but its functional effectiveness is lost when defensive operations are requisite. Older men are not going to allocate to young warriors the defense of their homes when attacked but will necessarily join in the action if they can. There is some evidence that age-set breakdown came earlier in the agricultural west, in Mbai, than in Sapiñ. For one thing, *pinta*-based settlement continued longer in the latter area. When plantain cultivation began to invade the western slopes, the land was settled by clans. These became the essential defensive unit and gained in importance as a social unit at the expense of the age-set in Mbai. It was only for the Mbai that I was told of the particular clans involved in wars. I was told also that persons of Mbai, who lacked clan affiliations were in constant danger from others: the "clanless man" might be summarily killed. Sebei treated this as if it were a difference in personality attributes between the Mbai and Sapiñ, but it was basically a difference in the structural situation; a pastoralist in dispute can move away from his antagonist, but a farmer cannot.

A second difference between Mbai and Sapiñ with respect to age-sets may at first seem trivial but is relevant to the altered ecological situation. I was told that Mbai men often married before they were circumcised in the days when circumcision took place at age twenty-five or later. In a pastoralist society, a young bachelor has a role to play; as a herdsman, he has his own resources and his own activities, even though he may remain dependent upon his father in many ways. Even if he does not engage in the traditional raiding pattern, he still is involved in constant military alertness. But where the productive economic activity is farming, which is in the hands of the women, the single adult male lacks both significant function and adequate resources. He is dependent, actually, upon his mother. It is reasonable, therefore, that he would seek marriage and independence. There are two solutions, either undergo initiation at an earlier age or marry before initiation. The Mbai chose the latter, probably because circumcision was a coordinated ritual that started from the still pastoral east, which set both the timing and the attitudes. Significantly, as the whole of Sebei became increasingly agricultural and sedentary, the second solution was adopted and men were circumcised while still in their teens and less motivated to establish their independence.

I was told that the people of Kapsirika laid more stress on *pinta* affiliations, and, quite clearly, the parents there make much more of these ceremonies than do the people of Sasur and are more assiduous in meeting the associated *pinta* obligations. Among the Mbai, I was told, men inherited the widows of their fathers, young wives who were not their mothers, but, among the Sapiñ, this was viewed as wrong. For the agricultural Mbai, such an arrangement makes good economic sense, for the father has allocated to his younger wives some of his land, which might be lost to the son if the father's wives were inherited by the paternal uncle. No such economic motivation would exist among pastoralists.

Evidence for the emergence of a new kin-based set of structural relationships may be seen in the comparison of Sasur and Kapsirika. In Sasur, there are three major "dynasties" of patrilineally related kinsmen living in close proximity. Lewendi Satya, Kezekia Boror, and Psiwa Kapchemesyekin were men of Chumo I *pinta* who had inherited land in Sasur; each was surrounded by married sons and, in some instances, grandsons, whose positions in the community derived from their fathers' heritages. They did not form a lineage in the traditional sense, though perhaps at some future date some such formalization will take place. But, meanwhile, these grandsons and great grandsons of original settlers enjoyed the privileges of this continuity. In Kapsirika, such units were also beginning to form, not represented by men who had inherited their positions, but by men who had pioneered their own. Nevertheless, the vicissitudes of pastoralism, especially when accompanied by patterns of raiding and warfare, render such continuity unstable; by the time of our visit in 1972, these local entities in Kapsirika had been destroyed. This last comparison seems to me to be a parable for the differential between pastoralists and farmers. Not merely are structural aspects of the situation different, but more importantly the dynamics. The men in Sasur and their descendants inherited a relatively secure position, unlike the pastoralists, for whom success is much more a result of personal achievement. The Culture and Ecology thesis anticipated that formalized offices and inherited social roles would appear in the farming areas, but not in the pastoral ones. There are no formalized offices in Sasur at the local level (other than governmental positions) but the beginnings of inherited social position have appeared.

Chapter 5
The Role of Livestock Among the Sebei

Sweet is the cow of debt.

Sebei proverb

The Sebei were once predominantly a stock-keeping people. Informants' statements, comparative ethnography, and internal evidence all suggest that at one time the animals kept by the Sebei provided their basic livelihood and set the pattern and tone of their lives. Animals are still important to the Sebei economy and even more so to other aspects of their culture.

CHARACTERISTICS OF THE HERD

To appreciate the character of cattle-keeping as an occupation, it is necessary to understand some of the complexities of a herd, complexities arising from the nature and needs of the animals as well as from the social definitions and involvements to which the Sebei subject them.

First, cattle are differentiated by age and sex and a proper herd must be balanced in accordance with these variants. Sebei terminological distinctions with respect to cattle are presented in Figure 8. There is a basic distinction between calves (moka) and grown animals (toka), and the former are not distinguished lexically by sex, but by their age, or more precisely by their eating pattern. Cows are distinguished also by age: those having their first calves from those in middle years and those that have had many calves, eight being the figure I was given. Bulls are distinguished also by age, the *wunwet* being one who is "practicing to serve cows," while the *piyosyet* is one that has become too old to serve. (The term is also applied to castrated animals. The word is used jokingly to refer to old men as well, just as boys who are acting childish may be called ŋariantet.) Castration normally takes place in the bullock's third year, but sometimes a calf is castrated while still suckling, in which case it is called *chilaktatitap kwot*. *Kwot* is the term for the substance that the mother licks from the newborn calf; *chilaktatita* is the term for castrating.

112

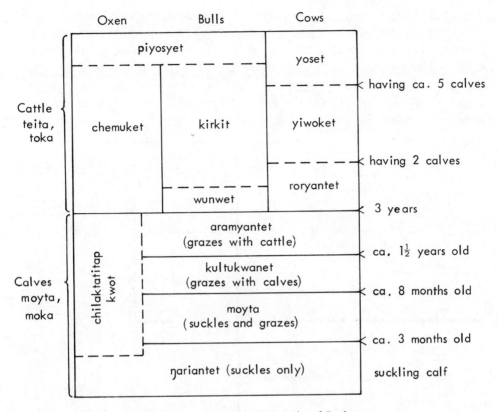

Figure 8. Age and Sex Categories of Cattle

I did not make actual herd counts, but I asked three highly competent herders the ideal ratios in a herd of a hundred animals — a question that was readily meaningful to them. Their responses ranged from three to six bulls, seventeen to twenty-four castrated males, and the remainder divided between cows and calves. These herdsmen say that cattle perform sexually after three years, that bulls serve normally for six to eight years, after which they are too old, and that if not killed by disease, the average cow will produce fourteen calves. The record reported was of a cow that died in the delivery of her twentieth; twelve of her calves lived to adult status. The herdsmen claimed that a cow reproduced annually on the plains but less frequently on the escarpment, though a general estimate is that three calves are born every year for every four mature cows.

I was told that no more than one bull in a herd should be left uncastrated in any one year, for two bulls of the same age would fight; furthermore, it is useful to have animals in different stages of virility. A bull can serve longer if the grazing is good and if it is not overtaxed with too many cows.

Sheep and goats are classed together as *warek* (*warwet*, sing.), a term that in its more specific sense means goats. Goats are also called *nororyet* (*norotik*, pl.); sheep *kechiryet* (*kechirek*, pl.).

Three other sets of distinctions among the animals within a herd are based upon legal and social definitions. The animals owned by a man are *sekonik*;

those that form a herd (are together as a group of animals under the control of one man) are called *yeidyeta*. Cattle-keepers engage in two types of contract that result in their placing some of their *sekonik* in other men's kraals while having cattle belonging to other people in the herd they are caring for (see Figure 9). The latter are spoken of as *namanisiyek* and *kamanakanik*, depending on the kind of contract; the former as being in *namut* or in *kamanaktay*.

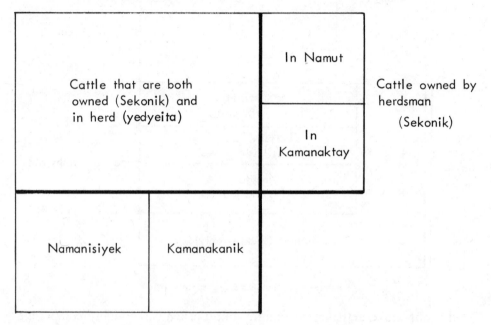

Figure 9. Cattle Herds and Ownership

A man's *sekonik* are distinguished between those allocated to his respective wives (*toka che kichenkochi korket*, literally cattle which have been smeared by wives), and the *tokapsoi*, in which the owner has retained full rights. Finally, cattle are also recognized as belonging to certain animal families or lineages (*kota*, *korik*, pl., literally house, the same word as used for human lineages). These are established when an animal enters the herd as gift, inheritance, or in exchange for property other than a cow already in the kraal. Lineages follow the female, no record being kept of the bull that has served her, and include not only her progeny, but animals received in exchange for them or bought with money acquired from their sale.

NUMBER AND DISTRIBUTION OF LIVESTOCK IN SEBEI

The continued importance of animals in Sebei economy is expressed in Table 14, which gives the numbers of livestock owned by Sebei in total and

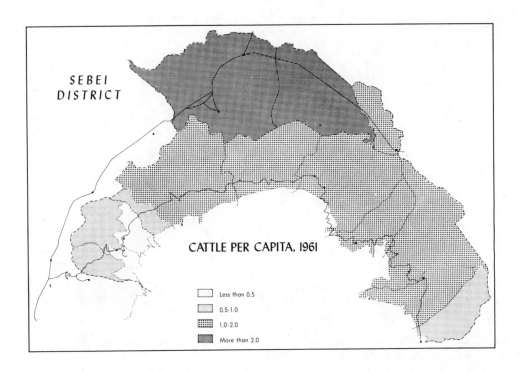

SEBEI
DISTRICT

CATTLE PER CAPITA, 1961

Less than 0.5
0.5-1.0
1.0-2.0
More than 2.0

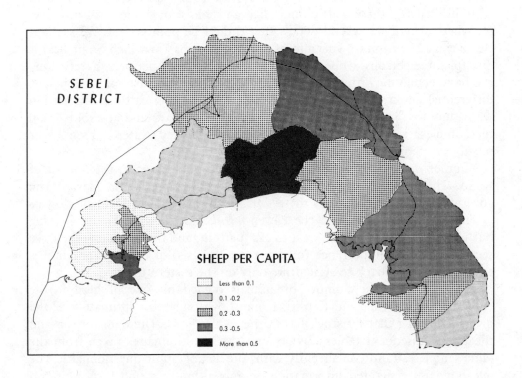

SEBEI
DISTRICT

SHEEP PER CAPITA

Less than 0.1
0.1 -0.2
0.2 -0.3
0.3 -0.5
More than 0.5

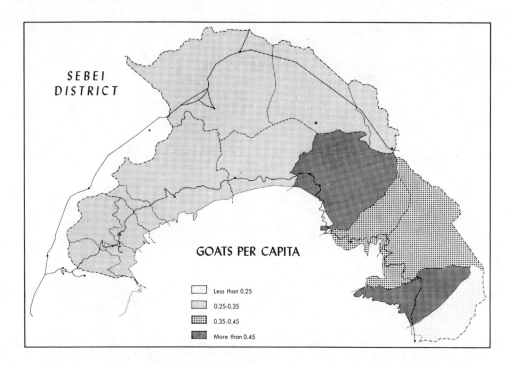

SEBEI
DISTRICT

GOATS PER CAPITA

Less than 0.25
0.25-0.35
0.35-0.45
More than 0.45

for each miruka. It must be emphasized that this tabulation is a delineation of *ownership*, not location, i.e., the 5,578 cattle in Sipi are owned by men who live there; these cattle may be, and most of them probably are, elsewhere. There are several details that should be pointed out. We see that the average per capita ownership of stock in Chema (in which Sasur lies) is one for three persons, while in Sundet it is nearly three per person, reflecting the basic economic difference between the farming and pastoral section. The differential among *warek* is negligible. Most of the Sipi cattle are located in the combined Kaserem and Kobil *mirukas,* a shelf of land at about 5,000 feet of elevation jutting northward that is less well watered than other portions of Sipi and is still mostly in bush.

Another detail is the unusually large sheep population in the Miruka of Kono. These are mostly in Benet, the major community in Masop. The government has banned goats there, but sheep thrive in the highland downs.

The four *gombololas* and the eleven *mirukas* of the escarpment (leaving out Ngenge) are arrayed in a west-to-east pattern, and by examining them we see the increased importance (on a per capita basis) of cattle as one moves eastward, shifting back to agriculture only on the eastern fringe.

Table 15 gives the number of animals owned by size of herd in the communities of Sasur and Kapsirika, and shows on a more intimate level the diverse meaning that livestock has in the two regions. The data for this and the three subsequent tables was obtained by questionnaires taken from the same sample as (and concurrently with) the demographic questionnaire. The questionnaire generated information on animal holdings and ownership, on

TABLE 14
Distribution of Livestock Ownership, 1961

Gombolola and miruka	Cattle			Sheep			Goats		
	No.	Per person	Per sq. mi.	No.	Per person	Per sq. mi.	No.	Per person	Per sq. mi.
Sipi total	5,578	.397	153.2	2,132	.152	58.6	4,268	.304	117.3
Kapeywa	739	.207	144.9	1,013	.283	198.6	844	.236	165.5
Kaserem, Kobil	3,501	.543	150.9	260	.040	11.2	2,114	.328	91.1
Chema[a]	1,338	.332	165.2	859	.213	106.0	1,310	.325	161.7
Kaptanya total	8,818	1.086	150.2	1,088	.134	18.5	2,323	.286	39.6
Tegeres	2,803	.947	438.0	253	.085	39.5	926	.313	144.7
Kaptaret	6,015	1.167	115.0	835	.162	16.0	1,397	.271	26.7
Kabruron total	10,997	1.291	108.5	3,512	.413	34.7	3,600	.423	35.6
Kabruron	3,878	1.264	81.0	861	.281	18.0	1,639	.534	34.2
Kono	4,340	1.598	122.6	1,757	.647	49.6	889	.327	25.1
Chesower	2,779	1.028	155.3	894	.325	49.9	1,072	.394	59.9
Bukwa total	12,647	.918	145.2	3,566	.259	40.9	5,021	.364	57.6
Kabei	4,984	1.050	107.0	1,612	.340	34.6	2,026	.427	43.5
Chepkwasta	5,009	1.174	229.8	1,173	.275	53.8	2,000	.469	91.7
Suam	2,654	.557	141.9	781	.164	41.8	995	.200	51.1
Ngenge total	20,782	2.927	158.9	2,122	.299	16.2	2,044	.282	15.6
Kapkwot	10,990	3.857	145.9	696	.244	9.2	836	.293	11.1
Sundet[a]	6,148	2.639	142.3	803	.345	18.6	707	.303	16.4
Greek River	3,644	1.896	296.3	623	.324	50.7	501	.261	40.7
Sebei total	58,822	1.141	142.0	12,420	.241	30.0	17,256	.335	41.7

SOURCE: Data on stock from June 1961 government census. (For information on population and area, see Table 2.)

[a]Includes villages of intensive study.

cattle contracts of the kind to be described below, on allocation of animals to wives, on cattle sales, and other matters. Though Sebei are said not to count their animals, those who have but a few can tell you the number and are generally willing to do so. There was evidence of a slight tendency to give round figures for numbers over ten, and I suspect also some tendency for poor men to claim more animals than they have and for rich men to claim fewer. The greatest error derives from the fact that the richest man in Kapsirika refused to discuss his herd with me. Thus, I conclude there is some underenumeration. The tabulation demonstrates the great diversity between the two areas; livestock are universally held among Kapsirika household heads but rarely appear in any numbers in Sasur.

Since Sebei contractual arrangements place cattle in other men's kraals, the animals in a man's possession are by no means the same as those he holds

TABLE 15

Size of Herds: Sasur and Kapsirika

Size of herd	Sasur				Kapsirika			
	Cattle		Warek		Cattle		Warek	
	Owners	Animals	Owners	Animals	Owners	Animals	Owners	Animals
0	17	0	8	0	1	0	14	0
1	5	5	3	3	3	3	5	5
2	3	6	12	24	3	6	3	6
3	1	3	5	15	3	9	1	3
4	2	8	4	16	1	4	1	4
5-9	9	59	7	45	9	64	11	71
10-19	2	30	1	14	8	110	5	73
22-29	1	24	...	...	8	192	2	53
30-39	...	...	...	...	1	38	...	...
40-49	...	...	...	...	1	49	...	...
50 up	...	...	...	...	4	392	...	...
Totals	40	135	40	117	42	867	42	215
Stock per hshld[a]		3.38		2.92		20.64		5.12
Stock per capita[b]		.58		.50		3.18		.78
Community est.[c]		260		225		1,115		276

SOURCE: Data for Tables 15-18 are based on livestock questionnaire taken in 1961-62.

[a]Average per household reporting livestock data (40 in Sasur; 42 in Kapsirika).

[b]Assuming these households have average for community (Sasur, 5.82; Kapsirika, 6.49).

[c]Corrected for total number of households in community (Sasur, 77; Kapsirika, 54).

as property. The forty-two men who claimed ownership of 867 cattle in Kapsirika held a total of 1,016 animals in the kraals, or an additional 17 percent. When we examine the distribution of livestock by size of herd, we find a reduction in numbers at the upper end, suggesting that large owners put more cattle in the kraals of others to spread the risk and perhaps also to distribute the milk more widely. We also find fewer animals in herds of 4 or less, suggesting that small units are best put with larger units, presumably as a labor-saving device.

In Sasur, nine of the twelve men having five or more head of cattle reported that they kept them elsewhere, either establishing herding camps on the plains, or making contractual arrangements with herders in areas of less intensive cultivation (information was not available for the other three). The men of Sasur who own cattle keep at most two or three near their homes, preferably a freshened cow and her calf. Some of the Sasur men share a cattle camp with others — not necessarily kinsmen — on the plains and take turns herding the stock.

These data offer an important correction to the information of the distribution of livestock as presented in Table 14, which assigns animals by ownership rather than distribution. Cattle are kept on the plains either through the establishment of cattle camps, through contractual arrangements, or occasionally because a man has two households, one on the plains and one on the escarpment (there were two divided households in Kapsirika). Thus the 7:1 ratio of per capita ownership as between Kapsirika and Sasur would expand to a ratio on the order of 20:1 on the basis of location.[1]

CARE OF LIVESTOCK

Cattle must be provided with food, water, salt, and protection. Sebei law, though it recognizes private rights to cultivated land, treats grassland as public property, and any man has the right to graze his cattle anywhere in Sebei territory and to provide them with natural flowing water and salt from available salt licks. Even privately held land may be grazed by anybody after the crop has been harvested. The problems of providing for the needs of animals varies regionally and seasonally.

Cattle are kept penned in a kraal each night; the calves, goats, and sheep are kept separately, sometimes in a small house of their own, sometimes at the back of the domicile, and sometimes in a separately fenced off pen. They are all released in the morning (Plate II:5); after the cows have been milked and given the calf, calves and small stock are separately herded by young boys, the cattle supposedly by the men but not infrequently also by boys. (Calves must be kept from their mothers to prevent their suckling, which would not only reduce the milk available but would, according to Sebei, cause illness in the calf.) Not only is it the responsibility of the herders to find appropriate grass for the animals, but they must endeavor to protect the stock from hyenas, leopards, and lions and make sure that all return to the kraal in the evening. The frequent failure to do so was indicated in Kambuya's herd, where ten of the 548 mature cattle (and many calves) were said to have been taken by animal predators. On those portions of the escarpment where cattle are kept in numbers, this responsibility falls heavily upon the boys, but, on the plains, it is more frequently the responsibility of young men. Where several men share the use of a kraal, the men take turns at keeping the stock. I was told that in the plains area a man can herd as many as 200 animals alone, though some said 100 is about the right number, and another claimed he could handle 400. A man with a large herd walks ahead of them backwards as they move over the grass. He is assisted by several lead

---

1. This situation changed in 1972 as a result of Pokot and Karamojong depredations. Many more small herds are now encountered in the farming area, and contractual relationships with plainsmen are less frequent because of the fear of loss resulting from these raids.

cows. These are not trained but are "natural leaders." The Sebei used to herd their cattle in tight groups, like the Masai, as protection against predators, but no longer do so.

When graze is scarce in areas like Kapsirika, the cattle are taken to a swampy area, just south of the Greek River, known as Soset, where grass and water are almost always available. They may remain there throughout the dry season which can extend from January to April, under the care of younger men whose wives or mothers bring food to their temporary shelters. In years of greater precipitation, the cattle may be grazed on the lower slopes of Elgon, remaining in the area overnight, with the herders in temporary shelters and the cattle protected in thorn bush kraals. Every second or third day, the cattle are taken to the Sundet for water, or all the way to Greek River.

One of my informants described the operation of a cattle camp (*kaptuken*) from his childhood memories dating to the mid-1920s, when he was a boy of seven or eight years. Five men owned nearly two hundred cattle, which were herded together. Two of the men were brothers, and all but one were of the same clan. They lived together in a *manyatta*, but they had a separate camp about three miles away where two boys remained with the stock. They alternated herding the calves and the cattle. In the evening the elder brothers or the wives of the herd owners would bring food to them and would help with the milking of some sixty producing cows, remaining overnight to get the morning milk as well. The evening milk was consumed in the camp, but the morning milk was taken for household use. Some of the women came during the day with food and would clean the kraals. Men who share in cattle herding, which is a mutual arrangement of indefinite duration, consider themselves neighbors (*latyet, latyosyek*). Cooperative action is not without its problems, which are expressed in terms of the relationship among cattle. Thus, if one man is losing cattle, the others may not want to keep their cattle with his, saying that his animals have "bitter urine." They may herd the cattle together, but will not keep them in the same kraal, for when the animals awaken in the morning, the vapor of the urine suffuses the atmosphere and cows with stronger urine will harm the others. There are certain clans that cannot share kraals for this reason.

Fields may be fenced, and a man is expected to fence the margins of a field bordering on a cattle trail, but the legal responsibility for damage to crops rests upon the stock man. The landowner can expect the replacement of food lost to animal depredations and may go to court to obtain satisfaction. Only on the rare occasions when extreme drought forces Sebei men to dig step wells in the bed of Greek River is there any private control of water. It is notable, however, that there are no quarrels or legal cases in my records directly attributable to conflict over access to land, water, or salt for livestock. However, in earlier times, in the cattle-keeping areas of the escarpment, the people of a *saŋta* might clean out and fence off a spring for the cattle and under such circumstances they may keep out the cattle of men who have not assisted in this work. The Sebei say that cattle prefer standing water which contains leached salt, to the sweeter flowing water, which is cold.

In many parts of Sebei there are no salt licks to which animals may readily be taken, and it is then necessary for men to gather salt and bring it to their kraals. The salt is dislodged with iron picks (*lotwet*), which play an important symbolic role in circumcision and other ceremonies. There is a large salt content in the rocks that form the many caves on the escarpment. When cattle dominated the economy there, the Sebei took their cattle to the caves for salt, but nowadays they generally bring salt to the few animals they hold and increasingly are purchasing salt for their cattle. Even aboriginally, salt was brought back to the calves, who cannot be taken to salt licks.

Some men are recognized for their special knowledge of curing cattle diseases, of delivering calves when there are difficulties, or of drawing blood from cattle. I talked to one man who had acquired specialization in delivery from his father, through helping him when he was a youth. For a breach delivery of calves, a very soft and greased rope, kept in a bamboo case along with the bleeding arrows, is used in lieu of forceps. The rope is looped around the neck of the fetus to draw it out. If the calf is too large to deliver, specialists are able to skin part of the fetus *in utero* and sever the head and if necessary the limbs to remove it in pieces. My informant had never performed this operation, but he had frequently assisted his father in its performance. An extruded uterus, after carefully being cleaned of adhering dirt, is induced to contract into the vagina by crackling a dried goatskin; it cannot be replaced by hand. After such operations, the vagina must be cauterized with a hot iron. Traditionally, there is no pay for such veterinarian services but a gift of tobacco at the time of delivery and the rights to some meat, whenever and wherever an animal is slaughtered, serve as compensation for such specialists. No ritual accompanies these activities.

The Sebei know cures for black quarter fever and pleuropneumonia but not for East Coast fever and rinderpest. For black quarter fever, a glutinous mass is made from the crushed roots of a plant (identification unknown), mixed with water, and poured down the throats of the animals. The whole herd is treated if one animal has the disease. The informant's father had acquired the medicine and passed the knowledge on to his son. The medicine is given a second time, after an interval of about a month. Between the two dosages, the family is under restriction and cannot offer milk to persons not a part of the household. This restriction is lifted with the second application. A person performing this service is given a "dew payment," *cherewontet* (to compensate him for getting his feet wet from the dew while collecting the medicines). Payment consists of a chicken or two shillings; later he will be given beer and perhaps 10 shillings more. If the disease continues to attack the herd, the family will prepare beer for a general party and will bless some of the roots of the medicinal plant with that beer.

Sebei cows are herded together with the bulls that service them. No control over servicing is exercised, and a bull may, if opportunity exists, service another man's cows. In selecting a bull to serve the herd, a man will seek one whose dam was known to produce many viable calves and give much milk. No other selective breeding practices were reported, but many Sebei said they culled animals by selling or exchanging those cows that were not producing calves or milk.

Calf mortality is high; estimates based upon data obtained from Salimu Kambuya (*KC* Appendix E) indicate about 30 percent, and informants' statements suggest that this is low. Little wonder then that newborn animals are surrounded with restrictions, particularly as protection against the evil eye. Hair is shaved from the head of a newborn lamb, and two parallel marks are branded on the left side of a kid, while for calves there are diverse kinds of protective medicine. Tobacco, chewed by women and spit into the calf's mouth, is its first medicine, given in its first or second day; other infusions are given at a later time. These animals are hidden from sight when they are young and vulnerable (except that sheep cannot be tied down and hence are not covered).

The first milk taken from a cow is not consumed but saved in gourds for about a week; it is eaten as curds by a senior member of the family. He or she must eat all of it, must not eat it at the same time as other foods, or eat away from home until the milk has been fully consumed. Breach of this restriction is thought to cause the calf to die.

LIVESTOCK AS ECONOMIC RESOURCE

Sebei herds and flocks were once the major source of their food supply and furnished their clothes, bedding, and many other articles of daily use. They remain today an important economic resource, supplying milk, meat, blood, and skins and serving as a source of money as well. Their importance to the domestic economy varies from region to region.

While the pastoral Sebei do not normally slaughter their livestock unless there is some special purpose, meat is an important element in Sebei diet. All animals that die are consumed, whether the death is due to disease, predator (if the carcass if found in time), or stillbirth. Small stock are more frequently slaughtered.

It is possible to get a rough estimate of beef consumption in Kapsirika. If a herd of 100 animals approaches the ideal and nearly 60 are mature cows, then one may expect an annual crop of about 45 calves. Probably 15 of these calves will die, of which 10 or more will be eaten by the Sebei, with the remainder lost to the hyenas and other predators. In addition to these 10 calves, some mature animals will be slaughtered (or marketed), either for ceremonial purposes or becasue they are old. If 75 of the 100 animals are mature and the life expectancy of mature animals is 15 years, then another 5 animals per 100 will be eaten each year.

The 42 families in Kapsirika reporting on cattle ownership held a total of 867 cattle. At the rate of 10 calves per 100 animals, this would mean that they consumed a total of 87 calves; at 5 mature animals per 100 this indicates an additional 43 head consumed; in round figures, 2 calves and 1 mature animal per household per annum. Two factors reduce these figures. First, the Sebei suffer more losses from raiding than they gain in similar actions. Second, nowadays, many mature animals are marketed and provide beef for the towns of Uganda and the mountain-dwelling Sebei, who have fewer animals but more cash. Even relatively wealthy men said they slaughtered cattle only rarely, perhaps two or three times in a decade, but that they frequently ate meat of animals that had died. Most consumption of beef takes place on special occasions, and most is eaten by men. Small stock are more frequently slaughtered. In Kapsirika, I judge this to be more than two animals per household per year.

These data must be taken as approximations; they suggest that meat is an important element in the diet, though I think conversion into pounds per person would give a spurious sense of accuracy.

Sebei men formerly engaged in a kind of beef-eating orgy called *korta*, in which a group of men agreed to slaughter animals in succession and consume them together. The men did not invite guests, except for a man to serve them, and also, I was told, uncircumcised girls. The feasts may follow one another with a lapse of a few days or may be delayed a year or more. A portion is given "to the *pororyet*," and men who come near to the scene of the feast may be given some food, but essentially the whole animal is consumed by the participants themselves. The feast serves no ritual purposes.

A similar feasting, *kochek*, found only among Kony does have a ritual function; it is initiated by a man "who wants to become rich." It also leads to blood brotherhood. The man who initiates the *kochek* invites a person of the same *pinta*, but if he is of the first subdivision, the friend must be of the second or third, while if he belongs to one of the latter, the friend must be of the first. Two other men are invited, but they may be any friend.

After the animal has been slaughtered, the doorway of the house is smeared with cow dung and set with apples of Sodom, which have been gathered by young girls. A palm frond and a branch of a koresyontet tree are placed by the door. An old man blesses bits of meat from the ox and gives it four successive times to the person who initiated the *kochek*. Each man will later make a ring out of a loop of the hide, which he will wear on the little finger of the right hand. There are certain restrictions with respect to drinking that are not entirely clear but apparently involve drinking milk. Though the four men consume the animal, they will throw some meat to persons they favor. This ceremony is much like the Sebei ritual for establishing friendly relationships between half-brothers born at about the same time. The quasi-kinship between the two men leads them to call one another *ŋiyawey*; they are not supposed to quarrel or to speak coarsely before one another's wives but must be circumspect, as with a mother-in-law. When the *ŋiyawey* visits, he must always be provided with a stool that is for him alone, be fed, and given beer. The sons and daughters of the two men may not intermarry but regard each other as siblings.

Milk is more important to the Sebei diet than meat. Sebei estimate that a cow produces between 1 and 2 quarts of milk per day. My single attempt to measure production gave an average of about 1 quart each for 21 cows measured for the combined morning and evening milking for one day in October (a dry season of low milk productivity). Using this conservative figure, and assuming half of the cows are fresh at any one time and that a herd of 100 cattle contains 60 cows, we obtain an average daily milk production of 30 quarts per 100 animals. There are about 1,000 cattle in the kraals of the 42 Kapsirika households reporting on this matter, who thus produce 300 quarts per day, or 7 per household.

This milk is consumed in different ways: it is drunk as fresh milk (*kayonik*); it may be allowed to sour for two or three days (*kwey riyonik*); it may be allowed to form into curds (*kasorkut*); it may be allowed to form into a thick and ripe cheese (*mentikliliyenik*); or it may be mixed with freshly drawn blood. (Women generally drink blood with sour milk, men with sweet milk.) Milk is also made into butter, but this is used only for anointing on ceremonial occasions and not as food. Nowadays ghee is also made.

Cheese is made by accumulating milk in a large gourd and letting it thicken, pouring off the liquid whey, and removing the top mold before adding more milk. It keeps for a long time — until the calf that drank of the same milk will be ready to be served. This is considered a great delicacy and is very rich; it is offered to special guests and to brides and initiates during their seclusion period. Pastoral Sebei do not sell their milk, nor does there appear to be much exchange in this commodity; essentially, it is all consumed within the household of the woman who does the milking. They recognize this element in their diet as the counterpart to "vegetables," which properly accompany the plantains or maize mush that is the staple food elsewhere.

Milking, which is done mornings and evenings, is women's work (Plate II:1), though men will milk when at a cattle camp or if no women are available. Morning milk is preferred because it is sweeter and is specifically required on certain ceremonial occasions. The gourd into which the milking is done is sweetened by rubbing the inside first with a charred stick of a particular kind and then with a palm frond stem (Plate II:2). The loose pieces of charcoal are shaken out. This treatment is said to improve the taste of the milk as well as to prevent worms.

The cows are each called by a name when they are to be milked. They are first given the calf, which is then tied so that the mother stands with her head over it while she is being milked. The calf may be allowed to suck a second time and the cow again milked. Calves are allowed to have all the milk for about the first week or two. When the calf gets diarrhea, it is known that the cow has enough milk for human use. If a calf dies, its skin is put over a heart-shaped basket frame and salt water poured on it, which the cows licks. It induces her to let down her milk, but the length of time milking can continue and the amount of milk the cow will give are both reduced. How many cows a woman milks depends upon her husband's wealth; the men said that if she has ten to fifteen "she considers herself a proper member of the family," and that a woman "who is not lazy" can milk twenty to twenty-five cows, but the women we talked to who were milking about five cows found that to be enough.

It is even more difficult to get estimates on the consumption of blood, which has been much reduced as a result of missionaries' disapproval. Bleeding is done by putting a tourniquet on the animal's neck, so that the jugular vein swells, and shooting a blocked arrow into the vein to produce a lengthwise cut in it (Plates II:3,4). An estimated gallon of blood may be drawn at a time, and animals may be bled as often as once a month, but more likely twice a year. It is considered good for a pregnant cow to be bled, but one should not bleed a cow that is giving milk. While it is not good to bleed cattle during a drought, a little blood can be taken if there is a food shortage. Aboriginally, blood contributes a significant supplement to the Sebei diet. It is now never used in Sipi and rarely used anywhere on the escarpment, but it still is a regular element in the diet on the plains, particularly when other foods are scarce. Blood may be mixed with milk, drunk as a liquid, or coagulated and eaten. It is sometimes very briefly boiled.

In Sasur, if an animal is to be slaughtered for a ritual, it will normally be a sheep; cattle are not even slaughtered at the funeral of a reasonably well-to-do man. On the other hand, meat is available there in the market and perhaps as much beef is consumed over the year there as on the plains. I had a clerk record the volume of sales of livestock and other commodities at the Sipi market each week over a period of 31 weeks from April 14 to November 10, 1962. During this period, 224 cattle, 51 sheep and 30 goats were slaughtered — an average of 7.72 cattle and 2.62 *warek* per week, which would mean about 400 cattle and 135 small stock per year. This market serves a large and concentrated population, but one of unknown size, so the figures cannot be converted to a per capita basis. The price was consistently 1.5 shillings per pound, which is nearly the value of a day's services as common labor at the time (2 shillings).

It can be seen that livestock make a significant contribution to the Sebei daily diet on the plains and, through the modern market system, to the people on the escarpment as well.

LIVESTOCK AS PROPERTY

Domestic animals are legally the private property of individual men, who have the right of use and disposal of the animals and liability for any damage they do. Clansmen can pressure a man to contribute to a ceremonial or assist in the payment of wergild, but this does not constitute a right to his animals. Indeed, the *pororyet* may also exert a similar claim.

A man may — and, indeed, is expected to — give subsidiary rights to each of his wives. The cattle so allocated and their progeny will ultimately be inherited by each wife's sons. She will also milk some of those cows kept by her husband and allotted to her. The cattle anointed for a wife cannot be used by the man for exchange, brideprice, or other purpose without the express permission of the woman who holds this subsidiary right. He may ask to use them, and she is expected to acquiesce in this as in other matters, but she has the right of refusal. Sebei believe that if a man uses a wife's cow against her wishes, the animal will not prosper; it will die or not reproduce. Yet, a Sebei does not like to be thought of as dominated by his wife and will often exchange an animal against her wishes. The wife cannot dispose of the animals allocated to her without his permission, nor does she take them with her in case of divorce. She really holds these animals in trust for her sons; she wants her share of the herd to prosper in order to protect their interests.

The anointing was described by informants. In the morning, after the cattle have been released but before they are moved out to graze, the wife and her mother-in-law collect cow dung in a skin of the kind formerly worn by the men. The mother-in-law points to the cattle (and sometimes goats and sheep) that have been assigned to the wife by her husband, and the mother-in-law smears some of the dung on each animal's back. There is no feast or other special blessings, but a wealthy man may provide beer. The woman's father should be present, if possible, as well as her husband and neighbors, who serve as witnesses. Her father may request an additional animal for his daughter and select an appropriate one, as may the husband's father or even neighbors. The husband may plead his case on the basis of need, but he cannot refuse an insistent request. The wife "is made happy" by this allocation of the stock, as she "is no longer a minor thing in the home" because something has been given to her. She expresses this by opening the kraal ceremonially four times; normally, it is the man who opens the kraal for the animals to leave or enter. There is no set time for this ceremony; the wife does not need to have borne children; and it is appropriate that it be done soon after the marriage rituals.

A woman may acquire animals in other ways. She may demand one from her brother-in-law during the wedding ceremony and one from her husband before permitting intercourse on her wedding night. She may occasionally bring cattle with her, animals given by a relative during circumcision, for instance, but this is rare, and I know of no specific occurrence. A woman may acquire an animal in exchange for a granary or for serving as midwife, and such animals are treated as part of the man's herd but are recognized as hers and as part of her sons' inheritance.

The decision whether or not to allocate cattle to his wives is the man's though, if he has a large herd, public opinion will pressure him to do so. If he has but few cattle, and particularly if he has but one wife, the matter is relatively unimportant. In Kapsirika, 23 of the 42 men interviewed on this subject had given a total of 159 cattle to 44 wives, or an average of 3.6 per woman. Goats and sheep were occasionally given to wives also. If a man allocates cattle to one wife he generally does so equitably, but not identically, to other wives. In three instances known to me, the last wife had not yet received any. One man had allocated 13 cattle to his first wife, 5 to the second, 6 to the third, and 1 to the fourth, presumably reflecting his declining economic circumstances. In Sasur, cattle are rarely allocated to wives. Only seven men had allocated cattle and 1 a goat; 2 men gave more than a single animal, and, all told, the 8 men gave 9 wives a total of 11 cattle and 6 goats.

The rights of minor sons to their father's herd, like the rights of women, are subsidiary and dependent. A man is expected to provide the animals for his son's first wife, and the son will later get his share of his father's animals. A boy may begin in various ways to build his herd, being given animals at specified times, such as when undergoing tooth evulsion or circumcision. He may not sell or exchange such animals, however, for until circumcision he is a legal minor. Yet, these animals and their progeny remain his. The son's rights to the herd are not impaired by the father's death, for the man who inherits the wife (or an older brother if no wife is to be inherited) will hold the stock in trust for the sons of the deceased. (I was told that, among the Kony, a youth whose father dies will undergo circumcision as soon as possible in order to attain legal majority, but this is not done among the Sebei.)

ECONOMICS OF HERD MANAGEMENT

Exchanges, sales, and other transfers of ownership and control of livestock play an important role in herd management. Economic exchanges are those transfers undertaken with a contractual obligation for a quid pro quo, as distinct from gifts or prestations. The Sebei have three different contractual arrangements: the *namanya* contract, direct exchanges (*walwet*) of animals, and sale or purchase. The first is clearly an aboriginal practice; the last is dependent upon modern currency. In addition to these transactions, which result in transfer of ownership, the Sebei engage in contractual arrangements (*kamanakanik*) in which the animals belonging to one man are taken care of by another. These may be viewed either as the hiring of a service or the rental of an animal. The frequency of all of these transactions indicates they form an important element in the daily lives of those Sebei who own cattle in any numbers.

The *namanya* contract is essentially the exchange of a bullock for a heifer, but the detailed character of the contractual arrangement makes it far more complex than a simple transfer of goods. Furthermore, it involves a set of enduring social obligations and relationships. The *namanya* contract may involve other considerations than cattle: other animals, land use, crops or food, and even money. Its essence lies, however, in the transfer of a viable and productive female animal in return for the consideration desired. The prototype for this contract is undoubtedly the exchange of bullock for heifer.

Namanya is initiated by the man who wants a bull, normally because he wants to slaughter it for some specific occasion. He is called *yenkintet*. He may need an animal of a specific color or character, but even if this is not a problem, it is considered proper for him to seek one outside his kraal, and a good herdsman does so when he can. In return for this bullock, he offers a heifer to the owner of the bull (*chitapteita* in this relationship), who will keep this animal until she has produced a heifer. The dam remains the property of the *yenkintet* and will be returned to him when her daughter is ready to bear, along with any bull calves she may have produced in the meantime. Thus, an immediate bullock is exchanged for a fertile cow at some later date. The time between the initiation of the contract and its ultimate fulfillment may be very great. The average is probably well over ten years. Formerly, the heifer promised was not yet born; nowadays, it is normally a very young calf. The contractual obligation remains with the herd and is transferred at death, and the funeral hearings will involve these matters. The period can be extended by delaying tactics on the part of each owner but involves the time for the first heifer to mature and be serviced, the gestation (with further delays if the calf is a male or dies) and the maturation of the daughter, for she should be pregnant before her dam is returned. Abnormal vicissitudes, such as the death of the cow before she reproduces or her barrenness, further delay matters. Time is not the essence of this contract; rather, its essence is the absolute obligation to provide a viable and reproductive cow at some future date. "A debt," the Sebei say, "never rots," and grandsons not infrequently settle affairs initiated by their grandparents.

The *namanya* contract entails a social relationship as well. The men who enter into the contract establish a bond that takes on the quality of a kinship tie and address each other as *tilyenyu*, which interpreters translate as "my kin of the cow." They are obligated to provide one another hospitality at all times, particularly when they slaughter an animal or have beer available, and they are explicitly enjoined from sexual intercourse with each other's wives. These obligations are expected to continue for the rest of their lives (and ideally devolve upon their sons), though I have heard modern Sebei from the farming sector argue that they apply only until the return of the original heifer to her owner.

Namanya arrangements were formerly hedged about by proprieties that border on the ritualistic, though these elements of protocol no longer are practiced. An informant gave me a detailed account of the customary way of establishing a *namanya* contract. The man seeking a bullock sends an emissary to say that the man wants to become a son-in-law of the house, so that the bullock owner must inquire — though very likely he is fully aware of the answer — "of the house or of the kraal?" If the animal sought has been allocated to a wife, the negotiation takes place in her house after proper refreshments are served. Although she does not enter into the discussion, she indicates her sentiments by her treatment of the guest. Should she disapprove, the husband might, if he can, supply an animal from his herd or that of a more favorably inclined wife. The man who is to receive the heifer does not yet ask to examine it. At some later date, by prearrangement, he will go or send an emissary to pick it up. If the animal does not suit him, he may request another. Once agreement has been reached, the original owner will send along his wife (and perhaps a neighbor) when the animal is taken by his *tilyet*, for the owner receives a portion of the neck, the hump, and the first four ribs of the right side, as well as some of the blood of the slaughtered animal. Before the animal is slaughtered, it should be sprinkled with milk and blessed by the wife or emissary of its former owner.

A man is not supposed to take his *tilyet* to court over matters pertaining to a *namanya* contract. They are, after all, kin and should behave as such. If continued pressure fails to get performance, he may use subterfuge by stealing in some obvious manner a personal possession, such as a spear, and thus bring the man into court. When this matter is under discussion, then a public airing of the real issue can bring pressure on the *tilyet* for contractual performance (*SL*:183-84). The Sebei also recognize that some debts are simply not collectible.

These arrangements are not affected by kinship considerations or other standard social parameters. Men may, and frequently do, engage in such contracts with their fathers, brothers, fathers-in-law, brothers-in-law, more distant kin, and persons who stand in no known kin relationship. They may or may not be age-mates; they may be from the same village or a distant one. There is no legal or social barrier against entering into such a contract with members of other tribes, but the absence of mutual trust, the difficulties in policing such matters, and the disconformity of customary procedures make this unlikely unless some close ties (such as intermarriage) also exist. At the opposite extreme, one man got involved in a *namanya* exchange between two parts of his own herd — *tokapsoi* and those anointed for one of his wives — under circumstances I do not now recall.

The *kamanakan* contract is an agreement between an owner and another man for the latter to care for one or more animals belonging to the former. In return, the herder takes the milk and blood. No feeding costs are entailed, as grazing land is open and unrestricted. If the stock increases over the years — and the arrangement may continue for a long time — the owner is under a moral obligation to give one or more animals to the herdsman, but there is no legal requirement to do so. Because an increase would suggest that the herder has been both diligent and honest — by no means universal attributes, in Sebei opinion — the owner is very likely to meet such an obligation if he wants to continue the arrangement. One informant told me that when an owner goes to visit his animals in *kamanaktay* (as they are then called), he will stop along the way to visit neighbors of the herdsman who are also his friends. His purpose is to pick up gossip about local events — raids, animal depredations, and the like — before he talks to the herder about the condition of his animals. In *kamanakan* arrangements, the herdsman has no legal obligation with respect to the cattle; if they are stolen, killed by predators, or die of disease, it is the owner's loss. The herder is merely expected to preserve such evidence of loss as he can, for instance keeping the skin of an animal killed by a leopard, for he does not have the right to slaughter them, as he may be tempted to do, and as he may well be accused of having done. These niceties are not always observed, and quarrels and legal cases arise over such matters. The social constraints of the *namanya* contract do not apply here. One man claimed that herders sometimes threw boiling water on the animal to kill it and claim that it had died of disease. Adequate performance is presumably assured by the constraints of the marketplace, for a man who does not exercise reasonable caution will not be entrusted with future contracts.

The *kamanakan* contract is an arrangement between equals; the herder is not seen as the servant or worker of the owner. Indeed, many men are on both sides of this arrangement. The Sebei do hire men to herd for them, usually persons from other tribes, frequently Bahima. They are paid in kind, distrusted, and looked down upon. I know of no Sebei who work for other Sebei under such an arrangement, though it does occur, and mention it here only to clarify the distinction between the *kamanakan* contract and the employment of labor.

The data in Table 16 attest to the importance of these contractual arrangements in everyday Sebei life on the plains. Frist, with regard to *namanya* contracts, we see that they are frequent in both Sasur and Kapsirika. As livestock are relatively unimportant in Sasur, the number of contracts per household is not great, but their importance to stock management is comparable to that of Kapsirika, with one such contract for every four or five animals held in each community. There is an even balance in each community between contracts bringing cattle and *warek* into the kraal and contracts placing them in the kraals of others. *Kamanakan* contracts are found in similar proportions in Sasur and Kapsirika, but in Sasur many more men place cattle in the kraals of others, while in Kapsirika men more frequently care for cattle belonging to others. This is a statistical reflection of the ecological differences between the two areas — of the fact that men living on the escarpment keep their cattle on the plains by means of this customary contractual arrangement. With *warek*, however, there is no comparable differential between Sasur and Kapsirika. Figure 10 shows graphically the effect of these contracts on the distribution of cattle.

The importance of these contracts for herd management can best be appreciated by examining more closely the handling of cattle by Kapsirikans. Table 15 shows that the 42 Kapsirikans reporting owned a total of 867 cattle (i.e., animals that were classed as *sekonik*). Table 16 shows that 213 of these animals were in other men's kraals either in *namut* or in *kamanaktay*, hence they were herding only 654 of their own animals. However, they also had in their kraals 385 animals belonging to other men under these contractual arrangements, so there were a total of 1,039 cattle in the Kapsirika herds (i.e., *yedyeita*). Hence only 63 percent of the average number of animals each man was herding belonged to the "owner" of the herd. The herd represents a network of economic ties and social relationships. Indeed, the 42 Kapsirikans had a total of 329 contracts of one kind or another, or about

TABLE 16
Current Cattle Contracts: Sasur and Kapsirika

| | Sasur | | | | Kapsirika | | | |
| | Cattle | | Warek | | Cattle | | Warek | |
Type of contract	Contracts	Animals	Contracts	Animals	Contracts	Animals	Contracts	Animals
Namanya contracts								
In kraal	17	33	10	13	74	99	27	32
Out of kraal	15	21	13	13	92	103	25	53
Total	32	54	23	26	166	202	52	85
In/out ratio	1.13	1.57	0.7	1.0	0.81	0.96	1.08	0.6
Contracts per hshld	0.8		0.6		4.0		1.13	
Contracts per 100 animals	23.7		20.4		19.1		23.3	
Kamanakan contracts								
In kraal	5	7	2	2	59	286	8	9
Out of kraal	15	25	5	8	40	110	5	15
Total	20	32	7	10	99	396	13	24
In/out ratio	0.33	0.28	0.4	0.25	1.48	2.60	1.60	0.60
Contracts per hshld	0.5		0.6		2.4		1.3	
Contracts per 100 animals	14.8		20.0		11.4		23.3	

NOTE: *In kraal* refers to animals belonging to somebody else that are in kraal of respondent; *out of kraal* refers to animals belonging to respondent that are held by others. *In/out ratio* is the number of animals in respondent's kraal that belong to other men divided by the number of animals respondent owns that are in other men's kraals. *Contracts per hshld* is the ratio of contracts to the number of households reporting on livestock (40 in Sasur, 42 in Kapsirika). *Contracts per 100 animals* is the ratio of contracts to the total number of animals owned by all the respondents in the village. Base figures for cattle: Sasur 135, Kapsirika 867; for *warek:* Sasur 118, Kapsirika 223 (see Table 15).

8 per household. With fewer animals at their disposal, it is to be expected that the number of contracts is much smaller in Sasur than in Kapsirika, yet significantly on a per animal basis both *namanya* and *kamanakan* contracts are somewhat more frequent in Sasur than in Kapsirika; that is, they are equally salient as aspects of herd management, though herd management does not loom so large as a whole.

I do not have a comparable corpus of data on outright exchanges, but the evidence indicates that they represent a significant element in the transfer of ownership and herd management and may result in profits to the astute trader (Goldschmidt, 1972c).

Cash transactions originated when Swahili caravans came to Sebeiland in the decades prior to Jackson's visit and traded iron wire and other exotica for grain and stock. The sale of cattle and grain still is an important aspect of Sebei economy (Plates II:33,35). The data on cash sales of livestock are more tenuous than those on contracts, for a sale is an event past, while the

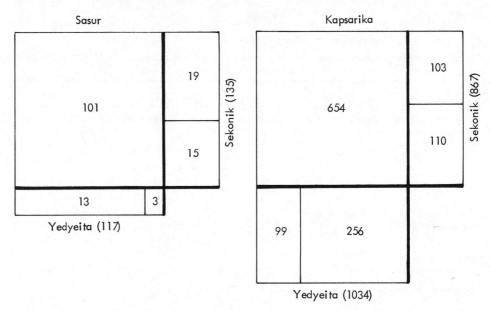

Figure 10. Diagrammatic Representation of Cattle by Categories
of Holding in Sasur and Kapsirika

contract exists in the form of an animal still possessed or owned. When asked, a respondent may or may not remember the date of a sale or even if it occurred within the past year. Table 17 summarizes the data on cash sales of livestock for the two communities, showing that cash transactions were a significant aspect of Kapsirika economy (accounting for half the total cash income), whereas stock sales have no important place in Sasur. Table 18 compares livestock numbers, contracts, and sales of the two communities, showing that, in Kapsirika, cattle ownership is more than six times more important than in Sasur and that virtually every Kapsirika household possesses cattle, which are a major source of income there.

Sebei exchanges and sales of livestock have important economic and social functions for the management of their herds. I have elsewhere (*KC*: Appen-

TABLE 17

Cash Sales of Livestock: Sasur and Kapsirika

Livestock	Sasur			Kapsirika		
	Hshlds rptg	No. of animals	Value	Hshlds rptg	No. of animals	Value
Cattle	4	4	600	18	43	11,460
Small stock[a]	3	3	134	0		
Chickens[b]	3		34	0		
Total value			768			11,460

[a]Small stock in Kapsirika not reported.

[b]Value of chickens in Sasur not reported; number and value not reported in Kapsirika.

TABLE 18

Summary Comparison of Livestock Economy: Sasur and Kapsirika

Livestock and contracts	Sasur (40 households)	Kapsirika (42 households)
Total number of cattle owned	135	867
Cattle per household	3.4	20.6
Households reporting cattle	23	41
Percent of households reporting cattle	57.5	97.6
Total cattle namanya contracts reported	32	166
Cattle involved in *namanya*	54	202
Contracts per household	0.8	4.0
Contracts per 100 head cattle owned	23.7	19.1
In/out contract ratios	1.13	0.81
Total kamanakan cattle contracts	20	99
Cattle involved in *kamanakan*	32	396
Contracts per household	0.5	2.4
Contracts per 100 head	14.8	11.4
In/out contract ratios	0.33	1.48
Total number of warek *owned*	117	215
Households reporting *warek*	32	28
Percent of households reporting *warek*	80.0	71.8
Warek per household	2.92	5.12
Total warek namanya contracts	24	52
Contracts per household	0.6	1.3
Contracts per 100 head of *warek*	20.0	23.3
Number of *warek* under *namanya* contract	26	85
Persons reporting cattle sold during year	4	18
Number of cattle sold	4	43
Cash value of cattle sold (shillings)	600	11,460
Average value of cattle sold (shillings)	150	266
Cash income per household (shillings)	15	273
Number of warek *sold during year*	3	0
Cash value of *warek* sold (shillings)	134	0
Cash value per household (shillings)	3.35	0
Men reporting anointing cattle for wives	7	23
Number of wives for whom anointed	8	44
Number of cattle anointed	11	159
Cattle anointed per wife given cattle	1.4	3.6

dix V; Goldschmidt, 1972c) shown that they further the growth of the herd and enable the owner to draw off profits in cash and to engage in important prestations.

One function of the *namanya* is to extend through economic ties the network of social obligations and rights. A man who stands to many others in the relationship of *tilyet* will find life richer and easier by virtue of these ties, though perhaps also fraught with special sources of anxiety. An explicit function is to spread the risk of cattle loss, and it is said that a man who has many such contracts will be rich, even though "he loses all his cattle," since disaster — especially in the form of cattle raids but also in the form of disease — tends to strike locally. This is, in fact, the case, for a man can reestablish his herd by collecting from his debtors. There is an obverse side of the coin, which I observed but never heard expressed: it is advantageous to have other persons interested in one's kraal because, if it is emptied by an enemy raid, they will have an interest in undertaking the difficult and hazardous task of retrieving lost stock.

Both the *namanya* and *kamanakan* arrangements have the effect of redistributing stock in relation to resources, on the one hand, and need, on the other. Small herds are wasteful of labor resources, and, if one cannot or does not want to share a kraal, the *kamanakan* arrangement is an obvious solution. If a man has too many animals to herd as a unit or too many cows for his wives to milk, contracts may relieve his situation, while giving an adequate unit and sufficient milk to his contract partner.

Another reason a man likes to have his stock scattered over many kraals is that it obscures his wealth. No man, I was told by a perceptive Sebei, likes to reveal how many cows he has any more than a European will tell you how many shillings he has in the bank. Thus, the envious eyes of one's neighbors can be avoided. The scattering of stock also obscures a man's wealth from the tax collector. Though taxes are a Western contribution to Sebei social life, native custom called for assessments for diverse reasons and it may be that these, too, could be lessened by obscuring the size of one's holdings.

Finally, the Sebei say that "sweet is the cow of debt." By this, they express the belief that the cow under *namanya* contract will grow fatter and become more productive. That is, they believe it not only right but good to engage in exchanges.

Other commodities may also enter into the *namanya* contract. For there are no separate spheres of economic activity among the Sebei like those Bohannan (1968:227-33) found among the Tiv. It is possible to parlay chickens into goats and goats into cattle and cattle into wives; agricultural products also enter into this network of exchanges as do both land and money. One Sasur man told me he had started his small cattle herd (large by Sasur standards) with one hen. Sebei recognize that this is the proper way for a poor man to become rich. Such Horatio Alger plots may not be frequent, but they do occur. (Kambuya initiated 7 separate families of cattle through exchanging goats, either directly or under *namanya* contract, for the heifer that originated the line, and these accounted for 86 of the 700 animals recorded as having been owned by him.) The building of a herd by exchange is not a recent innovation. I was told of a curse a Maina man had laid on his son who was trying to claim a heifer. The son had beaten the father, and that night the old man went naked into his kraal, placed the blade of his spear against the animal's flank, and said, "These cattle are descended from a cow my grandmother bought. She dug the land and planted nompuk [a yam-like root]. When the nompuk was ready, she traded it for a goat. When the goat multiplied, she sold the offspring for a bullock. The bullock was slaughtered by someone in exchange for a heifer, and that heifer multiplied and these cattle are her descendants."

Nonstandard exchanges (i.e., between two categories of goods, including the use of cash in *namanya* contracts, as distinct from direct purchases) are also viewed as normal.

Mixed exchanges are indicated in Table 19. These eighty-nine instances were offered by informants and do not represent a sample, but their number indicates the importance such exchanges have in the Sebei economy. I found three special cases, a bicycle exchanged for a cow, the acceptance of school fees by the teacher, and the exchange of a field of plantains of unspecified size for two cattle needed in brideprice.

The following account, given to me by a man of Sasur, shows how a Sebei can build his herd while drawing a profit in food, cash, and the creation of social obligations.

> Ananiya and I each had 100 shillings from coffee in 1948, with which we bought a cow. We took a bull for this cow as *namanya* and sold the bull for 250 shillings. We traded in goats until we had forty of them and sold them all in 1952 and got 1400 shillings, from which we each took 700. Ananiya added other money to this and put a tin roof on his house; I added some money to mine to pay the brideprice for my second wife. The cow has come back to us and has produced two bulls and two heifers, and Ananiya and I have one of each. My heifer is now *namanya* with Salimu Mire; she has not yet released herself.

TABLE 19

Mixed Livestock Exchanges: Sasur and Kapsirika

Livestock traded[a]	No. of exchanges		
	Sasur	Kapsirika	Total
Chickens for goats, *namanya*	8	1	9
Chickens for goats, direct	3	1	4
Crops for cattle, *namanya*	6	4	10
Crops for cattle, direct	2	32	34
Goats for cattle, *namanya*	13 ⎫	5	26
Goats for cattle, direct	8 ⎭		
Cash for cattle, *namanya*	3	2	5
Cash for goat, *namanya*	1	0	1
Total	44	45	89

[a]Some exchange ratios are: 12 - 15 chickens for a *namanya* goat, 5 - 6 goats for a heifer *namanya* or a bullock, 60 shillings for a heifer *namanya*, 8 shillings for a goat *namanya*.

Such a partnership arrangement is called *sankanya*. This relationship would make the two men *tilyet* to one another, but, as they are closely related (Ananiya is mother's brother's son to my informant, i.e., *mama*), they do not address one another as *tilyenyu*. Ananiya took the first heifer and the milk, as he was caring for the cow, not because his was the senior position in the relationship. In the old days, my informant said, they would have taken turns with the milk.

In sum, livestock transactions are a part of the intricate manipulation of property, which involves everything from minor chattels to the use of land and the acquisition of wives. They are important in the farming sector, as well as in the pastoral sector, to the degree that the farmer owns livestock.

SOCIAL USES OF CATTLE

Cattle and other livestock play a vital role in the structuring of Sebei social action. A man's herd is structured as is his household, reflecting the pattern of social relationships between himself, his wives, and his children. A line of animals is likened to a lineage, with the use of the same terms and a recognition of indefinite continuity — the ideal for both humans and animals. (The disconformity between the thoroughly agnatic character of Sebei lineage and their calculation of animal lineage by the female line does not impair this analogy for the Sebei). This lineal continuity is expressed in the patterns of inheritance and the recognition that the continuity of the herd reflects and reinforces the continuity of the family line. The exchange of cattle under *namanya* contract establishes a social bond that the Sebei liken to a kinship bond. Clan earmarks for cattle, while not reflecting a concept of ownership, reflect in symbolic form the larger unity of social relationships that so deeply influences Sebei attitudes.[2]

Three basic institutions express the role of cattle as elements in the structuring of the social order: wergild, brideprice, and the inheritance of stock. Wergild was formerly paid as a compensation for murder; it was in cattle and small stock, and the animals were transferred between clans. With British overrule, wergild disappeared from sight, if not from practice. It is not clear how many animals were regularly or normally transferred — figures given varied from six to eighty — possibly reflecting the degree of affluence of time and place. More was paid for a male than a female victim, and the amount paid for a woman varied with the probability of her bearing children, with twice as much for a newly married wife as for a barren old woman. The number probably was around fifty animals for a young adult man in a time of cattle prosperity.

In payment of wergild, the stock was accumulated from the clansmen of

---

2. Men like to herd their animals near where there is beer, so they can go there from time to time. "The people will never refuse a man beer because he is doing inportant work, and people say that the cows do not merely belong to him, but to everybody, for they may want to exchange for them in the future."

the murderer and paid to the clansmen of the victim. Richer men had to pay more than the poorer ones; most or all of the animals remained in the lineage of the victim. It is clear that livestock were used as social counters between clans, that clansmen shared the obligation to make such payments and the right to receive them, and that after such a payment the emotions were expected to have been allayed. The most important implications of this custom for the Sebei — and I daresay for any other place where it is found — are: (1) The concern with the strength of the social unit as an entity, which is impaired by the loss of a person; (2) the recognition that individuals and stock are interchangeable counters; and (3) the idea that each person has some calculable worth in livestock.

Bride payments, even more than wergild, can be seen as the prototypical use of stock as a counter in social interaction. The most important point about brideprice (*konewik*) is that they are the quintessential element in legalizing a marriage and legitimizing the children. Nothing could more explicitly express the social importance of cattle.

The third important social nexus expressed in the transfer of livestock is the process we think of as inheritance, but it is more accurately conceived as the ultimate right of a man in the herd of his father. In conformity with the idea of individual ownership of stock, only a man's sons will inherit the animals he owns. If there are no sons, the stock will go to the next younger brother. If a man dies when his wife is young enough to be inherited (which is normally before she has circumcised sons), the man who takes his wife will also take over his herd, but he keeps the animals in trust for the true sons of the deceased, who are their real owners.

The right of a son in his father's herd does not wait upon the death of the latter. His first right is to have enough animals to acquire his first bride. Later, he will be given his share of his father's *tokapsoi*, as if the total were being divided equally among all the father's sons at that time, together with his proportionate share of those anointed for his mother. (The latter group will most likely have been used for his brideprice, so that it would be unlikely, if he has younger full brothers, that he would get more of his mother's cattle.) Once a son has his share of the herd, he has no further legal claim on his father's animals, except for a cow given to him upon the father's death "for crying." If the father had many cattle, each brother will receive such an animal; if not so rich, only the son "who buries the father" will get one. In actual practice, these idealized regulations may be flouted. The last son is the residual legatee (*kontintet*), caring for his father and his father's herd until, when the father dies, he takes it over. It is apparently the father's decision as to when he will give a son his share of the stock. It does not normally take place upon marriage, for each son acts as his father's herds-man; it tends to take place when the next son is ready to take over this task, which would be after the younger brother has been circumcised and more likely after he has married.

Psiwa, the only man in Sasur who is wealthy enough in cattle to be concerned with the matter, described how he had allocated cattle to his adult sons (Table 20). Concerning the older sons, Psiwa said: "I gave them *warek*, plantain *shambas*, and land, and so I am rid of them and they cannot come back to me. They will inherit nothing from me. They are *kyichepyita* (persons who have inherited their share). If Sirar wants to marry a second wife and hasn't enough cattle, I can give him one more — but only one. If Noibei wants to marry again, I would help." Concerning Andyema, he said, "He, being the last one, is now my herdsman and keeps the cattle for me. I haven't given him any, and I'm not going to give him any, as he is still in the house and sharing the cows. The time will come when I die, and all these cows will automatically be his. He may be kind enough to give Noibei one or two. They could not bring a legal case for any, because they have had their share. They could only ask my young son kindly to give them one cow, 'for we have been crying for our father.' The older sons couldn't even ask for one. If Andyema gives a cow to his brothers, it should be [the descendant of] one that was received in brideprice."

Emphatically, Psiwa would not give any cattle to his daughter: "I sold her, why should I give her some cows? Those who do that have very many cattle, and they think their son-in-law is too poor, so they give him cows to milk. A daughter might be given a cow 'for crying [when he dies].'"

There are other occasions when a man will make a gift of cattle. Most gifts are either directly or indirectly to agnatic kin. (By indirectly, I mean the gift of an animal to his bride or the bride of his son or brother, for such gifts ultimately devolve upon her sons, who are clansmen.)[3] Such gifts may also be made to the sons of brothers or to grandsons. I have a record of only one instance where an animal was given to a nonclansman. A woman may be given cows by her father or uncle (mother's brother), which she then takes with her at the time of marriage. A daughter does not inherit her father's cattle, even if there are no sons, and she has no rights in her father's herd.

TABLE 20
Allocation of Cattle to Married Sons

Son[a]	Brideprice payments		Direct gifts	Total
	1st wife	2d wife		
Lazima	5	5	4	14
Sayekwa	5	0	2	7
Salimu	5	5	4	14
Sirar	6	c	2	8
Noibei	6	c	1	7
Andyema[b]	5	c	0	5

[a]Sons are listed in order of birth.

[b]Andyema was his father's herdsman and thus was in charge of the animals his father owned.

[c]Only one wife.

---

3. I found that Kambuya's prestations were in all sixty-nine ascertainable instances made to members of his own clan, either as gifts or for brideprice (Goldschmidt, 1972c: Table 5).

The use of cattle in prestations has the effect of both strengthening the clan as an entity and reinforcing existing kinship ties. This latter point is not to be taken lightly. A deep-seated sense of basic clan unity in both legal institutions (*SL:passim*) and economic institutions (Goldschmidt, 1972c) underlies the structure of Sebei behavior. The strategic use of prestations not only serves as a means for clan continuation by enabling sons and grandsons to marry, but also helps to reduce the rivalry and tensions within the group.

CEREMONIAL INVOLVEMENTS OF LIVESTOCK

The Sebei do not seem to be certain whether or not cattle dwell in the land of the spirits, but they are quite clear that the spirits, and spiritual forces in general, are integrally related to the cattle. They recount the following myth of man's original involvement with cattle:

> In the beginning, all the animals and Lightning lived together with Man. Lightning had wings and used to fly slowly over the people in the night, when everyone is asleep so they would not know. He found that Man was sleeping near the fire, and that Cow was attracted by the fire. There was father, mother, and child in each family, and every kind of animal and insects, and all spoke the same language. When Lightning saw Man have fire with Cow near by, he became frightened by Man, and said to Elephant, "Let us go up and live in the air." But Elephant said, "Why do you fear that little thing that you can step on?"
>
> The next night, Lightning flew over as before and saw Man sitting near his fire sharpening something and thought that this man might do something treacherous. The following day, Man speared the elephant calf and hid it, and when the Elephant returned, he couldn't find his calf. Lightning said, "I warned you not to stay near Man, for he does things that nobody knows."
>
> So Lightning decided to go away, and when the animals and the birds saw that Lightning had left the country, they scattered also, for Lightning was their chief. Only Cow stayed with man.
>
> One day, Man decided he wanted butter from Cow. He told Cow that his child was so ill he needed butter, though the child was not really sick. Cow said, "Take your gourd and milk me," and told him to keep the milk two or three days and to stir it a long time. So Man did this.
>
> Later he decided to eat Cow, and said to it, "My child is still ill and needs some blood." Cow showed Man how to make a bleeding arrow, and so he got blood. The next day, he said, "My child is very ill and needs some cud." So Cow turned the chyme out of its mouth.
>
> The following day, Man came to Cow saying that his child was so ill he needed marrow but Cow remained silent. That is when Cow lost speech; that is the day Man decided to slaughter his first cow. But before he was slaughtered, Cow said that he would remain in the middle and everything in the world would like Cow, warning Man that he would be in trouble; unless he defends his cows, they will go away. That is why everything competes for cattle; that is why cows understand words but do not speak.

A sick man may be advised by the diviner to dedicate an animal to the spirits (*oyik*). The bull designated will be castrated for him by a man he calls *papa* (father), who ties sinentet vine around its neck and blesses it by spitting. The bull is henceforth kept in the kraal and will not be sold, exchanged, or slaughtered until it is very old, at which time it must be slaughtered at the same home by the same man. Bits of meat are taken from each part of the animal and placed on pieces of potsherd or basket after sundown, as a gift to the spirits, and chyme is thrown at the same place. The bull's skull is kept on the kraal fence for the spirits to see. A man may also be advised to slaughter an animal of a particular kind and color — a chicken, ram, goat, or bullock — and make a soup in which he takes the required medicine. For all important rituals, an animal should be slaughtered and the mode of killing is usually specified.

Various animal substances are used for purification purposes. The chyme of a slaughtered animal is smeared on initiates before circumcision, strewn on the path of the mourners at a funeral as a purification, and smeared on the parents of twins at the twin ceremony. Fat, either from the tail of a ram or the kidney of an ox, must be smeared on a dead man's belongings before others can take them and on the instruments and weapons initiates will use after their period of seclusion. Butter is used for anointing initiates after they have completed their circumcision and again when they are to be released from their exclusion, and is also used on brides. Milk is spewed as a blessing, along with beer, fat, or moykutwek root, in various ceremonies. It is also used as a ritual refreshment when negotiating a *namanya* contract or a marriage and is sprinkled on animals that are undergoing ritual transfer. Cow dung is used to anoint the cattle being transferred to wives; it is also smeared on the doorways for rituals of friendship between brothers and formed into "kraals," in which milk and medicines are put when performing certain *korosek* ceremonies. The fetus of a ewe is an essential ingredient in the ritual for the release of the parents of twins. The blood of sacrificial animals is rarely used but does play a role in the ceremony of removing bad *oyik*.

Cattle, and sometimes other stock, are involved in the rituals for fertility, rain, and the settlement of disputes between clans after a murder and in the purification of a murderer, and they may be used in oathing ceremonies as well.

Two rituals are undertaken for the benefit of animals. One is a counterpart to the ritual for human twins or breech births, for cattle can be *tekeryontet* (see Chapter 9), just as people can. An animal that is a twin or otherwise so viewed is specially marked by cutting the skin on the neck so that it hangs down like a wattle. Such animals should not be used for brideprice or payment of other debts.

We participated in part of a ceremony for a breech-born calf. Its dam had not been confined but grazed with the other animals until the day of the ceremony. The calf was not to be seen by a person who was a twin. None of the milk that the cow had produced could be drunk; it was set aside and allowed to solidify and was eaten after the ceremony was over by the group who attended it. A woman who had had a baby by breech delivery prepared the medicine and acted as ceremonialist. The medicine is the same as that prepared for people.

The morning of the ceremony, the cow and calf had been kept in the kraal and were garlanded with vines. While tying on the vine, the participants sang a special twin song and beat together the iron pick and ax as they do during circumcision ceremonies. The ceremonialist came early with medicines and prepared them in the kraal. She then covered herself with a cloth and approached the cow, similarly covered, without seeing it. As she came up to it, she separated her hood, somebody opened the cow's cloth, and she spat medicine on the cow and smeared it around. She then drank some of the cow's milk. Thereafter, the animals were released and the people gathered to enjoy the feasting and beer drinking that followed. The men arose to sing praise songs for their cattle, and other relevant songs were sung. One sentiment expressed in song was that twin births are particularly fortunate and lead to the increase of both lineage and herd. The songs also express the pleasure of the participants because the birth has brought the "fat" ceremony they are enjoying. Similar ceremonies are performed for sheep but not for goats, "because they are animals that climb trees."

The second ritual specifically for animals is to establish amity between two herds that are to merge when one man inherits the herd of the other. Until the inheritor undertakes the ceremony, he should not eat the meat nor drink the milk of the herd of the deceased. Before the ceremony, the inheritor builds a new kraal to which he will bring the cattle of both herds. In the ceremony, the ritualist is a person who has obtained cattle from a brother; he is assisted by the wives he married and those he inherited. He brings bamboo from the forest and a palm frond, places these on either side of the gate, and ties them together at the top with the sinentet vine. The following morning, a large fire is lit in the middle of the kraal and, as people arrive, they throw into it *korosek* plants and the fat and chyme from a slaughtered ram. The principals then line up outside the kraal in the following order: the ritualist, his real wives, the widows he has inherited, the inheritor, his own wives and their children in the order of their marriage and age, then each widow and her children in the order of marriage and age, followed by the herd of the owner and the herd he is inheriting. The procession goes into the kraal, striking together an ax blade and a pick, circles the fire and goes back out, circles about and reenters the kraal, making the circuit four times. The people in the procession then enter the house of the senior wife and partake of milk from cows in each herd, to which fat from the ram's tail and beer are added. Each person in succession drinks from the gourd ("a child carried on a woman's back will not drink from it, as it will get it from the mother's breast"). The gourd is passed around four times. A beer party follows.

CATTLE AS INDIVIDUALS AND AS LINEAGES

Sebei animals have an individuality in appearance, temperament, and social role, and the Sebei has, with his livestock, particularly his cattle, what can best be described as a personal relationship. Most young animals are kept in the house to protect them from the evil eye and other sources of danger. There is no sentimentality in this, and stock are sold or slaughtered without the qualms we tend to feel in relation to our pets, nor are they treated as pets.

Sebei cattle are always named. Most of the names relate to colors or particular color combinations; some relate to the configuration of the horns; and some are named after circumstances of acquisition. Those cows obtained in exchange for goats are often called Chepkware (daughter of goats). One cow was called Buganda, because it was purchased from a Muganda. Sebei cows recognize their names and come when called to be milked.

One man told me of two animals that had become *sokoran*, a word that can best be defined as sinful. One of them began to suckle herself. The other mysteriously began to change color, which so alarmed the owner that he immediately exchanged it for another. But even this much continuity was too distressful, so the second animal was rapidly disposed of for cash to an itinerant Somali trader and the money "consumed," so as to remove all trace of its baneful influence. A similar fate was recommended for a cow that had gored the man's daughter in the vagina, but I'm not sure it was heeded.

Each herdsman has a special bull, *kintet* or *kirkitaptoka* (bull of the herd), in which he takes special pride and which should be slaughtered for a funeral feast on the third day after his death. His sons should not partake of this animal, but his grandchildren may. A larger herd may have other bulls to serve the cows, but only one has this special relationship. The history of the animal should be known, for its dam should be one that produced much milk and many calves; hence it cannot have been bought in the market. Nor should the bull have been received in bride payment, for it is not proper to allow such an animal to service one's cows. A man can sell this animal when it gets old, but he will prefer to keep it until it gets very old and then slaughter it ceremonially and place its skull on the kraal gate.

Men brag about their important animals around the beer pot, and women — a man's sisters or wives — sing praise about them, mentioning them by name and mentioning the owner, and this is said to make the man feel proud. Men have songs that praise the cattle of their clan as well, such as the following for the clan of Muntarit:

> Ours of Kaptenge [*kota*] ;
> Ours the cow with long horns;
> Ours the cow exchanged for ivory;
> Ours of the people come from the east;
> Ours of the clan of soft hair;
> Ours of the clan of the soft grass hair;
> Ours of the clan of Muntarit
> Ours of the clan who do not cut trees;
> Ours of the clan who cut bamboo. [4]

---

4. References in the song relate to the clan's derivation from the east, where they used bamboo vessels rather than wooden ones; the reference to hair was not explained.

Cattle are seen as belonging to lineages. The same word, *kota* is used for both. The recognition of lineages is most important to the Sebei conception of the herd, for a *kota* of cattle is treated as a legal entity. A lineage is initiated when an animal enters the herd, whether as a gift from the father, a payment in brideprice, or an acquisition by exchange for something other than cattle. The progeny of the cow first acquired, as well as any animals received in exchange for her offspring, are viewed not only as belonging to the lineage, but as having the same legal status. Thus, if the dam had been smeared for a wife or allocated to a son, these rights would also apply to the offspring or exchange animal. This even applies to animals bought with money obtained from selling one in the market. This subordination to its lineage does not destroy the individuality of the animal but desentimentalizes it. I had early to learn that when a man said he had a cow from some pre-European raid, he was not referring to its longevity but was expressing this sense of lineage continuity. The use of the word *kota* for both human and animal lineages is not coincidental. In both instances, unity is seen as being of overriding importance. The ultimate purpose of Sebei social action is the *kota's* preservation through time, its projection into the future. In this sense, the corporateness of Sebei social structure, and of Sebei cattle, has a psychological dimension.

SOCIAL STRUCTURE OF A SEBEI HERD

To Western eyes, a group of animals feeding off the lush grass of Kapsirika, or moving to water at the Sundet river, is so many head of stock, a total dressed weight of so many pounds, commanding on the market under fair conditions such and such a price. But when a Sebei contemplates his herd, he sees much more.

There is, first of all, the fact that some of the animals are his alone, to do with as he wishes without further ado, while others belong to his several wives. These animals he can use only if the wife agrees and in some of his cattle he will see aspects of his relationship with the particular wife who has smeared them with dung. These, too, are destined to be given to the sons of the wife in question. Has the wife with many sons also many cattle descended from those he anointed for her years ago, or have the fates been ironic and been more bountiful to her in cattle than in sons? Some cattle, indeed, may have already been given to this son or that — perhaps as a forfeit he had demanded before allowing his mother to anoint him at circumcision.

Then, again, there are cattle in his herd that do not belong to the man or his wives; they are not *sekonik*, but are held under contract. These cows are *kamanaktay* and belong to a relative on the escarpment; perhaps they are doing well, and he will get one of the calves to be dropped this coming year. Others are under *namanya* contract, and he is reminded of his desire to visit the owner and enjoy the beer of his *tilyet* when the maize is being harvested on the escarpment, more importantly because his *tilyet's* daughter is about ready for circumcision and might be a suitable wife for one of his recently initiated sons. Good *tilyet* relationships, he knows, make for good in-law relationships.

As a Sebei looks at his cattle, he sees families of cows, each a distinct line like the men of a *kota*; each originating with some particular event of the past. Here is a cow that came from the herd of his father — indeed, had been anointed for his mother as a gift from his father's father before he could remember. This cow of course is not that old, but she is the daughter of a daughter and thus is part of the same gift, a continuation of a tie that links him to ancestors from long before his time. Her calf, a young bullock, would be very good to use in brideprice, should his son marry (as he soon should) and provide him with grandsons.

Each animal has its own history, its own link with the past, perhaps reminding him of the deal he made a few years before when he was given a goat — a single magnificent he-goat that he exchanged for a bullock and then turned that through *namanya* into a heifer, this cow's mother. And he remembers perhaps that he should really give another goat to the man who exchanged that bullock, even though that is not a real debt.

Among these lines of animals are some that entered the herd as payment for his sisters and his father's sisters, as well as one bullock recently acquired from the man who married his sister's daughter. This animal would perhaps make a good replacement for his old *kintet*, his bull of the herd, but unfortunately he can not use it thus, for it is not proper to keep a bull from an animal received as brideprice.

There are also some special animals. The bull of the herd, with those fine horns, has sired many calves and is now growing old, and he may contemplate whether he should be killed ceremonially now or later and whether any of the bullocks could really take his place — a thought that may well remind him of his advancing years for, like most men, but particularly Sebei men, he fears death. And then there are the two cows he dedicated to the *oyik* when his wife became ill.

He also knows each animal by name, and, whatever its source, whatever its family line, whatever rights he has in it or has given to his wife, he knows it as an individual animal, with its particular habits, its virtues and faults. This one gives much milk but has difficulty in calving, that one tends to stray from the herd, a third one is a natural leader, and so on. Each animal, whether there be a mere handful or a hundred or two hundred in the herd, is known and recognized.

We see, therefore, that a man's herd is a complex organization of individuals tied to one another in diverse ways; quite as complex as the community of people in which he lives, and in many ways reflecting that community. His herd reflects the household structure, the lineage, and the clan; expresses the network of social relationships as they extend to his father's father and the yet unborn son of his son; and reflects also the ties that have been established through the marriages of his aunts and his sisters and the no less tenuous ties arrived at through contractual relationships, all of which bind him to widely scattered fellow tribesman.

These considerations do not render him sentimental about the animals as such. His overriding interest is to preserve the herd as a whole and, within that, to assure the continuation of each *kota* of animals, for it is that line of animals and not the particular beast that stands before him, that establishes his ties. Thus, he will trade, give away, or slaughter his animals as circumstances demand, for only by doing so can he build his herd and further his social ties. The herd as a whole stands for what he is, not by virtue of size alone — though a large herd is a measure of his success in the past and the nearest thing he can get to an assurance of his future — but by what it represents as a set of particular social relationships. In the final analysis, his herd is his autobiography and his monument; through it he will gain such immortality as may come to a Sebei herdsman.

Chapter 6
The Role of Agriculture

Dig yams my sister
Herd cattle my brother
We children shall meet tonight

Courting song of old Sebei[1]

HISTORIC DEVELOPMENT OF FARMING

The Sebei at one time raised millet and sorghum in a pattern of shifting cultivation that characterized all the Kalenjin peoples. To this agricultural base, they have in the course of time added many cultigens acquired from diverse sources. They claim to have brought under cultivation a native plant, nompuk (*Labiatae queer*), which still grows wild on the mountainside, and to have acquired plantains, potatoes, and beans from the Bantu and maize from the east before Europeans arrived. Later acquisitions include white potatoes (a staple in Masop), wheat (in Bukwa, and by 1972 throughout the escarpment), cassava, cabbage, tomatoes, and other vegetables (cultivated for the local markets). Cash crops have also entered Sebei agriculture. The most important of these is arabica coffee, which was introduced around 1920 and has become a major (and growing) source of income in the better watered areas.

Technological innovations have also played a part in the evolution of Sebei cultivation. Older informants stated that at one time all cultivation was done with hoes made of the shoulder-blades of buffalo or elephant, but that these were replaced with a crude native-made iron hoe they presume was brought by the Swahili. Every Sebei woman now has a broad iron hoe, purchased from the market and hafted on a short tree-crotch handle, which she swings from a bent position, her torso almost parallel to the ground (Plate II:23). Men, when they cultivate at all, use a lighter, long-handled hoe,

---

1. The youths sang this at gatherings, mentioning names of a boy and girl; if the girl did not like the youth, she sang the next verse: "Don't tie me to the centerpost, brother/ Don't tie me to the housepost." This form of song disappeared in Sowe times.

146

working more nearly upright. Where the land is reasonably flat, these implements are replaced by the ox-drawn plow (Plate II:24), which came to Sebei in 1933.[2] As early as the 1940s, some men were using tractor power in Bukwa, but this remains the rare exception. The government has provided a few combines for harvesting wheat, but most work is still done by hand. Whether the Sebei aboriginally used donkeys for transport is not clear, but they have known them since Swahili days and they are a regular means for the transport of goods. Much more important is the lorry, and its necessary accompaniment, roads. The road up the escarpment was built shortly after World War I but was not extended across the mountain to Kenya until about 1960. Powered transport has been an essential element in the furtherance of crops produced for the national market.

The aboriginal method of grinding was with a hand-held pebble and a flat grinding rock (Plate II:11). In 1954, the hand-cranked maize mill was found in most homesteads where maize was cultivated (Plate II:6). These are still to be found, but power-operated mills, to which the women carry their grain, have further lightened the burden of flour-making in the more populated areas. The influence of this technological development on the use of grains for food, and particularly for beer-making, must be considerable. Stone-grinding is now generally done only in special circumstances, as for instance, in pulverizing groundnuts.

These historical developments have impinged upon a landscape of great diversity, with the inevitable result that there is considerable regional variation in the character of the agricultural enterprise and the uses of the land.

Porter estimates there are 36,300 acres in cultivation in Sebei District. This is 13.7 percent of all land, but sub-county percentages vary from 3.6 percent in Ngenge to 76.0 percent in Sipi. These differences strike the eye of the most casual observer. In Sipi, one moves from house to house under a canopy of plantains, relieved here and there by a maize field or a piece of fallow land. In Ngenge, one follows cattle trails through dry brush and occasionally glimpses long, narrow plowed fields. This regional variation is expressed in the three maps showing, respectively, the percentage of land under cultivation, the distribution of plantains throughout Sebei District, and the acreage per capita under cultivation in crops other than plantains and coffee. In all these measures, we see the thinning out of agriculture as one moves eastward along the escarpment and the minimal involvement in farming in Ngenge.

EVOLUTION OF LAND OWNERSHIP

A basic principle in aboriginal Sebei law is that natural products (grass, water, salt for cattle, wild plants and animals, for example) are public

---

2. According to Hays, 1949. He reports there were 331 plows in use in Sebei County in 1949.

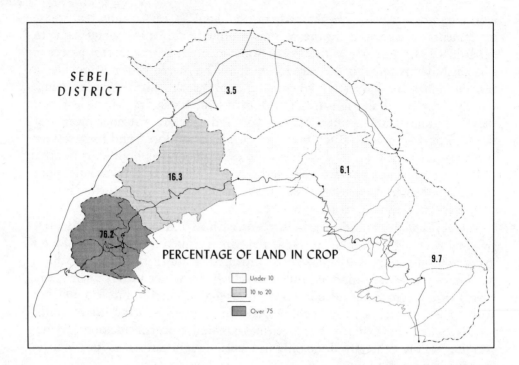

SEBEI
DISTRICT

3.5

16.3

6.1

76.2

PERCENTAGE OF LAND IN CROP

Under 10
10 to 20
Over 75

9.7

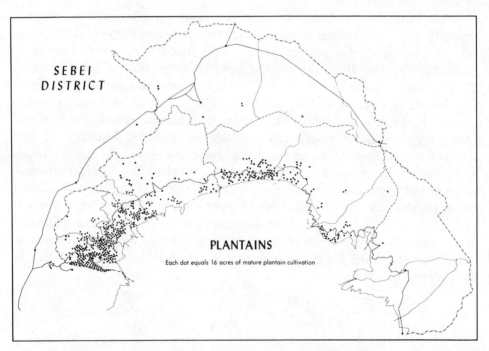

SEBEI
DISTRICT

PLANTAINS

Each dot equals 16 acres of mature plantain cultivation

property and not subject to private control (*SL*:143). When human effort
has been expended to make such products useful (dislodging salt, trapping an
animal, digging a well), then that product is the private right of the person
who expended the effort. This principle is applied to land and is in func-

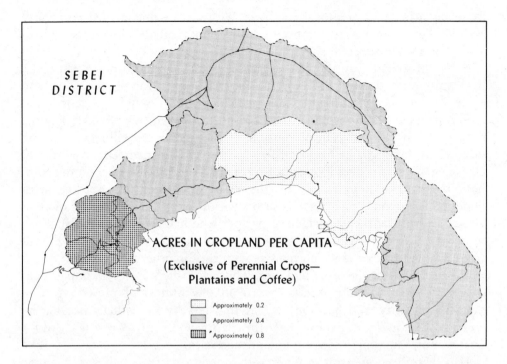

tional conformity with the needs of pastoralists: the grasslands are available to anybody, but cultivated lands belong to the cultivator and are private rights.

This basic rule, when applied to the diversity of environmental conditions and land usage of the Sebei leads to such confusion that Saza Chief Aloni Muzungyo could reasonably say, "As long as I have been chief, I have been trying to find out what is native custom regarding land." In these matters, Sasur and Kapsirika stand at opposite ends, for in the former all the land is in private hands and land disputes are frequent whereas in Kapsirika the land was taken up by in-migrants very much as it was needed, and land disputes are all but unknown. A dynamic view of the Sebei historical development is necessary to resolve Chief Aloni's dilemma.

By the middle of the nineteenth century, the northern escarpment was sparsely populated, while the plains below were used only sporadically for hunting or by groups going down together for mutual protection to cultivate contiguous plots of land. Cultivation was of limited extent and shifting in character. Each person claimed a private right to the lands he cultivated, in accordance with the basic Sebei rule of property, but, because land could only be used a few years in succession and potentially arable land was plentiful, ownership of land as a basic capital asset could not have been meaningful. As Gisu pressure drove Sebei out of the southwestern quadrant of the Elgon massif, those who fell back to Legene and Sipi tended to settle as clan group. In Sipi, villages often have clan names and are said to belong to a particular clan, but this pattern is not found elsewhere in Sebei. Later arrivals, often members of the same clans, "bought" land with an animal or by giving a feast for the local residents. With clans living in close contiguity and with the growing importance of cultivation, there developed the appearance, but not the substance, of clan landholdings.

Some informants say the clan owned the land. One informant said that a man who wanted land could go to the clan elders for it, but I have no evidence that this was a regular practice anywhere in Sebei. The fact is that each individual had private rights to the portion he cultivated, including the right to sell it without clan permission. If clansmen were willing to meet his obligations, he might instead transfer the land to clansmen. The objection of clansmen to a sale does not appear to have been motivated by a desire to hold the land as a unit, but by the desire to prevent the settling in of undesirable persons, e.g., persons suspected of witchcraft, members of clans viewed as bad clans, or clansmen of persons who had refused them daughters in marriage. A man would not — and still will not — purchase land without the presence of a seller's clansman as witness, for otherwise the clan might deny the sale after the seller had died. Thus, this rule was not an impairment of private right to land; it was control in the interest of preserving community solidarity and harmony. Land transfers by individuals became increasingly frequent, and nowadays the clan can do no more than exert a diffuse moral suasion in seeking to halt such sales.

Had there been an ethnographer with Austin's party in 1898 to examine land tenure patterns, he would have been justified in projecting an evolutionary development of corporate landholding in the clan, in analogy to practices elsewhere in Africa, citing the strength of the clan and the functional effectiveness of such a program. Instead, Sebei commitment to the ideology of private property applied to the control of livestock prevailed; land ownership was fully analogized to cattle ownership, though this was a functionally less effective solution.

Two old customs contributed to the formulation of these land rights: the ritual slaughter of an animal when a man joined the *pororyet,* and the exchange of an animal for crops in the ground. When a man exchanged a heifer for a plot of land that enabled him to harvest the nompuk or yams still in the ground, he acquired a kind of rental right. When this concept of exchange was applied to land in plantains, this right became one of indefinite duration and often ended up being a de facto transfer of property. By Maina times, men in Sipi were acquiring rights to uncultivated land through giving an animal. At least by 1910, men were using the senchontet plant as boundary markers, for I have data on a dispute over encroachment that dates back that far. A man made an oath[3] that he had been falsely accused of uprooting these markers.

---

3. The men gather around the hole, and the accused, pointing his spear at it, says, "If I have uprooted this plant, may this land eat me." The plaintiff then says, "If I falsely accuse you, may this land eat me." The men of the *saŋta,* also pointing their spears, then chorus the statement (*KC*:180). The curse was later removed ceremonially by the slaughter of a ram, and the clansmen of the deceased were smeared with chyme and mud taken from the hole where the oath had been sworn.

By the 1920s the Sebei had begun to use money instead of livestock for land acquisitions. Nowadays, in those areas where land is scarce, all transfers are by purchase with money, though the custom of giving animals for crops still in the ground continues.

The evolution of Sasur landholdings can be seen in the history of the family of a man I will call Chemengich (Chumo I *pinta*), whose father settled there in retreat from the Gisu in the 1890s, when Chemengich was a small boy. The father acquired two pieces of land with three goats and a bullock, which Chemengich subsequently inherited. These were fairly extensive tracts, not single *shambas*. Chemengich now claims thirteen *shambas,* only four of which are in Sasur. His three married sons claimed a total of twenty-six *shambas* of which fifteen were inherited from Chemengich, eight purchased, and three rented. In order for Chemengich to give so much property to his sons, he had to purchase extra land. He did so before each son married; the first piece when his oldest son was a boy (1920s) for three female goats, the next when his third son was a boy (1940s), paying 400 shillings for a piece largely in bush, and the last when his fourth son was circumcized. His second son is cultivating land that Chemengich had inherited, on which there are still plantains Chemengich's father had planted. When Chemengich's sons' sons are ready to marry, it will be far more difficult to supply them with adequate land.

This application of rights in cattle ownership to rights in land involves more than merely ownership, sale, and purchase. It involves the notion that land, like cattle, is owned by individual adult men, not women. It involves the expectation that rights to some of the land will be transferred to sons when they marry, just as cattle are transferred. It involves also the man's allocation of land to his wife for use, and to each of several wives in cases of polygyny. In short, what our older literature called a "culture complex," a set of interdigitated elements of standardized behavior, was transferred as a unit to a new set of circumstances.

This transfer of property concepts from cattle to land creates certain disharmonies, for land is by nature a very different kind of property. First, while cattle herding is the responsibility of men, farming is women's work and, though the men own the land, the *shambas* belong to the women in a practical, everyday sense. This means that, while ownership is transferred from father to son, the actualities of the transfer are from a woman to her daughter-in-law. If the family has a limited amount of land, either the son must delay his marriage until he can accumulate enough money to buy land, his father must buy land, or some of the land worked by the mother must be turned over to the daughter-in-law. Getting money to buy land is not easy for the ordinary person, while the last solution can be a source of conflict, since the mother must continue her productive activities. I was told that an avoidance relationship was developing between a woman and her daughter-in-law but could not confirm this — traditionally, the older woman is supposed to act as a surrogate mother to the bride.

Second, cattle holdings expand with natural increase — surpluses may be accumulated, put out to contract, and called in as needed — but such flexibility does not exist with respect to land. Difficulties arise when land becomes scarce. Some men with adequate land are able to hold some back as *soi,* comparable to the *tokapsoi* in cattle holdings, so that when they take a second wife, they have land for her to work, but most men are not so richly endowed. This scarcity of land has two effects. It makes it difficult for a man to have more than one wife, for before he marries he must have adequate land for his new wife to cultivate. (Some men were seeking sources of income to buy additional land for this purpose.) Second, it creates tensions between co-wives and between half-brothers. Half-brothers will be concerned with the lands allocated to their respective mothers, as this will determine what plots they will acquire. This problem is exacerbated by the fact that there is no ceremonial transfer and hence no public record of such secondary rights.

Finally, the need to acquire land for a wife does not replace the need to acquire cattle for brideprice. This puts the young man who wants to marry — or his father — in double difficulty; he must raise both the brideprice and the land in order to establish an independent household.

These dysfunctional characteristics of the system could be overlooked when the syncretization was taking place and land was still relatively abundant, when a man could keep land he claimed as a private right as *soi* and thus provide for a second wife or a marrying son. Only the increased involvement with the cash economy makes it possible for the system to continue to operate: money to buy land can be obtained through employment or the sale of coffee. (I was told in 1972 that there is a growing dichotomy between a landed and landless class of Sebei.)

Despite these disconformities, land rights are held by the man throughout most of Sebei District and land passes patrilineally to his sons. Rights are allocated to a man's wives, just as with cattle, and, likewise, the land allocated to a particular wife will be taken by her sons and not by the sons of her husband's other wives. Some land is given to the son when he marries, and some parents treat the youngest son as residual heir to the land, again as with cattle. When a man dies, the land he owns will belong to his sons and, if the widow is inherited, her new husband merely holds this land in trust, restoring it to the natural sons of the deceased when they have been circumcised. One Sasur man did not invest in planting coffee on the land he obtained from a deceased brother, because that man's sons, though living in Bukwa, might want to take the land back. He paid nothing for its use but recognized a moral obligation to furnish the real owners food, should they request it.

The next logical step in the evolution of land rights would be for women to own the land and pass it to their children, but the strong patri-orientation of the Sebei stands in the way of such development. A few women are beginning to acquire landholdings. In 1962, two sisters purchased land in Sipi, against considerable resistance from their father and uncircumcized brother and, in 1972, we learned of several additional instances. The circumstances and the resistances to such action indicate that the development will be slow in coming.

CULTIVATION PRACTICES

Farming is seen as women's work. Women do virtually all the soil preparation and sowing of seeds and generally do the weeding and the harvesting; when men do such work they think of themselves as helping the women. Men always clear the land and always do the plowing where the plow is used; they frequently help in weeding and in harvesting. Men also set out plantains and coffee trees and are in charge of coffee production. Though the land is owned by the men, each *shamba* "belongs" to a woman who is responsible for the production of the crops from that land. She may take some of the produce to market to sell and generally keeps the money, unless it is a substantial amount. The cash crops of coffee and maize are always marketed by men.

Each woman normally has a *kapterok,* a kitchen garden in which she may grow a variety of vegetables and sometimes tobacco. This is to the north of the doorway. The house and courtyard are swept out toward this garden, and the dunging of the floor of the house and outdoor drying space provide manure. The Sebei are fully aware of the value of such manuring, though they rarely apply it to their broader fields. The courtyard will also normally include a few chickens of variegated plumage, eating whatever scraps they may find. Chickens are particularly useful in providing meals for an honored guest, such as in-law, a visiting chief (or perhaps an ethnographer); they may be given alive as presents rather than prepared for a meal, if circumstances warrant. Women formerly did not eat chickens and eggs, but most of them now do, although some eat chicken but retain the tabu on eggs.

Plantains are a highly productive crop. The shoots may be put out over a period of 6 months (April to September); the plantains will start bearing after 2 years, and a well-tended *shamba* will produce for as long as 50 years. Each plantain shoot produces one stem of plantains; if the suckers are cut back, the stem will grow larger. The Sebei do not cut the suckers back severely; they prefer more, smaller stems, so as to spread the harvest over a longer season. Plantains are harvested by cutting down the entire stalk. The leaves and stems (aside from many other uses) serve as a mulch, which helps to hold the moisture in the soil and recycles nutrients. In addition the leaves may serve as fodder for goats. They are also used in cooking. The *sufuria* (aluminum pot) is lined with them, and the tops are folded over the peeled bananas so as to seal in the moisture during steaming. Aside from mulching, cutting off leaves, cutting weeds, and occasional ridging to hold back run-off water, there is little work in maintaining a plantain *shamba* or in harvesting. Plantains may be harvested virtually throughout the year, with a peak after the rains begin (April and May) and the lowest yield during the dry months of January and February. Proper pruning makes it possible to have some plantains at this time. Though bananas are sometimes dried, this is not very successful, and long-term storage is not possible.

An acre of plantains produces four to five tons of fruit, but half of this is lost in peel and stem, and the remainder is largely moisture. The carbohydrate production is about 800 pounds per acre. Plantains are low in protein, yielding only 1.4 percent of the peeled fruit.

Plantains as a crop have two characteristics that have profound effects on the social ecology of the cultivators: (1) they give a high yield per acre; and (2) they are, by human life-expectancy standards, a permanent crop. The carbohydrate yield is only about a third greater than that of millet or maize, but because the land does not require fallowing, the yield per land unit (as distinct from cultivated acreage) is twice or more that of millet or maize — depending upon the fallow requisite for grain crops. Thus, plantains allow for high population density. The fact that the land is in permanent use means that the population is permanent and settled, not subject to repeated movement and reshuffling, as under shifting cultivation. The social implication of a third aspect of plantain cultivation are not so self-evident; namely, the low labor demand. The only difficult tasks are clearing the land in the first place and keeping out the weeds until the plants provide the moist shade that limits weed growth. Once this investment has been made, only a few hours a week are required to provide the carbohydrate needs for the family. The social effects of whatever leisure time results are hard to determine because in most of the plantain area of Sebei the women cultivate other, more labor-demanding annual crops. Alternate sources of food are important, because plantains are low in nutritional value and require supplemental dietary elements. The cultivation of annual crops necessitates the difficult tasks of preparing the soil, usually two weedings, and harvesting.

Hand tasks are regularly undertaken in a work party, *moyket,* which will be described in the following section. It is thus possible for each woman to cultivate her whole field at one time, helping others in turn when they are ready for their *moyket.* Plowing requires two men, one to handle the plow, the other the oxen. Not only must the land be level enough to enable the oxen to pull the plow, but there is an additional loss of land in crops because of the necessary wide turn rows. Not all men own plows and oxen, and those who do may hire out their equipment for cash, or may allow others to use it in return for plowing their land. The latter is the rule when the work involves near kin, especially an old father (for whom the work would be very difficult) and his sons. The capital value of a plow was given to me in 1962 as 1,000 shillings; the value of a pair of good oxen must be about the same. The economics of this operation is indicated in the following case.

Lewendi, an old man of Sasur who owned a plow and team of oxen, agreed to prepare land in Kobil that had not previously been cultivated. He charged the owner 50 shillings for the first plowing in January, 30 shillings for the second plowing, and 10 shillings for the third. His two sons performed the work for 50 shillings, receiving 20 shillings each for the first plowing, nothing for the second, and sharing the 10 shillings for the third. Thus, 50 shillings went for labor and the remaining 40 shillings Lewendi kept as rent for his equipment.

I was told that when millet was a staple crop, it could be planted no more than two years in succession; as there were no alternate crops for rotation. On the eastern slope of Elgon, cultivation was followed by a grass take-over and a long fallow period; westward of Cheseperi, the fallow period was short because the land reverted quickly to bush and, after two or three years, it was no longer possible to tell that a *shamba* had been there. Modern Sebei have learned rotation techniques that require little or no fallowing. I was given the following data on the escarpment area:

> 6 year cycle: 2 years millet, 3 years maize and beans, 1 year fallow.
> 6 year cycle: 1 year sweet potatoes, 1 year millet, 3 years maize and beans, 1 year fallow.
> Continuous cycle: 1 year white potatoes, 1-2 years maize and beans, 1 year sweet potatoes, and back to white potatoes.

Though the Sebei recognize the effectiveness of fertilization on their *kapterok* and in the manure dropped by grazing animals, they still do little purposeful manuring. The only exception I know was a neighbor who manured his maize field and said he had grown maize successively for five years on a large plot with increasing yields. Sebei do not mulch in green manure except in the plantain *shambas*.

The Sebei never practiced irrigation. I am intrigued by this total failure to irrigate in Sebei. Surely they must have known of the practice in Marakwet and, to a layman, there seems to be both the need for such irrigation in parts of Sebei and the opportunity to do so.

The Sebei build granaries on low stilts, woven out of lianas and covered with loose conical thatched lids. Maize is stored on the cob (seed maize is kept inside the house), and millet is stored in the ear. Sweet potatoes and plantains are sometimes dried and stored in the granary above the grain.

Granaries vary in size and somewhat in function. I measured a group of nine belonging to Sabilla Arap Labu in Kapsirika, as shown in Table 21. Sabilla indicated that the very small one was used to store the fried beer mash, and occasionally also millet. The slightly larger one was used for storing maize cobs of small size. The next six represent pairs of *choken nyewo*, large granaries, for the contents of which he indicated the exchange rates in cattle, giving us a rough estimate of the relative value of grains and animals. The value is calculated in the same way for maize and millet, though the latter is more valuable per unit of volume. The very large granary is traditionally viewed as the famine-relief granary; it is the first to be filled and the last to be used. Sabilla indicated that he would require two heifers outright if he were to exchange it — clearly a measure of the important psychic value of this traditional Sebei anchor to the windward, as it is only half again as large as the preceding pair. Granaries are a more prominent feature of the social landscape in the mid-escarpment area and on the plains than they are in Sipi. A household may have a dozen or more granaries set out in rows in the former area; there are apt to be only one or two where plantains are the major crop.

TABLE 21
Size and Value of Granaries

Granary name	Size			Function	Value
	Height	Diameter	Capacity[a]		
Kutakut	27"	29"	10	fried beer, millet, yams	Not known
Kiterit	37"	37"	23	small maize cobs	Not known
Choket nyewo[b]	44"	53"	56	maize, millet	Must also give she-goat when exchange is for *namanya* heifer
Choket nyewo	49"	43"	41	maize, millet	
Choket nyewo	55"	60"	90	maize, millet	Exchange for *namanya* heifer
Choket nyewo	56"	64"	105	maize, millet	
Choket nyewo	52"	74"	129	maize, millet	Exchange for heifer outright
Choket nyewo	58"	68"	122	maize, millet	
Choket nyewo	57"	84"	183	family relief store	Exchange for two heifers outright

[a]In cubic feet.
[b]The various sizes are distinguished in terms of their value as indicated at right.

THE WORK PARTY

One afternoon early in my first visit, I heard a sound so nostalgic that it gave me a sense of *déja vu* until I recognized that the murmur of conversations, the high-pitched laughter, and the shrill voices of the women were precisely what one heard on coming rather late to a cocktail party. A turn in the path and I was in the midst of precisely such festivities, in conjunction with a *moyket.*

No institution is so central to modern Sebei life as the *moyket,* the work party for which the payment is beer — so everyday that one is apt to overlook it. Most Sebei host a number of these each year, and there is one somewhere in the vicinity virtually every day. It is the basic means by which the major tasks are accomplished, and it is the regular social gathering of the neighborhood, in which the interactions, both friendly and hostile, between neighbors and kinsmen take place. Its chaotic external appearance, abetted by a rather free flow of alcohol, masks an underlying structure.

Whenever a person has a task of major proportions to accomplish, he — or more accurately, she — initiates the action by preparing a supply of beer, a process of no small undertaking in itself, even when the maize has been ground at the mill. Beer may be made of honey, plantains, or maize, the latter now being the most usual. Various malting agents, including the fruit of a local tree, are known, but nowadays the most common is sprouted millet. The ground maize is mixed with water, and the mash is laid down under the eaves of the house in a pit, lined with leaves, which are folded over the mash and covered with earth (Plate II:14). There the mash ferments for about two weeks. It is then taken out and "fried" on a large metal sheet over an open fire (Plate II:15). The fried mash is put into pots with water to soften for a short while, after which the water is squeezed out and the mash is piled on a mat. (The water can be drunk by children and old people, but not by women of child-bearing age, for that would make the beer taste bad.) Sprouted millet is mixed in with the mash, the correct amount being determined by texture and appearance. The mixture is then placed in large pots, filled with water, and a bit of the millet is sprinkled on top (Plate II:16). It is kept in a warm house — preferably that of an old woman who likes to keep her home warm — where it ferments for one or two days. The beer is served in the same pots. As the level of liquid goes down, additional hot water is added two or three times.

A *moyket* may be held for planting (*lokisyo*), clearing bush (*temisyo*), weeding (*putisyo*), second weeding (*korukisyo*), harvesting (*kisisyo*), making thatched granary covers (*posowosyek*), building fences (*kerisyo*), or for various stages of house building (Plate I:22). The *moyket* appears to be more important in the mid-escarpment area, where annual crops are of greater importance, than in Sipi, where plantains rarely require a *moyket,* and fences and granaries are less important, or than on the plains or in Bukwa, where the land is prepared by the plow. But everywhere there are many occasions for *moyket* (Plates II:17-22, 26).

No formal invitation and no formal announcement is made of the time, place, or purpose of the *moyket*; it becomes a matter of general knowledge through the grapevine. Though there is no formal delimitation of who may or must work, a person is normally expected to work for those who have worked for him or her. Both the amount of work and the amount of beer expected for the work are, however, clearly understood (SL:211-14). The Sebei are very fond of beer; older people see it as a day lost when no beer is available. They will freely and vociferously complain if the beer is in inadequate supply or of inferior quality. A woman who does not complete her stint of work will be given the same treatment — not only by her hostess, but by others. Workers frequently complain that some women have not done adequate work. The implicit contract between the host-employer and the guest-worker is too trivial to be enforceable in law, but it is effectively enforced by the sanctions of the marketplace. Every person is tied into a network of such mutual obligations; each knows that he will have the opposite role another day; and each is dependent upon these mutual obliga-tions for both the personal satisfaction and the work performance that are seen to be essential to everyday life. I was told that a woman might refuse to let another work, but there are pressures against such action, unless it is for a good reason. If there is enmity toward the hostess, a woman will not normally attend a *moyket.*

If a person needs work done at a time when he cannot provide beer, he engages in a contractual obligation (*kwoloyit*) to provide meat as well as beer at some future date. Under these circumstances, there is a person (*kwoloyin-tet*) to organize the workers and see that they later get paid.

When cultivating a *shamba,* the stint of each person is measured out by a man (*kochak*) not of the host's family, who sees that the work is fairly divided and adjudicates quarrels. He has a place at the beer pot. At a Binyinyi *moyket,* the *kochak* measured off plots about twenty-two feet by forty feet on the part of the *shamba* that had been cultivated the previous year, and fifteen feet by twenty-five feet on some newly opened land, which is harder to till.

Some work may require cooperation (such as thatching or clearing bush), but much is individual work (like hoeing or bringing a load of thatching grass). In the latter case, each person comes and works his allotted amount when he pleases in the morning. Normally, a woman will come after her morning household chores are done, bringing her own hoe, and will work until she has completed her stint. Women help each other; uncircumcised girls often work for their mothers or grandmothers. After the work has been completed, the workers return to their homes, clean up, and appear for beer around 2:00 P.M. Most beer parties end before dark.

Beer is served in large pots and drunk through straws, with aluminum or woven grass filters. These tubes are taken from one or two kinds of liana that are plentiful in Sebei, and each person has one or more of these, often carried in a long, reamed out bamboo pole. They may be as short as 3 feet, but those who do not like to crowd around the pot may have them 8 or 9 feet long. The men and women gather around the pot 2 and 3 deep, with 20 to 40 around a pot (Plate II:19). There is a master of the pot, whose duty is to lead the discussion and conversation and quell any tendency to quarrel. A respected man who is a good talker should be selected. Proper decorum permits each person to speak without interruption. The leader's efforts are not always successful; many of the legal cases I recorded arose out of quarrels around the beer pot.

The hosts of the *moyket* will invite others to partake of the beer. The workers may also invite others. Sometimes, the hosts will plan to have a larger party for their friends and the women will generally retain a small pot for those who helped prepare the beer, which they drink inside the house after the others have gone home.

Chemtai obtained detailed information on 10 *moyket* and 3 *kwoloyit* held by 8 men from the Bukwa and Sipi areas. The *moykets* analyzed varied in size from 11 workers to 40, from a minimum of 40 shillings worth of beer to a maximum of 120 shillings.[4] While the value of beer available per person varied from 1 shilling to 3.82 shillings, the former was clearly substandard ("The workers were not happy because there was too little beer."), while the

---

4. The value was calculated in *debes* of beer, at 12 shillings a *debe* (A *debe* is a 5 gallon oil tin.) The data were recorded in 1972.

latter was so lavish that, when the same man later held a *kwoloyit,* no one complained although he provided no meat and very little beer. The average amount provided to the 295 workers, in these 10 *moyket* was 2.08 shillings. (The standard viewed as proper is 2 shillings' worth.) Six men indicated they had separate pots for men and women, and, when they did so, they usually provided more beer for the men than the women (2.52 shillings per man; 1.86 shillings per woman).

The 3 *kwoloyit* varied. In the one involving the same group that enjoyed the lavish *moyket,* the host provided beer worth only 2.84 shillings per person for the two days' work, and no food. He said: "This was very little beer, but because the workers had much beer before, they did not complain; they were happy." But they did not invite others to share the pot. In the two other instances, 25 persons were employed and received 120 shillings' worth of beer, together with 3 chickens in one and a goat in the other, but because the men had worked for 3 days, they were not satisfied.

These work parties were organized for a variety of tasks. Most involved weeding and other agricultural functions. Others centered around house-building operations, fencing, and building a kraal. The sample is too small to give us an accurate estimate of costs but does serve as an indicator. One man said he had 2 acres of millet weeded for 120 shillings, but another, whose beer was quite inadequate, said he had a similar size field weeded for 40 shillings. A third provided 80 shillings of beer for a single acre.[5]

When a *moyket* is held, the host will invite certain persons to partake of the beer. While many different "meats" are recognized, the host is limited in the number of invitations he may make to share the workers' pot. The standard is 3, but, in the 13 instances recorded, in 2, 4 guests were invited and in 2 others none was. Thirty invitations were made in all, which is about 10 percent of the 295 workers in the *moykets* analyzed. Of these, 16 went to kinsmen (6 to brothers or clan brothers, 4 to fathers or father surrogates, and 5 to in-laws). One man invited the man he calls *lekwet ap lekwet,* the son-in-law of his *senke* (father's sister). The other 14 were not kin (5 *tilyet,* 5 age-mates, and 4 personal friends).

The actualities of a beer party are complicated. A man may come by to beg beer and be offered a tube; he will then sit on the edge of his chair and suck until others around the pot complain. Another may come with roasted bits of liver or other meat to sell, or some cigarettes, and may be similarly treated. The host may have some beer he holds back, so as to invite his friends and kinsmen in for a party that night (as did several in the cases recorded by Chemtai), he may have a pot for sale (thus discouraging beggars), or he may have a pot for friends separate from those available to the workers.

My neighbor Lasto held a *moyket* employing 8 men and 8 women for cultivation, and 4 men for pruning coffee. Around the workers' pot were 6 others. They were not identified as having "meats," but as follows: (1) a man who helped pour the beer; (2) Chemongoi, who was circumcised right next to Lasto and, because he has Lasto's blood on his body, "he cannot pay for

---

5. These are not cash outlays, for much of the cost is in labor, *i.e.,* making the beer and providing the products of the field. I did not make a cost analysis of beer production.

beer in my house"; (3) a man of Lasto's age-set invited for no special reason; (4) the man who furnished the special plantain leaves used to line the hole in which the mash is buried while it ferments; (5) an elderly neighbor and classificatory mother's brother invited because "our wives are of his clan"; and (6) a man who, seeing it was about to rain, built a shelter of poles and banana fronds to protect the drinkers. The last man was invited by the workers; the others were Lasto's guests.

Inside the house was a noisier pot — perhaps because these guests had not worked and were not so tired. Lasto identified them for me: his brother ("the one who will bury me"); a man with the same name as another brother ("his *oynatet* is the same as my brother's, and he would have had the brother's share if he had come first"); Lasto's father-in-law; the wife of his father's brother (who is like a mother and therefore has the mother's share), and his wife's mother's sister's son and daughter-in-law (with whom Lasto and his wife have a long-standing reciprocal beer-sharing relationship). Those who were not kin included two age-mates and a special friend and their respective wives, an old woman of the neighborhood, a Pokot woman "out of kindness," a *tilyet*, a neighbor, and the quasi-brother already noted. My cook had bought the right to participate; another man was sent away because he was "merely begging."

These rituals of everyday life are the vital center of Sebei social interaction, where cattle exchanges and diseases are discussed on the plains and coffee prices and yields in Sipi, where the gossip of social interaction takes place, trysts are arranged, and disagreements aired. No little part of the discussion involves the quantity and quality of beer, the pleasures of a fat ceremony, or the disgruntlement with a niggardly host. Men may refuse to sit with others because of some past insult, and, as the alcohol takes effect, new animosities may arise. Not to participate in *moykets* is not to be Sebei.

RITUAL ASPECTS OF AGRICULTURE

Agricultural production enters into Sebei ritual life in two ways: by rituals concerned with agriculture and by symbolic use of farm products in nonagricultural rites. Farm-associated religious performances include a *korosek* ceremony held each year by each *pororyet* when the new crops are still in the field, a ritual for opening up new *shambas*, which appears to be derived from the *korosek* ceremony, a domestic harvest ritual variously called *misisi* and *mukutanik*, and a ritualized cooking of each new product as it appears seasonally. In addition, there is a rite to increase the fertility of plantains, manifestly a recent introduction by the Bumachek. Farm products enter symbolically into other rituals, most notably the regular use of beer as a libation, but also initiates' ritual bite of bread (actually thick porridge) after their circumcision, and the use of millet pellets in rites designed to placate the spirits (though this may be a Gisu custom). When women have emerged from their period of seclusion after circumcision, they are symbolically reintroduced to their agricultural tasks. In ritual life, aside from the use of beer, which may have more symbolic associations with alcohol and its effects than with agriculture, there is less symbolic use of cultigens than of products associated with livestock or even uncultivated plants.

The most important rite dealing with agriculture, the harvest *korosek*, involves putting branches or leaves of every cultigen (as well as other things) in a ritual fire (Chapter 3). Though it has many attributes of a harvest rite, its express purpose is to ward off evil. Though *korosek* in that form has not been performed for many decades, one informant described a rite he called *korosek*. He had been involved with the rite on the plains of Ngenge on three separate occasions. The ceremony differed from the traditional *korosek* in that it was not Sebei-wide in occurrence, but local, in that it involved the *saŋta* but not the *pororyet*, and in that it was not directed by the prophet. My informant first saw it performed in 1944, when his father furnished the animal and they lived in the village of Mokutu. He was involved again in 1949, when his family moved to Kapsirika, and again in 1971, after they had been driven out of Kapsirika and settled in Kabumboi. The fact that this renewal of the ritual took place after each successive move to new territory suggests that the old ritual form, which had been an annual affair and was thus associated with the harvest rather than the land, had become associated with the taking up of new lands in a new area. If this is the case, then perhaps the ceremony described to me for the opening of a new plantain *shamba* represents a similar adaptation. Some time after the plantain shoots have been set out but before any crop has been harvested, the owner should slaughter a ram and build a fire in the garden. A bit of the chyme from the ram is thrown at each shoot, and the word *anyiñ* (sweet) is repeated. The people present bring the *korosek* plants to throw on the fire. Some of the plantain are then cooked, and this and the ram (roasted on the fire) are eaten or taken home by the guests.

With millet, nompuk, and plantains, a ritual to placate the *oyik* is performed as a kind of first-fruit ceremony each year. Each wife, as she cooks the first of the crop to be harvested, will give her husband some of the food first to scatter to the good spirits with his right hand inside the house, and then with his left will scatter some away from the house for the bad spirits. The first nompuk should be boiled with ram's tail fat and chyme (presumably from the *korosek* fire). I was told that such ceremonies were not used for maize — "That is too recent."

A ritual called *misisi* takes place annually after millet has been harvested. On the escarpment, the ceremony occurs in the month called Twamo (about October) but it is earlier on the plains, where millet ripens sooner. Millet is spread on the ground to dry, and the stalks are later picked up and placed in granaries. The word *misisi* refers to the grain that falls off the ears and remains on the ground because it is too small to be gathered and stored. By extension, it refers also to the cobs of maize that are too small to be worth storing. The *misisi* beer was made of this grain, though, if insufficient, it could be supplemented from the granary.

The essence of the *misisi* ritual is a small feast to which specific close relatives are invited, its purpose being, according to one informant, to strengthen the friendship among those who share the feast. This purpose takes on special meaning when we examine the guest list proper to *misisi*: an age-set mate, a *tilyet,* sister's daughter's husband and his brothers, and, for each wife, her father, brothers, mother's brother, and their wives, and her daughter's husband. These kin may all be characterized as persons with whom there is a sense of mutual obligation and respect, but also a certain degree of tension. Thus, both the uncle to whom the man has given the *kamama* payment in brideprice and the nephew from whom he receives such payment are included, as well as the son-in-law and father-in-law from or to whom the basic brideprice payments are made. From the woman's standpoint, the son-in-law is a relationship of deep respect. Little wonder then that the songs they sing around the beer pot are all circumspect, not those sung during initiations.

The *misisi* feast includes, in addition to beer, maize meal steamed plantains (*matoke*) and some meat, a bullock, if the host is rich, or a ram or chickens. There is no anointing with chyme. The ritual aspects are limited to libations of beer for the good and bad spirits; the libation should be poured by the host's father but may be poured by any elder who, after offering it to the *oyik,* drinks from the libation gourd (*mwendet*) and hands it to a friend, who then becomes the other man's guest. "By brewing this beer, we say that there has been darkness and now light is coming with the new crops." The libation is accompanied by such words as, "Please accept this beer; I am still alive and let us enjoy it together." The good spirits are offered beer inside the house or kraal and are mentioned by name; they include the host's fathers, brothers, mothers, mothers' brothers, grandparents, fathers-in-law, brothers-in-law, and all the deceased members of the host's clan whose names are known and who have living descendants. A failure to mention an ancestor might annoy the spirit. Libations are poured for the evil spirits away from the house or kraal, using the left instead of the right hand. Evil spirits may also be mentioned by name and will include those relatives who have died without progeny and are therefore jealous, or those who cursed a kinsman when he was alive. They are thus placated but kept at a distance.

This ritual, somewhat changed in character, is now called *mukutanik* and takes place at Christmas. The change from *misisi* to *mukutanik* reflects a deemphasis upon the harvest, as such, and upon millet as a crop. The word *mukutanik* is built on the root word for a share or portion (*mukut*). A group of families establishes a pattern, and, on successive Christmases, each in turn serves as host, making the beer and providing the food. Each participant provides his share of grain for beer and food and may furnish shares for other guests. The hosts may invite two guests as compensation for their labor in making the beer. There is a lessened sense of obligation to particular kindred in this system, though many of those collaborating are related, just as was the case in the older *misisi,* and libations for the ancestors are not omitted. *Mukutanik* brings together neighbors rather than kindred.

The group of people around a *mukutanik* beer pot behaves differently from the participants around other beer pots, in that they tend to be quiet and subdued, singing songs in small groups but without the quarreling and boisterousness of a work party or other ceremonial pot. Christmas, incidentally, is a time when wives expect new clothes, and children, too, are given clothing. There is no other regular ceremonial associated with Christmas. The result is that adults have a quiet good time, but the children stand along the road, and at such other places where they congregate, with nothing to do.

The plantain area of western Sebei has acquired a ritual, referred to by Sebei as *kapturin,* to insure the fertility of plantains, brought to them by the Bumachek and performed by a member of this group. The ritualist, also called Kapturin, is a member of the Kamorok lineage of Kamnongore clan, the only lineage that may perform the ceremony. Kapturin claims that it was performed by his great grandfather, by his father, by his elder brother, who performed it twice, and by himself. The ritual takes place over several months, starting in December during the dry season. It is the only ritual that starts in the west and moves eastward. It formerly was performed every three years but has not been performed in decades — Kapturin was not clear just when it was last undertaken, but I think around 1940.

The ritual is initiated by a request from members of Kaminwa, Kamnaṭyemi, Kapsirikwa, Kamnatui, and Kamnongore clans — all Bumachek. They make the request by descending in a group — men, women, and children — upon the ritualist's house, attacking him with spears and knives while he is asleep, and bringing the iron rings worn on necklaces (*mukuranek*), which were formerly a part of his compensation. They press the Kapturin against the floor and announce that he has been "arrested" to those outside, who then begin to beat drums and shout. He then surrenders to their demand, and they dance through the night.

The plants necessary for the ritual are collected the next day. They are pounded in a mortar and mixed with water, and this infusion is placed in a leather bag of the type used for collecting honey and left to ferment for two days. Twenty-five native plants are used in the ritual. When asked what the basis of their selection was, the Kapturin said that some of these plants bear very much fruit and some very little, so if we mix them together in one container, the weaker plants will gain strength from those that bear too much. Eleven of these plants are said to bear fruit (only five of which are eaten by the Sebei), and four are said to bear no fruit at all. Eight plants are ingredients in various medications, one is used in *mumek* (oaths), and some have practical uses (as brooms, hoe and axe handles, arrow shafts, spoons, charcoal, salt, and the like). These uses were not, however, specified as reasons for their inclusion.

On the third day, the Kapturin, wearing bells on his legs and accompanied by a drummer and many others, begins to go through the plantain *shambas,* starting with those of the five clans who requested his services. Using a whisk made of a small plantain shoot whose roots have been crushed, he sprinkles a bit of the medicine on each stem. Water may be added to the infusion as needed. The group accompanying him sings special songs. There is a particular order of progression, starting with the Kapturin's clan's lands,[6] that will

---

6. The order is Kaminwa, Kamnatui, and Kapsirikwa; Kamoko, Budadarema (mostly Gisu), Kaptui and Kapkwedja; Kamnarongo, Kobil, and Kapchai; Kapkwirwok; Kapchuinai; Kapkaben and Tangwei; Sasur; Kapsombata; Chema and Tegeres, and Kamin. The ritual is not carried beyond this point.

take as long as three months. Each day, as he completes his work, he selects good stems of plantain and this, with an animal slaughtered by an owner of the land for whom he has performed the ritual, provides a meal for himself and his entourage. Chyme is not used in this ritual. In early times, the ritualist was paid in iron rings, but more recently he has been paid in shillings (5 per clan).

In the fourth month, when the ceremony is completed, the Kapturin and his entourage go to a cave called Wuyi near the confluence of the Chebonet and Sipi rivers, which may be entered only by members of Kamnongore clan. It is inhabited by snakes of diverse kinds, and these crawl over him and lick his body. After spending most of the day there, he goes to the Siroko River and washes out the leather bag, which concludes the ceremony.

This ritual is totally different in every particular (except the extensive symbolic use of particular species of plants) from other Sebei rituals — an indication of its alien cultural source. Some major points of difference are: its association with a particular clan, the specialized status of the ritualist, the manner of initiation of the ceremonial act, the purposes for which it is performed, the direction and order of precedence, the failure to extend it Sebei-wide, the complete absence of any ritual involvement of livestock, the use of the leather bag, the absence of a libation of beer, and the ceremonial use of caves and snakes.

Sebei have but slight ritual involvement with agriculture, hardly in keeping with the present-day economic importance of farm products or the personal involvement with the farming enterprise. There is no garden magic, there are no garden shrines, no special spirits inhabit the land, and land is not sacred to the ancestors or hallowed by the burial of the dead. The obvious borrowing of the *kapturin* agricultural rite fills a kind of ceremonial vacuum in Sipi life that has resulted from the transition to plantain cultivation, but its close clan control (and perhaps also its alien symbol system) has prevented it from becoming truly Sebei, and perhaps that accounts for its decline in recent decades. While agricultural products appear occasionally in rituals, farming as a process appears symbolically only briefly in the closing rites of women's initiation. Otherwise, land and farming have no symbolic expression in circumcision, marriage or death rites, nor in the rituals of the *pororyet*.

LAND USE PATTERNS IN SASUR

Details of land use and landholdings in Sasur were obtained by schedules, usually taken from women. Data recorded included the number of *shambas* each woman cultivated by the type of crop planted, how the land was acquired, and other ancillary information. It was not possible to measure farms, so our data must be based on that inexact unit, the *shamba*. We must therefore face the concept of *shamba,* the Swahili word that refers to any cultivated garden or field. In Sasur, the *shamba* is simply a unit of cultivation, marked off by metes and bounds, or perhaps only retained in memory. The size of the unit depends upon many things, such as aspects of the terrain, the availability of land to the individual, the type of crop being cultivated, probably the size of the work party that brought it under cultivation, and perhaps other factors. On land cultivated to annual crops, the size of a *shamba* may change from one year to the next. Nevertheless, because the Sebei measure their holdings in terms of *shambas,* unfortunately we must also. We cannot use the Uganda Government sample of *shamba* size, for no Sebei fields were measured and one cannot extrapolate from one culture or one type of terrain to another. I have therefore based *shamba* size on measurements Porter made in Sasur. The *shambas* he measured were not a random sample (they were measured for other purposes), but they are the best basis for estimation we have. The results of his measurements are indicated in Table 22. We will use these averages and will assume millet (for which we have no measurements) to be the same as maize. The map of the farm of Sayekwa shows a characteristic layout for a successful Sasur farm operation.

The data in this section and the section on farming in Kapsirika derive from the questionnaire on agriculture taken concurrently with the demographic questionnaire. In this we obtained information on the number of fields each cultivator held, the crops grown on each, the means by which the field was originally acquired, and some details on cultivation practices. We obtained data on the *shambas* of 51 women.[7]

In order to get an estimate of land in crops in Sasur, we must extrapolate from this sample to the total population in the community. There are 77 households in Sasur (Table 3). There are 70 wives currently living in the 60 households sampled in the demographic questionnaire (Table 9) and an additional 10 widows or unmarried men engaged in cultivation. Therefore, we find 80 cultivators for 60 households, or 4 cultivators for each 3 households. Correcting 77 households by this factor, we estimate Sasur has 103 cultivators.

Not all cultivate the same amount of land. Table 23 shows the distribution of the number of *shambas* cultivated by the Sebei women of our sample, an average of just under 7 per woman and a cluster near the mode of 6, exclusive of land still in bush or fallow. The women with more land tend to be wives of older men. The average age of those men whose wives cultivate 10 or more *shambas* is 47 years, while the average age of the men whose wives cultivate only 3 or 4 *shambas* is but 30 years. Two factors are at work in making more land available to older men. Most of them inherited their land, and a generation ago such inheritances tended to be larger parcels than are generally available now. Some of these older men, however, had acquired land through purchase. One of the larger landholders, a uniquely avid cultivator, had purchased 12 units. At the other end of the scale, the 4 cultivators with the least amount of land included 1 of the 2 unmarried male cultivators, 2 second wives (one a recent bride and the other an inherited wife) and a woman married only a few years earlier. These data show the dynamic effects of population increase in this part of Sebei. The tendency for older men to inherit land, the effect of efforts by some astute men to

---

7. Actually, two men who did their own farming were included. One had lost his wife, and the other was a bachelor.

TABLE 22
Shamba Measurements in Sasur

Land use	Shambas measured	Measurements (acres)		
		Largest	Smallest	Mean
Plantains	20	2.36	0.04	0.48
Coffee[a]	15	0.62	0.03	0.17
Coffee and plantains[b]	35	1.27	0.02	0.34
Maize[c]	25	0.85	0.01	0.26
Kapterok	4	0.04	0.01	0.02

SOURCE: Measurements made in Sasur by Porter in 1962.

[a]Includes five fields that had beans or sweet potatoes intermixed.

[b]Includes seven fields that also had taro, beans, sweet potatoes, castor beans, or onions.

[c]Includes ten fields that were interplanted with beans.

build up their holdings through purchase of land, and the lessened availability of inherited land in recent years, all make it difficult for young men to acquire adequate landholdings, and exceedingly difficult to engage in polygynous marriage.

Table 24 lists the number of *shambas* by type. For this analysis, we have double-counted the 30 units that were double-planted to plantains and coffee. Almost every cultivator has land devoted to plantains, coffee, and maize; about half the cultivators have millet and yams; and most have a kitchen garden (*kapterok*). There is very little land devoted to other products, though the *kapterok* produces a wide variety of vegetables, and other commodities are interplanted in the fields but were not regularly noted in our questionnaires, and therefore have not been included in this analysis. A typical woman has units devoted to plantains, coffee, maize and either millet or yams, and a kitchen garden. There are obvious advantages to diversification in terms of diet, sharing of work, cash needs, and work load.

Our sample of 51 respondents accounts for a total of 88.3 acres of cultivated land. If we assume that the average amount cultivated by these persons applies to the 103 cultivators in Sasur, then the total land under cultivation there would be 178 acres. Porter estimates that 75 percent of the 256 acres within the Sasur boundary, measured by planimeter, or 190 acres, is under cultivation. These two estimates are reasonably close, but we must recognize that they do not represent quite the same universe, for the people of Sasur do not limit themselves to cultivating within the land area of the village, while outsiders cultivate within Sasur. Sasur residents probably cultivate more land outside Sasur than those outsiders cultivate in Sasur, for the Sasurese utilize some of the lightly populated lower escarpment area of Kobil. Porter (personal communication) believes that the difference between our two estimates results from respondents underreporting *shambas*, because he found such underreporting in the area he mapped in detail.

On the basis of my data, the average cultivator has 1.73 acres of land in cultivation; using the total acreage of Sasur as measured by Porter, the

TABLE 23

Distribution of *Shambas* by Number Held: Sasur

No. *shambas* cultivated	Cultivators reporting		*Shambas* reported	
	No.	Pct	No.	Pct
2	1	2.0	2	0.6
3	3	5.9	9	2.6
4	7	13.7	28	8.0
5	6	11.8	30	8.5
6	10	19.6	60	17.1
7	3	5.9	21	6.0
8	6	11.8	48	13.7
9	7	13.7	63	17.9
10	4	7.8	40	11.4
11	2	3.9	22	6.3
13	1	2.0	13	3.7
15	1	2.0	15	4.3
Total	51	100.1[a]	351	100.1[a]

SOURCE: Data for Tables 23-27 and 29 are based on farming questionnaire taken in 1961-62.

[a]Totals do not equal 100 percent because of rounding.

TABLE 24

Number of *Shambas* per Cultivator by Crop: Sasur

	Distribution by number reported											
	0		1		2		3		4-6		Total[c]	
Crop[a]	Cult[b]	Units	Cult	Units	Cult	Units	Cult	Units	Cult	Units	Cult[b]	Units
Plantains	1	0	21	21	22	44	5	15	2	9	50	89
Coffee	2	0	24	24	18	36	6	18	1	6	49	84
Maize	2	0	26	26	15	30	7	21	1	4	49	81
Millet	28	0	18	18	2	4	3	9	0	0	23	31
Yams	21	0	25	25	5	10	0	0	0	0	30	35
Kapterok	8	0	30	30	12	24	1	3	0	0	43	57
Other	47		22	2	2	4	0	0	0	0	4	6

[a]The 30 *shambas* double-cropped to plantain and coffee have been included in both columns.

[b]*Cult* means individual cultivators.

[c]Persons engaged in cultivating type of *shamba*.

average would be 1.84. Comparable figures calculated on a per household basis would, by my calculations, be 2.31 acres and by Porter's, 2.47 acres. Eight percent of this land is double-cropped to plantains and coffee. Other double-cropping (especially beans) was not recorded.

The proportion of land devoted to various major crops (Table 25) is as follows: plantains (either alone or in combination with coffee), 43 percent; maize, 24 percent; and coffee (either alone or with plantains), 22 percent.

While neither yams nor millet involves much land, each yields an important increment to the diet.

Table 26 shows the location of lands cultivated, treating Sasur and Kamingong separately, to give a measure of the localized village as an operating entity. From the standpoint of landholdings and land use, community lines are unimportant, as a third of such lands lie outside the village of residence. The fact that both *kapterok* and coffee are rarely away from home reflects a concern with theft. Cultivation in other villages sometimes represents an effort to use an alternate environment. Sasur people frequently plant millet and maize in Kobil where they can cultivate by plow. They also plant millet at the very upper edge of the inhabited escarpment (below the forest line). Thus, the use of different environmental zones increases the likelihood of a successful crop. Not all outside cultivation is motivated by such ecological considerations. In some cases, an individual has merely acquired land elsewhere.

LAND TRANSFERS IN SASUR

In the latter half of the nineteenth century, when Sasur was sparsely populated, the first two or three clans that pushed into the area from the west simply appropriated land, in at least one case driving off existing people, and settled in clan units. As others came in, the new residents were not powerful enough to drive away the first expropriators, and so they bought land. From Maina times until the 1920s, land was acquired in exchange for livestock; a larger amount for a heifer or a bull, smaller amounts for goats. Although the size of the land units is not known, apparently they were bush land rather than cultivated *shambas*. In one instance, land was transferred (or taken) in compensation for a murder. One old man told me he had traded goats for pieces of land on two occasions, the first between 1910 and 1915, the second in 1927. In each instance, five *warek* were paid.

The transition to cash purchase and sale was not sudden. As late as the 1940s, men simply allowed others the indefinite use of the land. One man said of a piece of his land: "I just asked Maunya [his father's friend and neighbor, but a man of a different clan] for it, and he gave it to me and I planted coffee on it. When I got back from the Army in 1946, he asked for pay and I gave him 53 shillings."

Land prices have obviously gone up and continue to do so. We were told of one plot of nearly an acre near Sasur, which the owner had bought in 1930 for 200 shillings but valued at 500 shillings in 1954. Another man had purchased a piece of land upon his return from World War II for 200 shillings and sold it in 1959 for 500 shillings.[8]

---

8. The current cash value seems low at the 750 shillings per acre we found on measured plots of land. Sebei earned approximately 20,000 shillings in 1961-62 on about 20 acres of coffee land. (See also the discussion of coffee economics, Chapter 7.)

TABLE 25

Proportion of Land Devoted to Major Crops: Sasur

	No. of *shambas*			Estimated acreage	
Type of use	No.	Pct	Factor[a]	No.	Pct
Plantains	59	16.8	.48	28.32	32.1
Coffee	54	15.4	.17	9.18	10.4
Plantains and coffee	30	8.5	.34	10.20	11.6
Maize	81	23.1	.26	21.06	23.9
Millet	31	8.8	.26	8.06	9.1
Yams	35	10.0	.26	9.10	10.3
Kapterok	57	16.2	.02	1.14	1.3
Others	4	1.1	.31[b]	1.24	1.4
Total	351	99.9[c]		88.30	100.1[c]

[a]For explanation, see text and Table 22.

[b]Average of all fields.

[c]Total does not equal 100 percent because of rounding.

TABLE 26

Location of Agricultural Activities: Sasur

Type of crop	Total units	Units in village	Units out of village	Pct units outside
Plantains	59	36	23	41.1
Coffee	54	42	12	22.2
Plantains and coffee	30	23	7	23.3
Maize	81	49	32	39.5
Millet	31	1	30	96.8
Yams	35	20	15	42.9
Kapterok	57	53	4	7.0
Others	4	1	3	75.0
Total	351	225	126	35.9

Present landholders in Sebei have acquired their acreage through both inheritance and purchase. The relative importance of inheritance (70 percent) is shown in Table 27. Nobody currently operating land asserted that he had merely appropriated it, or "opened" it, as the Sebei say. One man did claim that he opened bush land in Kobil, but he said that this land had belonged to his father. There are few important differences with respect to the source of land by type of crop grown, though the permanent crops are more frequently on family estates than is maize.

Another form of land exchange is a kind of rental or "borrowing." Table 27 includes a column showing the frequency with which *shambas*

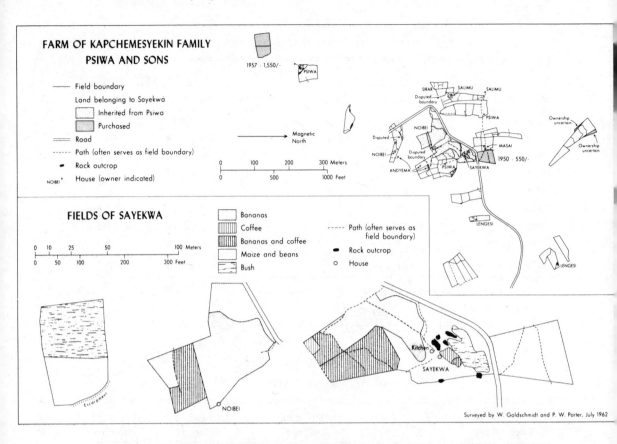

FARM OF KAPCHEMESYEKIN FAMILY
PSIWA AND SONS

1957 · 1,550/-

—— Field boundary
Land belonging to Sayekwa
☐ Inherited from Psiwa
▨ Purchased
══ Road
---- Path (often serves as field boundary)
• Rock outcrop
NOIBEI• House (owner indicated)

Magnetic
North

0   100   200   300 Meters
0   500   1000 Feet

FIELDS OF SAYEKWA

0 10 25   50   100 Meters
0   50   100   200   300 Feet

☐ Bananas
▥ Coffee
▦ Bananas and coffee
☐ Maize and beans
▨ Bush

---- Path (often serves as
      field boundary)
• Rock outcrop
o House

NOIBEI

Surveyed by W. Goldschmidt and P. W. Porter, July 1962

belonging to other people are being used under some kind of agreement, presumably *namanya* exchanges. Sebei do not exchange one type of food (i.e., staple starches such as plantains, maize, and the like) for another except in very small amounts for immediate emergency use, but they do exchange animals for such foods. Maize and millet enter into such exchanges after the harvest, while root crops are exchanged while still in the ground. Because root crops may be stored in the ground, the buyer tends the land for a year or more. Land may also be borrowed without any payment. This is normally done only when there is an established good relationship between the two persons. Such borrowing is not circumscribed by specific rules of kinship or residency, though one who has adequate land should loan it to a brother-in-law or son-in-law who needs it. Though there is no formal payment in such cases, the borrower should brew a pot of beer and kill a chicken for the owner from time to time, and, if he does that the loan may be extended, but the owner is free to terminate the arrangement at any time. The brewing of beer not only compensates the owner but reassures him that the true ownership is recognized.

A detailed examination of land transfers in an extended Sasur family provides further insight into land operations. Psiwa Kapchemesyekin was very likely the richest citizen in Sasur. He had two wives; the first bore him six sons who lived to adulthood; the second also bore six sons, only two of

ALBUM II
Economic Activities

1-5 Animal husbandry: (1) milking in Masop; (2) cleaning milk gourd, Masop; (3-4) bleeding a young bullock; (5) men examining a cattle herd resting in Kapsirika.

6-13 Women's work: (6) grinding maize with a hand mill; (7) drying maize and sprouted millet in Kapsirika; (8) fixing leather handle on a gourd; (9) weeding millet; (10) hauling wood; (11) the old way of grinding by hand; (12) woman of Masop weaving a basket; (13) women peeling plantains and gossiping (the girls standing at the right are preparing for circumcision and are inviting relatives to attend).

14-16 Beer making: (14) digging up the fermented mash; (15) frying the mash on a flat iron pan; (16) laying down the beer in pots.

17-21 Beer party: (17) libation at the kraal gate; (18) adding water to the beer; (19) group enjoying beer; (20) old men on way to beer party; (21) young man recently returned from military service repairing a beer straw.

22-26 Agricultural tasks: (22, 26) *moykets* for preparing fields in Binyinyi, 1954, and Sasur, 1962, respectively; (23) the thrust of the short-handled hoe requires great strength, but (24) is now often supplied by oxen; (25) harvesting millet with a small knife, Kapsirika, 1962.

27-31 The smithy: (27) Mamadi and (28) his son; (29) general view of the smithy; (30) the son works the bellows while (31) Mamadi shapes the iron.

32-37 Markets: (32) market on the lower Chebonet River, now abandoned, showing imported merchandise; (33) closing a deal at that market; (34) a large *duka* on the escarpment; (35) portion of the cattle market at Ngenge; (36, 37) scenes from the market near Sipi, the former displaying cattle entrails, the latter, vegetables.

1

3

2

4

5

6

7 8

 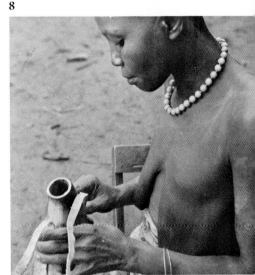

9 10

11

12

13

14

15   16

17   18

19

20   21

22

23

24

26

25

27

29

28

30

31

32

33

36

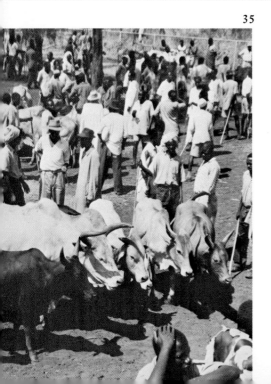

34

35

37

TABLE 27
Source of Land by Crop Use: Sasur

Type of Crop	Father		Purchased		Borrowed		Other		Total
	No.	Pct.	No.	Pct.	No.	Pct.	No.	Pct.	No.
Plantains	42	71.2	16	27.1	...	...	1	1.7	59
Coffee	41	75.9	13	24.1	...	...	...	...	54
Coffee and plantains	25	80.6	5	16.1	...	...	1	3.2	31
Maize	50	61.7	24	29.6	4	4.9	3	3.7	81
Millet	24	80.0	3	10.0	...	...	3	10.0	30
Yams	15	42.9	2	5.7	17	48.6	1	2.9	35
Kapterok	47	82.5	9	15.8	...	...	1	1.8	57
Other	2	50.0	2	50.0	...	...	...	...	4
Totals	246	70.1	74	21.0	21	6.0	10	2.8	351

whom were adults at the time of our research. He had inherited a large portion of his present holdings from his father. Our endeavor to map the large estate of Psiwa and his sons was never completed because of the owners' growing disenchantment with the project, but our attempt taught us a great deal about the manipulation of lands and the attitudes and conflicts that landownership can engender in Sasur (see Map). Table 28 sets forth the lands mapped, by type of use, for each son. From conversations with several men, we obtained reasonable estimates of the total holdings. Not all of the land mapped was in Sasur.

While making these maps, we discovered that these men had purchased 17 parcels of land between 1949 and 1962, involving 12.7 acres of 43 percent of the mapped land. They spent a total of 9,440 shillings or an average of 750 shillings per acre. The price paid varied widely, from a low of 285 shillings per acre for poor land to as much as 1235 shillings for good land. These data do not demonstrate a secular trend for the period in question, but one of the pieces purchased by this family rose in value from 200 to 500 shillings in a period of about 15 years. It is not clear what criteria, other than the desire to buy and sell on the part of the two parties, entered into the determination of price. Land on which plantains are growing does not regularly command a higher price than open land; an old growth may actually reduce the value.

Psiwa and his sons volunteered no information on whether they also sold land, except that Psiwa said he never sold land he had inherited, though he wanted to exchange some that was very high on the escarpment for land nearer home, because his wife was getting old and it was difficult for her to walk there. Psiwa was not manipulating in real estate; he was accumulating wealth for his family.

In several instances, the owner's motivation to sell land to Psiwa and his

TABLE 28

Landholdings of Psiwa and His Sons

	Plantain[a]		Coffee[a]		Maize		Bush		Total[a]		Unmapped[b]	Total
	Sh.	Acres	Sh.	Acres	Sh.	Acres	Sh.	Acres	Sh.	Acres	Acres	Acres
Psiwa	6	2.15	5	1.65	0	0	3	.49	9	2.64	2.0	4.64
Lazima[c]	. . .	. . .	. . .	. . .	. . .	. . .	. . .	. . .	. . .	. . .	8.0	8.00
Sayekwa	8	3.42	7	1.46	2	1.06	3	2.11	16	7.27	1.5	8.77
Salimu	6	1.70	4	1.27	3	.47	4	.53	13	2.70	0.0	2.70
Sirar	4	.56	1	.20	2	.26	1	.18	8	1.20	0.0	1.20
Noibei	5	.90	5	.44	3	.96	3	.96	13	2.96	1.0	3.96
Andyema[d]	3	.42	1	.20	1	.26	1	.20	5	.88	2.5	3.38
Masai[e]	7	1.92	5	1.31	4	1.35	6	3.41	18	6.76	2.0	8.76
Lengesi	6	3.28	3	1.69	5	.76	4	1.25	15	5.29	.5	5.79
Disputed	0	0	0	0	1	.08	0	0	1	.08	0	.08
Totals	45	14.35	31	8.22	21	5.20	25	9.13	98	29.78	17.5	47.28

[a]Twenty-four double-cropped *shambas* (7.12 acres) counted as both plantain and coffee; hence totals are not sums of crops listed.

[b]Estimates made by Porter on basis of discussions with each son.

[c]Lazima had no land in Sasur; he did not participate in our mapping.

[d]Andyema inherited Salimu's senior wife, who brought an additional 1.18 acres of Salimu's land with her.

[e]Masai inherited Salimu's junior wife, who brought an additional 1.52 acres with her.

sons was given. In three instances, the seller needed money to pay a son's brideprice (one had two sons marry the same year); two others needed money to pay indemnities resulting from a court case; and three cited various other purposes (school fees, wife's illness). In two instances, the seller was leaving the area and, in a third, the land (which he had acquired in a court compensation for the killing of his cow) was too far from his home. There were two cases where the land had been acquired from a father-in-law and another in which Psiwa had planted the land of a clansman to coffee, and his kin had agreed to sell the land to him. The motivations for purchase were not often expressed, but in one instance the buyer wanted to have land in a separate place for his second wife, as the two women were quarreling too much, and in two other instances purchases were made in anticipation of taking a second wife.

Land is not a part of brideprice bargaining anywhere in Sebei, but if a man has land and no cattle he will endeavor to sell some of his land. Psiwa said that, occasionally, if the groom's father cannot find a buyer, the bride's people will take some of the land in lieu of cattle — though he had never seen it happen but had only heard of the practice.

We observed Psiwa help his son Andyema buy a piece of land from a man who needed money to pay his taxes. The owner, Musani, had already borrowed money from Andyema, using land as security, and had now decided to sell. I came upon the preliminaries of the bargaining process by accident in searching for Musani, whom I found with his friend Seswet at the home of Psiwa. Andyema was also there. Joined by three of Psiwa's other sons (Lazima, Sirar, and Sayekwa) and by a neighbor named Ndiwa, we proceeded to the piece of land in the nearby village of Taboŋoŋ. The local chief came by — by chance, he said — and remained through the session. The land looked very good, a *shamba* sloping somewhat steeply up from a stream, with a large rock outcropping at the top.

Some plantain had been newly planted on the north border, and Musani immediately asserted that there had been encroachment onto the land, so a search was made for the senchontet plants that marked the border. Some plants were found that had just got a good start in growth, and it was said that the boundary had been moved over, all agreeing as to where the boundary had been. Down at the river was a large clump of senchontet, which had full luxuriant growth, in line with the old *shamba* planting on the lower side. As we walked back up, somebody noted a senchontet on the old border, but they had all already been convinced. Musani now marked off the old boundary by cutting the bush and putting stakes in every fifteen or twenty feet up to the top. The owner later claimed that, except for two plantains that were slightly over the line, the land was his, having been given to him by Musani's father. Bargaining proceeded on the assumption that the whole piece was involved, without reference to this potential impairment.

After marking the boundary, the land was paced off by Ndiwa, as a neutral party. It was thirty paces wide and fifty long (about .3 acres). Everybody watched carefully, and representatives of both sides noted down the data on pacing. Musani said that it should be wider, as the land extends to the top of the large rock, but Psiwa pointed out that this was not land that one could cultivate.

> *Musani:* "If somebody came and built a house on that rock, would you object?"
> *Psiwa:* "That is a part of the land that you can keep."

The men gathered at the upper boundary, Musani and his friend Seswet stood up on a rock; Psiwa sat hunched up to one side below them, while Andyema (the purchaser) stood farther below them with his brothers; Ndiwa and the chief were behind them. After some banter, including the suggestion that if there were arguments later they could write to me in America, they said there should be two sides with three men on each side. I declined an invitation to serve, so the seller asked my interpreter, Chèmtai, and Seswet. On the buyer's side were Ndiwa and the local chief, Bunyo.

Somebody said that the seller should first name his price, and Musani indicated 1,000 shillings. Ndiwa offered 300 shillings. Seswet was next asked to speak, but he deferred to Chemtai who said 600 shillings. Bunyo took time looking over the land; he finally announced 350 shillings as the right price.

> *Seswet:* I am always attending bride purchases bargaining, and they always give examples and that is why I'm going to tell you what I will say: you should realize that this will be your land for good, but that the money will be spent and finished. The people will agree with me, and I will say that the land should cost 750 shillings. I have sold many *shambas,* and I know how to bargain the prices.
>
> *Andyema:* I will give 450 shillings.
>
> *Musani:* Please pay me the 750 shillings.
>
> *Andyema:* Give me an example before charging me like that. Also, this land has banana weevils on it.
>
> *Seswet:* I sold my own land of 21 by 43 paces and got 650 shillings.
>
> *Andvema:* You got that high price because many people were buying.
>
> *Seswet:* Also another piece of land 31 by 71, and that cost 650 shillings.
>
> *Andyema:* I insist on 450 shillings.
>
> *Musani:* I insist on 600 shillings. You will keep the land forever.
>
> *Ndiwa:* If you agree, make it 500 shillings.
>
> *Musani:* No. One can buy a cow for 500 shillings and eat the meat and it is finished; yet this land is permanent.
>
> *Sirar:* Prices of cows have now dropped. Lazima bought land from Andyema for 500 shillings.
>
> *Musani:* I paid 500 shillings for a piece 9 by 21.
>
> *Seswet:* We won't ask for all the money right away; we will take pay in installments.
>
> *Andyema:* I agree to 500 shillings.

At this temporary impasse, a number of side remarks were made; Andyema spoke of the lasting friendship that the sale would create between them (apparently in analogy to the *tilyet*). One of the brothers suggested that, if Musani did not like the price, he could seek another buyer.

> *Seswet:* Lazima is ruining the conversation by telling his brother not to buy the land! He is not happy to see his brother get the land. You must realize that Musani has dropped from 1000 to 600 shillings.
>
> *Psiwa:* How many cows would you have to sell to get 1,000 shillings? It is mere bush. You should accept 500. You can buy three head of cattle for that. It's enough to buy a wife.
>
> *Musani:* I already have taken 250 from you [on a loan, using this land as security]. Are you going to give me only 250 more?
>
> *Psiwa:* I agree my son should give 500 shillings. He will have to sell something to raise the money. Don't take too much argument on this bush. If there was to be a *moyket* on the land, it would only take ten people to do the cultivation. Some of this land is covered with rocks.

The bargaining continued, with buyer and seller reluctantly inching toward one another between 550 and 600 shillings. The conversation occasionally moved away from the bargaining, to relieve tensions. It continued:

> *Musani:* O.K. at 550 shillings if cash, but not in installments.
>
> *Chemtai:* You should agree to 580; he is giving you a long time to pay.
>
> *Psiwa:* It is still a debt to be paid.
>
> *Seswet:* Bartega bought land at 100 shillings and sold it at 1000; don't you remember that?
>
> *Andyema:* Perhaps we will give you a bull to cover this amount.

Seswet: How big a bull to cover such an amount? Pay the 580 shillings. You will have no quarrel with any of your wives, for they will have land to cultivate.

Andyema: After paying you, the chiefs will arrest me for not having money for paying my poll tax.

Seswet: Psiwa knows where to get money for your poll tax.

Psiwa: No, I've already sent him away [i.e., given him his inheritance; though he had not, as everybody must have known] He has his own property.

Sirar: It is a very small piece of land.

Seswet: Do you mean to say that a man who is very small can't serve his wife right? I never heard of bargaining over a wife where they belittled the daughter as you are belittling our land here.

Musani: The money I get will be divided so many ways there will be nothing left; I'm giving 20 shillings to you. Give me the 580. My people have asked 600, and I have broken them by charging only 580. I've been too lenient.

Lazima: If our people insist on the 350 shillings that they started with, what would you say? But the buyer has been anxious to buy and has raised to 550. If it weren't for that rock, we would agree to a higher amount.

Musani: I know you, Lazima; you always want to buy at a cheaper price. If you were selling, the price would be 1,300 shillings.

Psiwa: In the old days, this would have only cost one he-goat.

Seswet: In the old days one could borrow land for 3 years without paying anything and could sell the millet for a cow and become rich.

The bargaining continued, without new arguments and slowly arrived at the price of 560 shillings. A contract was recorded, which the two principals and their representatives signed:

I, Ignatio Musani, have sold my land to Mr. Andyema, son of Psiwa Kapchemesyekin. The land is at Katoko area. The size of the land is thirty by fifty paces, and the price is 560 shillings. He has paid 304 shillings with a balance of 256 shillings.

We see in this bargaining the appeals to precedent, the analogies with wife bargaining, the use of cattle as a kind of standard of reference and value, the use of independent negotiators, and the use of delayed payment to increase price. Although there is only one buyer and one seller in this negotiation, the general market as potential competition lies in the back of the negotiators' minds. Of course, there are not many persons in the market at any one time and Musani's situation is hampered by the fact that Andyema has already loaned him money on the property. Because Musani needs money now, he would have to get a larger payment from an alternate buyer to cover the loan.

Nobody seemed very exercised over the land encroachment matter; it was seen as Musani's problem to resolve.

The practice of borrowing money with land as security is a recurrent theme; it was involved in both the sales we witnessed, was mentioned frequently in other discussions of sales, and was expressed in the moots that accompany funerals. Closely associated with this is the practice of taking options (*ketiŋye*). The custom derives from aspects of bride wealth; I was told that, "If you have a girl you love a lot, you give her parents a cow with calf to give milk for your future bride and that is included in the brideprice; that is *ketiŋye.*" The literal meaning of the word is to hold something down — as a paperweight holds down paper.

The use of written documents in contractual negotiations among the Sebei is now widespread but by no means universal. I have seen them used for bride payments (among more acculturated individuals) but not for *namanya* exchanges. They seem to be generally used for land sales. The use of witnesses is general and an essential element in contracts. There must be a witness from the seller's clan as well as a person not related to either, "to represent the *pororyet.*"

It is characteristic of all contractual agreements — whether land sale, brideprice negotiations, or *namanya* contract (at least, traditionally) — that the negotiations be carried on by representatives. The principals are normally present in these actions. Although they are supposed to allow the negotiation to take place between their representatives, they often intercede.

It is important to note that the different classes of contractual arrangements are treated essentially the same; I think the Sebei see them as a single class of events. When a man comes to arrange for a *namanya,* he uses the same formula as when he seeks a bride: I want to be a son-in-law of this house. The host must sort out what the true mission is. Similarly, land sale negotiations make reference to the proprieties of wife bargaining and the value of cattle.

CONFLICT OVER LAND

Conflict over land is a major concern in the heavily cultivated area, and encroachment (or a neighbor's accusation of encroachment) is a source of legal disputation that goes back well into Sebei history. The Sebei handling of land makes it particularly vulnerable to conflict: the loosely defined and irregular boundaries, the free lending, the distance of *shambas* from homes, land left indefinitely in bush, and a past tendency to undervalue land as an asset.

In mapping the landholdings of Psiwa, we obtained a picture of the conflicts within the family constellation and with outsiders. The first group of conflicts is the more numerous, and regarding most of them we had confirmation from both sides.

1. The first dispute expressed the hostility and jealousy between co-wives, the widows of Psiwa's son, Salimu, who had been inherited by two other sons. Psiwa had given the land in question to Salimu when the son married his first wife, and when Salimu took the second the land was divided between the wives. Now, five years after their husband's death, when the former senior wife was pregnant with twins, Yapyego, the younger wife, proceeded to uproot the senchontet and cultivate the whole plot, right in front of everyone, for this was what might be called the home field.

According to her father-in-law. Yapyego felt that she was more *poswama*, harder working and more productive, and that Salimu should have divorced his first wife. Yapyego, who had two sons, also denigrated the first wife for having only one son. Yapyego's husband Masai tried to stop her by shouting she was wrong, but she paid no attention. Ultimately, the matter was decided before Psiwa, some of the original witnesses, and the local chief and the senchontet was replaced.

2. A second dispute, about which little information was obtained, also involved these co-wives, as well as Salimu's brother, Sayekwa. It concerned a piece of inherited land that had remained in bush.

3. A major confrontation took place between Psiwa and three of his sons regarding the lands that Psiwa reallocated — or that they claim he reallocated — between his own co-wives. Psiwa claimed that the land was actually *soi*, and that he had given each of his sons their land, except for the youngest, who would inherit the remainder of his mother's land. Furthermore, he was concerned about the adequacy of land for the still junior sons of his second wife. The sons attacked Psiwa physically; he took a case against them, and each was fined 50 shillings. The sons of the second wife as well as the first wife's oldest son (who had been given more land than his brothers) did not enter into this dispute. The sons' complaint was that Psiwa was taking away land that was due to come to them.

4. Lengesi forced land (0.4 acres) from his father. He first planted coffee on it and then tried to straighten the boundary to enlarge the field, but Psiwa stopped him. However, Psiwa has now accepted the loss and recognized Lengesi's right to this larger *shamba*. Lengesi was undoubtedly motivated to act because he had not been given his share of land, and Psiwa's recognition of the justice of his son's case may have led to his ultimate acquiescence.

5. A brief reference to a small piece of land across the road from the main holdings, of which Psiwa said, "Lengesi took that from me before he was married — forget about that."

6. A boundary dispute between Sirar and Masai, involving perhaps 0.2 acres, the precise nature of which was not clear. The land had been bush and was being brought under cultivation, and it was expected that their father could clarify the matter.

7. A claim by Sirar that his two half-brothers were helping themselves to the plantains in a *shamba* he had acquired that was far from his residence, but near their homes. His solution was to sell the land at the first opportunity and to buy some closer to his house. Psiwa's family was not unique with respect to such conflict. Elsewhere, however, it was expressed by accusations of witchcraft as well as conflict over land; no charges of witchcraft surfaced in this family. It may be that antagonism was kindled because Psiwa chose, for his own reasons, not to treat his sons equitably with respect to land, as he had with respect to cattle. Probably also, Psiwa and his sons, to an extent found in no other Sasur family, were actively engaged in building up landholdings by converting income into real estate. Conflict over prop-

erty is a malady the rich suffer more than the poor. On the whole, however, Psiwa was generous with his sons, both in land and in cattle; I think he was genuinely interested in the preservation of his family line.

Not all the conflicts we uncovered in mapping Psiwa's land were intra-familial. Three pieces of disputed land in the acreage we mapped involved outsiders. One did not involve Psiwa's family directly; the man who had sold them the land would have to settle the dispute. The second was a boundary dispute between Psiwa and his neighbor, Boror, a man his own age. It concerned an area of land Boror had bought six years earlier; he claimed Psiwa had moved the senchontet plants. The dispute seemed more related to antagonisms between these two senior men of separate powerful clans than to the economic value of the land. The third boundary dispute also involved a man of Boror's clan.

We examined in detail the landholdings of another family, a Chumo I man I will call Chemengich and his several sons. When Chemengich married his first wife some time after they were circumcised in 1910, his father gave him the piece of land. He said "I am cultivating my father's plantains." He was also given land in Kobil then still in bush, and which he brought into cultivation. About 1934, he acquired the remainder of his father's property. When Chemengich married his second wife (about 1916), the two women shared the *shambas,* even after they opened the Kobil land, for Chemengich did not divide the land between his wives before his first wife died, around 1934. When Chemengich told me of the three parcels of land he purchased, he dated each of these in relation to the circumcision of his sons and gave these parcels to them as they married. Even so, those who married two wives found it necessary to purchase additional land upon their second marriage.

Examining the landholdings of Chemengich and his sons, fewer disputes emerged. Only two were made explicit. First, using a very small piece of land as security, Chemengich took 10 shillings from a man, who now claims this piece. Second, a triangular piece of land now being used by an old widow is being claimed by her son. Long ago, Chemengich brought the matter before a moot made up of the elders of the clans to which the two men belonged and of two neutral clans. Chemengich had given a cow to the deceased husband of the old widow, taking the disputed piece of land as security. "The agreement was that if he [the deceased] brewed six pots of beer for me, he could have the land, but now that he is dead, I have forgotten that." But his sons do not agree that the debt — either beer or a cow — is forgiven.

A third dispute was mentioned. One of Chemengich's sons had a legal case involving land in Kobil, but the details were not given to me.

The family of Chemengich was not free of internal conflict, and these conflicts also involved land, but I was not able to discover their precise nature. Others told me that one of Chemengich's unmarried sons by his second wife claimed some of the land that was being farmed by one of the sons of the first wife, but I do not have particulars. There were rumors of hostility between father and sons.

It was not possible to get at these disputes because the relationships were fraught with suspicion. One son's wife had borne no children, and when this happens in Sebei there is usually a suspicion of witchcraft, which was manifestly the case here. Thus, while there was no doubt that tensions existed among the men in this family, and more particularly among their wives, there is only indirect reference to their involvement with land.

The Sebei are cognizant of the potential conflict between co-wives over land and endeavor to give each equal amounts. Of the five two-wife households in Sasur, three reported that both wives had the same number of *shambas* (five, six, and nine, respectively). In the fourth household, the junior wife had been inherited, while in the fifth she was a new wife whose husband had not yet been able to acquire additional land for her. By contrast, in the two instances where the man's mother lived in the compound with her daughter-in-law, there was no such equivalence. In these households the older woman had six *shambas* and the younger ones four and five respectively.

AGRICULTURE IN KAPSIRIKA

The plains area is fertile but relatively dry. In the latter half of the nineteenth century, its capacity to sustain a horticultural economy was not so much limited by rainfall or soil conditions as by the depredation of more warlike pastoral tribes. The area between the base of the mountain and the Greek River become a kind of no-man's-land, furtively farmed in groups at the edges and periodically hunted.

The term *shamba* takes on a different meaning in Kapsirika; here it is accurately glossed as field. It refers to an area of contiguous plowed land, which may be several acres in extent. The Kapsirikans plow in fields as long as 500 to 800 yards, running in an east-west direction to minimize run-off, for the land slopes down gently to the north. The arrangement of farm land is shown in the map of the farm of Sabilla Arap Labu. Each *shamba* is

FARM OF SABILLA ARAP LABU, KAPSIRIKA, SEBEI

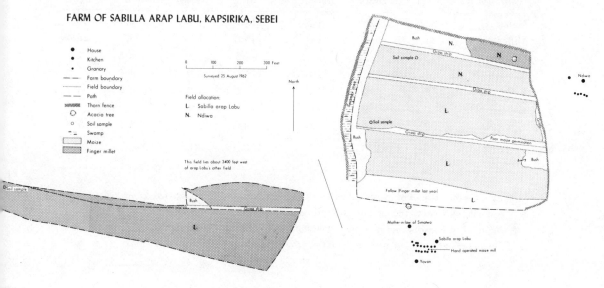

●	House
●	Kitchen
●	Granary
—·—·	Farm boundary
··········	Field boundary
— —	Path
※※※※	Thorn fence
۞	Acacia tree
○	Soil sample
⁼₋	Swamp
▢	Maize
▨	Finger millet

0   100   200   300 Feet

Surveyed 25 August 1962

Field allocation:
L.   Sabilla arap Labu
N.   Ndiwa

This field lies about 3400 feet west of arap Labu's other field divided into strips running the length of the field, which are separated by a narrow uncultivated hedgerow (Plate I:18). These units are called *baringos*. (I have no idea of the origin of this imported term or whether it has reference to the lake of that name.) Each woman has her own *baringo,* and each such unit is generally sown to a single crop.

While taking schedules in Kapsirika, I was given the dimensions of 14 units of maize and 16 of millet. The former averaged 7,900 square yards (or more accurately 7,900 square paces) and the latter 5,500. In view of the evidence elsewhere in Uganda on pacing measurements, it is reasonable to reduce these by about 20 percent, to 1.5 acres for maize and 1.0 for millet.

The information on land use in Kapsirika was supplied by the men and refers to total use per household (rather than per woman cultivator, as in Sasur) in conformity with cultivation practices. I obtained responses from 37 of the 54 household heads. The Kapsirikans do not cultivate in neighboring villages, but 2 or 3 had second residences (and other wives) on the mountain; data on these are not included. Two men had no land in cultivation in Kapsirika, 4 had but a single *baringo* most (22) had from 2 to 4 under cultivation, and the remaining 9 had from 5 to 9 *baringos.* I did not count land currently fallow.

Table 29 shows that virtually every cultivator has maize and millet, that few report anything else, and that the *kapterok* is rare. The data from Kapsirika were obtained on the basis of households rather than individual cultivators, as in Sasur. The households had an average of 4.6 acres. To make the data more nearly comparable to Sasur, we must calculate the amount of land per woman. In Kapsirika, there were 65 wives currently in the 43

TABLE 29
Land Use in Kapsirika

Land use	Persons rptg	Units[a]	Size factor[b]	Acreage		Est. total	Acreage Pct[c]
				Total	Average		
Maize	33	76	1.5	114.0	3.1	166.4	66.9
Millet	31	45	1.0	45.0	1.2	65.7	26.4
Cotton	2	3	1.5	4.5	.1	6.6	2.7
Cassava	1	1	1.0	1.0	1.0	1.5	.6
Sorghum	2	2	1.0	2.0	1.0	2.9	1.2
Kapterok[d]	2	2					
Unknown	2	4	1.0	4.0	1.0	5.8	2.3
Total	37	133		170.5	4.6	248.9	100.1[e]

[a]In *baringos* (see text).

[b]Basis for calculations of maize and millet explained in text; other crops based on analogies.

[c]Applying averages to the total of 54 Kapsirika households.

[d]*Kapterok* in Kapsirika not measured; their number and sign would not significantly alter totals.

[e]Total does not equal 100 percent because of rounding.

households of our sample (Table 9); in addition, there were 5 widows in this group of 43 households, or a total of 70 cultivators. The average amount of land is therefore 2.8 acres per cultivator. The estimated total acreage in farms in Kapsirika is about 250 acres, as against between 178 and 190 for Sasur. Hence, in terms of land used in farming, the pastoral community had a larger total area and a larger per capita acreage than the farming village. Acreage is not, however, the significant measure. while 75 percent of the Sasur land was devoted to crops, only about 3 percent of Kapsirika land was so used. Kapsirikans estimate that, in a good year, 520 pounds of maize or 430 pounds of millet are produced per acre, yielding half as much carbohydrate as plantains. Furthermore, while coffee sales constitute a major source of income in Sasur, agricultural products (mostly maize) constitute only 10 percent of Kapsirika's cash income.

While Sasur cultivation is intensive, Kapsirika's is extensive. All cultivation in the latter involves the use of the plow on new land properly cultivated with two plowings as soil preparation and one at the time of seeding. Millet is planted broadcast without covering; maize is sown in covered rows. The major tasks are weeding (Plate II:9), which should be done twice, and harvesting. These may be done by *moyket;* women do most of this work but men help. A stick may be used to help in weeding millet. A crop rotation of two years of millet, followed by two to four years of maize, and three or more years of fallow is practiced. After fallowing, the land is treated as new land in preparation. Maize ears are pulled; they are shucked and stored in the cob; millet heads are cut off with a small knife, and millet is stored in the head (Plate II:25). Harvesting may also be done in a *moyket.*

Though farming does not require the input of energy in Kapsirika that it does in Sasur, and though the Kapsirikans think of themselves as primarily cattle keepers, they are involved heavily and increasingly in farming and produce a surplus in good years. The year of our study was a reasonably good year; twelve of the forty respondents had sold maize valued at 1,732 shillings, and three had sold millet valued at 242 shillings.

The most important aspect of the Kapsirika scene is the free availability of land. Fifteen of the thirty-one men reporting said they had opened the land themselves (60 percent of the acreage); only 10 obtained land (24 percent of the acreage) from their fathers. Many had simply borrowed their land. As one man said: "The former owner left this place. When I first came to Kapsirika I lived in his old house. It is now my permanent land because that Kitosh man has moved away."

We uncovered only one land dispute in Kapsirika; it was a quarrel between two leading men, in which one claimed that the other (a newly arrived outsider) had taken some of his cultivated area, which the courts decided in the plaintiff's favor.

While the men prepare the land, they regard the individual *baringos* as the province of their wives. In Kapsirika, not Sasur, I was told that each wife should have the same number of *baringos.* However, the women do not possess their *baringos,* in the sense that women possess *shambas* in Sasur;

Kapsirika sons are not going to be concerned with the lands their mothers cultivated. What is relevant to this equity is the husband's service as cultivator, not his allocation of property.

In Kapsirika, Porter analyzed the agricultural operations of Sabilla Arap Labu, a man of over fifty whose father had pioneered the area, and from whom he claims to have inherited his land. Sabilla has never bought or sold any land but has loaned or given some that he considers his to his brothers and sons. His two wives have borne several sons, and he works collaboratively with one of the sons, who lives nearby with his own wife. Two of Sabilla's daughters are married; three sons have houses near to his own; and his remaining household consists of his two wives, the old mother of one of these, and three remaining children.

Sabilla and his son had about 8.6 acres under cultivation in 6 separate *baringos,* 3 (5.6 acres) in maize and the remainder in millet. They were in two distantly separated parcels and represent not more than 4 percent of the approximately 160 acres that Sabilla claims as his own. He estimates that he gets 430 pounds of cleaned grain per acre of millet and 520 per acre of shelled maize in a good year. He had 17 granaries at his house (his granaries are the subject of Table 21), which could hold about 1,500 cubic feet of grain, and his son has an additional 5. In 1962, Sabilla sold 4 200-pound sacks of maize for 120 shillings and another amount later to pay 20 shillings in school fees. This represented his total cash income for the year. These sales are made to itinerant merchants, who pick up the grain at his door.

The seasonal round of agricultural work starts in January with the cutting of the bush, which dries for a month and is burned on the ground. The ground is then plowed by Sabilla's married son assisted by the unmarried one. The land is left open until after the first rain in April, when it is planted in rows by his wives, who drop three or four grains together about a foot apart. The seeds are then covered by girls who follow. One weeding is necessary in June, and the harvest takes place in August or September, usually with a *moyket.* Finger millet requires two weedings.

Another major differential between Kapsirika and Sasur has to do with the amount and distribution of labor. Unfortunately, the task of measuring labor is so formidable that we did not undertake it. It appears, however, that the total amount of work (both farming and stock keeping) required per person is less in Kapsirika than in Sasur, because of the utilization of oxen as a source of energy. Oxen are utilized not only for plowing, but also for hauling sledges of grain from the field and carrying water (in 50 gallon drums). Woman are the chief beneficiaries of harnessed animal power, for they would otherwise cultivate the land and carry the loads. Their work is increased by a burden of milking, but this is by no means the equivalent of hauling loads in time, energy, or onus. Men, on the other hand, in addition to caring for the stock (with which they burden themselves very lightly) engage in the quite demanding task of driving the oxen; they also help in the weeding and the harvesting.

Despite the difference in landholdings between Sasur and Kapsirika, Sebei consistently see landholding as more significant to individual welfare than livestock. When Edgerton asked what a man should choose if he could have anything he wanted, thirty-four of those responding placed land first as against forty naming cattle, and the Kapsirika men were the ones who particularly selected land (fifteen) as against cattle (seven). Similarly, when asked how a poor man might become wealthy, forty-six in each community said by cultivating land. In view of the traditional background of the Sebei and the current reality situation, I find these responses surprising; they demonstrate the degree to which Sebei have become psychologically attuned to farming, even though Kapsirika men tended to identify themselves as cattle-keepers.

SUMMARY AND COMPARISONS

Though farming is of economic importance to the plains people and its role is increasing, it does not have the saliency for the social order that horticulture has in Sipi, and our contrasts will point up some significant differentials. These rest on one crucial element that contrasts Sasur with Kapsirika; in Sasur all land is privately owned and controlled, whereas in Kapsirika land is available for the taking. In the general context of Sebei institutions, everything else follows. Furthermore, this differential can be seen to represent, despite some important developments in Kapsirika, a spatial differentiation that corresponds to changes taking place in time. Undoubtedly, the social role of agriculture in Kapsirika today is much closer — though not identical — to its historical role than is true of Sasur. Not only do the Sebei tell us that this is the case when the recount aspects of Sebei history, but it is manifest in a good deal of internal evidence. The most important pieces of evidence are the patterning of their institutional arrangements relative to property, which are more fitted to cattle than to land, and the fact that the Sebei constantly though unwittingly draw parallels between their behavior with respect to land and their behavior in cattle operations.

One of the crucial elements in this analogizing process is so obvious that it could easily be overlooked; namely, the individual and private rights to the land. These notions of private property are as deeply engrained in the Sebei psyche as they are in that of Western man, and the true sense of freehold is a point of departure for Sebei attitudes toward land. These attitudes toward landholding are unusual in horticultural societies with shifting agriculture. Among tribal peoples falling in this economic category, land is more often either freely available or held by the clan or community and allocated to cultivators as they need it. Evidence suggests that the Sebei, as pastoralists in cultural background and origin, have a traditional commitment to the notion of private rights and personal independence; individual rights in private property take precedence over their commitment to clan, even though such commitment continues to be a strong underlying theme in Sebei attitudes. They have enjoyed some benefits from these traditional attitudes, but they have also had to meet some costs of this cultural intransigence.

There is explicit evidence of a syncretism between old pastoral patterns and new agricultural conditions in the details of Sebei institutionalization of land control within the framework of private rights: the patrilineal inheritance of land, the allocation of land to wives and the retention of some as *soi*, the way in which sons are given their heritage, and the use of land in *namanya* contracts and outright exchanges. These arrangements often create dysfunction, particularly to the degree that land becomes a scarce commodity.

There have also been some failures to syncretize; notably the lack of ceremonial observances to sanction the allocations of land, and the failure to utilize land transfers as elements in brideprice. People devoted to the land almost universally endow it with sacred properties, with spirits of the locale, with ritual acts. But the Sebei have not done so; such ritual as pertains to agriculture focuses on the crops and the processes, not on the land. The strong Sebei spiritual identification with cattle rather than land creates the anomaly, among others, that the young man who wants to marry must acquire not only the *shambas* his wife needs to provide him with food, but also the cattle and other goods for her brideprice. The double burden creates no small strain; I doubt that it would be possible if coffee production did not provide some flow of cash into the area.

The treatment of land as property is also beginning to have another effect: within one generation of the secondary influx of population into Chema, men were purchasing land with stock; in a second generation, they were purchasing it with money, culminating in land manipulation. While these men are not buying and selling land for profit they are clearly building up their holdings and those of their sons, while taking a profit in the form of a living and thereby translating their commercial competence into status, influence, and the welfare of their family line. There is a difference between amassing land and amassing cattle. The size of one man's herd does not directly affect the size of another's. Indeed, feedback factors tend to make the growth of stock self-limiting (Goldschmidt, 1972c). But when one man accumulates *shambas* within a community with a finite area of land, somebody else must necessarily be the loser.

So far in Sasur there is no clear evidence of awareness of these effects. Yet, the effects are there, and we see men who are less astute or less calculating, less energetic or less provident, selling their patrimony — acts that Psiwa, like a good New Englander who would never dip into capital, specifically rejects. I have no way of knowing whether the Sebei recognize the implications of these land control changes for the ultimate character of their social order. (I expect not, for so many more apparent changes have come to Sebei, and they have no census bureau to announce, as ours in America did, that the frontier was gone.) These changes place and conflicts directly within the family structure, especially in the relationship between co-wives and among the half-brothers who are sons of these co-wives, but also between fathers and sons.

The people of Sasur did not invent conflict; intrafamilial conflict in relation to property finds expression in Kapsirika as well.[9] A man knows what sector of the herd belongs to his mother; once the original allocations have been made, the size of the herd is presumed to be the function of external, fatalistic forces. Matters are neither so clear nor so external with respect to land, partly because of the failure to ritualize the legal arrangements, but largely because the father's actions are so deterministic. Land allocation sits there, inert and unchanging — very different from a herd of cattle.

Land problems involve relationships among neighbors. In my brief investigations, we uncovered some half-dozen explicit disputes over land boundaries between neighbors in Sasur, but only one in Kapsirika. The people of Sasur, particularly when they have invested in plantains and coffee, are committed to their location. They cannot, as do the Kapsirikans, move away from conflicts but must live with them from day to day and year to year.

These differentials are mitigated by two circumstances. The first is the growing importance of farming in Kapsirika. The second is the existence of a cash crop in the farming area, which enables men like Chemengich and Psiwa to build up their landholdings for the benefit of their sons — utilizing, in fact, the labor of their sons. Despite these two economic influences that tend to reduce the contrast between Sasur and Kapsirika, basic differences in the social and behavioral characteristics of the two communities suggest that underlying economic factors have a potent influence on the pattern of social relationships.

---

9. The major intrafamilial conflict witnessed in Kapsirika (*KC:passim*) was between full brothers. This difference relates to the structure of potentially conflicting situations.

Chapter 7
Compensation, Craftsmanship and the Cash Economy

Do not collect all your debts, but save some for the morrow;
when indebtness comes, you will have a source of supply.

Sebei proverb

HOMO ECONOMICUS SEBEIENSIS

Transactions of an essentially economic kind are a pervasive element in the Sebei social order and ideology. An exchange of goods or services may be considered to be economic when there is an expected quid pro quo, in contrast to transfers of goods and services that are expected because the two persons stand in a particular relationship in the social order, however effective these may be in assuring an appropriate redistribution of goods in times of availability and need. Economic transactions play an important role in Sebei life.

Sebei economic transactions are universalistic; the chain of exchanges can link together all exchangeable goods and services. One class of livestock may be traded for another, and these may be traded for food in the ground or in the granary, or for land. A hunter may acquire a cow for the tusk of an elephant he killed, or for the poison he concocted that made the elephant hunt successful. Nothing so clearly demonstrates the universalistic character of Sebei economic transactions as their extension to brideprice. Among the Sebei, as elsewhere, sentiment and social considerations clearly enter into marital choices, but economic considerations are also involved. The fact that Sebei have traditionally used the same bargaining pattern for *namanya* exchanges and brideprice negotiations and now analogize their land purchases to them suggests that the Sebei see a continuity from one to the others.

This pattern of economic exchanges extends to services as well. An essentially economic contract for services is exemplified in the herding sphere by the *kamanakan* arrangement, in which one man cares for the livestock of another for the privilege of using the products, and in the

186

agricultural sphere by the *moyket,* where there is a clear expectation that work will be compensated for in beer, or, if payment is delayed, in beer and meat. The same applies to the construction of houses. The contribution of labor is not merely the "roofing bee" known to pioneer America; there is a definite expectation of compensation for the work performed. The fact that roles will be reversed on a later occasion does not satisfy the workers on the current project, it merely serves as a means of insuring performance through the law of the marketplace.

Table 30 shows that this pattern of payment applies also to professional and ritual services. The tabulation lists all instances in which an informant expressed the idea of a payment or expected compensation, whether he was describing a specific incident or generalizing about customary procedures. In some instances, the person performing the service for which payment is demanded stands in a kinship relation to the recipient; in most other instances, the persons may also be related, but in either case the expectation of a proper reward overrides such social ties.

It may be argued that this pattern of economic transactions is a result of the Westernization of Sebei culture and the monetization of their economy. I find the evidence to the contrary compelling. In the first place, some of these exchanges, notably the *namanya,* the *kamanakan,* and the *moyket,* are clearly aboriginal in character; their very form is so different from anything

TABLE 30
General Pattern of Compensation for Services

Service	Compensation
Ordinary labor	
1. Agriculture (clearing, cultivation, weeding, harvesting)	
a. *Moyket*	Beer worth 1.50 - 2 shillings (now sometimes cash)
b. *Kwoloyit* (delayed compensation)	Beer plus meat of slaughtered animal
c. *Kwoloyintet* (person in charge of party)	Same as worker
2. Housebuilding (furnishing poles, thatch, construction, thatching, and other unskilled labor)	Same as *moyket* or *kwoloyit*
3. Cattle herding (*kamanakan*)	Use of milk and blood. If successful increase, an animal may be given
4. Cattle herdsman	Milk from selected cows
5. Carpentry work	Cash payment (usually by contract)
Skilled services	
6. Midwife (for difficult delivery)	Calabash of sour milk mixed with blood

(TABLE 30 — *Cont.*)

Service	Compensation
7. Circumcision; person who performs operation	5 shillings. Extra compensation if girl is pregnant, initiate cries, or there is excessive bleeding.
8. Treatment of illness	"Dew payment" of a chicken or about 2 shillings at time of treatment; beer at time of recovery
9. Sale of medical knowledge	Small stock (10 - 20 shillings) plus beer
10. Treatment of animal illness and sale of such knowledge	Same as for human treatment
11. Veterinarian services (chiefly difficult deliveries)	Share of beer and meat at any pot or slaughtering

Ritual services

Service	Compensation
12. Twin ceremony ritualist[a]	12 shillings plus beer
13. Cutting helix of twin (performed by mother's sister)	Pot of beer
14. Twin ceremony (children who dance on roof)	3 shillings each
15. Twin ceremony Sister who takes spear Clan brother who digs hole	 Goat or 10 shillings Beer
16. *Kisa* ceremony[a]	Pot of beer
17. Sponsor for initiates at circumcision[a]	5 shillings
18. Persons who hold down initiate who cries	Ram shared by the four men who do this
19. Bride's aunts who admonish bride during seclusion	Beer, food, and usually 2 - 5 shillings
20. Ceremony for pregnant wife after first wife has died[a]	Skin, head and half the meat of slaughtered ram
21. Funeral: man who spears bull	Compensation required but amount not indicated
22. Fertility of plantain *shambas*	5 shillings per clan; formerly rings for necklaces
23. Divination (all kinds of diviners)	Various charges

[a]The person performing this service must previously have been the subject of the same rite.

European as to preclude the notion of borrowing. Many of the other payments are made — or were made — in kind, independent of the availability of a medium of exchange. Some of them, like brideprice and payment for ritual services, extend to realms in which payment is antithetical to the European ideal. Finally, the very pervasiveness of the pattern suggests that it reflects deeply held attitudes and strongly felt sentiments among the Sebei.

The Sebei manifest a concern with the appropriate reward in every social nexus, expressing an underlying assumption that material things are an essential extension of the individual as well as a measure of his worth. This is elegantly expressed by the Sebei who say that a woman feels "she is no longer a minor thing in the house" when cattle have been allocated to her. Property concepts are deeply imbedded in the Sebei psyche, as they are in Sebei social institutions.

Exchanges are one functionally effective means of redistributing goods that for some reason are not evenly distributed. The interdependence between the farming area and the plains area today involves interchange of services if not commodities, while there is a constant traffic of goods along the escarpment. Much of this interchange of goods and services can be satisfactorily accomplished in ways other than by purchase and sale, even when money and markets are available. For instance, whenever a woman who lives in the east visits a friend or relative in Sipi, she usually brings some gift and takes home a stem of plantains. Much redistribution is accomplished in this kind of informal exchange. Conant describes a considerable movement of commodities among the Pokot, where internal environmental differences are even greater. Thus, although economic exchanges are a functionally effective means of achieving traffic in goods and can be shown to have that effect among the Sebei, they are by no means the only way redistribution can be achieved.

CRAFTSMANSHIP

Craft specialization also requires institutions for the redistribution of goods. Although the Sebei recognize that some individuals are more skilled at making particular things than others, there is very little craft specialization among them. In fact, the Sebei are not much given to craftsmanship, with the result that their material culture, which had always been spare, has become very lean indeed since Western manufactured goods have become available.

One craft of limited distribution is the basketry of Masop women (Plate II:12). They bring their baskets to the escarpment to exchange for foods or to sell for cash.[1] Most baskets are made of split bamboo, which is

---

1. The baskets fall into the following categories: *montit,* a five- to ten-quart split bamboo basket with bilobed base, small mouth, and leather bale, used for carrying and storing grain or flour; *chemulyankut,* a small round basket of softer material, used for carrying native tobacco; *sweswet,* a flat lyre-shaped shallow basket of split bamboo, which may be used for eating, for shelled maize, or

readily available in Masop. Basketry does not supply a woman's livelihood but only supplements the family income.

Gourds are very much used,[2] particularly on the plains, where they are important as milk receptacles (Plates II:1, 8). Milk storage gourds are normally capped with a leather lid and often have handles sewn on the gourd. Both handle and cap are often decorated with cowries or trade beads. There is no specialized personnel for making these things.

Men still occasionally dress skins, which were formerly used for clothing and are still used by many as sleeping mats, but they now play only a minor role in Sebei material culture. Men also make hide sandals and formerly made very elegant shields (*loŋet*) of buffalo or boar hide. These are no longer carried but are required for certain rites.   In woodwork, the men fashion tripod stools out of logs, bows, arrows, and spear shafts and a few men have the carpentry skills necessary to set up roofs and to install prefabricated doors and windows. These items are rarely carved or painted, nor do the Sebei make any carvings. I was told there was one potter among the Sebei, but I never met him; the ubiquitous and highly important beer pots are all purchased in the markets.

Though people make many of these things for themselves, a good many objects find their way to the local market. Thus, over a period of 8 months, the following items appeared repeatedly (but not each week) in the Sipi market: bows, 2 shillings; arrows, 2-2.50 shillings; ropes (of a length for tying cattle) 70 cents; beer tubes, 2-5 shillings; baskets, 1-3.50 shillings; and reed mats, 1 shilling. More rarely reported were iron knives, 1-1.50 shillings; stools, 2.50 shillings; folding chairs, 2 shillings; tables 5 shillings; and brooms 30 cents. These constituted all of the available products of local craftsmanship in the Sipi market.

The Sebei utilize native crafted iron implements regularly today. These include knives, arrowheads, the blades and butts of spears, axes, picks, bells for cows and goats, and iron ornaments, chiefly bracelets. The wide variety of ornaments, especially iron neck rings with flat iron pieces spiraled around them, are now worn by only a few of the older women. Iron hoes were made for awhile, but were abandoned with the introduction of manufactured hoes. Other implements are rapidly being displaced by imported goods; only arrows, knives, and spears are sought from the smith in any quantity.

The blacksmith is the only true craft specialist among the Sebei today. Because the smith has a special place in Sebei life (as he does throughout Africa), and because I, too, find the craft of special interest, I will describe the smith and smithy in some detail (Plates II:27-31). My interest was

---

for winnowing; *kulunkut,* an oval or tear-shaped basket of split bamboo, used for carrying things or as an eating vessel; *kenepet,* a round basket with narrow opening and concave base, designed for carrying on the head; and *tempet,* a woven split bamboo mat used for drying millet, or as a door closing.

2. *Mukuntut,* large gourds for brewing beer or keeping milk; *sotet,* middle-sized gourds for milk storage; *tarket,* small gourds for carrying milk; *saket,* gourds with narrow necks cut in half lengthwise and used as water dippers; *koteriet,* a small dipper used as a cooking spoon; *rarakta,* extremely large gourds used for beer; *rimarit,* gourds with large bulbous necks used for carrying beer, and *sapaywet,* eating bowls.

enhanced by the character of Mamadi, the one remaining smith among the Sebei. He was a man apart; sharp, with a kind of insouciance, yet friendly; most important, he seemed proud of his craft.

Mamadi is a member of Kamnongora clan, the only clan now performing this function, since one smith formerly working in Bukwa died out. The work of the smith is not only a clan monopoly, it is also a family affair. The sons of the smith serve as apprentices, making the charcoal, working the bellows, and ultimately learning the trade; they begin with simple things, such as arrowheads and knives, and only later make larger and more complicated implements.

Mamadi's wives have their gardens, but Mamadi and his sons spend most of their time at the smithy, and I judge it to be an important source of income. Mamadi's son, Amisi,[3] is learning the trade and now makes knives and spears; another son now regularly pumps the bellows. Mamadi has a large family, and other adult sons are farmers.

Strong pressures deter any person not a member of such a clan from taking up the trade:

> If a man whose father or grandfather was not a smith wants to become a smith, he will not be able to because he will become ill. A man at Sipi wanted to become a smith but a smith cursed him, saying that he was trying to do business that wasn't his. He died. That was before the Europeans came. We don't do anything except say, "If you do the smith work and the smithy is not of your *aret,* then you will die" and work the bellows without using the clay funnel. That man is given a year to die. If the clay funnel is used with the blacksmith's curse, our clan would die too, but if we take away the funnel, then the air will go out and kill the man.

The right to engage in the craft, however, extends to the sons of a daughter of the clan — the sister's sons, as the Sebei say. "There is one man named Chemonges Arapkisa whose mother belonged to our *aret.* His *aret* is Kapchesaga. He can be a smith because he has our clan's blood."

Psychological pressure also works to keep some sons in the craft: "If a man of my *aret* refuses to become a smith, every night he will get questions, he dreams: Where are the knives? Where are the spears? Where are the arrows? If he doesn't become a blacksmith, he will become ill. But if he does, he will get well very quickly." Mamadi recounted his own experience:

> I was pumping when my father was a smith. If a boy doesn't pump, he may become sick; then his parents go to the witchdoctor, who says that the boy must become a smith, and they spit beer before he can become one. When I was practicing with my father, I used to make arrows only. In 1928, I went to Kenya and returned in 1930. When I returned I didn't want to come here because it is a dirty place. In 1932, I fell ill. I had no strength, and there were pains in my joints. I went to a witchdoctor, who said that my father, who had died in 1928, wanted me to become a smith. They were ordered to make beer and this was spit on me. Then I became a smith.

---

3. In 1972, Amisi had taken over the operations of the smithy, because Mamadi had become too old to do the work.

The eldest son is expected to take over the work; second sons are not supposed to set up rival shops, but the brothers should work together, or at least operate from the same smithy.

Mamadi remains a person apart, but I could detect no outward signs of either fear or respect, despite the blacksmith's control of special oathing techniques (see Chapter 11).

> During the olden days, all the blacksmiths were feared and if there was war between two tribes and the enemy came here while I was working, everybody would be killed, but I would be left alone. They think that if the blacksmith is killed an evil will kill them all.

Mamadi is not dependent on other persons for any of his equipment. He obtained his original equipment from his father but has had to replace all of it. He replaced the anvil his father left him in 1930. Though the one he was using is still serviceable, he took us to his source — a hill southwest of Soroti — to get a new one. The appropriate clay for the funnel is found in a stream bed in Bugisu; the present owner now demands payment for the clay. Mamadi also makes the bellows and prepares his own charcoal. He is thus dependent only on scrap iron, which is sometimes brought to him by his customers, sometimes found, and occasionally purchased.

The smithy (*kitainy*) is a small, open, thatched structure, about 100 yards from Mamadi's houses. It is a gathering place for the men and boys of the community, and, whenever a stranger appears, Mamadi takes the opportunity to show how he can weld two pieces of iron or break apart a large piece by doubling the pace of the bellows to create a higher temperature. The stroke of welding or breaking scatters a shower of sparks and provides great excitement. But it is important, Mamadi says, to have no other metal in the fire: "They want to be alone there." The double-bowl-shaped wooden bellows are covered with goat skins, to which sticks are attached. They force air through a separate Y-shaped, unbaked clay pipe into a small charcoal pile. The bellows are worked by one of Mamadi's sons. The smith and his helper sit on stools (or banana stems) at either side of the fire. They handle the iron with wooden sticks into which the hot iron has been thrust. Mamadi has three iron hammers: the large and middle made of sections of crowbars left by roadworkers, the smallest made by himself. They have no handles but are simple rods with one end serving as head. Stone hammers were abandoned in 1930. The anvil is of stone. There is also a tapered iron piece that serves as anvil for shaping the sockets of spearhead and butt.

At one time, the Sebei knew the art of smelting, but nobody today knows how to do this, nor where the iron-bearing gravels are to be found. Although Mamadi claims his father (a Nyonki age-set man who died in 1928) knew how to smelt ore, he has never seen it done himself and implied that it was a somewhat secret process. The Sebei say that, prior to Nyonki times (up to circa 1865), hoes were made of buffalo or elephant ribs (never of cattle bones) or of hard wood but describe a hoe with a heavy shank of native iron of reddish brown color. Hobley (1929:248) says of the Elgon region that the

Bantu-speaking Samia were particularly adept at smelting and manufactured hoes of native iron, which had become a form of currency throughout the area north and east of Lake Victoria. Swahili traders of the late nineteenth century gave a great impetus to the use of iron, according to the testimony of historical documents and Sebei informants. The heavy use of iron ornamentation began with the coiled wire carried by these traders. Iron was much in demand according to Austin (1903:76), who found that beads were useful as a medium of exchange only on the southwestern border of Sebeiland.

The spears, like those of the neighboring Nilotes, are made in three parts: head, shaft, and butt. The lanceolate blade has knife-sharp edges (encased in a small, hide sheath when carried) with a tapered stem broadening into a conical socket. The butt is tapered from a similar socket to a dull point. The pointed ends of the wooden shaft are inserted in the sockets of butt and blade and fixed with glue. The Sebei spear is 6 to 7 feet in length, in contrast to the 8 to 10-foot spears of their plains neighbors, and is not so handsomely crafted as those carried by the Pokot and Karamojong. The Sebei on the plains prefer the Pokot spears and generally carry them. Apparently the shorter spears are better adapted to the rough mountain country; the Sebei say they are less likely to break when hunting pigs or hyenas than the long ones. The Gisu are said to like their spears even shorter than the Sebei.

Arrowheads are made by the smith, but nowadays they may also be hammered out of a large nail by anybody. They are also lanceolate in form and may either have a tang or a socket. Axes and knives have a tang, which is inserted into a wooden base; both are still regularly used, though the purchased *panga* (bush knife or machete) is much preferred and universally carried by the men. The pick is used for detaching salt rock from caves. The prices for iron products were quoted by Mamadi as follows: ax head with handle, 2 to 3 shillings; picks, 5 shillings; knives, 50 cents to 1 shilling; spears (with shaft), 4 shillings; arrowheads, 30 cents — all generally less than market prices. Bells are contracted for individually. Today, the arrowheads and spears are brought to market by members of Mamadi's family, and Mamadi says he has a relative who is his agent on the plains, where the greatest demand for such armament exists. Until about 1940, purchases were made by special order.

THE CASH ECONOMY: INCOME

Exchanges of a more commercial nature began with the Swahili traders who were using the Mount Elgon area as a provisioning center by at least the 1880s, mostly acquiring iron and cowry shells. When Austin came to the mountain, he intensified this trade, and by 1915 the rupee had entered into the brideprice. The use of cash has grown ever since. The information in this section on Sebei income derives from schedules taken in Sasur and Kapsirika on items sold and wages earned during a one-year period (roughly 1961).

Despite the difficulty of assessing a time limit, I think the data are reasonable approximations. As most of this information came from men, there is an underrepresentation of the women's casual market sale of plantains and other agricultural produce, but this would not have any great effect on the total amount of cash available to the households — though it would be important to the individual women.

Table 31 gives the results of responses from forty-five Sasurese and forty

TABLE 31
Cash Income by Source: Sasur and Kapsirika

Source	Sasur (45 households)			Kapsirika (40 households)		
	Persons rptg	Income (shillings)	Pct	Persons rptg	Income (shillings)	Pct
Livestock						
cattle	4	600		18	11,460	
warek	3	134		0		
chickens	2	34		0		
Total livestock		768	2.4		11,460	49.7
Produce						
maize	6	403		12	1,732	
plantains	9	269		0		
millet	0			3	242	
cotton	0			1	160	
coffee	44[a]	20,100		0		
other[b]	4	62		2	54	
Total produce		20,834	65.8		2,188	9.5
Wages and salaries	16[c]	4,978	15.7	2	1,620	7.0
Commercial enterprise	3[d]	1,360	4.3	3[e]	7,100	30.8
Other						
beer and miscellaneous	23	2,752		9	706	
miscellaneous	2[f]	950		0		
Total others		3,702	11.7		706	3.1
Total income		31,642	99.9[g]		23,074	100.1[g]
Income per household		703.16			576.85	

SOURCE: Data from Tables 31 and 32 are based on economic questionnaire taken in 1961-62.

[a]The one man reporting no sale also had coffee *shambas*.

[b]Vegetables, a calf skin, milk.

[c]One man working full time in Nairobi not included; his wife did not know his income.

[d]Sale of land in two instances; buying and selling coffee in one.

[e]Operation of maize mill, 1,500 shillings; operating *duka*, 4,800 shillings; trading in cattle, 800 shillings.

[f]Brideprice, 900 shillings; given by son, 50 shillings.

[g]Total does not add up to 100 percent because of rounding.

Kapsirikan households and shows that there was a substantial amount of cash entering into the local economy. The sums available per household in Sasur were 22 percent greater than in Kapsirika; indeed, this understates the case.

In Sasur, coffee accounted for two-thirds of the total cash income and was a resource in virtually every household. (Porter found that 96 percent of the adult males in the Sipi area were members of the coffee cooperative and that the average farmer had 0.4 acres in coffee from which he obtained an income of about 260 shillings per year.[4] Wages account for another sixth of cash income. This figure is somewhat inflated by the salaries I paid. The sale of beer accounts for a surprising 8.7 percent of the total income.

In Kapsirika, just half the income is from the sale of cattle; nearly another third was earned by three men who engage in commercial enterprises; and nearly 10 percent was derived from the sale of agricultural products, mostly maize. Only two persons reported cash income from wages and salaries, most of this being the salary of 1,560 shillings of the local chief.

Cattle sales have been treated as income, without regard to costs of production. Many of those who sold cattle, however, used a part of the money to buy young animals, so that not all the cash income was used to meet cash demands or purchase consumer goods. This makes the differential in cash available for consumption between Sasur and Kapsirika even greater than appears in the tabulation.

Table 32 gives the distribution of total reported income among households in Sasur and Kapsirika. Compared to Sasur, the Kapsirikans varied widely in the amount of cash available. Four persons claimed no income, and nearly half the population (46.2 percent) reported less than 200 shillings or

TABLE 32
Distribution of Cash Income: Sasur and Kapsirika

Income bracket (Shillings)	Sasur						Kapsirika					
	Reporting		Amount				Reporting		Amount			
	No.	Pct	No.	Pct	Ave.		No.	Pct	No.	Pct	Ave.	
No income	0	0.0	0	0.0	0		4	10.3	0	0.0	0	
1-99	1	2.3	60	0.2	60		4	10.3	220	1.0	55	
100-199	3	7.0	417	1.3	139		10	25.6	1,374	6.0	137	
200-399	10	23.3	3,169	10.0	317		6	15.4	1,566	6.8	261	
400-599	5	11.6	2,574	8.1	515		2	5.1	946	4.1	473	
600-699	14	32.6	11,561	36.6	826		7	17.9	5,065	21.9	724	
1,000-1,499	7	16.3	8,327	26.3	1,189		1	2.6	1,040	2.6	1,040	
1,500 and up	3	7.0	5,502	17.4	1,834		5	12.8	12,923	55.9	2,585	
Totals	43	100.1[a]	31,610	99.9[a]	735		39	100.0	23,134	100.2[a]	593	

[a]Totals do not add up to 100 percent because of rounding.

4. Some of the discrepancy between his 260 shillings and my average of 447 shillings may derive from double sales: small growers sometimes sell to others, who take the cured beans to the market.

7 percent of the total. At the other end, five persons had incomes of more than 1500 shillings and obtained well over half the total income reported. Those who reported no incomes were generally young men who said their fathers paid their taxes, while those with high incomes were the chief and the commercial operators. One of the men with the highest income had sold eight head of cattle for 2,910 shillings during the year, but he purchased five animals with 990 shillings of that sum.

THE ECONOMICS OF COFFEE PRODUCTION

Inasmuch as coffee accounts for nearly two-thirds of Sasur cash income, I will examine its production economics in greater detail. The information for this analysis was obtained in 1972, but no major changes in production costs or techniques had taken place since 1961, except that spraying and the use of commercial fertilization had increased, and it became against the law to bring more land into coffee production. The data here analyzed were obtained from a former secretary of the Sebei Cooperative Society and from two growers.

Coffee prices are set by the government and always have been established by the marketing agency (variously the Coffee Trust Fund, Coffee Board, and Coffee Union). In 1971 and 1972, 4.46 shillings per kilo was the price for first grade arabica, which is the variety Sebei farmers produce. The price per kilo was as high as 5 shillings in the late 1950s, and in 1962 was 4.40 shillings. For many years, the Uganda Government endeavored to induce the Sebei to produce coffee and established nurseries on the mountain from which young trees were furnished below cost at 15 shillings per hundred to "progressive" growers as against 30 shillings on the regular market. The government has also had field assistants to advise individual growers regarding the planting and cultivation of coffee, and it still subsidizes spraying and pruning, as well as providing marketing facilities.

To find the production cost of coffee, it is necessary to separate out the cost of preparing the orchard (long-term investments) from the annual costs of production. The land must be prepared, the trees planted, and the orchard tended for three years before a crop is produced in the fourth year. These costs may reasonably be estimated. An acre of land should have 680 trees set 8 feet apart; these are furnished by government nurseries at 15 shillings per 100 and therefore cost 102 shillings per acre. The original clearing of the ground, ridging, and setting out the trees can be generously estimated as costing 100 shillings. Holes 2 feet deep and 2 feet in diameter must be dug for the trees, and the topsoil then replaced in the holes until after a rain. The cost of digging the holes is 20 cents each, or 136 shillings per acre. Fertilizer (4 ounces of amonium sulphate per tree) should be applied each April and September, and the cost (at 78 shillings per 220-pound sack) for the six applications during the period of immaturity, including labor, would be about 400 shillings. There should be 3 weedings each year at an average cost of 70 shillings, or another 630 shillings. The total investment, exclusive of land cost, adds to an estimated 1,368 shillings per acre or about 2 shillings per tree (the amount generally added to the price of land when a man sells land with mature coffee trees). An orchard has a productive life of about 20 years, and these costs (exclusive of interest) may thus be amortized at about 70 shillings per acre per year. These costs are in terms of ideal practices; they represent chiefly the value of labor, much of which the farmer himself may provide.

To these investment costs will be added the annual production costs incurred in maintaining the orchard and picking and preparing the beans for market. Field work includes weeding three or four times a year, removing suckers, pruning every third or fourth year, mulching, and maintaining ridges. Coffee ripens as cherry-red berries in November and December. The "cherries" must be picked, the pulp removed, seeds ("beans") sundried, with the poor beans removed by hand, and the crop taken to market. For small operations of a hundred or so trees, most work can be done by the farmer and his family, but for larger operations much will be done by paid labor or by *moyket*.

Annual costs will be estimated on the basis of the actual operations of Andyema, the son of Kapchemesyekin in 1971, when he had a good crop (see Table 33). By selling about 900 kilos at 4.46 shillings per kilo, he earned

TABLE 33
Analysis of Andyema's Coffee Production Costs

Item[a]	Costs (shillings)	Income (shillings)
Production costs		
Weeding	300	
Pruning	70	
Fertilizing	100	
Spraying (government rate)	5	
Picking (@ 1.50 per *debe* cherries)	380	
Pulping (@ .30 per *debe* cherries)	75	
Total annual production costs	930	
Investment costs		
2.8 acres @ 70 shillings per acre	200	
Total costs	1,130	
Gross income (@ 4.46 shillings per kilo)		4,000
Net income[b]		2,870

[a]Background facts: 1,900 trees owned, of which 1,500 are mature; estimated acreage in coffee; 2.8 acres; 1971 coffee production of 900 kilos.

[b]Net income here does not take account of family labor nor of value of land.

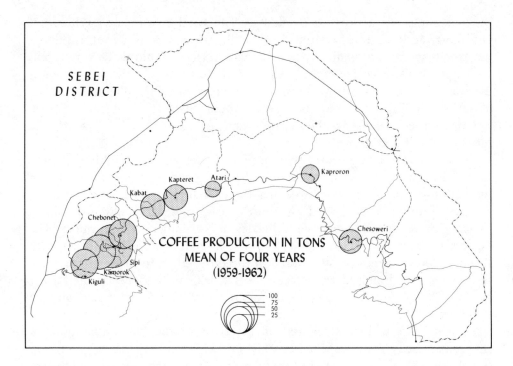

SEBEI
DISTRICT

COFFEE PRODUCTION IN TONS
MEAN OF FOUR YEARS
(1959-1962)

roughly 4,000 shillings. He weeded four times: the first three cost him 75 shillings each in cash; the fourth he paid by *moyket,* with beer (purchased for 75 shillings) as that was the only way he could induce his neighbors to work when they were busy on their own land. Picking is paid on a piecework basis, usually 1.50 shillings per *debe* of cherries. As a *debe* of cherries makes 3.61 kilos of beans, harvesting cost is .42 shillings per kilo. Assuming all coffee was picked by hired labor at a cost of .42 per kilo, his total harvesting cost for 900 kilos was about 380 shillings. In the past year, Andyema contracted to have his whole orchard pruned for 200 shillings, but, because this cost is borne only every third year, the annual cost would be about 70 shillings. He fertilized only 500 of his trees during the year, spending 96 shillings for the fertilizer and hiring two brothers to help him at 2 shillings each. He purchased a pulping machine in 1971 for 900 shillings and lets others use it at 30 cents per *debe* (and had already retrieved over a third of this investment). In calculating his costs, I am charging 30 cents per *debe* of cherries for pulping. The government charged him a standard fee of 5 shillings for spraying his whole orchard. All other tasks were done by Andyema and his family. The result of these calculations indicates a net income of 2,870 shillings or about 1,000 shillings per acre.

Andyema's net income would be allocated by economists in part to interest on his investment, in part to the land, in part to the labor of Andyema and his family, and the rest to "entrepreneurial skill." I will leave to others the making of such allocations. I should note, however, that a good deal more than hired labor is involved. Putting out and taking in the beans in order to dry them requires much vigilance and a great deal of work. The whole time Andyema was discussing these figures with me, he and one of his wives were sifting through beans on a mat, and removing defective ones, a necessary task if the coffee is to be accepted as first grade. His wife must have had to carry the 900 kilos of coffee on her back about two miles to market. These tasks are in addition to the family labor of mulching, ridging, and removing of suckers. Furthermore, we cannot take the year 1971 as typical; Andyema had a much poorer yield in 1972 as a result of pruning. He intends in the future to prune the orchard as necessary during each weeding, so as to avoid such fluctuation.

While Andyema is by no means unique, most men do not operate with such enterprise or have so much land and capital available. Those men who have but few trees often use their coffee as a kind of legal tender, selling or exchanging it in small quantities. One man slaughtered an animal and was exchanging beef for coffee cherries, refusing to accept money because he received greater value in coffee than his customers would pay in cash. In such ways, as well as in the hiring of labor, the economy of coffee suffuses the whole of the Sebei population wherever coffee is grown.

THE CASH ECONOMY: MARKETS

With the levels of cash available to Sebei, marketing facilities are inevitable. The Sebei did not have markets aboriginally; I do not know when they entered Sebei territory. In 1954, a biweekly market was held on the Chebonet River in Kapeywa, along the old road that led to the escarpment (Plate II:32). A wide array of goods was available from the outside — soap, sugar, tea, razor blades, cigarettes, household goods of various kinds, as well as a variety of native foods and livestock. African and Asian merchants appeared at this market, both to sell manufactured articles and to buy cattle, plantains and maize. By 1962, the market along that stretch of road had been abandoned.

In 1962, regular markets were held on the plains at Ngenge (Plate II:35) and on the escarpment at Sipi (Plates II:36,37), and farther east at Kaptaret, and in Bukwa. The market at Ngenge was held twice a month and was primarily for the sale of cattle. Many outside traders came to buy cattle and to sell manufactured goods. I attempted no analysis of the Ngenge market activities.

The market at Sipi was held each Saturday. People from a wide area started collecting there as early as 8:00 A.M. and by 10:00 it was often quite crowded; it was usually over by 2:00 P.M. Beer and food was available in local shops, and a festive air frequently prevailed. Merchants sometimes came in lorries to buy goods, chiefly plantains. Several persons, mostly women, sat on a grassy slope under some shade trees, with their wares in front of them. There is not much evidence of haggling over prices, nor any frenzy of activity. The most active part of the market is provided by the butchers. Animals are slaughtered at the market, their carcasses laid open on banana fronds, and the butchering done by men with the ubiquitous *panga*. Meat is purchased by the pound, weighed in a hanging balance, and wrapped in banana leaves for the customer. Entrails and other special pieces are often bought to be broiled and resold for immediate consumption.

A clerk made a regular inventory for a period of thirty-one weeks, from April 14 to November 10, 1962, at Sipi market. He was asked to list all items available at the market, the quantity available, and the asking price. I do not know how many of these goods were sold nor the prices finally received, but in general Sebei hold to the asking price.

Table 34 includes only those food commodities most frequently sold at the market. Slaughtered cattle and goats, chickens, eggs, maize, millet, and plantains are present virtually every week, while cassava, groundnuts, beans, yams, sorghum, cabbages, fish, and mutton are found most weeks. Other items, especially fruits, appear seasonally. Not included in the tabulation are items that appeared infrequently, sporadically, or in very small quantities, such as sugar cane, passion fruit, tomatoes, and onions. Occasionally, a local fruit called lobotik, bamboo shoots, the fungus called katonik, and mushrooms were sold. Maize in the ear (both raw and cooked) appeared on one market day, as did a *debe* of wheat, which was offered at 10 cents a bowl. On two successive weeks, ducks were available, priced at 15 shillings each. The tabulation also shows the amount of goods offered, and the price range, and, where one price generally prevailed, that figure is listed in the right-hand column.

Some prices are quite constant; others fluctuate widely. For instance, over a three-week period, chickens were successively priced at 4.50 shillings, 6 shillings, and 3 shillings. Efforts to correlate these prices with the quantity of items offered for sale or with the quantity offered the preceding week were not generally rewarding. Maize is an exception. It started at 6.50 shillings per *debe*, rose to 7.50 shillings in late May, held at 7 shillings for the following three months, and then declined to 4 shillings in October and November. This drop was related to the quantity available, which rose from about three sacks per week to about eight, with the new harvest. There was also some negative correlation between quantity and price in cabbages: an average of seventeen heads was available when the price was 1.50 shillings; thirty-six when the price was 80 cents or 1 shilling, and thirty-seven when the price was 50 cents. A similar relationship could not be established for chickens or fish.

I was not able to obtain a full year's record, but the major changes in both the character of the market and the prices charged appear to have been seasonal. In Table 35, the sequence is divided into three periods of eleven, ten, and ten weeks, and shows that many prices tended to rise during the summer months and all (except millet) are lowest in the fall, when crops are being harvested.

The market declined in amount and variety of goods in this last phase, but I do not know whether this reflects availability of goods, lack of need in the postharvest season, or other factors. The decline may be related to the

TABLE 34
Commodity Offerings at Sipi Market

Commodity	Goods Offered			Price (shillings)[c]		
	Frequency[a]	Ave. Amt.[b]	Unit	Low	High	Standard[d]
Meat, chickens, eggs						
beef	29	7.28	head	1.30 lb.	1.50 lb.	1.50 lb.
goat	30	1.70	head	1.50 lb.	1.50 lb.	1.50 lb.
mutton	21	1.57	head	1.25 lb.	1.50 lb.	1.50 lb.
chickens	29	16.30	head	2.50 each	6.00 each	
Grains, starches						
maize (shelled)	31	4.20	sack	4.00 *debe*	7.50	7.00 *debe*
millet	31	9.48	sack	10.00 *debe*	13.50	12.00 *debe*
sorghum	19	2.13	sack	.50 bowl	.50 bowl	.50 bowl
plantains[e]	30	128.70	stem	1.00 stem	4.00 stem	
beans	22	1.91	sack	.50 cup	1.00 cup	.50 cup
cassava	25	3.16	sack	.04 each	.25 each	
sweet potatoes	14	2.00	sack	.03 each	.40 each	
yams	21	21.70	yam	.15 each	.50 each	.20 each
Fruits, vegetables						
cabbages	26	33.40	head	.50 each	1.50 each	
oranges	18			.02 each	.03 each	
ripe bananas	14			.10 for 14	.10 for 8	.01 each
lobotik	10	.63	lobotik	.10 for 30	.10 for 3	.10 for 5
ground nuts	20	1.83	sack	.50 bowl	1.00 bowl	.50 bowl
Miscellaneous						
fish	22	30.00	fish	.50 each	2.00 each	1.00 each
milk	26	10.60	gourds	5.00 gourd	12.00 gourd	
beer	7	7.43	*debe*	.50 bottle	.50 bottle	.50 bottle

[a]Number of times commodity offered between April 14 and November 10, 1962 (31 market days).

[b]The average amount available for sale on days commodity was offered. Data not available for some commodities.

[c]The unit offered in this column is that on which amount available was indicated.

[d]For those commodities which fluctuated occasionally, but were usually offered at the same price. It is not an average price.

[e]Plantains varied in type and pattern of sales. From April 14 to July 21, the number of stems varied between 150 and 285, and these were, I believe, sold to itinerant merchants and went to the towns. After that the clerk recorded 12 stems each week with widely fluctuating price and diverse varieties. I suspect the absence of plantains one day to have been a clerical error.

change in the sale of plantains. In the first half of the period (until the end of July), many stems were brought to market and sold to itinerant merchants, the number varying between 150 and 285 (average 231), and the price ranging from 2 to 4 shillings (average 2.71). After that date, only a dozen or so stems were brought for sale locally, their price varying from 50 cents to 3.50 shillings, according to size and variety.

Objects of local craftsmanship, native medicines, curry powder, and a few

TABLE 35

Variations in Average Prices of Selected Commodities

Period (1962)	Prices (shillings)					
	Chicken	Maize	Millet	Cabbage	Fish	Milk
4/14-6/23	4.54	6.85	10.41	1.00	1.30	9.85
6/30-9/1	4.67	5.33	12.10	0.98	1.00	10.85
9/8-11/10	3.11	4.90	11.60	0.66	0.56	7.25

other miscellaneous goods were also available. One day, some women brought loads of wood that they endeavored to sell for 2 shillings each.

Aside from the periodic markets, goods are available in small shops, *dukas*, several of which are found in each town, and occasionally elsewhere along the road running across the escarpment, more frequently in the densely populated west and less so in the east (Plate II:34). Because Asian merchants were not allowed to establish such stores in the district, *dukas* are all operated by Africans, chiefly Sebei. The Indian merchants act as wholesalers, bringing goods by lorry. They offer nonperishable items such as cloth, soap, razor blades and other cosmetic goods, kerosene and kerosene lamps, cigarettes, and the like. A few *dukas* sell either native or bottled beer and have informal beer parlors attached. More rarely, they are what are called hotels in rural East Africa, shops that serve prepared food. I made no effort to analyze the operations of these *dukas*. There is also some sale and purchase not connected with the more formal institutions of exchange, such as itinerant butchers who purchase an animal, slaughter it, sell most of the meat to consumers, and sell the head, feet, and internal organs to another man who will cook them and peddles this food at beer parties.

SUMMARY

Basic Sebei attitudes toward exchanges, regularly recognizing payments for goods and services, established a climate in which the adaptation to cash transactions was easily made. As a result, cash is a regular element in Sebei daily life. It has entered into such traditional exchanges as the *namanya* contract and the brideprice and is used as payment for services that were formerly paid for in beer or food. The people of Sasur are more deeply involved in the cash economy than are those of Kapsirika in that they have more money, more of them regularly use cash, and they are more dependent upon purchased goods. But this is only a differential in degree, for the Sebei everywhere are dependent upon the cash economy for imported goods and regularly use it in internal economic transactions.

Chapter 8
Women and Men

Our fathers have come,
Have come very slowly
To cut for me my spear.
I shall spear my enemies,
The enemies of my hearth.

Sebei circumcision song

RELATIONSHIPS BEFORE MARRIAGE

In olden times, I was told, girls slept in the house of their grandparents, sleeping next to their grandmothers as a protection from the boys. Only uncircumcised boys or wizards could enter a house and have intercourse with a sleeping girl. Youths, after they were circumcised, built a bachelor's house (*sikerointe*) where several slept together each night. Here they brought their sweethearts to talk, enjoy one another's company, and make love. The boy would lie on the girl, stimulating her sexually by playing his hands over the breasts and caressing the rows of keloids that ran down her abdomen, while she played her hands over the boy's back, ultimately arriving at mutual climax. The penis would be against the girl's vagina and ejaculation between her thighs, for it was not proper for a girl to permit penetration, and most of those not circumcised would fear the public exposure and ridicule at the time of their initiation. The youth was also under restraint, for he would have to pay a fine of two cows for getting an uncircumcised girl pregnant, and, if she died in childbirth, the fine was five cows for "having killed her with his spear." The boy who caused a girl's pregnancy before initiation also had to pay a sheep or goat or tobacco to the woman doing the operation.

A pregnant girl would not be circumcised in the line with the other girls of her group and was expected to become a junior wife of an old man. A young man who married her would be subject to restrictions in warfare — the same as would apply if he married a girl who had cried during the circumcision.

The Baganda, it is said, predicted that when Sebei girls started using soap, eating salt, and wearing European clothes "they would all become harlots," and, according to some, that has happened. The loosening of the sexual code was said to have taken place during Koronkoro times; that is, in the 1930s.

It is doubtful if nowadays any normal boy or girl reaches circumcision a virgin, though it is still considered very bad for an uncircumcised girl to be pregnant, and, if she is, she should not be circumcised with other girls. A pregnant girl is forced by her parents and brothers — by beating if necessary — to name the man responsible. They then call together the boy and his parents and neighbors and force him to pay a fine. If he does so, the child belongs to him. He is not forced to marry the girl, and nowadays her marital opportunities are not affected by this circumstance. If the boy denies paternity, the parents may take a legal case against him. They usually wait until after the child is born, when a number of women determine if it resembles him. The boy may suggest an oath, but this is generally avoided as being too dangerous.

> L's daughter became pregnant and said it was my son. L became angry and demanded payment, but I refused as she had had intercourse with many young men. So L arranged an abortion, and now she is married to H.

If she has the child, and the father has not been determined, it will be given to the grandmother if a girl, but left to die if it is a boy.

Despite these constraints, sexual activity is a major preoccupation of adolescents of both sexes. It is occasionally observed and freely discussed and has the general approval of the parents.

> Parents are always asking to find out if their son is petting with many girls — if so they are very proud. They are also very proud if their daughter is petting with a boy of a very good family. If she is petting with a boy of a bad family, they beat her to make her stop.

As one girl said, if a girl has a clever mother, she can "tie the girl's blood" so that she will not become pregnant. Trysts frequently take place in the home of older people, sometimes the boy's grandparents.

> When you are in the house with an old woman, you wait until the fire goes down, but the old woman may sit and listen to you talking and hear you breathing — but she only smokes her pipe, she doesn't mind. The girl may be shy and want to wait until the old woman is asleep before she agrees to have intercourse.

Arrangements of premarital liaisons have something of the sparring character described among American college students of an earlier era, with no little playing of games and trickery. One man described his activities thus:

> I wait until I see the girl I want along a path and grab her by force and ask her to make a date to pet. The girl may set a time but not keep it. She will promise, "If I don't come, may I sleep with my brother or my uncle." This is a strong oath, but I don't believe her and tell her so. She then says, "If I don't come, may I have intercourse with my father," but I reply, "Your father saw your vagina when you were a young girl; I still don't believe you."

I then ask for the beads she wears around her waist, and if she gives me them, I know she will come. As she has worked all day with nothing to eat, I know she is hungry and will agree if I argue long enough. Then she meets you, and she asks, "Have you brought my beads back?" "Of course," you reply, and then you pet, but if you want more intercourse, you don't give them back until she gives you what you want.

A sixteen-old girl said,

He will send me a note asking me to come to his house, and I will go to find out why he has invited me. He says, "I am anxious to talk to you; when can I pet with you?" and I may refuse, or I may arrange a time. We will arrange to meet in someone's house, where there are other girls; we have the house privately.

We talk together; the boys try to persuade you to have intercourse with them by saying they will marry you. Some girls will agree, others will not. If I refuse intercourse, we just talk. It may take a month to convince the girl to have intercourse, or as long as a year. I may give the boy the beads I wear around my waist as an agreement for future marriage, or my nicest dress. (Boys also try to take these beads by force.) I take his handkerchief or wristwatch.

If you have intercourse right away, you are shamed. You should not do it quickly — and only with one boy. Boys do not fight if their girl is petting with another — they just forget you. If you really want to have a boy marry you, then you should not have intercourse with him or you will come to want it, and if he goes away, you will want to see another boy. If another boy comes near me, I will be excited and have intercourse with him!

These premarital activities bespeak an ambience of tension — tension and deceit between the sexes, tension between the satisfaction of libidinal desires and a concern with pregnancy. This latter relates to the rules with respect to circumcision, with the result that girls are undergoing the rite at an earlier age now than formerly. It also relates to the strong belief that a person — particularly a male — should be of the clan of his genitor. For this reason, uncircumcised girls commonly resort to abortion or allow male children to die. Yet, both sexual prowess and sexual desirability are strongly held values. Some of these attitudes were expressed in answers to Edgerton's questions and values test, as indicated in Table 36. These data show that two-thirds of the respondents believe that men should have premarital sex and nearly half believe that women should; most feel that when a girl is pregnant nothing more than verbal abuse is called for, though the father should either marry the girl or pay a fine. This openness with respect to sex perhaps explains why most respondents did not imagine a sexual outcome to the scene of a man lurking in the bushes watching a woman come down the path.

The attitudes vary somewhat between Sasur and Kapsirika (but there are no significant differences in the responses of men and women to these matters). The Sasurese are generally more permissive than the Kapsirikans toward premarital sex but are more severe in their concern with pregnancy. In conformity with this relative permissiveness, of those who saw the scene

TABLE 36

Attitudes Toward Premarital Sexual Activity

Question asked or scene shown	Sasur	Kapsirika	Total
Should a man have premarital sex? (36)			
Yes	43	33	76
No	15	25	40
Should a woman have premarital sex? (32)			
Yes	35	17	52
No	23	42	65
Action against a pregnant girl (34)			
Scold or do nothing	38	48	86
Be circumcised/get married	19	7	26
Beaten	7	0	7
Action against the father (35)			
Scold or do nothing	7	27	34
Made to marry or fined	57	30	87
Killed	0	1	1
Scene of man hiding as girl passes (VP 7)			
Seen as potentially sexual	19	30	49
Not seen as sexual	45	29	74
Scene of couple on bed (VP 8)			
Seen as adultery	9	28	37
Seen as nonadulterous sex	34	14	48

NOTE: Data obtained by Robert Edgerton. Parenthetical numbers refer to questions asked in RBE, Appendix I and II. VP means value pictures. There were 64 respondents in Sasur and also 64 in Kapsirika. Irrelevant answers are omitted.

of a couple on the bed as being sexual, the Kapsirikans tended to see it as adulterous while the Sasurese more frequently said they were lovers or married.

While in general these responses show a high degree of permissivness (all respondents were married), they do express some of the internal tensions engendered by premarital sexuality among the Sebei, particularly in the double standard in Kapsirika and the greater concern with adultery expressed there, and the greater Sasur concern with establishing marital stability.

CHOICE OF SPOUSE

With increasing frequency, young people marry persons of their choice, though this choice is limited by regulations of kinship, the authority of the woman's father, and economic considerations.

A person may not marry into his own clan, that of his mother, or those of certain great-grandparents. Sometimes, but not always, these regulations apply also to linked clans. Furthermore, a man cannot take a second wife from the clan of his first, and he is not supposed to marry a clan sister of his brothers' wives, but the former rule is sometimes and the latter frequently disregarded. Men from the same lineage should not marry full sisters. In addition, some clans are viewed as generally disadvantageous for marriage and, in particular, some clans are thought to be bad in combination – in the sense that they will not produce children. Finally, a man is specifically enjoined from marrying any daughter of a man of his age-set.

In theory, and in accordance with the whole complex of brideprice negotiations, the father decides who his daughter will marry. Clearly, even the theory was never absolute, for bride capture, on which more below, was a means for circumventing his wish. Nowadays, many couples establish a liaison prior to getting parental permission and a large proportion of recent marriages are of this type. Parental choice of husband was outlawed by the British colonial government, but whether this or other socioeconomic forces brought about the change is not certain. Efforts to control a daughter's marriage certainly have not disappeared entirely (Goldschmidt, 1972a), but I have no true measure of their incidence. I have a feeling that in this the pastoralists are more conservative.

Gale talked to twenty women, mostly around Binyinyi, in 1954 about circumstances surrounding their marriage, the character of choices available, and the way in which the decision was reached. The women ranged in age from the mid-sixties to one who had been married in the preceding month. Three of these women said their parents had forced them to marry against their will; seven said the arrangements had been made by the parents but the women had agreed with nothing more than formal objection; three replied that they had reached an agreement and then gone to their parents; and five had started to live together before arrangements were made. (Information was unavailable on one case, and in the other the parents were dead and arrangements had been unusual.) The three women forced into marriage had all been married by the early 1930s, the five who eloped were married in the early 1940s or later; while the ten for whom marriage was arranged were evenly scattered throughout the period. How did they perceive the alternate possibilities available to them and the manner in which a decision was reached? Of those who were forced by their parents to marry, one said her parents "wouldn't wait for me to find the right man. It took four men to carry me to my husband's house, and they had to come and get me a second time." Another said that she had objected to her husband because he was not baptized, "but my father forced the marriage because this man was ready to pay all the brideprice at once. My mother came to comfort me, saying that I must remain, as the man had already paid everything."

A woman who married a man of her own choice had had six previous offers and said she had rejected them because she did not love them. Concerning her marriage, she said: "We knew each other and decided to marry. After I gave consent, he asked his father to discuss arrangements with my father, and an agreement was reached. Then he brought men and captured me. I fought and cried to show I didn't want to be married, even though I did."

Another had had offers of marriage from four men, of whom two were single and two had prior wives. Her father had objected to her marrying either of the ones she wanted, both of whom were already married, and she had refused to marry either of the single men, saying she did not love them. She and her husband had talked about marriage prior to her final circumcision ceremony, and she was willing but her father had rejected him and told her that if she would not marry the man he chose, she would have to wait a long time. She waited two years. A third had not married three of her suitors because "one of the men was known as a thief, one was known to beat and mistreat his wife, and the third, also married, was unable to pay the brideprice." Though she preferred to be a first wife, the woman would have liked to marry the third man, had he been able to pay, for he did not beat his wife but was known to be kind to her.

A number of women who had begun staying with their husbands before any arrangements had been made reported that their father, rather than the father of the groom, as is customary, had initiated discussion regarding payment.

When Edgerton asked the basis for choice of spouse, he found no significant differentiation between Sasur and Kapsirika, but the answers are of interest (Table 37). Men overwhelmingly answer that women want to marry a rich man; women also say so, but not so frequently. Women consider love

TABLE 37
Basis of Desirability of Marriage Partner

| Basis of choice | Choice for husband (21) | | Choice for wife (29) | | Total |
	Male resp.	Female resp.	Male resp.	Female resp.	
Rich/good family	28	13	0	1	42
Love	10	27	12	23	72
Handsome/pretty	7	6	9	13	35
Sexuality	5	1	18	9	33
Character/hard working	3	5	8	4	20

NOTE: Data obtained by Robert Edgerton. Parenthetical numbers refer to questions in RBE, Appendix II. Rich for husbands; good family for wives; handsome for husbands, pretty for wives. Sexuality refers to sexual competence or fertility.

to be the most important basis for choice, both in choosing their husbands and in being chosen. (By contrast, 120 of 125 Kamba respondents expressed preference for rich husbands, while 182 of 245 Pokot responses expressed preference for pretty/handsome spouses.) Sebei men, on the other hand consider sexual competence, by which they usually mean fertility, to be the most important criterion for a wife. Edgerton also discussed the basis of choice with several boys and girls and gained the clear impression that behavioral traits are more important than either physical ones or economic status. Politeness, kindness, ability to speak properly, and capability are most often mentioned. This is not to say that they do not have criteria for beauty and discuss members of the opposite sex in these terms. "We consider each girl as we meet them and agree on how pretty they are. If I do this alone, other boys would not agree with me and they would tease me."

In one of the women's accounts, we saw an example of bride capture. This was once a regular form of establishing a marital tie, though it is not possible now to get any true measure of its frequency. In the instance noted, the couple had apparently made the arrangement as a means of pressuring the parents. The tactic does not always persuade the parents to accept a marriage the couple desires. The following description of a raid in about 1915 is that of one of the men who participated in it. Perhaps the girl acquiesced to the plan; at least, she accepted the results.

> Sikoria lived near the Chaptui River. He thought of marrying a girl named Koibi from Kamogo, but not of settling the matter with her parents first. He brought together a group of thirteen boys, some for taking the girl and some for preventing the neighbors from stopping them; he did not take more because most of the people in Kamogo were of his own clan.
>
> They first sent a spy, who went very secretly so as not to be seen and found that the girl was home with her father and mother. Before they could attack the girl, they had to determine which man had no *tekso* [tabu] relationship with her mother, so he could hold her. Sikoria remained behind. The others went very quickly; the man selected held the mother, somebody else the father, and the others disappeared with the girl. Nobody followed, but they knew who the young man was who wanted to marry this girl. The mother wanted to curse the route they took, but the father refused, saying, "They aren't going to slaughter your daughter. If we don't want them to marry, we will get her back."
>
> Koibi did not mind. Though she cried in alarm when she was seized and made no sign of love, she nevertheless went on eating and serving meals. If she had not wanted to marry the man, she would not have done that and would have found an opportunity to run away.
>
> In those days, when a girl was captured in this manner, the man was not supposed to have intercourse with the girl, though they sleep together on one hide. If the mother objects to the marriage, she will send for her daughter, but, if not, the boy's family will initiate arrangements to pay the brideprice after three or four days have passed. Then they can have intercourse, though the girl will first demand to be given an animal, normally a bullock or a heifer, before she consents. The mother did not object later, and they were married. Sikoria paid a brideprice, but in those days it was very low.

But not every wife capture was based upon such an agreement; in the next description, the husband (who told the story) made secret arrangements with the girl's father.

> I went to the parents of the girl and tried to arrange to marry her; they accepted me and I paid half the brideprice, but she didn't want to come with me. So I got together four friends. The parents let me take her; nobody

helped her. My four friends carried her, and I went behind and picked up things that fell down — clothes and beads. I had to kill two hens for them and the next day had to buy beer for them. I had to stay with her night and day until she became pregnant — that was her handcuff.

Because it is now illegal to force a daughter to marry against her will, and also because women can now, with adequate cause, initiate divorce proceedings that would require return of the brideprice, it is not easy to find examples of parents forcing a daughter into an unwanted marriage. I was witness to two attempts, both of them ultimately unsuccessful. In both instances, the father had accepted part of the brideprice and was using both persuasion and beating to try to make the girl agree; in both instances, the girl had a strong aversion to the man her father had chosen and was more concerned about avoiding that marriage than about marrying a man of her choice (each preferred another man). In both instances, also, it required great personal strength and obdurance on the woman's part to withstand the sustained pressure. In each instance also, the mother appeared essentially to side with her daughter but took no overt action in her behalf. (Goldschmidt, 1972a)

The weakening of parental authority, however, is best expressed in the increased pattern of "elopement," to use the interpreters' gloss for those instances in which the couple establish their liaison and legalize it later. In the sample of brideprice payments recorded in 1962 and covering the preceding fifty years, the first elopement took place in 1936. Elopements were rare in the 1940s (five instances) and became frequent in the 1950s (nineteen out of forty-two contracts, or 45 percent). They were somewhat more frequent in Sasur (seven of thirteen) than in Kapsirika (twelve of twenty-nine), but the difference is not statistically significant.

Neither the wife capture in the past nor the elopement of today entirely destroys the authority of the father, though both certainly diminish it. The fact that legalization of the marriage, with its important implications for the social position of the children, depends upon negotiating the brideprice, leaves some leverage to the father.

The dominant theme in the interpersonal relationships of the unmarried is antagonism; sexual relationships are enjoyed not only in a libidinal sense, but as counters in this battle of the sexes. Men are always on the make, and are willing to use any means for the conquest of the women. Rape is not recognized as possible among the Sebei unless more than one man is involved, and this kind of rape and subsequent gang shag is not an infrequent occurrence (*SL*:136). The taking of the beaded girdle is more than a mere pawn, which would prove embarrassing to the girl when her mother found it missing; it is highly vulnerable to efforts at magic and no simple token of affection or earnest on a promise. The girls play into this game; they also score by having the boys want them and tease them along with wiles, promises, and duplicity. Since they also want the libidinal satisfaction, believing that once they have had sexual relations with a boy they can no longer control their passions, they ultimately acquiesce. In these attitudes, the young people are encouraged by their elders. (Seduction has with justification been defined as persuading a person to do what he wants to do.) The old woman sucking on her pipe while the couple is making love a few feet away is undoubtedly obtaining vicarious satisfactions and must be seen as encouraging them. The popularity of children is important to parents, who encouarge this sexual gamesmanship.[1]

Edgerton's investigations showed that men most often say that women seek a rich man as husband, while women respond that they seek a man they love and assume that they are sought on the basis of this personalized motivation (though the men do not say so). Love is a word not easily defined, but we get some insight from women's discussions with Gale. Sebei love is not the singular, made-in-heaven attachment of Western romantic fiction, because these women spoke of loved ones in the plural. It must indicate the importance of personal choice and attachment. Yet, the men credit the women with only ulterior motives.

NEGOTIATION OF BRIDEPRICE

The amount and character of the brideprice is the result of negotiations between representatives of the man and the father of the woman. The brideprice is necessary to legitimize the marriage and, more importantly, the children. The amount varies widely, as does the way in which an agreement is reached, but a transfer of goods, and particularly of cattle, is essential (though during the terrible years around 1900, many contracts called only for *warek*). Even for inherited widows, or for a divorcée who may still have children, one cow should be transferred. If the couple has eloped, or if the woman has been captured, the negotiation takes place subsequently, but in the same manner and with the same presumption that an agreement may not be reached. In some instances (usually involving divorcées) there is no true negotiation, though a payment is still made. After an elopement, the woman's family may take the husband's or his father's cattle in a raid; this was also sometimes done in earlier years after a woman was taken by force.

Traditional Sebei brideprice consisted of cattle, a sheep or goat for the mother's brother, an iron hoe and an iron bracelet for the mother, beer, tobacco, and perhaps some clotted milk. Many other items have become standard additions. Cash was introduced at least by 1915, where it first appears on my schedules. Blankets, army coats, cloth for women's dresses, and *sufurias* (aluminum pots) were generally used in the 1920s. Other items appearing in the schedules include hats, *kanzus* (men's robes), iron pans, mosquito nets, lamps, kerosene, and *waragi* (native gin).

In truly polite and traditional usage, the boy's representatives will call on the girl's father during her seclusion after circumcision and speak his purpose

---

1. If these attitudes and activities seem familiar, it is because they are characteristic of our own culture (see, for instance, Henry, 1963). Ethnography is so often the depiction of the exotic that really familiar events may be overlooked, a kind of ethnographic "purloined letter."

only after being asked at the close of the visit, and then by circumlocution: "I have come to beg something from this house." And after further prodding: "I want to have kinship with this house." When the host enquires if he wants a bullock (in *tilyet* exchange, for the protocol is the same), he replies, "I came to see about a lamb whose tail has been cut." He should bring beer and might also make presents, such as a bullock, which ultimately becomes part of the brideprice. Such preliminary enquiries give the family ample time to discuss the candidacy and learn more about the family, if necessary.

Modern practices generally appear to be more informal. While three of S's daughters (who lived in Kapsirika) were still in seclusion, a suitor for one of them appeared one day when I was present, along with S's two sons. According to S (who may have been exaggerating somewhat to impress the suitor or me), four men had called on him for the first daughter, three for the second, and two for the third. None of the girls wanted any of the men, for each had a man she favored who had not yet declared himself. S said he was prepared to meet the desire of the first girl, whose mother had just died, because he "didn't want to upset her," but the other two would have to obey him and marry the men he chose — perhaps the new suitor would be the husband of one. At this, the sons became very angry, describing the new suitor as a bad man who mistreats his brothers-in-law. They added that his clan had "married many of our daughters, including one who is our real sister, so we don't want to give this clan any more of our daughters." To this S responded angrily that the sons should not interfere with matters pertaining to his daughters — "Have your own daughters and do what you like with them." The suitor pointed out that S's clan had a daughter of the suitor's clan and added, "If you don't let us have one, I will curse your sister." One son responded that he had already heard the suitor was going to bewitch the family if S didn't let the suitor have a daughter, and the other son turned to S and said: "If you force the girl to marry, we will arrange with a young man to elope with her." With that, the two sons stalked off.

I had described to me another custom that expresses symbolically the girl's growing freedom of choice. The custom was borrowed from the Bantu in the 1950s, but I do not know how widely it is used. After the brideprice has been negotiated, the man sends her a new basket containing the following items: 60 shillings, a 2-shilling bar of soap, two pounds of sugar, two cakes of Sunlight soap, one bar of Lux soap, one box of matches, one package of Crownbird cigarettes, a 2-shilling jar of vaseline, a 5-shilling piece of cloth, a 3-shilling purse, and a 1-shilling handkerchief. A single cigarette is put on top. When this package is given to the girl, she will light the cigarette before looking at the contents if she is willing to marry. She is then anointed with ghee and garlanded with vines and given over to her husband. The practice is apparently limited to the Sipi area.

If the father of the girl agrees, he will arrange to have the groom's representative — his father or brother — appear for a bargaining session (*koyeito,* or *koryet ap ketik,* breaking the sticks). The suitor is not supposed to be present. The representative brings beer to the house of the bride's mother, where he will be greeted by the girl's father and a neighbor and such others as may be desired. There is a kind of adversary character to the negotiation of brideprice; the bride's father tries to maximize his satisfactions, while the groom is justly fearful of excessive cost or even defeat.

In 1954, I had had no opportunity to observe a negotiation for brideprice, so I induced a number of Sebei men to enact one. This role-playing proved an effective device for getting the Sebei view of standard expectations in such an event, actually more appropriate to generalization than the particular instances recorded on my later visit, and I therefore reproduce the protocol.

We gather in the small house and settle ourselves. Two suitors' representatives are to appear and ask to "break the sticks." The girl's father has invited his brother, who lives at a great distance, and told him that both suitors want to marry his daughter and the brother should send one of them away. He has also invited a neighbor. The suitors' representatives arrive at the same time but are dealt with separately.

After some discussion, the brother rejects the first offer, telling the representative, "There is nothing to say but that Mangusho should be sent away and Yona should remain, because Yona is a very kind man and very generous to his friends." Mangusho's representative: "That is all right; I am not sorry. I will leave as ordered, but if this other man is defeated by the brideprice, then I will come back." He leaves, and Yona's representative, his father, enters, accompanied by his neighbor.

The girl's father's brother goes out to get ankurwet sticks from the bush, breaks them into six-inch pieces, and places them by his side. He puts eight sticks in front of him: five to represent heifers that have never calved, one to represent a cow with a calf, one for a bull, and one for the bull for the mother's brother.

The boy's representative and neighbor discuss this and then indicate acceptance of three heifers, the cow, and the two bulls but push aside the other tallies. The neighbor of the girl's father asks, "Why do you push these away? Perhaps you are not really going to come to this house to marry our daughter."

The boy's representative then cites precedent, saying he has always visited houses where the number is four, to which the girl's father responds, "If you are unable to pay, you may go away." But the boy's neighbor tells the girl's father that in a recent bargain two men had agreed to take that many cattle, and that his daughter's marriage did not mean he would no longer receive anything [for a man continues to be obligated to his father-in-law]. He urges the girl's father to agree.

Both sides finally compromise on the four heifers, the cow with calf, a bullock, and a bull for the mother's brother. (In an aside, I was told that the price is charged according to what the person can afford to pay.)

After this agreement has been reached, the tallies are set aside and the goats and sheep are discussed. The neighbor of the girl's family sets out six sticks in three pairs, a seventh stick (representing a castrated he-goat) alongside them, then an eighth stick, and finally one for the mother's brother. The boy's representative pushes away one of the original sticks and one of the last three. They finally agree on a total of eight, and these tallies are put aside.

The girl's father's neighbor next puts out six sticks to represent 600 shillings, the boy's representative takes three away, indicating a willingness to pay 300 shillings, but the girl's father's neighbor quickly puts one back, saying, "You eat me too much." After further discussion, they agree on 400 shillings, and these tallies are put to the side.

The girl's people then put out sticks representing 40 shillings for the mother and 20 shillings for the mother's brother. There are no arguments, and these sticks are put with the other tallies. Then the girl's father's brother takes more sticks, which he identifies as follows: two to represent heavy blankets, one for the girl's father and one for her mother; one representing the blanket for the girl's grandmother [this usually goes to her mother's mother but in the case of a second daughter may go to the father's mother]; one for sheeting six yards long; one for a *kanzu* for the father. He starts to add another stick for a pair of trousers. All but the last are readily accepted. Next, two sticks are put out, one for a big aluminum pot and another for a hoe; neither is questioned.

Then he puts down a stick indicating thirty chickens and another for five chickens for the girl's mother's brother. Because this has been done since Sowe times, there is no discussion. Similarly with a five-gallon tin of tobacco. Again sticks are put out, two for two bags of dried beer mash for the girl's father and one for her mother's brother, and are accepted.

> *Father:* Now you have seen that we agree that people should marry our daughter but perhaps later on somebody might bring complaints.
>
> *Grandmother [Who had remained silent at the back of the house]:* Really, as you have judged the brideprice, I am not one to say anything, but if I had any opinion, I would not have accepted it.
>
> *Father [angrily]:* Why do you say that you would not allow this to take place? By what means do you say that?
>
> *Grandmother:* At the time that the Baganda came here, some women were appointed to go help on the job. We were all being made to carry things but the father of this man here saw me with a little girl who was sick and he went right on beating me and didn't pay any attention to what I had to say, and he didn't think that this little girl of mine would grow up and provide a wife for him.
>
> *Boy's father:* I was just a government servant and was doing that for the sake of the government.
>
> *Girl's father's neighbor:* Doesn't the government know that nobody can compete with illness?
>
> *Grandmother:* My opinion is that these people should not be accepted because, though you have judged the price between you, they did that very bad thing a long time ago.
>
> *Girl's father's neighbor:* Truly, grandmother of this girl, if what you have said is true, you should have said it before the sticks were broken. Now that these things are arranged we should not send this man away, but we

should ask him to pay a fine because he could not see that the child was sick. What do you think, Uncle?

Girl's father's brother: This man did a very shameful thing, beating a woman when her child was sick. I think the suitable fine is one heifer.

Boy's father: Some people make mistakes without knowing the future. Since this is so, why not just fine me a goat.

Grandmother: This was a really bad thing. If I had died or if my daughter had died, where would you come to get a wife? If you want to accept this, well I don't want a goat. It will just end in the house of a hyena. If you want me to accept this, I will agree on one heifer.

Girl's father: It is up to you to say what you will do. This was your mistake. You have seen the girl's grandmother refuse the goat. It is up to you to pay the heifer or to go away.

Boy's father [addressing aide]: What shall I do, neighbor?

Boy's father's neighbor: Sometimes we do things and we do not know what will happen in the future. Let us accept it.

Grandmother: The heifer for the fine should be the first one that we receive.

Girl's father: When there is bargaining, there should always be beer and tobacco. We should have some tobacco and beer. So long as no one has provided us with beer, let us have tobacco.

With this I realized that the bargaining was over, it was up to me to supply the tobacco.

Both negotiations witnessed in 1962 followed this course of action, the real ones taking little longer than the enacted one, and both were characterized by the same formality. In one, the representatives of the groom had anticipated higher charges against them and the possibility of a fine, but the bride's father, an old man who had served as a chieftan in the early days of European contact, was mellow and kindly and asked for fewer cattle than his representative had proposed. A man of wealth, he had six wives (and had had many others) and one of his sons estimated he had about a hundred siblings. There was no talk of a fine, and the groom, according to whispered conversations while the hosts were out of the room, paid less than he and his representatives had agreed they were willing to pay. Still, they engaged in the bargaining with vigor. I felt that perhaps the father's generosity was for my benefit.

The other instance involved a school teacher who had eloped with a schoolgirl — both were thus relatively acculturated. After the agreement had been reached (*SL*:44n), the bride's father raised the matter of a fine as follows:

Bride's father: I think you have finished [the negotiations] now, but I have something to say. There is a case I want to take against these gentlemen. Here is the case: these people have snatched my daughter, and I have lost my year's school fees. I started to take a case against them in the gombolola court, but I have decided not to do so, and to bring the case here. I had best bring this case here because, if you do not settle the matter, even though the sticks have been broken, nothing will be done [i.e., the marriage will not take place]. I can refuse everything that has been discussed. I have sent my daughter to school for many years. I spent a lot of money on school fees for

her. I sent her to school so that if she got married and then the time came
that she wanted a divorce, she would be able to earn a living for herself.
Last year she finished primary schooling and went on to secondary school. I
spent the fees for the whole year. In the middle of the year, my son-in-law
waited by the side of the road and persuaded her to remain away. He is an
educated man who should know better. He could have arranged the marriage later and written to her, instead of spoiling her schooling. So you must
agree on this matter. This is the only meeting place where we can settle this.

Groom's brother [who was in charge of negotiations]: My father, I am
pleased that you were patient enough to wait until today with this matter.
Had you brought this before the government, my brother's job might have
been spoiled.

The girl's father then told how his wife had tried to bring a case in court
but was refused, and concluded by saying: "In all my years I have seen many
boys and girls, and you never find girls fighting with their father, but the
sons do. I sent my girl to school so she could help me when I am old."

The groom's brother admitted the mistake, appealed to the precedent that
a person who pleads guilty before a court is sometimes excused, and asked
that the fine be waived.

Father: Don't think that I don't want the girl to marry this boy. I am only
complaining about my money. If I could arrange for her to continue her
schooling and get her certificate, that would be all right. A certificate
would be valuable to my daughter. She may be insulted in the future
because she has no certificate. Had she finished, both of these young
people could be working and they could help their children. These two
young people are now good friends because they were just married, but
later they will get annoyed with one another and the girl will be abused.
People will blame me for not educating her properly. That is why I must
have my money returned; it is only part of what I would get for her. If I
ask her for something, her husband might fight her over it. But if she were
earning money, she could give me as she wishes. I have already told you
that I have been very kind; I could have taken a case before the school
officials or the court. Therefore, I am not going to excuse you.

You must realize that she has lost her chance for a school certificate.
Therefore I regard my daughter as one who has been speared. When they
quarrel, she will come home crying, "Father!" But I will send her away for
she has asked for her trouble, and then she may go out and hang herself.

After extensive discussion by all persons present, a fine of 450 shillings was
agreed upon.

Father: I want this money before the brideprice is paid. If it is refused, then
I will take a case against my son-in-law. If you do not pay the 450 shillings, I will not accept the brideprice. This case has been heard in my
house. If it is not paid, I will take it to another house. My son-in-law is a
grown man and has an education; he has been hearing people cry about
nurses and so on that are needed, and now he has stopped her education.
This brideprice is a normal one even for a girl who has not been educated.
But compare this girl to one who is not educated — this is really a great
loss.

In both instances, the bride's father and the groom had others negotiating, and neither bride nor groom was present. This is the general custom but is often not followed. In a series of schedules on brideprice (on which more below), I asked who was present at the negotiation. My informants could detail for me the participants in 61 instances on the groom's side and 52 on the bride's. These data reveal the following:

1. Bride's father is generally present (80 percent); groom's father usually for groom's first marriage, but only in 55 percent of all marriages.

2. Bride's father's brothers are almost always present (92 percent), but groom's father's brother is infrequently so (25 percent).

3. The groom was present in thirty-five instances (55 percent) but most of these were second marriages.

4. Neighbors representing the bride's father were present in 67 percent of the cases; those representing the groom came less frequently (35 percent).

5. The groom's brother is frequently present (30 percent) particularly for second marriages but also as a surrogate for an unavailable father. The bride's brother is rarely present (21 percent).

6. There is very little participation by more distantly related members of either clan (six instances on groom's side, eight on bride's).

7. The mother's brother is present very rarely (one instance on each side), and the only other representatives of the mother's clan were the mothers themselves (13 percent of groom's and 10 percent of the bride's) and, in one instance, the mother's sister.

8. The sister's husband was present in five instances on the groom's side and two on the bride's.

9. Women take a very small part in these negotiations (about 7 percent of all participants). Two of these were senior wives of the groom.

In bargaining, the sex of the animal may be specified, and in Sipi they specifically request one cow along with her new calf, but the particular animals are not examined.[2] As with contractual exchanges, if the animal dies or is not productive, it must be replaced. The cows will be turned over at a later time. The delay in the payment may be quite extended; I knew a man over forty with three wives who, after some fifteen years, had not completed the payment for the first. The cattle are not transferred in the dry season, and they are taken to their new home so as to arrive in the evening, after the birds are asleep, for the birds, they say, might fly in from behind and bring an evil omen. If the distance is great, the trip may be made as if they were being grazed, but they are not brought to the kraal until dusk. The bulls received in brideprice should not be retained as bulls but should be exchanged for heifers or used in turn for brideprice by the recipient or his sons.

The negotiations result in a formal contract — nowadays often signed (Plate III:29). Between whom is this contractual arrangement? One way of

2. Certain cattle should not be paid in brideprice: those without horns (*karo*) or with cropped tail (*chemutul*) or ears (*chemichir*), striped (*somu*), with mixed black and white hair tails (*lilet*), or brown cattle with black around eyes (*tuweich konya*).

answering this question is to determine who pays and who receives the stock and other goods transferred. It is the obligation of a man's father to furnish the cattle for his son's first wife, and nobody is obligated to help him. His brothers or other kin may either loan him stock or give an animal, but this is not an obligation. For subsequent wives, a man is expected to furnish the cattle himself, though frequently his father will assist. It is proper for a man to request animals from his brother or uncle, but neither is obliged to comply. Table 38 shows that almost all the animals were provided by either the father or the groom, and that in only four instances were other kindred directly involved. (The instances of the use of sisters' brideprice are those that went almost directly from one contract payment to the other; in other instances, cattle were used that had once been part of a brideprice.)

TABLE 38
Source of Cattle Used in Brideprice Payments

Source of cattle[a]	No. of contributors[b]			Cattle contributed[c]		
	Sasur	Kapsirika	Total	Sasur	Kapsirika	Total
Father	14	17	31	55	98	153
Self	9	20	29	22	103	125
Inheritance	1	5	6	1	35	36
Sister's brideprice	2	1	3	6	2	8
Brother or other kin	1	3	4	1	8	9
Totals				85	246	331

SOURCE: Brideprice questionnaires taken in 1961-62 from men on marriages in Sasur and marriages in Kapsirika.

[a]In relation to the groom.

[b]Some payments had more than one contributor. Information on this question obtained on 22 Sasur marriages and 37 Kapsirika marriages.

[c]Excludes payments still due and other instances where information is lacking.

The recipient of the cattle is chiefly the father of the bride; he is supposed to give one animal to his brother, but this is not regularly done.[3] One bullock (formerly a ram) is given to the bride's mother's brother, and, as other items have entered into the formal obligations, other near kin (always the mother, but sometimes the siblings of the girl's parents, or her grandparents) are given something. The mother is now frequently given an animal ("for the mother's milk"), but nobody else receives stock directly. These patterns suggest that the contractual arrangements are between the immediate kin of the principals, not the wider kin-groups. The largest heifer or cow, called *chemwai*, is supposed to be allocated to the mother of the bride, or if she is dead, to the woman who has been the bride's surrogate mother. The

---

3. A woman who has neither father nor brothers will simply go to live with a man; there will be no ceremony and no brideprice, for somebody outside her family would receive it. She cannot be a first wife but will be second wife even to her husband's wife by a subsequent marriage.

second largest (or the largest one of the second daughter) is called *syema*, but there is no specific allocation. The bull received, no matter how fine, cannot be used to service cows, for if it produce offspring the bride would be prevented from conceiving, so it must either be slaughtered or castrated. This animal (or the one received in exchange for it) is to be kept among the father's *tokapsoi.* Within the household, each wife should receive (or at least have the use of) one heifer produced by the brideprice animals, as these are born. However, this is not regularly done now.

Though the contract involves immediate kin only, it is true that her husband's clan has a right to the woman. She will be inherited by his closest possible relative. The clan expects to receive the product of her potential fecundity. While the immediate purpose of a man's marriage is to acquire a spouse, the broader aim is to preserve and strengthen the clan.

Brideprice is by no means standard, though the Sebei will speak as if it were. It varies with the time, place, and circumstance of the marriage, and also ,with the prevailing sentiments regarding the liaison. On the series of schedules involving seventy-nine negotiations, I found payments ranging from one to seventeen cows and brideprice values ranging from 288 shillings to 2,943 shillings. Detailed analysis of these data has appeared elsewhere (Goldschmidt, 1973a, 1974), so I will merely summarize the conclusions.

1. Over the fifty-year period, there is a general upward trend from 2.4 cattle and a total value of 654 shillings in 1910-19 to 8.5 cattle and 1,540 shillings in the 1956-60 period. A slight dip in the 1930s appears to reflect depression conditions.

2. Livestock is a relatively constant proportion (about 60 percent) of the total brideprice but increases in relative significance in Kapsirika and declines in Sasur. Cash increases in importance from about 10 percent of the total brideprice in the early period to nearly 25 percent in the last.

3. Men in Kapsirika pay a consistently higher brideprice than men in Sasur, reflecting the greater scarcity of women in Kapsirika because of the higher incidence of polygyny on the plains. In general, women from areas where pastoralism is more important than horticulture require higher payments than women from areas where farming dominates, presumably for the same reason. In response to these differentials, Kapsirika men marry women from the farming area, but Sasur men rarely take wives from cattle areas and never from the plains.

4. All men defer payments, but the outstanding indebtedness in Sasur is nearly twice as great (34.3 percent of the contracts of the final decade) as in Kapsirika (18.4 percent).

5. When the couple elope prior to negotiations, the brideprice is somewhat higher, but the difference does not meet tests of statistical significance.

6. When the bride's brothers raid the groom's kraal for cattle after elopement, the number taken are consistent with the total brideprice of the period or, if not, negotiations will follow to make it so.

7. Divorcées consistently command a lower brideprice than girls marrying for the first time.

8. Sebei believe they pay more for polygynous than for first marriages, but this is not consistently the case. They pay less for second marriages but more for third and subsequent ones. Men often take divorcées for polygynous unions to reduce the cost. The highest payments, however, are found when older men take a young woman as a third or subsequent wife.

9. Men who take additional wives are in measurably better economic status than those who do not. Men with two wives were more affluent than those with one; men with three or more wives were still more affluent.

All of these conclusions are consistent with the thesis that brideprice reflects economic factors. Sentiment is not irrelevant. A man who falls in love with a particular woman will marry her if he can possibly afford it ("the brideprice was very high, but I wanted the woman very much"), and a daughter with strength and determination may override the will of her father. Yet one cannot help but be impressed with the strong element of economy-mindedness that characterizes this important aspect of interpersonal relationships.

RITUAL ASPECTS OF MARRIAGE

The full panoply of wedding rites involves a series of events that begin when the groom brings the bride to his house and end when she has made a ceremonial visit to her natal home. In between, the bride goes through a period of ritual seclusion and restriction reminiscent of the liminal period of initiation. The rituals involve specific kindred and clearly express the altered social relationships that the marriage brings about. This account is based on generalized descriptions, on what several young women told Gale in 1954 about their weddings, and on the final ritual of one, which we witnessed.

After the brideprice has been settled, the groom goes with a close friend to bring the bride to his house. She goes with a show of reluctance, whether or not she desires the marriage, and they proceed slowly. She brings along a friend, or friends, ideally unmarried age-mates. As they cross a stream, she refuses to continue, demanding from her new husband a gift, ideally a heifer that will be part of her sector of the herd. When she enters his house, the bride will continue to demonstrate her reluctance by refusing to eat. She is fed by her mother-in-law and should be well-treated. The groom is expected to seek a calabash of clotted milk, a great delicacy. If the bride does not want her husband, she may have to be watched so that she does not run away.

The bride is in a period of seclusion and tabu (*chekerteko*). She is under dietary restrictions, particularly against eating meat and native salt; she is not supposed to do any useful work such as milking, fetching water, or cooking; she is not supposed to bathe, be shaved, nor speak in a loud voice. She should remain inside the house, but it is not clear whether or not she may be seen by others. The bride has sent to her home for a couple of young girls who act as *mwenik* and take care of her personal needs. During this period, the couple engages in sexual intercourse. This period should last at least four days (three for a twin).

Partial release from seclusion (*yotunet*) involves a series of minor ritual acts on the fourth day or some time later. The small ceremony (*ŋololyunet*) involves neighbor women or kinswomen of the groom or his mother. (In this, and in all other matters, the role of the groom's mother may be taken by his senior wife in polygynous marriages.) These women are fed by the mother-in-law and tell the bride: "We want this man to marry you and you must regard him as your husband; anything he demands you must give. Don't let your husband go without food or he may become weak. Don't be rude to your husband but obey all his orders. During your menstrual period, don't sleep with him on the same skin but sleep away from him." (In the Sipi area, she is not supposed to cook for him, but this is not the custom in the east.) A sister of the groom brings lepeywontet plant, which is boiled in water; cow's urine is added to this, and the sister, the bride, and her *mwenik* all bathe in this mixture. The sisters-in-law of the bride then "instruct" the bride in the performance of household duties; together they prepare a thick porridge, some of which is tied with sinentet vines to the stirring paddle and taken outside the house. A brother of the groom takes this away and eats it. Thereafter, the bride may engage in normal work but she still may not eat meat or speak in a loud voice.

The brother of the groom then or later engages in a small but highly significant ceremonial act of changing the bracelets (*kokewolyi karik*). I was told that this ritual marks the legalization of the marriage; after this ceremony, dissolution of the marriage would require divorce proceedings. The brother removes a bracelet from the bride's right arm and puts it on his; he then moves one from her left arm to her right arm. If she has no bracelets, sinentet vine may be substituted. The groom's father may not be present; the groom may be there, but usually is not, as "he is not interested." The act must certainly be viewed as binding the woman not merely to her husband but to his clan.

At some time during the bride's seclusion, especially if she shows great reluctance in her new role, the groom's mother will invite the sisters of the bride's mother and other female kin to a small feast called *kapokerto*, a term implying retaliation. For this, a goat should be slaughtered and beer provided. Presents are given to the girl's aunts. (In 1954, the standard amount was 5 shillings to a true sister of each parent and 2 shillings to others; aboriginally, it was bracelets or neck rings.) The women admonish the bride to remain with her husband because they have received things.

The closing of the period of seclusion may be delayed for weeks or months. It begins with a most important ritual, the return of the bride to her natal home (*kawoktayet*) (Plates III:27-29, 31-33). We witnessed this ceremony in Atar and Tuban in July 1954.

When we arrived at the groom's house about noon, we learned that the bride had returned alone to her natal home early in the morning because of the death of her father's brother to be smeared with chyme from a he-goat slaughtered by her father. When she returned to her husband's house (about 1:00 P.M.) ritual bathing took place in that part of the house where the goats are kept.[4] The groom's mother cooked large quantities of maize meal, which was served with sour milk mixed with sweet milk. After eating, everyone went outside and the groom's mother brought three large gourds of sour milk and decorated them with sinentet vines. The groom's sister, the bride, and the *mwenik* wore garlands across the chest, and the groom's mother, his senior wife, and his father's sister arranged a crown of the vine upon their heads. The bride, her sister, and the groom's sister had the gourds of sour milk loaded onto their backs. A bottle of sesame oil, in lieu of butter, was brought and the groom's mother anointed his sister, the bride, and the *mwenik,* as well as the five girls who had recently been circumcised at this home. The neighbor women and the small girls of the household were given sesame oil and green vaseline with which they anointed themselves. The group formed a procession and went about 100 yards before stopping to sing a clan song.

The party arrived at the bride's home after 6:00 P.M., having walked several miles (Plate III:31). As they heard the singing in the distance, the relatives and neighbors of the bride's mother took up green sticks and practiced mock fighting in a good humored way; when the party came to within about a hundred yards, the bride's relatives and neighbors went out to meet them and struck at their legs with the sticks. The women — only women are involved — went at this with considerable zest and vigor (Plate III:32).[5] After about 5 minutes of scuffling, the bride's relatives and neighbors lined up on the path and her mother's mother placed a stick across the path (Plate III:33). The bridal party began to sing, but the local women stopped it. An old woman said, "Don't keep on singing. Pay us first before you sing." The groom's women replied that they hadn't brought anything but finally came up with 1 shilling, which they handed to the bride's mother's mother. Other women called out, "Don't agree to accept 1 shilling," and the old woman threw it down contemptuously but finally picked it up, agreeing to accept it. The stick was removed from across the path and the groom's mother moved on down toward the bride's mother's house.

The bride was now covered with a cloth (as she should have been as she left her husband's home). The bridal party formed a line and began singing and moved forward along the path. Near the house, they were met by the local women and the groups faced each other. First the bridal party advanced, while the other women retreated; then the reverse. The lines went back and forth, four times, singing the standard Sebei song of welcome. The bride's father's brother's wife danced with a basket of maize in her hand.

Everyone then stood around uncomfortably, especially the three women who were burdened with the heavy gourds of milk, while a long argument

4. The order of bathing was: classificatory sister of groom, bride, bride's full sister, bride's half-sister, bride's classificatory sister, three *mwenik* (all bride's classificatory sisters).

5. I was told that the severity of this mock battle was dependent upon how the bride had been treated. I felt it reflected an attitude of hostility, which was later given verbal expression.

took place. The groom's party demanded money for the milk the bride had brought, and the ceremonies could not proceed until this was settled.[6]

Ultimately, the bride's father walked up and in a loud and angry voice said, "Unless you pay the 5 shillings, you may not take the milk. Someone who has 5 shillings may take it." The groom's father's second wife then harshly said to pay quickly, because the bride was very tired. The bride's mother's brother's wife promised to pay.

Everyone then sang briefly the song of uncovering the bird, and the bride's father's clan sister uncovered the bride and anointed her with sesame oil. The groom's sister was next anointed, then the groom's mother and the *mwenik*. The gourds of milk were removed from the three women and taken into the house. Beads were then placed around the head of the bride, and a piece of serechontet grass was stuck into them at the center of the forehead and pressed down so they lay over the head.

Now the groom's party could enter the house. The old woman who was supposed to spew milk (from a black cow) on them as they entered had refused to do so because she had received nothing from the brideprice, so a young woman performed this duty. The party entered and backed out four times, each time receiving a blessing, and then they were asked "to bend their knees," i.e., to sit down. They did so, but the *mwenik* soon rose and ran out.

When all were settled, the bride's father's brother's wife asked the groom's women for tobacco, claiming the bride's relatives had been neglected. The groom's women responded that they had sought to buy tobacco but could not find any. If the bride's women wished, and knew where tobacco could be purchased, they would go home and fetch the money (obviously now quite impossible). The bride's father's brother's wife said to the groom's father's second wife, "I have never had your beer or your tobacco." Response: "Have I ever closed my door to you? You haven't had my beer or tobacco because you have never come to my house."

At this point in the rituals, the two families eat together, after which the bride has an opportunity to complain to her family about any mistreatment she may have suffered at the hands of her husband, mother-in-law, or co-wife. If she has any complaints, her parents will admonish the representative of her husband's family, saying that if she is not treated better, they will take her back. Maize, plantains, and sour milk furnished by neighbors were served, but, after eating, the bride's mother again brought up the matter of tobacco, demanding either tobacco or money with which to buy cigarettes. She then initiated a long discussion about the grievance of the bride's father's mother, who had refused to be present. The grandmother had demanded 4 shillings. Both families agreed that they had never heard of a grandmother demanding anything (though if she paid a visit to the bride's new family, and the groom was generous, he might give her something). Nevertheless, the bride's mother asked her daughter to bring 4 shillings, to

---

6. Aboriginally, this was the gift of a bracelet or neck ring; in 1954, the standard was 10 shillings.

which the bride replied that if her grandmother wanted money she would have to come and ask for it herself. Then the bride's mother brought up the fact that although a brideprice blanket for the father was too light and had been returned, no new blanket had been given the father, nor had the one for the grandfather been paid.

The bride's mother then started to talk about how much a mother's brother was given these days, and other women present pointed out that he now receives a bullock, goats, chickens, and even shillings. The mother then said to her brother's wife, "Since you get so much, you could at least pay 5 shillings to the bride for the milk." There was no response.

Finally somebody asked, "Is there anything to talk of?", a reference to the bride's treatment. The bride's mother said that it wouldn't do any good to talk about any misunderstanding between the bride and her mother-in-law; "If we settle now about the quarrels of the past, will we be there in the future to settle quarrels?"

There also was extensive discussion of the payment to ten different relatives of the bride, amounting to some 30 shillings. The money, which came from the groom though it was not considered a part of the brideprice, was distributed by the bride's parents.

As the party inside the house broke up, the group teased the bride about her sinentet vine, for all the others who had been decorated had now taken theirs off. She said she would demand a heifer of her husband before she removed hers. The bride was then laden with the traditional gifts of a gourd of clotted milk, a palm frond (*sosyontet*), a stick for cleaning gourds, and a basket of cooked maize meal, and the party began the long walk back at about 10:00 P.M., after singing a song of departure.

According to tradition, a brother of the groom demands these gifts, (milk, food, palm frond and stick), stopping her on his return to her husband's house, but the bride will not release the gifts until she has been offered an appropriate present in return — a she-goat or perhaps a bullock. The groom, who has stayed at home, and his friends eat the food and drink the milk that return with the bride. The women in the groom's party remove their garlands of vines and place them on the house roof over the door, but the bride continues to wear hers, as well as a leather rope (made from the hide of a slaughtered bullock) around her neck. She will refuse to remove the garlands and rope and to have intercourse with her husband until she has again extracted the promise of a gift. They are supposed to have intercourse that night.

The couple remains in the house the next day; on the following day, the wife and her friends have their heads shaved. The husband should find a bullock or ram to slaughter, for now his bride can again eat meat. This is the final ceremonial act in the release of restrictions. The husband should then start to build a house for his bride for "now she is a full woman." Only after this is done will there be an effort to collect the brideprice payment.

A number of features in this ritual cycle demand our special attention, particularly attitudes that the various rituals reflect or reinforce in the minds of the principals, particularly the bride. A number of elements combine to convey the notion of a transition from one status to another. The period of seclusion, with food tabus and restrictions on other normal activities, is reminiscent of the liminal period associated with circumcision. Significantly, the bride is instructed in proper wifely conduct by representatives of her new family and emerges from work restrictions with ceremonial induction into her all-too-familiar tasks by her husband's sister. Thus, when the bride returns to her natal home and is uncovered, she appears there as a married woman, a member of her new family, a stranger to her own home, and must be blessed by them before entering, just as she had been after her circumcision seclusion.

The extended links of her new involvements are also expressed in these rituals. It is not the mother-in-law or senior wife who instructs her, but other women of the kin and community. More importantly, it is not her husband who changes the bracelets, but his brother. And again it is his brother — some say the same one, some a different one — who takes her gifts from her and promises something in return. Noteworthy also is the fact that these should be true brothers, for the ties to the clan as a whole are secondary, the immediate kin are primary.

With the exception of the role of the groom's brothers, the ritual aspects of marriage involve only women. The men negotiated the brideprice and will subsequently pay it; the women see to the transfer of the bride. The bride undergoes the liminal period; there are no restrictions on the husband. When men are present at all, they are largely outsiders, hanging about as men may do at bridal showers in our own society, being bored or feigning boredom.

Though these are women's activities, the sides are drawn as with clans, and it is not irrelevant that the bridal party sings the husband's clan songs. There is clearly a sense of confrontation. The groom's mother has two feasts — one for each set of kindred — but the real confrontation, dramatized by the mock battle and the public discussions, takes place when the bride returns home. This sense of confrontation takes on real meaning in the discourse in the bride's natal home. Though clearly her family wants the marriage to continue, and though in many ways the bride has a new set of allegiances, the purpose of this aspect of the ritual is to demonstrate her family's support and protection in the event of improper treatment by her new relatives. If they no longer have a legal right in her, nevertheless, they have a moral responsibility for her — or should have.

I am impressed here, as in so many other facets of Sebei life, by the degree to which the exchange of goods enters into the interaction patterns between these two families. It is not merely that gifts are given and received, which is common enough, but rather that they are negotiated, demanded and quarreled over, and ramify outward from the principals to involve others. The receipt of such gifts seems to contain a psychic load entirely out of keeping with their intrinsic value.

In this context, the bride's demands of gifts have heightened significance. There are three separate occasions when she can refuse to proceed unless her demands are met — when she first goes with the husband, before crossing a stream (i.e., entering his community); when she brings gifts from her family and these are taken by her brother-in-law; and before she consents to sexual intercourse after returning from her mother's house. Whatever else these acts indicate, they certainly reinforce a pattern of constant negotiation between bride and groom, and the importance of goods as recompense for social compliance.

If rituals have the purpose of conveying or expressing social sentiments, then clearly Sebei weddings show the reluctance of the bride in her new role, the subordination of the bride to her new kindred, and a marriage relationship that involves essentially hostile negotiations between husband and wife, as well as between their clansmen.

THE MARITAL RELATIONSHIP

The standard expectations are that the man is dominant in the marital relationship and the woman subservient. This order is maintained through major institutional regulations and minor but demeaning customs. The major aspects of Sebei law that enforce male dominance have already been examined: the thoroughly patri-orientation of the organization of kindred, the holding of all property in the hands of the men, not only the livestock but also the land that the women work, and the brideprice payments which render the woman's father and brothers reluctant to support her in issues vis-à-vis her husband. Moreover, the woman is viewed as legally incompetent to engage in contracts; she is not even supposed to collect a debt owed to her for the sale of a granary if her husband is alive or if she has a grown son.

Many minor regulations reinforce this dual standard, preserving male dignity and demeaning the woman. The husband's stool is all but sacred, and a woman may not sit on it. She may not drink from the milk gourds, as her husband does, but must pour the milk into another vessel; she is not to handle the gourd with which libations of beer are poured, nor the husband's drinking gourd. She may not call the name of her husband's prize ox, nor play the mandolin (*bugandit*), nor step over spears or bows or arrows or a walking stick of her husband. To pass wind in front of her husband is a great insult. Many of these regulations apply also to minor sons, thus placing her as an incompetent socially, as she is legally. Her husband, on the other hand, is enjoined from removing the ashes from the fireplace or cooking his food if she is away on a trip; he does these things only after her death. A woman must always serve her husband first.

So goes tradition. These items are in varying degrees important still and in varying degrees observed. They are less firmly enforced in Sasur than in Kapsirika, where men are much harder on their wives. Yet, I observed that the Sasur, women, to some extent freed from these regulations, must actually work harder than those of Kapsirika. Certainly in both communities, all domestic chores — gathering firewood, cooking, housekeeping, baby tending — are women's tasks, along with most of the work in the fields.

It is taken as a matter of course that the husband beats his wife ("beating and quarrelling are common"), and, unless he does so without cause, too severely, and too often, the wife is expected to accept beatings without open complaint. Routine beatings are not now and have never been grounds for divorce. The fact that women beat their husbands less frequently is seen by the Sebei as a result of the women's inferior strength. Only when the husband is lying down drunk can a wife beat him, they say — and we drove one man to the infirmary whose wife had cut him in the head with a *panga* while he was drunk.

Women are expected to be obedient. When Edgerton asked if women ever disobeyed their husbands and whether such disobedience was right, only five respondents (four of them women) indicated it was not necessary for a woman to obey her husband. Most (forty-nine men and thirty-three women) said that wives did not obey but should do so; the remainder (twenty-seven women and thirteen men) said that they did obey and this was right. The Kapsirika responses were proportioned like those of the women; the Sasur ones like those of the men.

Yet women are not without power; they have two weapons. Women are frequently referred to by the Swahili word *kali*, fierce or sharp. They use their tongues effectively, insist on their rights, and press their point of view. Where they have specified rights, no husband would be willing to deny a *kali* wife. They are known to fight back physically as well as with verbal abuse. In such fights, women seek to grab the man by his genitals, a matter of great concern among the men, who believe this causes weakness. (When it happens, a man must slaughter a ram before he can enter that wife's house or have intercourse with her.)

Women also possess magical means of controlling their husbands. This knowledge is imparted to them in the secret session that closes the initiation ritual cycle. There they learn of the "leopard," receive their age-set membership, and are taught the nature of medicines. The men have no such medicine, but they are quite convinced that their wives not only know these black secrets but use them. I suspect that this fear led one husband to prevent his wife — quite improperly — from attending one of these ceremonies.

According to men, a woman may do magic against a man (*ntoyenik*) by urinating in his food, by putting a bit of her excrement or some menstrual blood in his milk calabash, or by passing wind into it. Such acts sap the man's strength. Men say: "He has no strength for fighting or for competing with people. In a cold season, he quickly feels cold, or he will be helpless in the mountains. He has no power in his home; he will be controlled by his wife. He will not be a smart man. He may become ugly in the face. The men have power, and the woman wants to be over her husband, and this is why she does such a thing. The women also use medicine. These medicines are not used by men; men cannot do such a thing." One woman told Gale that she knew potions that could make her husband love her, make him stop beating her, and make him grant her the favors she asked — an import from Bantu peoples. There was formerly a ritual (*chepserer,* Chapter 3) designed to cleanse the community of witchcraft. A gourd dipper (of the kind used in libations) of the water taken from the pool where the ritual takes place will be hung in the house above the fire or taken to where the people are drinking beer. A woman who has engaged in *ntoyenik* and drinks this beer will not expel the afterbirth at her next pregnancy — only water will flow instead of blood. Drinking beer in a house with such a dipper will also affect a man who has done witchcraft; his stomach will become swollen. Only the guilty will be affected; they may be left to die, or may be saved by eating the fat of the tail of a ram slaughtered for them.

All of these matters display a lack of mutual trust between husband and wife. This is substantiated by responses to questions asked by Edgerton. Given two choices of persons trusted, 12 women selected their husbands but only 1 man named his wife. (A total of 126 responses favored agnatic kindred — father, brother, son — 24 selected friend and 16 mother.)

Sexual intercourse plays an important role in the marital relationship for both the husband and wife, and either has a legitimate complaint if the other fails to meet this need. A wife may complain, "My house has leaked for a long time" (in reference to continued menstrual periods), or "It has been a long time since my husband has had a meal in my house" (eating is a polite way to refer to intercourse).

There are many traditionally proper regulations of sexual activity. Foreplay is engaged in; a man will stroke the vagina with his left hand. Intercourse may take place at any time; it is usually done lying on the side, but the husband may also lie on top of his wife; entry from the rear is considered very bad. It is also evil to try to fornicate with a woman while she is asleep.

There is a tabu against a man seeing his wife's vagina, and one woman went to court to complain that her husband had forced her thighs apart to see if she had engaged in adultery. A man coming into the house where his wife is sleeping is not supposed to build up the fire lest she be exposed. Very young girls learn to sit with their legs together. Only at the time of women's circumcision is this rule overlooked. There is no counterpart reluctance to expose the penis. Though men now characteristically go clothed, they formerly wore a skin over the shoulders, which only intermittently concealed them; boys of eight or ten still often wear no clothes whatsoever (though with increased schooling they now usually wear khaki shorts), and men are frequently seen micturating alongside the road or path.

Sexual intercourse is forbidden under diverse circumstances. It is considered very shameful for a menstruating woman to engage in sexual intercourse because it would cause her husband to get a "rough, black face," to become soft and womanlike, and to be unable to fight in battle or to hunt. (In the Sipi area, the menstruant woman is also enjoined from handling utensils or cooking, except that, when necessary, she may use a banana leaf to hold them.)

The couple may engage in intercourse through the fourth month of the wife's pregnancy if the woman is having her first child, but only through the third month in subsequent pregnancies. Thereafter, only *coitus interruptus* may take place, as it is believed that the sperm forms a tough coating on the fetus, which often causes boys to die, makes girls weak and susceptible to disease, and sometimes causes the mother to die in delivery. Too much sexual activity causes disease in the woman; she vomits and white matter like semen is discharged through the nose and mouth; the baby has semen covering his body; and delivery is difficult. The couple should not engage in coitus until two months after the baby is born, but should do so "before he smiles." Failure to meet this latter obligation requires the slaughter of sheep to avoid the deleterious effects. Intercourse is to be avoided (1) when there is a sick man or a sick animal (cattle, sheep, or goats) in the household, or when a person is about to visit a sick friend, lest the illness become more severe and lead to death; (2) when a man takes his cattle to the salt lick, lest the cattle fail to get the necessary benefit from the salt; (3) when beer is being made, especially during the time it is buried in the ground; or (4) when one's daughters are being circumcised. If a couple wants to engage in sexual activity a second time during the night, the man should urinate first "in order to clean out the penis."

Edgerton obtained data that show intense anxiety over sexual performance. Both men and women respond almost univocally to the question as to whether men and women worry about satisfying their spouses sexually (see Table 39). Only one of the twenty responses indicating no anxiety in the matter was obtained in Kapsirika, suggesting that while anxiety levels are

TABLE 39
Anxiety Over Sexual Performance

	Husband satisfying wives		Wives satisfying husband	
Response	Men	Women	Men	Women
Express concern	61	47	57	45
No concern	3	3	7	7
No response	0	14	0	12

SOURCE: Questions 39 and 40 (RBE:310).

universally high, they are greater among the pastoralists than the farmers. This anxiety may relate to the expectations expressed of an average frequency of intercourse of more than three times per night. (Men expected a greater frequency than women, and Sasurese expected more than Kapsirikans.) Respondents also indicated that frequency of intercourse was at the husband's wish (twenty-seven responses); none indicated that it was the wife's choice.

The Sebei are also very concerned with having children, a matter of greatest importance to both husband and wife. If a couple is childless, the general assumption is that it is the woman's fault, but if the man takes a second wife who also remains childless, people recognize that the evidence points to the man. But women are said to know how to tell if the sperm is "weak." The sperm is placed on the leaf of the ankurwet plant; if the leaf turns dark, the sperm is fertile and the wife will seek medicines. If the semen stands like water, the blame falls upon the husband and the wife conveys this information to her mother, who transmits it to the husband's mother and she in turn to his father. The father then arranges for the husband to get medicine. If such medication is unsuccessful, the people of the *saŋta* will suggest that the husband take another wife, so that a true judgment can be made. If the second wife produces children, the fault is seen to lie with the first wife, but if both wives have no children, that means the fault is with the husband. A sterile person of either sex is called *son.* If a man is born *son,* no medicine avails, but if his sterility derives from disease, medication can be effective.

Nowadays, if a woman finds that her husband cannot make her pregnant, she leaves him, but that was not the old Sebei way. It was Sebei custom for the man to ask his wife to find some other man of his clan to impregnate her. The children would be considered the husband's. The substitute had to be a clan brother of the husband but not his real brother, for it is regarded as very wicked to have intercourse with a real brother's wife. Such arrangements are viewed as strictly private ("People say that she got it from her husband even if they know better").

A woman accused her husband of impotence in a court case I witnessed. She claimed that he could not have an erection, that when he ejaculated it felt cold, and that his semen was watery. She had previously brought the matter to court but had only recently made the leaf test. She also claimed that her husband forced her to have intercourse during her menstrual period and during the daytime. "He is very strict with me and doesn't like me to have other men. A woman doesn't like to have to stay with a hopeless man like that."

Extramarital sexual activity would appear to be the norm among the Sebei. Though a woman is ideally supposed to be faithful to her husband, there are no severe sanctions against her having adulterous relationships. If she continues a liaison with one man too long, then the husband may be enraged and perhaps even divorce her for it, but that appears to be more a concern with a potential transfer of allegiance than with the sexual infidelity itself. To be sure, the woman would be beaten if her husband learned that she had engaged in sexual activities, or even suspected that she had, but then she may be beaten for more trivial offenses. Men said that they might kill the wife or her lover if caught *in flagrante,* but no cases could be brought forward (either past or current) and no evidence exists to indicate that this ever happened. The husband is more likely to demand a payment from the man; Gale was told in 1962 that the standard fine was 168 shillings.

One Kapsirika woman spoke of extramarital affairs as follows:

> Every one of us has a boy friend, but we cannot tell who. Every single woman has a friend. My husband cannot serve me strongly enough. But even if my husband could satisfy me, I still must have someone outside. This friend outside will give me money and soap and please me in many ways. We do have affairs with unmarried men, but we do not trust them because they may spread the story to all their friends. A married man will keep the secret. Also, if I have intercourse with such a young man, he may later want to marry my daughter, and my husband would not understand why I refuse him.

One man who has spent time in Sipi as well as Kapsirika characterized the difference as follows:

> Every wife in Kapsirika has a boy friend, but in Sipi every wife has three or four boy friends. There are more unmarried and divorced women in Sipi because intercourse is so available that men are not eager to marry. In Kapsirika, the couple pet and talk all night but in Sipi they have intercourse right away. The women get drunk and have intercourse in the daytime.

If a woman has intercourse with several men successively, she must be cleansed by a ceremony, for the mingling of semen is considered harmful, both to her and her husband. To cleanse herself, she must drink the fat of the tail of a sheep specially slaughtered or, if her husband is rich, the kidney fat of an ox.

Men do not consider themselves bound to marital fidelity, and most men engage in sexual activity with unmarried girls and other men's wives, respecting only such more stringent regulations as avoidance of daughters of one's age-mate, wives of one's neighbor or *tilyet* relative, and woman from clans standing in a tabu relationship. This is not to say that women do not object to such infidelity, but rather that they have no effective weapons against it, except the power to express their resentment and perhaps the potential of their sorcery. They can, of course, withhold their favors, which one man's wives were doing, in a Lysistrata-like strike. They may also refuse to cook for him, saying he should be getting his meals outside as well.

POLYGYNY

"A man with but one wife is a friend to the bachelor," according to a Sebei proverb, for if his wife should be sick or die, he must engage in household chores he finds demeaning and onerous. Traditionally and currently, men place a high value on having multiple wives; chiefs and other leaders usually have four or five and some of the older men had ten or more. The incidence of polygyny is associated with the degree of involvement in pastoralism. In

Kapsirika, I heard young men exhorted to take additional wives, but not in Sasur. There does not appear to be any diminution of plural marriages, though this is impossible to demonstrate.

In a society in which polygyny is found, every man remains in the marriage market so long as he has such interest. His every social contact with an unmarried girl or woman has the potential of leading to a permanent and legitimate sexual liaison, in a manner that is not possible (or at least not proper) in a monogamous society. This fact is quite clear when one is in the company of Sebei men, who openly flirt with the unmarried girls they chance to meet on the path or at beer parties, particularly those who have just emerged from their postcircumcision seclusion and are on the prowl for a husband. The flirtations I observed carried with it elements of both sexuality and the hostility that so characterizes marital relationships. Once when our path crossed that of a group of recently circumcised girls, my Sebei companion demonstrated to me how a fully initiated person can haze the uninitiated (they had not yet completed the ritual cycle) by pressing their wrists between two sticks, painfully reaching a tender nerve. Afterward, he tweaked and stroked the full breasts of one girl, peeking through gaps in the top of her dress, which was then regularly worn in this manner for its titillating effect.

When a man marries a second wife, there is no special ritual like the one performed to bring amity to the two herds amalgamated when a man inherits his brother's widow or the one to create amity between brothers of the same age born to separate wives. This is all the more surprising in that a ritual (called *chemunwuch misikok,* removal of hearth) is requisite when a widower remarries. When this new wife is pregnant, shortly before delivery, a ram is slaughtered by suffocation, the stones are removed from the hearth, the chyme is put around the fireplace, and the stones are returned. A circle of skin is taken from the ram and worn by the man — on the right arm if his first wife has died, on the left if his second. A ritualist, any person (related or not) who has undergone the ceremony, blesses the husband and wife by spitting beer on them. The ceremony is performed so that the children of the marriage will be healthy, presumably because the spirit of the deceased wife may do them harm. The ceremonialist receives the skin, head, and half the meat of the ram.

In general, subsequent wives are married after some interval of time. The data in Table 40 are based on the assumption that marriages regularly took place immediately after the woman was circumcised. They show that this delay is longer in Sasur than in Kapsirika, and is longer on the average between second and third marriages than between first and second ones. I was told that the old custom was to take a second wife when the children of the first wife are about to undergo initiation, but my data on early polygynous marriages do not support this contention.

There are no explicit rules defining the man's conduct toward his several wives, but he is expected to behave equitably toward them, furnishing each with a separate house, an equitable amount of land, and treating them alike,

TABLE 40
Spacing of Polygynous Wives

Time difference[a]	Sasur wives[b]	Kapsirika wives[b]	
	1st & 2d	1st & 2d	2d & 3d
None	0	6	0
1-3 years	2	4	1
4-5 years	3	2	1
6-10 years	4	4	2
11 or more	4	3	2
Average difference	7.2	5.2	8.7

[a]Based upon circumcision year.

[b]Data refer only to wives not previously married.

including meeting their sexual needs. A man will not generally admit to having a favorite wife (*kirotet*), because he is not supposed to show favoritism, but it is recognized as a frequent occurrence.

The first wife is regarded as senior wife. She is supposed to take the role in subsequent marriages that the husband's mother plays in the wedding rituals of a first marriage. She is also expected to instruct junior wives in their household duties. When a man is sick, he is to be treated in the house of his senior wife, and if he dies, she is the chief mourner. An inherited widow cannot be a first wife, and none of the re-married divorcées in my sample were first wives.

In Gale's interviews with women from Binyinyi in 1954, she found that women differ in their feelings about polygynous relationships; some wanting to be first or only wives, some not caring or preferring to be junior wives. Where attitudes toward co-wives were expressed, they were, by and large, more friendly than hostile. One of the women said with respect to her junior wife: "I just saw him coming with her one day, and we became friends and love one another." Another said she wanted her husband to have another wife, but they were too poor to buy one, and a third claimed she had selected her husband's second wife, for whom her husband paid more than he did for her, as the brideprice had gone up by then.

Men consider it very bad for a woman to try to prevent her husband from taking additional wives. Nevertheless, a wife has many ways of blocking a second marriage; she may tell her husband bad things about the girl (that she is lazy, her mother rude, and so on), complain to the girl about him, saying that he is sexually impotent, or she might use treachery to break up the marriage before the final ceremony, perhaps by defecating in the new wife's house so that when the husband finds the evidence he suspects his new wife of witchcraft.

Women also have magic to make themselves the favorite wives of their husbands — though the Sebei say that the *kirotet* often is the one who has no children, while the sons of those not favored (*chesesan*) are the ones who become rich. One old man told me that the wife, Cherimur, of his father's father, Chepsongel, had the *ntoyenik* of making her husband love her. She was the first wife, but she was barren. He loved her so much that he divorced his five other wives. Finally, Chepsongel's clansmen came, dug out the roof of their flat mud house, and threw all Cherimur's belongings out through the roof — her clothes, baskets, gourds, and everything else. Digging the hole in the roof was to show her that she should leave; without a roof, she had no place to stay. Then Chepsongel married four other women, two of whom he earlier divorced, and, the old man continued, "They had children, one of whom was my father. Nowadays a man must send his wife away himself, but in those days the clan helped a man do that."

Wives are expected to collaborate on domestic chores and usually do, yet, by and large, they operate separate establishments. Each is concerned with milking her cows, cultivating her *shambas,* and caring for her children. Thus, the women remain as independent of the other women in her husband's menage as they find congenial. Each is legally and economically only directly concerned with the husband and their mutual interdependence is secondary or derivative from their common interest in and involvement with him. But it is of the greatest importance to each wife for the welfare of her children that she establish her subsidiary rights to cattle and land. Because of such interests, she engages in the gentle blackmail of demanding gifts from her husband and his family during the wedding and whenever else the opportunity arises.

These arrangements work out more easily with respect to livestock than land; a wife cannot press her husband for a gift of land as she can for livestock, and her *shambas* will not multiply. In Sasur, disputes over land are recurrent between co-wives and between son and father over land allocated to different wives.

The Šebei, with the strict patriliny derived from their pastoralist tradition, demonstrate the advantages of matriliny in a horticultural society. Where cattle are the primary resource, a daughter-in-law does not erode her mother-in-law's rights; in fact, she provides the continuity of line that is so important. The cattle that a woman gives up for her son's brideprice have been acquired for that purpose. But where the productive activity is farming, the mother-in-law continues to need land to perform her primary social and economic functions and the daughter-in-law cuts into her resources. The inheritance of young widows by a man's sons and the tendency for old widows to live with their sons are partial but unsatisfactory solutions to these problems. The growing but still minimal tendency for divorcées to establish independent households may pressage a future pattern. But the more likely long-range solution will be peasantization. That is, with increased commercialization of farming, men will take a more active and controlling role in agricultural production, as they already do with coffee and plowing.

DIVORCE

A man has cause for divorce under the following circumstances: (1) his wife's laziness, (2) her repeated adultery, (3) her refusal or inability to have sexual intercourse, (4) her refusal to cook, (5) if she curses or abuses him, (6) if she has killed her children, (7) if she uses magic against him, (8) if she uses a weapon against him, (9) murder, theft, or other behavior bringing discredit to his reputation, (10) if the relationship proves to be illegal, or (11) if her vagina is black. Childlessness is not grounds for divorce, nor is her insanity. A woman may obtain a divorce if her husband (1) does not provide land for her, (2) is impotent, sterile, or refuses to have intercourse with her, (3) engages in "unnatural" sex relations with her, (4) mistreats her by beating her too often without provocation, (5) is mad, or (6) curses her or spreads bad rumors about her (for further details, see *SL*:54-59). These regulations reenforce the sexual-reproductive obligations of both spouses and their economic roles — the husband to provide land and the wife to fulfill her work obligations. I do not understand the differential standard regarding madness.

Traditionally, domestic difficulties were handled in local moots. A wife who feels mistreated must go to the home of her father and complain. The husband and his friend or neighbor will be summoned and, together with her father's neighbors, will listen to the complaints several times. If the wife is deemed at fault, her brothers may whip her on the thighs with a small walking stick. If the husband is seen to be at fault, his father-in-law will warn him that he may lose his wife. The couple is then sent back home, unless there have been repeated complaints, in which case the matter will be taken before representatives of the *pororyet*. They will determine whether the couple should divorce, and, if so, will decide that the dowry be returned to the husband. The same animals given in brideprice, including their issue, should be returned, and, if they have been exchanged, the wife's father should endeavor to retrieve them. Cattle may be substituted for the *warek* that had been transferred, but not the other way about, and nowadays shillings are acceptable. If the woman has had children, the husband must leave a bull with the woman's father if there is a boy child and/or a cow if a girl, "or else the family can curse you." The children belong to their father and will be sent to him when they are old enough to herd goats.

Men in general complain that these traditional procedures have been eroded by the modern courts, for (at least under colonial rule) a woman could bring a case against her husband, and the courts do not demand the return of the dowry. Some detailed instances demonstrate current attitudes and actions; they took place in the gombolola court in Binyinyi in 1954.

A lean, handsome woman, stylishly dressed, but with concern on her face has brought a divorce case against her husband. She claims that her husband beats her every night when he returns from drinking beer and at other times.

The husband, poorly dressed, denies this with an unconcerned air. When asked, she replies that this is the second time she has brought a formal complaint, but the defendant points out that the earlier case had been decided against her.

> *Court:* Does your father know you are being troubled by your husband?
> *Plaintiff:* Yes.
> *Court:* Perhaps you are planning to leave your husband without the knowledge of your father?
> *Plaintiff:* No. Whenever he beats me, I go to my father's house.
> *Court:* Are you sure that your father will support you in the matter of divorce from husband?
> *Plaintiff:* Yes, because I go to his home when my husband beats me. [*They look for a note from the dispensary that the plaintiff claims she gave the court as evidence of beatings but fail to find it.*]
> *Assessor:* Have you heard your wife's claims and that she wants to leave you because of your treatment of her?
> *Defendant:* Yes, I have heard her, but I am not willing to have a divorce, for I never did anything wrong to her.
> *Court:* Will your father-in-law agree that you haven't mistreated your wife?
> *Defendant:* Yes, he will agree.
> *Court:* If your father-in-law agrees to his daughter getting a divorce, what will you decide?
> *Defendant:* I will demand the brideprice back.
> *Assessor:* Let us have the father say what he thinks.
> *Father* [*Standing between the two*]: I have two things to say: yes, he beats his wife every day, and when he is quarrelling with his wife, he comes to me demanding the brideprice back. [*It is improper for a husband to mention the brideprice when he quarrels with his wife.*] Even if I were foolish, I wouldn't give the brideprice at home, for the court might not assess me as much, or the man may deny I have done so. I say the couple should leave one another.
> *Court:* You have heard the word of your father-in-law; do you have anything to say that will overcome him and make your wife go home with you?
> *Defendant:* No.
> *Assessor:* What about the brideprice?
> *Court:* According to new regulation, if we judge against the husband, he can ask for brideprice, and, if he is not given full property, he can bring action in court.
> *Assessor:* Since they don't get along and something bad might happen, I think they should separate. [*Other assessors agree*]

The court holds in favor of granting the divorce. Shortly after the decision has been rendered in the woman's favor, she returns, complaining that her husband had taken her cowry girdle and expressing fear that he would do her harm by means of it. The man denies having taken it and the court indicates that that action will require her to bring a separate case.

In the second case, a woman has complained that her husband has removed the ashes from the fireplace, perhaps because he was wishing that she would die. He has run off and has not been heard from for three years. One of the assessors rises and makes a speech, putatively in a joking vein (with much laughter and repartee by the audience) along the following lines: "You women are silly; as soon as your husband disappears, you cry for a divorce. Why not work hard and have *shambas* and make friends with someone who will make you pregnant, and then when your husband comes home he will find you have children?"

The court holds that the woman should bring her father to the court to indicate if he would return the brideprice, should the husband return.

The third case was brought by a junior wife who has not produced a child after three years' marriage. Before testifying, she goes outside and draws from under her dress the notes from the dispensary to prove she has been treated for beatings. Then, with much gesticulation, she describes incidents of beatings, concluding as follows.

Wife: Later, I returned home. The fire was dead, and I went to a neighbor to get an ember. When I returned, the lock was broken and my husband's blanket had been stolen. I was very worried, but then in my heart I decided it was my husband's other wife who had done this, for otherwise my things would also have been stolen; she was trying to undermine me with my husband. I was afraid I would be beaten by my husband, but he did not beat me. He abused me, saying I am barren and a harlot going after many men. Perhaps it is my husband who is barren, because the first wife has not produced any children either. I have been called many names, and now I want to leave this man.

Court: Do you agree to what your wife said, that you beat her and that you called her a harlot and barren.

Defendant: I never called her those things. I did beat her. When I asked her to get my beer straw, she pushed me, so I beat her. [*Laughter*] When I was coming home, I wanted my wife to take my beer straw, but she refused upon an oath. She jumped over the straw and went away a few yards. I asked her why she threw away my straw, and she pushed me, and that is why I beat her. [*More laughter*]

Court: Have you any witnesses who saw your husband abusing you?

Plaintiff: No. He does this when we are alone.

Court: Did your husband's other wife hear?

Plaintiff: No, the other wife is not troubled by our husband; only myself.

Court: Why does he trouble you if the other wife doesn't give birth?

Plaintiff: I don't know. Perhaps he doesn't trouble his other wife because he didn't pay a brideprice for her; they just ran away. [*Laughter*]

Court: You are the wife that the man paid a lot of wealth for; you are the one he fears; how can he care for the one he didn't pay for? How often have you accused your husband?

Plaintiff: This is the first time.

Court [*Addressing husband*]: Why didn't you collect your own beer straw and not fight when you were drunk but bring a case against her the next morning?

Defendant: That defeats me; if I had known, I would have done so.

Court [*Summarizing*]: This woman accuses her husband of beating her, but it is her first accusation; she says her husband calls her barren and a harlot, but she has no witnesses; you judge if this woman should be given a divorce or made to go back to her husband.

Assessor: As the husband has agreed he beat her on the back, the woman wins the case, but not a divorce. The husband should pay 10 shillings compensation; 5 shillings fine, and 2 shillings court costs. [*Other assessors agreed.*]

Court [*Lecturing*] : Everywhere in Uganda, the most women you see in court are Sebei women. This was not the case in old times; they are trying to leave the old way. If there is a quarrel, they should bring it to the people nearby until those people are tired of judging the case. If women run to court all the time, it makes court just a play. Husbands shouldn't accuse their wives unless they have seen them sleeping with another man. When you quarrel with your husband and then go home, the neighbors there might mislead you, saying that he is unable to serve you. Go home and cooperate and if he troubles you again come back, and the court will have a decision to make about divorce.

These cases indicate that the courts provide an avenue of escape for women from the oppression of their husbands; they also indicate the reluctance of the courts to approve divorces, unless the woman's father agrees and is willing to return the appropriate part of the brideprice.

A divorced woman takes with her only her personal things: clothes, personal ornaments, cowry belt, knife, pipe, hoe, drinking gourd, cooking pots, and such things as may have been given her by her parents. The animals allocated to her (and even any given to her by her parents) will be given to the surrogate mother of her children (co-wife or husband's sister), who will use them to feed the children. Her sons will retain the subsidiary right to the cattle that were anointed for her, just as if she were not divorced. The sons also retain the right to the use of their mother's land. When they are circumcised, she must provide the beer and anoint them; when her daughter marries, she gets the goat and other things specified for the mother, and the bargaining should take place in her house.

Divorce is by no means an infrequent occurrence. Our analysis of the schedules taken in Sasur and Kapsirika indicates that, of the 165 women married to the respondents, 25 had had previous marriages and 16 had left their husbands. (Table 41) Of these 41 instances, 32 had been divorced, 4 were inherited widows, and 5 were separated. Some of the women had had more than one previous marriage. It is thus difficult to calculate a "divorce rate" with precision, but it is on the order of 20 percent. There was no significant difference between Sasur and Kapsirika in these rates.

A divorced woman has little difficulty in remarriage. A few divorced women now live alone by choice. In 1962, I learned of two sisters who had bought a piece of land with that plan in mind. They later accumulated seven pieces of land. They said that people were "jealous" of their owning land, fearing that "it encourages women to leave their husbands when they do not like the treatment they get." They had been subjected to many difficulties: encroachment by a neighbor, for which the case they brought has not been decided; an accusation of using witchcraft against this neighbor, who was killed in an automobile accident shortly after he had taken land from them; severe injury from a broken bottle thrown at one of them by a son of the dead man; the spreading of false stories about them, for which they brought

TABLE 41
Multiple Marriages of Sebei Women

Wife's marital history	Sasur	Kapsirika	Total
No prior marriage	71	69	140
Prior marriage (not related)	10	11	21
Prior marriage (inherited)	3	1	4
Total	84	81	165
Subsequently divorced	6	5	11
Separated	3	2	5

NOTE: Data on all marriages contracted by household heads. Frequency of prior marriages or subsequent marriages not indicated.

and won a suit, though the defendant has not paid the 377 shillings in damages; a severe illness characterized as "blood moving upward at great speed, accompanied by sweating," which was diagnosed as being caused by witchcraft; the theft of coffee and plantains from their land; and general harassment, including mistreatment of the twenty-one-year-old son of one of them.

On the other women who have set up independent households, we have less information. One had served many years as an ayah for a European family in Kenya, had saved some money, and, after divorcing her husband (a policeman in Kampala) bought land and set up a household on the road. She claimed many men had tried to marry her, but she felt they were only after her land and refused them. She endeavored to establish a bar, but harassment from the men made this difficult, so she turned to cultivating plantains and coffee and feels that she is generally accepted now that she is engaged in the more usual kind of woman's work. Another woman was a school teacher, had a large house with an iron roof and a number of children, the oldest a boy of about seventeen, and was successfully cultivating land with the aid of her unusually cooperative and efficient children. A third had set up a bar in Kapchorwa and was purchasing land in Bukwa, but there was no opportunity to interview her.

Since women do most of the productive work, as well as the housework, it is not difficult for a woman to make a living in the agricultural area without a man. We heard of no instance of such a pattern of existence on the plains, and I doubt that it would be possible for a woman to make such an adjustment there, where cattle keeping is important and agricultural production is dependent upon the use of the plow. Nor could female independence have taken place under aboriginal conditions, for, without the protection provided by modern laws, inadequate as they appear to be, the men would not have permitted such behavior, nor could there have been any means of acquiring land.

INHERITANCE OF WIDOWS

Although the marriage contract is essentially between the two immediate families of the principals, the clan of the husband acquires a right to the woman and to the progeny produced by the union. This means that, if the husband dies, his widow will be inherited by one of his relatives, as a legal right. The proper heir is the next younger brother of the deceased, failing this the next older brother and older brothers in reverse order of seniority, younger adult brothers in order of seniority, half-brothers, and more distant relatives (SL:69-70). Junior wives may also be inherited by the sons of a senior wife. This custom is limited to Mbai and is not old; it is disapproved in the eastern sector of Sebei.

Many factors may prevent the order of inheritance; a man may not inherit a woman whom the general rules of marriage would forbid him to marry. For instance, he could not inherit a woman who belongs to his wife's clan, his wife's mother's clan, his mother's clan, his mother's mother's clan, and the like. Other elements may intervene — the fact that his mother had been inherited, or certain ritual involvements of his with the deceased husband's household (SL:72). The determination is made in a public moot at the final ceremonies connected with the husband's death.

To some extent, the woman's feelings in the matter are taken into account, though, in theory, and I think in tradition, these are supposed to be disregarded. I have cases of acquiescence to the widow's desires as to which brother would inherit her, as well as instances in which the proper brother refused to take the widow. An inherited wife who is again widowed cannot be inherited again. A woman who has grown (circumcised) sons will not be inherited but establishes a household near her son's house and maintains her own gardens.

The widow never becomes the first wife of the inheritor, even if he is not already married; when he does take a wife, that wife legally becomes the first wife, and her sons take precedence over the widow's sons by the inheritor.

If a man inherits his brother's widow he will, some time after they have had a child, undergo a ceremony not unlike that for fertility. The couple passes underneath the stomach of a bull or, if he is too wild, they will slaughter the animal by suffocation, remove the large intestine, which two persons will hold up for the couple to pass beneath. In any case an animal will be slaughtered and the chyme smeared on the couple and their children, and they will be blessed by spitting beer. It is thought that such a couple's failure to have children means that they are not in peace and suffer from "bad birds." The ceremony involves no medicine, but beer is brewed. The husband wears a circle of skin from the animal on his right wrist.

The property of the deceased, land and livestock, belong to his sons, if he has any; the inheritor uses the estate as if it were his until these sons gain their majority. Any sons the inheritor has by the widow will have no claim on the property of the deceased man. These rules have important legal and metaphysical implications. The entity that a man creates — his land, livestock, and sons — continue as a viable unit and a projection of himself. In practical ways, land, livestock, and sons may be subject to the vicissitudes of the inheritor's actions but, in theory, at least, they remain unimpaired by the fact of his death. The inheritor receives only the widow, and his progeny by her are a part of his continued social existence, not a furtherance of that of the deceased.

SUMMARY

Men and women are drawn into marriages because the ultimate fulfillment of life rests on having children. For the woman, not to have children is to be viewed as useless, to be despised and unfulfilled and to suffer a personal sense of inadequacy. One of our neighbors in Sasur was an attractive childless wife whose desire for children was frequently manifested; she could get but cold comfort from her accusations that her co-wife and mother-in-law had "tied her blood" and rendered her barren. For the man, having sons is essential not only for the continuation of his line, but for his own postmortem existence. Marriage, therefore, is as deeply structured into the psyche of each individual as it is into the institutions of the social order.

But the relationships between the sexes are overwhelmingly manipulative, lacking in trust, and hostile. In courting procedures, male force and pressure are countered by feminine wiles and deceits that are institutionalized in the marriage negotiations and wedding rites, where the men determine whom the woman shall marry and the women try to protect their interests by manipulation. Manipulation, distrust, and hostility continue into the marital relationship, within which a standard of mutual deceit preserves the pleasures of infidelity.

These attitudes and activities operate within the framework of two institutionalized patterns of behavior; male dominance and mutual distrust. Male authority is simply a basic assumption of the relationship. Distrust is institutionalized in the form of witchcraft belief and was given direct expression in response to the questionnaire. Hostility is given expression in the high incidence of physical violence, particularly in association with drinking. It is also manifested in a recurrent tendency for older women, after their sons are grown and established, to move away from their husbands, often living in a separate ménage in close conjunction with one of their sons.

The institutionalization of the two major elements in husband-wife inter-action — dominance and distrust — suggests that the character of the relationship between men and women is an old one; not a result of acculturative forces. This does not mean that the situation has been unchanging, but only that present behavior has roots in the distant past. When the Sebei were heavily engaged in pastoralism, and the age-set system was functioning as an important element in local political action, the household unit had less importance in the daily lives of the people. Under such conditions, the disharmony of domestic relationships would not have had its present in-sistency, even if it had the same character.

The information on the differences between Sipi and the plains suggest that there has been some amelioration of domestic life as a result of the increased involvement with agricultural production and the productive role of women. This is suggested by the testimony of one Sebei observer, the general disinclination of women to marry men of the plains, the lower incidence of polygyny, the reportedly greater degree of sexual freedom of the women, and the independence of some divorced women from husbands or fathers. These differences have not eroded the strong male orientation of Sebei culture that lies deep in Southern Nilote tradition. There is no shred of evidence that matri-oriented institutional forms, or even bilateral tendencies, are manifesting themselves; male domination is deeply institutionalized and internalized.

Chapter 9
Infancy and Childhood

If your mother loves me, then I love you;
If your mother hates me, then I hate you;
I throw you away.
Mother has gone to beg food.
Mother is near; Mother is near.

Lullaby sung by *mwet*

THE IMPORTANCE OF CHILDREN

The Sebei say that a man who dies without children is forgotten; his name is thrown away; his spirit is dead. Worse, his spirit becomes an evil *oynatet*, bent on doing harm to the living. When food or beer is given to such spirits, it is cast away from the house with the left hand. A man with many children will be remembered, his spirit fed happily. Perhaps, if he has many cattle or much land, he will become the founder of a lineage. There is a strong urge among Sebei men to have progeny. The motivation to bear children is even greater among women, though its basis is more mundane. A barren wife is scorned and shamed, for reproduction is seen as her prime purpose. Although her husband may not divorce her because she has no children, he will normally treat her badly.

The strength of these motivations is revealed in Edgerton's data. When he asked Sebei to choose the two best thing that can happen to a woman, children was one of the choices 126 times, a near unanimity. Among men, there were only 37 choices of children as the best thing that could happen to a man, but having a wife won 65 responses. If the two are combined, it would appear that reproduction remains high on the list of Sebei priorities. Moreover, 102 Sebei thought that having no children was the single worst thing that could happen to a woman. The Sebei are not unique in the importance they attach to having children, but Edgerton found that they are

243

unique in their reason; they speak of the need to "produce more children" in order to "increase the population." Specifically, 73 Sebei answered something like, "I must produce more children to add to the Sebei population." Not one person in the other three tribes in Edgerton's study gave this answer. (*RBE*:121) When asked if they preferred sons or daughters, most (62 percent) said both, and most of the remainder preferred to have boys (34 percent of the sample). There was no significant difference between the responses of men and women or between those of farmers and pastoralists. These evaluations generally accord with my observations and discussions. Men particularly want sons to preserve and further the clan and lineage, but they also want daughters, in no small measure because the brideprice they receive for daughters is used to obtain wives for their sons.

One would think that the great desire for children would mean that babies would enter a world of love and warmth, but observations belie this assumption. It would appear that progeny are desired, but children are not particularly wanted. Even the desire for progeny appears to be tempered by practical considerations. Modern Sebei women are not uninterested in birth control, as many indicated by queries to Gale. The more acculturated and educated men, too, are concerned with the costs of raising large families, particularly school fees. The Sebei deny engaging in infanticide as a regular practice, but it is apparently not infrequent and there is no penalty against it, though a man may divorce his wife "if she has children three times and kills them each time." A kind of infanticide through neglect (to which the above statement may well refer) appears to be recurrent. Very rarely, for instance, does one find both twins living to adulthood, and the middle child among triplets "never survives."

Information on the frequency of childbearing is presented in Table 42, which summarizes fertility and mortality information obtained by the demographic schedules.[1] Individual women in the sample had from one to thirteen live births; eleven in the sample had given birth ten or more times. Though two women had no living children, none had failed to bear at least one child. This is a flaw in the data, because infertile women tend to leave their husbands. Thus, average reproductive rate of all Sebei women is probably somewhat lower than the 7.24 figure indicates. Because Sasur women have a significantly higher fecundity than those of Kapsirika and there is a much greater incidence of mortality on the plains, Sasur women have on the average 2 more living children than the Kapsirika women do. The fewer births in Kapsirika and the higher death rate are largely accounted for by the fact that life on the plains is more difficult and disease more prevalent. In some measure, however, the data may have been influenced by the better medical facilities in Sipi, particularly the presence of the Catholic Mission there.

---

1. Women of Koronkoro or earlier age-sets were analyzed because, with possible rare exceptions, they were past childbearing age by 1961. Abortions and stillbirths are not included because Sebei are reluctant to speak of them; they are viewed as evidence of disease.

TABLE 42
Fertility of Women Past Childbearing Age
and Childhood Mortality

	Sasur	Kapsirika	Differential[b]	Total
Women reporting[a]	22	20	—	42
Livebirths reported[c]	172	132	76.7	304
Births per woman	7.82	6.60	84.4	7.24
Living children	123	70	56.9	193
Children per woman	5.59	3.50	62.6	4.60
Deceased children	50	68	136.0	118
Mortality rate[d]	29.1	51.5	177.0	38.8

SOURCE: Demographic questionnaires taken in 1961-62.

[a]Women of Koronkoro age-set or earlier. It is barely possible that some of these women could have another child.

[b]Kapsirika as a percent of Sasur.

[c]Stillbirths not recorded.

[d]Children who have died as a percent of all children born.

PREGNANCY AND BIRTH

Although a pregnant woman (or perhaps the embryo) is seen to be in some special danger, the restrictions on her activity are not severe and she continues to work and engage in normal household activities. She may not eat meat from an animal that has died but may eat meat from the hind legs of an animal that has been slaughtered. She is also under some sexual restrictions; semen is viewed as harmful to the fetus. In the seventh or eighth month of pregnancy, an old woman who has special knowledge may visit the mother and rub her abdomen with butter. If she believes that the fetus is not properly positioned, she manipulates it from the outside into a position that will avoid difficulty in delivery.

The mother normally has the child in her own house. She will ask her husband to leave, for no men (not even a boy over the age of about three) may be present. Some women have their babies unassisted, but, if there is any difficulty, women of the neighborhood are called in. The mother may pull on the posts that hold up the storage rack inside the house, but, if another woman is present, she may pull on the mother's hands. A leather cinch-belt of buffalo hide is pulled tight around the abdomen to help push the fetus out. It is acceptable for the mother to yell in pain; "She does not have to be brave as during circumcision." Either the mother or the woman who is assisting her receives the infant, cuts the navel cord immediately, and cleanses the child with a cloth or leaves of the aukurwet plant. The placenta may be taken out and buried, but it is often buried on the second day after the child is born, under the part of the house where the goats and sheep are kept, for it is feared that if it is buried outside a person may take it for purposes of witchcraft. Because it is felt that the woman who assisted in delivery has dirty hands, she may not milk cows until a cleansing ceremony is held on the second day after delivery, after which the women have a small feast. This is a very simple ceremony in which the mother and the woman who has assisted in the delivery wash themselves and the infant with water in which lepeywontet leaves have been boiled. The husband remains out of the mother's house until she has cleaned it thoroughly and resmeared the floor — a matter of perhaps weeks.

INFANT CARE

The mother wears a tight thong or cloth around her abdomen until the infant is old enough to sit up, taking it off only when she eats. This girdle makes more or less permanent stripes on the mother's skin, and these are referred to in song as a symbol of the burden she has borne. The father is expected to have provided food for his wife during her postpartum confinement, the proper food being blood (taken from a bull for a boy and a heifer for a girl) mixed with sour milk. This is cooked, but not brought to a boil. It is for the wife to drink, but a second bleeding should take place at the time of the cleansing ceremony to provide a feast for the women (men do not partake of it) and a calabash for the midwife to take home.

If the mother does not have milk at first, which the Sebei say often happens with the first pregnancy, a few spoonsful of milk are boiled and fed the infant. The child begins to take cow's milk along with the mother's milk from the very beginning; indeed, the Sebei believe that a child should have both forms of milk in order to grow strong. At first, the mother dips her fingers in the milk and puts them in the baby's mouth; later, she cups her hand around the baby's chin and pours milk into it so that it covers the mouth and the child draws it in in gags. It does not appear to be a very happy process, but it is effectual (Plate III:4). The infant may also be fed thin gruel in this way, though normally children are not given food other than milk until they are old enough to drink from a calabash. If there is insufficient milk available, the mother may dip cooked plantains or sweet potatoes in vegetable broth, so that the infant can swallow them easily.

Edgerton remarks on the readiness of nursing mothers to meet the demands of their infants. He writes in his field notes:

> Having now seen some 45 infants at the breast (up to 2.5 years at a guess, but mostly under 18 months), I must say that these children are most demanding, display almost no frustration tolerance, and are highly aggressive. The mothers indulge their every demand. The infant wails; quickly the breast. The infant demands; quickly the breast. If the baby bites, the mother squeals but does not punish. It seems to take delight in attacking the breast, pulling, pushing, squeezing, before relaxing for a contented sucking. It usually plays with the unused nipple, often pulling it in a most savagely aggressive manner.

The mother meets these demands with minimal social contact with the infant: some other task may engage her attention; she may be in conversation with other adults; or she may just be abstracted (Plate III:1). There is little eye contact, vocalization, caressing, or other apparent communication between mother and child. The only fondling of babies that I saw was when a childless or unmarried young woman held another woman's baby. The mother's detachment is expressed in the characteristic manner in which she holds the infant, whether seated or standing, whether nursing or not. The mother encircles the child with her arms, giving it support with her forearm, not with her hands. Even when she is doing nothing and has no other distractions, she does not look at her child, whether it is nursing or not. Characteristically, she does not use her hands to caress or play with the child; occasionally one hand supports or holds the child, especially when she is standing.[2]

If the mothers show little emotional involvement with their children, the fathers show even less. I do not believe that I ever saw a father meeting an infant's needs or playing with his child. One man, in talking about the values picture showing a man holding up a baby (*RBE*:307), said, "The father very rarely picks up or dandles a child. He does make it dance sometimes and holds it up in the air to please it." The responses to this picture, which was intended to show a father playing with his child, are analyzed in Table 43. About half do see the child as playing and/or the scene as happy, and some commented that this was right, that they play with their children, that the man is admiring the child or showing it to God, and one said, "More people should play with their children instead of neglecting them. The child is not yours but belongs to everyone." But significantly, about half also feel that this scene requires explanation: the child is sick; it is crying; it must be held because the mother is working. Ten persons saw the man as a woman, or an ayah, or in one instance a Nandi tribesman. In short, the scene seemed so unusual that it had to be accounted for. Women, in particular, find it necessary to explain why a man is handling an infant. The "other" category consists of three extraneous explanations (doing exercises, teaching the child something, and crossing a river). There are very few negative statements, but these are startling: the man is angry and throwing the baby down; he has quarreled with his wife and is holding the child to keep her from leaving.

The baby is regularly carried on its mother's back, held by a cloth sling under its buttocks, which is tied over the mother's breasts. Thus, the baby remains close to its mother's body while she is awake and working; it learns to sleep and to observe the world over her shoulder. At night, it sleeps with the mother, lying at her front so long as it has no younger sibling, or until it is three or four years old. The woman may put a child down while she is working, but normally it remains on her back. We observed at length a Masop mother making a basket and her naked toddler trying to get at the breasts and fussing about until she finally let it play with the knife she had been using (Plate III:2). While women are working about the house, infants

---

2. A detailed analysis of photographs substantiates these generalizations (Goldschmidt, 1975).

TABLE 43
Attitudes Toward Father's Relation to Infants

Response[a]	Total		Sasur		Kapsirika		Men		Women	
	No.	Pct	No.	Pct	No.	Pct	No.	Pct	No.	Pct
Playing/happy	58	48	29	48	29	48	35	57	23	38
Because wife working	8	7	7	11	1	2	5	8	3	5
Child is sick/hurt	26	21	11	18	15	25	9	15	17	28
Child is crying	11	9	4	7	7	12	7	11	4	7
Not seen as father	10	8	8	13	2	3	3	5	7	12
Harming child	5	4	2	3	3	5	2	3	3	5
Others	3	2	0		3	5	0		3	5
Total	121	99[b]	61	100	60	100	61	99[b]	60	100

[a]Responses to Values Picture No. 6 (RBE:307). Answers offering no explanation have been eliminated (128 responses possible).

[b]Totals do not equal 100 percent because of rounding.

and toddlers are usually put on the floor; they frequently are allowed to cry and fuss without attention until they fall asleep.

Sebei women believe that suckling pains them in the breast when they become pregnant (though not all feel such pain and others disregard it) and that the milk smells or tastes bad to the child. Hence, they usually wean their children at the onset of the next pregnancy. If there is no subsequent pregnancy, they will continue suckling the child until it leaves the breast of its own accord or because it is being teased by its friends for continuing to nurse. Thus, the child may leave the mother's breast after four or five months or may continue to suck for as many years.

Gale interviewed a number of women in 1954 regarding child-rearing practices in the Binyinyi area. Thirteen, with about forty-five infants among them, reported on weaning, revealing a diversity of practices, including variations in the way each woman handled her several children. They use different methods to wean their children. The most frequent is to smear red pepper on the nipple, but one woman used the juice from her tobacco pipe on her five children, two women pinched the children's cheeks, and one weaned a somewhat older child by talking to it. Some mothers claim that the child simply refused the breast, often when the mothers had again become pregnant "and the milk tasted bad." The use of pepper must be repeated several times, and the child usually cries a great deal. One woman said, "Pepper doesn't kill the child, so it isn't bad." Some women reported comforting the crying child, others said they merely told the child, "I don't want you any more." The mother who had used tobacco juice said her oldest child was walking and talking when she became pregnant, and the child washed off her breast five times and then asked, "Why won't you let me anymore? Do you have another baby?" She responded only that she didn't want him any more, and when he cried she beat him and sent him outside. She laughingly claimed she had behaved similarly with all five of her children.

A woman who used neither pepper nor tobacco nursed her first infant until the second was born, when she told her, "You must stop nursing now because there is another child who will take your place at my breast, and I cannot nurse two." The baby tried to push away its younger sibling, but the mother would not permit it. The older girl later returned to the breast when her younger sibling died and continued nursing until her friends began to tease her. One woman did nurse two children at the same time but was criticized both for having children so close together and for allowing them to feed at her breasts simultaneously.

Seven of the thirteen mothers reported on weaning practices indicated that one or more of their children continued nursing until quite old. Usually this is the last child, though it need not be if the next pregnancy has been long delayed. Mothers seem to feel that, if there is no pregnancy, a child should be suckled as long as it wants and that it is easier to let it be weaned by the teasing of other children than to go to the trouble of putting pepper on the breasts.

Only two of the women reported differences between children who are weaned early and those who are allowed to continue at the breast. One said: "The child who nurses a long time is not clever. He will step on a new baby and harm it if he finds it lying alone." Another said that the child who remains on the breast will cry and refuse to do chores until it is beaten and will only discover later from his friends that he can avoid beatings by meeting his obligations. She denied that late weaning affected the infant's later behavior, noting that the child would not be any more likely to cry at circumcision.

The mother takes for granted that her dress and back will be soiled from time to time, and she merely washes her cloth and wipes off the baby with ankurwet leaves. Similar soiling about the house is treated with equal casualness when done by infants. After the age of about six months, however, the mother endeavors to guide the child outside when it is about to defecate, and if she is unsuccessful in her training she will put the feces on its head. The child is allowed to soil at night without training or punishment until it is old enough to go outside on its own. If, however, a child continues to soil beyond the time it is expected to know better, it is beaten, both at night and on the following morning. It was not possible to get a statement of the age at which training is supposed to be accomplished. One method of training the child to stop urinating in bed is to tie a snake skin (one that the snake has shed) around the child's middle while it is asleep at night and tell it the next morning that "the snake has come and tied itself around your waist because you do not go outside." The Sebei hate snakes; they kill them whenever they see them, whether they are poisonous or not.

An infant is bathed daily in the house, in a basin, usually in the late afternoon either before or after its supper. When the child is old enough to walk, it goes to the river to be bathed.

While mothers take their infant out to the field as they work, toddlers who are too old to carry on the back are left very much alone. An older sibling is expected to serve as *mwet*, taking care of these infants (Plate III:3). If there is no older sibling, a girl is borrowed from another relative, preferably the mother's younger sister or the father's younger sister or a child of one of the parent's siblings. One frequently sees a young girl of five or six years out playing with another child of one or two years on her back. This is not very popular with the nurses, but one simply said, "My mother would beat me if I didn't." The sentiment is reflected in the lullaby sung by these nurses, which appears as an epigraph to this chapter. Sometimes the *mwet* becomes an adopted child remaining in the household until she is ready for circumcision. She uses parental terms for the baby's parents and is prohibited from marrying their son (if indeed the marriage is not forbidden by rules of kinship). Her true parents receive a goat in return, but if the child remains in the household until circumcision, the adoptive parents should be given one of the brideprice animals. I did not investigate actual cases of such adoptions.

While child nurses are employed everywhere among the Sebei, the custom is less prevalent on the plains, where the women do not spend day after day in the fields or attend beer parties virtually every afternoon. Parental neglect of older children is exacerbated by Sebei eating habits. It is customary for the Sebei to take a main, cooked meal, in the late afternoon or early evening, eating the leftovers for breakfast. Thus, to inattention is added hunger. The problem in the Sasur area is so great that the school provides porridge and sugar for the children.

A disobedient child will be chastised by inattention, teasing, threats of supernatural sanctions, abuse, curses, or a beating. Weaned children are often left to cry until they stop of their own accord or are sent out of the house. When a child falls down or otherwise fails to behave appropriately, it may be laughed at; when this happens, the child cries. Children are expected to learn not to cry when they hurt themselves, however, and very young children frequently showed great stoicism in the face of pain and discomfort.

The infant is vulnerable to outside influences; it may not be seen by a twin or by a person with the evil eye. Because nobody can determine whether a person has the evil eye, mothers generally do not allow their newborn infant to be seen by any outsider until it has gained a measure of strength. For proper protection against the evil eye, the infant should wear a cowry shell, an iron neck ring, and a medicinal herb that has been mixed with cow's milk. Friends and neighbors may see the child, but they are expected first to give the child a small gift, formerly a cowry shell or other bead, but nowadays usually a copper coin.

There is an elaborate set of concerns about the order in which teeth erupt, and certain teeth are considered "*oyik* teeth," i.e., representative of malevolent spirits. If the canines or molars erupt before the incisors, this is considered a sinful (*sokoran*) circumstance. A canine or molar must be removed, and others will emerge all right. A goat must be killed to remove the "bad birds" that result from such a circumstance. If the upper teeth erupt before the lower teeth, there is something wrong with the parent: the mother for a girl, the father for a boy. Medicine is tied on the jaw and rubbed on the gums when these swell to prevent this from happening. The Sebei believe that such teeth will cause diarrhea, vomiting, and watering of the eyes, and that, if the teeth are not removed, the child will die.

When a woman has a series of misfortunes with her children and loses a number of them in succession, she may "throw away" a new-born infant. There is no ceremony involved, because "one does not want to remember the child," but it is merely put into the bush where, presumably by prearrangement, the foster mother "finds" it. The new mother is addressed teknonymously (e.g., Yapchemoŋoyo, mother of the Pokot).

NAMES

The Sebei normally have a succession of different names. Each child is given a name associated with some circumstance of birth; he or she is shortly thereafter given the name of an ancestor, which may later be changed; another name is added at circumcision; and nowadays there may be a Christian or Muslim name as well. Finally, every woman is known teknonymously as the mother of her oldest living child until she has grandchildren, when she is named after her oldest living grandchild. Men are also sometimes called by the teknonymous name, though only in the immediate family. Men frequently add to their given name that of their father, preceded by *arap*, meaning "son of." Thus, during his or her lifetime, a Sebei person may be called by a half-dozen different names, depending upon age and context.

The first name given to a child is based on some circumstance of its birth; the place where born (on the veranda, in the plantain field, on a visit), the time of birth (as the cows were returning, just before daybreak), some special event (during circumcision, when a plane flew overhead), some special aspect of the birth (born before full term, breech birth, the mother went to sleep after delivering), or some ordinal position of the child (a twin, following a twin, following a series of children who died).

A divinatory ceremony determines which ancestor will give the child its second name. The divination must be done in the late afternoon, when the spirits are out. It should be done on the fourth day after birth, except for twins and other special children, when it is done on the third day. An awl is stuck in the floor of the house and encircled with a ring of beer or milk. A hard, round, hollow pod is filled with water and balanced on the handle of the awl. The names of deceased relatives of the infant, first those belonging to his father's clan and then to his mother's are called out successively. Men's names are called out for boys, women's for girls. If the pod fails to balance, it is because another spirit has knocked it off. When the pod balances on the handle four successive times, the child is given that relative's name because the spirit wishes to have the child named after him or her. It is said that the spirits frequently quarrel over this privilege. If the fruit does not balance, it is assumed that many spirits are seeking the child, and he is given the name Kiteyo, "many spirits." Only names of a man who had been circumcised, married, and had children, or a woman who had had children, may be used. [3] The person who performs the ceremony must be of the clan of one of the child's parents; he or she need not be old but must know names of the deceased relatives.

If a child subsequently becomes ill, it may mean that he is refusing the spirit he was named for, or that several spirits are fighting to have the child named after them. The balancing ritual is repeated, and the child may be renamed. If the child still does not become well, a diviner will be consulted. He may thus discover that the illness is caused by disease, or by spirits who demand the slaughter of a cow. The parents will then kill a proper animal and, put the meat out on sticks or broken pieces of gourd on the rock outcropping. If the meat disappears, they know that the spirits are pleased and the child will get well.

Children are sometimes named after an ancestor whom they resemble in some respect. One child had a drooping eyelid recalling that of an ancestor. The spirit of the ancestor was said to have caused the child's eye to open because he was pleased to have a child named after him.

SPECIAL CHILDREN

Twins are recognized by the Sebei as special children; they are introduced into the world by special ceremonies and are hedged about by special treatment. Special children (*tekeryontet, tekerisiyek*, pl.; from *tekeret*, ear-mark, because the helix is cut with a blocked arrow) include multiple births, a breech-born child (*chemongich; mongich* is ram), a child following twins (*kisa*), a child following the death of a previous child if conceived after the first subsequent menstruation of the mother, or a child born after a number of successive prior siblings have died (*cheptai* or *chemaket; maket* is hyena; the implication is that the child born had "eaten" his older siblings). Twins and breech-born cattle and sheep are also *tekerisiyek*, and a special ceremony is held for them.

When twins are born, the mother is immediately placed in confinement in her house; she may not leave the compound at all, may go outdoors only to relieve herself, or perhaps to sun herself if she has been careful that nobody can see her. Her husband may not see her or the baby; he must go about covered with a cloth (Plate III:18). Neither father nor mother should be seen by a person who has had a twin or a breech birth, is a twin, or was a

---

3. One sequence observed was: FaFaBrSo, FaFaBrSo, MoFaBr, MoBr.

breech-birth baby, or by a woman who is menstruating, pregnant, or known to be barren. The husband is not to hear his wife's voice, though she may hear his, so she must carry on conversations in a low voice. If she needs to attract attention, she does so by pounding the floor with a stick. Her children may see her, but no men enter her house, and most women must stay away. She may not eat meat of an animal that has died (only one that was slaughtered), eggs, milk, bamboo shoots, mushrooms, chicken, fungus, plantains (except two varieties, ŋeriontet and naŋesyet), or use native salt. The plantains she does eat must be brought with the whole stem, including the phallus-shaped flower at the end, which is also peeled and eaten. No ashes may be removed from the house during the period of her confinement; the same applies to plantain peels. Breach of these tabus is said to cause skin disease or even death of the mother.

Because the child is important, it wears special iron jewelry, a twisted iron necklace called *semointet* and two plain bracelets on each arm and anklets on each leg, as well as bells on the legs. Ideally, the child should have a necklace of cowry shells strung on a rope made of black monkey fir, but it will certainly have at least one cowry shell to ward off the evil eye. The mother also will wear special beads around her head for several years to advertise her importance. These restrictions continue until the coming-out ceremony, *yotunet,* is performed (Plates III:20-26).[4] A special drum, made of zebra skin, is required for the subsequent ceremony.

The medicines are prepared and the ritual supervised by a woman who has had twins of the same combination of sexes and raised them to maturity. Like most Sebei ceremonies, the *yotunet* must take place when there is a moon. After the husband has found a woman to prepare the medicine, he must acquire a pregnant ewe and provide beer.[5] One informant of considerable standing had prepared eighteen pots of beer, though in the two instances we witnessed there was no such generosity, but instead a babble of complaint about the insufficiency of refreshments. The affair starts in the evening. Neither parent may partake of the festivities, and the mother remains secluded.

The ritualist is greeted by the women of the host's clan with a song of welcome (as at circumcisions and weddings); they dance backward to the house where the parents of the twins are being kept (Plate III:19). The ritualist prepares the medicine over a special fire inside the house. A clan brother of the father makes an opening in the side of the house large enough for a person to crawl through and digs an oval hole about fifteen inches deep and two feet in diameter a few feet from this opening. The mud from the hole is taken into the house by a clan sister of the wife, while a mother's

---

4. This account of the *yotunet* is based on observation of two twin ceremonies (Atar, 1954; Sasur, 1962), a full description by an informant who had the ceremony for one of his children, and general discussions.

5. One informant had three pots each for his own clans, his age-set members, his wife's father, his wife's brothers, and ceremonialist and her clansmen, and the men who married his sisters. He paid 12 shillings to the ceremonialist, 3 shillings to each of the children who danced on the roof, 10 shillings in lieu of a goat to the sister who took the spear, and beer to the clan brother who dug the hole.

brother's wife smears the inside of the hole with cow dung and mud to make it impervious. The medicine, compounded of diverse leaves, roots and bark, cow's milk and beef, is given to the wife to drink to release her from food restrictions. Some is placed in the hole, and some is kept to be taken over the next few weeks by the mother.

As the pregnant ewe, fully concealed by skins or cloth, is brought to the house by a group of men, it is greeted by the women in the same manner as the ritualist had been. The songs give thanks to the mother for bringing twins, referring to the fact that she has produced a tree with two branches, and often have lewd sexual references. The ewe enters the house through the special hole and is slaughtered by suffocation, the mouth and nostrils being held shut while the animal is swung back and forth. The mother is given some of the amniotic fluid to drink and the grub of the Mount Elgon tick (*seperyontet*, found in cow's dung) to eat. (This grub is normally eaten roasted or dried, not raw.) The chyme is removed from the ewe's stomach and mixed with some of the dirt taken from the hole. The skin, carefully cleaned of all blood and also rubbed with the dirt taken from the hole, is worn by the father of the twins during the subsequent ceremonial. While the animal is being skinned, the women sing and dance inside the house, accompanied by a zebra hide drum, beaten with the ewe's front hoof (Plate III:20). The husband and wife, hidden from the others and each other, are now carefully garlanded with beads and sinentet vine. The father also wears a cowbell over the shoulder and sometimes carries a similarly garlanded spear. The mixture of chyme and earth from the hole is used to anoint the mother, father, and ceremonialist. The ceremonialist and the mother (in one instance both the father and mother) then emerge through the hole, and women who have had twins or breech births smear chyme on their head and face as they appear outside. They also try to smear one another and to avoid being smeared with the nauseous mixture.

Meanwhile, the hole in the ground has been filled with water and the lamb embryo put into it and two uncircumcised children (ideally a clan brother of the father and a clan sister of the mother) have climbed on the roof of the house in which the mother has been confined. They are dressed up, garlanded with vine; one has a bow and arrow and the other a spear, if the surviving twin is a boy, a basket if it is a girl (Plate III:23). A circumcised clan sister of the father is given a shield and spear to hold.

As the principals come out of the house, they are joined by the people present and all dance counterclockwise around the hole; the ceremonialist carefully steps into it and dances for a few minutes on the embryo while the others are dancing and singing around her. She is followed by the father, who is later joined by his wife. After a few minutes, they are again replaced by the ceremonialist. The two children are also carefully dancing on the roof. The dancing continues for 15 to 20 minutes, with the couple dancing on the embryo three or four times. At the close, the whole group dances around the woman's house; the two children on the roof are helped down and run about making charges and thrusts with their weapons, as if in a fight, feinting at those present and the house. The father's sister, who is holding a shield and spear, likewise dashes about pretending to spear people (Plates III:22, 26). Now, people greet the parents in the normal and appropriate manner. People may also insult the parents with remarks that would normally start a fight: "May devils circumcise you," "You are like tapeworms," "Eat feces," and so on. We saw precircumcised boys do this.

While drinking beer later on, those who are so minded may spit beer in blessing on the couple and are similarly blessed by each in return. The beer party continues with all present free to partake, though certain special pots are provided, one for the husband's clan, one for the wife's clan, one for the ceremonialist, and one for the wife's sisters' husbands.

The day after the ceremony the father's brother puts sticks over the hole, the embryo being left there to rot away in the unfilled hole. The ashes are removed from the house by the ceremonialist and hidden where the parents will not come upon them accidentally, for to see them would render one piebald. In the future, both the ritualist and her children should always receive food whenever they visit the house. On the third day, each twins has the upper helix of one ear severed with a blocked arrow (the right one of the first born and the left one of the second) by the mother's sister, who receives a pot of beer in the name of her husband.

When both twins die, the father is supposed to slaughter a ram and rub the fat from its tail on his wife and on his own feet to purify him so he can go about; otherwise, people would say he was cursing the land, for the cattle will not fatten. The parents must do without food or water until a ceremonialist whose twins had also died arrives. She provides the leaves of a plant called kelelonik, which are crushed in water and drunk, and a root of cheplelyontet, which is chewed. After that, most of the restrictions are lifted.

In one case, twins were born to an inherited wife who was not, I think, much wanted by the heir. The first twin had died at birth, the second after ten days. The ceremony should have taken place three days later but was delayed two weeks because the husband had not obtained the services of a ceremonialist, in part because of the reluctance of the appropriate old woman. Gale joined the ceremonialist at 10:00 A.M. on the way to the home of the mother of the dead twins. They were greeted by the father of the twins and his mother, but she left after a few minutes and reappeared only once hours later to bring food to the ceremonialist. A long delay, presumably waiting for the ceremonialist's sister to bring some additional medicines, ended when the ceremonialist made it known that she wanted 24 shillings before beginning to cook the medicines (2 shillings for going down the mountain, 2 shillings for cooking, and 10 shillings each for herself and her sister, who never showed up), and two pounds of sugar, and tobacco and cigarette papers. The husband took a very long time seeking these resources at his brother's house and the house of his first wife, ultimately returning with the money and only one pound of sugar (he had used one pound of sugar for the ceremony).

The ceremonialist unwrapped the medicines (roots cut in pieces, tree fungus, and tiny white mushrooms), placed them unwashed in a small pot, and boiled them in about two cups of water for about forty-five minutes. The liquid was poured into a cup with a few ounces of milk and placed in front of the mother. She did not pick it up for about fifteen minutes, saying she "feared it" and did not like having had twins. "Don't say you don't like twins. If you do, you'll get them again," was the ceremonialist's response. The husband did not participate in this, as it was said he should have. The women present then ate the food provided by the husband's mother. The mother was told to cook the same medicine twice the following day.

When both twins die, the child following the twins (*kisa*) is treated much as a twin. The mother of the *kisa* and her child are confined, and a *yotunet* ceremony for their release must be performed. Some time after the ceremony for the *kisa*, the family visits the grave of the twins (twins were buried aboriginally, though other persons were not) to disinter their bones. One man who had performed the ceremony said that he and his wife were accompanied by his full brother and his wife and others. While the others sang and danced, the brother dug up the bones of the twins, sprinkled beer on their burial place, smeared mud from the grave on the mother and *kisa*, and then took the bones in an old basket and hid them in a dry hollow place in the rocks. Subsequently a ceremonialist and her sons shaved the *kisa* and her mother, leaving a small patch (*sukunyet*) which is not shaved until just before circumcision, when the same woman (or if she is dead, one of her children) will again shave the *kisa*, this time taking off the *sukunyet*. Beer must be provided for the ceremonialist, the father's clansmen, and the mother's clansmen.

When the *kisa* or twin is to be circumcised, the following persons (who are represented by their children if they are dead) must be present: the ceremonialist, the sister who held the shield and spear, the two who danced on the roof, the brother who dug the hole for the embryo, the mother's brother's wife who smeared the hole, and the person who cut the helix of the ear. There must be a shield, a spear, and a basket present at the circumcision. The night before he (or she) is circumcised, he must go to the place where the hole was and smear himself with some mud from that hole. The surviving member of twins is also expected to visit his sibling's grave and smear himself with dirt taken from it. When a twin dies as an adult, he is supposed to be buried, but later his bones should be dug up and placed in a dry cave to release the spirit and enable the clan to have more twins. Other minor special elements in the subsequent ritual life of a twin or *kisa* have been noted in context. One recurrent feature is that ceremonials generally take place on the third rather than the fourth day. A *tekeryontet* may not participate in funerals.

The Sebei do not expand on the symbolism and meaning of the ceremonial activities surrounding the *tekeryontet*. They speak of the joys of having twins, of the status it gives the mother, and express these sentiments with special decoration for both the mother and the child. At the same time, the ceremony is recognized as a hardship on the parents, because of expense, the confinements, and restrictions, and the ritual activity emphasizes the fact. Both in words and expressions, it is made clear that such items as the smearing, the wearing of the wet skin, the dancing on the embryo, and the drinking of the amniotic fluid are repugnant to the Sebei. To this is added the express permission to heap the gravest of insults on the principals and to allow young people, who would normally be beaten for expressing such thoughts to an older person, to join in the insults. It seems that those who have been so "lucky" as to have had twins, and by extension any other *tekeryontet*, must suffer for it and pay the community through a form of hospitality that is often beyond their means.

One other feature of the twin ceremony is the expression of the close identification between humans and livestock, particularly cattle. In human ceremonies, we have seen slaughter of a pregnant animal and the presence of its embryo, the use of the cow bell, and other symbolic representations suggestive of the herding life. Not only do counterpart ceremonies take place for animals, but the women who serves as ceremonialist is a woman who has undergone the same circumstance, not a woman who merely has a cow that has done so, and she gives the animal the same medicine that is given to a mother of twins. While the human celebrations of the *yotunet* for twins were largely dolorous affairs, the one for the calf was cheerful, with happy references to the benefits the special calf brings humans. There may be sound breeding reasons, rather than any magical purposes, for the belief that a twin calf should not be paid in brideprice or exchanged in *namanya* contract.

The role of the *tekeryontet* is enigmatic. He is a special person, marked off from infancy and childhood for the rest of his life in many special ways. He is viewed as particularly vulnerable to harm, and he must be protected by special amulets, medicines, and treatment: As one man said, "His *oynatet* is weaker." His friends are warned not to hit him on the head, because it was bad for him to bleed. One said:

> Other children would tease me because I was wearing rings on my arms and legs, and some would try to pull them off, but I was strict and didn't like them to break these things. I would wrestle with other children but not fight.
>
> I was specially treated by my parents. When I was annoyed, I would cry, and they would come to me, saying, "Keep quiet, my *tekeryontet*." When they spoke politely to me, mentioning that I was *tekeryontet*, I would become quiet, or if they asked me politely, I would do what they wanted. My father beat me only once, when I was grazing cattle and they destroyed somebody's crops. Before the circumcision, they came and shaved me, applied butter on my head, and spit beer on me.

A *tekeryontet* was traditionally not supposed to hunt; he might not lead in warfare but could engage in war. Enemies were not supposed to kill a *tekeryontet*, but the Karamojong did not honor this rule. A *tekeryontet* was not allowed to be a *kirwokintet* but was permitted to speak in council meetings. Today, he is not to go into the house where the beer is fermenting because it would spoil the beer. The most important fact about the *teker-*

yontet is that he participates in the leopard ceremony of the women rather than the lion ceremony of the men at the close of the initiation cycle.

Is it good to be a *tekeryontet*? One man said, "People like to be *tekeryontet* because whenever beer is to be brewed in the family of a *tekeryontet*, there must be extra beer, and when people start singing, they praise his name." Another said that the status was good because he was treated with special consideration and politeness. A non-*tekeryontet* said it was not good for a man "because you are despised and cannot join the lion ceremony."

FRIENDSHIP CEREMONY FOR HALF-BROTHERS

When sons are born to two of a man's wives at about the same time, a ceremony called *chichomnko lekok* is held to cause friendship (*chom*) between the children (*lekok*). This ceremony is performed for boys when the senior one has not learned to walk before the second is born. (If the boys should see one another before the ceremony, it would make them very ill of diarrhea.) Such brothers are in some ways regarded as twins (though they are not *tekerisiyek*), and the ceremony has many aspects of a twin ceremony. There are also similarities to the Kony blood brotherhood ceremony. The two boys may not stand together when they are circumcised; somebody must be between them. Yet they and the person between them must stand on the same cowhide so that their blood will mix together and thus make all three of them friends. Because it is important that boys who have undergone this ceremony "forget" any quarrels between them, whichever one who feels mistreated should find an old man (father, father's brother, or unrelated neighbor, not necessarily the ritualist) to review their problems and establish peace between them.

I observed one such ceremony at which Psiwa Kapchemesyekin was ritualist, for two of his now grown sons had undergone the ceremony. The ritual took place in the home of the second wife, the mother of the younger sibling. Psiwa's party demanded beer before starting the ceremony, which was brought, since "We must obey Psiwa's family as they could do harm to the children." A ram, covered with a blanket, was led through an opening into the house, just as the ewe is handled in the twin ceremony, and was suffocated in the same way. Its throat was then slit with an arrow, the ventral side opened, and the intestines put into pans. No augury was made. Meanwhile, mud was chopped away from the door posts and lintel and palm fronds placed in the openings thus made on either side of the door were mudded over with fresh cow dung by Psiwa and his wife. Apples of Sodom were studded along either side of the door. A small basin of mud was made on the door sill; it was filled with apples of Sodom, and chyme was placed inside the mud basin. Sinentet grass was put around the pot of beer and on the roof and was later worn by Psiwa, the father, and the two mothers. A number of different plants brought by Psiwa and his wife were used to make an anointing whisk. The scrotum of the ram was pulled over a small gourd, in which was put milk from cows belonging to the two wives, beer, and bits of the slaughtered ram's tail and penis. Some of the ram's meat was cooked so that the children could be given a piece from each part of the ram.

When these arrangements had been completed, each mother brought her covered child and sat near the doorway, the senior one to the left of the door and the junior one in front. The children were uncovered, and Psiwa spat a mouthful of the contents of the gourd on each child several times in succession. With each spitting, he and others said *anyiñ* (peace) and other things not recorded. In the interval between repeated spittings, the older child looked over at the younger and took his hand, which amused all, for these two children had never before seen one another. Psiwa then took bits of the meat, chewed them slightly, and put them in the mouths of the two children. The mothers then exchanged children and suckled them (though the younger refused the breast, to everyone's amusement but no one's consternation).

A procession now formed of Psiwa, the father, and the two wives carrying the children (Plate III:17). One of Psiwa's sons for whom the ceremony had once been performed anointed the husband, wives, and children, by dipping the whisk into the chyme in the basin on the threshold. Chyme was then smeared on the head, face, body, and legs of each person. After the anointing, Psiwa led the small process went around the house, banging an ax head against a pick head beneath the blanket he wore. They circled the house four times, stopping in front of the door each time to be anointed again.

Plantain mush and boiled mutton were served to the guests. While they were eating, Psiwa fed the mothers and the two children bits of meat. This closed the ceremony, and Psiwa and his guests returned to the beer pot.

CHILDREN'S TASKS

Children from their earliest years are expected to handle serious chores and are inducted into their responsibilities with stern measures. One woman described the work of girls as follows:

> When a mother goes away from home she may leave a girl of four or five years. She gives her a small gourd to fetch water in and tells her to sweep the house, bring firewood, collect vegetables, and look after the younger children. A few years later, when the girl is seven or eight, she will start to dig in the gardens. She will start to cook and make the fire by the time she is eight. She is taught to do exactly as her mother does, so that when the mother goes anywhere, she will return home to find the work done. If the mother finds the work improperly done, she only abuses the girl the first time, saying: "I hope that you have stomach pains and dysentery." Mothers are concerned that their daughters learn proper housekeeping so that their husbands will not beat them for neglecting their duties, and so it will not be said that they failed to learn proper behavior from their mother.

When one of the herd-boys near Binyinyi was asked what chores a boy had to do he said:

> Some of them plow the fields with oxen [if the family has them] ; some go to school; some hunt; some weed the maize and millet; some scare birds and monkeys away from the fields; some help harvest; some help build houses by cutting poles and vines and by tying the small sticks together that form the walls; some build fences around the kraal or gardens; and sometimes down on the plains, when boys are alone with the cattle, they milk the cows, but never when the women are present. My grandfather taught me to herd when I was four or five years old and I taught my younger brothers. My paternal grandfather also taught me how to make a bow, but I learned how to make arrows from the older boys, who also taught me how to hunt.

His younger brother expanded on the herding chore, which was their principal task. The boys take turns herding the cattle of their fathers. On the days that the boys are not herding, they look out for the proper grass so that they will know where to take the cattle. When one of the goats was eaten by a hyena, his father merely abused him, because it was his first offense. ("You foolish child, why do you sleep while the hyena eats my goats? I wish you would disappear and die. You just played with your friends and let my goat die.") Later, when one of the cattle got into another man's field, the boy hid in the bush for three days, sleeping in the home of a friend, "Until my father was happy again," and again he was only scolded. He was beaten once for refusing to herd the cattle and going to school instead. Older men recalled childhood experiences with pain. One told of having his hands tied to the housebeam and being beaten on the thighs, "Until they were as dry as bark of a tree," for losing a cow. When he let the sheep get into the house and eat the potatoes prepared for supper, he had to go without food while watching the others eat. Another time, he was whipped for not keeping his younger brother from eating out of the pot of honey.

The herding chore normally passes from son to son as these grow older, and a son continues to look after his father's herd until after he has married and a younger brother can take over. Thus, the relationship established in youth continues until adult status is achieved, and the father continues to berate and occasionally curse the sons for delinquencies and inefficiencies. Curses are extremely dangerous and rare but stand as an ultimate threat.

Edgerton asked a series of questions about what a child should learn or know at various ages (*RBE*: 310), and the responses consistently point to the performance of tasks. When he asked what was the most important thing that parents should teach toddlers, tasks were mentioned in 28 of the 168 responses (only the Pokot used this response more frequently), and this was the largest category of response. Obedience and politeness were mentioned 15 times. The responses to the question, "What is the first useful task a boy/girl is given," are set forth in Table 44. These show most clearly that the work expectations for the sexes vary. Care of children was not specifically mentioned even for girls. Neither herding nor skill with the bow and arrow is really important to Sasurese, though there is some care of goats, but parents still expect their children to have these capabilities.

Edgerton also asked what were the two most important things a man or woman should *know* before marriage — here not suggesting work, but asking for any kind of knowledge. For women, farming, housework, or simply "hard work" accounted for 121 responses (52.2 percent); for men, care of farm, cattle, or property for 97 (49.5 percent), and "get wealth" an additional 40 (20.4 percent). Learning obedience accounted for 9.9 percent and 8.7 percent of responses for girls and boys, respectively; learning bravery was mentioned once, and care of children was not mentioned at all.

Work appears as the basic imperative of life, not as a moral value. There are virtually no responses indicating how persons should interact with one another, other than to learn obedience, not even how to care for babies, though two persons thought that learning to please their husbands sexually had such priority.

One of the ubiquitous products of Western influence is the school (Plates III:5-6). The Catholic Missions operate large schools in Sipi, Kabruron, and Bukwa and smaller ones elsewhere; the Anglican Church and its affiliates operate numerous primary schools, which now are fully under government control. There was no secondary school in Sebei until about 1960 and no college (high school) until several years later. The first generation of leaders was unschooled or educated in conjunction with military service. The leaders in the 1950's were generally mission-educated away from Sebei; there were but a handful at that time, and they remain a small cadre. Increasingly, however, school is seen as a necessary means of advancement and more and more children are getting some education. (One of the more remarkable changes observed in 1972 was the fact that, although few adults speak English, the younger children were learning it in school. During the colonial period, instruction was in Luganda; since independence, teaching has been in English.)

In 1962, interest in education had not suffused the general population and the level of education in the villages was still quite low. Evidence on the level of education appears in Table 45. This information is presented in three sets: (1) household heads of Kwoimet age-set or younger, (2) circumcised sons and daughters of all households (who would have completed their schooling), and (3) uncircumcised children who have had some school. A comparison of the data on Kapsirika and Sasur men shows that more Sasurese have an education and also that educated Sasurese have spent more time in school. The data base for the third set includes all children, from new-born infants to circumcision, and hence 40 to 50 percent of them are not ready for school. Thus, the data do not tell us the proportion of school-age children in school. They show that almost as many Kapsirika as Sasur children go to school and that the differential between boys and girls in school continues among the younger children in both communities.

TABLE 44
First Tasks for Children to Learn

Learning experience	Boys			Girls		
	Sasur	Kapsirika	Total	Sasur	Kapsirika	Total
Herding	44	53	97	0	0	0
Farming	4	0	4	43	15	58
Housework	0	0	0	17	45	62
Bow & arrow	10	6	16	0	0	0
Obedience/morality	1	0	1	0	1	1
Other/no answers	5	5	10	4	3	7
Total	64	64	128	64	64	128

SOURCE: Questions 5 and 9 (RBE:310).

TABLE 45
Educational Attainments: Sasur and Kapsirika

Respondents	Sasur				Kapsirika			
	Male		Female		Male		Female	
	No.	Pct	No.	Pct	No.	Pct	No.	Pct
Household heads[a]								
No schooling	19	63.3			21	77.8		
Some schooling	11	36.7			6	22.2		
Average years[b]		4.1				3.5		
Circumcised children[c]								
No schooling	24	47.1	21	72.4	8	42.1	16	80.0
Some schooling	27	52.9	8	27.6	11	57.9	4	20.0
Average years[b]		4.6		2.6		3.7		3.0
Uncircumcised children[d]								
No schooling	71	71.0	73	83.8	50	68.5	60	88.2
Some schooling	29	29.0	14	16.1	23	31.5	8	11.8

SOURCE: Demographic questionnaires taken in 1961-62.

[a]Younger men, Kwoimet age-set and younger. Data on education of wife not obtained.
[b]Average of those who had any schooling.
[c]School attendance usually completed.
[d]All living uncircumcised children, whether of school age or not.

CHILDHOOD PLAY

Children make diverse toys: hoops and poles, jackstones (tossing a rock upward rather than bouncing a ball), wheel push-toys made from plantain trunks, dolls fabricated out of parts of the plantain blossom, and a wheel-barrow-like wagon in which they push each other about. At certain seasons, the boys fabricate elfin-like hats out of fleshy leaves, which they press together, shaping them over their knees, and wear about for days (Plates III:7-9,11,13-14). From time to time, we came upon children making minia-ture houses, playing house, or pretending to bargain for cattle or wives (Plates III:15-16). Three young informants described these activities as follows.

> We use the small stones for young cattle and the big ones for bulls; we find stones of special colors, and we give them the names of cows of that color. We exchange cows. If one of us wants to borrow a bull [in imitation of the *namanya* exchange], he asks for it and pays a heifer for it, and then when the heifer has a calf we pay it back. We also pretend that we are going to ask somebody for his daughter to marry, and then we pretend we go back after months and talk about payment. We use sticks to represent the cows and goats in counting what we will pay; we put down the bull for the uncle and then the sticks for the cows, and if we have no goats, we will add another cow, and so on. We pretend we have beer; once when we go to ask, once when we are counting out the sticks and once when we come to get the daughter. We find a rock that represents the pot and we take long grass for beer straws. Then two of us will drag the girl home, telling her that her father has taken all the payment and that she shouldn't refuse, and we beat her with small sticks. When we get her home we have her cook food for our visitors and give her something to eat, but sometimes she refuses. We fear she will try to run away, and we watch her. We sometimes build a house so she will stay. We don't demand the "cows" back; we don't play to win or to get anything. We also play we take the cows to where they are kept in other men's kraals. Sometimes we slaughter them and sell them or pretend to eat them. We put the sticks down in a line and say we are circumcising boys; we pretend to be the fathers. We take a certain kind of grass and make a "knife" out of it and pretend to be cutting them. We also dance and pretend to slaughter a sheep and use mud for the smearing. Sometimes, one of them cries and we pretend to hold it down, and then we must bring a stone, for one has to pay a cow to the circumcisor for crying.

Boys also do a good deal of hunting, especially in the drier areas. They early learn to make crude but effective bows and several different kinds of arrows for shooting rodents, birds, and the like. The animals they kill are cooked and eaten by the children while in the bush. Early one morning at Atar, after the "leopard" ceremony closing the initiation cycle, we watched a group of children playing (Plate III:10). After they had been scolded for playing with the friction drum in obvious imitation of the ceremony that they had been forbidden to watch, they played with a bird that had been stunned with an arrow (Plate III:12). A stick was tied to its leg, so that when the bird was released the weight prevented it from escaping; as its burden became entangled in the bushes, the boys would catch it over and over again; later they broke its leg and ultimately killed and ate it. We rarely saw children fighting, though they did quarrel a good deal. We saw them play no games of skill except jackstones, no games of chance, and no team games, except at school. Sebei adults do not play; the game of *mweso*, sometimes called African chess, which is common throughout Africa, was known to some informants, but we never saw Sebei play it. The contests formerly associated with boys' seclusion after circumcision — throwing spears, throwing clubs and wrestling — have been largely if not entirely lost to modern Sebei youth.

Girls of about eight cut scars on their bodies in rows extending from just below the ribs to the abdomen and raise keloids, which are considered sexually exciting to their lovers later on. Boys cut marks on their faces, usually one or two on each cheek, and darken them by rubbing soot into the wound, while girls make beauty spots in the same place by means of a leaf that leaves a permanent black mark on their brown skins.

At about the age of eight, shortly after the eruption of the second teeth, both boys and girls have the two central lower incisors removed. The evulsion is performed by any person skilled at the operation, and he may be given something like tobacco, but there is no pay. There is no demand for the bravery that characterizes circumcision, but the family would be ashamed if the evulsion had not been done by the time of circumcision. A person who has not had these teeth removed would not be allowed to bite off the ceremonial "bread" that is given to initiates after the cutting.

GENERAL CONSIDERATIONS

The two most significant aspects of child training among the Sebei are the insistence on obedience — young to old, females to males — and on the importance of the performance of tasks. The Sebei share the Southern Nilotic tradition of age-grades, and age-grades always carry with them not only the identity of age peers, but the superordination of the older over the younger. Among the Sebei, the latter aspect is the more important. It is also important that this is a generalized obedience, not just obedience to one's parents or other particularized individuals. Obedience is also inculcated through circumcision, which provides a powerful sanction for all adults to control all children. The unobtrusiveness of Sebei children suggests that the children internalize this lesson at an early age.

Work is the second major feature of Sebei child training. One of the harassments initiates undergo before their final ritual is to be asked to perform tasks of exaggerated difficulty; when they refuse, they are punished. The Sebei attitude toward work is devoid of the sense of moral good. The child is not made to feel that it is good to be busy, that idleness is evil, or that work is its own reward; rather, work is something that must be done

ALBUM III
Parents and Children

1-4 The care of children: (1) characteristic way of holding child; (2) child nursing mother who is making a basket; (3) child nurse (*mwet*) and her charge; (4) feeding baby cow's milk with cupped hand.

5-6 School scenes: (5) *al fresco* in Kapsirika; (6) classroom in Sasur.

7-16 Children's activities: (7) child shooting toy bow; (8) children at Benet; (9) boy mimicking our picture-taking; (10) imitating the use of the friction drum on the morning after the *melilo* ceremony; (11) home-made wheelbarrow; (12) teasing bird on a string; (13) herdboy with mushrooms collected on a stick, wearing a leaf hat; (14) of the kind being fashioned by another child; (15) fantasy play of household activities; (16) fantasy play with stones representing cattle.

17 Psiwa Kapchemesyekin leading procession in ceremony for half-brothers.

18-26 Twin ceremony: (18) father of twin remaining concealed while seeking a pregnant ewe: (19) dance procession of the women upon arrival of the ceremonialist; (20) women awaiting for the mother of twins to emerge from the ceremonial door; (21) woman anointing the mother as she emerges from the ceremonial door; (22) man demonstrating to a young woman how spear should be handled; (23) children dancing on roof; (24-25) the parents of twins dancing on the embryo of the lamb, and (26) woman engaging in mock fighting. (Numbers 19-21 taken in Sasur in 1962; numbers 22-26 in Kaptanya in 1954.)

27-33 Wedding party: (27) preparing the bride; (28) anointing members of the bridal party; (29) loading a *mwet* with a gourd of milk; (30) signing the contract; (31) bridal party arriving near home of bride; (32) scene from the mock battle; (33) confrontation between bridal party and bride's family.

34-35 Ceremony for digging up the bones of the prophet: (34) an offering of beer; (35) offering a goat.

36-38 Ceremony for removal of a curse: (36) anointing members of the cursed family; (37) weapon upon which curse was made; (38) preparing the anointing mixture in a 'kraal' formed of cow dung at the threshold.

2

3

4

5

6

8

7   9

11   12

10

13   14

15

18   20

19   21

22

23 24

25

26

27

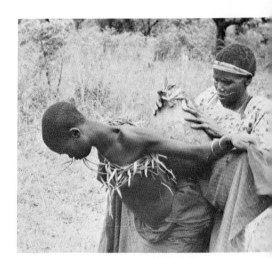

29

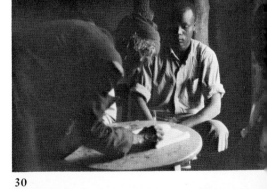

28　　30

31

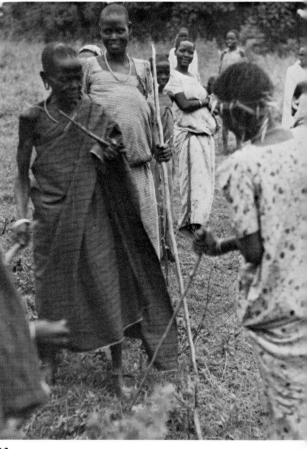

32   33

34 35

37

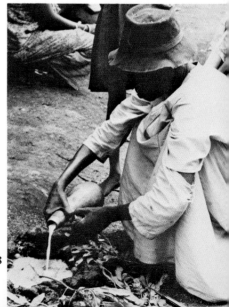

36 38

and failure to do it leads to abuse and chastisement. Children are punished for failure, not praised for fulfillment. Moveover, the Sebei display a notable lack of the spirit of workmanship. Few Sebei make things; fewer still take pride in craftsmanship, and one does not see children engaged in elaborate fabrications. The rapidity with which the Sebei gave up their limited technical skills — tanning, pottery, for instance — is a case in point. Work, then, is a task, not a source of personal satisfaction or an expression of moral worth.

The lack of moral content in the concept of work reflects the small role moralizing plays in child training in general. Neither morality nor specific moral precepts are thought necessary for children; they are taught to be obedient rather than good. Bad spirits are specifically not the result of bad people, but of unfortunate ones; they are to be placated, not condemned. The tales that are told are neither cautionary nor moralizing. If any one behavioral theme predominates, it is that people are not to be trusted. Many begin with such standard openings, "Hare and elephant were friends," and conclude with one doing the other in.

The child learns early that, so long as he obeys the demands of his elders and fulfills his duties, he is free to do very much as he pleases. Those Sebei who found their way into more advanced schooling and became leaders seemed to do so because they wanted to, not because of coercion by their parents or because they sought to please them. Parents do withhold schooling, but if they do so it is because they do not want to pay the fees or because they require the services of their children, not because they want to direct the child's future. There is little pressure on the children to conform to specific parental standards.

Perhaps this absence of pressure, either moral or social, is responsible for the relative absence of competitiveness among children. Even the competitive sports that once characterized the initiation period for boys have quietly dropped from sight. This quality also makes for the absence of quarreling and fighting among children. So long as they have met their duties as housekeepers and herd boys, they are free to play their replicas of adult life, circumcising, trading cattle, and beating the wives for which they bargain.

One thing all children clearly learn in early childhood is the sexual role they are to perform; boys and girls each have their tasks. Occasionally, a boy will serve as *mwet*, taking care of a younger sibling, but this is really a girl's job, as are farming and household chores, while the boys are taught to care for livestock even when these are an insignificant element in the economy. They not only learn the appropriate sex-related tasks, they also learn the sex-related social roles, as their fantasy play indicates. They also indulge in sex play.

Underlying all these elements in Sebei childhood is the essential affectlessness of their personal environment. The infant suckling at the breast receives nurturance and bodily satisfactions from his mother, but he gets very little of her personal attention, no matter how hard he kneads the other teat with his little fist. Later, he avoids abuse and punishment by fulfilling his duties but he receives no special commendation for work well done; accomplishment neither increases the love he will receive nor improves his self-image. Perhaps the shift from the indulgence of the suckling infant to the demand for obedience that he internalizes a few months later does not create the trauma that theory would suggest because it is not accompanied by any change in affect. From infancy on, the child is surrounded by indifference, not cruelty.

This indifference is evident when the child hurts himself, for he is not comforted but only teased or mocked if he cries. From this, he learns to be a little stoic, enduring pain without complaint or demonstration. The absence of empathy toward misfortune expresses itself in childhood interaction, for, though children rarely fight or quarrel, they do tease one another mercilessly for any evident failures.

Though by Western standards childhood is relatively carefree and with few parental pressures, it is not a happy period, and the Sebei do not view it as one. Of the 128 respondents, only 7 (3 men) said that childhood was the happiest period in a man's life, and only 14 (8 women) said that "before circumcision" was the happiest in a female's. Young adult status, particularly that between circumcision and marriage, was the most frequently expressed ideal.

We did not compare childhood and child training in Sasur and Kapsirika. I think infant care and childhood is essentially the same in terms of parental attitudes; expectation of work, insistence on obedience, slight concern with moral bases for behavior, lack of empathy and low expression of affect. Boys in Kapsirika are more apt to perceive their work as meaningful but have more work to do, and girls have fewer and generally less onerous duties, except that hauling water is often burdensome. There is a slightly greater tendency to view childhood favorably in Kapsirika (fifteen as against six such responses), and I think this reflects these experiential elements rather than variation in treatment by adults.

Chapter 10
The Ritual Transformation from Child to Adult

My stomach is churning;
Mother is very worried,
I do not think that you will be brave tomorrow.

Mother's circumcision song

The ceremonial activities (*meriket*) that mark the transition of Sebei boys and girls into adult status are the most important and dramatic events of Sebei life today and probably have always been so. The ceremonial cycle may take one to six months to complete. Boys generally undergo the initiation at eighteen to twenty years; girls a couple of years younger. There are two major and several minor elements in the cycle: the first has as its central feature the circumcision of the boys and a counterpart operation, involving the severing of the whole labia minora, for the girls. (This is also called circumcision locally, and I shall follow this practice, although it should perhaps be called labiodectomy, for it is not merely a clitoridectomy.) There follow minor ceremonies of shaving, painting, and partial release from seclusion tabus. The cycle culminates with the second major ritual events, allocating the initiates to their appropriate age-sets and signalizing their reentry into the normal activities of society.

Our presentation is built on several sources. We watched six first ceremonies involving the circumcision of thirty-three girls and ten boys. These were in Atar, Kabruron, and Bukwa in 1954 (all girls); in Sasur, Kapsirika, and its neighboring village of Nyelit in 1962, the first of girls, the second coeducational, and the third of boys. We watched the shaving, painting, and release ceremonies once each, and we watched, to the extent we were permitted, three closing ceremonies. In addition, we held many discussions with informants about the ceremony and the subjective aspects of their experience. There was little objection to our observing the first and middle phases of the ceremonies, but we were denied permission to observe the ceremonies in which the secrets are imparted or to see the "animals" (*tiyonik*), as the medicines are called. We were disappointed not to have

267

observed the final ritual, in which the initiates receive instructions, for this would have given us insight into Sebei values and attitudes.

Like most initiatory rites, this one demonstrates the themes associated with death and rebirth: the initiate enters into a period of nonexistence from a social point of view; he does not use his name but is referred to by his ordinal position; he is rigorously secluded from his opposite-sexed parent; and he emerges with a new name, receives new clothes, and must be reintroduced to the familiar items of everyday life. These themes are now given no overt expression, even by implication, either in songs or in conversations. For instance, although the painting on the body of the initiates could easily be interpreted as representing a skeleton, no Sebei made such an indication; informants repeatedly denied that the marks had any significance and merely said that initiates were painted so that even a mother could not recognize her child.

The dominant overt theme of the initiation is that of an ordeal — a trial and proof. In songs, in exhortation, in concern over preparation, in avoidance of evil forces is the reiterated theme of the hardships to be faced and the necessity to be brave. An initiate of 1920 retains a dubious notoriety through the song created when he cried at circumcision:

> Chemokey was cut to cry the alarm,
> Chemokey was cut to bellow.
> As a cow seeking calf; as a cow delivering calf.
> In Chepkasta.

PRELIMINARIES

Sebei children start to attend initiation ceremonies as infants on their mothers' backs and, as we have seen, they enact the ceremony in their childhood games. One of their childhood songs refers to the bitterness of the experience. As they reach puberty, they become increasingly anxious to participate in the ceremony that will make them a man or a woman.[1] As boys, they will want to avoid being rejected by women because they are "dirty"; as girls, they will begin to fear pregnancy. The boys especially begin to resent the constant irritation of being viewed as a "mere boy" by the men and women in their community. They find that those with whom they have been herding cattle and sharing fantasy play now treat them with disdain. Thus, one informant reports:

> I was refused permission in 1938 [when fifteen]. I returned from school and found my brother suffering from the circumcision, and I went to see his sores. He was with his friends, all initiates. I asked them to tell me about it, but they would only say that it is very painful: "The cutting, that is a very small thing, but the pain of the sore one feels very strongly." My brother told

---

1. They are called boy (*wirit*) and girl (*chepto*) until they are circumcised; thereafter, they are warrior (*moran*) and young woman (*koket*). While the man's transition from *moran* to elder (*pontet*) is gradual, a woman is called *muraret* after marriage and *chepyos* after menopause.

me that, if I was ready, he would have no objections to my being circumcised in the same year as he was, but one of his friends said: What is that child saying?" So I started to cry and lost my temper and tried to force my father and mother to circumcise me in the same year. But they refused.

Later the same year, when another group of boys was being circumcised, this informant sneaked out during the night and tried to join them as they were undergoing their precircumcision rituals, but his father spoke to those in charge and he was stopped just as they were arriving at the place to be cut. He refused to eat for two days. Similar behavior was often reported, for both boys and girls; in Sasur, a girl of fifteen tried to join the group but was stopped by her father who did not want her circumcised when he had not prepared beer, though another girl's father did not mind.

In earlier times, the circumcision ritual for boys took place every six or seven years at a time determined by the prophet on the basis of when the sietet plant (*Mimulopsis* sp.) flowered. The initiation started at the eastern end of Sebeiland and continued, *pororyet* by *pororyet*, across the territory. At that time, apparently, very large groups of boys were circumcised to-gether, giving a sense of unity to the initiatory rite; the total ritual cycle received a kind of Sebei-wide coordination that it now lacks. By the late 1920s, such coordination had declined. While circumcision now officially opens in the east, each small group of self-selected boys is initiated without regard to east-west precedence. By the mid-1930s, a two-year schedule was established in governmental regulations and timed to minimize disruption in the boys' schooling. Nowadays, there is a tendency to have the ceremony on Saturday for the same reason. No such consideration applies to the girls, who are now circumcised every year, usually if not always in the spring. As luck would have it, the boys' circumcision fell in December when we were not in Sebeiland, but we were privileged to see it because some plains area men disregard the regulations.

For some neighboring tribes, there was reportedly a tendency for the established age-sets to try to hold off the initiation of a new one, because it threatened their controlling functions, but no such attitude was expressed by the Sebei who, in remembered culture never had such age-set functions anyway. Nevertheless, all informants agree that men were formerly initiated at a much later age — after they had beards — than is customary today. In those days, men might go on raids before they were circumcised. In the Mbai area, they also sometimes were married before circumcision but this was not Sapiñ custom, and some consider it very shameful (*KC*:67-68). The earlier age of circumcision, I was told, began with the Chumo *pinta*, between 1910 and 1920.

Though many of the youths make last-minute decisions, most of them prepare in advance for the ritual. Youths ready to be initiated get together and perform a dance (*chepkwoyet*) to announce they are ready to undergo the rite; this has the effect of bringing pressure on their elders to make arrangements. A week or so before the date set, they put on the beads and other paraphernalia associated with circumcision and go the length and breadth of Sebeiland extending invitations to relatives and associates of their parents (Plates IV:1-2, also Plate II:13). The girls used to go naked on such excursions (contrary to the nonnudity of girls and women generally), but the missionaries early induced them to be clad, and they now wear very short skirts in addition to their beads. Boys also used to go naked, but in earlier days men generally exposed themselves; nowadays, they go fully clad. Those expected to attend are the siblings of each parent and the married siblings and grandparents of the initiates. The man who stood next to the father in initiation is particularly enjoined to be present and should furnish a ram for slaughtering. A twin or *tekeryontet* has other special persons to invite.

Gale talked to Siret's three daughters, who were to be circumcised together, regarding their peregrination inviting kindred to their initiation. One of them detailed the places they had gone to; together, the girls had spent seventeen days circumnavigating Mount Elgon, a good deal of it on foot but some by bus, received gifts and promises of gifts from about a dozen relatives (brothers and sisters of their fathers; brothers of their mothers), sung and danced at each place, and generally enjoyed themselves.

In addition to making up the invitation list, preparing beer, and arranging for food, the parents must decide who is to be initiated, who the instructors are to be, who is to do the operation, and the order of precedence among the initiates. Some of these decisions cannot be made until after the ceremony has begun because of late entrants and dropouts.

The unit now initiated together is very small; the number we saw ranged from five to nine. They need not belong to the same clan or village, though they will normally live close together. Once a small nucleus has formed, others attach themselves to it up to the very last minute. And some drop out at the last minute, too.

Some parents take the opportunity of an initiation to put on a lavish display; some do not. It is considered particularly appropriate to do so when the first child is initiated, but feasting really depends on parental attitudes. It is, in fact, one of the major differentials between the plains and the escarpment. As one plainsman said, "down here we compete." Siret, who was planning the circumcision of two sons and three daughters, said disdainfully, "I wish I lived in Masop, where the people aren't troubled. As soon as the circumcision is over, they just walk away to find where the beer is. A friend of mine in Kapturu, who had his girls circumcised, made beer, but when the time came he sold that beer and went out to find beer for himself" (*KC*:45). In 1954, in Atar (near Binyinyi, in the central escarpment), the beer laid on by one of the fathers was less than social expectations demanded, while another did not have any beer, though his daughter was a *tekeryontet*. In Sasur in 1962, there was even less concern with meeting these social obligations. Only one of the six parents furnished a ram for slaughter, and there was no feasting. The senior father quite clearly had no intention of killing an animal, or even providing beer, and made no preparations for his daughter's initiation. This was not unusual; three men were tied up during the circumcision as "prisoners" of their *pinta*-mates because they had failed to provide beer for their age-set when their children were circumcised earlier.

The contrast in the plains is extreme. There, parents often give a feast that can be likened to a Northwest Coast Indian potlatch. Arrangements go on for weeks in advance. One man claimed to have already spent 4,000 shillings (*KC*:44) for an initiation that was to take place four weeks later. He was accumulating animals to slaughter, laying down beer, and buying sugar in 100-pound sacks and tea in quantity. He set forth for me a guest list of more than thirty men who would receive specific invitations; they would bring their wives and children, and many others would "push in." He described enviously the arrangements made by the leader of the next village to the east.

> Koboloman had a circumcision ceremony, and we stayed at his house a month. If you had taken pictures, you would have run out of film. This time [he was then planning a second circumcision], he has prepared 40 sacks of maize and I think he wants people to stay at his home for two months. Koboloman is very proud of himself because he is rich in food. Everybody respects him, for he buys respect in this way. Last time he killed six oxen. This man will brew so much beer he hasn't room in his house and must rent his neighbor's houses. When such a person is around the beer pots, people will dance and speak his name, tell the amount of beer, and say that he kept people at his house for such a long time.
>
> Down here on the plains, we don't have persons who furnish rams and bullocks; nobody must help, it all depends on me. We despise those people in Masop who put their children together, select one of them to slaughter a ram, and after the circumcision get one or two pots of beer, or just buy a 20-shilling pot. They cannot boil tea, never kill a cow, don't buy English beer or even *waragi*. Nobody in Masop tries to compete with another . . . so that he would come to be a person who is known.

Each initiate (*chemeryontet*, *chemerik*, pl.) has an instructor (*moteriyontet*, *motriyonik*, pl.), a woman for girls, a man for boys. The *moteriyontet* provides the medicines and administers them; goes with the initiates during the ceremony; instructs them in the dances, songs, positions to assume, and other aspects of behavior; and ultimately teaches the initiate the secrets imparted during this period. During the cutting of the girls, she encourages them to be brave; after the cutting, she disposes of the severed parts and the blood, which must not fall into the hands of hostile persons. The *moteriyontet* must be a person who has a good relationship with the initiate and his family; he or she may or may not be kin. I was told that the *moteriyontet* cannot belong to the initiate's *aret*, nor can a mother act as *moteriyontet* for her daughter. Yet, I have instances where the *moteriyontet* is of the same clan as the initiate or is married into the clan and one instance where a woman served as instructor for a younger half-sister. The father's sister is particularly enjoined from engaging in this role. Usually *motriyonik* are relatively young adults who have been initiated for ten or fifteen years, for it is a rigorous activity. A permanent role, reminiscent of godparenthood, is established, and the initiate will address his instructor as Moterienyu (my instructor) throughout his life and will be called son or daughter by him. The *moteriyontet* is usually paid something for the activity (now normally 3 shillings) and at some subsequent date the father should brew beer for him or "he will be cursed [by the *moteriyontet*] and will have bad luck." The *moteriyontet* must be a trusted person, for his failure to dispose of the blood and severed parts properly could harm the initiate later on. A man may not marry a girl for whom his wife has served as *moteriyontet* "because they might quarrel at some later time." Another consideration in selecting an instructor is the bravery of the youths he has sponsored. The selection of *moteriyontet* is thus a matter of importance. He or she in turn selects the assistant (*sayantet*) who performs the more onerous task of finding the medicinal plants that are vital to the ceremony.

The locale and order of precedence for the cutting are subject to a good deal of controversy among the parents. Early placement confers some status; it is based upon the seniority of the father and, within the family, the seniority of the respective mothers, the relative age of the children being irrelevant. During the period of seclusion, the initiates are known by their ordinal position: *kaporet*, the first; *arapkaporet*, after the first; *kamayai*, the third; *arapkamayai*, after the third; *kaplatum*; *arapkaplatum*, and so on. (*Arap* is used for "son of." but here it has the meaning of following.) The several pairs are expected to have particularly close relationships throughout life. If there is an odd number, the final person associates with the preceding two. A person circumcised alone is called *kamukur*, alone. A pregnant girl is circumcised after all the rest. Two brothers (sons of the same man) must not be next to one another in line. If necessary, a child will be asked to stand there, as we saw happen to a frightened and protesting boy of about ten. He was not, of course, circumcised then. Twins are an exception; they must stand on the same skin next to one another; even if one is a boy and the other a girl, they should be circumcised together. The *kaporet* has seniority, and men want their sons or daughters to have this position, if possible. It is said that if he or she is brave, then the others will also be. However, the *kaporet* position does not mean that he or she will later be a leader of the group.

Formerly, circumcision took place in an open grassy area; nowadays, it generally takes place close to a house of one of the principals and, in the plains, it is considered proper to have it in the kraal, though this is a new custom. A chief consideration in Sasur was whether the place was known to be lucky. In the Nyelit circumcision, the two principal fathers agreed that, though the initiates would spend the precutting ceremony together, they would be circumcised separately in two groups, one in each kraal. Koboloman, the leader of the Nyelit group, was anxious to have his son be first in line, but one of the other boys was son of a man, now dead, who was his senior. Koboloman and the other boy's guardian resolved the conflict by having separate cutting groups, with two *Kaporet*, (though the boys went through all the preliminaries together and shared the same circumcisor). The reason given me, however, was that, if the boys were circumcised only in one place, the *oyik* of the other clan would be annoyed and cause excessive bleeding. A similar dispute occurred in Sasur, with more apparent acrimony. Many such matters are sitll subject to debate during the night before the cutting, long after the ceremonial activities have begun.

The circumcisor (variously, *korkoptum, kepintet,* or *mutintet*) must also be selected. Some time before the date set, the father will get in touch with a specialist in these operations, giving him a part of his pay and taking the knife back with him as a kind of security. No Sebei men and only two women perform this operation. Girls are usually circumcised by a Pokot or Nandi women (Plate IV:13) (though we watched one old Sebei woman perform the operation in Atar), boys always by men from the Gisu, Kitosh, or some tribe other than Sebei. Sebei men once performed the circumcision but now disdain this work. I was told that a man once refused to take any cattle for his daughter's brideprice from a circumcisor as they had been acquired by the blood of circumcision (with a symbolic appropriateness, he accepted a spear). Informants were disdainful of Gisu who make a trade out of being a circumcisor and have a saying that a cow bought with money thus earned will certainly die. By 1972, there were several Sebei circumcisors of both sexes, some quite young. Circumcisors are now given biennial medical examinations and are certified by the government. I was told in 1962 that they received 20 shillings for the operation, 2 shillings for their appearance and 50 cents "to wash their hands." If the girl is pregnant, the fee may be as high as 40 shillings, and extra is also paid for a *tekeryontet.*

CIRCUMCISION

The ritual of circumcision starts at dawn, continues through the day and night, and culminates with the actual cutting just as the sun breaks the horizon the following morning. Except for the operation, and perhaps some of the secret medicines, it is identical for boys and girls.

The initiates (*chemerik*) usually have been together through the night; they gather behind the house where they have stayed with their instructors and put on their costumes, then kneel on the ground and a strong purgative is administered by the *moteriyontet.* A special flexible stick (*syomyet*) is cut from the cheptuyet bush by the sponsor or his assistant, and the initiates and others carry one or more of these throughout the ritual. They now get their first instructions, a series of tabus on their behavior for the next twenty-four hours: do not laugh, do not touch the ground, do not put down the long sticks, do not spit on the ground but in the handkerchiefs they are given. Then their instructors raise them one by one, they sing their first song, and dance in front of the house (Plate IV:30), observed by sleepy youngsters and a few adults who have come out:

> The circumcision knife is in the house for you.
> It is not for the slaughtering of a cow,

> But for your slaughter.
> The leopard is in the house in need of goats.

After a few more songs, they adjust their costumes, adding some beads or other decoration loaned to them by some woman (a relative, a sweetheart, or even a mother), "For we do not fear [respect tabus] at this time" (Plate IV:31). These must later be retrieved by some small payment. Let us follow the coeducational Kapsirika group through the day, because we have the best data about it during this phase of the activities. The above events took place between 6:30 and 7:30 A.M., followed by some desultory dancing and a lengthy delay consumed in part by much discussion concerning two Kitosh circumcisors who were being rejected because they had circumcised one boy who had died. At 8:30 A.M. the initiates again danced, made more adjustments to their gear, and went to another house in the compound to dance for about ten minutes. Then they marched off single file with only one *moteriyontet*: first to the house of the circumcisor to pick up his knife and dance, then to the home of another Sebei where they danced and rested before proceeding to the home of a man married into the clan of the father who was sponsoring this initiation, where they again danced briefly (Plate IV:33).

By now, it was early afternoon; they rested in the shade of one of the houses and were twice given a mixture of milk and water to drink (Plate IV:36). (One Kitosh girl, who had decided to be circumcised, was given nothing because she was not allowed to drink milk.) After a rest of about an hour and a half, they danced again and then marched off to the Sundet River. Here, they were painted (*seret*) with white clay (*woryontet*) by their instructors, who by now had all joined them (Plate IV:34). During and after the painting, there was much teasing and taunting; they were asked if they wanted water teasingly, to which they responded with proper stoic silence. A large group of both initiated and preinitiated young people joined the *chemerik* at the river, all of whom engaged in a great deal of sex play. There was also some very free-flowing dancing by the men near the river. The group left the river at about 5:00 P.M., arriving about an hour later at the home where the circumcision was to take place.

Meanwhile, a white banner had been raised over the house; the circumcisor had arrived shortly before the initiates and was greeted by a group of women, who danced her and her party back toward the house in a manner similar to that of the arrival of parties at the twin ceremony and the final marriage ceremony. This return home marked the beginning of the festivities. People had by then gathered in great numbers around the beer pots. As the group returned, they were met by the mothers, who sang a song of welcome (*serot kumaganga*):

> Welcome with some bread.
> Where have you delayed until sunset;
> Where have you delayed until dawn.
> Welcome with some bread.

The girls' reply in song, referring to the palm fond rib, *sosyet,* a sign of peace.

The initiates then gathered to dance a couple of dances (Plates IV:35,37) and retired behind one of the houses, where they were given instructions, while the men and and women began highly spirited dances. The mother's brother of one of the girls slaughtered a ram, and he, the father's brother, and the mother's sister's husband anointed the initiates with the chyme. The *chemerik* then went back for more instructions, and the people continued to dance and to drink beer, so that as the night continued they became increasingly gay. Perhaps two or three hundred Sebei were present at this "fat" ceremony.

This night is one thing for the *chemerik*, another for the guests. For the initiates, it is a constant and demanding performance of dances; they go from one house to another — in no special order except as dictated by convenience — throughout the night; they should visit the house of each initiate at least once. At one point, the Kapsirika group went to the grave of one girl's mother, who had committed suicide a few months earlier; there, some of the dirt from the grave was smeared on them. The father, who had accompanied them, then poured beer on the grave so that the mother's spirit would know she had not been forgotten, lest she might cause bleeding or death to one of the girls. They also went to another relative's grave.

At the Bukwa ceremonial, the girls visited their relatives during the night and were welcomed by the women at each home with the *serote kuman-ganga* song; at two homes, a relative slaughtered a ram and anointed the girls with chyme. The scrotum of one ram was cut off, leaving a loop of skin by which it was hung around the girl's neck and lay between her breasts. (My informant denied any symbolic meaning.) We did not see this done at any of the other ceremonials, and I was told that the custom had been adopted from the Bok. The smearing in these instances is always done by old people, for it is a wish for a long life. The animal is usually furnished by the mother's brother but may be furnished by other relatives or by the father's age-mate. The night's activities are considerably more demanding than those of the daytime; large crowds exhort the *chemerik* to dance and sing, and they are kept on the move for hours at a time, resting only during periods when medicine is administered.

Minor differences in many ritual details mark the initiation of a *tekeryon-tet*. The most important differential for the boy *tekeryontet* is that he must be taught the women's medicines or "animals" and receives his medicines from a woman, for he learns the woman's secrets, though he may not impart them to other men. His *moteriyontet* must take him away from the other boys at various times to administer these to him.

For the guests, the activities are very different. It is a time for drinking, dancing, general gaiety, and a high degree of license despite the serious and sober central purpose of the event. A proper initiation involves the parents in great expenditures of time, goods, and money. Siret's party in Kapsirika lasted for three days after the cutting, with hundreds of guests of all ages present. Beer flowed freely, and there was an unusual spirit of camaraderie. Normal tabus are dropped, and a man can say anything, even in front of his mother-in-law. Sexuality is in the air and often in the bush as well. Men proposition women openly though not always with success, and, on some occasions, women approached me in ways that were at least suggestive. A group of girls anticipating circumcision in the near future, dressed like *chemerik* in short skirts and beads with bare, budding breasts, were fair game for a group of boys or unmarried men who sought to abduct them with more noise than apparent success. One old man shouted, "You young girls showing your breasts makes one's prick stand on end; you boys go grab those girls and get them down." Smaller children ran about making sexual gestures or mocking the movements of intercourse. One girl of about ten was crying bitterly and apparently very frightened; some of her male contemporaries, having caught the spirit of the occasion, had also caught her, making efforts that she was not old enough to appreciate. One man exhorted the group, saying that no person who had had intercourse should be at the circumcision, lest he make the initiate bleed excessively. He added that a child conceived on the night of such a fat ceremony would never become rich. I was told that, though people talk about sexual matters and make propositions to other men's wives, nothing of that sort happens; yet some men try to keep their wives away from the ceremony out of jealousy. It is said that a barren woman should have intercourse with a man that night, suggesting that the ritual has some fertility implications.

Several forms of dance are associated with the circumcision rituals. The *kapkompet* is limited to this ritual occasion and is found among all the Sabaot people. Initiates line up on one side; all the people gather round and sing; and young men dance in front of the initiates with high stiff leaps straight in the air. *Tumdo*, which means drum, is a dance to the accompaniment of drumming, the men on the "lower" side and the women on the "upper." A part of the *tumdo* is called *chemundarai*: this is when a man and women enter the circle and dance with a hopping step, clapping hands. This is a peculiarly Sebei dance and takes place at all ritual occasions. The third is called *serio* and was borrowed from Kenya; it consists of two parts — *ndyolit*, an undulating back and forth movement of the circle of dancers, and *kironget*, a leaping dance.

The night of the ceremony at Bukwa, a large crowd gathered at the house where the circumcision was to take place. Suddenly, one of the men let out a shout; a kind of response was made by others, and gradually a song emerged. Men, two at a time, danced out into an open area, going up and down in wild hopping leaps, holding their left legs to the front. Gradually, a circle developed around them and the dancers began a sinuous, undulating movement, thrusting the hips forward. Then, two women entered the circle and two men confronted them, exaggerating their leaps when they were face to face. The movements were sensuous and arousing. At another dance, I entered a very crowded room with my interpreter; the men and women were dancing packed together. My companion began to dance with a woman present, holding her in an embrace as close as copulation, each clutching the other's buttocks. Many of the songs reiterate the theme of sexuality: "Offer yourself that you may have children; what is the use of a barren woman?" "Open out your vagina that you may take the banana blossom." Many of the songs integral to the initiation refer to the sexual organs, the crimson buttocks of the baboon, or the secretions of the glans penis. Verbally, as well as in action, sexuality is strongly expressed. Of course, the focal point of the whole ceremony is the genitals of nubile youths.

While guests and principals have such differential involvements in the events, they are not separate. When the initiates are not taking medicine or stopping at one of the houses, or visiting the grave of a dead relative, they are outside the house dancing, and the guests, or some of them, are dancing with them. When the *chemerik* are dancing, they dance side by side in a line, with the others filling out a large loose circle. From time to time, the girls come out in pairs and dance back and forth in the circle, each staying on her own side and turning inward, describing a long figure eight. After some time, one or two persons, either men or women, join the circle and confront these two, and the four do a leaping dance facing one another. Once I saw a boy of about eight engage in this part of the dance and then melt back into the circle. Sometimes these dancing confrontations also take place while the initiates are at the side of the circle.

Songs of warning are most likely to be heard in association with these dances in particular. Some songs give encouragement:

> Although the knife is bitter, who will fear it?
> Someone did not die;
> The grandparents did not die.

Others are discouraging, like the one used as epigraph to this chapter, or are taunting:

> Approaching is the daybreak;
> If you be afraid,
> Go join the Suk,
> Go join the Teso;
> Tie up your heart.
>
> Catch for me the youth.
> The country smells of daybreak,
> The country smells of dawn.
>
> Tell us, young man.
> At daybreak, young man.
> Dawn is upon you, young man
> Dawn is upon you, dirty one.[2]
> Don't take the trouble, youngster.

Some have responses built into them, such as the following:

---

2. The word here, *kumaret*, has reference to the secretion of the sexual glands; uncircumcised youths are considered sexually dirty — hence my rendition.

I warn you, oh, youth;
I warn you, dirty one;
I warn you, youngster;[3]
I warn you, dirty one;
I warn you, fearful one.
The daybreak is upon you.

Responses: It cannot kill a person.
Why did not our ancestors die?

Tis dawning, oh, youth;
Tis dawning, *chirachir*.[4]
We are helping you now,
But tomorrow it is yours.
Separate from your countrymen.
Separate from your clansmen.

Response: Defend yourself men!

These expressions in song are reiterated in other contacts; we came upon one *moteriyontet* earnestly talking to a *chemeryontet*: "My daughter, don't make me ashamed. Nobody has died of circumcision. It will be painful, but nobody has died. It is not too late; you seem to be afraid." And she went on to say that the girl should not cry as her grandmother had. We also heard an old woman address two *chemerik* at great length beside one of the houses; she was the sister of one of their fathers and seemed to be annoying them deliberately, telling them how painful circumcision would be, frightening them with all kinds of remarks, and even striking out at them. They responded with silence.

After many hours, the festivities die down; some of the older people traipse back home; many others find a place to lie down and catch a few hours' sleep; the *chemerik* continue to dance from time to time but spend more time in instructions and medicines. These medicines are the most secret elements of the ritual; we were not allowed to observe their administration. The initiates are given both purgatives and emetics for the specific purpose of cleansing them. The instructor chews one medicine and spits into the nostrils of the initiates; it is said to make their eyes steady, so that they will not blink during the cutting — and most initiates have a glassy look during the operation. One medicine is formed into pellets, which one informant likened to goat dung, and swallowed. Another involves the scrapings from an elephant's tusk. At one point, the boys are asked to urinate on a red-hot pick and adze blade. Toward morning, the *chemerik* are led off to bathe in a stream; they clean the secretion from under the foreskin or behind the hymen with a stick and apply stinging nettles to their genitals. Such are the "animals" they "catch" during their periods of respite in the 24-hour activity. By the time they are ready to be cut, they are purged, exhausted, and probably to some extent drugged.

---

3. Here, the Gisu word for uncircumcised boy was used, presumably for elegant variation.
4. A word meaning to push penis in and out of foreskin.

Shortly before dawn, the parents and *motriyonik* make preparations at the circumcision place. A ram is slaughtered by suffocation, one man holding its mouth and nostrils closed while two others bump its back against the ground or swing it back and forth until it dies (in Muslim-dominated areas, they now kill it by bleeding). The ram is brought into the house covered by a blanket as it must not be seen. Two spears, the blades crossed, have been set in the ground, and a whetstone is placed between them. This is to warn off anyone who would do magic to make the *chemerik* cry or bleed excessively. In some areas now, Sebei also make a kind of flimsy pole fence over which blankets or plantain fronds are hung to screen off the circumcision place, but this was instigated by British officials and does not impede the view. There was no fence when circumcision took place in the kraal.

When the *chemerik* come to the place of circumcision, they sing and dance briefly. They then file up to two or three old men (not necessarily related), who take some of the chyme of the ram and anoint each initiate in turn, rubbing it across the forehead, down the side of the cheeks, across the shoulders, down the arm, and along the body and legs to the feet, expressing wishes of sweet long life (Plates IV:3-4).

The chyme, still warm from the ram's body, stiffens on the boys' skin and "makes it tough." The old men also tell the *chemerik*, "Your father has killed this important animal and if you fail to keep still while they cut, it will be a great shame." After each initiate is thus anointed, he darts through the arch of spears to the circumcision place (Plate IV:5). Here, the ceremonies for the two sexes differ somewhat.

The boys line up, with the *kaporet* to the east; they face the north, standing rigidly side by side, looking with unblinking eyes straight in front of them. The people crowd around and watch the operation intensely (traditionally, people knelt on the ground in silence during the operation). In the west, where marriage sometimes precedes circumcision, mothers-in-law are kept away out of respect, but the wife may be present. Also kept away — in fact tied to the center post of their houses — are women who have cried during their circumcision.

The circumcisor's assistant dusts under the foreskin with ordinary dust; the operator pulls the foreskin forward and cuts around it with one cut; the assistant catches the head of the penis between thumb and forefinger; and the operator then cuts the foreskin off. The boy is told at this time to start raising his hands slowly so that by the time the operation is finished his arms are raised straight above his head (Plate IV:38). He holds them there until the second boy has been cut, when he lowers them to rest on his head. When the second pair has been cut, the first pair sits down, each person holding in his left hand the skin just behind the cut, pulling the skin forward so that it does not shrink away, and also so as to stop the flow of blood. The *moteriyontet* cleans the blood and bits of skin and keeps these; the blood is allowed to fall on the ground (Plate IV:39). A *tekeryontet*, however, stands on the hide of a slaughtered bullock. The initiates remain there until all have been cut, when the women raise a high-pitched ululation (*sikarkarta*), the drums are beaten, and relatives and friends run and skip about and begin to sing and dance. If a first-born child has been circumcised, people go around pulling their ears, pinching one another, and telling jokes. Shortly afterward, the mothers of the boys come with cowhorns filled with butter, and with this they anoint their sons on the forehead (Plate IV:40). The sons will frequently refuse this anointment until the mother has promised them a gift; perhaps a heifer, possibly something less. In a short while, they file off to the hut in which they will live in seclusion. The group, now joyous and happy, turns to singing, dancing, feasting and drinking, if there is food and drink still left. The *motriyonik* and the circumcisor share the slaughtered ram.

The girls are similarly smeared and pass under the spears[5] and enter the cutting area at a trot. Procedures differed somewhat; I will describe events at Atar (Plates IV:6-9). The six girls sat on the ground, facing south, the *kaporet* on the east, their *motriyonik* behind them, and the circumcisor and her assistant in front. Many women (Gale included) crowded into the fenced off enclosure; men (myself included), children and other women leaned on the flimsy fence. The assistant then carefully positioned each girl in turn, laying her down, drawing her knees as wide apart as possible, flattening them against the ground by bringing her feet together, then adjusting her body so that it was firmly against the ground, and wiping off her vagina with a cloth. Then the cutting began. Using a native curved knife with a wooden haft, the operator cut the labia minora off in one piece, sawing and pulling, for her knife was not sharp enough. While she was cutting, the assistant and the girl's *moteriyontet* spoke firmly but softly to her, the latter tapping her with a forefinger as she spoke. After each girl had been cut, the assistant raised repeatedly a homemade flag to signal success, amid shouting and ululations from the women. (The flag, incidentally, was an innovation made by this circumcisor's assistant, who proudly told us that she had introduced the idea four years earlier, saying that it was red as a symbol of blood. By 1962, banners were sometimes carried by the dancing *chemerik* and a white flag fluttered on a long pole over each house where circumcision was taking place.) The circumcisor, rinsing off the knife with some water from a battered enamelware teapot went to the next girl. After each girl was cut, her left leg was put over her right and she was helped to turn on her side. Though there was no little complaint that this circumcisor was "too slow," none of the girls flinched or showed pain during the operation. When all six had been cut, the operator began to sing in a high plaintive cry and dance with a running motion; the dancing and singing lasted more than ten minutes, with all the women joining in; while the *chemerik* sat in pain (Plates IV:16,17). Before the women filed out of the enclosure, each girl was given a bite of thick porridge massed on a wooden stirring paddle and some clotted milk (Plate IV:15). They have eaten nothing for at least twenty-four hours, and the food is a ritual expression not only of their release from fasting but

---

5. Spears are not used in the western part of Sebei.

also of their unity, for all bite from this single piece of "bread." "The taking of bread is an agreement among the *chemerik* that they must honor one another, that they should be friends." For the men at least, it signifies that they should always share their beer or their slaughtered animals and should not make sexual advances to one another's daughters. Blankets were then placed over the girls' shoulders, and they walked about 100 feet to the shade of a tree, where they rested to gather the strength to walk to their places of seclusion. Two girls were to be quartered separately from the others; they had to walk about two miles to their place of seclusion. They walked painfully, the blanket held between their legs to catch the blood. The *motriyonik* removed the severed pieces and blood for later disposal (Plate IV:18).

Nowhere else was the operator so inept; the cutting of both boys and girls was over before one was aware it had started, and the careful positioning of each girl did not occur. Otherwise, the ceremonies were essentially the same — though, ironically, not with the same self-control.

"CRYING THE KNIFE"

The ceremony of initiation is clearly regarded by the Sebei as a test of fortitude. It is rare for a man to show fear or pain. (I was told that the Kapsombata clansmen have a tendency to cry when one was reported as having done so in 1972.) Women express pain or fear more frequently. The men consider this evidence of the relative weakness of the women, but I am inclined to think the test far more severe for girls, though painful enough for both. Ideally, the initiate is not even to blink or flinch. Moreover, if a girl bleeds excessively, if the drum that makes the *melilo* ("leopard") sound breaks during her initiation, if the stick she carries breaks, her neck-ring comes off, her skin skirt tears, or other seemingly chance events occur, she is subject to the penalties for crying.

A woman pays several penalties for crying. First, she is not allowed to be a man's first wife, but must marry an old man. Young men are needed for fighting, and her husband cannot fight in wars as he would be weakened by such a wife. Also, it is the duty of the first wife to care for her husband whenever he is ill; if the woman who cried at circumcision were a man's first wife, she would endanger his life at such time. The second penalty is that, during all future circumcisions, she must be tied to the center post of her house so that she cannot move. She is kept away from the circumcision because she might bring bad luck to the initiates or perhaps might curse them. She is also "despised" by other women. One informant whose father had married a woman who had cried told me that he entered her house quite late the night one of her children was being circumcised and found her tied by her hands to the center post. A group was taunting her with songs about her having cried and suggesting she join the Karamojong, where they do not circumcise. "I sent those people away, cut her off the post, and told her to remain there quietly." Such severe treatment would end only when her own children had become *chemerik*.

Crying the knife frequently takes the form of refusal to permit the operation to continue after it has been started. A *chemeryontet* may refuse to go through the ritual at any time, even after having entered the circumcision area, but once the cutting has started, he or she must allow it to be completed. If not, four men must hold down the *chemeryontet* while the circumcisor finishes the work. Extra payment must also be made to the circumcisor and the men must be given a ram. The person who holds one girl down must also hold three others down on subsequent occasions lest he die of the ill luck.

We observed one situation at Kabruron where a girl cried the knife (Plates IV:10-14). A tall handsome girl, the *kaporet* of her group, refused to allow the circumcision to continue. The operator was a Pokot woman married to a Sebei ("Therefore I am a Sebei," she said), and much more swift and skillful than the Sebei woman at Atar. However, the girls were not laid out carefully but flopped on the ground one or two at a time, the later ones turning to watch those ahead of them. Under these circumstances, things happened much faster than I had anticipated on the basis of our previous experience. I only learned of the *kaporet's* refusal from the great hue and cry raised by the crowd, and by this time the third girl was being cut. The circumcisor continued, and after each operation the assistant helped the girl roll over on one side, her left arm appropriately placed over the waist of the preceding girl. One of the girls seems to have bled heavily; the second to the last girl in line watched those preceding her and, when her turn came, flopped down on the ground, quite anxious and brave, though her legs did jerk during the operation, as those in Atar had not done. No notice was taken of this. The last girl in line then refused to lie down, remaining adamant after some heated discussions, whereupon the women present stripped her of her paraphernalia and she disappeared. I was told, with an air of full causal explanation, that her mother had cried the knife; however, the girl may undergo the initiation at some later date with no loss of status. About this time, a woman dashed up to the circumcision area from the east, behind where the girls were being circumcised; she had cried the knife and had therefore been tied up since the preceding morning. Now she had been released and was in a position to celebrate, in a sense vindicating herself through her daughter, with a great display of pride and satisfaction in the outcome.

By now, there was a great hullabaloo. Some women danced, sang, and shouted in glee at the joyous results with respect to those who were closest to them. One woman became concerned about the girls whose operations had been completed, and who should have been moved to a resting place. She succeeded in getting them down the trail, holding their blankets between their legs.

The *kaporet* stood up. Her paraphernalia was stripped from her by the women. Her father, a handsome and aging man, was literally fit to be tied, with four men restraining him and others holding banana frond strips with which to tie him if necessary. The girl's sister and another relative began fighting, one apparently accusing the other of responsibility, until they were stopped by the appointive chief. The *kaporet* stood in the enclosure, looking forlorn and beaten and silently crying. Many people stood around, arguing with her that she should lie down and let the operation continue, but she was adamant. The chief tried to talk to her. This discussion and shouting and shoving and hauling went on for about half an hour. Finally the girl left, darting down the path, followed by the taunts and jeers and a few thrown sticks from the crowd, some even running a way after her. As she ran she looked back, a haunted thing.

The crowd's response was diverse. Some were laughing, with a laughter that conveyed sadistic pleasure; others were taunting; some were disappointed for they had had varying degrees of hope of winning this handsome girl as a wife; one woman was crying; and the enraged father wanted to beat the daughter who had so shamed him; a few expressed some empathy, particularly one girl who was about to be circumcised herself.

We had to leave; four men would have to hold her down while the cutting was forced upon her, and our credentials were not sufficiently untainted with official connections to make them feel they could proceed. Had we not been there, they might have gone ahead immediately. As we went away, the father was venting his feelings on a man who owed him a ram; as he would need it to pay the men for holding his daughter. Groups were standing about in knots, discussing the morning's events. A group of men pursued the girl after we left, found her in a tree threatening to commit suicide, brought her down, and completed the operation according to custom.

A week later I called on the *kaporet*. It was shortly after the painting ceremony and her torso was still covered with the pale paint; she was living in seclusion alone, away from the other girls, in the care of her father's sister. She claimed her seclusion was solitary because her home was too far away, and the girls who were to serve her would have too far to go if she stayed with the others, which is, in fact, a basis for separating initiates. Her *moteriyontet* came from time to time to look after her. The girl still claimed to be the *kaporet* of the group and presumed she would join the other girls in later ceremonies, such as the ceremonial release. I did not find out if she was correct.

She was embarrassed at her failure but not unwilling to talk about it. She had climbed the tree because she wanted to commit suicide; she felt that, because she had cried, life would not be worth living, but the men arrived too soon. Now that they had completed the circumcision, she was glad that she had not killed herself. To my questioning she replied that she first felt fear when the knife began to cut; had she felt it earlier, she would have dropped out of the group. Then she explained her actions:

> It was_____who caused it. About four months ago, I went with two other girls to fetch water and this young man tried to stop me. I refused to stop because I thought he wanted to break my pot, and so I disobeyed him and

went on. I thought about this after the ceremony and decided he had caused me to fear. I told some of the women, and one of them said she saw him afterward hiding in the bushes. He was getting away for he feared the people would get after him. There is nothing I can do about him, but I will always consider him a wizard.

My impression was that the *kaporet* had succeeded in externalizing her failure and that she would survive the trauma with minimal psychic cost. In this day of changing culture, it is not unlikely that she may even become a first wife, as she intimated. At any rate, the Sebei say that, even though a girl who cries the knife cannot be a man's senior wife, nevertheless, they are the first to marry, for the old men seek them for their wives, and they are the ones who have cattle. Their status is said not to affect the brideprice.

MAGIC IN CIRCUMCISION

One of the things initiates learn is the use of certain kinds of magic. Women in particular learn the magic performed against men, but all initiates learn how to make the *chemerik* cry during circumcision. It is one of the sanctions men and women have in the use of authority against a person who is not yet adult. Presumably, such an influence resulted in the tragedy for the *kaporet* at Kabruron. I was told how this magic is performed.

> Suppose some boy has been misbehaving or insulting you, or has said things that prevented you from getting a wife, then you watch him privately. When you see him urinating, you take some of that. You put it in a *murkuyontet* [a small cylindrical iron ring that is worn on the iron neck rings], which you close up at both ends with a piece of skin. At the time of circumcision, you hang that ring by a piece of string from a tree or over the edge of a cliff so that the wind can blow on it. When the wind blows, then that boy will begin to shake his head and say he doesn't want the knife. When it stops blowing, then the boy is again willing. If there is no wind at the time, you can go there and shake it. Or, again, you can put that neck ring in a place where the urine will dry out; then you put that ring between your toes and as they start cutting him you shake your foot and he will start jumping about.

It is against just such magic that the crossed spears are intended to act — not as countermagic but merely as a warning. There is, however, a more direct preventative method. The night before the cutting, each boy is taken aside and asked two things by his *moteriyontet*: whether he has had sexual intercourse with a married woman or insulted or misbehaved toward any person. Some of the boys do not like to mention the woman's name, but they should tell it so that the girdle may be taken from the woman and worn by the boy to prevent bleeding. One man reported:

> During our circumcision, two boys had had intercourse with married women. One didn't mention it, and he later bled very much and had to tell later, and they brought the girdle, though her husband could do nothing except abuse his wife for having had intercourse with a dirty uncircumcised boy. I told

about a man whom I had insulted, and the *moteriyontet* told my father about that, and then that very night they sought him out and kept him so that he would have no chance to do magic against me. My father's age-set mates all watched over him carefully and told him that if anything happened to me, he would be stabbed to death, but he swore he had not arranged such a thing. If my father had not been a strong man, he could have said: "Yes, I have done that, for the boy did wrong and insulted me, and I demand payment so I can undo that thing." Then my father would have had to pay and he would have had to take apart [the thing that contained the magic] in front of the men and the matter would be finished.

INTERMEDIATE CEREMONIES

When the *chemerik* leave the circumcision area they go to a house that has either been built or set aside for them (*mentyet*). The *chemerik* are secluded in these houses, eating food prepared for them by their mothers and served by uninitiated girls. During this period, the boys are not to be seen by their mothers or any initiated woman; the girls are not to be seen by any man. They undergo a series of rites that lead to the final ceremony, shaving and bathing on the fourth day, and a special ceremony to be described shortly. There is no absolute calendar for these activities, and some of them are elided. The girls or boys circumcised together remain in the same house but frequently break up into smaller groups for reasons of convenience. Their food, now called *nentet* (clay given cattle for salt), is brought in baskets referred to as *loŋet* (shield); and what they do not eat may be eaten only by their servants (*mwenik*).

During this period of their seclusion, the *chemerik* are under many specific restrictions. They are not allowed to take baths but cleanse themselves with a leaf that exudes liquid when put by the fire. They may not sit or sleep on skins but only on the wuswet leaves, (during this time called trientut), or on those of the ankurwet. When these leaves dry out, they are replaced, but the dried leaves are placed in the far part of the house and are burned at the close of the ceremonial period. The *chemerik* may not touch food with their hands but eat with a sharp stick and cut it with another sharp stick. They may not eat meat, but they may drink milk and eat vegetables, as well as maize or other starchy food. The girls must sleep on their backs, for if they sleep on their sides the vagina will not heal properly. They have been given a special robe, called *artit*, dressed cowhide with the hair removed. They swear by this skin because they may not swear in the usual ways — by their mothers or their cattle. They continue to carry the circumcision stick (*syomyet*); they also decorate themselves with seed beads (*tilek*) and big iron rings (*merenket*). One informant said that they were moved out of their special house because they were dreaming very much and their wounds were getting worse. He claimed that there were spirits (*oyik*) like maggots that cause these dreams. Some of the *oyik* did not want the boys to stay in the *mentyet*, and made bad dreams that drove the boys out. These ceased when the boys left the *mentyet*.

Four days after circumcision (or three if one of the initiates is a *tekeryon-tet*), they have the shaving ceremony, which should be accompanied by a beer party that the father gives for his age-mates. We observed the shaving at Atar (Plates IV:19-21). The girls bathed themselves, one at a time, from a pan of water and then rubbed themselves with vaseline. In earlier times they were supposed to char castor beans and rub this on themselves. After all had bathed, they came out and were shaved. Each *moteriyontet* shaved her initiate with an ordinary double-edged blade held in the hand. The *tekeryon-tet* in this group was supposed to have milk on her head, but because there was none, beer was spit on her head four times. She refused to be shaved until the *moteriyontet* gave her a present of 2 shillings "because I am an important person." The hair was let to fall on the ground but carefully placed in a pile and later taken up; should it remain a cow might snuff it up, which would cause the girl to waste away. The hair is later burned along with the severed portion of the vagina.

While the shaving was taking place, some native tobacco was brought out and placed on a stool to be used by the women present. Because a *tekeryon-tet* was present, an oval basket was brought and held by one of the women during the subsequent singing and dancing. A drum, also associated with ceremonies involving the *tekeryontet*, was also used.

The men stayed away from the narrow place between two houses during the shaving and while the women later danced. Each song was initiated by one woman, with others taking up the chorus. The *chemerik* did not join any of the dancing, for they were still in no condition to do so. The first song anticipated the final ritual of the cycle, making reference to the "leopard" that will appear on the veranda.

The lyrics of the songs have a very different character from those of circumcision night; they are largely songs of praise and thanks. One, for instance, praises the *tekeryontet*, a gift of the *oyik*. Another lauds the *kaporet*:

> Thanks to our *kaporet*;
> Greetings, *kaporet*.
> Had you feared the cutting, others would do the same.
> As you kept still, others did also.
> You are very brave.

A mother's song refers to the stripes on her stomach from the tight thong she wears after childbirth:

> My waist is striped from the binding-cord.
> Had you cried it would have disappointed me.
> But now you have completed your initiation.

Another tells of a girl about to be initiated who is told she is not old enough, however, she continues to beg and the mother agrees but warns her to be brave. The mother is about to jump off the cliff in fear, but just before she does so she learns that her child has been brave.

After all the girls had been shaved, they were made to stand up and the song was sung of the uncovering of the bird that expresses release from seclusion in various ceremonial contexts — though the period of seclusion was far from over. This ceremony is referred to as butter, "for butter is a precious thing; it implies peacefulness, and this is a peaceful ceremony." One other song expressed the sentiment that children are precious, too, because if there were no children people could not enjoy rich ceremonies such as this.

As the dancing gathered in spirit, the women found the area between the two houses too confining and moved to an open area. The girls remained behind, either to avoid too much walking or to preserve their seclusion. In the dance that followed, two women danced out in front of the line in apparent imitation of the men's way of dancing, which aroused a great deal of laughter and amusement in the crowd. One woman pretended to be a man, dancing as the men do "because there used to be a lot of men around at these rites," according to my informant, but I suspect that there is deeper ritual involvement in such mockery. (On another occasion, when the girls were being partially released from their seclusion, a woman placed a maize stalk in her belt in such a fashion as to make it look like a penis in erection, and danced about with highly amusing vulgarity.) Beer appeared, and there was some drinking, but the proper beer party was to be held the next day.

Bread was brought out on a paddle held by an old woman — old as a wish for a long life — and offered first to the father, then to the mother, and then to each of the *chemerik* (Plate IV:21). Each took a bite, and this was repeated four times. They were very careful not to spill any crumbs, for this would cause bad luck. At this point they were asked to leave, as the Sebei generally do not want their medicines to be known to the uninitiated.

The initiates begin to learn during this ceremony the true identity of the "animals" they first met during the circumcision night, though not all of them. They also learn medicines to help them cure themselves, though the men told me that women do not need the medicine as much as the men, for women can urinate holding their legs together, and the urine will heal wounds. I do not know if the women agree. The *chemerik* also begin to learn magic that can be performed against others: the magic that will make an initiate cry, ants come out of a person's head, a man's skin as rough as the bark of a tree, or will make his feces come out in foot-long pieces. The women are also inspected at this time to be sure that they are healing correctly. Because the Sebei are unlike some peoples who infibulate their women, with the specific purpose of having the vagina heal partially closed, the Sebei insist that girls not lie on their sides so that the vagina will remain open.

Four days after the circumcision of boys at Nyelit, I observed their shaving ceremony to the extent permitted the uninitiated. The boys left their seclusion together and went into the small calf kraal where they bathed. They washed first their heads and then their bodies with soap; then they washed their penises with cow urine and then again washed their bodies with water in which urine had been mixed, as well as some medicine that had been boiled. The urine causes the penis to hurt very badly. One old man present kept saying that they should put more on, "as this boy has refused to bring firewood." After the boys were finished, the *motriyonik* washed themselves and then the boys washed their beads in the same solution. An examination of the genitals was made to determine if any additional cutting was required, and I was told that the scab from one boy's wound should be scraped off with a thorn. The *chemerik* returned to their house, which had been swept clean by one of the women, and the shaving took place there. Milk was poured onto the concave seat of a native stool and applied to the head as a kind of shaving cream. The boys were shaved three at a time; there was no rule as to who shaves whom, except that a boy cannot be shaved by the age-set mate of his father.

After the shaving, the boys went out to the cattle kraal, made a fire and burned up the hair (and presumably the severed foreskins) while all six stood around, together with their *motriyonik*. The group again returned to the house, and, after some extraneous discussion about some missing beads, the two circumcisors came. Each boy was brought to the door of the house, over which a skin had been hung, this skin was placed over him and he was given a small lecture by the circumcisor, who occasionally emphasized his points by hitting on the skin with his circumcision knife:

> I am cutting you and want you always to behave yourself. You must obey your father and your mother and do what they ask when they send you for water or wood, also all persons older than yourself, and you should respect your age-mates. When somebody's wife invites you to her house, saying that her husband is away, you should not go there. Take the woman into the bush, and, after you have had intercourse with her once, go away. If you sleep in somebody's house, you may be arrested, after which your cows must be sold. I wish you good luck and that you may find a wife who will brew beer for me.

He also told one of the boys always to speak the truth.

After each boy had had such a lecture, his father and mother were asked to go into the house to spit beer on the initiates in blessing. Though I was not in the house, I was told that they say something like the following: "You boys, if one of you runs mad or becomes sick, never blame your parents, for they are spitting this blessing on you. You may misbehave yourself, but never blame your mother or your father. I ask you to behave yourself well." There was no dancing while I was there. As the mothers are not supposed to see their sons, I assume the boys remain covered. It was made clear that my presence was no longer desirable, so I left.

A few days after the shaving ceremony, whenever they feel sufficiently comfortable, the *chemerik* will paint their faces and bodies with white clay (Plates IV:22-24). They now may go about and visit their friends, but they are still under some restrictions. They still may not walk on the paths, and, if they must cross one, they must break off leaves and step on them. They may not cross a stream, lest it dry up. They may not visit in people's houses, and, if they want to go into their own house, they go in by the entrance for the goats and remain in back, away from the fire. If a girl sees her father, she must cover her head. Boys may not be seen by any married woman. The girls, and their mothers as well, tie strings of beads around their heads, across the forehead; nowadays they use commercial beads, but formerly they used seed beads. They may not shave themselves again until after the final ceremony, except at the nape of the neck. They do not touch fresh blood or meat, nor do the mothers or the *mwenik*. The father is not bound by this restriction, because he does not make or handle the food they eat. During this period, a *chemeryontet* should not drink beer and must be careful about what he eats, as it is very bad to vomit. Similarly, he should avoid any physical damage to himself, especially drawing any blood, or his marriage will be much delayed. Sexual intercourse is not permitted. Initiates should not call an alarm or speak in a loud voice; if they need to attract attention, they must whistle. They do not greet anyone, not even one another, by mouth. Two *chemerik* meeting should greet one another by caning each other severely around the legs with the sticks they always carry. An initiated person will greet them by taking their sticks and squeezing the wrist between them; the severe pain must be endured without a murmur. If they have been disobedient, the older person will press so hard that tears will come. The instructors also use this method of punishing *chemerik* who disobey them.

Before the *chemerik* are healed and can walk about freely, but after they have been shaved, they have a custom, called *andayet*, of rising at dawn and going outside and singing songs. The songs are intended for other *chemerik* in seclusion, whom they will call out by name. There are apparently three standard songs. The texts of these as I obtained them are too cryptic to render into meaningful English. One says that the women's task is to make thongs for the calabashes, the men's is to make rope for the cattle; a second refers to the white scar that sometimes appears on the penis and both girls and boys sing that it will go to others and not themselves; the third refers to the holes the ground rat digs for excrement. The last two are considered vulgar and the kind of thing that should not be said aloud where one's *tekso* relations might hear it. Where a number of *chemerik* groups are within earshot, each tries to be the first to sing these songs. They sing again in the evening.

Some time after the boys begin to heal, I was told, they find a sharp thorn, which they poke through a piece of wood. They hold the back of the penis very tight so that the blood accumulates at the head and then they beat the head with this instrument until it bleeds. This, they say, makes the penis sharp and small so that if they lie with a virgin their penis will be able to penetrate. During this period, the boys used to gather together from time to time to dance and play games. Among the latter are mock fights, in which one boy tries to strike another with his stick while his opponent wards him off with a specially-made wooden shield. The game is seen as practice and as a means of unifying the circumcision group; apparently groups contest with one another.

Following the shaving, the father of the *chemeryontet* is supposed to give a beer party. There should be a pot for (1) the *motriyonik*; (2) the clansmen of the father; (3) the age-mates of the father (two pots, one for the first subset of the *pinta*, the other for the other two subsets; the section to which the father belongs receives a small pot; the other sector a large one); (4) the mother's brothers of the *chemeryontet*; (5) the men who have married women of the father's clan, referred to as the sons-in-law of the clan; and (6) a special pot for the special friend of the father (usually the man the father was next to in his circumcision), who is supposed to have supplied the family with a bullock. No animal is slaughtered.

At Atar, the beer was made available the day after shaving and, while it was not quite so lavish as indicated in the demands laid out, there were four or five pots, some with as many as thirty-five participants. The heads and shoulders of the women married to the host's age-set were garlanded in vines. The group danced and sang songs of the same kind as on the preceding day; there was gaiety in the air and some ribaldry, as when a woman jokingly asked a man of her husband's *pinta* to come out to the bush with her.

For some time after the shaving, the initiates and their *mwenik* will collect basketfuls of a round yellow fruit called apples of Sodom. One night when there is rich moonlight, usually about a month after the operation, the *chemerik* take these baskets and, followed by their *mwenik* and any other uncircumcised boys and girls, go to each house in the *saŋta*, singing and whistling in a distinctive pattern and pelting the doors of the houses with the apples of Sodom. The woman in the house then brings them some maize, millet, milk, or other food, which they collect in the baskets. They do not pelt a house where a *tekeryontet* lives but will only sing and whistle. The children on such occasions are in high spirits; the whole is so reminiscent of our "trick or treat" of Halloween as to be positively eerie. This ceremony releases the *chemerik* to walk on the paths and to cross streams, and they may even engage in some work, though they are still under the general restrictions of the seclusion and go about painted with clay, visiting their friends. The ceremony is called *kokisiraran* or *kolakta tukap lopot*, which means literally throwing cattle of fruit.

CLOSING CEREMONIES

The ceremonial cycle for initiates closes with a set of ritual activities, normally from two to five months after the circumcision began. The rituals for both boys and girls start with a highly secret ceremony held throughout one night, followed the next day by a ceremonial adoption into the age-set to which they belong, and closing four days later with shaving and the final induction into normal adult life. The secret ritual that marks the emergence from initiate's status is separate for the boys and the girls; indeed, this separateness is its major import. The boys are introduced to the "lion" (*ŋetuindo*); the girls to the "leopard" (*melilo*). The males meet in the bush away from houses, the females in a tightly closed house.

The lion is a bull-roarer, which makes the sound the initiates have heard in the past, but the source of which they did not know. It is also a representation fabricated out of a monkey skin, I was told. I did not see a bull-roarer, but it was described as being black, about a foot long and five inches wide. It is swung by a thong to which a handle is attached.

While some of the older men are operating the bull-roarer out of sight of the initiates, one or more of the *motriyonik* hide in the bush. Each initiate is taken individually to the "lion" in the dark and made to take hold of it. A *moteriyontet* scratches the initiate with bent thorns. He is then shown the bull-roarer. When all the *chemerik* have been introduced to the lion in this way, they are made to twirl the bull-roarer for a long time, until they become very tired. It is considered a very evil omen for the blade to come loose while it is being twirled, and I was told that the father or brother of each *chemeryontet* should be present to ascertain that the thong is in good condition, for a person of evil intent may cut it part way through. The instrument is not supposed to die down gradually but to be damped suddenly if it is to be stopped at all.

After the *chemerik* have been introduced to the lion, they are given final information about all the "animals." This they are supposed to remember, especially inasmuch as they will be asked to demonstrate their knowledge before being allowed to attend subsequent ceremonies. They are also given instructions on how to use the "animals" to cause fear in others but advised to use such knowledge with restraint. Moreover, they are lectured on such moral values as the avoidance of stealing, lying, and adultery. One tradition-oriented elder improvised the instructions for me:

> First of all, it is I who am your master; it is I who have led you to this lion ceremony; and it is I who am your *moteriyontet*. Never insult a person's child; never be greedy for the riches of your brother, even if he is richer than you; never be jealous of him, thinking that he could die so you can inherit his property. That is bad. Stay in peace. Pray to God who created you. Respect your mother; respect your father; respect your grandfather, who is the father of your sons. Be always pleased with your children, your wives. I wish you to have many children, and these children will look after you when you become old. Remember the proverb: "The sperm is liked, the grey hairs are not liked." Finally, never mention what you have learned here.

The ceremony concludes with an oath called *kachesochiŋ*:

> If you mention it, it will mention you;
> If you neglect it, it will neglect you.

It is a very powerful oath. One man said: "Nobody ever tells; not even mad people tell. They may tear their clothes or eat feces, but they never tell."

The *melilo* ritual is the counterpart ceremony for the girls. The leopard is a "friction drum"; sound is produced by twirling a stick on the drumhead. There is also, presumably, a representation of the leopard, for each girl receives two parallel scars on her forearm from the animal's scratch. I was told that the *melilo* ceremony was not performed in the Sipi area until the 1940s; older women there do not bear these cicatrices.

The rite inducts a girl into the world of womanhood, imparting to her the special secrets of the world. Also imparted are knowledge of the other "animals," of how to perform acts of magic that will make noninitiates cry at circumcision, and of the *ntoyenek*, witchcraft against men — or so men firmly believe. The rite is also a reaffirmation of womanhood for those already initiated, a ritual expression of their unity in the world closed to men — or almost closed.

Among the enigmatic elements of this rite is the fact that a *tekeryontet* man may participate in it — indeed should participate in it. Any *tekeryontet*, even a boy, may join the women in this role. He may not participate in the *melilo* rites when either his wife or his mother is present; if one of them is already there, the other is not permitted to enter. If a husband and wife are in the ceremony together, they will have no children. They never speak to one another about these matters, each acts as if the other does not know. (*Tekeryontet* women do not have the counterpart privilege; they, too, participate in the leopard ceremony.) A *tekeryontet* man may also purchase (for 10 shillings in 1962) the privilege of participating in the lion ceremony at a later time. He may wish to do this to avoid teasing by other men at the time of initiation. I was told that one part of the woman's rites was closed to the male *tekeryontet*: the knowledge of the witchcraft performed against men.

Gale sat outside the house where the ceremony took place in Kapsirika and her observations give some insight into the ritual. When she came to the place at about 5:00 P.M., a group of women were singing and dancing about 50 yards from the house; they were the *motriyonik* and were bringing the "animals" from the bush. One of them threatened to beat the observers if they did not leave. Most went into a nearby house, but one man remained behind, as he was a *tekeryontet*. He was not permitted to join the women until later. Another woman could not enter the house as she had not "caught the animals"; she was asking permission to buy this knowledge.

Gale asked to purchase the right and was told, "If you want to lie down and be cut, we will be willing to let you catch the animals." Her interpreter would not enter the house because, she claimed, she had forgotten all but the main animal, and her local clan sister said the interpreter would be refused entrance. One *moteriyontet* said: "This is a very serious matter; if we showed the animals to others, harm would befall us as well as the person to whom we showed them. It would mean death to everybody concerned."

The *motriyonik* had gone into the bush the previous evening to "catch the animals," had danced all that night, and had then "released the animals" in the early morning. Later, they had caught them again and were now just returning, stopping frequently to "feed them." The women approached slowly, the drum constantly making its roaring sound; from time to time women would shout, "Keep our animal; don't let it out!"

The women then went inside the house, where they sang songs with lyrics like the following:

> We are attacking the leopard,
>   But don't tell it out;
> Look after the leopard,
>   For you shouldn't see it;
> Look after the leopard;
>   For no man should see it;
> Look after this fanged one,
>   That no man may see;
> Guard the side of the animal,
>   That no man can see it;
> Guard the animal,
>   That no man can steal it.

Their songs also warned that looking upon the leopard would cause a man to die and that one should be of strong heart when catching the leopard. After a half-hour or so a *moteriyontet* leaped out of the house brandishing a stick and shouting: "If anyone steals our animals or looks at them, he will suffer in the future! If you see them, you will die and everyone will die!" She then admonished the women gathered outside to dance, and they formed a line, made a few circles, and entered the house. From the time the animals had appeared the friction drum had not ceased its roar.

The rituals of the lion and the leopard are in some sense a further test of bravery and the endurance of pain. Some Kalenjin people have such post-circumcision tests of manhood. Roscoe (1924:76-77) so viewed the matter, but Sebei informants denied it, although one informant did refer to seeing the lion and twirling the bull-roarer as "a punishment." I found no evidence of anticipatory fear; the period is one of heightened ritual danger, but the danger arises from mischance or bad magic, rather than from inadequate personal performance.

There is a strong sense of secretiveness in this phase of the activity; though many individuals thought we should be permitted to see the ritual, our efforts to do so were consistently and effectively thwarted. For instance, at Atar, we were told that the ceremony would not take place on a certain night, but when we arrived the next morning, we discovered it had been held the night before. When the *chemerik* greeted us, they had bandages around their arms where the "leopard" had scarred them. "What bandages?" was their devastating reply to our obvious question. A group of children, with much sniggering and self-conscious naughtiness, was imitating the playing of a friction drum; the women studiously ignored their behavior, but when the father of one of them appeared, he scattered them with some withering abuse. When Gale sought to purchase entrance into the *melilo* ceremony at Kapsirika, her interpreter, who is from Sipi, said that her brother had been killed by the women of that very village; we heard other accounts of such induced death. The curse laid on one Kapsirika man caught peeking at the ceremony two years earlier was that he should not marry or have children, as indeed he did not have, though he was neither too young nor too poor. The women had taken him out in the bush and grilled him, for he claimed to have bought the animals; he proved that he knew them quite well, Yet, he had been caught peeking again and they intended to curse him again.

Despite the fact that *tekeryontet* men join in the women's rites, the rituals celebrate the worlds of men and of women, respectively, and give institutional expression to the hostility and mutual distrust between the sexes. The leopard ritual reinforces the sense of womanhood among women of all ages at the same time that it inducts the neophytes into the secrets. Edgerton, on the basis of his investigations of individual behavior and attitudes, offers us insight into the psychological load this ritual carries.

> The Sebei ... focus upon the malignant power of women. It is not simply that the Sebei are hostile toward women. ... The Sebei *fear* their women. They fear their supernatural power as witches, and their secular power as shrews. ... Fathers caution their sons not to fall under the malignant spell of their mothers, and women admit that men fear them, with good reason: "A man must treat me well; if he does not ... well, he will regret it." A most characteristic Sebei response involves suicide. The typical Sebei suicide is said to be one in which a man is caught in an attempted theft; when he returns home, his wife berates him, heaping invective upon him. He says nothing, but meekly goes to bed. During the night, he murders his wife while she sleeps, then kills himself. Women, say the Sebei, "are worse than anything ... except death." [*RBE*:120-21]

The lion ceremony has the same sort of significance for the men. If there is less overt expression of sexual hostility in the men's activities, it may well be that because men are dominant, they are not so emotionally pressed in the matter. Though we never were as close to a lion ceremony as we were to the leopard, it is manifest that the leopard and the lion express the opposition between the sexes. There is also symbolism in the locale of the two ceremonies.

On the day following the lion or leopard ceremonies, an open ritual inducts the initiates into the world of regular affairs and establishes their age-set membership. It is essentially the same for boys and girls. I will describe events at Atar in 1954. The girls, covered with their initiation cloths, went about fifty feet away from the house, and got on their hands and knees, and crawled toward the house in single file, with much direction from the men and women watching, while the senior wife of the host danced backward in front of them, with a basket of maize on her head (Plate IV:25). This crawling is considered a form of punishment, and the distance depends upon whether the *motriyonik* feel that the *chemerik* have been misbehaving; the fault of one brings on the suffering of all. The girls were then turned, still hidden under their cloths, to face north. They held the poles they were carrying so that they overlapped one another and made one long stringer. An old woman, age, not kinship being relevant, then queried their proper age-set by asking, "Are you such and such *pinta*?" giving the wrong one, at which the girls rose slightly and shook their heads. When she called the correct one, they raised their heads about eighteen inches off the ground, lifted their poles, and assented by intoning an extended "Hmmm." She went down the line four times repeatedly asking her question, once each time asking the right name. Then she took dried beer, chewed it, and taking a mouthful of milk from a gourd, sprayed this mixture on each of the girls, going again four times down the line. The mother of the *kaporet* then took pink vaseline (in lieu of butter) and smeared some on the top of the cloth on the back of each girl, then lifted the cloth and smeared some on the girl's forehead (Plate IV:26). The group sang the song of uncovering the bird while this was being done; it was the mothers' first view of their daughters since circumcision.

Each girl receives new clothes (Plate IV:28). After the mothers had carefully helped the *chemerik* take off their old cloth and put on the new one, the girls stood up, and the mother of the *kaporet* again anointed each with vaseline. The girls danced in position for a few minutes and then, led by a young and vigorous *moteriyontet*, ran in single file at a great pace over a grassy area and around the houses several times until they were breathless (Plate IV:29). Thereafter, the people began to dance.

According to descriptions received, the boys' ceremony is essentially the same. After each mother places butter on her son's head, the father or his brother is supposed to take it off and place it in the mother's cloth. The *chemerik* refuse to allow them to do this until they have been promised a present. I was told that when a boy's father is rich he may get as many as three cattle in this way, and he is permitted to take them that very day. The boys open the singing with a song that goes as follows:

> What is the age set,
> The age set that will never end?

Henceforward, the initiates are no longer *chemerik* but are now called *ŋunik* (*ŋunantet*, sing.), which means wet, in reference to the butter that covers them. The boys are now very proud; they are not allowed to do any work or to eat meat or vegetables but must restrict themselves to milk and starchy food. They may go to any home and sit outside, and the people should furnish them with food. Any girls being initiated will now come and live with the boys, though informants insisted that in the old days they did not have intercourse at this time but only petted.

The final element in the ritual cycle is a shaving ceremony, which takes place at the home of one of the parents on the fourth day. The girls in Atar were shaved in order of their circumcision by one of the *motriyonik*, who should have been shaved first but was not. Each girl first washed her hair in soap and water and rinsed it off, then fresh milk from a black cow was poured over her head. The shaving started on the right side, moved to the back and around the left side, and finished across the front. The eyebrows were also shaved off. Each girl carefully picked up all the hair and made it into a little ball, which she placed in front of her. The whole procedure was very matter-of-fact and unceremonious. People then directed the three last girls to collect wood and, when they came back with sticks, the *arapkaporet* built the fire and the *kaporet* placed all the hair in the fire; the girls stood around while it burned. There was then some horseplay, in imitation of an animal, and loud laughter; it was the first time they were permitted to laugh since the day before their circumcision.

The girls now went through a series of ritual introductions to normal activities: they were supposed to get grain out of a granary, but, because neighbor woman was taking maize which she had just bought from the host out of one, each girl merely pretended to take grain out, stepping up on the granary posts four times, each time being spat upon with beer by one of the *motriyonik* as she did so. Then each girl took a hoe and cut a few strokes in the turf while again being spat upon with beer; the *kaporet* only was given a *panga* and she cut at the grass while being blessed with the beer. Grinding stones were brought and each girl pretended to grind some maize while being spat upon (Plate IV:27). Finally, the *kaporet* peeled a single plantain with a *panga* while being spat upon with beer. The girls then cooked some beans with native salt (salt had also been on their restricted list). Later, when the father kills a ram for the newly released sons or daughters, the *moteriyontet* is supposed to cut four pieces, spit a blessing on them, and feed them to the new men and women to remove the restriction on meat. Though it was not done at Atar, before an initiate may enter his or her mother's house, an old woman is supposed to sit at the door and, using milk from a black cow, spit a blessing as the *ŋunantet* enters four successive times. An initiate must be thus blessed at the entrance of his or her mother's house, all the father's wives' houses, and the father's neighbor's house. The *motriyonik* close the ceremony by asking each initiate what name he or she wishes to take, for initiates receive a new name. "Now they are free, and tomorrow, or perhaps even this evening, some man will come to start to arrange the marriage."

Men are introduced to the items they will use: the stick for herding cattle, bows, arrows, spears, clubs, and shields. These things are also blessed by the *moteriyontet*, who spits on them with beer and chewed moykutwet root and smears them with fat. At the close of the shaving ceremony, a *moteriyontet* who is still strong and agile will take these implements and run with them, while the initiates, also carrying these items, run after him. They are supposed to run as far and as fast as they can. They also have contests in throwing clubs and spears. This is the last action of the cycle of circumcision rites.

CHANGE AND VARIANCE

There are some differences between initiations of girls and boys, some changes that have taken place over time, and some regional variations.

Certain changes are responses to the declining importance of the age-set in Sebei social life, a set of changes that had begun long before Europeans entered the area but intensified during colonial rule.

The most significant change has been the elimination of the mass rites, involving the whole *pororyet* as a single group of initiates, and the substitution of rites for small groups of half dozen or so initiates, drawn from a local area. The *pororyet* was once the military unit, and the unification of the young men in a common circumcision activity must have reinforced this sense of community as well as created a stonger bond among the initiates. The only formal *pinta*-oriented concern is that each father is supposed to entertain his age-mates and that the special age-mate of the father should provide an animal for the initiate — even these customs are often honored in the breach.

A second change is the reduction of the five- to seven-year interval between initiations to two years. This not only has obscured the age differentiation between successive sets but means that the fathers are now members of widely divergent *pintas*, thus reducing the potential unity there.

A third important change has been the elimination of sporting contests among the initiates. Formerly, the boys were supposed to wrestle and otherwise practice "manly sports," such as spear-throwing and club-throwing. These were engaged in as late as the Sowe initiation (1920s), but no longer occur. The relation of this change to the declining military functions is obvious; the change must also have affected the initiates' sense of mutual involvement. Another associated change is the elimination of restrictions against taking as a first wife a woman who had cried during circumcision, which was thought to be dangerous for the husband as a warrior.

There has also been some decline in the degree to which ritual details are observed. The erosion of old practices is far greater in the Sipi area than in the east or on the plains, but to some extent it is also associated with education. Among the more educated men, there is some tendency to have circumcision performed in the hospital, an option that is not open to the women. (Some Sebei leaders suggested to me that the circumcision of women should be abandoned.)

The decline in traditional practices was remarked on by both Bomet and Chemtai, who saw a greater decline in Sipi and Kaptanya on one hand than in Bukwa and the plains on the other: "In the west, the initiates dominate the *motriyonik*, while, in the east and on the plains, they obey them." Among the specifics they noted were that initiates in the western region insisted on taking food and drink and did not take the medicines; they often refused to be painted; they do not dance as hard but "are lazy"; they laugh and make noise, as they are not supposed to do; they bathe during the period of their seclusion and repaint themselves (if they paint themselves at all) rather than forego baths. In addition to the erosion of ritual restrictions, the people in the west have ceased to use the crossed spears and whetstone;

they have substituted vaseline for butter for anointing; and they do not demand and receive livestock from their parents and other relatives. The people in Bukwa and on the plains continue to use animal skins for clothes during circumcision, but the westerners have substituted cloth. They have also substituted a flannel cummerbund for the cowrie shell girdle traditionally worn. One girl in the Sipi area told me that she had spent her circumcision eve listening to phonograph records.

Certain elements have been brought in from the outside. The Gisu have introduced the use of the Colobus monkey headdress; this is more prevalent in the west but is now rather widespread. The use of banners is also a western innovation that has spread throughout Sebei. The use of the ram's scrotum, borrowed from Kenyans, has not, however, spread to the eastern area.

Another change throughout Sebei has to do with the comportment of the observers; people formerly kneeled at some distance and watched the operation quietly; now they crowd around and make a great deal of noise. There also appears to be a general tendency to drop the ritual involving the throwing of the apples of Sodom.

(In 1972, the rituals we observed in Sipi and Kaptanya showed further deterioration, largely as a result of the increased use of native gin, for Muslims maintain greater decorum. In one instance in Sasur, there was no positioning of the girls but each came up separately to the circumcisor. People were pushing and shouting and crowded the operator so closely that she had to brandish her knife to drive them back. In another instance, the older people had so little concern for their duties that, when the boys arrived at the home where the initiation was to take place, they could not be smeared with chyme as no ram had been provided, and there was not even an agreement as to where the initiates were to undergo the operation.)

Some differences between the plains and Sipi reflect economic variation. Chief among these is the lavish display that characterizes the plains initiation in contrast to one in Sasur and elsewhere in the plantain area. Lavish display reflects the greater emphasis upon the initiate as a person and particularly the parent's stronger sense of personalized status. Another feature that differentiates the plains rituals from those of Masop, and particularly those of Sipi, is the acquisition of gifts by the initiates. Three plains boys indicated that they had received animals, a bull in one instance, a heifer in the other two, and a ewe in each case. These animals were given by their fathers and brothers (cattle) and the husbands of their sisters (sheep). They also received money in amounts ranging from a few cents to 10-shilling notes and totaling about 20 shillings each. In an earlier circumcision, one boy had received two cattle and another three. Diverse relatives and friends gave money only to the four girls I spoke to, in amounts ranging from about 40 shillings to 100 shillings — the larger amounts from each mother's brothers. While gift-giving and demanding are not entirely absent in Masop, they are far less extensive, and there is nothing comparable to the giving of cattle.

SUMMARY AND CONCLUSIONS

The manifest function of the rituals associated with circumcision is to transform boys and girls into men and women. During the liminal period, the initiates are symbolically nonpersons, numbered instead of named, hidden, denied certain regular amenities and privileges, and vulnerable to the fates.

Circumcision also confirms the initiates' relation to their age-sets and reaffirms the age-set affiliation of the adults and the system of seniority. As the circumcision rites have become less involved with matters of age-set affiliation, they have increasingly functioned as local community ritual.

Nowhere in the circumcision ritual do we find any rationale for undergoing this painful experience; nor could we elicit from informants either secular or religious explanations. No origin myth accounts for circumcision; that bane of ethnographers is the only response: we have always done it. Men's circumcision can be rationalized in terms of cleanliness, but this cannot be made to apply to women and hence becomes suspect as an explanation at all. Elsewhere, female circumcision is related to the protection of virginity, particularly where the vagina is closed by the manner in which the wound is permitted to heal, but such results are carefully avoided by the Sebei. Europeans often try to expalin clitoridectomy as an effort to reduce the level of sexual desire in the women, but the Sebei offer no such explanations, and the behavior of the women, and what Sebei men expect from their women, renders such an explanation implausible. Neither do men or women claim that circumcision enhances the sexual experience. Men say they cannot feel any difference, except when caressing the vagina. The continuing tenacity with which the Sebei adhere to circumcision for both men and women, despite the decline of the age-set system and the efforts of the government and the missionaries to discourage its continuation, stands in marked contrast to their treatment of most other traditional rites. Such tenacity suggests that some overriding social importance of these rituals remains unverbalized by the Sebei themselves. The functional importance of circumcision may well be the affirmation of sex identity. This focus on sex identity relates to the conflict between the sexes among the Sebei. This identification is particularly important to the women, who undergo a test of courage and fortitude at least as demanding as that of the men. The Sebei are very snide toward those who are uncircumcised, whether because they are still too young, of an alien tribe, or fear the knife. They chide men for undergoing the operation in the hospital. In 1972, I had a conversation with one of Bomet's sons, a high school youth, who was to be circumcised in a few days and did not want to undergo the ritual because he felt that it had been emptied of its social meaning. His father, highly traditional in outlook, was adamant; his son capitulated because of one argument: if he were not circumcised, he would suffer the jeers of his fellows would say that he had been afraid. The Bumachek adopted circumcision because the Sebei "despised" them and refused to drink beer with them.

Because the Sebei strongly value courage, it is important for a person to demonstrate this quality — especially so for women as a countermeasure to male dominance. Even more important is the strong sense of social unity that the ritual engenders in the women. The magic that they learn in the women's rites is directed at the men. The age-sets may have become virtually meaningless and military action minimal, but the confrontation between the sexes continues to be a major feature of daily life.

The variations in the ritual confirm these implications. In the more pastoral sections, such symbols as spears and animals remain and have even been augmented. The eroding of ritual activities in the west, such as the failure to take the medicines, does not merely make for an attenuated ritual; it eliminates the sharing of secret knowledge with members of one's sex and deprives the women of participating in the ritual unification by which they express both their unity and their sexual antagonism toward men.

I do not believe that the current differences in circumcision rituals are merely a matter of "acculturation." In agricultural matters, Bukwa has changed more than Sipi. Even Kapsirika, though less influenced by the money economy and schooling, has engaged in more and earlier innovations in brideprice payments. There is certainly no less involvement with witch-craft in Sipi than in Kapsirika. I believe, rather, that the differential must be responsive to the difference in the economy — the relative unimportance of pastoralism and associated masculine pursuits in comparison to farming, and the consequent enhancement of the women's economic role. The absence of military threat and the lack of cattle alter the whole stance of men in Sipi: the functional importance of the values of bravery and stamina has been lost, and the men retain their interest in circumcision out of traditionalism and the psychological sanctions that come from other Sebei men, with whom they must interact. Their unity as men has been rendered unnecessary by these changes, and their economic and social welfare has become dependent upon their individual households. They also, we are told, treat their women with more consideration — or at least less harshness. The women have not only more responsibility but also more freedom, and under these circum-stances there is less pressure upon them to assert their unity against their men. I do not mean to imply the relations between men and women in Sipi approach equity or are ideal, but only that there has been some relaxation. Above all, women need no longer contend with the ritualized unity of men.

In Kapsirika, on the other hand, and to a lesser extent in eastern Sebei, the men engage in traditional cattle-keeping and continue their military activity. Even if this warfare is only defensive and half-hearted, nevertheless, it does reinforce traditional masculine values. On top of this, in Kapsirika and Bukwa, the agricultural pursuits involve the plow, reinforcing men's association with livestock and lessening the economic importance of women. Under these conditions, the functional importance of age-sets is retained; the Kapsirika women continue to ritualize their unity and ceremonialize their antagonism toward men.

Matters are not entirely unchanged in the east, however. The Kapsirikans have added something new to the circumcision rite: the potlatch element. I do not have any evidence that this rivalrous use of the circumcision feast was part of traditional practice. A man was expected to slaughter an animal at least for his first child's initiation, and men of substance probably did a good deal more. But the competitive aspect that appears in Kapsirika could not but have had a deleterious effect on age-set unity and would therefore have been destructive to a crucial institution for traditional Sebei pastoralism.

The development of rivalrous feasting does, however, relate to two important elements in the climate of attitudes that prevails among pastoralists: individualism and the free expression of feeling (*RBE:* 272-83). The initate or the father or both are praised — as individuals — around the beer pot. The custom also represents an open expression of rivalry and this is in direct opposition to the covert expressions of hostility in the form of witchcraft found in Sasur.

Chapter 11
Sebei Metaphysics

Lightning and moon used to live on the earth with elephant and man, and they were all friends. Moon and lightning came to realize the behavior of man, and they decided to leave the earth and live up in the sky. When they were up in the sky, they called back to elephant, saying: "We have seen that the customs and manners of man are bad. Would you like to come up to the sky with us?" "No," the elephant answered, "I am very strong and man can do nothing to harm me." After a short time, man invented the arrow and arrow poison. He made a kind of stick, and on one end there was the poisoned arrow and on the other a kind of club. He threw this at elephant, and he speared the elephant. Elephant felt the pain of the poison, and he cried up to moon and lightning: "Help me! Please help me! I am hurting." But lightning and moon refused to help elephant and said, "We told you that you should leave man and come with us, but since you did not heed us, we will not help you." So elephant died.

Sebei perceptions of the world will involve us with their cosmology, their efforts to avoid evil influences that inhere in the world and to harness these unseen forces for their legitimate and nonlegitimate purposes. As religion is not a separate domain of social life but is a component of virtually every item of behavior, I have presented rituals in the social contexts in which they occur. Here I want to summarize the perceptions and understandings that form the underlying stratum of belief out of which action emerges. This it seems appropriate to call their metaphysics.

The Sebei are inarticulate with respect to these matters. They are genuinely uninterested in speculations and theories, and although some would discuss witchcraft freely — certainly the most tabu Sebei subject in modern times — persons who were pointed out as having such esoteric knowledge either denied it or refused to talk about it. This is not merely reticence. Verbal speculation and theorizing are generally absent in Sebei culture; the contrast with American Indian cosmological material is impressive. For instance, the verbal accompaniment to Sebei rituals usually repeats words like "peace," "sweet," and "good," or merely requests the bad spirits to leave and the good ones to remain. Such statements tell us something about attitudes but not very much about beliefs. There is little or no moralization. Sebei men and women do not engage in storytelling, and I could never get anything like an origin myth in any detail. As men and women become old and inactive, they join groups around the fire at night and tell tales to the grandchildren. But these stories are chiefly animal stories, not cosmogenic myths. The story at the head of this chapter is one of few exceptions, and it does not penetrate deeply into either understanding or morality. This paucity of verbalization, which leads to a vagueness in formulation and a lack of consistency among the Sebei in their metaphysical understandings, is, to judge from ethnographies of the area, characteristic of Kalenjin peoples. It relates to another Sebei characteristic: the almost total absence of visual or plastic arts. There is, one might say, little institutionalization of fantasy. We will therefore be compelled to attend to the character of Sebei ritual life for clues to their perceptions of the world, along with items from everyday gossip.

COSMOLOGY

The Sebei share with other Kalenjin tribes the recognition of a high God associated with the sun, called Asista. Asista created the universe; he is the ultimate source of all power and is viewed vaguely but essentially as good. ("He only loves; he does not hate.") But Asista is not involved in the affairs of men; no prayer or libation is directed His way; He does not respond to prayers and needs no placatory action but may be thanked when good fortune befalls. The Sebei make relatively little reference to Him. Some interpreters occasionally translated as god the plural term for spirits, *oyik* (but sometimes also used the singular, *oynatet*).

Of the other cosmic phenomena, mention should be made of the moon, lightning, thunder, and the rainbow, which causes a particular disease. These may be spoken of in personalized terms. Moon, though it tricked man into undergoing death, is essentially good. Ceremonies (other than one of the death rituals and certain oaths) should never be performed when the moon is dark. Lightning and thunder are essentially harmful. They are sent by spirits and require a prophylactic ritual in which specially made spears (*palipalis-yek*) are thrown at the place where lightning has struck a house, animal, or person. This is not an effort to kill lightning but to chase it away. Spears are set about the area in such a way as to protect it, some to "meet" the lightning, some to intercept it, and some to "show it the way." The spears are left in place to rot away. The spear thrower must be a left-handed man who has not suffered from lightning. He and the owner of the destroyed property or the victim's brother (if a man has been killed) say, "You are wrong to destroy this; I have paid you compensation." The ritual takes place between sunset and dark two days after the event, and no work should be done by anyone of the *aret* or the *saŋta* for five days after lightning has struck.

A genealogical myth accounts for origin of the Sebei and their relationship to their neighbors, but few men know it. The presumed genealogy is reproduced in Figure 1. It appears to have been heavily edited — if not essentially created — for political purposes. Occasional stories account for some phenomenon, but no consistent effort is made to explain nature or man's customs in cosmogenic terms.

A description of the cosmos was pieced together from statements by two or three informants, though other old men denied such knowledge. Above the surface of the earth (*ŋuñ*) is the sky (*tarat*), which one can see. Beyond that is *polyet* or *polyetnyetui* (a black cloud). The sun and his neighbor the moon live beyond *polyet*, in an area beyond the range of human vision and variantly called *wom* or *araraita*. Lightning lives there also. The sun goes below the earth to the south, where it nourishes itself. Beyond *araraita* is *chakai* — "So very far away, nobody could know." Below the earth is an area of darkness called *sililoy*, where the *oyik* dwell. *Sililoy* rests on an underground lake or sea, called *tampayayet*. These descriptions lack detail and imagery and do not suffuse the thoughts and attitudes of the Sebei in their daily life, as do the *oyik*.

The most coherent and consistent strain in Sebei religious belief has to do with the human soul. Each living person has a *soponto*, which we might call an essence or life itself; it resides in his heart and disappears upon death. He also has an *atotoito* or soul. (Animals have *soponto* but not *atotoito*.) The soul does not leave the body, even when the person is sleeping, except upon death, when it becomes an *oynatet* and lives among other *oyik* underground. It looks like a man, "but it cannot be touched — like the wind."

In general, the circumstances of the *oyik* reflect those of the living; as one man said, there are rich and poor *oyik*, and they can make a man rich or poor. *Oyik* are seen to be either good or bad; the good *oyik* "let people live and have a long life and get rich," while the bad *oyik* harm the living. The *oyik* retain their relationship within the clan, and they largely help or harm the living of their clansmen; a person may also be affected by the *oyik* of his mother's and his father's mother's clans: "It follows kin relationships." The *atotoito* may be reborn, but the *oynatet* nevertheless remains among the spirits. There is no evidence that the spirit's postmortem existence is affected by the conduct, personality, personal attributes, or economic circumstances of his bodily counterpart during life. Rather, the character of the ancestral *oynatet* is established by the circumstances of the survivors. If they are rich and powerful, it is evidence of the strength of the *oyik*; if ill luck befalls them, then the *oyik* are ill-disposed. It is perhaps more in accord with Sebei sentiment, however, to think of the *oyik* not as individual souls of particular ancestors but as a collectivity representing the totality of clan spirits. Thus, when informants use our word god for the *oyik*, they are not without reason, for this collective will is operant on the survivors of their *aret*. The strength and wealth of the spirits in their postmortem existence do not rest upon the strength or wealth of the individual, but upon the strength of the kin group. Libations and other ceremonial acts addressed to the *oyik* usually refer to them in the plural as a collectivity, though good and bad spirits are separately treated; the good given beer with the right hand at the threshold, kraal gate, or centerpost of the house, while beer and food for the bad *oyik* is cast away from the house with the left hand. One person even likened the *oyik* to a court presided over by a head *oynatet* but subject to the collective will of the "assessors." He hastened to add, however, that "one bad *oynatet* can kill a man." The *oyik* live under the ground, existing — some say — much as men do. Not only do they want beer and food from their descendants, but they may demand that a cow or bull be given them, not slaughtered, but dedicated to them. Thus, while the bad *oyik* are simply malevolent, the good ones are also potentially so and require constant attention lest they become malicious. These spirits also, apparently, want to reenter the world through a descendant; at least, this is the implication of the naming ceremony, where the determination of the name is based upon the desires of the *oyik*. So far as I can judge from Sebei actions and statements, the Sebei do not believe in any form of reincarnation. The ancestor is not reborn in the child, nor does the ancestor's spirit enter the child. It is more as if the child were dedicated to him, as cattle are dedicated to the *oyik*. The child serves to preserve the ancestor's existence in the spirit world by keeping alive his memory.

Through their conception of the *oyik*, the Sebei assert the clan's unity, identity, and continuity through time, reinforcing the clan's role as a jural entity. The clan identification provided through the commonality of its ancestry as conceptualized in these ancestral spirits is one of the more compelling elements in Sebei belief.

The sense of fatalism suffusing Sebei action is implicit in such concepts as the evil eye, "bad birds," and luck and is expressed in the pervasive use of omens, diviners, and prophets. Because some persons possess the evil eye, others can be harmed unwittingly by the simple act of looking at something on which a spell has been cast. Infants (especially a *tekeryontet*) and young animals are particularly subject to dangers from this source. Amulets are used as a means of protection against such influences, and a small gift, like a copper coin, may be requested, apparently as a kind of earnest of good intentions. Persons may also be possessed of "bad birds" (*taritek che miyotech*) and occasionally good ones. There is a tendency for these to be associated with clans, but essentially they express a commonly held notion that certain individuals are endowed with good fortune and others with bad. One informant said that "bad birds" were indicated if a woman failed to perform certain rites, as for instance proper mourning for a death in her husband's clan. Another kind of fatalism was expressed after a fugitive from jail survived a fall over a cliff; it was said that he would live to a very old age, for any person (or animal) who has one narrow escape is charmed.

Sebei thoughtways also have a set of attitudes analogous to our genetic explanations. Certain qualities are thought to be inherent in certain clans — "in their blood," as Westerners might say.

ILLNESS AND DEATH

The Sebei lack a consistent and unified theory of illness and the causes of death. While probably no serious disease or, for that matter, any other misfortune, occurs without some suspicion of witchcraft, it is by no means true to say that all deaths are attributed to this source. More often, such suspicions are but fleeting sentiments. Illness may be seen as deriving from any of a number of causes: inheritance in the clan blood, infection or "natural" causes, ill luck brought by rainbow, failure to comply with any of various behavioral restrictions (such as an improper marriage), an oath directed at the person's clan or one made by a clansman against others which may return upon the clan. Recognizing diverse sources, a Sebei who is ill may seek various kinds of treatment — native or patent medicines, bleeding, and rituals designed to remove the effects of an oath. Sick persons also tend to go to several diviners to find the cause. If witchcraft is suspected, four diviners must so diagnose it, implicating the same individual, before appropriate action may be taken. I first learned of one man's illness when he asked me to read the labels on several packages of patent medicines. He went to at least two medicine men, took the medicines they prescribed, and was twice in European hospitals before he undertook the ceremony for the removal of a curse — or more accurately, two separate curses — which finally cured him. This experimental approach to treatment is also found among the curers, who are not the prisoners of formal rules but retain a pragmatic, open-ended, and almost experimental outlook.

Some clans have a tendency to inherit certain diseases, e.g., mental retardation, goiter, blindness, and neck sores, but the Sebei distinguish between inherited disease and disease caused by some external event — between being born mentally defective or sterile, for example, and having been made so. Some diseases are thought to be brought about by contact with those who are ill. Thus, a person having an epileptic seizure must be avoided, as it is thought that others can contract the illness through contact with the saliva of the epileptic at such a time. Leprosy may be contracted from the sleeping skins of a leper.

The Sebei distinguish between the diviner (*chepsokeyontet*), whom interpreters call witch doctor and who only determines the cause of the malady, the curer (*psakichantet*), whom they call medicine man and who knows the medical treatment for one or more diseases, and the specialist (*muswokintet*), who can bleed, set bones, and the like. Though I was told that the *psakichantet* may be so specialized as to make his or her living from the practice, I never met one who did so. It is recognized that the *muswokintet* requires very special knowledge and skill ("can only be done by a very senior person"), but it is not a full-time specialty.

Most cures are administered by persons who have been cured of the illness and have bought the knowledge from the person who cured them. A person may also learn the cure when his child or animal has been successfully treated, and some persons learn to cure many diseases. The most professionalized medicine man I met discussed his skill as follows:

> I inherited some medicines from my father, and some I got myself. I know medicine for *kweremon*, which is a disease like gonorrhea, for *chepkalasyet*, which is a disease we believe comes from the rainbow and is very much like chronic malaria, for *kisor* or *kisortit*, an infection that attacks mostly toes and fingers, and the medicine for infected eyes, *sakechetap koinyek*.
>
> The medicine I learned myself I obtained from an old woman. First I fell ill and was treated by this old woman. After recovering, I paid for the medicine; 2 shillings for the "dew" and two female goats. Then I asked to know the kind of medicine and that woman charged me 30 shillings and some beer for blessing it. So I made beer. I gave one big pot to the woman and one gourd.
>
> Rainbow disease always comes when it is raining. The rain brings it to a person's body whenever it rains and a rainbow is in the sky. The rainbow has many colors and will affect a person through the rain. A medicine man can determine that a person is suffering from the rainbow. He can tell by seeing if they have a serious headache or a heartache. The appearance of a child will be different; the skin will be tight on the face, and the patient will be vomiting. I have treated very many for this, and all recovered; nobody dies of this disease. I charge 2 shillings for the "dew" payment and 20 shillings when the patient is cured. He must pay 10 shillings extra plus the beer to learn the medicine. I have cured more than thirty people and sold medicine to about ten. There is no rule about whom to sell it to — I can even sell it to a Gisu if I wish — except that the man must have been ill of the disease. If a child falls ill, the father can have the medicine.
>
> When I see a person is suffering from rainbow disease, I go to the bush and collect medicines. I take a root about a yard long from a tree and if the person doesn't get cured, I take another root from a different stem. After taking the root, I spit and bless the spot I have taken it from. In my heart, I say the blessing that it will be good; I don't speak out loud. I boil the root, pour some in a mug or a calabash for the patient to drink, and instruct him to use any remaining liquid to wash his face in the mornings and his hands before meals and to sprinkle on his bed or sleeping skin. I leave the instructions for the person taking care of the patient. A patient can choose to take the medicine by itself, in soup, or in beer; it doesn't matter what the soup is made of.

Although an animal must be slaughtered for many medicines (and its intestines examined for prognosis), the details vary and seem to be without significance. This doctor orders a white goat both in accordance with the instructions received from his mentor and because "I believe if I use a white one, it is like a light in the house and will light up the dark body and cure the disease." He uses male animals for men and female for women but does not feel it matters whether the animal is slaughtered or suffocated, as was formerly the practice, or what meat is used, except that neither the liver nor the spleen should be used and the head should be the last portion cooked for medicine. He recognizes variant practices: "So long as there are many doctors, there will be many different ways of applying medicine," and, "If a person does something, I want to do it better."

A death is announced by the women of the household, who go outside and make a special high-pitched cry, used for no other purpose, which carries a great distance and is repeated by other women, to spread the announcement. If a man dies early in the morning, he may be buried that day, but if it is later in the day, he will not be buried until the following morning, as stock should not be released from the kraal until his body has been disposed of. The delay also enables his brothers and sons to examine the body for evidence of witchcraft. The body should be placed inside the house of the first wife in the area set aside for visitors.

Like many of their Kalenjin neighbors, the Sebei used to place the body in a bushy place and allowed the hyenas to devour it, but prophets and twins were interred and their bones removed from the grave after two or three years and placed in caves. Burial, thus, was not unknown; its general practice came very rapidly with European influence. As I have described Sebei funeral practices elsewhere (Goldschmidt, 1973b), I shall merely summarize them here.

When arriving at a funeral, people exchange no greetings but may speak freely of other matters. The relatives, particularly the women, may keen before the body or at the grave (Plates IV:41-42). The grave is dug near the house of the first wife, in the area where refuse is thrown, by brothers or clan brothers of the deceased. The brothers remove the personal ornaments, wash the body, and place it in the grave (Plate IV:43). After interment, the widows of the deceased remain in the house of the first wife, attended by another widow and accompanied by the man who will inherit the widows. They may not work, eat certain foods, or engage in sexual intercourse and must remain unseen. Nor may they use sleeping mats, scratch themselves with their fingers, touch their food, or remove ashes from the hearth. These restrictions are essentially the same as those for initiates. The man who is to inherit the widows, properly the husband's next full brother or the first son the first wife of an old man, is chief mourner; he is spoken of as the one who "buries the deceased" — a phrase that may also express the close relationship in ordinary conversations while both are still alive. All clansmen, all members of the mother's clan, and all the people of the *saŋta* are expected to observe a four-day period of mourning (three days for a *tekeryontet*) by refraining from all work, except milking and herding cattle, and no ceremonies are to be held "as far as the next stream, in either direction." Clansmen, but not fellow villagers, are also expected to refrain from sexual intercourse.

Mourning ends with *kopuntoyet ap met*, chasing away death, which combines the most important funerary rites with a moot in which all creditors must make a public claim upon the estate and the inheritance of widows and property may be decided. If the deceased is a man wealthy in stock, his herd bull (or another animal) will be slaughtered by spearing and the chyme strewn on the path to the stream at which the mourners bathe; if the deceased is a twin or the father of a twin, the chyme will be smeared upon the mourners. In farming areas, a ram is slaughtered. The man who spears the animal must be compensated.

After the slaughter but before the distribution of the meat, the mourners are shaved: first the brother who buried the deceased, then other brothers and their wives, and finally the widows (Plate IV:44). Women of the clan who have married are not shaved. The widows are shaved behind a screen by a woman who has lost her husband; she leaves tufts of hair, so that people will know they are in mourning. Ashes are sprinkled on their heads, down the right side, and in the vagina. When all have been shaved, the widows go to the stream to bathe, scattering their hair in the bushes. When the mourners return, the personal belongings of the deceased are smeared with fat and spewed with beer by a clan elder.

Now the moot is held. Most items are readily taken care of, but heated debate may take place over who will inherit the widows or how the cattle are to be divided.

That evening a kind of stew is made of all the tabu foods, together with a bit of each part of a slaughtered animal, to be eaten by the widows, their children, and the man who is to inherit them. That night, the man has sexual intercourse with each widow in order of her seniority, an act known as "cleaning out the ashes." This makes them *keyanyiñ*, good or clean and concludes the mourning customs, but some time later, if the deceased and the inheritor both have herds of cattle, the ritual of amity between herds will be performed.

A woman's funeral is handled by her husband's clansmen. Her corpse is placed on her left side. If she is pregnant, the fetus is removed and either buried beside her or, if after the seventh month, placed in a separate grave. The husband is under restriction until the cleansing ceremony four days later; someone is appointed to cook for him, as his other wives should not do so. As women own no significant property and have no debts, there are no hearings.

Twins and the parents of twins evoke certain special considerations. Only those quite closely related cease to work during the period of mourning; the personal ornaments are not removed but are buried with a twin; the shaving ceremony takes place on the third day rather than on the fourth; a ram is slaughtered and tail fat placed in the mouth of the dead twin, who is smeared with its chyme; and the grave is marked so that the bones can subsequently be removed and placed in a cave. Twins and parents of twins cannot take any principal role in the rites connected with funerals: "They are free of everything; they cannot even weep." During the night of circumcision, a surviving twin or, if both are dead, the child following twins (*kisa*) goes to the grave of the dead twin and smears earth from it on his face.

A man or woman who dies at a very old age has what is known as a sweet death (*kolil*), and none of the funeral rites described above is performed. An old person's body is laid out in an open place or under a tree, on his sleeping skin, with his beer straw, his spear, and his pipe beside him. His grand-children and great grandchildren are told to go and see him that they may enjoy a long life like his; they may laugh and enjoy themselves; they sing the song of welcome as at a wedding or after a circumcision. Such a death is a feast (*sakwet*), not a funeral.

Infants who die at or shortly after birth are buried unceremoniously by the mother near her house or in that area where goats and calves are kept, but older children are buried with more ceremony. When a child of nursing age dies, the father digs the grave and the mother is the one to step inside and arrange the body. There is a crying as for an adult, but not many attend and strict mourning is not kept. The father remains with the mother at night, but they do not have sexual intercourse and the cooking is done by another wife or a young girl.

Two elements are paramount in mortuary rites: the sense of pollution and its attendant danger to the survivors, and the almost total disregard for the dead, either as a body or a spiritual being. The very name "chasing away death" turns attention away from the particularity of the deceased to the general problem of deathness. The Sebei, having come to utilize the sanctify-ing ambience of a funeral to settle matters of property, force the mourners to behave with unseemly self-interest whenever an important relative dies. This awakens their sense of guilt. The situation brought about by the death, rather than the dead man, evokes this cupidity and its attendant guilt, thereby creating a sense of pollution that the rites are designed to cleanse away.

The Sebei have an inordinate fear of death. Edgerton (*RBE*:119) found this the most prominent Sebei characteristic in his psychological investiga-tions. It is not a fear of the dead, but of death, just as Sebei funeral rituals do not exorcise the spirit of the deceased but sweep away death. Death among the Sebei is very nearly a total anihilation, since there is no coherent theory of afterlife. The Sebei are quick to dispose of the body; it is buried in the refuse area nowadays and was formerly placed in the bush for the hyenas to devour. (Sebei do not say, as other Kalenjin do, that the soul finds its way to immortality through the hyena's intestinal tract.) The soul, too, is dropped into an abyss and the survivors attend not to it, but to death — their own death. Perhaps this sense of annihilation at death relates to the general low level of affect among Sebei kinsmen, which is expressed in the tendency to see *oyik* in general terms, rather than as spirits of particular ancestors.

PROPHETS, DIVINATION, AND AUGURIES

The Sebei have diverse techniques for determining the course of events and the causes of misfortune, techniques for peering into the unseeable forces that work upon man's fate. These vary from the all-important work of the prophets and include a class of semispecialized diviners, more generalized forms of divination by diverse methods, and also a number of minor omens.

The secular role of the prophets and their social position have been discussed in the context of Sebei social organization. Since prophets have not actually functioned for thirty or so years, I can give very little information on how they determine future events. I was told that they dreamed, which I presume means that they entered into a trance state, and that their auguries were presented in parables. Always using eliptical statements, they predicted not only disasters such as epidemics, locust plagues, and military invasion, but also hunting success and other details. The prediction of the Europeans' arrival was described as follows: They were called butterflies, because of their colorful dress; they would carry fire in their mouths and hollow sticks that could kill a man. One description suggested that some prophet engaged in legerdemain ("He would throw his clothes in the air, and they would stay there."). The advice passed on by the old men indicates a certain ambivalence toward prophets:

> There are good prophets and bad ones. If an outstanding young fighter is killed, perhaps the prophet wanted this, and then the prophet would be killed. They told us that for some *pinta* the prophets were good and that we should watch our prophet, obey him if he is a good man. If a prophet is good, he may dream about elephants and about how the people go hunting and kill them. He may have a medicine for the people to throw at the enemy and weaken their strength. Then you will know that he is a good prophet. The bad prophet will say, "Go to such and such an area for elephants," but instead, people will find enemies and the survivors will report this. When a bad prophet gives medicine, it will not overcome the enemy. Such a prophet should be beaten until he is dead.

Specialist diviners (*chepsokeyontet*) are consulted in cases of death, illness, and failure to produce children. Unlike the prophets, whose auguries foretell events, the diviners use diverse means to determine the cause of the problem. Muslims "read the book"; men toss sandals and read the manner in which they fall (a practice they claim was recently acquired from the Karamojong). Both men and women may be diviners; the latter are usually consulted by women who fail to become pregnant.

The diviner never directly names the person responsible but identifies him indirectly by some means, which the questioner must read. A diviner told me that if he accused the person directly, then he would suffer retaliation.

I visited a *chepsokeyontet* myself on behalf of my neighbor, Charles, a pleasant, outgoing man of about thirty with no children by the wife to whom he had been married for some four years. Still in many ways a youth, he was a favorite around the beer pot, an avid dancer and drummer. One day in April he visited me. There were puncture wounds on his knee where he had been bled and cupped, with black spots where the medicines had been applied by a neighbor. The medicine was to counteract bewitched substances that had been placed along the path, and while it had helped him sleep (most of the bad blood had been removed), he was still ill. Somebody suggested he had rheumatism (*mokonkyontet*) and recommended the services of a woman who provided medicine.

Charles at first denied that he had any enemies who might want to bewitch him, but, as I questioned more closely, a complex, but not entirely clear story of intrafamilial discord emerged. He had recently built his house on land where his father's younger brother had formerly lived because "my father had kindly let him use it." But, when Charles married, his father chased the uncle off the land. The uncle complained to the father and took a case before the local chief, "but my father refused to listen." When Charles got sick, his neighbors warned him. Furthermore, one of his sister's sons came to him after spending the night with this uncle, from whom he had been trying to collect a debt, and urged Charles to make peace with the uncle and give him the land. Since the father's brother had never had beer in Charles' home, there was reason for Charles to be suspicious. He thought he might ask a neighbor to visit the *chepsokeyontet* named Samweri, for he should not go himself. Charles's good friend Mwanga and I offered to go.

Samweri was nervous at our arrival, though he continued the enquiry he was engaged in. After objecting to my presence, he said, "I have been told that you were hunting for me," and demanded a shilling. Samweri was very small, frightened rather than unfriendly. He soon began to query the *oyik* in Charles's behalf by means of his *rupet*, a shallow wooden bowl with nine colored stones in it. He shook the bowl so the stones rattled around, while asking questions. When the stones stick together at the bottom when he holds the bowl at an angle, it means that the *oyik* respond affirmatively in answer to his question; if some fall out, then "the *oyik* cannot agree" on this cause. Samweri had obtained the *rupet* from his father and believed his grandfather had made it. He had found the stones. There can be any number of them, from three to about ten. The spirits do not reside in the stones; the *oyik* express themselves in the actions of the pebbles. The role of *chepsokeyontet* is a Karuma clan skill; were he not to perform this function he would become ill. When he dies, his "*oynatet* will catch somebody" of his clan to do the job.

> *Samweri* [shaking the *rupet* and addressing *oyik*]: Please do come because an old man has come here from Europe. Don't be idle. Why are you *oyik* not awake? Please let me know what is the matter with Arabusi's son [i.e., Charles] — he is a son of Kapchai [Samweri's area in Sebei]. I understand he beats a drum.
>
> I wonder if this is a kind of *mumek* [oath]. *Oyik* of Kapsombata [Charles' clan], please let me know if this is *mumek*. Please let me know what is the matter with that child who is sick. He has pain on his arm, wants to know if somebody bewitched him; please, my *oyik*, let me know. Let me know what is wrong with Arabusi's son. [After some further queries I did not catch, he stopped shaking and stones fall from the *rupet*. He addresses Mwanga.] Are you a neighbor of Arabusi's son?
>
> *Mwanga*: Yes.
>
> *Samweri*: Do you know that a member of Arabusi's clan killed a Gisu man? That Gisu said something wrong.
>
> *Mwanga*: Yes.
>
> *Samweri*: So, my *oyik*, please let me know the person who bewitched this man.

If this is *panet* [witchcraft] let me know. Please my friends [*oyik*], let me know. [Two stones fell out.]

But, *Oyik* of Kapsombata, if this is not a man of Kapsombata, please also let me know. This man played the drum until his arm got paralyzed. If this is a disease of the bush, please let me know. Let me know if it is sheep or goat. If it is no disease, please let me know. [Again, two stones fell out.]

Please let us know if Kapsombata people stole somebody's cow or ate somebody's goat or stole somebody's money. Please let me know. Tell the *kota* of Kapchai, for this man is suffering in one arm and one leg.

[At this point, Samweri stops shaking the *rupet* and begins to rock back and forth.] They have eaten — killed a goat — father is clan member who knows — killed a dog and this dog was taken to person who killed the dog someplace where they hunted — dog belonged to Matei — burned the dog as one does a rat — must spit blessing on the dog — dog taken into cave of Kapenmet — this was bewitched. That's it.

[Mwanga agreed that this had happened. The dog was shot with an arrow. The stones had kept quiet, which means that this was the truth.]

Samweri: First, he has two different diseases — first, a Gisu was killed by a Kapsombata man, and second, the dog has been bewitched. Ask Satya, the son of Matei, who shot this dog and took it to the cave. They should ask the dog's owner to dig up the bones and bless them, and Charles will get better. The dog was put in the fire, and when it burned, its arms and legs curled up like this [gesturing] and that's why it hurts. Must find ram and kill it and apply the fat on the sore places. Please ask Satya, son of Arabasi, to do the ceremony. Satya is the one who owned the dog that was killed. Let him show you where it was kept.

The matter of the dog, rather than the ancient murder, was the real cause, Samweri later explained. A good hunting dog belonging to Matei, a grandfather of Charles, had been killed during Maina times, and, when Matei discovered this, he became angry and took the dog to the fireplace to singe off the hair and make an oath called *kusekut*, and then buried the animal in the cave called Kapenmet. Samweri did not know who killed the dog, but the owner did, as did Charles's (classificatory) father, who should perform the ceremony of removal. "He should get earth from the place where the bones are buried, even if bones cannot be found, and apply them on the sick person and spit a blessing on him." The dog was now turning on the clan that made the oath.

Some days later, Mwanga and I reported to Charles and his wife Joyce what Samweri had told us. Charles confirmed the story of the dog's death and agreed that the curse had been made by a member of his lineage. Joyce was particularly concerned. She seemed relieved when Mwanga assured them that it was not witchcraft, particularly after she had been further assured that Mwanga had not suggested the matter of the dog and that the diviner "had found out about it by himself." In the course of the recountal, I discovered that Charles was not on good terms with his father ("though he did come to visit me while I was sick") and that a grandchild of Satya had recently died ("I think this was also the cause of his death").

Charles, who had sat quietly through the account, finally asked Mwanga to repeat exactly what Samweri had told us. After the second recountal, Mwanga ended with:

> Have you understood this clearly, Charles? The reason you complain about your arm and knee is because of the burning of the dog and because its leg acted the same as you are now. That is all he said.

Though quite perturbed, Charles seemed to resist initiating the necessary action. Finally he said:

> I will send somebody to ask Satya to come up from Soi. When he comes here, I think he will ask his brother [Charles' father] to decide what they should do regarding this matter. I think they will agree and perhaps all contribute some maize and then brew beer and dig out the dog and sweep away this matter. There was a time when they did say they would sweep this away, but they did not do it. I will ask you to explain to him all you have told me.
>
> I know thoroughly well that such things have been done before and can kill a child, even a full-grown man, so it is a very important matter and should be swept away. When he comes here, I'll ask him to encourage his brother to see that beer is arranged. I'll also offer one *debe* of maize. We must sweep this thing away.

While the cause of disorders and the necessary actions for cure are the province of specialist diviners, the determination of what will happen may be established by a variety of divinatory techniques and auguries, known widely to the population. The most important of these is the use of entrails of slaughtered animals. Many older men are able to read the entrails. For an important action, such as arranging to collect a debt, a man may slaughter an animal to determine whether the time and circumstances are auspicious. If the augury is inauspicious and the action can be postponed, it will be. But the augury may be avoided by refusing to partake of the sacrificial animal (which may be eaten by others) and slaughtering another. Of the specific readings, I was told that a deep depression in the animal's liver indicates that a sick man will die; if the liver is nearly flat, he will get well; a large yellowish intestine without gas is also bad; if the animal was slaughtered for a guest, it means the guest will become ill; a sharp protrusion on the animal's bladder indicates that an expected child will be a boy; its absence a girl; a section of the intestines called *peywat* (unidentified) will foretell whether a man will suffer losses or will prosper. An old man told the following story.

> One day I visited Greek River with ex-*saza* chief Wandera. An ox was slaughtered for us and the intestines examined, and they were very bad. We refused to eat it entirely. Another bullock was slaughtered and examined; it was all right, so we used that one. The intestine doesn't cause the disease; it merely tells the future. If you refuse the flesh of the animal, then by good luck people will recover. That ox was eaten by other people but not by the guests.
>
> A man here named Chepsigor visited his nephew in Bukwa, and a he-goat was slaughtered for him. They examined the intestines. It was seen to be *kame* (dead), and he was warned not to use flesh of that goat. He refused, saying that we now follow the Baganda custom and don't worry about such things. He fell and died very shortly after that.

A variety of omens is also found. Some of these are personalized. Once, en route to a beer party, I stumbled slightly and a companion asked me what my luck was about this. Each person determines for himself whether it is good luck to stumble with his right or left foot, or to meet a man or woman first on the path when starting on a trip. Thus, my informant said that he was lucky if he met a woman first and noted that the fact his first child was a daughter had been good luck for him. Owls also predict events. If seen on the left side, there will be trouble; if on the right, good luck; if behind, the visit will be short; if in front, you will see something dead before you return.

OATHING

The oath is a powerful instrument of Sebei ideology and behavior. It stands as a great equalizer, rendering all men potentially dangerous; it underlies all legal action and becomes the ultimate sanction for the enforcement of law; and it is the ideological cement that binds clansmen to one another, for they share vulnerability to the oaths sworn against any of them. The Sebei distinguish between oaths and sorcery or witchcraft. The distinction is clearer to them than it is to me, and I cannot but feel that one man's oath is often another man's witchcraft.

The Sebei are much given to maledictions. Fathers berate sons, husbands swear at wives. Men assert their innocence by calling upon matters sacred or tabu at what seems but slight provocation. These are merely words, though when a man swears on his mother's vagina, his cattle, or the skin robe he wore at circumcision, these words take on great power and may reach the level of an oath.

Beyond such informal swearing, the mildest form of oath is *chepisyo* or *chipot*, a formalized cursing. It does not use things; it is still "mere words." It is a curse a father may make against a son, clansmen against one another, or may occur between neighbors or age-mates. It is used, therefore, in cases of hostility within groups where amity should prevail. Unlike other forms of oathing, *chepisyo* is not an instrument in legal action, but an adjunct to internal authority.

An example of *chepisyo* took place in Kapsirika. K had cursed Chemisto saying, "Even though you are married to the daughter of my *pinta*, you will have no children. If you do, they will die." Chemisto's wife of two years was pregnant with his first child, and the baby died after two months. The motives for K's actions are unclear but in some way involved Chemisto's relationship with K's wife — either suspicion of adultery or a quarrel. Chemisto's father became concerned and brewed beer, and K came and anointed Chemisto and his wife with beer and mud and sprinkled medicine on them, retracting the curse. Even *chepisyo* should be chased away.

Oathing in general is called *mumek*, (*mumyantet*, sing.); the term is also used specifically for those forms of cursing in which the victim publicly swears that he has been harmed by the accused and the accused publicly swears he has not injured the victim. It is a particularly dangerous form of oathing, because the accuser puts his life, or more accurately that of his clan, on the line.

The second class of oath is *surupik*. It is also a public oath, but it is not directed at any particular subject; it seeks out the appropriate victim. Since *surupik* does not require that the accuser swear against himself, it does not carry the same degree of danger — though it, too, may return to the clan of its perpetrator.

Sekutet is an oath carried out in secret by the person harmed (or his clansmen) against the individual, whether known or not, who casued the loss. It often serves as a counteragent to witchcraft, but *sekutet* can be used against persons whose delict is straightforward and clearly known.

Oathing has a number of characteristics. True oathing always involves things — either some portion of the matter in dispute (a feather from the stolen hen, ashes from the house in arson cases, portions of the man who died) — or of the intended victim. Even verbal oaths involve things in name. Although oaths are directed at the individual who caused the damage, they act upon others as well — his progeny in particular, but also upon the whole clan. Indeed, I was told that the man who committed the act "will be the last to die." However, when oaths are allowed to remain too long in effect, they will work against those who perpetrated them (as occurred in the case of Charles and the oath perpetrated upon the dog). Thus, those who initiated a curse have an incentive to remove it at the victims' request. Finally, there are ritual means of removing curses. Though even the mildest form of oathing is apt to be hidden from the ethnographer, the ceremony for removal is not, and through it we can get some insight into the attitudes attending the uses of *mumek*.

Mumyantet in its more restricted sense involves bringing together the accused and the accuser, normally accompanied by their clansmen, and performing the oath in front of people of the *saŋta*. The classic form of Sebei *mumyantet* was described for me by a group of old men. Members of the two clans, those who have suffered a loss and those accused, gather by the path near the house of the accuser. A hole is dug, a number of posts from trees are implanted in it. They are tied with an unidentified poisonous liana called rarawet, and the whole is encircled with stones. This will be left in place so that people can see it "and know that something bad has taken place there." The accuser, the accused, men from their clans, and unrelated men gather naked around this alter. They hold their unsheathed spears against the base of the altar, or lunge at it, and swear as follows (in an instance involving arson):

> *Accused*: If I have burned your house, it will eat me.
> *All*: Will eat you.
> *Accused*: And if you libel me, it will eat you.
> *All*: Will eat you.
> *Accuser*: If I falsely accuse, it will eat me; if you have burned, it will eat you.
> *All*: Will eat you.
> *Accuser*: And if you have burned, it will eat you, and also your treasury [children and cattle].

All: Will eat you, my fellow; if you have burned, it will eat you; but if you have not burned, it will not eat you. That thing will eat the owner of that house and, my friend, if you have falsely accused this man, it will return upon you.

They sing a song that could not be translated and, at the close, thrust their spears at the base of the altar and then scatter in all directions "as if an animal were chasing them."

If the accusation has to do with arson, the altar may be placed where the center pole of the house was located. Alternatively, the principals each shoot an arrow into the place where the house had stood. It is said that if the accused was guilty, he would die and turn black as cinders after death.

These are variants of *mumek*:

Kirosyet. A branch of the kirosyet tree may be used for accusations of theft. The two parties jump over the branch.

Kotet ap mwan (poisoned arrow). The parties spit on the place burned, the container from which something was stolen, or the horn of the stolen animal and then put the point of the arrow on this place. Each then twirls the arrow, as if making fire, asserting the other's guilt and his own innocence. The object on which this is done must be kept, presumably to enable the curse to be removed.

Keich ap taita (swearing on a cow or bull). There are several ways in which oaths may be performed on cattle. They may tie the disputed animal for bleeding and each shoot a blocked arrow at its vein. It is said that the guilty person cannot make the blood come, so the one who succeeds takes the animal. Swearing may also be done on certain bones of a dead animal — the rib or thigh. Each endeavors to break the bones with a stone while swearing. An oath may also be made by twirling an arrow on the animal's horn, bringing up shavings upon which the oath is expressed.

Cheptoimet (razor). If an animal has been killed and a person is suspected of having caused the death by witchcraft, the animal is cut into pieces and shared with the people of the *saŋta*, but the accuser and the accused eat a portion that has been cut off with a razor and swear upon that.

Kiroset ap mukuntut (swearing on a calabash). A new calabash called *mukuntut* is used. It is filled with beer, or the two persons urinate or defecate in it, and then swear upon it, breaking it with a stick on the fourth stroke.

Kochech musarek (swearing on porridge). A sick person is given a sponge bath, and the water is then used to make a porridge, which both the sick person and the accused eat. This is a recent innovation.

Swearing on a dog. A dog is held by the two persons (one clutching the forelegs, the other the hind legs) and an elder cuts it in two through the stomach until it is pulled apart. This is viewed as a particularly dreadful form of oath and is generally used only between people of different tribes.

The blacksmith makes a form of *mumyantet* called *chesuket*, which is considered especially powerful. When something is stolen from a smith, he makes a completely new bellows (new wooden bellows bowls with new skin diaphragms, a new Y-shaped clay pipe) on which to swear an oath. He fans the fire with it to burn something of the stolen item (e.g., feathers from the stolen hen) or something left by the accused (e.g., the mud or dust in which he left his footprints) and repeats such curses as, "The person who stole this thing should die; let this [object burned] eat you and your family." Those who witness such an oath repeat the refrain, "Eat you and die." The bellows and pipe are hung up in the smith's house and not used again. Mamadi described the following instance:

> A blacksmith had four sons, one of whom had some plantains stolen. So the father made a new bellows and performed *chesuket* at the place. It didn't take very long before five children of the thief died. The skin of the children who died looked as if it had been burned in the fire. The man then showed that he was the thief and agreed to have the removal ceremony (*kapyipuyito*, it has been rubbed off). Somebody who was not a member of either clan dug a hole where the plantains had been. The clan gathered and brought a sheep, which was suffocated. The blacksmith smeared its chyme on all members of the clansmen of the thief and also threw some of the chyme in the hole, saying: "*Anyiñ*," [sweet] which the people repeated. The sheep was roasted without being skinned, it was cut into small pieces by the ritualist, and all present, including the clansmen of the thief and of the owner, ate some of it. The bellows and other things were burned on the fire where the sheep had been cooked, so that this death would end.

Most of these variant forms of *mumek* may also be used for *surupik*; the distinction lies in the social situation. *Surupik* requires the presence of the people of the *sayta* or *pororyet*, and was described to me as follows:

> A dried acacia post, of a kind the termites will not attack, is implanted in the ground, and a number of other plants are attached to it. The people of the *sayta* gather round. If it is a man's affair — e.g., a stolen cow — then the men perform the oath and the women remain in the background. Naked, they lunge at the post with their spears four times, on the fourth hitting it and swearing, "If there is anybody here who has done this wrong, let this spear eat him." If it is a matter concerning women, such as a sick child, then the women do this and the men are not present. They also do this naked and strike the post with the cowry-decorated girdle women wear beneath their dress. This is not done when a person has died but only for sickness or theft.

Sentiments surrounding the use of oathing emerged when Kilele lost all his cattle in a Pokot raid, the second raid he had suffered in about six months. Kilele, convinced that his neighbor Megawit was responsible for these raids by directing the Pokot raiders to his kraal, called together the men of Kapsirika to air the matter. Kilele's daughter was married to Megawit's son, but Megawit had not paid the brideprice and Kilele had stolen some of his cattle in a manner sanctioned in Sebei custom but not calculated to make friends. Megawit was said to have threatened to recover his cows "by the red stick." During the hearing, old matters were brought forward, as well the fact that Megawit had a Pokot wife and had behaved oddly the night of the raid. The legal aspects of the case do not concern us here, so I will excerpt only those matters that offer insight into attitudes regarding oathing. Kilele came immediately to the point:

> *Kilele*: I can't really prove Megawit stole my cattle or planned to arrange for thieves to take them. The only thing I believe, and that must be discussed, is that my cows have been stolen from time to time. Is this the only kraal where they can find cows? Let us find out what to do to help me — whether to curse people. But my main point is to fill a new gourd with beer, defecate into it, and say that the man who did this act should not live for more than a month. If this is done, I want the suspected person to be present, and I will break it and he will break it. The next day we will crush the gourd and say that whoever is wrong will die on that gourd.

The discussion that followed was directed to two main points: discovering the evidence against Megawit (which was impaired by the absence of Kilele's chief witness during the night of the raid), and dissuading Kilele from this course of action. Toboyi, a young member of Kilele's clan, immediately sought to stop Kilele when he heard Kilele's plan to perform an oath.

> *Toboyi*: If we break the calabash, it will be *mumyantet* and it is we young people who will be the ones to die. You old people are finished. It may be that the suspect hasn't done this and, if that is the case, it will come back to you and your family will die.
>
> *Toboyi* [later]: You are going to do this. But if the suspect didn't do this, don't you realize your sons will die?
>
> *Kilele*: Keep quiet. I'm no uncircumcised boy.
>
> *Toboyi*: Don't think your kraal is the only one attacked twice by enemies. I don't think you should be so hot and so quick. [Later and more specifically]: I don't want these two men to do this for we young men will be the ones to die.
>
> *Megawit* [after justifying his behavior]: But the last thing to say is let us do this *mumek*. This kind of oath must be performed, and, if I'm the one, I wish to die quickly. [Later, with a show of bravado, he called for a stronger oath.] I am thinking the breaking of the gourd will take a long time. I want to bring a dog; each of us will hold it and we will cut it and kill it. That will take less time than a month.
>
> *Seperia* [the local appointed chief]: In 1948, Kamwatil lost his money and said we had stolen it. They investigated and couldn't prove it. Kamwatil went to the diviner many times, after which he was told to buy a hen, pull of its feathers, put it in granary, and feed it medicine. Look, we are still alive but Kamwatil is now shaking with that featherless hen.
>
> *Toboyi*: This is important. I won't agree so quickly to do this thing. Another example, Kapchege and Kapsilut did this because Kapchege suspected Kapsilut of having burned his house, but as he did not do it, the Kapcheges have all died and Kapsilut is still alive.

After much testimony and the airing of many old quarrels and accusations of witchcraft, some of those less concerned in the affair began pressing for another solution.

> *Seperia*: I advised Kilele to ask the people of the *sayta* to come here and ask them what we can do about this without accusing one person. I think if you

want to break the gourd, do it for any person in the *sayta*. [i.e., make an open oath rather than a specific accusation, namely *surupik*.] It will find the [guilty] person. There is nothing to prove the case against Megawit; it is mere rumors. The *sayta* should make *mumek* by not pointing to any one person. After that, we can ask the sun to look upon us and then, if somebody dies, the identity of the person responsible will come out of itself. Asista is guiding us. I don't want one *aret* to do this *mumek* against another. I don't like that.

Kilele finally agreed to this course of action.

Sekutet is done in secret and in its form and character certainly borders on witchcraft, though for the Sebei the two remain distinct.

Sekutet done in retaliation against somebody who has killed is done secretly and alone by an old man who is a member of the clan and lineage of the deceased, particularly his lineage. An old man removes from the body of the dead man his tongue, the end of his penis, his anus, his navel, all his finger and toenails, and hair shaved from the top of his head. He dries this flesh. Each night during the dark of the moon he goes out naked after dark and opens the packet containing these parts and incants over and over again the following:

> Person who killed you for nothing
> eat him and his children
> and all his clan. Finished.

During the *sekutet* period, the old man must not drink beer or eat from the same dish with any clansman of the suspected person nor may he have intercourse with his own wife. If the deceased has been burned, then the ashes may be used instead of the body parts and *sekutet* may be performed at the grave or where the burning took place. For some cases of *sekutet,* the body parts are hidden at the base of a simotwet tree. An old woman of the clan goes to the tree naked each night and urinates and defecates where the things are hidden: 'She opens her buttocks to that tree." The men keep some of the bone in the house and rub it with an arrow in the manner of a firedrill, incanting over it to kill the person responsible.

The complexities and attitudes invoved in Sebei oathing emerge most clearly in a ritual for their removal we observed in 1954. S, a man then of about forty, who had just been appointed to a high government post, suffered from a wasting disease that brought him to the brink of death and a suicide attempt. The ceremony was the last of two months of diverse efforts to diagnose his illness and find a cure: the services of at least three native diviners and curers, visits to both a general and psychiatric hospital, the use of patent medicines, many rumors about (if not actual accusations of) witchcraft, the diagnosis of rainbow disease, evidence of anxiety with respect to his new appointment, and at least two instances of suspected *sekutet* (for which the ritual was undertaken).

A large, handsome man of commanding presence when I first met him, S's condition grew progressively worse, though there were periods of improvement. At times, he was in a state of virtual coma; at other times, he did not recognize his friends and relatives; he sometimes behaved irrationally. In addition to general debility and a gradual wasting away, his symptoms included headaches, vomiting, and delirium. His behavior while delirious offered clues: he sometimes referred to his new government position and to his rivals for it; he whistled and made gestures characteristically used by Sebei while herding cattle; and he waved his arm in the sinuous and characteristic pattern of an elephant's trunk.

This last caused the elders to consider a dispute that had taken place some forty or fifty years earlier between one of S's ancestors and a member of another clan over the rights to a slain elephant. There were other difficulties. S's father had recently suffered a stroke, and a number of clan members had died. S's sister had become sick, for which a ceremony was performed, and five head of cattle were paid to the victim's clan to remove the *sekutet* for an unspecified murder. Since then, "We haven't seen anything except these elephants that have been making trouble." S had made an unsuccessful effort to clear away the matter before he became ill.

The senior man of Kapkeich, S's clan, said the elephant matter had happened when he was very young. His father a man named Psiwa who, according to clan genealogy, was the grandson of the clan founder, went hunting with Chepkarwa of Kapchoik clan, using elephant poison prepared by Mwotil, also of Kapchoik clan. Psiwa, I was told, was the first to spear the elephant, but he made only a small wound and Chepkarwa killed the animal. Chepkarwa therefore claimed both tusks. (Presumably one of them went to Mwotil for furnishing the poison, but this was not stated.) Psiwa said nothing until the Baganda established their authority, but then he took a case before the new courts and was awarded a heifer in compensation. Apparently this action was anticipated, or took place very shortly after the hunting expedition, for the Kapchoik people made the curse, using the spear, the bones, and the earth darkened by the elephant's blood as the oathing substances.

When S made the elephant gestures and requested the ceremony, his clansmen made contact with the descendants of Chepkarwa and Mwotil of the Kapchoik clan, offering to make restitution and asking for the removal of the curse. Chepkarwa and his people had migrated to Pokot and his descendants were not represented, and Mwotil had died, but the Kapchoik clan was represented by the following persons: Mwotil's son, Andyema, his uncircumcised son, Kamwendui, and two brothers of Mwotil, Chemonges and Myogos. The *sekutet* had been made before Andyema, who was in charge, was born. After Mwotil's wife had died, Chemonges' wife had urinated and defecated on the materials; Andyema's wives could not do this because they were still bearing children and would therefore have destroyed the effectiveness of the curse.

There was a further complication: members of the Kapchesi clan, led by senior elder Mirime of Bukwa, came to clear up another matter disturbing the Kapkeich. It had no connection with the elephant, but apparently the Kapkeich clan was hedging its bets. One of the wives of S's father had lost several successive children and had "thrown away" the subsequent child. She gave her baby son to a couple belonging to the clan of her husband's mother. One day, while the boy was still small, he was left alone at the cattle camp and had disappeared when the family returned that evening. The actual father took a case against the foster parents, and the court awarded him three heifers and two bullocks. When the Kapchesi people paid this debt in 1926, they cursed the Kapkeich clan, saying: "If we did something to this child, then truly these cows [given in payment] will do well, but if it was eaten by something and we did not kill the child, then these cattle will come back to us safely." Mirime, the Kapchesi clansman present, had been at the cattle camp at the time and was beaten and accused by S's father; he had also been present at the court decision. The Kapkeich clan now wanted to make restitution.

The removal of the curse is called *keprekei korosek ap sekutet* (brushing away *korosek* of the curse). It began toward 11:00 A.M., after a youth had brought the sheep that was to be slaughtered. Saulo, the head man of the Kapkeich clan, started the formal discussion by recounting the elephant hunt, the situation with S and the desire of his people to make a settlement. Andyema, the spokesman for the Kapchoik clan, said that as long as the Kapkeich clan was willing to pay, his clan was willing to take one cow and one ewe. Both animals should be present, and both clans would spit a blessing upon them and each other.

The Kapchoik people were sent to gather *korosek* plants, six apples of Sodom, milk from the morning's milking, and beer.

When the *korosek* plants had been brought, everybody moved some hundred yards away to the home of S's senior wife, where the women made fires to heat water for beer and the men lit another behind the house. The piece of elephant bone and the arrow (Plate III:37) were brought out by Kapchoik men. Each was separately wrapped in skins. It was explained that only a piece of the elephant bone had been brought; the rest would be burned at home. The Kapchoik men first put the bone into the fire, then slaughtered a ram with a clasp knife, one man holding the ram's muzzle closed while another slit the throat. They severed the head, skinned it, and took out the chyme. The arrow (only the fore part of the shaft, with some of the hafting and the stub of rusted point; the rest had broken off when the elephant was killed) was placed in the fire after the sheep had been slaughtered. Portions of the *korosek* plants were also put into this fire. When the bone and arrow had burned for a while they were taken from the fire, placed on a chip of bark, put on a skin, pulverized with a handy piece of wood, and set aside.

After some further delay, the head of Kapchoik clan formed a "kraal" of fresh cow dung about a foot in diameter on the veranda, to the left of the doorway of the senior wife's house (Plate III:38). Into this he put some of the chyme, some beer, some milk, a bit of earth scraped from the threshold of the house, some tobacco and, finally, the pounded remnants of the bone and arrow. Some of the *korosek* branches were tied into four little bundles, carefully using some of each plant for each bundle, and a stick from one of them was used to stir up the mixture in the "kraal." All the members of S's family were brought round in a circle, including children and married-in wives. Three members of Kapchoik clan and one of the Kapchesi clan each took one of the brushes, dipped it into the mixture in the kraal and sprinkled it on each Kapkeich person in turn four times, lightly on head, shoulders and chest, while repeatedly calling out the following, "*Anyiñ, anyiñ* [sweet], *baibai, baibai* [happiness], *karram, karram* [good] *chomnyot, chomnyot* [friendship] " (Plate III:36).

After the sprinkling, tail fat of the ram was taken from the fire by the old men, cut into pieces, and passed around to all present to eat. All then went to where the calf and the ewe were tied. A piece of the sinentet vine was tied around the calf's neck, beer was spat on it by the Kapkeich elder, and milk sprinkled on it by S's senior wife. The same was then done to the ewe. The meat of the ram was roasted and eaten by all present, after which three pots of beer were furnished, one shared by the Kapchoik and Kapchesi clans, one by the Kapkeich, and the third by the *pororyet*. This closed the ceremony.

The ritual had done double duty, establishing peace for the Kapkeich with both the Kapchoik and the Kapchesi. The difference between the two actions reveals the difference between the Kapchoik's *sekutet*, which had involved the use of things, and the Kapchesi's curse, which had merely been words. The Kapkeich had carefully established the fact that the Kapchesi had not removed hairs from the tail of the cattle before they had paid them; i.e., they had not oathed on objects and preserved them. The two clans were closely related by marriage and on generally friendly terms. It was therefore not necessary to perform the *korosek* ceremony in this instance (though they did take the opportunity to sprinkle with the *korosek* substances) and the animals to be repaid would not have to be anointed. Why did the more serious action require the lesser payment? Basically because the oath had had its effect; Kapkeich people had died as a result of it and thus had repaid in blood.

The heifer that was anointed with fat and milk was taken by Andyema, the son of Mwotil whose poison had killed the elephant, and will eventually go to his son, Kamwendui. The ewe was taken by Chemonges, whose wife had relieved herself on the *sekutet* items. As the ewe reproduces, the lambs will be shared between her children, with Mwotil's surviving brother receiving the first female and the first male. The heifer was compared to compensation paid for damages, the ewe to a fine paid to the government. S, the man whose life had been endangered, eventually regained his health and held governmental appointments.

SORCERY

"For as long as I have been chief," Aloni Muzungyo, the *saza* chief of Sebei, said to me once, "I have been trying to discover who was a witchcraft person, but nobody will tell me." Nobody will admit to knowing a witch, let alone to being one, for the matter is shrouded in secrecy in native sentiment. Moreover, actions of witchcraft are serious delicts in modern law and thus not to be freely discussed with an outsider. Even the diviners obscure their divinations by circumlocution and indirection to avoid responsibility for accusing a specific person.

The Sebei do not make the distinction found in anthropological literature between the involuntary witch or wizard and the purposive sorcerer. Some persons possessed of "bad birds" or the evil eye involuntarily cause harm to others but are rightly not considered witches. The Sebei regard as witch or wizard one who engages in the practice with evil intent.

While not every death is attributed to witchcraft, the suspicion is always there, and no person should conduct himself so as to let it fall upon him. I was firmly advised to go to my neighbor's beer party, lest I be suspected. When a man dies, all the neighbors must visit the home of the deceased to avoid suspicion. These sentiments were expressed and demonstrated in Sasur; I did not hear them in Kapsirika. The Sebei credit neighboring tribes with greater powers of witchcraft and stronger cures than they themselves possess. They spoke to me about witchcraft that causes intrusive objects (rocks, pieces of glass, or gourd). It had entered Sebei from Kitosh in 1938, they thought, by way of a Bumachek woman. Only two Sebei had learned how to remove these substances, and one of them had died. The patient is made to vomit the objects with specially collected grass.

When the Sebei refer to witchcraft as a special practice, they will say there are two kinds, and these must be seen as the major forms. However, two other categories are also recognized. The four types are as follows:

1. *Panet* is the major category of witchcraft from the standpoint of the Sebei, in the sense that it is the ultimate in evil intent and action. When the Sebei say that they do not know who engages in witchcraft, they refer to the *ponintet*, the man or woman who knows how to influence the supernatural forces to cause the death of another out of personal malice. This form of sorcery does not have to be provoked by some more or less just cause; it works, therefore, without respect to any action of the victim and kills outright rather than through a wasting illness; it is not operative on the clan but directly on the subject. It is suspected when a man suddenly dies.

2. *Kankanet* is the second major form of witchcraft. It is used only in retaliation against a person who has done harm or failed to meet an obligation and works only if the victim is guilty. This form of sorcery causes the victim to become ill by a wasting disease and can be removed if he rights the wrong he has committed. Like *panet*, but unlike oaths, it works on the individual rather than on the clan (though it may work on his children). This form of sorcery is known only to the members of two clans, both of which are centered in Sipi. One informant thought it might have been learned from the Gisu but was not certain. The practitioners are known (or at least clearly suspected) and members of the clans involved freely discuss such activities. There was free and open discussion of the fact that one senior Kamechage had taken action to recover some cattle from a son-in-law, who now looked

healthy but was actually wasting away. He had asked his persecutor to release him and given the old man a goat as an earnest of his intent to pay the cattle. The attitude toward the elder's action was approval and respect — tinged with fear.

3. *Ntoyenik* is the witchcraft of women against men. Women learn it during their final circumcision rite (or from their mothers). It is the focus of Sebei men's fear of women, for they can weaken and debilitate the men, make them unfit for warfare, and force them to love the practitioner better than their other wives or even refuse to take additional wives. Women can also perform *ntoyenik* on other women; in particular, they can render them barren. No childless woman is without suspicion that some neighbor is responsible and will go to considerable expense to discover who it is.

4. Witchcraft against initiates. Each Sebei learns the means of causing persons undergoing circumcision to hemorrhage, tremble, or cry.

The Sebei do not express any belief in "familiars" in the form of animals or incorporate beings, nor is the action of the witch taken against the spirit of the victim. The *oyik* are involved only in that a man's spirit may, if it is strong enough, act to protect him against such action. The problem of how witchcraft works does not seem to trouble the Sebei.

Panet is perceived as a major crime, but witches cannot be apprehended by ordinary means. A death is attributed to witchcraft only when four separate diviners' statements point the finger at the same person. When this happens, the suspected witch is subject to a poison ordeal, which is administered in a special location in Sebei by members of the clan of Matui. The suspect must drink an intoxicating concoction while sitting in the hot sun. If the accused cannot answer simple questions ("What do I have in my hand?" "How many fingers is this?"), he is found guilty, and the members of the victim's clan will beat him to death, as his kinsmen stand by. So far as I am able to tell, the ordeal is administered only for *panet*: I never heard of a women being subjected to it for *ntoyenik* nor of a person undergoing it because he made initiates cry.

Witches act at night, in the dark of the moon, and use elements belonging to the victim. Among these are blood, feces, urine, hair, nail clippings, footprints, leavings of food eaten by the victim, such as bones or corncobs, and items of clothing, particularly those in close contact with the body, such as the beaded girdle women wear under their clothes, modern underwear, or the stained portion of a man's collar. Such elements are hidden in caves or rock crevices or buried near the victim's home. To these may be added the body parts of the deceased. Certain symbolic actions, such as making the witchcraft stuff tremble to induce fear in the initiate, may be undertaken. Such data place Sebei behavior in the context of sorcery practices elsewhere but do not provide us with any real insights into their understanding of how these forces work.

Though there is a good deal of talk about sorcery, witchcraft is not much in evidence and the Sebei are not obsessed with the subject. The only ritual activity I saw that involved witchcraft was an effort to exorcise the spirits that were troubling a young woman. Maria, as I call her, was part Gisu and junior wife of a Sebei man, and the Sebei believed that Gisu *oyik* were troubling her. The attendant ritual appears to be some kind of syncretization of Gisu and Sebei beliefs. The sacrifice of chickens is alien to Sebei behavior, and apparently the two shrines used represent the two ethnic groups. Maria accused her senior wife of witchcraft, but the people saw the problem as jealousy because Maria had not been given adequate land. She described her symptoms as follows:

> At night I have bells ringing in my ears; people tell me it is the *oyik*. The *oyik* don't allow me to eat— I can take only three bites of plantain porridge. When I get the lamp ready at night, I can see shapes coming toward me and going around and around on the wall and on the roof, and they tell me this is the *oyik*, too. I never have seen these things before. The people tell me they are Gisu spirits. At night, I hear the *oyik* running outside and I know I am going to die. One day I bought beer and sprinkled it around the house for the *oyik*, but that night they came and beat me all night and in the morning I vomited blood. Also some *oyik* had intercourse with me. I can't sleep; the *oyik* come and say, "Wake up! Wake up!" When I sleep in the house, my feet become swollen and my head very hot. If I sleep elsewhere, I am also very afraid but the *oyik* come only once to where I sleep and it feels a little better. When I sleep in my own house, it feels very cold at dawn and I cannot pull my bedclothes over me because my hands are shaking with fear.

The ceremony followed immediately after the hearing on Maria's complaint against her co-wife (*SL*:123-28). Two small houses were constructed. One was flat-roofed, like those still found in Masop, and was built at the right of the entrance to Maria's house by her husband's brothers and their wives; the other, with a pointed roof, was constructed at the back of the house by members of Maria's paternal and maternal clans. A black hen was offered to the *oyik* by Maria's husband's brother; a white hen was offered to the *oyik* by Maria's mother's clan. A member of Maria's own clan spoke to the black hen, saying: "Our *Oyik*, we offer you this to enjoy with the food that has been prepared for you. Please let our families stay free. All old men and all old women, our *Oyik*, please help the children of this house." Maria's mother's brother came and said four times to the white hen: "Here is a hen given to you, old men and women. Don't trouble our child. Let her be at peace. This hen is here for you." He then poured a libation of beer inside the house and did the same outside, but with his left hand, asking the bad *oyik* to leave. Then again, he poured beer inside the house and made a similar prayer, this time specifying dead ancestors and concluding: "If it is you who followed her here from Bugisu so that you may be recognized by the people of this family, please enjoy this beer and go away." Maria's brother did the same. Maria's mother's brother then spit a blessing of beer on Maria, with similar expressions.

The black hen was killed by the husband's brother; blood from it was dribbled on both of the shrines; and its feathers were plucked and some placed on the roof. Meanwhile, thick finger-millet porridge and the cooked

ALBUM IV
Initiation

1-2 Tour of invitation: (1) *chemerik* dancing at the home of relatives while on tour of invitation; (2) girls before initiation.

3-9 Circumcision: (3) procession of *chemerik* coming from stream to the circumcision area; (4) being anointed by old men; (5) passing under the spears and (6) being laid into position; (7) women watching the cutting; (8) the circumcision taking place; (9) lying on the ground immediately after the operation.

10-14 "Crying the knife": (10) watching the cutting; (11) the *chemeryontet* (center) standing and refusing to continue; (12) the girl who refused, ten days afterward, while in seclusion; (13) the circumcisor and her assistant; (14) the reaction of the crowd (the girl at the upper right will be ready for circumcision the following year).

15-18 After circumcision: (15) first nourishment; (16, 17) after the cutting; (18) removing the blood and severed pieces.

19-24 Intermediate ceremonies: (19) women gathered for the ceremony; (20) shaving; (21) a bite of ritual bread; (22-24) painting the face and body.

25-29 Final ceremony (Atar and Kabruron, 1954): (25) crawling to the ritual area under cover (the uncovered girl is a *mwet*); (26) anointing the *chemerik*; (27) ritualized reintroduction to household duties; (28) dressed in new clothes after the ritual; (29) running as expression of freedom from restraint.

30-37 Initiation in Kapsirika and Nyelit, 1962; the day before initiation: (30) early morning dance instructions; (31) accepting the beads from a friend (they will be ransomed after successful completion); (32) youth who invited us to the Nyelit circumcision (see also 38 and 39); (33) marching from a relative's homestead; (34) painting the *chemerik* at the Sundet River; (35, 37) dancing in late afternoon; (36) a controlled sip of milk for the *chemeryontet*.

38-40 Circumcision at Nyelit, 1962: (38) *chemeryontet* at moment of cutting; (39) after the cutting; (40) anointing *chemeryontet* with butter in cow's horn.

41-44 Funeral: (41) sister prostrating herself before the body of the deceased; (42) one sister holding another in paroxysm of grief; (43) washing the deceased; (44) shaving a mourner.

1

2

3

4

5

7

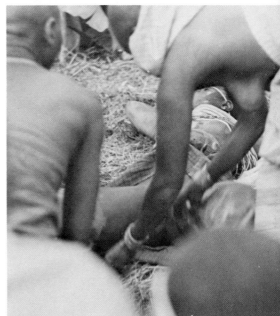

6   8

9

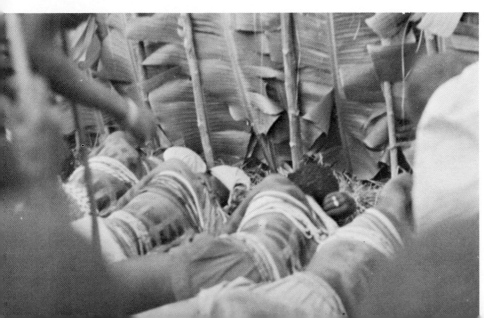

10

12

11

13

14

15   16

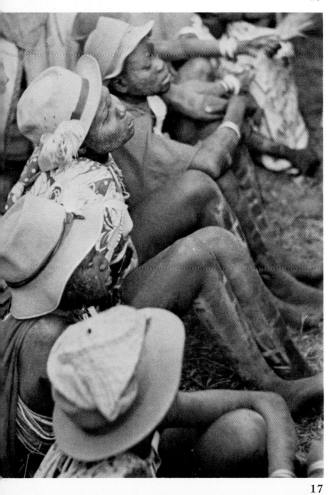

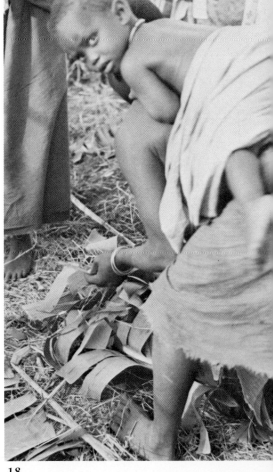

17   18

19   20

21   22

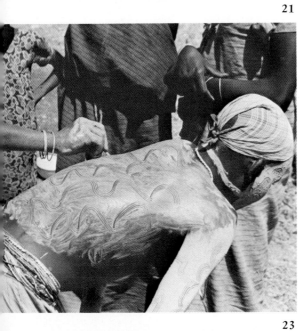

23   24

25

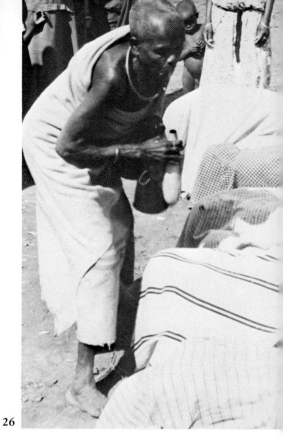

26

27

28

29

30

31　　　　32

33

34

36

35   37

38

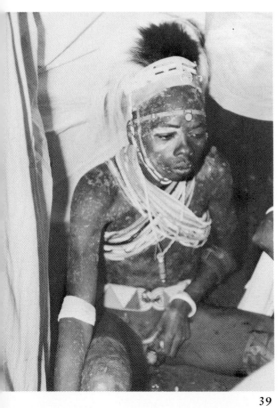

39

40

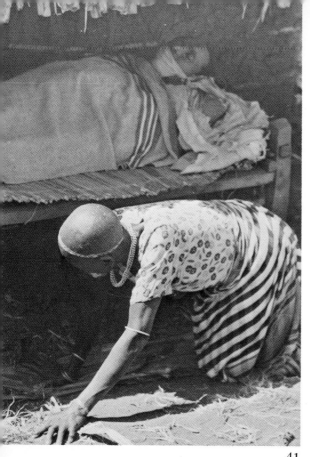

41   42

43   44

chicken were put into a basket. Small balls of porridge with little pieces of meat inserted, called bread of the spirits (*kumik ap oyik*), were distributed to two groups. One, consisting of the husband's brothers and his mother, moved about ten yards away from the house and threw their pellets into the bush to the east, while the other group, consisting of Maria's kinsmen, simultaneously did the same, moving to the west. The mother's brother inside the house threw some on the ground, saying: "Shoo, go away." The remaining porridge and chicken were eaten. The spoon used to stir the porridge was put on the roof of the house so that the spirits might eat from it and be happy. Two small pots of beer were brought and placed by the two houses, and people of both sides drank this and then gathered around the three beer pots (one for Maria's relatives, one for her husband's, and one for members of the *saŋta*).

Sorcery and oathing have essentially the same content: both call forth supernatural forces to perform actions harmful to others for the satisfaction of the self; both utilize objects significant to the social situation that evoked the act and involve actions with relevant symbolic meaning. The effectiveness of each is explained in the same metaphysical perceptions about relationships between things, words, and actions, on the one hand, and human responses on the other. Yet the Sebei assert that sorcery and oathing are different classes of events, and I think they are right. They are different psychologically, sociologically, and perhaps historically.

Two "persons" (in the legal sense) are involved in every act of oathing and witchcraft — the perpetrator and the victim. In witchcraft, the perpetrator is acting in unprovoked malice or more accurately, in malice improperly provoked by jealousy, hatred, or some personal emotional state. In oathing, the perpetrator is acting in retaliation against a person who he believes has caused him harm. It is important that a Sebei oath is not effective on a person who is innocent of the act. It is therefore retributive. But of greater interest is the different state of the victims. In witchcraft, there need be no actual perpetrator. The essence of witchcraft lies not in the act, but in the suspicion of the act; it is, to use Theodore Schwartz's happy phrase, "institutionalized paranoia" (1973:155). Following Clyde Kluckhohn (1967:88-90), this projection of hostile acts on others is an expression of the witchcraft "victim's" hostility, a means of coping with his own antisocial sentiments. The person engaged in oathing, on the other hand, is responding to a harm that has befallen him rather than expressing hostility. If the victim of an oath responds to its influence, he does so in guilt, for if he is not guilty the oath is not effective.

That the Sebei perceive witchcraft as the expression of hostile impulses is suggested by a recurrent element in their regulations. It is quite improper to engage in an act that properly takes place when another person dies. The clearest example is that a man must not have intercourse with his brother's wife, particularly the wife he would inherit; the Sebei regard such an action as tantamount to witchcraft against the brother. A married man should not remove ashes from the hearth, because he will do so when his wife dies.

Co-wives must not bathe together, for they will do so at their husband's funeral. The act is the expression of a wish: James Joyce might have called it wishcraft.

Sociologically, sorcery and oathing are even more distinct: witchcraft is an abhorrent antisocial act that warrants severe retribution, while oathing is an honored adjunct to the maintenance of the social order. If the oath response appears to be stronger than the original delict warrants, it is not seen by the Sebei, whose punishments under *chomi ntarastit* also rather exceeded the crime (*SL*:106). Furthermore, it has its own constraints, for the oath is a dangerous instrument, capable of harming those who perpetrate it. There is a further sociological difference: sorcery is the act of individuals — a single perpetrator and a particularized victim — and is therefore socially disintegrative. Oathing is a group act and its target is not a person but the clan. Its social effect is therefore integrative. It enters into every phase of Sebei social action in one form or another; it is a major instrument in legal sanctions; the dread of oath preserves the integrity of *pinta* secrets and binds clansmen to one another inextricably. Even *sekutet*, which shares more the character of sorcery than other forms of oathing, serves this positive force.

Witchcraft is an old element in Sebei culture. *Ntoyenik* and the magic to make initiates cry are deeply embedded in its traditions, and *panet* is found under the same name and form as among the Nandi (Huntingford 1953:107-111). *Kankanet* is probably a recent addition to the armament of magical practices.

It was part of our general hypothesis that witchcraft would be more prevalent among farmers than herders because farmers are forced to live in smaller and more permanent communities and therefore must suppress their hostile impulses, while pastoralists can act out their hostility and remove themselves from the scene if the local situation becomes untenable. The quantified data gathered by Edgerton support this distinction among the Sebei (*RBE*:178-83,326). Thus, the frequency of witchcraft in Sebei responses to his questionnaires was nearly twice as great among farmers as among pastoralists (1.88 versus 1.01 mentions per person). Edgerton relates this difference to the farmers' greater concern with hatred (9.59 versus 6.25 mentions) and with insults (6.60 versus 4.15), and their greater need to avoid direct conflict (1.98 versus 1.51).

It was not possible to obtain comparable data on the incidence of witchcraft in Sasur and Kapsirika, but certain anecdotal material corroborates Edgerton's findings. The most dramatic and obvious evidence for the pastoralists' disinclination to attribute misfortune to malevolent acts was their response to an epidemic of meningitis that struck Kapsirika when we established camp there. I heard no accusations or suspicions of sorcery but was besought to help secure government medical aid in their behalf. My timid suggestions that malevolence might be responsible were brushed aside. Yet, in Sasur, every illness — even lorry accidents — carried with it at least the suspicion of some human agent. Contrast the actions and attitudes of Kilele in Kapsirika with those of Chemengich and his family in Sasur. Kilele brought his conflict with Megawit into the open; the family of Chemengich engaged in indirection and gossip: Chemengich's wife was causing his daughters-in-law to be barren; the sons were bewitching their father; the brothers suspected each other. The only secret gossip that came to us in Kapsirika was directed at a man who had recently moved there from the farming area by another who was a traditional herdsman.

Two deaths, those of S in Sasur (Goldschmidt, 1973b) and Kambuya in Kapsirika (*KC:passim*), offer a similar contrast. Rumors and gossip of witch-craft came with news of S's death, but there was no open confrontation and we heard only allusions in public discussion. In the hearings on Kambuya's estate, the sons charged that their brothers caused their father's death, but such accusations never evoked a response; from all outward appearances, they were not taken seriously. A similar contrast appears in two conflicts between co-wives, one near Sasur and the other in Kapsirika. Maria's case, just described, is a classic projection of hatred stemming from jealousy and envy. Sibora (*KC*, Chapter 8) did not complain of witchcraft; her mother brought the accusation openly, just as had the sons of Kambuya, for personal advantage. (Interestingly, the major "evidence" brought against Sibora's co-wife was that she had visited an uncle in Sipi, the farming area, where Kapsirikans presumed she could obtain the necessary "medicines.")

I do not want to overstate the contrast: on the one hand, open accusa-tions of witchcraft of the kind made in Kapsirika imply a belief in the possibility of witchcraft, and instances of surreptitious suspicion probably could be found there; on the other hand, Sasur was not suffused with witchcraft. Yet, these contrastive instances support S. F. Nadel's point (1952:28): "Witchcraft beliefs . . . are causally as well as conspicuously related to specific anxieties and stresses arising in social life."

CHARACTER OF SEBEI RITUALS

More than forty separate rituals have been described in this monograph, some important and extended, others minor and brief. I described them in their social context because they illuminate the nature of that social action — and because this is the way the Sebei see them. I define as a ritual or ceremony any event in which a group of Sebei join together and perform traditionally sanctioned acts designed to harness supernatural forces in order to influence human affairs. (Major elements of these rites are summarized in Appendix D. Page reference to the description of the rituals discussed below is given in this Appendix.) I divide these events into five categories:

1. *Rites of transition.* Rituals designed to bring individuals through crises. These include both the classic *rites de passage* and others that share the same characteristics.

2. *Rites of protection.* Community-oriented rituals conducted to ward off disaster and evil forces.

3. *Rites of retaliation*. Rituals that seek supernatural redress for a wrong done a person; they tend to be clan-oriented.

4. *Rites of conciliation*. Rituals that remove expressed or feared sentiments of antagonism or hostility.

5. *Domestic rites*. Rituals of a minor character, mostly involving domestic matters.

The rites of transition include the life crisis ceremonies of birth, initiation, marriage, and death. All involve a period of seclusion and release. They include also the twin ceremony, the ceremony for cattle twins and breech births, and rituals for a person who has killed a man, because these share the essential feature of seclusion and release and thus share basic psychological and sociological elements. It is recognized that the person undergoing these periods of transition is in danger — "like a sick person." Seclusion is a protection. The ritual aspects mostly celebrate the "release to the sun," or, to borrow from the song associated with these rituals, "the uncovering of the bird." There is also some element of seclusion in two other rituals — those of friendship between half-brothers (which is associated with birth) and amity between herds (which is associated with death).

Seclusion varies in intensity and character; it is particularly severe and extended for the mothers of twins and for initiates and widows; it involves restrictions on food, sexual intercourse, visual and vocal contact, and other elements of behavior. Only for initiates does one get the verbal inversions, but for others there are also such special rules as sleeping on special leaves, not removing ashes, food tabus, and so on. Restrictions on brides are less severe, and on animal twin ceremonies seclusion is only symbolically observed. Release rituals for initiates and brides share a number of features: feasting with beer, shaving, entering the mother's house with a blessing of milk spewed from the mouth of an old woman, and slaughtering an animal. Slaughtering is by suffocation, because these happy ceremonies should not involve the shedding of blood, but there are two significant exceptions; the mortuary sacrifice of a bull or ox and the slaughter of a goat for a murderer. The goat is slaughtered on two other occasions associated with disaster: the visit of the bride's relatives, which is likened to a raid, and the eruption of an infant's teeth in abnormal order (*oyik* teeth). There is no sacrifice for normal births, but there is for twins. Except for the murder ritual, beer and/or feasts are important adjuncts to the ceremonial occasion and are referred to as "fat" ceremonies. Even the murderer has a feast, but it is limited in scope.

In all ceremonies of transition, the major ritual role is performed by a person who has undergone the rite at some earlier time. Some special definitions of secondary ritual roles are based upon kin relationship to the principal. The brother plays an important role in the marriage and death rites and a minor one in the twin ceremony. The mother, insofar as she is not the object of the ritual, anoints initiates and bathes with her son's bride and accompanies her to her home. Sisters and mother's sisters have ritual roles in twin, marriage, and death ceremonies. Except in the twin ceremony, fathers have no ritual role; they are merely providers. There is no specified ritual role for the mother's brother. In general, one is impressed by the limited degree to which these personally-oriented rites involve kin, especially the extended kindred such as the mother's brothers and the father's sisters.

What I have called the rites of protection are those rituals directed at reinforcing the unity of the spatially based social entities, the *pororyet* and the *saŋta*. They all have the character of protection — either against the external forces of nature or the internal evils of one's fellow man. I have included in this group the *chomi ntarastit*, for it shares the essential social purposes, though its ritual form places it with the category of retaliation. Insofar as there are ceremonialists, they tend to be specially appointed by the prophet. Some clans claim to have the right to perform specified roles, but this is unclear and certainly not general.

The major rituals in this group, leaving aside *ntarastit*, are the *korosek* rites. The *korosek* category of rituals has the purpose of righting things, of readjusting relationships. These ceremonies usually involve feasting. The occasional use of streams in these rites is apparently a form of sympathetic magic rather than a cleansing agent as in funerals. *Korosek* rites are characterized by the use of a group of plants, which are burned as a kind of offering. *Korosek* plants reappear in other ceremonial contexts, notably for the removal of oaths, the unification of herds, and the fertility of new plantain *shambas*. The harvest *korosek* has the classic elements of a harvest rite and new fire ceremony — a kind of general thanksgiving and renewal — yet, significantly, the express purpose is to ward off evil and bad luck. The disease *korosek*, clearly a variant form, gives emphasis to this prophylactic character.

Rites of retaliation are oathing rites, involving the special oathing plants and ritualized swearing. Three of these are standard oaths with variant properties. The form and some of the oathing symbols are used for the ritualized splitting apart of clans, and, while this is not strictly retaliation, it is closely allied. The *chomi ntarastit*, sociologically community protection, is virtually identical with classic forms of *mumek* and *surupik* and involves the iteration of an oath. It uses an old ceremonial form for a new set of social purposes; whereas oaths in general are clan-involved and clan-oriented, the *ntarastit* is done by the *pororyet* and directed at *pororyet* members.

The major ritual element in this group of rites is the implanting of a group of special plants in the ground to form an altar. These oathing plants may be seen as the opposite of the *korosek* plants. The ritual involves swearing on them by men who must be naked, a recurrent element in oaths, and in witchcraft as well. Associated also is the use of spears by men. Women also may appear naked when they swear oaths and use for this purpose their cowry shell girdles, which are deeply infused with their personal spirit and are magically their most highly charged possessions. Absent from these ceremonies are all the items that are ameliorative, comforting, or expressive of amity, such as commensal food and beer and the various substances for anointing or spitting. Ritual roles and ritual leadership are in the hands of the persons most involved.

The rites of amity are directed specifically to the resolution of hostility or the avoidance of anticipated conflict. They are closely related to the *korosek* in many ways and generally use some or all of the *korosek* plants. All involve feasting and beer, for commensality is the prime expression of amity — one must even share food and beer with the dead. Ritual action and ritual leadership depends upon the groups involved with the conflict, clansmen when the clan is involved, the *pororyet* when it is involved, and so on. We find also in this group of rites the familiar activities of spitting beer, anointing, and blessing. Though chyme may be used to put into the fire or in some other way, it is not used for such anointment. Occasionally, persons who have formerly undergone the rite serve as ritualists. Of particular interest is the fact that essentially the same ritual forms are used to remove areas of potential conflict as are used to sanctify the resolution of an existing conflict. The ritual of friendship between two infants born contemporane-ously of two mothers by the same father is a recognition of potential conflict and, in view of our evidence on half-brother relationships in Sasur, a realistic anticipation. Even a potential conflict between herds is allayed by such a rite. I have included in this set the ritual of blood brotherhood among the Kony, for the basic form and symbols are identical. It, too, is a ritual of amity — not to resolve preexisting animosity, but rather to intensify a preexisting friendship. It is in keeping with Sebei cultural orientations that they should have transformed a rite designed to create special friendship into one designed to prevent antagonism. Included in this group is the ritual to remove bad *oyik*, for its purpose is the restoration of amity. Its form and symbols are quite different, however, suggesting its alien origin.

The remaining rituals are all minor and essentially domestic in character, except for the *kapturin* ceremony. I have divided them into three categories: those involving persons, those involving cattle, and those involving agricul-ture. The first includes a number of minor ritual ameliorative acts. A number are cleansing actions designed to overcome the breach of a tabu (after improper forms of sexual intercourse or when a woman has grabbed the testicles of a man) or to heal a person who sickened as a result of the *chepserer* ceremony. Others clearly placate the spirits of the dead (remar-riage of a widower, the inheritance of a widow, and, in a sense at least, the child-naming ceremony). The ceremonial removal of the baneful influence of "*oyik* teeth" and the ceremony to chase away lightning are directed at the more intense dangers from the external world. (This last ceremony stands out from all the rest in its ritual actions and symbols so that it appears to be of alien source, but I have no direct evidence of this.) These rituals character-istically involve the slaughter of a ram, and the use of either its tail fat or its chyme for ritual purposes. Being domestic in character, they include no beer or feasting. But then, this group of rites is not designed to establish amity among the living, but between the living and the spirits of the dead or other spiritual forces.

The three rites dealing with cattle are not the only ones centering on livestock (cattle twins and unification of two herds are the others), but they are essentially domestic. Two of them merely sanctify contractual arrangements; the third placates spirits.

Of the four remaining rites, *misisi* is the most interesting and the most important. It is unique in its specification of kin as participants and in the absence of the usual symbols of amelioration. The first fruits and new plantain *shamba* rites again use chyme as a symbolic element. The *kapturin* rite, like the ritual for lightning, stands out in character. It is the only rite that has an inherited ritualist or moves from west to east, and it involves none of the standard Sebei symbolism. There is no doubt of its extraneous origin.

SEBEI ICONOGRAPHY

There is indeed a "forest of symbols" among the Sebei, including not only a wide variety of wild plants, but also many artifacts of daily life and much use of animals and animal products. Cultigens are less used in the symbol system and wild animals hardly at all.

Two sets of wild plants are regularly used to represent what may be thought of, respectively, as virtue and evil: the *korosek* plants and the oathing plants. They are listed in Appendix E with botanical identification where available. Sebei recognize the associations of these plants with good and evil but could not give me reasons for such association, and, without such direct assistance, it was not possible for me to engage in an ethnobotanical investigation that might have provided further insights. The symbolism is not self-evident from their alternate uses. The association between the korkorwet tree, with its beautiful red blossoms, and suicide is more than coincidental, but I do not know why it is the tree of death.

Aside from these, a number of other plants reappear in ceremonial associations:

The sinentet vine, used to garland the mothers of twins and initiates, brides and their mothers, stock given in payment or *tekerisyek* animals, and beer pots filled with ceremonial beer.

The moykutwet root, chewed and spat as a blessing along with or instead of beer or ram's fat or milk on various occasions.

The lepeywontet plant, used as an infusion for bathing mothers of infants, initiates, and brides.

The palm frond (which has practical use for cleaning milk gourds), a symbol of peace in a number of ceremonies, including weddings (where it is a gift to the bride) and in several rituals of amity.

Apples of Sodom, collected by initiates and their friends and pelted against the doors of neighbors when demanding gifts and reappear studded in cattle dung or in the "kraals" filled with medicine in rituals of amity.

Domestic animals and their products play a great part in the symbolic expressions of Sebei life. Sheep appear to be more important than cattle, being slaughtered whenever supernatural danger lurks, whether because of a crucial transition or because of real or potential confrontation between individuals or groups (in one instance it must be a pregnant ewe; in another a virgin one). Sometimes a bullock or ox is substituted or called for (especially in the major *korosek* ceremonies). The goat retains its symbol of evil. Dogs are sacrificed only for the direst kind of *mumek* and for peacemaking between enemy tribes. Chickens appear in only two ceremonies, at least one of which is of Gisu origin. There is also a clear good/bad difference between suffocation and spearing or stabbing an animal; the latter two are done only with death-associated rituals or in the more dire rites of retaliation.

Virtually every part and every product of the sacrificial animals enter into the ceremonial actions. Indeed, for some sacrifices, it is specified that a bit of each part of the animal — however the Sebei calculate parts — be included in the ritual eating, as for instance the stew cooked by the widow or the parts fed to half-brothers. Among the other parts and products that may be found somewhere in ritual action are cattle dung, cattle urine, cattle horns, amniotic fluid, lamb embryo, and the scrotum of a bullock, but the following reappear on many ceremonial occasions:

Butter, used to anoint initiates and brides and explicitly recognized for its soothing quality.

Heart, sacred to the clan and to be shared only by men of the clan.

Milk (sometimes must be morning milk, and sometimes only from a black cow), used as a blessing, particularly when entering one's parental home after a period of seclusion. It is spewed from the mouth of an elderly woman of the family.

Ram's tail fat, for anointing (much as butter) to remove the essences of evil from spiritual forces — particularly the spirits of the dead.

Chyme, smeared on parents of twins and *chemerik*, on the path to the stream along which the mourners will go, and thrown into some ceremonial fires, appears to be a blessing for long life (though one person said it hardens the skin to make one impervious to fear).

Skin ringlets, fabricated from the slaughtered animals, are worn on the finger or wrist by widowers, participants in *korosek* and other rituals and by women on their necklaces. They preserve the sense of ceremonial protection as long as they last.

Wild animals play but a small part in Sebei symbolic representation. The leopard and lion are important elements in circumcision (though they appear only in representation); the leopard reappears as the robe of the prophet, Matui. The elephant appears only in that its tusk is one of the "medicines" of the initiates. The hyena is used in *chomi ntarastit*, and a snake in *chepserer* (and in the foreign kapturin ceremony), but along with the Mount Elgon tick, these are the only representatives of wild fauna that appear in my notes on Sebei ceremonials.

Cultivated plants and foods made from them appear most importantly in the harvest *korosek* and most frequently in the form of tabus during periods of seclusion. But most frequent of all and most important of all is beer. No beer is drunk without first offering an appropriate libation to the spirits of the dead and the ancestors of the hosts. Beer is also frequently spat as a blessing, often using the dried mash. Millet porridge (and now maize porridge) enters into some ceremonials, particularly for the initiates and for the bride, where it is eaten directly from the stirring paddle as an expression of close association, but also for the half-brother rite. The rites for plantain *shambas* are the only ones directly concerned with agricultural production.

Numerous artifacts have symbolic involvement. Only three things are made and kept for their ceremonial function: the bull-roarer, the friction drum, and the zebra-headed drum. Nowadays, there are also special head-dresses and banners for initiates. Some items recur:

The striking together of hidden ax and pick in the two rites involving brotherhood, the amity between cattle, and the ritual for a murderer; ax and pick are also associated with circumcision.

The spear, with its death association, in oathing and *ntarastit*, in circumcision as a warning against malefactors, and importantly but enigmatically in the twin ceremony.

The shield and the oval basket, associated with twins and other special children wherever they are involved in ceremonies.

Iron bracelets, ritually changed at marriage and taken off at death.

Other items that enter into ceremonies are: awl, beads, bellows, bleeding arrow, bow and arrow, cowbell, cowry shells, girdle worn by women, gourd cleaning stick and gourds, herding sticks, neck rings and spirals on neck rings, sleeping skin, stool, whetstone.

The house has its sensitive aspects, particularly the doorway or threshold. The door is a forbidden entrance to initiates, who can enter the house only by the doorway for goats; special doors are constructed for certain rituals, and the existing doorway is remudded, plastered with dung, and studded with apples of Sodom for others. The gate to the kraal may be similarly treated, and both these and the center post of the house are places for pouring libations to the good spirits. The hearth features in one ritual, and ashes from the hearth in several. The corpse is placed in the area set aside for visitors.

There are other symbols. Streams are particularly important; they feature in two rites (*korosek* for drought and *chepserer*), are used for washing in two (initiations and funerals), and express the limits of ceremonial action in several (funerals and *korosek*, but less significantly in other matters).

Directions are also significant. Initiates and the dead face east, and rituals move from east to west. The left side appears occasionally, as at death and in the lightning ritual, and as a minor element elsewhere. Paths also have ritual significance: an initiate or unanointed father of twins may not step upon them; oaths may be sworn at important pathways.

This examination of ritual behavior offers us a rich vocabulary of Sebei symbolism; to give it grammar is more difficult. I shall essay with no little diffidence a few generalities that I think the data sustain.

Dualism is a recurrent religious concept and is currently a focus of anthropological attention. Several symbolic expressions of duality are essentially trivial: left/right appears occasionally, most importantly in relation to the funeral path, with the left representing female, weakness, and danger. East is important ritually, but not in direct opposition to west, except as source and culmination of action. South/north, which in Sebei is up/down, is economically and socially important but receives no ritual expression.

There are two major expressions of opposition: the *korosek*/oathing botany and the good/bad *oyik*. In terms of their usage and treatment in ceremonies, I do not think they can be read to symbolize good and evil, in the sense that Western thought brings to this duality. They signify, rather, conflict and resolution, force and counterforce. Nor do I think the duality of the *oyik*, though reasonably translated as good versus bad, reflects a philosophy of duality in the Western sense. Good *oyik* are capable of doing harm, while bad ones are hopelessly evil; they do not confront one another; there is no battle of the hosts.

Remarkably little sexual symbolism is expressed in Sebei ritual, and even less sexual opposition, though the major ritual activity — circumcision — deals overtly with sexuality. Perhaps the very openness of the antagonism makes it unnecessary to express these matters symbolically. The battle of the sexes appears ritually in two places: the *chepserer*, which is essentially an effort to suppress women's witchcraft, and the opposition between the lion and leopard ceremonies. Both are overt. One can find phallic symbolism, for instance, in the spears, the plantain blossom, and decorated or special doorways, but these are hardly central to the rituals. There is more evidence of ritual unity in the common rites for most of the initiation cycle and in the fact that women may join in or separately engage in oaths. The tendency to treat the *oyik* collectively renders them androgynous; their gender is subordinated to the importance of patrilineal descent.

The third area of meaningfulness is the close association between the individual and his possessions. I have shown elsewhere (SL:236-38; Goldschmidt:1970) how important this is to the Sebei social order. This sense of identification is the essence of those forms of "sympathetic" or "contagious" magic in which acting upon the object affects its owner, the essence of most Sebei oathing. It appears in the uses of the men's stools and sleeping skin and the woman's girdle, in the fact that the possessed object acts upon the living, in the importance of sacrificing animals, making payments and gifts, and forcing gifts in the process of ritual performances.

Sebei rituals are much more involved with the pastoral side of life than with farming, an ancient emphasis out of keeping with modern economy. There is only one truly Sebei gardening ritual (utilizing a slaughtered ram!). There is no garden magic; there are no garden shrines. Sheep, cattle, and their products suffuse virtually every aspect of Sebei ritual life; agricultural products play a minor and subdued role, except beer, which has its own source of ritual efficacy. Wild plants play a more significant role than cultigens; wild animals are virtually absent. But slight interest is shown in the rich and dramatic fauna of this land.

SOCIAL AMBIENCE OF SEBEI RITUAL BEHAVIOR

It is axiomatic that ritual and beliefs function in the maintenance of the social order, but to know the function of ceremonials does not explain the ritual forms. Such knowledge does no more than enable us to ask the right questions: What is problematic about the social order that requires ritual and ideological support? Why should this be problematic here?

Sebei ritual life as a whole dwells on dangers, disasters, the immanent evil in the universe. These negative forces are not particularized; the emphasis is not on the evil of witches or other individual representations, nor on particular situations out of which danger arises, nor is it related to breaches of tabu or the commission of sins, though such may also bring disaster and are in the ambience within which the Sebei dwell. Most ritual symbols and symbolic acts are ameliorative in character: the spitting, libations, anointing, and cleansing are designed to remove unspecified but strongly felt contaminating elements that adhere to persons, things, and situations. Sebei ritual life is not concerned with good and evil, right and wrong, but with retaliation and amelioration.

The central element in the rites of transformation is the vulnerability of protagonists: the new mother, particularly the mother of a special child, the initiate, the bride, the widow. She (or he) is, as one man said, like a person who is sick, and must in varying degrees be protected by restraints on her actions, by denial of her impulses, and by literally hiding her from the sources of danger. The protagonist is also seen vaguely as a source of danger, a threat to others — as someone whose crossing of a stream would make it dry up, for instance. Rites of transformation are the most important Sebei rituals and the only major ones to survive the destructive force of acculturative influences. The same spirit animates the protective rituals engaged in by the *pororyet* and *saŋta*. Nothing in these ritual performances is designed to ennoble citizenship or extol the virtues of the locale. They are fat ceremonies, in the Sebei expression, but they are not joyous gatherings. The harvest *korosek* (and drought and disease *korosek*) might be expected to be a positive expression of community solidarity, a song to the bounty nature has provided. The Sebei see it, however, as ritual purification designed to counteract disease, drought, and bad luck. The other *pororyet* ritual, *chomi ntarastit* utilizes the dread oath as a means of providing social solidarity. The only unifying ritual of the *saŋta* is explicitly designed to combat evil acts.

The most important rite of conciliation is the *korosek* for sweeping away an oath. This and some of the rites of retaliation are the only clan-oriented ones. Thus, the only ritual reaffirmation of clan unity is negative in character, its function being to respond to threat or remove supernaturally sanctioned evil. There is no ingathering of the clan, no celebration — only placation — of clan ancestors, no reaffirmation of clan unity and continuity. The rites in this class have a common theme: the amelioration of potential hostility — between half-brothers, between parties who have resolved a conflict, even between two herds of animals.

Most of the minor domestic rites involving people are also placatory or ameliorative. Only among the minor cattle and agricultural rites are there exceptions; the most important is *misisi*. Among all the native rituals of Sebei, the most distinctive in character, personnel, social purpose, and ritual performance is this minor thanksgiving dinner. It reminds us of what rituals can be. *Misisi* is not a dramatic rite in the Sebei ritual calendar; except for the libations of beer and utilization of newly harvested millet, it evokes no spiritual forces and uses no ritual symbols. But, just as the ritual brings together specific kindred, its libations are offered to specific, named ancestors, rather than generically to the good and bad *oyik*. The shift from *misisi* to *mukutanik* involved a change from kin-specific personnel to neighbors and friends, reflecting the economic change that created greater tension among neighbors than among kinsmen; yet, it still draws people together in a spirit of amity and pleasure. Moreover, it is still directed at potential discord; the people invited are now those with whom there may be tension: "The purpose of *misisi* is to gather together and strengthen friendship." The shift from kinsmen to neighbors reflects the sedentarization of the Sebei.

Leaving aside *misisi*, Sebei ceremonies emphasize the dark side of life. Why this pervasive fear, this darkness of spirit in the land of the Sebei? The natural environment of the slopes of Mount Elgon is essentially benign; it is not without its dangers from wild animals and diseases, but the escarpment is relatively free of such endemic African scourges as malaria and bilharzia. It is, by any standard, a rich, beautiful, and healthy environment. The real dangers that the Sebei have been subjected to for more than a century are the virulent raids of more aggressive enemy tribes. The rituals make no reference, direct or oblique, to this source of difficulty, nor do they, circumcision aside, reinforce the institutions for combatting this scourge. They express rather a fear of nature and of their fellow Sebei.

This dark view of life is expressed directly by the Sebei. An outstanding feature of Sebei culture that emerged from the detailed investigations by Edgerton (*RBE*:119) was their inordinate fear of death.

> The Sebei have a virtual obsession with death. Thirty-four Sebei said that death was the worst thing that could happen to a man; only ten persons in the three other tribes combined gave this response. When asked the totally open-ended question about the worst thing that could happen to a woman, sixteen Sebei gave "death" as the answer, compared to only three such answers from the other three tribes combined. In the content analysis, the Sebei were conspicuous by their frequent concern over death · · · · ; they spoke somberly of burial, putrescent bodies, the agonies of serious illness. But the flavor of this concern is even more striking than the frequency of its expression. It is not a perfunctory concern: it is a fearful dread. For example, when Sebei become drunk, their most typical worry is about death. It is quite

common for a man in his cups — a quite robust man at that — to begin
weeping and.say: "Nothing is worse than death; I want life, I don't want to
die!" It is not the means of death that the Sebei fear: disease, violence, and
witchcraft are equally to be feared. It is death itself that terrifies them: "A
man should not die; what could be worse than that?"

This fear of death is associated with a general fearfulness of so diffuse a
nature that it can properly be called anxiety. The Sebei are fearful, not
merely of specific dangers, but of everything: "We are afraid of everything,"
or, "We Sebei are cowards, we are afraid even to fight. We are all afraid."

The second most important element in Sebei ritual life may be termed
commensality. Sharing food and beer is necessary to the conclusion of amity
after a dispute; a feast with beer normally concludes the return from periods
of ritual seclusion. *Misisi* is pure ceremonial commensality. The Sebei recognize a class of rituals as being *sakwet*, a feast and therefore a good ritual.
These rituals are good because food and drink are pleasurable. They are also
good because, for the time at least, dangers are allayed, suspicion is set aside,
and harmony prevails.

Seen in this light, the emphasis upon commensality perhaps aids our
understanding of the pervasive fear that characterizes Sebei ceremonies and
relates to a second major feature that Edgerton found characteristic of Sebei
culture: hostility/suspiciousness (*RBE*:120):

> Of all the tribes, the Sebei rank lowest on cooperation . . . .   . Their
> profound jealousy is not confined to wealthy men: "We are jealous of
> everyone!" And, "Everyone hates me — my clan, everyone." Or, this: "Per-
> haps my friends may plot to kill me. Who will protect me?"

What emerges from these findings is that Sebei ritual behavior relates more
closely to dominant psychological attitudes than to external reality. What
they celebrate and how they celebrate it express their state of mind; to
understand Sebei ritual, we must turn from economics and sociology to
psychology.

Three dominant and interrelated themes emerged in our examination of
Sebei childhood: the low level of affect that parents display toward their
children; the insistence on obedience and task fulfillment for its own sake,
supported by punishment for failure, rather than praise for accomplishment;
and the absence of a provision for a coherent, articulated moral code against
which to measure one's behavior and personal worth. Sebei children may be
said to enter a cold world rather than a hostile one, an empty world rather
than one beset by demons, a Daliesque landscape that provides no consistent
scale against which to measure the self. Sebei mothers are neither witches
nor sirens; they scold little and seduce less; they are remote providers of
sustenance. A neo-Freudian analysis would suggest that a Sebei's daily
satisfactions in sucking on the beer straw, drawing from a mammary-shaped
vessel a white, warm, soothing liquid that momentarily allays suspicion and
unrest, reflect infantile experience of a mother who gave of herself only
through the nipples. Such an analysis might further suggest that the bicker-

ing around the beer pot represents those active fists kneading the other teat. I would not be able to contest the analogy.

Sebei fathers are equally remote, sources of authority who demand obedience because the child is small and the father large, a pattern institutionalized so that all "large" persons — i.e., those who are circumcised — may demand acquiescence of any small one. All men are fathers, not in the kinship sense, but in the sense that all men have the right to demand obedience and to punish. Thus, the father is not a particularized focus of hostile sentiments; resentment suffuses to all men; it becomes generic. The child learns that he can do wrong but not that he can do right — certainly not what *is* right. The clan and *pororyet* rituals do not tell him what is good and right about those social groups of which he is a part, but only about what dangers he shares with them. This negative basis for personal identity parallels the negative basis for behavior in general. Disobedience or incompetence merits punishment; fulfillment of one's duty reaps no rewards. The bad *oyik* are bad, but the good *oyik* can but be prevented from doing harm.

Another theme in Sebei culture must now enter the equation: the individuated pattern of Sebei behavior. A person's success in life depends on his or her efforts, not on clan affiliation. This is a common theme in pastoral societies, as I have argued elsewhere (Goldschmidt, 1971a:132-42); it is highly relevant to the economic realities of the pastoralists' life and therefore certainly not without its virtues. But, in the absence of clear standards of behavior, with no guiding moral philosophy or even a precise definition of good work, with little satisfaction attained through social identification, individuation becomes an unbridled urge to self-aggrandizement. When the individual feels free to do whatever it is possible to do, he or she projects similar sentiments on others. Hence the pervasive hostility and jealousy of which Edgerton speaks — pervasive in the sense that they are not directed to particular others, but rather to the social ambience. Even at funerals, there is no personification or particularization of the source of fear.

The social order demands that each person pursue his or her welfare. This is guilt-provoking, particularly in the absence of a moral code that channels and justifies these acts, and such guilt is projected on others. For if a man is prepared to do what is necessary to satisfy his desired, then others will be seen to do likewise. Guilt pollutes, and Sebei ritual provides the constant and reiterative use of cleansing agents. Lady Mcbeth would understand.

The absence of specified ritualists fits this pattern of individuation and reflects also the nonspecific father in Sebei childhood. Ritualists are selected, even prophets are selected, on the basis of personal competence and trust — and trusted no further than necessary. Not only is there no priest, there are virtually no kin-based ritual roles. Nor is there anything that can be called a cult. The general absence of shrines, of ritual loci, and of localized spirits is perhaps a characteristic reflecting a more mobile pastoral state. Sebei ancestral spirits are clan-based and clan-unified, but to call their libations ancestor worship would be absurd; there is no ancestor cult. The *oyik* give spiritual unity to the clan but primarily as a negative force. Thus, the individual is entrapped by the spiritual force of clanship rather than being inspired with the joy of membership or comforted in its security.

Sebei rituals stand in meaningful relationship to the attitudinal sets of Sebei psychology, and these in turn can be seen as derivative from the experiences of infancy and childhood. Such "explanations" of institutional systems are, however, really assertions of cultural continuity — descriptions of feed-back loops. They do not tell us why these particular sets of interaction should occur among the Sebei rather than some *other* internally consistent systems of attitudes and belief. They are certainly not, in any simple sense, related to the particular needs that derive from the slopes of Mount Elgon and the surrounding predatory neighbors. They are a product of the dynamics that derive from the adaptive process, to which we will turn in the final chapter.

Chapter 12
Continuities and Adaptations

*The tribe had found somewhere to settle. In the middle of the
desert it had found a broad stretch of cultivable land, rich in
water, green fields and trees; and unconsciously, without anyone
actually proposing it, the tribe, instead of making one of its brief
sojourns there, had taken root in this Paradise; it had become
wedded to the soil, and the thought of moving on again did not
occur to it. Apparently it had reached that superior stage of
evolution which makes nomad existence impossible, and it was
now resting from the march of history. The tents gradually
changed into houses; every member of the tribe became a prop-
erty-owner.*

    *Years went by. Ali, a born warrior, and restless in the new
mode of life, saddled his horse and galloped all over what he
insisted on calling 'the Camp', shouting 'I'm leaving. Follow me!'
'And who will bring our beloved land with us?' they asked him.
Only then did they all realise that they had become wedded for
ever to that plot of earth; and Ali had to go alone.*

                    Italo Svevo, *The Tribe*, 1897

My primary purpose in writing this book has been to describe the culture
and behavior of the Sebei. But I also want to understand why the Sebei
behave as they do and to try to convey this understanding. This is an
exceedingly difficult task for any social order; the Sebei present a particular
challenge, in part because they make so little effort to explain themselves,
but more importantly because they clearly underwent major changes in their
patterned behavior in the century prior to the advent of colonial overrule.

Sebei society, like any other, may be viewed as a system; it is bounded,
self-perpetuating, made up of diverse parts (themselves systems), and the
component elements serve this perpetuation by complex interrelationships
that create feedback loops. The Sebei social system exists in an environment
of other systems, and between it and each of them there is an interaction.

342

Following Parsons (1968:459), we may recognize that the Sebei consti-tute two systems, a social and a cultural.[1] The social system consists essentially of the standardized and institutionalized interrelationships among individuals as they collaborate in the processes of food production, con-sumption, procreation, nurturance, protection, and whatever else they must do to maintain the social order. The cultural system consists of the shared and standardized perceptions, interpretations, and sentiments that charac-terize the population. The two systems interact and interpenetrate at so many points that they could be considered separate facets of a single system, but each has its own universe and its own mechanisms for self-perpetuation. Functionalist anthropology has traditionally concerned itself with the man-ner in which the social system operates and maintains itself. The psychologi-cal anthropologists have concerned themselves with the manner in which perceptions and sentiments operate and how these are perpetuated in the processes of socialization and enculturation.

Because the social and cultural systems are so closely interrelated, they must be mutually reinforcing; ritual is the major point of articulation between the two systems. A ceremony is by definition an institutionalized pattern of interaction. It communicates sentiments and therefore reinforces them. The sociologist would argue that ritual exists to reinforce the proc-esses of social interaction; the culturologist would contend that ritual rein-forces sentiments. Both are right.

As systems are always in interaction with other systems, they operate within an environment that has particular characteristics of its own. A society does not merely exist in an environment, with the passivity that such phraseology evokes, but is in dynamic interaction with it; societal operations are adapted to the exigencies the environment creates. This is the central point of the approach of cultural ecology. The ecological approach takes the problems of explaining a given system one step further; it argues that this set of institutions is the functionally effective means of maintaining the social order *in the context of a particular set of contingencies*. It also tells us why a particular institution is functionally appropriate. For instance, the *namanya* contract is an effective means of spreading the risk in a situation where raiders tend to strike a single kraal. Or again, private and individual owner-ship of property may be the best means of handling livestock where seasonal drought requires the scattering of herds in small groups.

The cultural systems, the system of sentiments, also has its ecological component. Attitudes of personal independence and responsibility are an important systemic element for a community of herders, each of whom must independently take care of his stock for months on end. Sentiments also may be common responses to situationally created circumstances. The heightened incidence of witchcraft involvement may be seen as an unin-

---

1. This disregards the other two systems he postulates, the individual organism and the individual personality, as being a different order.

tended consequence of the restraints necessary on Sebei farmers who must curtail more overt expressions of aggression.

The social system also articulates with another system: the human being as a physiological and psychological entity. Any effort to explain human social systems must involve a set of assumptions about the nature of the human individual. My first is that man is programmed for survival; when he perceives an opportunity for more food, more protection, more likelihood that his children will survive, he will tend to take advantage of it.

My second major assumption is that man is programmed to improve his self-image, which I attribute to what may be called affect hunger, or what I have called the "need for positive affect." (Goldschmidt, 1959:26-29). An individual can achieve self-image, or positive affect, only through interaction with others: as an infant in relation to his mother and others on the domestic scene, as a youth in the context of the peer group, as an adult in the achievement of status and power. This affect hunger may be satisfied by the kinds of behavior deemed appropriate in the culture or by the symbolic rewards that the culture has standardized — that is, by cultural values.

This quality in man is the source of both centripetal and centrifugal forces. It involves a need for positive identification with others and is the psychodynamic basis for group unity.

It is also a potential source of social disruption, for the individual searching for ego satisfactions is necessarily in pursuit of self-aggrandizement. The search can — and usually does — lead to conflict. One of the central tasks of any social system, therefore, is to harness these impulses for the maintenance of the social order and to utilize the energies that they create to advance and protect society, while at the same time restraining the naked aggression that may result from these impulses. The history of man suggests that this is no easy achievement.

In an orderly and unchanging world, there should be a perfect harmony within a system and between it and its environment, proceeding indefinitely through time. But, because the world is not orderly and unchanging and because the system is in dynamic interrelation with this outside world, such harmony is not what one usually, if ever, finds. Introduce a new people in the environment, as the Ngoni invasion did in Central Africa, and such equilibrium as existed is rapidly dissipated and internal changes are rapidly effected in the social systems. Introduce a new element of technology and, to the extent that it alters man's use of the land, the dynamic relationship with the environment has altered as well, for ecological relationships involve these interactions. Change the habitat so that the balance among existing exploitative techniques is altered, and the social order again will be out of joint with the times. Because such dynamic changes are constant elements in human history, equilibrium is at best an ideal condition — an expectation rather than a realization.

SEBEI ADAPTATIONS

When the ancient Kalenjin culture, forged over several millenia as an adaptation to the highlands of East Africa, arrived on the well-watered slopes of Mount Elgon, certain new opportunities were provided and certain new limitations were confronted. The cultivation of plantains and other intensive crops more appropriate to the new environment reinforced and furthered these opportunities and their attendant limitations. These were not minor environmental or economic changes; the two modes of economy are different in the extreme, requiring different daily patterns of life, different muscle use, different kinds of hardship, and many other specific matters. Such changes had repercussions throughout the organization of interpersonal relations and social sentiments.

I have brought together in tabular form three sets of data on institutional and attitudinal variations. Table 46 sets forth the major alterations in Sebei institutions through time. Some of these were specifically mentioned as recent precolonial social changes; others are inferred from comparative data on other Kalenjin peoples. Table 47 sets forth a group of lesser elements that distinguish the people of the agricultural west from the more pastoral east. Table 48 summarizes the detailed differences between agricultural Sasurese and pastoral Kapsirikans, demonstrating the specific kinds of adaptations. These tables represent three different orders of data, but all relate to the same basic differential — a shift in the economic order.[2]

The change in the Sebei economic infrastructure came gradually but essentially occurred in two steps: an increased dependence upon agriculture resulting from the use of traditional Kalenjin cultigens on the better watered slopes of Elgon, and the intensification of this process through the adoption of plantains, yams, and sweet potatoes. The first phase must have begun at least two centuries ago, possibly much earlier; the second phase must have begun in the nineteenth century and was still in progress when Europeans arrived on the scene.

The first consequence of the change was the sedentarization of the population. Even those who continued to graze animals did not have to move their stock far for grass and water and could keep their cattle throughout the year without going far from their homes. To the extent that they emphasized farming, their work was at their homes and they did not have to leave at all.

The second consequence was the placing of value upon all potentially cultivable land. Indeed, land became a commodity to be traded in, allocated to wives, and passed on to sons. The Sebei utilized existing laws pertaining to ownership of cattle in the handling of this new and vital commodity; more

---

2. They also represent different degrees of certainty. These tabulations represent the matrix of evidence, summarized from the text, upon which I draw to develop a systematic understanding of dynamic change among the Sebei.

TABLE 46
Major Changes in Sebei Institutions

Category	Ancient times	Recent times
Economy	Dominance of cattle pastoralism; millet and sorghum secondary	Animal husbandry secondary; agriculture dominant; acquisition of plantains
Property	Land publicly held except when cultivated	Land privately held and traded
Settlement patterns	Age-based concentrated communities; geographical mobility relatively free; local community secondary	Houses scattered over the land; mobility limited or restricted; local community primary
Authority	Age-grade of elders confers authority role	Charismatic *kirwokik* authority; increased power of prophets; *ntarastit* provides community authority
Warfare	Hit and run raiding; warrior age-grade	Defensive military action; all able-bodied men are soldiers; warfare organized by clans (west only)
	Acquisition of cattle major purpose	Defense of home and land
Age-sets and circumcision	Age-sets formulate age-grades, status levels within age-sets, internal (military) leadership in age sets; *tamokyet* ritual for age-set advancement; initiates engage in military practice	Initiated men undifferentiated; no status advancement markers; no differentiated age-set functions; no ritual of age-set advancement; military practice eliminated
Kinship and domestic life	Houses in close proximity; men much away from home; kin-oriented *misisi* ceremony; kin division of slaughtered animals; friendship enhancement ceremony (*kochak*)	Houses isolated; men much in home; neighbor-oriented *mukutanik* rite; functional division of beer "meats"; placatory ceremony for half-brothers

importantly, they also applied their attitudes and sentiments. The strong sense of private ownership of property that characterizes Sebei culture today is a trait deeply integrated into every facet of their culture and highly adaptive to the dry-land pastoralism from which they derive. As the essential productive resource shifted from stock to land, it was reasonable for men to begin to measure their worth in terms of this new source of sustenance.

A third consequence of this basic change was the change in settlement patterns. The concentrated *manyatta* organized on an age-set basis had functional meaning for a stock people. As land utilization increased, it was more important for each individual to live on his own plot of land, not only

TABLE 47
Special Characteristics of the Mbai (Western Sebei)

Category	Characteristic
Economy	Permanent boundary markers only found in west; absent or temporary ones in east. *Kapturin* land fertility rite only as far east as Chema
Settlement	Clan settlement reported only for western Sebei
Warfare	Clan military action only reported in west; territorial threats only in west; military action against invaders
Social organization	Long line of prophets reported only for Mbai. *Chomi ntarastit* introduced by western prophets. Clanless men said to be in greater danger in Mbai than in Sapiñ
Age-set and circumcision	Traditional ritual elements more frequently not observed in west than in east (or plains). *Melilo* ceremony for women not practiced. Failure to give feasts and provide beer for age-set mates. Absence of gifts to initiates
Kinship and domestic life	Mbai men marry before circumcision. Mbai men inherit their father's wives
Sorcery	Mbai clans are only ones to have *kankanet* sorcery

TABLE 48
Comparisons Between Kapsirika and Sasur

Category and Item	Kapsirika	Sasur
Economy		
Cattle per hshld	20.6	3.4
Percent land cultivated	3%	75%
Major source of income	Cattle	Coffee
Namanya contracts per hshld	5.1	1.4
Settlement		
Population density	25 sq. mi.	1,000 sq. mi.
Proximity of other villages	Separated	Contiguous
Geographical mobility	High	Low
Warfare		
Participation in raids	Occasional	None
Attitude toward warfare	Unfortunate necessity	Absolute refusal

TABLE 48 — *Cont.*)

Category and Item	Kapsirika	Sasur
Social organization		
Clan proximity	More dispersed	More concentrated
Family continuity	No family dynasties	Family dynasties
Community action	Occasional	Absent
Property		
Land acquisition	"Opened": 59.7%	From father: 70.1%
Land conflict	Rare	Frequent
Age-set and circumcision		
Circumcision feast	Elaborate	Rare or absent
Beer for age-mates	Regularly given	Often omitted
Age-set unity	More important	Less important
Domestic life		
Average household size	6.47	5.90
Polygyny rate	151 per 100	117 per 100
Live births per woman	6.60	7.82
Living children per woman	3.50	5.59
Infant mortality	51.5%	29.1%
Brideprice: cattle	6.6	5
Total cash value	1,400 shillings	1,214 shillings
Brideprice indebtedness	18.4%	34.3%
Co-wife relationship	Little conflict	Much conflict
Major sibling conflict	Full brothers	Half-brothers
Women's extramarital sex	One lover	Many lovers
Sorcery		
Mean frequency of mention	1.01	1.88
Social concern with	Little	Considerable

NOTE: These data only summarize the relevant major contrasts discussed throughout the volume; for more precise meaning, see text.

from the practical standpoint of farming operations but also to assure and reinforce the rights of possession and prevent the theft of crops.

A fourth direct consequence was a shift in military stance. Traditional military action had been the give-and-take, hit-and-run operations of the raiding party, for which the immediate motive was the acquisition of enemy cattle, though the indirect effect was to protect and even to expand territory. With cattle as an easily stolen good, these patterns of raiding were endemic in the dry highlands of East Africa. For that reason, it was essential that each people train its herders to take protective action against such depredations (as well as against the dangers of lesser animal predators). Inevitably, such a stance meant indulgence in aggressive raids as well. But the shift in economy meant that it was now necessary to protect a *territory* rather than merely the scattered herds of cattle, and this resulted in the adoption of a defensive posture. This change was undoubtedly furthered by other particularities of the Mount Elgon environment: the fact that the mountain offered them something of a bastion, the further protection afforded them by the extensive caves in which they and their stock could hide, and the increased difficulty of engaging in raids because of the distances involved. Where the economy became virtually totally agricultural, there was also a lessened incentive for raiding on both sides.

These four direct consequences of the economic change resulted in a major realignment of the social order, shifting emphasis away from the age-sets to the local territorial units. The age-set system in East Africa is a sociological device that is highly adaptive to the functions of governance, the maintenance of order, and the protection of property in a predominantly pastoral situation (Bernardi, 1952:331; Evans-Pritchard, 1940a:266). The age-sets, through common initiation, are highly integrated sodalities; they progress through time through a series of age-grades — soldiers, junior elders, and senior elders. The functional importance of the soldier cadre is crucial, for through it the internal integrity of the age-sets is reinforced. But the shift from hit-and-run raiding to defense of territory meant that *all* able bodied men had to engage in warfare when called upon. This blurred the lines of distinction between age-sets and, in doing so, also reduced the sense of social solidarity; the process had major repercussions for the Sebei polity.

A number of particulars in the age-set structure express this change: there was no internal structure in the form of formalized leadership roles within the *pinta*; the age-sets did not have internal status differentiation by attainment of higher levels; and the lines of distinction became so blurred that there were no longer ceremonial markers that indicated advancement to higher levels in the age hierarchy. The destruction of a warrior age-grade also had the effect of destroying the functional effectiveness of an age-grade of elders. The very lack of unity, delimitation, and structure of the warrior group would deprive them, a generation later, of the structural coherence necessary to serve as a group of elders with the functions of governance that characterize pastoral Nilotes in general. The destruction of the age-based *manyatta* must also have contributed to this declining functional role of the age-sets — or perhaps each contributed to the other. The total result was that the form of an age-set system was retained, but its substance was lost by the elimination of functional age-grades.

The decline of functional age-grades can be appreciated only in terms of the character of governance under pastoral conditions. We must assume that the clans served as jural entities in the *Urkultur* of Sebei and that any major dispute between two persons was potentially a confrontation between the two clans, with the ultimate possibility of a feud. Such a system can be very disruptive unless there is also some institutionalized means of settlement. The Sebei did not recognize offices, did not have third-party decision making. But with an established age-grade of elders there is a means of avoiding the escalation of disputes and resolving them, as Neville Dyson-Hudson (1966) shows for the Karamojong. The decline of the authority of a unified cadre of elders created a power vacuum which the *kirwokik*, dependent upon their personal charisma rather than on a formal structure of authority, could not adequately fill — particularly in the more densely settled agricultural areas. Two basic developments took place.

Those Sebei who dwelt in Legene and farther south in what is now Bugisu must have been in the vanguard of this set of changes, for agriculture in this area was particularly attractive and cattle-keeping was not. Furthermore, in this area, the Sebei were being subjected to a military pressure very different from the traditional hit-and-run raiding of the plains — a mass of land-hungry Bantu bent on expanding their territory. In response, and in the absence of a warrior grade, military action fell into the hands of clans (one does not hear of clans in military organization in the east). The result was the strengthening of the clans as a political force in the western sector, so that when they retreated to the Sipi area they tended to settle in clan units and to preserve the strength of clan unity in the use of internal power. This system is not calculated to maintain an orderly society, particularly in a densely packed, immobilized agricultural community.

In this situation and area, the prophets established new institutions for the maintenance of order. The prophets are an old element in Kalenjin culture, but their secular power was remote. The fact that they could be killed summarily when their prophecies were displeasing indicates the limitation on their role. But the Kapchai prophets, culminating in Matui, stood apart. For one thing, a long line of succession indicated that they had firmly established their authority. For another, they exerted, according to testimony, a good deal more executive control than any other prophet.

They established the basis of community law by creating the ceremony of *chomi ntarastit*. They harnessed the dread power of Sebei oathing, attached to it the pattern of east-to-west *pororyet*-centered ritual activity and many of the *korosek* plants, and topped the whole thing off with a stem of plantains, to assert the right of community judgment. They did this with the avowed purpose of protecting the weak against the strong, the clanless man against the powerful clans. They did not eliminate the power of the elders; indeed, they strengthened the hands of the *kirwokik* with this institution. Nor did they eliminate the role of the clans in initiating the *chomi ntarastit* rite, which at any rate they could not have done. This was a stroke of genius, marred chiefly by the failure to insist on holding the ritual annually to give it more constant reinforcement. This new institution effected a major shift in organization: the age-set system lost all functional significance; the territorial unit became the center of political action as it was of military action; the earliest beginnings of a kind of national integrity were established.

The economic developments, together with these alterations in the structure of Sebei polity, also had their effects upon the domestic ménage, on the functional roles of men and women, and on the relationships between them. The *pororyet* had changed from a military unit to a spatial division in which a kind of citizenship was established. The *saŋta* was created as a smaller entity, suggesting closer and more domestic unity. The households were isolated from one another, each man living with his wives on his own land, and the household became a more significant social unit.

The traditional life history of a Kalenjin man began when the boy left his parental household at circumcision to dwell with his age-mates. With them, he herded cattle and undertook military forays. Herding the *warek* socialized him to these tasks as a child; the rite of circumcision socialized him to the qualities of fortitude and endurance. He was also socialized to the qualities of obedience and deference to his elders, a pattern designed to create attitudes of hostility that would have the secondary effect of reinforcing his ties with his age-mates. He was also reared in a relatively affect-less environment, which further reinforced male bonding, was taught that men's and women's roles were essentially different and that at best women were enfeebling to men. Women served as a means of gratification rather than as an emotional haven — gratification of his sexual urges and a means of obtaining the progeny necessary for his immortality. The essential relationship between the sexes was therefore antagonistic rather than intimate, though, as everywhere, the sexes were locked into a system of mutual dependence. Thus, the Sebei herder, in pursuit of a normal career, began to amass livestock through good husbandry, successful raiding, and clever manipulation, working conjointly with his masculine age-mates. He translated his successs into wives by means of bride payment, and these ultimately into children and grandchildren to preserve his line. He was probably well advanced in his career before he gave up the not inconsiderable pleasures — as well as hardships and dangers — of bachelorhood for the life of an elder, a transition made easier by the fact that his age-mates made it at the same time.

With the decline of herding, the career pattern to which he had been socialized was closed to him, though much of the institutional socialization continued. The father remained remote; the commitment to initiation was too great to abandon readily; and the young Sebei was still expected to herd goats — even apparently when there was no real herding to do. This discontinuity in social conditioning is, I think, one of the important elements in understanding modern Sebei men.

His career opportunities curtailed by the altered economy, the young Sebei never really left home but built a *sikerointe* in the shadow of his father's — or, perhaps more significantly, his mother's — house. He turned naturally to early marriage — even before circumcision — and, if he was success-oriented, endeavored to maximize his landholdings. Several factors lessened his chances for plural marriages: earlier marriage made fewer women available; lessened military activity meant fewer of his rivals would be killed; and the dual responsibility for land and cattle often made the costs of plural marriages prohibitive. A successful career was more likely if his father had been wealthy and there was adequate land. But he was in the home earlier, more of the time, and more directly associated with a particular wife.

Women's careers were less affected by the change. They were still social-ized to domestic chores, engaged in essentially the same activities, and found status satisfactions in childbearing. Instead of acquiring rights to cattle upon marriage, they obtained a plot of land, and their work continued to keep them in close association with other women. The major direct effects on them were more insistent demands on their time because of their larger economic role, and, thus, their enhanced economic importance. It may be that the increased demands upon their time lessened their psychological involvement in mothering their infants.

Though husband and wife were thrown into close juxtaposition, and though masculine careers had been destroyed by the economic shift, men were reluctant to take on farming tasks. Men were still socialized to the old economic order; a strong sense of sexual separation and masculinity was induced in them as children and asserted by the initiation rites. It was bad enough for them to give up warfare and herding but worse still for them to take up "women's work." When jobs, such as plowing or handling coffee, later took on a different character as a result of European influence, they did not shirk these duties, and in fact they increasingly involve themselves with the more mundane agricultural tasks.

Social estrangement, the lack of affect in their infantile environment, continued to imbue the men with patterns of hostility toward and domi-nance of their women. Such sentiments were functionally relevant in the traditional economy and would not have been so insistent in daily life when men and women lived apart much of the time. When, however, men were forced into the home, when furthermore their ego-satisfactions were thwarted, and when they had to recognize that the work of their women was more important then their own, these traditional sentiments exacerbated the relationships between the sexes. Hence, the excessive fear of women, com-pounded out of resentment and guilt and built upon the assumption of innate basic sexual differences.

The women had traditionally not accepted their lot passively; the ritual of circumcision served to condition them to the physical demands of pastoral life. The strong sense of female bonding expressed in the *melilo* ceremony, in which they learned anti-male magic, gave them considerable power and the men a basis for their fears. The increased economic role of women, though intensifying rather than allaying men's fears, did reduce male authoritari-anism, with the result that the women's ritual of unification was dropped in the agricultural west, though later re-adopted.

The close settlement on the land and the importance of the land altered the patterns of jealousy and hostility and the manner of their resolution. Landholdings came to be carefully bounded by planting senchontet markers, and quarrels over boundaries were frequent sources of irritation between neighbors. Potential conflict between neighbors became more important than such conflicts among in-laws, transforming *misisi*, a ceremony of amity among kinsmen, into *mukutanik*, a ceremony of amity among neighbors. A similar transition took place earlier, when beer parties became more important than the slaughtering of animals, but the principle of allocated shares was continued. The "meats" of the beer pot symbolize the greater attention the Sebei give to functionally relevant patterns of interaction than they do to structurally defined kin relationships. Such rituals allayed many fears and hostilities, but they did not eliminate them. The imperative of continued close association among neighbors required the suppression of hostile sentiments, with the result that farmers avoided direct action in conflict situations and sought ameliorative techniques or suppressed their hostilities, which heightened suspiciousness and intensified sorcery.

DISEQUILIBRIA AND MALADAPTATION

Impressive as is the evidence for change and adaptation in Sebei institutions, it is also necessary to recognize that the Sebei demonstrate evidence of social disequilibrium. Two areas will concern us here: the failure of the Sebei to establish a social order capable of maintaining their boundaries, and the failure to develop a commitment to a relevant set of moral principles. The one is an institutional failure, the other an attitudinal one, but the two are closely linked. The former is evidenced by the historical fact that the Sebei were pushed back on all fronts by their neighbors; the latter is manifested by the absence of any consistent expression of moral sentiment, the fearfulness of the Sebei in general, and a pervasive alcoholism.

The Sebei failure to achieve a new and relatively stable equilibrium is not surprising. During the whole period of change, they were constantly harassed and pressed by their neighbors. They were clearly in the midst of a massive alteration of their economy, with attendant changes in their institutions, when suddenly, out of nowhere, came an alien and powerful rule. Caught off balance in mid-stride by the Baganda domination and the colonial government, which severely limited their freedom of action and any possible further organic growth of their native institutions, they have retained the disharmonies that the processes of change had made inevitable.

Why should disharmonies be an inevitable result of change? Men adjust their actions in terms of their perceptions; their perceptions alter as new actions create new situations. A man who decides that he and his family will be better served by living on his land and cultivating it to plantains sees the reward in greater leisure, more food, and healthier progeny; he does not anticipate the remoter consequences of his acts. The feedback loops through which a course of action is reinforced have varying periodicities. A person may perceive in two or three years the value of a new crop or farming technique; an institutional solution to new situations will take as many decades, while the attitudinal sets established through patterned practices of child rearing and ritual reinforcements will certainly take as many generations. The disruption that renders old institutions and attitudes obsolete creates a disequilibrium, and the formulation of a new balance and harmony takes a long time. The Sebei were not given that opportunity. As new patterns of social interaction developed, mostly in the agricultural west, the emerging institutions were inadequate to the task at hand. The limits of military unity were the *pororisyek*, areas averaging between five and ten square miles, with populations averaging no more than two thousand persons. Collaboration among such independent units required mutual consent. Internally, authority rested on personal leadership; there were no real lines of command. Internal solidarity was dependent upon shared fears rather than a positive sense of community.

The manner in which the Sebei were socialized made it difficult for them to establish the unity necessary for creating a strong government. Their system of socialization reinforced a sense of independence and individuation and failed to create strong bonds (except the obsolete one with male age-peers). The pattern of individual self-help, the assumption that a person should take advantage of his position of power, reduced willingness to submit to authority. There was no focused authority figure, but rather a diffused authority among all elders. This was reflected in and reinforced by the spiritual importance of the *oyik* as a collectivity of ancestors. The blind command to obedience in traditional socialization failed to provide positive guidelines to social actions and did nothing to reinforce a sense of community loyalty. The Sebei as an individual was not socialized to accept such institutionalized presuppositions as would make for a strong sense of community: group loyalty, recognition of responsible leadership, subordination to authority. The socialization process created individuals appropriate to the pastoral life, not a citizenry for an integrated and organized state system.

These same elements also created disharmonies within the individual. In a stable order, the measures by which a man guages his value are the qualities he internalizes as a child and a youth; these qualities should be attainable by the ordinary individual, and they should be manifestly purposeful to the needs of the social order. The qualities inculcated in Sebei men through early training and reinforced by the initiation ceremonies were independent achievement, fortitude, and endurance. Success was measured by the acquisition of cattle, wives, and children. Such values forged a population of tough-minded, expressive, masculine-oriented men, free-moving and ready to act. But Sebei society no longer rewarded such action or needed such personalities. Sebei men were socialized for frustration. This accounts for the excessive and unfocused fear, the regular and pervasive resort to the anodyne of the beer pot, and the low level of cultural commitment.

The poverty of Sebei expressive culture, the disinterest in the manifestations of supernatural forces, the failure to communicate either a religious rationale for behavior or a clear moral philosophy are also attributable in part to this general situation. Expressive culture in the form of a rich mythology, a devotion to aesthetic forms in the plastic arts or to intricate ritual forms, is not particularly characteristic of the Southern Nilotes, oriented as they are to the exigencies of their pastoral life. But the Sebei seem even less expressive in these areas than their cousins, perhaps because what they have been trained to believe has turned out to lack substance — so that, in a very real sense, they believe very little. The dominant theme expressed in their rituals is essentially a negation, a ritual expression of the fear they demonstrated to Edgerton, an institutionalization of their social dissatisfactions.

BASIC DYNAMICS OF SEBEI CULTURE

All is not change. Underlying the processes of adaptation is a basic continuity in the Sebei social order. The three basic themes that suffuse Sebei behavior and its institutional manifestations go far back in time and reach deep into the underlying structure of Sebei thought and sentiment. These themes may be labeled: (1) the strong sense of clan unity and continuity; (2) the right of the powerful; and (3) the deep involvement with things, with possessions.

When we speak of themes in a culture, we mean pervasive sets of attitudes that find expression in the various department of social life; they are important to everyday domestic affairs; they find expression in law; they underlie economic action and economic motivation; they are expressed ritually. They may be thought of as the presuppositions in the thoughtways of a people, the assumptions so much taken for granted by the citizenry that they are not subject to question in the course of ordinary life. They are therefore the very stuff of culture. Because these presuppositions are the basis for action, they are constantly reinforced and revalidated; it is the operation of what Robert Merton called the self-fulfilling prophecy.

Identity with the clan is the strongest social identification among the Sebei, and the presumption that this social unit exists continuously in time and space is one of these essential thematic elements. Each person is a member of a clan without wanting to be and without escape, assumes he has the characteristics he learns inhere in the clan, is liable for the actions of any clansman, past or present, and expects his clansmen to be liable for his actions. This continuity is expressed not only in the darker fears of Sebei oathing, where it has so central a part, but in the more ordinary expression of ritual libations, which give primary attention to dead clansmen. There is thus a spiritual as well as social unity to the clan.

Time extends forward, as well as backward; the Sebei interest in progeny, the purpose of their marriages, has as its very heart the concern with establishing descendants and thereby becoming an ancestor. When we examine the choices of action that lead a man to amass a herd, we find the ultimate rationale not so much in the maintenance of his immediate well-being, not so much in security for his old age — though there is no denying that these, too, are part of a complex system of motivations — but in the continuity and maintenance of a line. "This herd of cattle should not be dispersed," say the elders regarding Kambuya's rich legacy, knowing full well they will be but feeling they represent the continuity of the line that Kambuya had established.

The second basic theme in Sebei attitudes is the right of the powerful. This principle establishes the right of adults to dominate children, of men to dominate women, of strong clans to dominate weaker ones, of persons with the powerful magic of *kankanet* or with the capacity and will to pronounce an oath to instill fear in others, and of the *oyik* to harm the living. This aspect of Sebei culture finds its strongest expression in the relationship between old and young, where it is institutionalized in the age-set organization and more particularly in initiation rites. This authority, like that of clan relationships, can invoke the use of supernatural powers as an ultimate sanction. It is also expressed in the relationship between the sexes, where the ultimate basis for male dominance is specifically said to rest on masculine strength. Here no spiritual forces are evoked; on the contrary, the use of magic is, to the woman at least, a legitimate means for counteracting masculine authority.

It was against the naked use of this principle that *chomi ntarastit* was introduced. When I first learned of the custom, I was told that a powerful old man came to the place where a group had assembled and asked who a certain stranger was. When they said he was merely a clanless man, the old man speared this stranger to death, saying, "If he is a clanless man, then he is worthless and can do me no harm." When the prophet Matui heard about this, he realized that the power of the oath had been lost, and he called for the performance of the *chomi ntarastit* ceremony. The force of the principle that might is its own justification was counteracted only by invoking the strongest of maledictions, of ritual self-threats — not by the affirmation of loyalty and solidarity. The principle infuses modern political action, not only in the incipient age-grading of persons in authority, but in the generic assumption that persons with positions of power will use them to their own advantage.

The third central theme in Sebei culture is the strong personal identification between the individual and his possessions. This is not merely the concept of private property as a personal right, nor the tendency to measure status by ownership, nor the recognition that a person has liability for the actions of his livestock, though all these are important ingredients in the concept. Also involved here is a recurrent element in sorcery and oathing, the utilization of the thing involved to invoke the necessary spiritual force — the cow in dispute, the bones of the elephant involved in the case. This attitude is an expression of a metaphysical unity between the thing and the possessor, which we sometimes simply label sympathetic or contagious magic, but which expresses in fact a very deep sense of continuity between persons and objects.

Each man and woman has a value in property, a kind of Dun and Bradstreet rating of "net personal worth." Brideprice is certainly not a token prestation, nor is it merely a compensation to the father for the daughter; it is an expression of the value of the woman. Each man has his value, his worth in cattle, which his clansmen will accept as a substitute for him if he is killed. The premise that people can be translated into livestock, and vice versa, is a subtle but pervasive element in Sebei thought.

The most important manifestation of this theme is in the use of goods as expressive of social ties. When the wife has been given her cattle, she feels proud, for she knows that now "she is somebody." The use of a transfer of rights to express a social tie, meet an obligation incurred, create a social bond, or establish evidence of one's personal worth, occurs over and over again. The initiate demands a cow at a crucial point in the ceremony; the bride a heifer before she will proceed with the marriage or allow its ritual consummation. Lovers demand tokens of one another; the boy takes the cowry girdle as an earnest of the girl's promise; the girl lets the initiate have her beads for the ritual and retrieves them with a forfeit when he has proved worthy. Cattle ownership allocations within the household reflect the structure of the social relationships in a pattern so fraught with significance that it was applied to land as well.

Virtually every ritual performance, whether executed by a stranger or a close relation, involves the propriety of a proper compensation, aboriginally in native goods but now readily translated into money payments. The aunts urge their niece to remain married, because they have now received a gift from her husband; a man begs a cow from his father's legacy, "for crying for the dead father." The funeral is half ritual, half law court for the determination of property rights (Joyce might have written its propertyrites). This is not merely covetousness, though this is a sin not unknown to Sebei, but rather the expression of affect in goods. The *tilyet* relationship is pure pecuniary nexus, established through exchanges of property, turned into a bond of sentiment as strong as kinship. The *oyik* are not immune to the spiritual force of property. Cattle are given to them so that they will act favorably — or cease to act unfavorably. They are also given libations of food and beer.

Terms such as property and ownership, exchange and purchase, seem too narrow to convey adequately the role that material things play in Sebei perceptions; things as possessions and things as prestations are integral to the ordinary interactions and special relations that Sebei men and women have with one another.

These themes cross and intersect at many points because they are involved with the various domains of social life. They underlie the structure of social action and the organization of social sentiments and give a substratum of unity to Sebei culture despite the changes it has undergone through time and the variations that it expresses in space.

L'Envoi

To place a culture under scientific scrutiny is to expose its weaknesses as well as its strengths, to show the bad along with the good, to investigate the seamy side of life. When a people has been subjected to the pressures and tensions that have characterized the Sebei situation for the past century or two, the maladies of the social system seem to outweigh their strengths. Imbued with a personal command to honesty that is strongly reinforced by the scholarly tradition, I have been compelled either to describe them as I see them, or to abandon the project entirely.

If what I have written should offend the Sebei, I am sorry. Perhaps, however, they will take less offense if they realize that I find Sebei culture and behavior a parable for ourselves, a reflection of American culture and behavior as it manifests itself in the latter half of the twentieth century. The similarities are not fortuitous.

We, too, have been subjected to a massive social change not unlike that which took place on Mount Elgon. Ours was a culture forged on the frontier, where attitudes of independence, self-help, and great courage were necessary, and where these qualities reaped rich rewards, and we induct our children into this form of behavior. We have institutionalized motives of self-help so powerfully that we have lost the capacity to restrain the principle, even when we see it destroying the foundations of our sustenance. We have frustrated the satisfaction of induced cultural values to such an extent that uncontrolled violence, alcoholism, and the excessive use of drugs have been endemic. If the advertisements on our television reflect the individual anxieties of our population, we are beset with a host of inflictions that bedevil our flesh, despite our rich environment and our medical technology. Our national unity builds on such illusory fears, giving emphasis to an undefined concern with external threat, rather than celebrating the richness of our heritage and endeavoring to reform our institutions to meet present exigencies.

My friends, the Sebei, your problems are our problems, and perhaps through understanding you, we can somewhat better understand ourselves and can move a step closer to achieving a new equilibrium, a new harmony. *Anyiñ.*

Appendix A
Chronology

Year	Age-set	Event
1785-1804	Koronkoro period	
1805-24	Kwoimet period	
1825-44	Kaplelaich period	Diaspora of Sebei on account of famine (Sirikwa?)
1845-64	Nyikeao period	Gisu pressure begins in Legene area Bumachek establish themselves peaceably among Sebei in Western region Sebei of Legene move eastward to Chema area, bringing plantain and changed architecture Kabruron area depopulated by raids from Masai and others Pressure in southeast from Masai and Kitosh Prophet Namume establishes *chomi ntaristit*
1865 ca.	Nyoŋki I	
1871 ca.	Nyoŋki II	
1878 ca.	Nyoŋki III	Age-set nicknamed Kapsaror (descendants of the tail) because a star with tail (comet) appeared at time of initiation
1884 ca.	Maina I	Swahili traders arrive before this initiation and maintain a fort in Sebei
1890		Jackson and Gedge visit Sebei (February) Maina I famine
1891 ca.	Maina II	
1896		Hobley travels around north side of Elgon
1897 ca.	Maina III	
1897-98		Austin's headquarters in Sebei (November 1, 1897 - December 20, 1898)
1898-99		Maina III famine
1901 ca.	Chepilat circ.	Aborted circumcision; disease of penis
1902		Visit by Grant and Tidmarsh with Kakunguru's army (December)
1903-1904		Beginning of Baganda overrule in Sebei

Year	Age-set	Event
1908		European direct involvement with Sebei administration begins
1909-10 ca	Chumo I	Sebei men begin to enter King's African Rifles
1912-14		Military garrison in Greek River and Sebei begin settling in Ngenge
1914 ca.	Chumo II	
1918		Chumo II famine
1920 ca.	Chumo III	Coffee introduced about this time
1924 ca.	Sowe I	Establishment of Sebei as a *gombolola* (sub-county); Wandera appointed *gombolola* chief
1927 ca.	Sowe II	
1930 ca.	Sowe III	Mangusho, son of prophet Matui, arrested for allegedly seditious actions
1933		Sowe III drought and famine
1934	Koronkoro I	Sebei transformed to *saza* (county); Wandera named chief
1936	Koronkoro II	
1938	Koronkoro III	Prophet Matui dies
1940	Kwoimet I	
1942	Kwoimet II	Mangusho released from detention.
1944	Kwoimet III	
1946	Kaplelaich I	
1948	Kaplelaich II	Aloni Muzungyo succeeds Wandera as *saza* chief
1950	Kaplelaich III	
1952	Nyikyeao I	
1954	Nyikyeao II	(Our first visit to Sebei January-July)
1956	Nyikyeao III	
1958	Nyonki I	Road completed across escarpment to Kenya. Protest against treatment by Gisu District government begins
1960	Nyonki II	Roadblock as act of civil disobedience (December). Taxpayers' strike against Bagisu government. A. Y. Chemonges, first Sebei to be elected to Uganda Legislative Council
1961		(Our second visit, June 1961 - November 1962)
1962	Nyonki III	Sebei District established (February). Uganda independence (October)

Appendix B
Sebei Calendar

	Month	Season	Comments
January	*wakitaptai* (first of year)	Dry (*kamei*)	*Waki* — from Swahili *mwaka* (year), hence borrowed term
February	*wakitaplet* (second of year)		Women prepare fields for root crops; herding important throughout dry season
March	*roptui* (black rain)		Black because of charred fields; white ants collected; plant sorghum and millet on plains, yams on escarpment
April	*plelaipi* (white water)	Long rains	Sunshine and rain mixed; sunshine on rain makes white water; planting continues; weeding on plains; boys herd because grass is plentiful
May	*psundetaptai* (heavy rain)	(*yekat*)	Weeding is major work, but still some planting on mountains
June	*psunditaplet* (second heavy rain)		Still planting in upper regions
July	*teter* or *mukeyo* (too much rain)		
August	*mowo* or *psirwomo* (afternoon rain)	Dry	Millet harvest starts on plains; yams and *nompuk* harvested on escarpment; a time of dancing
September	*sirwomo* (or *teter*) (stars at night)		"Harvest has started climbing"
October	*twamo* (short rain)	Short rains	Little rain and much wind; no building, rituals, marriages, making beehives; only common work; a time of danger
November	*watkut* (short-grass rain)	*yekat*	Rains produce short grass; streams are low and raiding possible
December	*terit* (dust)	Dry (*kamei*)	Very dry and dusty; last of millet harvest

Note: Sebei informants are not consistent in delineating the calendar, partly because of regional variations (see Porter, n.d.) and acculturation influences. This calendar is summarized from the accounts of several Sapiñ informants, who were not in full agreement.

Appendix C
Kin Terminology

Sebei kinship terminology is presented with the nearest English equivalent (or key gloss) in the left column. The central column gives the Sebei term in the vocative, (marked with an asterisk), the first-person possessive, and third person; the right column shows the applicable kin. To the standard abbreviations, I have added two terms necessary for Sebei: Ar = *aret* (clan), meaning a clan affiliation, and Pi = *pinta* (age-set), meaning age-set mate, either as the subject of the term or connecting relative. (Footnotes are at the end of the table.) Blanks indicate the absence of a term in the first-person possessive or third person.

English	Sebei	Applicable to:
Father	*Papa* Papamwanyi Papanyi	Fa, FaBr, FaPi, MoSiHu, MoBrDaHu, DaHu, WiFa
Father	Kwan, kwaninyi	Fa (used in reference only)
Mother	*Yeyo* Yeyomwani, yeyonyi[a] Yeyit	Mo, FaWi, MoSi, FaBrWi, MoBrWi, MoBrDa, MoBrSoDa, WiMo, MoArWomen, FaPiWi (♀spkg)
Mother	Kamet, kamatyi	Reference only
Sibling	*Yeya* Yeyamwani Yeyanyi	Si, Br, FaSo, MoSo, MoSiDa, MoSiSo, FaBrDa, FaBrSo
Brother	*Mutapiya*[b] Mutapiya ani Mutapkwam, mutapkwamet[c]	Br, FaSo, MoSiSo, MoBrDaSo, FaBrSo
Brother	*Wonyo*	♀spkg: Br (address only) ArBr, MoSiSo
Sister, daughter	Chepiy, chepiya[d] – – – Chepkwam, chepkwamet	Si, FaBrDa, MoSiSo, MoBrDaDa, Da, BrDa, ArBrDa, MoSiDa Reference only
Uncle (mat.)[e]	*Mama* Mamamwani Mamanyi	MoBr, MoBrSo, MoBrSoSo, (all males of MoAr except MoFa)

362

English	Sebei	Applicable to:
Aunt (pat.)	*Senke Senkemwani, senkenyu Senkenyi	FaSi, FaMoSiDa, FaArSi[f], FaFaSi, BrSo (♀spkg), BrDa (♀spkg)
Son[g]	*Weri Werenyu Werenyi, weritap	So, FaSiSo, BrSo, BrDaSo, BrSoSo, SoPi (♀spkg), HuSo (♀spkg)
Child[h]	*Lekwet Lekwemwani Lekweni lekwet tap	Da, SiDa, BroDa, MoSiSoDa, FaBrSiDa, PiDa, SoWi, BrSoWi, SiSoWi, So, SiSo, BroSo, MoSiSoSo, FaBrSoSo, PiSo
Grandfather, Grandchild	*Kuko Kukomwani Kukonyi	FaFa, MoFa, FaFaBr, FaMoBr, MoMoBr, MoFaBr. ♂spkg: SoSi, SoDa, DaSo, DaDa, BrDaDa
Grandmother, Grandchild	*Koko Kokomwani Kokonyi	MoMo, MoMoArWomen, MoBrWi FaFaSi, FaFaBrWi. ♀spkg: SoSo, SoDa, DaSo, DaDa, HuSiSo, HuSiDa, HuBrSo, HuBrDa, HuBrSoSo
Grandchild[i]	*Muchokoret Muchokonyu Muchokorenyi	SoSo, SoDa, BrSoSo, BrSoDa
Husband[j]	*Pontoni Pontenyu Ponitet	Hu, HuBr, HuPi, HuArBr
Wife	*Chepyos Chepyosyani Chepyosyet	Wi, FaPiWi[k], PiWi, Mo
Wife	*Korkoni Korkenya Korket	Wi (disrespectful)
Co-wife[l]	*Chemnyo – – – – – –	HuWi
Co-wife	*Siyenyu Sentenyu	HuWi HuWi, HuPiWi
Son-in-law	*Santani – – – Santanyi	DaHu, FaSiHu
Brother-in-law[m]	*Kapikoi Kapikoyenyu Kapikoyenyi	WiBr, WiArBr, SiHu, SiHuBr, BrWiBr, FaSiHu, WiBrSo
Brother-in-law[n]	*Alaptani Alaptaninyo Alaptaninyi	(like brother-in-law, above)

English	Sebei	Applicable to:
Sister-in-law	*Pukot* *Pukotyenyu* *Pukotyenyi*	WiSi, BrWi, HuBr, HuArBr, HuSi, ♀spk: FaSiHu?
Brother-in-law, Sister-in-law[o]	*Limenyu*	SiHu, WiSiHu, WiSiHuSi
Sister-in-law[p]	*Arawe, arowe*	BrWiSi
Father-in-law	*Pontetapikoi* *Pontemwani popikoi* *Pontenyi popikoi*	WiFa, BrWiFa, HuFa, SiHuFa
Mother-in-law	*Chepyosyetapikoi* *Chepyosyemwan popikoi* *Chepyosyeni popikoi*	WiMo, BrWiMo, SiMo, SiHuMo
Co-parent-in-law	*Pomwai* *Pomwaimwani* *Pomwainyinyi*	SiWiFa, SiWiMo, DaWiFa, DaWiMo
Great grandchild, Great grandparent	*Kasanya* *Kasanyantenya* *Kasanyantenyi*	FaFaFa, FaMoFa, MoMoFa, MoFaFa, FaFaMo, FaMoMo, MoMoMo, FaMoMo, SoSoSo, SoDaSo, DaDaSo, DaSoSo, SoSoDa, SoDaDa, DaDaDa, DaSoDa

[a]Both mean my mother; *yeyomwani* would be used in reference ("This is my mother"), *yeyonyi* in address as polite form.

[b]*Mutapiya* (and *chepiya*) are used mostly in Sipi and very little in the east but are not Bumachek forms. Alternate version is *ŋatapiya*, only used in Sipi.

[c]"Your brother/sister." A reference term used for quarrels. "Let him have it; he is your mutapkwamet."

[d]*Chepiya* is polite form; *chepiy* is rude or cross and used "when you want her to stop doing something."

[e]These terms apply only to relatives of true mother, not to those of father's other wives.

[f]All old women of father's *aret* (except grandmother) are called *senke.*

[g]This term may be extended to grandchild generation but is unusual.

[h]Not normally used after this relative has been circumcised, but substitutes *karimonintet* for "sons" other than true sons and *korgemwani* for "daughters" other than true daughters.

[i]The more usual terms are those that are reciprocal between grandchild and grandfather and grandchild and grandmother; this term is used more rarely and only to grandchild.

[j]Not proper in public after wife has a child. *Pontoni* means old man; more usual address form is *pontenyu,* my husband.

[k]Used in respectful address to old women, even for own mother. *Chepyosyet* is most respectful.

[l]Most common form for address.

[m]Used reciprocally between a man and his father's sister's husband. Not frequently used by women but may be used for persons that husband would call by this term.

[n]Mostly used in the east and not frequently heard.

[o]From Bok, used only in the east.

[p]Used only in Sipi but not thought to be a loan-word. I am not certain of all extensions of this term. *Pukot* is the more common usage.

Appendix D
Analytic Summary
of Sebei Rituals

This appendix is an assembly of basic data on Sebei rituals described in the text and discussed in Chapter 11. Only recurrent items are tabulated; for details see text, as referenced in the tabulation. Where I did not see the ceremony, I cannot always be certain about the absence of nonreported items. Each major unit in the circumcision and marriage rituals is listed separately. A few definitions are in order:

Social unit refers to the group participating in or significantly represented in the ritual.

Ritual roles are those persons (other than the subjects of the rite, if any) who have a specialized function to perform. Many of these persons are selected because of their status as previous subjects (pr. subj.) of the rite.

Commensality indicates that either drinking beer or some kind of feasting is seen as integral to the rite.

Cleansing substance includes items, such as chyme, beer (often dried beer mash) milk, butter, or chewed moykutwet root, that are used to anoint a person or ritually relevant objects or are put into the fire.

Cultigens are ritually specified items, not food or beer as such. I have included instances where agricultural processes are ritualized or food restrictions are specified in this column.

Wild plants are those ritually specified. The *korosek,* oathing, and *ntarastit* plants are listed in Appendix E.

The remaining ritual acts and substances are self-explanatory, except for "axe and pick," which involves striking together these two artifacts, and skin rings, which are circlets of hide taken from the slaughtered animal and worn by the participants.

(Appendix D — *Cont.*)

Ritual	Reference	Soc. unit	Ritual roles	Commensality	Cleansing substance	Animal slaughtered	Cultigens	Native plants	Seclusion	Shaving	Bath	Fire	Spears	Axe & pick	Dancing	Skin rings
1. *Transformation*																
Birth	246	Neighbors	Pr. subj.	Milk, blood				Lepeywontet	*		*					
Twin	252	*Sagta*	Pr. subj., kindred	Beer	Chyme	Pregnant ewe		Sinentet medicine	*				*	*	*	
Kisa	256	Kindred	Pr. subj., kindred	Beer	Mud from grave				*	*						
Cattle twin	140	*Sagta*	Pr. subj.	Beer, milk				Medicine	*						*	
Initiation: Circumcision	273	*Sagta*	Pr. subj.	Beer, feast	Chyme, butter	Ram	Millet, bread	Diverse medicines	*				*	*	*	
Intermediate	285	*Pinta*	Pr. subj.	Beer			Millet, bread	Lepeywontet	*	*	*	*			*	
Closing	290	*Pinta*	Pr. subj., Mo	Beer	Milk, beer, butter, moykutwet	Ram	Agr. tasks, restricted foods		*	*	*	*		*	*	
Marriage: Beginning	220	Neighbor, kinswoman	Hu Br, Hu Si	Food	Butter		Millet	Sinentet, Lepeywontet	*		*					
Kapokerto	221	Kinswoman				Goat			*							

(Appendix D – *Cont.*)

Ritual	Reference	Soc. unit	Ritual roles	Commensality	Cleansing substance	Animal slaughtered	Cultigens	Native plants	Seclusion	Shaving	Bath	Fire	Spears	Axe & pick	Dancing	Skin rings
Closing	221	Kinswoman		Feast	Butter, milk, beer, moykutwet	Ram		Lepeywontet		*	*				*	
Death: Burial	308	*Sayta*, clan	Br kindred						*		*					
Funeral	308	*Sayta*, clan	Pr. subj.	Ritual stew	Chyme	Ram, bullock		Native foods	*	*	*					
Murder	68	Old man	Pr. subj.			Pregnant ewe		Medicines	*					*		
2. Protection Harvest korosek	65,161	*Pororyet*	Appointed by prophet	Feast	Smoke	Bull	All foods	*Korosek* plants				*				*
Disease korosek	66	*Pororyet*	Appointed by prophet *Teker-yontet*	Feast		Bull or ram		*Korosek* plants Palm fronds				*				
Drought	66	*Pororyet*				Ewe	Beer				*					
Chepserer	71	*Sayta*														
3. Retaliation Mumyantet	316	Clansmen, *sayta*						Oathing plants					*			

(Appendix D – Cont.)

Ritual	Reference	Soc. unit	Ritual roles	Commensality	Cleansing substance	Animal slaughtered	Cultigens	Native plants	Seclusion	Shaving	Bath	Fire	Spears	Axe & pick	Dancing	Skin rings
Surupik	318	*Sayta*						Oathing plants					*			
Sekutet	320	Clansmen						Oathing plants								
Chomi ntarastit	61	*Pororyet*					Plantains	Oathing plants						*			
Clan separation	90	Clan						Korkorwet						*			
4. Amity *Korosek* of curse	320	Clan, *pororyet*	Clan elders	Food, beer	Moykutwet, milk, beer	Ram		*Korosek* plants apples of Sodom				*				
Dispute settlement	90	Clan	Clan elders	Food, beer	Moykutwet, fat, beer	Ram		Korkorwet				*				
Join *pororyet*	64	*Pororyet*		Food, beer	Milk	Bullock		Palm frond								
Kochek	123	Friends		Feast		Bullock		Palm, apples of Sodom								*
Half-brothers	258	*Sayta*	Pr. subj.	Feast, beer		Ram		Palm, apples of Sodom	*					*		

(Appendix D – *Cont.*)

Ritual	Reference	Soc. unit	Ritual roles	Commensality	Cleansing substance	Animal slaughtered	Cultigens	Native plants	Seclusion	Shaving	Bath	Fire	Spears	Axe & pick	Dancing	Skin rings
Cattle herds	141	Domestic	Pr. subj.	Feast, beer	Chyme, fire	Ram		Palm *korosek* plants *sinentet*	*			*		*		
Oyik removal	326	Clansmen	Clan elders	Feast, beer		Chickens	Millet									
5. Domestic A. Persons Naming	251	Hshld	Old person		Beer or milk			*Chemakan-yontet*								
"*Oyik* teeth"	250	Hshld				Goat		Medicine								
For *chepserer*	234	Hshld				Ram										
Intercourse I	229	Hshld				Ram										
Intercourse II	231	Hshld				Ram										
Cleansing genitals	231	Hshld			Chyme	Ram										
Remarriage	232	Hshld	Pr. subj.		Chyme, beer	Ram										*

(Appendix D – *Cont.*)

Ritual	Reference	Soc. unit	Ritual roles	Commensality	Cleansing substance	Animal slaughtered	Cultigens	Native plants	Seclusion	Shaving	Bath	Fire	Spears	Axe & pick	Dancing	Skin rings
Widow inheritance	240	Hshld	Pr. subj.		Chyme, beer	Bullock										*
Spearing lightning	303	Hshld	Left-handed man			Chicken		House-bldg. plant					*			
B. Cattle Smearing for wives	126	Hshld	Mother													
Namanya contract	128	Hshld	Wife		Milk											
Dedicating bull	139	Hshld	Hshld head		Milk, beer			Sinentet								
C. Farming *Misisi*	161	Kindred		Food, beer	Beer libation											
First fruit	161	Hshld			Chyme		Millet									
Opening *sbamba*	161	Hshld			Chyme	Ram	Major cultigens								*	
Kapturin	163	Clans	Specialist	Food		Ram		*Kapturin*				*				

Appendix E
Ritual Ethnobotany

The following list of plants were especially mentioned in one or another ritual of three classes: *korosek, ntarastit,* and other oaths. Identification of plants was made courtesy of the East African Herbarium of Nairobi. Identification of trees was made by reference to Eggeling (1952). Plants used in these rituals that were also used in the *kapturin* ritual are marked with an asterisk. The greater frequency of *korosek* (twenty-six) than oathing (nine) plants results from more detailed information and a greater variety of *korosek* rites.

The tabulation shows that *korosek* and oathing plants are mutually exclusive but that each contributes to the *ntarastit* rite (five *korosek,* two oathing). Informants indicated that more of the *ntarastit* plants were used in oathing, but they did not appear in my notes. Of the twenty-five plants used in the *kapturin* ceremony, six appear in the traditional Sebei rites, five are *korosek* plants, and one is an oathing plant.

Sebei name	Identification	Korosek	Ntarastit	Oathing
chepaiwet*	*Cassia singueana* or *C petersiana*		x	x
cheptuyet	*Maba abyssinica*	x		
kepachichet				x
kaportit	*Maesa lanceolata*		x	
kochet	*Lasiocarys* sp. (?)			x
korkorwet	*Erythrina abyssinica* Len. (Uganda Coral tree)		x	x
koryantet		x		
kurosyantet	*Euphorbia candelabrum* (?)			
latapuchet				x
lepeywontet*	*Satureja abyssinica* Benth. (Savory)	x		
lopotwet	*Solanum incanum* L.	x		
mowet*	*Ficus glumosa* Del.	x		
moyetyet		x	x	

Sebei name	Identification	Korosek	Ntarastit	Oathing
moykutwet	*Oncoba spinosa* Forsk.	x		
murkontet		x		
mutuŋwet*	*Rauvolfia caffra* Sond. (?)	x		
nyechepwet		x		
nochekwa		x		
pisemwet	*Clematis simensis* Fresen (?)		x	
rarawet	a poisonous liana			x
sanotyet	*Hypowestes verticillarius* R. Br.	x		
semotyet			x	
sinentet	*Periploca linearifloria* Dill. et Rich. (silk vine)	x		
simotwet	*Fiscus natalensis* Hochst.	x	x	
sinetwet	*Cassia didymobotrya*	x		
soŋorchet	*Lasiosiphon lampranthas* Getz		x	
sonwoichet				x
sosyantet	*Dracaena reflexa*	x		
supulyantet		x		
tempuryantet		x	x	
tepachicho				x
toposwet	*Croton machrostachys*	x	x	
toratwet*	*Cissus erythrochlora* (?)	x		
torokyontet	*Junipero procera* (African pencil cedar)	x		
tororumwet			x	
tupuŋwet	*Vernonia holstii*	x		
wenetwet		x		
wuswet*	*Uclea* spp.	x	x	
yimit	*Olea chrysophylla*	x		

Glossary

Words in parentheses are plural forms.

aletairion	military leader; Masai loan word
ankurwet	*Coleus barbatus.* A fleshy-leafed bush used in many ways.
anyiñ	sweet, peace; used in prayers or libations
arap	following; son of; sometimes a prefix
arapañ	linked clans. Literally, sons of meat.
arèt (arosyek)	clan. Literally, path.
asista	Sun, God
askari	Swahili term for soldier
Atar	river in central Sebei, giving name to area
Baganda, Buganda	the people and country of dominant kingdom in Uganda. As general in Bantu languages, the prefix *ba-* means people, *bu-* means land, *mu-* means person, *lu-* means language.
Bagisu	the Bantu peoples living west and south of the Sebei. (See Baganda for usage.) *See Gisu.*
baringo	marked-off strip of plowed field, unit of land measurement on the plains
Benet:	village in Masop
Bok	tribe of the Sabaot group in Kenya
Boŋom	tribe of the Sabaot group in Kenya
Bugisu	the country of the Gisu. The district of which Sebei was a part until 1962.
Bukwa	easternmost *gombolola* of Sebei
Bumachek	ethnic enclave of Bagwere, largely assimilated to the Sebei
Chebonet	river east of village of Sasur. Market village on this river and general area.
Chema	*pororyet* in which Sasur is located
chemeryontet (chemerik)	initiate

Chepilat	special age-set, not part of regular cycle
chepserer	ritual to remove influence of witchcraft
chepsokeyontet	diviner
Cheptui	river in western Sebei
Cherengani	hills east of Sebei, inhabited by the Kalenjin Elgeyo and Marakwet tribes
Chesoweri	a *pororyet* in eastern Sebei
choken	granary
chomi ntarastit	ritual affirming right of community to punish person for crimes
chumo	one of the cycling age-sets
Debasien	mountain north of Mount Elgon. Also called Kadam.
debe	Swahili word for five-gallon oil tin
duka	Swahili word for small shop or store
Elgeyo-Marakwet	closely related Kalenjin peoples living in Cherangani Hills
Gisu	form now generally used to refer to the Bantu people living west and south of Sebei; properly Bagisu, Mugisu
gombolola	subdivision of a county (*saza*) in modern government. Luganda term.
Greek River	river forming the northern boundary of Sebei (Keriki in Sebei)
Kabruron	small market town about fifteen miles east of Kapchorwa; also the nearby region
Kalenjin	cluster of languages to which Sebei belongs
kamama	clan of the mother's brother. Also, goods paid in brideprice to the mother's brother.
kamanakan	contractual arrangement under which cattle are cared for by a person other than the owner
kamanakanik	animals held under *Kamanakan* contract
Kamingong	a village, once a part of Sasur, and included as part of Sasur in this work
kankanet	sorcery that affects only the guilty, known only to two clans
kanzu	a man's white robe, introduced by the Swahili
Kapchai	large clan living in Sipi; the area dominated by this clan, also called Kobil
Kapchorwa	town in which district headquarters are located
Kaplelaich	one of cycling age-sets
kaporet	the first in line of a group of initiates
Kapsenyis	clan of great grandparents
Kapsirika	village on the plains that was the subject of intensive investigation

Kapsirikwa	clan thought to be associated with the "Sirikwa holes" and a people who disappeared
Kapsombata	a clan of historical importance, well represented in Sasur
Kaptanya	area around Kapchorwa in the central escarpment
kapterok	kitchen garden
kapturin	fertility ceremony for plantains; also the ritualist for this ceremony
Karamojong	pastoral peoples living north of Sebei
Kaserem	*pororyet* west of Chema
kirwokintet (*kirwokik*)	Judge or elder
kisa	a special person (see *tekeryontet*) born following twins or after several earlier siblings have died
Kitosh	Sebei term for Bantu peoples south of Mount Elgon, consisting of various tribal groups
Klalmet	rectangular house now found only in *Masop*
Kobil	shelf of land in Sipi Gombolola at a lower elevation, used by people of Sasur
kochek	a cattle feast establishing ritual brotherhood among Kony
kok or *kokwet*	council (of *pororyet, saŋta* or clan); also, meeting place for council
Kony	Sabaot tribe in Kenya (Pronounced koñ.)
korkorwet	*Erythrina abyssinica* Lem. Red-hot poker or Uganda Coral tree from which suicides should jump.
Koronkoro	one of the cycling age-sets
korosek	ritual for the removal of curse or harm; also, plants used in these rituals
kota (*korik*)	lineage (subdivision of an *aret*); also, line of cattle descended from an original acquisition. (Literally, house.)
Kwoimet	one of the cycling age-sets
kwoloyintet	man in charge of arrangements in organizing *kwoloyit*
kwoloyit	work party where beer payment is delayed, requiring extra compensation of food
latyet (*latyosyek*)	neighbor; man with whom one shares kraal
Legene	area on the Sebei-Bugisu border; called Bulegene by Gisu.
lepeywontet	*Satureja abyssinica* Benth. Plant used in many ceremonies.
Maina	one of cycling age-sets
mama	mother's brother
manyatta	a brush-enclosed settlement. Masai term.
Masop	Mount Elgon; uphill as a direction; also, the inhabited region above the forest on Mount Elgon

Masopesiyek   people living in Masop

Mbai   the westernmost of the three tribes constituting the Sebei

Mbale   city serving as capital of Eastern Province, Uganda; center of government for Sebei until establishment of independent district

melilo   leopard; also, leopard ceremony in which initiated girls enter age-set

mentyet   house in which initiates are secluded

miruka   minor civil division in modern government; subdivision of the *gombolola*. Luganda term.

misisi   domestic ritual celebrating millet harvest

moran (*moranik*) warrior or young man. Masai term.

moteriyontet   ritual leader or sponsor for initiates
  (*motriyonik*)

moyket   work party

moykutwet   *Oncoba spinosa* Forsk. A plant widely used in ceremonies as a purification agent

mukutanik   neighborhood ceremonial sharing feast that evolved out of *misisi*

mumyantet   any oath but particularly an oath done in conjunction
  (*mumek*)   with the accused

mwet (*mwenik*)   child servant

namanya   used here in adjectival form for contract exchanging a bullock for future heifers

namanyantet   heifer exchanged for a bullock under *namanya* contract
  (*namanisiyek*)

Ngenge   *gombolola* of Sebei on the plains between Mount Elgon and Greek River

nompuk   *Labiatae queer*. A yam-like root cultivated by the Sebei and native to Mount Elgon.

ntoyenik   witchcraft engaged in by women

Nyelit   village east of Kapsirika; also, a salty grass (*Sporobolus marginatus* A.Rich.).

nyikanet   military leader
  (*nyikonik*)

Nyikeao   one of cycling age-sets

Nyonki   one of cycling age-sets

oynatet (*oyik*)   spirits of the dead; any spirit

panet   witchcraft act; also, witchcraft substances

panga   bush knife or machete. Swahili word.

pinta   age-set

Pokot   Kalenjin people living northeast of Sebei, formerly called Suk

ponintet   witch or wizard

pororyet (*pororisyek*)	territorial division of a tribe; the basic spatial unit of military action; also one of the "meats" of the beerpot
Riwa	a spur of Mount Elgon lying to the northeast
rupet	wooden bowl used by diviner
Sabaot	modern term including the Sebei, Bok, Boŋom, and Kony in Kenya, who share the greeting, *supay*
Sakwet	a ritual feast
saŋta (*soŋmwek*)	village; also, area in household compound where beer pot is placed
Sapiñ	the easternmost of the three tribes that make up the Sebei
Sasur	village in Sipi Gombolola that was subject of intensive investigation
saza	county. Sebei constituted a single county until 1962. Luganda term.
sekonik	cattle owned by a man, whether or not in his herd
sekutet	a curse made privately against a subject
senchontet	*Dracaena deremensis* Engl. A long-lived plant used as boundary markers.
shamba	field. Swahili word.
sikerointe	bachelor's house
sinentet	*Periploca linearifolia* Dill. et Rich. Vine used as garland in various rituals.
Sipi	westernmost *gombolola* of Sebei
Siroko	river forming western boundary of Sebei territory in earlier days. Sebei name is Ciok.
soi	downhill direction; also, the plains
sokoran	sinful
Sor	one of the three tribes that make up the Sebei
Sosyet	palm frond used for cleaning gourd and in rituals
Sowe	one of the cycling age-sets
Suam	river forming eastern boundary of present Sebei territory
sufuria	aluminum pot of Indian origin. Swahili word.
Sundet	river along which village of Kapsirika lies
surupik	oath against an unknown person
Tegeres	*pororyet* east of Chema
teita (*toka*)	cattle
tekeryontet (*tekerisiyek*)	a special child; twin, breach birth, or one born after several others have died.
tekso	tabu relationship between certain kin
tilyet	relationship between men who have engaged in cattle contract (*namanya*)
tinkyontet	iron bracelet
tokapsoi	cattle kept by husband and not allocated to a wife

Tulel	*pororyet* of Sapiñ
Uasin-Gishu	highlands east of Mount Elgon, occupied by Maa-speaking peoples known as the Uasin-Gishu Masai
waragi	native gin
warwet (*warek*)	collective term for sheep and goats
workoyontet (*workoyik*)	prophet
yedyeita	cattle herd; animals herded together but not necessarily owned by one man
yotunet	ceremony of release from ritual seclusion

Bibliography

Anon.
  1960? *Memorandum of Sebei People in North Bugisu to the Minister of Local Government.* Entebbe: n. d. Mimeographed.
Anon.
  1961. *A Report from Chepsukunya Police on 2/8/61.* Mimeographed.
Austin, Herbert H.
  1903. *With Macdonald in Uganda. A Narrative Account of the Uganda Mutiny and Macdonald Expedition in the Uganda Protectorate and the Territories to the North.* London: Edward Arnold.
Barber, J. P.
  1961. Female Circumcision among the Sebei. *Uganda Journal* 25:94-104.
Beadnell, C. Marsh
  1905. Circumcision and Clitoridectomy as Practised by the Natives of British East Africa. *British Medical Journal* 1:964-65.
Bernardi, B.
  1952. The Age System of the Nilo-Hamitic Peoples: A Critical Evaluation. *Africa* 27:316-32.
Bohannan, Paul and Laura
  1968. *Tiv Economy.* Evanston, Ill.: Northwestern University Press.
Chapman, Susannah
  1966. A Sirikwa Hole on Mount Elgon. *Azania* 1:139-48.
Chemaswet, Salimu
  1962. Eri Abasebei Awamu Nabagenyi Abakunganye wano Kap-Chai Sipi/Sebei District Leero Ku 11/11/1962. A meeting of the people of Sebei and guests held at Kapchai, Sipi, Sebei District on 11/11/62). Trans. from Luganda by Livingstone Walusumbi. Ms.
Dundas, Kenneth R.
  1913. The Wawanga and Other Tribes of the Elgon District, British East Africa, *Journal of the Royal Anthropological Institute of Great Britain and Ireland* 43: 19-75.
Dyson-Hudson, Neville
  1966. *Karimojong Politics.* Oxford: Clarendon Press.

Edgerton, Robert B.

1971. *The Individual in Cultural Adaptation: A Study of Four East African Peoples.* Berkeley and Los Angeles: University of California Press.

Eggeling, William S.

1952. *The Indigenous Trees of the Uganda Protectorate.* Rev. ed. by Ivan R. Dale. Entebbe: Government Printer.

Ehret, Christopher

1971. *Southern Nilotic History.* Evanston, Ill.: Northwestern University Press.

Evans-Pritchard, E. E.

1940a. *The Nuer; A Description of the Modes of Livelihood and Political Institutions of a Nilotic People.* Oxford: Clarendon Press.

1940b. The Political Structure of the Nandi-Speaking Peoples of Kenya. *Africa* 13:250-67.

Gedge, Ernest

n.d. Journal. Ms. (This journal was in the hands of the late H. B. Thomas, who copied the relevant passages from it for me; the ms. is now in the Oxford Colonial Records Project, Institute of Commonwealth Studies, Oxford, England.)

Goldschmidt, Walter

1959. *Man's Way: A Preface to the Understanding of Society.* New York: Holt, Rinehart and Winston.

1961. A View from the Far Side: A Document in Acculturation. In *Culture in History: Essays in Honor of Paul Radin,* ed. Stanley Diamond, pp. 241-52. New York: Columbia University Press.

1964. Pastoral Society as Ecologic Adaptation in Sub-Saharan Africa. Paper for Symposium on Pastoral Nomadism, Burg Wartenstein, August 1964. Multilith.

1965. Theory and Strategy in the Study of Cultural Adaptability. In Variation and Adaptability of Culture, A Symposium. *American Anthropologist* 67: 402-408.

1967. *Sebei Law.* Berkeley and Los Angeles: University of California Press.

1968. Game Theory, Cultural Values and the Brideprice in Africa. In *Formal Approaches to Social Behavior,* ed. Ira M. Buchler and Hugo Nutini, pp. 65-74. Pittsburgh: University of Pittsburgh Press.

1969. *Kambuya's Cattle: the Legacy of an African Herdsman.* Berkeley and Los Angeles: University of California Press.

1970. The Metaphysical Infrastructure of Sebei Social Behavior. *Proceedings of the 8th International Congress of Anthropological and Ethnological Sciences,* Tokyo and Kyoto, 2: 109-11.

1971a. Independence as an Element in Pastoral Social Systems. *Anthropological Quarterly* 44: 132-42.

1971b. The Theory of Cultural Adaptation. Introduction to *The Individual in Cultural Adaptation: A Study of Four East African Peoples* by

Robert B. Edgerton. Berkeley and Los Angeles: University of California Press.

1972a. An Ethnography of Encounters. *Current Anthropology* 13: 59-78.

1972b. Freud, Durkheim, and Death Among the Sebei. *Omega* 3: 227-31.

1972c. The Operations of a Sebei Capitalist: A Contribution to Economic Anthropology. *Ethnology* 11: 187-201.

1973a. Brideprice of the Sebei. *Scientific American* 229 74-85.

1973b. Guilt and Pollution in Sebei Mortuary Rituals. *Ethos* 1: 75-105.

1974. The Economics of Brideprice among the Sebei and in East Africa. *Ethnology* 13: 311-31.

1975. Absent Eyes and Idle Hands. *Ethos* 3: 157-163.

Greenberg, Joseph H.

1955. *Studies in African Linguistic Classification.* New Haven, Conn.: Compass Publishing Company. (Reprinted from the *Southwest Journal of Anthropology.*)

1963. The Languages of Africa. *International Journal of American Linguistics* 29 (Part II): 1-171.

Gulliver, Philip H.

1955. *The Family Herds.* London: Routledge and Kegan Paul.

1963. *Social Control in an African Society: A Study of the Arusha; Argricultural Masai of Northern Tanganyika.* London: Routledge and Kegan Paul.

Hays, T. R.

1949. Notes on Safari in Sebei Saza. Mbale District. *Agricultural Yearbook,* May. (Ms., District Commissioner's Office, Mbale, Uganda.)

Hennings, R. O.

1951. *African Morning.* London: Chatto and Windus.

Henry, Jules

1963. *Culture Against Man.* New York: Random House.

Hobley, C. W.

1902. *Eastern Uganda: an Ethnological Survey.* Anthropological Institute of Great Britain and Ireland, Occasional Papers, No. 1.

1929. *Kenya, from Chartered Company to Crown Colony.* London: H. F. and G. Witherby.

Huntingford, G. W. B.

1927. Miscellaneous Records Relating to the Nandi and Kony Tribes. *Journal of the Royal Anthropological Institute of Great Britain and Ireland* 57: 417-61.

1953. *The Nandi of Kenya.* London: Routledge and Kegan Paul.

Jackson, Sir Frederick

1930. *Early Days in East Africa.* London: Edward Arnold.

Kipkorir, B. E.

1973. *The Marakwet of Kenya: a Preliminary Study.* (with F. B. Welbourn). Nairobi: East African Literature Bureau.

Kluckhohn, Clyde
1967. *Navaho Witchcraft.* Boston: Beacon Press. (Originally published in the Publications of the Peabody Museum of Harvard University, 1944.)

LaFontaine, J. S.
1959. *The Gisu of Uganda.* In Ethnographic Survey of Africa series, ed. Daryll Forde: East Central Africa, Part 10. International African Institute.

Langdale-Brown, I., H. A. Osmaston, and J. G. Wilson
1964. *The Vegetation of Uganda and its Bearing on Land Use.* [Entebbe]: Government of Uganda.

Lewis, I. M.
1961. *A Pastoral Democracy; A Study of Pastoralism and Politics among the Northern Somali of the Horn of Africa.* London: Oxford University Press for the International African Institute.

Lind, E. M. and A. C. Tallantire
1962. *Some Common Flowering Plants of Uganda.* London: Oxford University Press.

Macdonald, Lieut. Col. J. R. L.
1899. Notes on the Ethnology of Tribes Met with during the Progress of the Juba Expedition of 1897-99. *Journal of the Royal Anthropological Institute* 22 (n.s., 2): 226-50.

Malcolm, D. W.
1953. *Sukumaland, an African People and Their Country.* London: Oxford University Press.

Montgomery, C. A.
1970. Problems in the Development of an Orthography for the Sebei Language of Uganda. *Journal of the Language Association of Eastern Africa* 1, no. 1: 48-55.
1966. The Morphology of Sebei. Ph.D. Dissertation, University of California, Los Angeles. University Microfilms, Ann Arbor, Michigan.

Murdock, George Peter
1959. *Africa, Its Peoples and their Culture History.* New York: McGraw-Hill.

Nadel, S. F.
1952. Witchcraft in Four African Societies: an Essay in Comparison. *American Anthropologist* 54: 18-29.

Odner, Knut
1972. Excavations at Narosara, a Stone Bowl Site in the Southern Kenya Highlands (with appendix by Alan H. Jacobs and Richard M. Gramly). *Azania* 7: 25-92.

Oliver, Symmes C.
1965. Individuality, Freedom of Choice and Cultural Flexibility of the Kamba. In Variation and Adaptability of Culture, A symposium. *American Anthropologist* 67: 421-28.

Parsons, Talcot
1968. Systems Analysis: Social Systems. *The International Encyclopedia of the Social Sciences* 15: 459-73.

Peristiany, J. G.
1939. *The Social Institutions of the Kipsigis.* London: Routledge and Kegan Paul.
1951a. The Age-Set System of the Pastoral Pokot: The Sapana Initiation Ceremony. *Africa* 21: 188-206.
1951b. The Age-Set System of the Pastoral Pokot: Mechanisms, Functions, and Post Sapana Ceremonies. *Africa* 21: 279-302.

Porter, Philip
n.d. The Ecology and Environment of East Africa. Ms.

Ravenstein, E. G.
1891. Messrs. Jackson and Gedge's Journey to Uganda via Masai-land. *Proceedings of the Royal Geographical Society and Monthly Record of Geography* 13: 199-203.

Roscoe, John
1924. *The Bagesu and Other Tribes of the British Protectorate.* London: Cambridge University Press.

Schwartz, Theodore
1973. Cult and Context: the Paranoid Ethos in Melanesia. *Ethos* 1: 153-74.

Sebei Kok Committee
1960?. *Memorandum Submitted by the Sebei Kok Committee to the Commission of Inquiry, Bugisu District.* Mimeographed.

Sutton, J. E. G.
1964. The Sirikwa: Archeology and the Kalenjin Traditions. *Uganda Journal* 28: 69-74.
1966. The Archeology and Early Peoples of the Highlands of Kenya and Northern Tanzania. *Azania* 1: 37-58.
1968. The Settlement of East Africa. In *Zamani: A Survey of East African History,* ed. B. A. Ogot and J. A. Kieran. Nairobi: East African Publishing House and Longmans Green.

Thomas, H. B.
1937. Capax Imperii — the Story of Semei Kakunguru. *Uganda Journal* 6: 125-36.

Thomas, Ioan
1963. The Flat Roofed Houses of the Sebei at Benet (Part II of the Brathey Exploration Group's Expedition to Uganda, 1962). *Uganda Journal* 21: 115.

Tucker, Archibald N. and M. A. Bryan
1962. Noun Classification in Kalenjin: Pakot. *African Language Studies* 3: 137-81.

Weatherby, J. M.
1962a. Intertribal Warfare on Mt. Elgon in the 19th and 20th Centuries. *Uganda Journal* 26: 200-212.

1962b. A Note on the Sebei Caves. *Uganda Journal* 26: 213-17.

1964. The Sirikwa in the Elgon Area. *Uganda Journal* 28: 61-66.

1967. Aspects of the Ethnography and Oral Traditions of the Sebei of Mt. Elgon, M.A. Thesis, Makerere University, Kampala, Uganda.

Were, Gideon S.

1967a. *A History of the Abaluya of Western Kenya.* Nairobi: East African Publishing House.

1967b. *Western Kenya Historical Texts.* Nairobi: East African Literature Bureau.

Winans, Edgar V.

1965. The Political Context of Economic Adaptation in the Southern Highlands of Tanganyika. In Variation and Adaptability of Culture; a Symposium. *American Anthropologist* 67: 435-41.

Addendum:

O'Brien, Richard J., S. J., and Wim A. M. Cuypers, M. H. M.

1975. A Description Sketch of the Grammar of Sebei. *Georgetown University Working Papers on Languages and Linguistics* 9: 1-108.

Cuypers, Wim A. M., M. H. M.

1975. A Sebei English Word List. *Georgetown University Working Papers on Languages and Linguistics* 9: 109-190.

Index

Abaluyia, 17

Abandonment of children, 321-322

Ability, as basis for status, 109

Abortion, 205, 244n

Adaptation: by Sebei, 345-353; study of, i; theory of, 31-32, 343-344

Adoption: of children, 251; to clan, 87

Adultery, 206, 230-231

Affect, lack of, 265, 344, 352

Afterlife, 304-305, 310

Age, social distinction in, 108, 268n

Age-grades, 264, 349

Age-mates; in harvest rite, 162; during initiation, 281; obligations of, 270-271, 290, 297; as quasi-kin, 98; tabus relating to, 99-100, 231

Age-sets: antiquity of, 13; changes in, 346, 349, 350; communities of, 75-76, 105, 349; comparisons, 110, 347-348; organization of, 102-108; and prophets, 311; relations between, 105-106, 269; ritual induction to, 294-295, 299; in warfare, 67, 105, 300, 349; women's, 108

Age-set cycle, 103-104, 269, 359-360

Agriculture: coffee production, 196-199; distribution of, 147-149; history of, 13, 19, 41, 146-147, 149-150; in Masop, 39; productivity, 154, 182; ritual for, 160-164, 336, 338, 370; seasonal aspect of, 361; techniques and practices in (general), 153-156, (Sasur) 164-168, (Kapsirika) 179-183

Alcoholism, 298, 353

Altar, for oathing, 62, 316, 331

Altitude: of Kapsirika, 47; of Sasur, 46

American culture and Sebei, 358

Amity. See Rituals, of reconciliation

Amniotic fluid, in twin ceremony, 254

Amulets, 250, 253, 257, 305

Ancestor, mythical, 16

Ancestors. See Genealogy; Spirits

Anglican Church, 261

Animals (wild): rights to, 147-149; symbolic use of, 334, 337

"Animals" of initiation. See Medicines

Anointing, 222-223, 279, 323, 332, 337. See also Blessing

Anvil, 192

Apples of Sodom: in blood-brotherhood cere-

mony, 123; in initiation rites, 290; in removal of oath, 322; for ritual of half-brothers, 258; symbolic use of, 333

Arapkoipot (prophet), 59, 107

Arapkuprukoin (prophet), 59

Arapta, D. P., xvi

Arrow: in oaths, 317, 322; manufacture of, 190, 193; sale at market, 190; as symbols, 335; use in wars, 68

Arson, and oaths, 317

Art, 190, 303

Artifacts, symbolic use of, 335

Arusha, 14

Ashes: at funerals, 309; removal of, 327; as symbol, 335

Attitudes: between sexes, 204-205, 210-211, 226-231, 238-239, 294, 352; to children, 243-244, 261, 266; to circumcisor, 273, 299-300; to death, 310; to divination, 313; to divorce, 237-238; and ecology, 343-344; to exchanges, 202; to farming, 181, 183; general, 338-339; to initiates, 278, 280, 281-283, 286; to in-laws, 222-224; to oaths, 318-320; to polygyny, 231-233; to smiths, 192; to twins, 256-257; to uninitiated, 268; to war, 69, 70; to weaning, 248-249; to widow inheritance, 240

Auguries, 314-315. See also Omens

Austin, Herbert H.: account by, 25-27; mentioned, 58, 75, 193, 359

Authority: on basis of age, 108; change in, 346, 349-350; and curses, 315; diffuseness of, 354; of fathers, 210, 238, 264, 340, 349; of prophets, 56, 58. See also Attitudes, between sexes

Avoidance, among cattle, 120

Avoidance, of mother-in-law, 97, 151

Awl, as symbols, 335

Axe: manufacture of, 190, 193; ritual use of, 69, 141, 259, 278, 365-370; as symbol, 335

Bachelor's house, 203, 251

Baganda: rule of, 27, 28, 58, 107, 353, 359; mentioned, 203, 214

Bagwere, immigration of, 22. See also Bumachek

Bahima, as hired hands, 130

Bamboo: mats, 39; ritual use of, 141

385

Chickens: (Continued)
by women, 153; in ritual, 326, 334; sale of, 200-201; as source of income, 194
Childhood, influence of, 339-341, 354
Child nurse, 82, 243, 250, 265
Children: care of, 260-261; dedicated to spirits, 305; desire for, 230, 241, 243-244, 355; play of, 263-264, 265, 268; tasks of, 259-262; terminology for, 96. *See also* Special children; Twins
Chilla (informant), 20, 25
Chomi ntarastit: as community law, 21, 61; mentioned, 328; organized by prophet, 58; plants used in, 371-372; as *pororyet* rite, 337; to protect weak, 95, 331, 356; ritual elements in, 368
Chyme, ritual use of, 65, 140, 141, 161, 162, 164, 221, 232, 240, 254, 259, 279, 309, 332, 334, 365-370
Circumcision: adopted by Bantu, 16; antiquity of, 13; changes in, 346; in children's play, 263; function of, 299; of married man, 279; and mourning customs, 309; nature of operation for, 267, 279, 280; payment for, 188; of pregnant girl, 203; preparation for, 273; prevention of by Gisu, 30; restrictions during, 229; ritual of, 273-281; as sexual symbol, 336; of special children, 256; symbols in, 335; and witchcraft, 325; and womens' attitudes, 352. *See also* Initiation
Circumcisors, 94, 273
Clan: changes in, 348; fission of, 90, 368; found in neighboring tribes, 18; in funeral, 308, 334; general characteristics of, 86-88; histories, 17-18; and inheritance of traits, 94, 306; joining *pororyet*, 65; legal role of, 91-94, 136-137, 349; linkages between, 89-91; as local unit, 71, 76, 149, 150; military functions of, 19, 67, 350; of mother, 95, 99-100; and oaths, 316, 321-323, 328, 331; occupational specialization of, 94, 191; and prophets, 60; rights of, 92, 159-160, 183, 219, 221; rituals of, 93-94, 163, 332, 337-338, 340-341; role in brideprice negotiation, 217-218; unity of, 94, 138-139, 304-305, 355-356; and witchcraft, 324-327
Clanlessness, 62, 94-95, 356
Clan songs, 142, 222, 223, 225
Climate: Kapsirika, 47-50; Sasur, 47
Clothing: given to initiates, 295; paid in brideprice, 211
Clubs, at initiation, 296
Coffee: control of by men, 153; distribution of, 43, 198; economics of, 194, 195, 196-199; influence of, 152, 184, 352; introduction of, 146, 360; land in, 166-169
Coitus interruptus, during pregnancy, 229
Colobus monkey, 298
Commensality, 339, 365, 366-370. *See also* Feast
Comparisons. *See* Pastoral-farming comparisons; Sasur-Kapsirika comparisons
Compensation, for murder, 92. *See also* Payment
Community: changes in, 348; development of, 350
Community law. *See Chomi ntarastit*

Competitiveness, absence of, 265
Conant, Francis P., xv, xvi
Conciliation, rites of, 330, 332
Contests, among initiates, 264, 289, 296, 297
Contracts: antiquity of, 187-189; and crops, 170; land, 150, 170, 184; livestock, 114, 117, 127-136, 263, 343; marriage, 217-220; work, 158-160; written, 176
Cosmology, 302-306
Cost analysis: of coffee, 197-198; of commodities, 200-202; of crafts, 190; in general, 187-188, 194; of grain, 155-156; of land, 168, 171; in mixed exchanges, 135; of work, 158-159
Cotton: cultivation (Kapsirika), 180; income, 194; introduction of, 41
Council: of clans, 87, 90, 92-94; at funerals, 309; for marital relations, 235; of *pororyet*, 55, 64; of village, 71
Courts: and land sale, 172; of *pororyet*, 64; use in divorce, 235-238; of village, 71
Co-wives: mode of address, 96; relation among, 79, 152, 176-179, 221, 225, 233-234, 237, 241, 281, 329, 348; restrictions on, 328
Cowries: as amulet, 250, 253; antiquity of, 13; as symbols, 335; as trade items, 27. *See also* Girdle, cowry
Craftsmanship, 189-193
Crafts, sold at market, 201
"Crying the Knife," 281-284, 297
Cultivation. *See* Agriculture
Cults, absence of, 340
Cultural evolution, 5
Culture, concept of, 1-3, 343
Culture and Ecology Project, xv, 5-7, 111
Curing, 307-308. *See also* Medicines
Curses: against children, 260; distinguished from oaths, 315; against witchcraft, 71. *See* Oaths
Cushites, influences from, 12, 14, 23
Customs. *See* Etiquette

Dance: at initiations, 269, 274-277, 287, 295; in rituals, 366-370; at twin ceremony, 254; at weddings, 222
Death: causes of, 306; and divination, 311; fear of, 310; obsession with, 338; in rites of transition, 330; and witchcraft, 324, 328. *See also* Funerals
Death and rebirth, theme of, 268. *See also* Initiation
Debasien, Mount, 37
Defecation, on oathing substance, 320-321
Defensive posture of Sebei, 67. *See also* Warfare
Demography, 50-54; of Masop, 39
Directions, as symbols, 335
Disasters, ritual response to, 337. *See also* Famines; Warfare
Disease: of cattle, 121, 134; caused by rainbow, 303; causes of, 252, 303, 306, 324; and oathing, 320-323; prophecies of, 57, 311; ritual removal of, 66, 337, 367. *See also* Curing; *Korosek*; Medicines
Disputes: between age-sets, 105; change in, 349-350, 352; and clan fission, 89; over land, 149, 176-179, 181, 185; ritual of settlement,

Time, in contracts, 128, 174. *See also* Space-time relationships
Time reference and tense, 5
Tiv, 134
Tobacco: paid in brideprice, 211, 214; as protective medicine, 122; in ritual, 65, 286, 322; for weaning, 248
Toilet training, 249-250
Tooth eruption, 250-251, 369
Tooth evulsion, 13, 264
Totemism: 88
Tractors, 44, 147
Trade: with Austin's party, 26-27; in *Masop*, 40; with Swahili, 24. *See also* Economics; Exchanges; Markets; Sales; Shops
Trance, of prophets, 311
Transition, rites of, 329-331
Tribe, meaning of, 5
Tribes of Sebei, 44, 63
Trophies, taken in battle, 68
Trumpets, 67
Trust: absence of, 241; between husband and wife, 228
Trysts, 204
Tumbuka, 14
Turkana, 14
Twins: dangerous to infants, 250; funeral rites for, 255, 308, 309; garlanded with vine, 333; at initiation, 270, 272, 275, 279, 286, 289-290; and leopard ceremony, 292, 294; rarely survive, 244; ritual for, 188, 252-258, 330, 335, 336
Twins (cattle), rituals for 140-141, 330, 332-333, 366

Uasin-Gishu Masai. *See* Masai
Ultimogeniture, 137-138, 152
Urine: as cleansing agent, 221, 287-288; in oathing, 320-321

Vegetables, 39, 146. *See also* Kitchen gardens
Veterinarians, 102, 103, 121, 188
Village: definition and description of, 46, 55-56, 71-77; development of, 351; and oaths, 316-318; and rituals, 304, 308, 331, 337. *See also* Sasur, Kapsirika, *Sanţa*
Vulgarity, at initiation, 287, 289

Wandera, Yunusu, xvi, 11, 28, 29, 58, 108, 360
Warek: definition of, 113; in exchanges, 130-131, 133; paid in brideprice, 211; in sales, 132; in Sasur and Kapsirika, 116, 118; slaughter of, 125; as source of income, 194. *See also* Goats; Sheep
Warfare: as age-set function, 105; attitudes toward, 21; with Austin's party, 27; change in, 346, 348-349; comparison, 347-349; de-fensive character of, 21; description of, 66-70; history of, 18-21; internal, 20; military pressure of on Sebei, 15-16; preparation for, 67; present day, 69-70; as source of leadership, 55; and territorial unit, 63-64
Wars, predicted by prophets, 57, 311
Water, access to, 120, 121, 147-149
Wealth: attainment of, 134, 135, 183; as basis for marriage, 208; display of, 271, 298; importance of, 55, 261
Weaning, 248-249
Weddings. *See* Marriage
Welding, 192
Wells, 41, 120
Wergild, 136-137, 357
Western influence on Sebei, 23-28
Wheat, 39, 146
Whetstone, at initiations, 279, 297, 335
Widower remarriage, ritual for, 369
Widows: inheritance of, 110, 240-241, 308-309, 370; mourning of, 308; in son's household, 83
Winans, Edgar V., xv, xvi
Witchcraft: attitudes toward, 302, 313; and authority, 356; and childbirth, 241, 246; comparisons, 347-348; description of, 323-329, 331; ecology of, 343-344; frequency, 325; in illness, 306; against initiates, 283-285, 287, 300; for murder, 92; and oaths, 315, 316, 327-238; ordeal for, 325; protection against, 71, 367; suspicion of, 179, 308, 311; by women, 227-228, 233-234, 292, 325, 326
Witchdoctor (as curer) 191, 306-307
Witches: attitudes to, 337; behavior of, 325
Womanhood, affirmation of, 292
Women: age-sets of, 108; changed role of, 238-239, 352; clan affiliation of, 87; after delivery, 246; as diviners, 311; funerals for, 309; and livestock, 125, 128-129; multiple marriages, 81, 238-239; and oathing, 320; powers of, 227, 294, 299-300; restrictions on, 226; rights to land, 151-153; role in warfare, 68; subordination of, 79, 87; and witchcraft, 227-228, 233-234, 292, 325, 336; work of, 80, 124, 153
Woodwork, 190
Work: of children, 259-262; value of, 260-261, 264-265. *See also* Agriculture; Craftsmanship; Herding; Smiths; Women, work of
Work party, 154, 156-160
World view, 302

Yams: adoption of, 345; cultivation of, 166-169; sold at market, 200-201; used in ritual of purification, 65

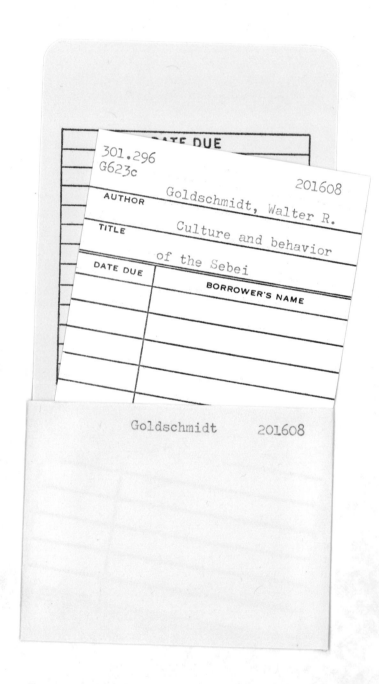